Routledge Revivals

Nationality in History and Politics

First published in 1944, *Nationality in History and Politics* unpacks the vagueness of terms such as nationality, national consciousness, national character, national will, national self-determination, etc. The phenomena underlying these terms are exceedingly complex, and writers frequently shift the sense according to the interest defended. National consciousness comprises a number of different aspirations which, however, can be summed up as a striving for national personality. The book investigates in detail the correlations between those aspirations and such factors as race, language, religion, territory and State, and examines in particular the social background of modern nationalism. The chapters give the sociology of national sentiment and national traditions, usually called national character, against a wide historical background. The latter part of the book treats the evolution of ideas on nationality and on supranational aims from the Middle Ages to our own time, and the influence of the doctrines of great thinkers on the national ideology of the principal nations. This book will be of interest to students of history, political science, sociology and psychology.

Nationality in History and Politics

A Psychology and Sociology of National Sentiment and Nationalism

Frederick Hertz

First published in 1944
by Routledge & Kegan Paul Ltd.

This edition first published in 2022 by Routledge
4 Park Square, Milton Park, Abingdon, Oxon, OX14 4RN

and by Routledge
605 Third Avenue, New York, NY 10017

Routledge is an imprint of the Taylor & Francis Group, an informa business

© 1944 Routledge & Kegan Paul Ltd

All rights reserved. No part of this book may be reprinted or reproduced or utilised in any form or by any electronic, mechanical, or other means, now known or hereafter invented, including photocopying and recording, or in any information storage or retrieval system, without permission in writing from the publishers.

Publisher's Note
The publisher has gone to great lengths to ensure the quality of this reprint but points out that some imperfections in the original copies may be apparent.

Disclaimer
The publisher has made every effort to trace copyright holders and welcomes correspondence from those they have been unable to contact.

A Library of Congress record exists under LCCN: 44005058

ISBN: 978-1-032-25150-9 (hbk)
ISBN: 978-1-003-28199-3 (ebk)
ISBN: 978-1-032-25192-9 (pbk)

Book DOI: 10.4324/9781003281993

NATIONALITY IN HISTORY AND POLITICS

A PSYCHOLOGY AND SOCIOLOGY OF NATIONAL SENTIMENT AND NATIONALISM

by

FREDERICK HERTZ

author of Race and Civilization

LONDON
ROUTLEDGE & KEGAN PAUL LTD
BROADWAY HOUSE: 68-74 CARTER LANE, E.C.4

First edition 1944
Second impression 1945
Third impression 1951

To
GEORGE P. GOOCH, C.H., D.Litt.
IN ADMIRATION, GRATITUDE AND FRIENDSHIP

Printed in Great Britain by
Lowe and Brydone Printers Ltd., London, N.W.10

PREFACE

This book is a study in human nature and human society. Its subject demands the combination of historical investigation with psychological and sociological methods. Though the scope of the book would seem to be more comprehensive than that of previous treatments of the problem, it must be emphasized that the book is by no means meant as an exhaustive discussion of all aspects and all materials available. Such a discussion would fill an encyclopaedia and would require the co-operation of many specialists. War-time conditions, moreover, impose strict limitations on the size of books. I was compelled to leave out several important chapters and to economize in space wherever possible. It should not be assumed, therefore, that questions not treated in detail, or at all, either escaped my attention or were considered unimportant. One of my principal rules in selecting the materials was to avoid treating questions in detail which have been widely discussed already and about which most readers may be assumed to be well informed, unless I had to put forward a new interpretation or significant supplementary arguments. Many problems of nationality, moreover, have already been dealt with in other publications of mine, and I intend to publish shortly further books and papers which will continue the investigations of this book. Space has also been saved by numerous references to books by other authors where the reader would find a more detailed discussion of certain issues than I could afford.

I should not have been able to pursue my studies and to write this book but for the generous help of the Society for the Protection of Science and Learning in Cambridge and All Souls College in Oxford, and I take this opportunity of expressing my warmest thanks to them. In particular I am most grateful to Dr. W. G. S. Adams, Warden of All Souls, Sir William Beveridge, Master of University College, Dr. George P. Gooch, and Mr. Alexander Farquharson, General Secretary of the Institute of Sociology, for all the kind interest shown to me and my work. I am also greatly indebted to friends who have read chapters of this book and have suggested corrections, in particular Mr.

Cyril Fox, Dr. R. Laffan, Miss Catherine Marshall, Miss Mary Baylay, Mr. A. T. Ashton and Mr. E. T. Turner. My special thanks are also due to Dr. Margaret Eisen, who devoted much work to typing and revising the manuscript of the book.

LONDON, *April* 1943

PREFACE
TO THE THIRD IMPRESSION

This impression gives the text as published first in 1944 and reprinted in 1945. In consequence, references are made to the facts such as the war from the standpoint of the time of the first publication, and no account is taken of later events. A detailed discussion of later developments would require a separate book. It may be said, however, that the view of nationalism expressed in this book has again been confirmed by many tragic experiences. Nationalism is such a widespread and powerful element in the spirit of our time, and often so evasive, that even many who recognise its dangers, and deplore its existence, may prove not immune from its infection. Again and again actions of intelligent and obviously well-meaning people of all nations evoke the thought: They know not what they do . . .

Every nation has its specific ideology, which is a mixture of truth and error, vanity and wishful thinking. Its function is to bind the nation together and to give it a certain unity of thought and will, and a certain feeling of solidarity and self-confidence. To many it is a sort of substitute for religion, others may be more critical, but public criticism on an effective scale is hardly possible, least of all in decisive moments when national passions are running high. Most believers in an ideology do not realise all its implications. In a great many questions people of different nations have the same outlook and standards of behaviour. But if issues of national ideology arise each nation seems to look at the world through spectacles showing it in a different colour and perspective.

The remedy would, of course, be to set up an international Reign of Law, based on conviction and agreement. Unfortunately we seem farther removed from this goal than we were fifty years ago. Its attainment would presuppose a much better understanding of the complex psychology of nations, a realistic view of the dynamics involved in collective mentalities, and a critical attitude to all ideologies. National megalomania naturally is the greatest enemy of mankind. But there are also friendly illusions which may have disastrous consequences. They often serve as a smoke-screen for useless activities, or encourage an opportunism closing its eyes before the most glaring violations of elementary human rights and of national self-determination. On such foundations a true Reign of Law cannot be built.

In the preface to the first edition I mentioned that further studies of mine on problems of nationalism were in preparation. In the meantime my book "The Economic Problems of the Danubian States, a Study in Economic Nationalism," has appeared. It gives ample supplementary materials and arguments to certain parts of this book, in particular to chap. V, 17 and chap. VII, 5.

FREDERICK HERTZ.

March, 1950
37 CORRINGHAM ROAD,
LONDON, N.W.11.

CONTENTS

CHAP.		PAGE
I.	THE STRUCTURE AND FORMS OF NATIONAL CONSCIOUSNESS	1–51
	1. THE MYSTERY OF NATIONALISM	1
	2. THE WORD "NATION" USED IN MANY DIFFERENT SENSES	5
	3. THE ASPECTS OF NATIONALITY AND THE METHODS OF ITS STUDY	8
	4. PROPOSED DEFINITIONS OF A NATION — THEIR INADEQUACY	11
	5. ANALYSIS OF NATIONAL CONSCIOUSNESS . . .	15
	(a) The Problem of Collective Mentality . .	15
	(b) Human Groups Actuated by Traditions, Interests and Ideals	18
	(c) The Four National Aspirations, their Forms and Antinomies	21
	(d) Nationality and Civilization . . .	24
	6. THE IDEA OF NATIONAL PERSONALITY . . .	26
	(a) Personality, Organism and Freedom . .	26
	(b) The Nation as a Natural Organism . .	29
	7. THE HISTORICAL ORIGIN OF NATIONALITY . .	31
	8. NATIONAL CONSCIOUSNESS AND NATIONALISM . .	34
	9. THE IDEA OF NATIONAL CHARACTER . . .	37
	(a) Popular Views and Scientific Theories .	37
	(b) The Structure of National Character . .	41
	(c) The National Ideology	44
	(d) The National Ideology and International Relations	48
II.	NATIONALITY AND RACE	52–77
	1. DIFFERENCES AND PARALLELS IN THE IDEAS OF RACE AND NATION	52
	2. NATIONAL AND RACIAL SENTIMENT	53
	3. THE SOCIAL ORIGIN OF RACIAL SENTIMENT AND ITS BEARING ON NATIONALITY	56
	4. THE RISE OF MODERN RACIAL IDEOLOGY . . .	61
	5. THE SOCIAL BACKGROUND OF GERMAN RACIAL DOCTRINES — RACIAL ANTISEMITISM	63
	6. RACIALISM IN BRITAIN	66
	7. RACIALISM OUTSIDE EUROPE	68
	8. RACIALISM AND RELATIONS WITH JAPAN . .	74

CHAP.		PAGE
III.	NATIONALITY AND LANGUAGE	78–97
	1. LANGUAGE AS A SYMBOL OF PERSONALITY	78
	2. NATIONALITY AND LANGUAGE IN ANTIQUITY AND THE MIDDLE AGES	78
	3. THE ORIGIN OF MODERN NATIONAL LANGUAGES	81
	4. LANGUAGE, ARISTOCRACY AND ENLIGHTENMENT	83
	5. THE ATTITUDE OF DEMOCRACY AND ROMANTICISM TO LANGUAGE	85
	6. LANGUAGE IN THE AGE OF NATIONALISM	87
	7. IRELAND AND HER NATIONAL LANGUAGE	89
	8. THE JEWS AND LANGUAGE	91
	9. CONFLICT OF LITERARY AND POPULAR LANGUAGE—GREECE AND NORWAY	92
	10. SCRIPT AND NATIONALITY	93
	11. SCRIPT, LANGUAGE AND NATIONALITY IN CHINA	94
	12. LANGUAGE AS A CRITERION OF NATIONALITY	95
IV.	RELIGION AND NATIONALITY	98–145
	1. RELIGION AS A SOCIAL FORCE	98
	2. JUDAISM	101
	3. THE BEGINNINGS OF CHRISTIANITY	103
	4. CHRISTIANITY FUNDAMENTAL TO MODERN FREEDOM AND NATIONALITY	104
	5. CHRISTIANITY AND NATIONAL DIVERSITIES	105
	6. THE NATIONAL CHURCHES OF THE EAST	107
	7. THE ATTITUDE OF THE GREEK AND THE ROMAN CHURCH TO NATIONALITY AND THEIR INFLUENCE ON NATIONAL CHARACTER—THE BYZANTINE EMPIRE	109
	8. THE ROMAN CHURCH AND THE ORIGIN OF NATIONALITY IN THE WEST	114
	9. THE NATIONALIZATION OF THE WESTERN CHURCH AND THE REFORMATION	117
	10. THE CHURCHES AND THE RISE OF LIBERTY	120
	11. MODERN NATIONALISM AND RELIGION	121
	12. THE INFLUENCE OF RELIGION ON THE NATIONAL CHARACTER	122
	13. THE SPIRIT OF CATHOLICISM AND ITS INFLUENCE ON NATIONAL CHARACTER IN ENGLAND, FRANCE AND GERMANY	123
	14. LUTHER AND THE GERMAN MIND	128
	15. CALVINISM AND NATIONAL CHARACTER	132
	16. THE BRITISH CHURCHES AND NATIONAL CHARACTER	133
	17. RELIGION AND THE SUPRA-NATIONAL SPIRIT	134
	18. RELIGION AND NATIONALITY IN INDIA	136
	19. ISLAM AND NATIONALITY	139

CHAP.		PAGE
V.	THE NATIONAL TERRITORY	146–206
	1. THE SIGNIFICANCE OF TERRITORY FOR A NATION	146
	2. IS A TERRITORY ESSENTIAL FOR THE CONCEPT OF A NATION? THE CASE OF THE JEWS	147
	3. HOME FEELING AND NATIONAL FEELING	149
	4. FACTORS DETERMINING THE FORMATION OF TERRITORIES	151
	5. EMPIRES AS CRADLES AND GRAVES OF NATIONS	153
	6. THE THOUSAND-YEAR STRUGGLE OVER THE HERITAGE OF CHARLEMAGNE	156
	7. THE SUPRA-NATIONAL EMPIRE OF CHARLES V	158
	8. NAPOLEON'S NATIONAL EMPIRE AND THE RISE OF MODERN NATIONALISM	162
	9. THE NATIONAL UNIFICATION OF FRANCE	165
	10. THE NATIONAL UNIFICATION OF GERMANY	168
	11. THE NATIONAL UNIFICATION OF ITALY	170
	12. THE DEVELOPMENT OF BRITISH NATIONAL UNITY	172
	13. NATIONAL PROBLEMS OF THE BRITISH EMPIRE	176
	14. THE ORIGIN OF AMERICAN NATIONALITY	182
	15. NATIONAL PROBLEMS OF INDIA	188
	16. NATIONALITY IN THE RUSSIAN EMPIRE AND THE SOVIET UNION	191
	17. NATIONALITY IN THE AUSTRIAN EMPIRE	196
VI.	THE NATIONAL STATE AND THE NATIONAL WILL AND CHARACTER .	207–250
	1. FEUDALISM AND NATIONALITY	207
	2. THE BUILDING OF NATIONAL STATES	208
	3. THE INFLUENCE OF PARLIAMENT ON NATIONAL UNITY IN ENGLAND, FRANCE AND GERMANY	211
	4. THE INFLUENCE OF WAR ON THE FORMATION OF NATIONS AND OF FUNDAMENTAL NATIONAL TRADITIONS	217
	5. THE DEVELOPMENT OF MODERN MILITARISM	223
	6. THE DEVELOPMENT OF TOTALITARIAN WAR AND ITS INFLUENCE ON POLITICS	227
	7. THE NATIONAL WILL	233
	8. NATIONAL SELF-DETERMINATION	240
	9. THE RIGHTS OF NATIONAL MINORITIES	247
VII.	THE SOCIAL BACKGROUND OF MODERN NATIONALISM	251–282
	1. OPINIONS ON THE CAUSES OF THE RISE OF NATIONALISM—THE INFLUENCE OF RULING CLASSES	251
	2. THE INFLUENCE OF CAPITALISM. WAR AND CAPITALISM	253
	3. THE RELATIONS OF NATIONALISM TO LIBERALISM, DEMOCRACY AND SOCIALISM	262
	4. RATIONAL AND IRRATIONAL FORCES IN NATIONALISM	270
	5. THE ECONOMICS OF NATIONALISM	275

CHAP.		PAGE
VIII.	POLITICAL THOUGHT AND NATIONAL IDEOLOGY	283–409
	1. THE INFLUENCE OF THOUGHT ON POLITICS	283
	2. MEDIAEVAL THOUGHT ON NATIONALITY, THE STATE, PEACE AND WAR	286
	3. NATIONALISM AND COSMOPOLITANISM IN THE TIME OF HUMANISM	292
	4. MACHIAVELLI AND ERASMUS	295
	5. HUMANISM AND NATIONALITY IN FRANCE. BODIN, POSTEL, MONTAIGNE	298
	6. HUMANISM AND NATIONALITY IN ENGLAND. BACON, SHAKESPEARE	302
	7. PURITANISM, MERCANTILISM AND NATIONALISM IN THE SEVENTEENTH CENTURY	305
	8. THE GROWTH OF PACIFISM AND INTERNATIONAL LAW	309
	9. NATIONALITY AND ENLIGHTENMENT IN ENGLAND, LOCKE, SHAFTESBURY, BOLINGBROKE	310
	10. NATIONALITY AND ENLIGHTENMENT IN FRANCE. LOUIS XIV, MONTESQUIEU, VOLTAIRE	314
	11. ROUSSEAU AND NATIONALITY	318
	12. THE FRENCH REVOLUTION AND NATIONALITY	323
	13. BURKE AND THE IDEA OF NATIONALITY	325
	14. GERMAN THOUGHT ON THE EVE OF THE FRENCH REVOLUTION AND AFTER	329
	15. FICHTE AND NATIONALITY	336
	16. HEGEL'S DOCTRINE OF THE STATE AND HIS ATTITUDE TO NATIONALITY	344
	17. ROMANTICISM AND POLITICS	353
	18. ROMANTICISM AND NATIONALITY IN GERMANY	355
	19. INDIVIDUALISM, ROMANTICISM AND NATIONALITY IN BRITAIN	362
	20. THE DEVELOPMENT OF FRENCH NATIONAL IDEOLOGY SINCE THE REVOLUTION	374
	21. MAZZINI	384
	22. GERMAN NATIONALISM IN THE NINETEENTH CENTURY	392
	23. HEINRICH VON TREITSCHKE	397
	24. PAN-GERMANISM AND RACIALISM IN TWENTIETH-CENTURY GERMANY	405
	EPILOGUE	410
	INDEX	414

NATIONALITY IN HISTORY AND POLITICS

CHAPTER I

THE STRUCTURE AND FORMS OF NATIONAL CONSCIOUSNESS

1. THE MYSTERY OF NATIONALISM

It has been remarked of certain theological controversies of the Byzantine Empire which gave rise to grave commotions that popular passions have often been roused to the highest pitch by disputes about subjects which were far beyond the understanding of the human mind, not to speak of the ordinary man. To a certain extent this could also be said of many political struggles of our time. In particular, the strongest factor in modern politics, namely, national sentiment, is also the most obscure. Nationalism has proved more powerful than any other political creed. Great empires have broken down under its assault, wars and revolutions have been started in the name of nationality which have changed the face of the world. Economic interests, morality, and religion were unable to stem the torrent, which seems to push our whole civilization towards an abyss.

Yet few people would condemn nationalism outright. English usage identifies it with national sentiment and the complete elimination of this sentiment would be widely deplored and resisted. The general view is rather that nationality and national feeling or nationalism have their value, but must be kept within bounds. In certain countries a sceptical or hostile attitude towards nationalism would indeed be regarded as little short of criminal. Nowhere, however, the average man would be able to give an adequate definition of nationalism or to state exactly where the line of demarcation between beneficial and harmful nationalism is. The most widely held view, obviously, is that nationalism means but love of the nation or people, zeal for its true interests, loyalty to the State, affection for the homeland, and that nationalism is about the same as patriotism. If this were correct it would be difficult to understand why a mere excess of love or zeal should in certain cases have led to a policy which ended in mass-slaughter of the people, and in the destruction of its wealth, civilization, and good name. Others would define nationalism as a policy actuated by national egoism, or as a mistaken, narrow-minded view of national interests. Such an interpretation again helps us little to understand the nature of nationalism. It is clear that nationalism is not merely a matter of ignorance or lack of judgement. Otherwise there would be no explanation for the fact that the rise of destructive nationalism has taken place precisely in an age of unprecedented spread of political knowledge, and that its protagonists and supporters are chiefly to be found among the highly educated classes of certain countries.

The use of the word nationalism for national sentiment, which is peculiar to English usage, and has also been adopted by many sociologists and historians, is very confusing. A significant illustration is offered by a speech by Ramsay MacDonald, then Prime Minister, on May 13, 1924. He said, according to a report in *The Times*, that his heart was with the small nations of Europe. He was a nationalist convinced and unbending. He respected national conditions and national characteristics. It would be a very bad day for the world if all the diversities of humanity created by so many different experiences of race, creed and clime were sand-papered into one feature. That was not his ideal, nor was it his ideal that they should run nationalism so hard that it became a pest to anyone trying to make peace. Nationalism was not aggression; nationalism was self-respect, and those who respected themselves best were the very best people to respect others.

MacDonald, in these words, claims to be a nationalist in a purely cultural and moral sense, wishing to preserve the national characteristics of every nation and to safeguard self-respect as a condition of mutual respect. He admits that there is also a less peace-loving mentality, that claims the name of nationalism, but this he regards as a mere exaggeration of true nationalism, and he would even deny it that name since nationalism was not aggressive. The theory of " wild nationalism " being a mere exaggeration of " mild nationalism " would, obviously, lead to the conclusion that Hitler stood essentially for the same aims as MacDonald, but that he was more radical or pursued his objects by mistaken means which could not have the desired results. Such a view certainly shows no understanding of Hitler's nationalism, and is rather apt to mislead public opinion in regard to the dangers of nationalism.

The lack of clearness, however, extends also to the concepts nation and national, and to composite words like national sentiment or consciousness, national will, national character, national self-determination, and so on. When asked what a nation is, most people would answer : A nation is a people. English usage, indeed, identifies the two terms. In a democracy, in particular, the nation is the possessor of sovereignty, the State is the machinery for implementing its will, and the Government is the management of the State appointed by the nation. In English the word national often designates something common to the whole people, for example, the national language. As the English language, furthermore, has no adjective derived from the word state, it employs national also for designating anything run or controlled by the State, such as the national debt or national health insurance. Now we even have national butter and a national loaf, i.e. a sort of butter or bread introduced by the Government in the public interest for the time of war. To nationalize a railway means that the State becomes the owner and controls it. The word national, according to this usage, easily assumes the connotation of " popular " or " democratic ". In democratic countries public opinion, therefore, has long been disposed to look favourably upon movements abroad which called themselves national. It was seldom realized that national had not everywhere abroad the same significance as at home. Parties have frequently used national as a label, for example, in compound words like National-Liberal, National-Democratic, National-Socialist.[1] It depended on the conditions of a country whether national was meant as a corroboration or a qualification of the second word. In German usage national is a much more emotional word than in English. The word nation conveys to the German mind the impression of a great, powerful and highly civilized people with its own State, and national is employed only for such lofty concepts as national honour, national unity, the national flag. The designation national butter would be impossible in Germany. For many things called national in English the German language employs other expressions, for instance, mother-tongue for national language, State-debt for national debt, the people's health for national health.

We shall show later that the word nation is also used in very different senses, and does not always simply mean the same

---

[1] That parties of the same name may stand for quite different ideals is illustrated by the fact that both Dr. Benes' party and Hitler's party called themselves National-Socialist.

as people. This divergency of usage is often rooted in the antagonism of ideologies or interests, and frequently it is due to a lack of critical sense. Even careful writers, however, are often compelled to use inaccurate terms because the public has become so used to employ the same word for different things that it would resent the introduction of new terms merely for the sake of scientific accuracy. Anyhow, the lack of a clear and stable terminology greatly contributes to the confusion of ideas. Powerful groups, moreover, have an interest in the vagueness of language, and the nationalists, in particular, must wish to maintain a certain obscurity about their aims. A frank programme of national aggression, an outspoken policy of prestige and domination, would not appeal to the broad masses of modern nations. But the assurances that nationalism means ardent love of the people, uncompromising, relentless fight for its true interests, protection against foreign aggression and intrigues, safeguarding of the national language, civilization, traditions, and customs, stressing of national unity and solidarity, subordination of particular interests to those of the whole people—these and similar assertions have always had a magic power.

The secret of the success of nationalism is that it appeals to some extent even to opponents of its aggressive aims, misleading them into fatal mistakes. Conservatives were often inclined to welcome nationalism as an ally against democracy and were convinced that they would always be able to control it. Too late they became aware that this was an illusion and that nationalism contained elements of an entirely anti-conservative, revolutionary character. Liberals frequently hailed national movements as a striving for freedom, and they were convinced that a free people would be peaceful, just and well-disposed towards other peoples. When these nations after their liberation often showed themselves intolerant and aggressive against minorities in their own territory, or aggressive against neighbours, this was ascribed by Liberals to their lack of political education and to the machinations of governments and the privileged classes. When at last the fanatical anti-liberalism of nationalism could no longer be ignored, many Liberals still consoled themselves with the delusion that all this was only transitory, or a product of economic distress and would disappear with the improvement of business and employment. Socialists usually were convinced that nationalism was a smoke-screen for capitalist interests, or a means for diverting the people from the struggle for social liberation. They believed, at any rate, that the working classes were immune against national slogans, and that the ideology of nationalism hardly required refutation. The orthodox Marxists thought that a vigorous class-war was the best remedy. The Bolsheviks, however, have also tried to make use of nationalism, especially among Asiatic peoples, by arguing that their capitalist oppressors were also their national enemies.

Can scientific research contribute to the practical solution of the terrific problems which nationalism has raised ? It is impossible to answer this question with assurance. The power of passions, prejudices and interests is so strong that the scientific elucidation of a problem of political sociology may prove ineffective for practical politics. Moreover, even scientific investigation presents great difficulties. A prominent scholar who has devoted much research to this problem, Professor Carlton Hayes, says : " What has given great vogue to nationalism in modern times ? We really do not know." [1] This confession of one of the greatest experts in this field indicates how complicated the problem is.

2. The Word " Nation " used in many Different Senses

Great confusion is caused by the fact that the word " nation " is used in many senses. Its meaning has changed in the course of time, different nations and different parties within a nation frequently do not connect the same ideas with it, and even the same politician or writer often changes its connotation according to the demand of certain interests which he defends. The concept, of course, is seldom clearly formulated and is mainly implied in practical conclusions. A critical analysis shows that a great variety of tendencies has been associated with the term " nation " and that the perplexing multitude of senses has developed through the fact that this or that element has been particularly emphasized by a specific nation, party, or philosophy. It will help to bring order into this chaos if we first indicate the principal lines of approach.

We may start with a glance at the historical development of the ideas connected with the word " nation ". The next step will be the investigation of present concepts of a nation and it will become clear that public law understands by it something

[1] Cf. Carlton Hayes, *The Historical Evolution of Modern Nationalism*, 1931, p. 302. This book gives an excellent survey of the development of ideas. Professor Hayes has also induced his pupils to investigate special problems of nationality. Among these studies is a very useful bibliography by Koppel Pinson, *Bibliographical Introduction to Nationalism*, 1935.

quite different than social psychology and sociology. There is a legal and a social concept of a nation, the first being expressed, for example, in a passport and the second in national consciousness. But what is national consciousness? Further analysis will show that it comprises four main aspirations appearing in numerous forms and combinations and closely connected with objective factors such as the national territory, language, and history. National consciousness can be defined as a striving for national personality and this raises the question of structure, i.e. the relations of a nation both to its organs such as churches, dynasties, ranks, classes or parties, and to the individuals composing the nation. It will be shown in the chapter on the " national will " that from the point of view of structure, there are four principal concepts of a nation which may be called the conservative, liberal, democratic and nationalist. A further problem consists in the demarcation of one nation from another. It is often a matter of fierce dispute between nations which criteria are in a specific case to be considered decisive for drawing frontiers, and any solution adopted implies a particular concept of a nation. Lastly, the problems of international relations have also a bearing on the question: What is a nation? The clear distinction of the various ideas of a nation is not merely of theoretical interest. If we wish to build up a system of international law securing peace we must begin with defining as clearly as possible the terms with which international law has to operate.

The word " nation " has a long history.[1] In former times the chieftain of an Irish clan was called " captain of his nation " and it was usual to speak of " savage nations ".[2] Gradually,

---

[1] Originally *natio* meant a backward, exotic tribe, approximately what we describe as natives, which comes from the same root. *Nationes ferae* (Sallust), *natio servituti nata* (Cicero), *innumerabiles et ferocissimae nationes* (Hieronymus). Varro uses *natio* for a breed of cattle. Great civilized peoples were called *gens*, and the Roman people as the bearer of sovereignty called itself *populus*. In the Vulgate *natio* and *gens* means the Gentiles, while the chosen people is the *populus*. In the Middle Ages English writers designate the English people usually as *gens Anglorum*, and it seems exceptional when Matthew Paris speaks of the English as a nation with a patriotic accent. Roger of Wendover calls the Scots and the Welsh barbarian nations and describes the troops of the Emperor Frederick I as *cohortes diversarum nationum*. Bracton uses *gens* for a great people while he speaks of *tribus* and *nationes* as subject to the judgement of lawyers. For German usage, compare, for example, Albertus Magnus, Theutonicus, nacione Suevus. In universities the students were divided in nationes which formed autonomous corporations. The divisions did not correspond to our present nations. *Natio* meant rather a certain tribal territory within the present boundaries of nations, characterized by common dialect, customs, etc. In the first centuries after the Middle Ages the word " nation " was used in Germany and France for designating the higher, ruling classes in opposition to the *Volk* or *peuple*, which corresponded to the English word " populace " or " common people ".

[2] This usage is sometimes found also in modern writers; cf. W. Bagehot, *Physics and Politics*, 1872, pp. 100, 106; W. H. Rivers, *Social Organisation*, 1924, p. 32.

however, the word became associated with the idea of power and sovereignty, the ruling classes were called "the nation" and at last nation meant a free, self-governing people.[1] Sometimes it was also used in the sense of a great, highly civilized or powerful people. Mazzini understood by nation a people with a mission, and spoke of the ascent of a people to the capacity and dignity of a nation.

A very widespread modern usage identifies a nation with a people constituted as a state. In this view every state forms a nation and every citizen is a member of the nation. This definition, of course, is an exclusively legal one, and like many other declarations of legal equality disregards factual inequalities. Many states were or are composed of different nations or nationalities. The Scots and Welsh regard themselves as nations, though they live in a common state with the English. In the former Austro-Hungarian Empire twelve nationalities were living together. Loyalty to the Empire and to the constituent states and countries and patriotic emotions were not lacking, but nobody would ever have spoken of an Austro-Hungarian or of an Austrian nation. In some cases the word "nation" was used for the people of a homogeneous state or for the ruling people, while "nationality" designated a national minority. It is important, however, to realize that legal and social nationality form entirely different ideas. An individual may legally belong to a nation which he fiercely hates or which does not regard him as a true national. This is particularly the case in states where an ethnical section of the people has a dominant position while the rest is more or less "oppressed". The moving force in modern history, however, is not the legal concept of nationality but the social force of national consciousness.

Most definitions of a nation take exclusively account of the criteria demarcating it from other nations, such as language, civilization, religion, race, historical rights, natural frontiers or economic interests. As a rule, the claim of a nation to a specific territory is founded on several arguments. It often happens, for example, that the criteria of language, civilization and religion coincide in a given territory. But none of them is absolutely indispensable for constituting a nation. A nation may speak several languages or comprise several religions, and the same

---

[1] When the Irish Parliament was restored in 1782 Grattan said: "I am now to address a free people.—Ireland is now a nation." Cf. Alice St. Green, *Irish Nationality*, p. 208. In 1757 Chesterfield said: "We are undone at home and abroad. The French are masters to do what they please in America. We are no longer a nation". The latter statement implies that prestige is the essential criterion of a nation.

language or religion may be found in different nations. In many cases each of several nations struggling for the possession of a territory founded its claim on different criteria of nationality, one, for example, on language, others on civilization or historical rights or security, and so on. Sometimes the spokesmen of a nation also put forward criteria incompatible with one another, for example, in one case stressing the argument of historical rights, and in another case rejecting it, namely, when it would have favoured the claim of a rival nation.

In opposition to those objective criteria the subjective fact of the wish of the people concerned is often declared to be decisive and a plebiscite is considered the best way of ascertaining that wish. But the result of a plebiscite largely depends on the fact how the territory in which it takes place has been demarcated.

International law recognizes nations alone as subjects possessing certain rights and, in particular, the right of national self-determination is exclusively open to nations. Primitive tribes or sections of a nation have no claim to it. Not every people is eligible for membership in the League of Nations, but only those recognized as nations, and this recognition depends on the assent of a qualified majority of the assembly. These examples show that the question of how to define a nation forms also a problem of international status.

A satisfactory idea of a nation must obviously take account of its various aspects. The fundamental issue is that of national consciousness. Without a sufficient measure of this consciousness there is no nation, but whether a specific people possesses this measure is often very difficult to decide. Further aspects are those of internal structure, external demarcation, and international status. These aspects, moreover, are to some extent interdependent. The four fundamental national aspirations correspond to the four theories of national structure, and these have their counterparts in the field of external demarcation and international relations.

3. The Aspects of Nationality and the Methods of its Study

The study of nationality must begin with agreement about a clear terminology. If we cannot always use a separate word for a specific idea it must at least be clear from the context in which sense the word is used. The phenomena which we are going to examine are partly objective or external facts like the national language, territory, state, civilization and history, partly subjective, or internal facts like national consciousness or sentiment. The external facts, of course, can be ascertained with a much greater degree of accuracy than the internal. One can explore the growth and the rules of a national language or the institutions of a national State with considerable exactness, and without interrogating members of that nation which may be an extinct one as the old Romans or Greeks. National consciousness or national sentiment, however, is an exceedingly elusive thing. Its manifestations can be studied in political literature, public speeches or national institutions, but the interpretation of such documents or objects in regard to the underlying national spirit is always more or less insecure. The interrogation of numerous individuals belonging to the nation in question about their national feelings or ideas would be very difficult and the results would be disappointing.[1] Legal nationality, cultural nationality, and the status of a people according to international practice can easily be ascertained. But political nationality is a very complicated matter as it depends on a sufficient degree of national consciousness which cannot be observed and measured by exact methods.

The elaboration of an adequate terminology requires an analysis of national consciousness, which has a complicated psychological structure and shows many historical and social varieties. Therefore we must not restrict our analysis to phenomena of our time and country, but must try to extend it to many times and peoples. Neither must we rely too much on our psychological intuition, and try to explain complex processes in the handy terms of inborn instincts, or indulge in fanciful constructions according to popular theories which claim to offer in a few formulas the master-key to the human mind. It would be equally misleading to embark on sociological generalizations before a careful study of a wide field of history. The historical study of nationality, however, is beset with peculiar difficulties. Since

[1] In States composed of different nationalities it is a difficult statistical problem to count their numbers. The question : To which nationality do you belong ? is inexpedient because many people would either understand nationality in the sense of citizenship, or could not answer it because they are between two nations (e.g. persons of mixed origin, speaking both languages, and having no preference for one nationality). In the former Austro-Hungarian Empire, therefore, the question was put which language a person used in daily intercourse. This solution was often criticized on the ground that the collectors of the statistical forms sometimes abused their position in the interest of their own nationality by altering the entries. Nevertheless, the solution was probably the best possible. The essential correctness of the Austrian statistics was later confirmed by the statistics taken in the Succession-States.

terms like nation, nationality, national sentiment, admit of different interpretations, it is not always clear which track the historian should follow. As a rule each historian selected those facts as relevant which accorded best with his own idea of nationality. The result was a one-sided picture which often disguised a political ideology.

Liberal historians who conceived nationhood as the status of a free, independent, sovereign people, and nationality mainly as a striving for political liberty, tried to solve the problem by describing the rise of freedom in nations and the liberation of nations from foreign domination. It is true that these strivings have been of the greatest importance for the growth of nationality. Yet this is only one of the aspects of the problem. We are faced to-day with a form of nationalism which denies all freedom both to its own people and to others, and according to the Liberal concept it would appear that a people ceases to be a nation under a totalitarian dictatorship. Other writers have seen the essential characteristic of nationhood in a wide and firm unity, comprising especially all peoples speaking the same language. They would deny, therefore, that small peoples, or peoples of the same tongue but living in separate states, such as the Greek city states, may be called nations. From this point of view the historian has to follow the formation of a strong central power and the amalgamation of small states into a big one. The prussianizing school of historiography tended to give the impression that there was hardly a German nationality before the Hohenzollerns created National Unity through their military power-state, and Bismarck imposed it upon the whole of Germany. Frederick " the Great " and many other princes who did their best to destroy the unity and strength of the old Empire, and who allowed large sections of the German people to fall under foreign domination in order to obtain foreign support for their own aggrandizement, appear in these histories as national heroes. But also many democratic historians regarded unity as the most important aim of national aspirations and believed that territorial centralization was necessary for social unification. This was the reason why the French Revolution abolished the historic provinces.

The Romanticists and traditionalists regarded a distinctive and original national character as the most important element of nationality. They believed that mediaeval institutions, popular customs, and old traditions contained the wisdom of the forefathers and expressed the true soul of the people. This concept of nationality inspired many writers, and among them eminent scholars, to interpret the history of civilization of their nation in the light of their idea of the national character. They tried to show that the whole history of the people was actuated by the same spiritual forces. Most of these constructions could not stand the test of historical criticism, and the whole concept of the national character has been discredited by these romantic phantasies. Still other writers saw the essential features of nationality in national power, honour and pride, and in hostility towards other nations. Most historians, however, followed no clear line in treating nationality. As a rule they touched upon it incidentally, using symptomatic illustrations which were often of doubtful significance. Others followed not the growth and spread of national consciousness in the mind of the people but the ideas of philosophers and political writers on what a nation, its ideals, and character should be.

Before the historian starts to describe the growth of nationality he must have a clear and comprehensive idea of its structure. The elaboration of such an analysis is the task of the social psychologist who, however, to a certain degree, must also take account of historical experience. This would lead to a vicious circle, only to be avoided by adopting a provisional working hypothesis which must then be tested by historical research and modified in its light.

The study of national sentiment and aspirations cannot be separated from that of supra-national or international ones.[1] In all the great thinkers and statesmen who have pondered these problems, both strands of thought are mingled and intertwined. If one of them only were taken account of this would give a one-sided and misleading picture.

4. Proposed Definitions of a Nation—their Inadequacy

Most writers who attempted to define the concept of a nation have pointed out objective factors as the decisive criteria, i.e. factors independent of the will of individuals. The most frequent and obvious criterion is language. Others have stressed the importance of race, religion, civilization, territory, or citizenship in a State. All definitions, however, based exclusively on one or several of these factors, are inadequate. None of them fits all cases of recognized nations and none explains the typical aspira-

---

[1] We prefer the word supra-national both to international, which is more frequently used but has a different meaning, and to supernational, which could also be misunderstood as excessively national.

tions called national. All these objectivist theories, moreover, were often used by nationalists for justifying annexations without consulting the people which they wished to annex.

The obvious inadequacy of all objectivist theories has induced many political theorists to define nationality as a community formed by the will to be a nation. This subjectivist view corresponded to the striving of Liberals for freedom and to the democratic concept of a popular will expressed by the majority. Amongst others, John Stuart Mill (1861) saw the essence of nationality in the mutual sympathy of its adherents and in their desire to be united under a government of their own, produced through a community of history and politics and through feelings of pride and shame, joy and grief connected with experiences of the past.[1] Ernest Renan expatiated upon the same idea in a famous lecture in 1882.[2] It is not race, religion, language, State, civilization or economic interests, he said, that make a nation. The national idea is founded on a heroic past, great men, true glory. Common experiences lead to the formation of a community of will. More than anything else it is common grief that binds a nation together, more than triumphs. A nation, therefore, is a great solidarity founded on the consciousness of sacrifices made in the past and on willingness to make further ones in the future. The existence of a nation resembles a plebiscite repeated every day. Renan's view was in accordance with the principle of self-determination proclaimed by the Revolution. Moreover, this was also the decisive argument of the French nation in demanding the return of Alsace-Lorraine to France. For this very reason the spokesmen of victorious Germany scornfully rejected it.

The subjectivist definition of a nation is essentially correct, but it needs a careful formulation. National aspirations are neither always, nor merely, a striving to be united under a national government, nor do they always imply the cult of traditions. The Scotch and the Welsh, for example, claim to be nations, though they do not aim at independent national governments. The Soviet republics and the Turks of to-day have broken with fundamental traditions of their past. If Mill saw the nature of nationality chiefly in the mutual sympathy of its members, he overestimated one of its elements. True, people of the same language, religion, education, colour, etc., find it easier to develop mutual sympathy than others. But the

[1] J. S. Mill, *Considerations on Representative Government*, 1861, p. 287.
[2] Ernest Renan, *Qu'est-ce qu'une nation ?* 1882.

motive power of a national movement is not so much sympathy for the individual members of the nation as devotion to the same aims. The arch-nationalist of our days, Adolf Hitler, in his book *My Struggle* does not conceal his profound contempt for the masses of his own people. His seizure of power was followed by the introduction of a system of the most ruthless terrorism and intimidation against all those Germans who were not in agreement with Nazi policy, and who at that time certainly formed the majority of the German people. It may be that nationalists aim at uniting the whole people in fraternal love, but surely their methods are often such as those described in a German couplet : *Und willst Du nicht mein Bruder sein, so schlag ich Dir den Schaedel ein* (If my brother you will not be, your skull shall soon be smashed by me). Modern nations, however, have to a large extent really been brought together by this method.

If the subjectivist theory stresses the will to be a nation, it is usually not explicit enough about the meaning of will and the meaning of nation. Will is often conceived in a too rational way. It is not so much a clear outspoken will which actually lives in a whole people but a multitude of feelings and vague ideas, animating a large and influential part of the people, that tend to crystallize in a will in certain conditions. In the history of national development, moreover, this will was at first only that of a minority which in the course of time succeeded in gaining more or less the assent of a majority. In firmly consolidated nations everybody knows to which nation he belongs ; but if a people has not yet reached this stage, or if an old loyalty has been destroyed by historic events, there is no spontaneous national will but merely a welter of conflicting aspirations. The subjectivist theory, moreover, needs to be supplemented by allowance for objective factors, among which the national territory at least is indispensable. A community without a territory is not a full nation though it may possess unity, solidarity, mutual sympathy and the wish to live under a government of its own. A Church or a party shows these traits too. There are even communities with a territory which are not nations such as a city or a county.

The subjectivist theory must not be stretched so far as to obliterate the significance of the objective factors. The mere will does not yet make a nation. A nation cannot be founded like a company or a club. It is a community of fate, to a large extent brought together and moulded by historical events and natural factors, and the individual has practically little opportunity of choosing his nationality or changing its fundamental traits. An emigrant may legally give up the citizenship of his native country and after some time acquire that of the country where he has founded a new home. But this is not enough for being a real member of the nation. He must also assimilate its social outlook and its national traditions, and even if he, or his children, succeed in this task, it is not yet sure whether they will be accepted by the national community as real nationals.[1] Jews have been living in Germany for a very long time—in some parts even for a thousand or perhaps two thousand years; they have made a tremendous contribution to German civilization, and most of them were completely assimilated. Nevertheless, the present Nazi regime has branded them as aliens and treated them as outcasts.[1]

What is primarily wanted as a starting-point for our study is a clear notion of the spirit of nationality. It does not take us much farther if we hear that this spirit is inherent in a nation and rooted in its traditions, and that nationality consists in the will to be a nation. This no more explains the specific nature of the community called a nation than the community of a Church is explained by the will to belong to it.

An attempt to formulate the spirit of nationality has recently been made by Arnold Toynbee.[2] He defines it as "a spirit which makes people feel and act and think about a part of any given society as though it were the whole of that society". This definition contains a great truth, but it seems rather vague. One can feel and act and think about society in many different ways, of which some have nothing to do with nationality, or are even opposed to it. Moreover, many views are possible about what forms a whole and what a part. Some people will think that mankind is the whole, others may regard a race, or a nation, or a civilization, or a religious community, or a class as the whole. If we accept a civilization as the whole (which is Toynbee's view), the further question arises how to define and delimit this term. Have all civilized nations of to-day essentially the same civilization, or is there, for example, a

[1] The problems of assimilation and naturalization would demand a careful comparative treatment which is outside the scope of this book. Cf. a collection of Nationality Laws of various countries edited by R. Flournoy and Manley Hudson (Publication of Carnegie Endowment for International Peace), 1929. This endowment has also published Americanization Studies, ed. by Allen Burns (10 vols., 1920–4). In the course of this war enormous migrations have taken place and others will follow. A part of the migrants will probably remain in their new countries and the problem of naturalization and national integration will be of great importance.

[2] A. Toynbee, *A Study of History*, vol. vi, p. 407. This great work contributes much to the study of nationalism, though Toynbee seldom uses the word, and rather calls it parochialism.

distinct English, French, Japanese, North-American one? Does Hitler's "New Order" belong to the same civilization as the ideals for which England is fighting?

The well-known psychologist, Professor William MacDougall, finds it hardly possible to give a definition that is applicable to all nations.[1] He prefers, therefore, to describe the ideal type of a nation which combines all the attributes of nationhood to a high degree, and then to class each nation according to its approximation to this ideal. We need not enter into a discussion of the subjective and objective traits which he describes. His idea that nationality is a complex structure and a matter of degree is certainly true. Max Weber has shown that the method of drawing an ideal type is a better way of investigating complicated social structures than the usual sort of definitions.[2] MacDougall's attempt, however, demands a qualification. Neither an abstract unhistorical definition nor an ideal type of a nation, assembled of traits observed in different nations, leads to a deeper psychological understanding of national dynamics. No static definition can explain concrete, historical, dynamic facts like national sentiment, the national character or nationalism. It seems to us more fruitful, therefore, to start with describing the dynamic factor of national consciousness as observable in typical modern nations, and then to define a nation as a people possessing national consciousness which, of course, is also a matter of degree.

5. Analysis of National Consciousness

(a) The Problem of Collective Mentality

National consciousness is a specific kind of group consciousness, or group solidarity, which constitutes a bond between the members of a group in regard to the pursuit of certain aims. It is of a very complex structure, embracing many strands and variations, extending from a subconscious, latent state of mind to a clear-cut ideology. It greatly varies both in nations and in individuals, and the definition that nations possess it does not mean that all individuals belonging to a nation have it to a large degree, or at all.

The psychology of groups is a much-disputed problem. Sociologists and psychologists have developed many theories about the

---

[1] Cf. W. MacDougall, *The American Nation, Its Problems and Psychology*, 1925, p. 4.
[2] Cf. Max Weber, *Wirtschaft und Gesellschaft*, 1922, pp. 3, 10.

relations between individual and collective mentality.[1] We need not discuss the more general questions here as this would lead too far from our immediate subject. It is clear that instincts or quasi-instincts [2] play a great rôle in forming and actuating social groups, though in the shape of complex combinations. Some writers, like Giddings, MacDougall and Trotter, assume that group consciousness or gregariousness itself is an instinct. Many psychologists have attributed a more or less instinctive character to certain types of behaviour which are of great importance in forming groups, such as the impulse to imitate actions of a multitude, liability to suggestion, sympathy, pugnacity, self-assertion, self-subordination. A large literature has been produced about mass psychology, i.e. the behaviour of individuals under the influence of a crowd to which they belong.[3] It is widely agreed that unorganized crowds, and to a lesser degree even organized ones, show an increase of suggestibility, emotions, impulsiveness, and a decrease of reasonableness, responsibility, inhibitions. A nation, of course, is not a fortuitous crowd such as gathers on a square and listens to a speaker. It is a highly organized society, of great extension in time and space. Nevertheless, Hitler's success in seizing power demonstrates that even a great civilized nation can be degraded to a mob by skilful use of all technical means of propaganda for arousing latent instincts.[4]

Nationalists often regard national sentiment as a natural instinct which needs no explanation or justification, and they look upon people lacking it, or rather lacking the nationalist brand of it, as perverse, degenerate creatures.[5] Liberals sometimes rather optimistically assume that true national sentiment

[1] Cf. especially M. Ginsberg, *Psychology of Society*, 1933 ; W. MacDougall, *The Group Mind*, 1920 ; F. Giddings, *Principles of Sociology* (first published 1896) ; L. Geck, *Socialpsychologie im Ausland*, 1928 ; *Socialpsychologie in Deutschland*, 1921 (very useful surveys of many theories) ; G. Tarde, *Les Lois de l'Imitation*, 1890, *Les Lois sociales*, 1898 ; W. Bagehot, *Physics and Politics*, 1872 ; W. Trotter, *Instincts of the Herd in Peace and War*, 12th ed., 1940.
[2] The word instinct is not used here in a strict sense. It is even doubtful whether higher animals are moved by true instincts. Cf. Johannes Loeser, *Animal Behaviour*, 1940.
[3] The best known, though not the first, exponent of this doctrine was G. Le Bon, *Psychologie des foules*, 1892. For criticism, cf. Geck (2), p. 32, Ginsberg, p. 128, and W. Pillsbury, *Psychology of Nationality and Internationalism*, 1919, p. 164.
[4] The theories of Le Bon and other writers on mass-psychology obviously tended to discredit democratic movements, and have doubtless contributed to the development of the ideologies of Fascism and Hitlerism. Many traits of these totalitarian systems, however, show the closest possible parallels to Le Bon's descriptions, for example, the hypnotization of the masses by the leader and the suppression of intelligence and morality by mass emotions.
[5] A well-known German psychologist, Professor E. Jaensch, has written a voluminous book developing this thesis. He employs the most modern apparatus of psychological research for demonstrating that everybody who is not a Nazi is a degenerate. Cf. E. Jaensch, *Der Gegentypus*, 1938.

is of the same nature as our feelings to our family, which certainly contain a considerable instinctive element. Freud thinks that group sentiment in general is the product of *libido*, the instinct of love in a wide sense, focused on the leader.[1] As regards national sentiment, however, many writers believe that it is chiefly rooted in the striving for power and prestige and in pugnacity.[2]

That the motives of human groups are to some extent offshoots of a gregarious instinct is made probable by the example of many animals living in herds or groups. Gregariousness consists not only in associating with others but also in excluding outsiders, and this tendency often leads to conflicts without any other motive than group feeling. Many animals live in closed societies.[3] A stranger, though of the same species, getting somehow among a group, is attacked, roughly treated or killed. If the new-comer survives he may after some time be admitted to the group. This behaviour is not due to any racial aversion springing from the difference of kind. Sometimes, for example, in mixed colonies of ants, different species may be citizens of the same state, and hold together through thick and thin against non-citizens. Animals also conclude friendships with others of quite different species and kinds, and with men. Neither can hostility against strangers always be explained as rivalry for food or as sexual jealousy. Sometimes the behaviour rather suggests a will to dominate and pugnacity. Certain dogs may live in concord with cats and other animals in the same house but attack every dog passing near the house, while they are much less quarrelsome far away from the house.

Life in herds seems to increase pugnacity. Herds or groups often have a sentiment of owning a certain territory upon which foreigners must not trespass. In Oriental cities every street and alley has its own pack of half-wild dogs which never leave it. If one of these dogs enters a strange alley, the dogs domiciled there fall upon the stranger and tear it to pieces unless it saves itself by speedy flight. One could see in this behaviour the beginnings of nationalism. In some animal societies an individual is recognized as the leader, and enjoys special authority.[4]

[1] Cf. Sigmund Freud, *Massenpsychologie und Ich-Analyse*, 1923.
[2] This theory has been excellently stated by Professor Walter Sulzbach in an article " Begriff und Wesen der Nation ", published in the *Dioskuren. Jahrbuch für Geisteswissenschaften*, vol. ii, 1923, pp. 128-59, and in his book *Nationales Gemeinschaftsgefühl und wirtschaftliches Interesse*, 1929.
[3] Cf. Fr. Alverdes, *Social Life in the Animal World*, 1927, p. 107.
[4] I remember having read an article in a German zoological paper in which a scientist described with enthusiasm the wonderful sense of leadership and loyalty to the leader which he had observed among certain animals in Central Asia. It read like a

Sometimes even a sort of hierarchy or an order of precedence exists which accords the superiors certain privileges.[1] Individuals are more active, energetic and daring when acting together with their fellows, but they are also subject to suggestion and panic. When separated from the group some animals ail and die. It would be wrong, however, to generalize the pugnacious instincts. Instances of indifference, friendship, or mutual help are frequent.[2] Likewise we must not assume that primitive men are usually warlike and savage. Many of them seem to be comparatively peaceable.

(b) Human Groups Actuated by Traditions, Interests and Ideals

In spite of these parallels between the behaviour of human and animal groups the instinctive factor actuating human groups must not be exaggerated. Not even animals are moved merely by instinct. Human groups are mainly kept together and actuated by three types of motives, namely traditions, interests and ideals. Traditions are patterns of behaviour which are regarded as values simply because they are a collective heritage regardless of any reasons of utility, beauty or supernatural sanction. A nation clings to its language even if it would have more economic profit and cultural stimulation by adopting another language which opens access to a greater literature and is much more widely spread. An interest is an aim regarded as useful to the existence and well-being of the group, such as everything conducive to safety, health, wealth, mental or bodily fitness. What is considered a national interest, however, largely depends on the national ideology, which varies according to country and age. An ideal is an aim which is not a direct interest of individuals. It is regarded as possessing a high authority, and thereby has the power to command obedience and the sacrifice of individual interests. Traditions, interests and ideals form a complicated framework. The traditions connect a nation with its past, the interests with its present, the ideals with its future. In most cases, however, they are not strictly separated but form parts of a psychological structure. The idea of the national territory,

---

homage to the leader of the German people, though there may have been some irony in it as the animals described were wild asses.

[1] Among hens some enjoy the respect of others because they show a certain aggressive disposition, and easily peck the more timid ones. Experiments have proved that this was due to the larger share of male hormone in them. Cf. H. Munro Fox, *The Personality of Animals*, 1940, p. 102. It would be interesting to know whether human aggressiveness has a similar cause. Hitler, anyhow, does not seem to have too much male hormone.

[2] Cf. Peter Kropotkin, *Mutual Aid*, 1908 (tr. from Russian).

for instance, combines all three elements. The territory is regarded as a heritage of the national past, and is the basis for the whole present existence of the nation, while its further development forms an ideal in the future.

The traditions, interests and ideals predominant in a nation are often called the national character. Some of them are directly related to the idea of the nation and these form the national ideology and the national aspirations. They are differentiated according to localities, social classes, religions and parties, and each section has its particular traditions, interests and ideals, though many elements are common to all. The regional, local, social and denominational peculiarities within a nation are often so strong that they might menace national unity and lead to the development of various types of particularism. But the national ideology tends to decrease differences and even to utilize sectional interests for its purposes. The broad masses of the people, for example, have little knowledge of the national history and civilization,[1] but they cling to their language, religion, customs and local traditions. The national ideology, therefore, tries on the one hand to spread the cult of national heroes and pride in national exploits, and on the other to give a national significance to local or sectional facts such as old customs, popular ballads, folk dances, etc. In Germany, for example, King Frederick II of Prussia, was by means of intense propaganda elevated to the unique position of Frederick the Great. To the non-Prussians he was represented as the pioneer of German nationality, to the Protestants as the champion of Protestantism, to Catholics and free-thinkers as the herald of toleration, to the intellectuals as the philosopher-king, to the soldiers as the ideal warrior, to the people as the friend of the common man. The national ideology consists of numerous legends which appeal to the specific mentality of every section of the nation. Its instruments are the schools, literature, art, music, the press, festivals, emblems, and so on.

Every national ideology has made great use of two types of myths, that of the noble descent of the nation and that of its great mission.[2] It is doubtful whether there ever was a people which did not claim a particularly noble origin, at least at a certain epoch of its evolution. Even rather primitive peoples

---

[1] Some years before the last war educational tests were taken on recruits for the French and German armies. In France they were asked, for example : Who was Joan of Arc ? and in Germany : Who was Bismarck ? Very few had any idea.

[2] Many examples of the myths of noble origin and the great mission of nations are given by Robert Michels, *Der Patriotismus, Prolegomena zu einer soziologischen Analyse*, 1929.

harboured this belief, they often designated themselves alone as " men " and other peoples with a derogatory name, or they traced their origin to gods or semi-divine eponymous heroes. The old Teutons claimed to descend from Mannus, the son of the god Tuisco, who had been born out of the earth. The Athenians too were so proud of their autochthonism that Antisthenes compared them to the slugs which were also earth-born. In the Middle Ages the ruling class, believed to descend from Trojan heroes and the Franks, were traced back to Francion, a supposed son of Hector. The part played by the idea of race in modern nationalism is generally known. The idea of a Divine mission entrusted to a chosen people forms the backbone of the history of the Israelites as told in the Bible. But they were by no means the only people who were taught that they were endowed with a mission from God. All great nations, and even small ones, have at certain times cherished the idea of having been chosen by God for a special task.

The counterpart to beliefs exalting the excellence of one's own nation are the national prejudices tending to discredit other nations. National prejudice is so widespread and difficult to suppress that probably very few people are quite free from it. If one looks through great collections of proverbs and popular sayings one finds countless curious beliefs about other peoples or certain parts of the same people.[1] Most of them are prejudices or taunts for alleged peculiarities. It is interesting to find that many of the present ideas of the characteristics of certain people are very old, and this fosters the fallacy of a racial character.[2] Other views have greatly changed in the course of time. Fre-

---

[1] Cf. for example, Vincent St. Lean, *Collections of Proverbs*, etc., vol. i, 1902 ; D. E. Marvin, *Curiosities in Proverbs*, 1916, p. 237 ; M. Plaut, *Deutsches Land und Volk im Volksmund*, 1897 (contains also many judgements on other nations) ; W. Wachsmuth, *Geschichte der deutschen Nationalität*, 1860, i, p. 126 ; H. Floerke, *Deutsches Wesen im Spiegel der Zeiten*, 1916. Since Bacon remarked that the genius, wit and spirit of a nation could be discovered in its proverbs, numerous attempts have been made to follow this track. The results, however, have been disappointing. Cf. A. Taylor, *The Proverb*, 1931, p. 164.

[2] It is of great interest to study the development of views which a people holds of another people, and to trace the origin of prejudices. For views of foreigners on England, cf. Malcolm Letts, *As the Foreigner saw Us*, 1935 ; Edward Smith, *Foreign Visitors in England*, 1889 ; the bibliography, " Travellers Descriptions of Great Britain ", in the Bulletin of the British Library of Political Science, Nov. 1921 ; Georges Ascoli, *La Grande Bretagne devant l'opinion Française depuis la guerre de Cent Ans jusqu'àla fin du 16. siècle*, 1927. Opinions of the English on the Germans are compiled in Willi Radczun, *Das Englische Urteil uber die Deutschen bis zur Mitte des 17. Jahrhunderts 1933*. The views of mediaeval French of the Germans were treated by Fritz Kern in the *Historische Zeitschrift*, vol. 108, 1912. German views of the English from the sixteenth to the nineteenth century are surveyed by Franz Muncker, " Anschauungen vom englischen Staat und Volk ", in *Sitzungsberichte der Bayerischen Akademie der Wissenschaften Phil. Kl.*, 1918, 1925.

quently historical events have given rise to opinions of certain peoples and these were generalized and survived as traditions. Prejudices tend to strengthen national pride and may have an influence on national solidarity. Professor Pillsbury says that in the U.S.A. national prejudice is one of the strongest forces compelling the foreigner to assimilate.[1]

(c) *The Four National Aspirations, their Forms and Antinomies*

National aspirations are composed of four elements, namely :

(1) The striving for national unity comprising political, economic, social, religious, and cultural unity, community and solidarity.

(2) The striving for national freedom, which comprises independence from foreign domination or interference, and internal freedom from forces regarded as un-national or derogatory to the nation.

(3) The striving for separateness, distinctiveness, individuality, originality, or peculiarity. The most significant example is the value attributed to a separate national language.

(4) The striving for distinction among nations, for honour, dignity, prestige and influence, which easily becomes a striving for domination. The striving for distinction is, probably, the strongest of all four aspirations, and seems to underlie them all.

An important factor in nationality is also the striving for a certain measure of equality within the nation. Equality is indispensable for unity and liberty and is implied in these aims. There cannot be any real unity and solidarity between masters and slaves, a highly privileged class and downtrodden serfs. The creed of the French revolution, expressed in the words " Liberty, Equality, Fraternity ", summarized essential elements of national aspirations.

National consciousness consists in the combined striving for unity, liberty, individuality and prestige. The concrete aims of these aspirations have shown many historical changes. The Reformation implied a national striving for liberty and individuality, but soon religious and political unity became the paramount national aim. Then political freedom, cultural emancipation, economic independence and social equality became the aim of national movements. The various national aspirations were often conflicting and thwarted each other. Too much national liberty has often resulted in the weakening of national unity, or

---

[1] Cf. W. Pillsbury, *Psychology of Nationality*, 1919, p. 140. On the rôle of ideals in forming a nation, cf. Pillsbury, pp. 224, 246.

in the complete loss of independence. National unity and equality were exaggerated to such a degree that liberty was wiped out, and the nation was degraded to a mere machine producing power. National separateness or prestige have frequently been stretched so far that liberty and unity were jeopardized or destroyed. History shows that many national movements have defeated their own aims and have become destructive for the nations concerned. Nationality is full of latent antinomies, i.e. possible conflicts between its principles. The religious revolution of the sixteenth century aimed at liberty, but in a large part of Europe it led to great intolerance and the rise of despotism, and the religious wars almost destroyed national unity. The French Revolution overthrew absolutism, but soon anarchy paved the way for the despotism of Napoleon and the rise of nationalism. In our time the antinomian tendency inherent in nationality has expressed itself in the policy of isolationism which corresponded to the principle of absolute national independence but resulted in the total loss of independence of many nations.

Besides the general spirit of an age, the ideology of every nation has given a special sense to the principles implied in nationality. The meaning of political liberty, for example, was not always and everywhere the same. Modern German nationalists deny that England and France have anything like real freedom. In their eyes only the Germans are a free nation, and their ideology teaches the dogma that real freedom means submission to the leader. Hitler boasts of having restored German freedom, though the rest of the world is inclined to call the state of the German people slavery. The ideas of originality and prestige too have shown the greatest variations. In some nations it is assumed that national individuality is compatible with the fundamental unity of morality, just as individuals may show differences of character and education and still recognize certain common standards of conduct. Some German romanticists, however, have contended that each nation has quite different ideals, even in morality, and modern nationalists have alleged the innate, indelible and fundamental racial diversity of nations. The spokesmen of many nations believe that the national prestige depends on their social and cultural achievements, on their success in establishing a peaceful and progressive system of government, while others cannot conceive of any other prestige than that of power and domination. In former times the Germans were proud of being called by foreign students of their civilization the people of poets and thinkers, while now the children in Nazi schools are being taught that a regiment of good soldiers is much more important than a Goethe.

National consciousness is very fluid and appears in the most various forms and degrees. It is not the same or equally strong in all members of a nation. Many have very little of it or none at all, at least in normal times, though it may be latent in them and only break forth in a time of national emergency under the impact of a great wave of national emotion. It is mainly certain sections of a nation which cultivate national aspirations, and which are more or less recognized as national leaders and spokesmen. Sometimes they have even claimed to be the nation. Those sections, however, which are not consciously " national ", or are even opposed to every sort of pronounced national sentiment, are bound by numerous invisible bonds to the nation. Without knowing it they are imbued with the elements of the national ideology. Marxism taught that the proletarian had no fatherland and that the workers of all countries were to unite and put an end to wars, exploitation and oppression all over the world. National sentiment was declared to be a mere screen for capitalistic interests, designed to divert the workers from the struggle against their real enemies, the capitalists. The socialists of all countries were quite sincere in their internationalism. Nevertheless, many of them were unable to resist a sudden surge of national sentiment. In 1911 Italy undertook a war for the conquest of Libya, actuated merely by lust of prestige and aggrandisement. The war was very popular, even on the Left, and some Italian socialists like Labriola glorified Italy's mission to spread her civilization.[1] In 1914 the German Government plunged the world into war and attributed its outbreak to a treacherous attack by Russia. The German Social-Democrats were completely swept off their feet and voted the war credits demanded by the government. A national ideology tends to enmesh a whole nation in a gigantic network which is hardly noticed before a crisis stirs up national sentiment. However, national consciousness is not necessarily of the aggressive type. Many nations have developed a thoroughly peaceable form of it.

National consciousness constitutes a nation in the political sense. A nation is best defined as a people possessing a developed national consciousness, though it is often very difficult to say whether a people has a sufficient measure of it for nationhood and whether the four elements of nationality are so shaped and poised that they will not destroy one another and that the nation

[1] Cf. Benedetto Croce, *History of Italy*, 1929, pp. 259, 263.

has a chance of living. The mere fact that a people has a certain degree of civilization or has produced great men is not enough. The decisive criterion is whether there is sufficient solidarity among them, whether the idea of a duty to sacrifice particular interests to the national has become dominant in the people. The modern idea of a nation implies the duty of unlimited solidarity, of unconditional loyalty overriding sectional and individual interests. Religion, morality and international law, of course, demand that the policy of a nation should keep within certain bounds and that loyalty to the nation should not transgress them. Democracy, moreover, puts the power of deciding what the national interest is into the hands of a majority of nationals. In practical politics the ideal of unlimited solidarity can never be fully realized, but this applies to all political ideals, including democracy.

(d) *Nationality and Civilization*

It is a very popular view that each modern nation has grown out of a common civilization and that the foundation of unitary national states fulfilled the longing of small peoples for unity created by their cultural community. The word Civilization however, has various senses. On the one hand, it is used for any community of traditions, interests and ideals, however primitive, and on the other it means only an advanced phase of cultural development. In the first sense one speaks of the civilization of the Stone Age, while in the second it is declared that only a civilized people may claim to be a nation. Sometimes the term is also used in a still more restricted sense referring merely to the higher spiritual achievements such as literature or art. Now it is clear that great diversities in language and traditions hamper political unification, though this factor was of less importance before the rise of the principle of nationality in the nineteenth century. It is also true that the development of national consciousness presupposes a certain level of civilization, the diffusion of schools, a literature, an interest in the past and the future, the existence of an intelligentsia. Nevertheless, a community of civilization and its high development alone are not able to bring about the political fusion of different peoples into one nation. First of all: not every type of civilization seems to lead to the formation of nations in the modern sense. Modern nationality primarily developed on the soil of Western Christianity and then spread farther and farther to the East. India, China and the Islamic peoples brought forth great and comparatively homogeneous civilizations, but the idea of modern nationality was alien to them before they were permeated by European ideas. Many pioneers of modern nationality in Asia have frankly confessed that their peoples could not yet be regarded as nations [1] and that their national aspirations were imitating European models. But even in Europe the progress of civilization alone did not initiate national unification in the political sense. Ancient Greece, or Mediaeval Italy and Germany, possessed very high civilizations while there was hardly any national solidarity between the different peoples into which each was divided. Their city-republics and other tiny states had on the whole a common language and civilization and the sentiment of kinship among them and of common interests against foreign nations were not lacking. But all this was not sufficient to create a strong sense of political solidarity between those small peoples and they had no desire to abandon their separate nationalities for a common one, however advantageous this would have been. A high level of civilization was even adverse to national unity on a wide scale. Athens, Florence and Nuremberg were proud of the splendour of their own achievements and looked down upon their backward kinsmen in other cities. Most great thinkers, poets and artists of all nations were cosmopolitans and showed no interest in the national aspirations of their time, though some of them dreamt of a great spiritual mission of their nation. History shows that the progress of civilization was often accompanied by a weakening of national sentiment. In the late Roman Empire civilization was high and comparatively widespread. Yet there was neither any political liberty nor much unity and solidarity. Many historians ascribe the fall of the Empire to the insufficient development of national consciousness. The Romans and Greeks had become so civilized that they regarded military service as beneath their dignity and left it to barbarians, which led to the desintegration of the Empire. A thousand years later a great Mohammedan statesman and thinker, Abd'ar Rahman Ibn Chaldun, looking back upon the rise and decay of Arabian civilization, developed a philosophy of history, focused on national solidarity.[2] He found that hardy barbarian nomads possessed it and, therefore, succeeded in building up great states, but that the progress of civilization necessarily destroyed it, and brought about the downfall of every Empire and civilization itself. About half a thousand years

[1] Cf. Sun-Yatsen, *The Triple Demism*, translated by P. M. D'Elia, 1931, p. 64.
[2] Cf. A. von Kremer, *Ibn Chaldun und seine Culturgeschichte der islamischen Reiche*, 1879.

later, after the defeat of France in 1871, Ernest Renan,[1] pondering the causes of the catastrophe, came to conclusions which in some respects remind us of Ibn Chaldun's views, though he did not despair of a national revival.

6. THE IDEA OF NATIONAL PERSONALITY

(a) Personality, Organism and Freedom

The four strivings for unity, liberty, distinctiveness, and prestige may be called a striving for national personality. This term is used here by analogy with human personality, though the parallel must not be stretched too far. Personality in an individual, as in a nation, is a combination of unity, freedom, distinctiveness and distinction. Each of these traits is indispensable for the idea of personality. It has been objected to applying the term personality to groups that these do not possess the same degree of unity as individuals. This may be true, but the individual personality too is not a strict unity. It usually comprises antagonistic forces, and reason is constantly needed to bring them into harmony. Another analogy which is often applied to groups is that of an organism. This term signifies the specific form of unity which characterizes living beings. It is a diversity in unity, a number of different organs functioning and co-operating in close unity.[2] Personality, however, is more than an organic unity. A plant or a fish is an organism, but not a personality. This idea implies besides unity also freedom, a certain spiritual distinctiveness and prestige, i.e. ideas which form the objects of national aspirations.

The idea of national personality, irrespective of its reality, is a very potent factor in political ideology. It has a great significance, moreover, for constitutional and international law. The ideas of the national will, sovereignty, self-determination, responsibility, presuppose personality. Only a person can have a will, or be responsible. This personality, of course, is a legal fiction; but its practical application is often strongly influenced by the image of national personality prevailing in the ideology

---

[1] Ernest Renan, *La réforme intellectuelle et morale*, 1871.
[2] The comparison of society with an organism or a person is much disputed. It has certainly been grossly abused for political purposes. In particular, the idea of a collective mind has given rise to fanciful speculations. Cf. the criticism by M. Ginsberg, *Psychology of Society*, 1933, pp. 46, 119, and by P. Barth, *Philosophie der Geschichte als Soziologie*, 1922, i, p. 105. Further cf. W. H. Rivers, *Psychology and Politics*, 1923, p. 59, E. Hanbury Hankins, *Nationalism and the Communal Mind*, 1937, and for the historical side, O. Gierke, *Political Theories of the Middle Age*, 1900, with an important introduction by F. W. Maitland, and E. Barker, *Church, State and Study*, 1930, p. 160. H. Laski, *Foundations of Sovereignty*, 1921.

of the nation concerned, and this image usually exaggerates the unity and stability of national personality.

The longing for personality is expressed in the use of symbolic figures personifying the nation, like the classicist images of Britannia, Germania, Italia, and the more popular ones of John Bull,[1] the German Michel, the French Marianne, Uncle Sam. We may add the British lion, the German eagle, the French cock, the Russian bear, the Chinese and Welsh dragon, the German oak, the Slav lime tree, the Irish shamrock, the Welsh leek, and so on. This national mythology, zoology and botany supplement the abstract notion of a nation by more concrete images able to arouse warmer emotions than a mere abstraction. Such images are the stock in trade of orators, poets, journalists and artists.[2]

The striving for national personality often implies the sacrifice of individual personality. We are compelled to subordinate our spiritual and material interests to those declared as national interests and to conform our mentality and behaviour to the so-called national character. One of the principal reasons of this attitude is that the individuals are overawed by the power, greatness and fame of the nation and hope to enlarge their individual personality by merging it in the collective. It is a sentiment which shows certain parallels with religion, and the growth of national sentiment in modern times was certainly encouraged by the decline of religion and the rise of mass-mentality. It would be a mistake to ascribe this process merely to the conscious policy of the State or the pressure of economic interests, though both, of course, are potent factors. But the influence of the atmosphere of national aspirations surrounding and permeating the individual mind is much more powerful.

Membership in a nation is as a rule not a matter of choice. The great majority of people are born into a nation as into a family. Foreigners may have a chance of being naturalized, but

[1] The image of John Bull seems to have undergone a curious change. In our time the figure is widely understood in Britain as a symbol of doggedness in fighting out a struggle, while other nations often associate it with pugnacity, or aggressiveness. John Bull is usually accompanied by a bulldog. Arbuthnot, who in 1712 created the figure, however, used it for combating the doggedness of the Whigs in fighting out the war against Louis XIV. In his *History of John Bull* the hero symbolizes the plain common sense of the middle class which is for some time misled by sophisticated politicians and intellectuals, and entangled in long quarrels, but at last sees through their game and finishes the strife. Beattie says: in John Bull the nation of shopkeepers could view their own likeness. Cf. Lester M. Beattie, *John Arbuthnot*, 1935.

[2] The national colours, too, have great emotional significance. In France the revolutionary government of 1848 was faced with the conflict between those who demanded the red flag as national emblem and the adherents of the tricolour, and in 1873 a fierce struggle raged over the question whether the white flag of the Bourbons or the tricolour should be adopted. In republican Germany the issue whether the national flag was to be black-white-red or black-red-gold aroused incredible passion.

this does not result in making them shortly full nationals; and in many cases they never overcome the difficulties of assimilation and admittance. The ways of thinking and feeling recognized as national may differ widely from those of many individuals, but these will seldom have a chance of altering or successfully resisting them. No nation can freely reject its past. The attempt was sometimes made in a great revolution, but the final result usually was that certain traditions of the past re-emerged, though in a changed form. In many respects, therefore, a nation appears as a community of fate, endowed with a life and personality of its own, and not subject to the will of individuals.

The Greek philosophers discussed already the question whether society was an artificial construction or an organism, and the dispute has never come to an end. Modern nations are very widely regarded as historical organisms, though this is usually more implied than explicitly stated. The national territory, for example, is looked upon as an organism which cannot be mutilated without the risk of destroying the whole nation, body and soul. When in 1871 France was forced to cede Alsace-Lorraine to Germany, both Michelet and Renan put forward this argument.[1] Restrictions of immigration and other measures against foreigners are often defended on the ground that these formed an inorganic element which the national organism was unable to assimilate. Nationalists like to defend their striving for expansion by conquest with the argument that every youthful organism is bound to grow, and they compare those nations which they want to annex or rob to senile, decaying organisms.

In the ideology of all movements for national liberation and unification a nation was conceived as a community not created by the will of individuals but by God, nature, or the genius of race, and this origin was used for justifying the demand that the individuals must be willing to sacrifice everything to the nation. The protagonists of national aspirations were never discouraged by the fact that the majority of the people whom they wanted to liberate, unify or make powerful often showed themselves quite indifferent if not hostile. They believed to have a mission from an authority higher than any individuals.

Political thinkers of all nations have worked out the doctrine that the State was a spiritual organism, the result of historical growth and the embodiment of the experience of all ages. Montesquieu, Burke, Hegel, de Maistre, Royer-Collard were some of

[1] Cf. Jules Michelet, *La France devant l'Europe*, 1871, p. 113; Ernest Renan *Qu'est ce qu'une nation ?* 1882.

the defenders of this thesis. Though they held in many points divergent views, they agreed in the rejection of the view that a nation was merely the people living in a state, and maintained that both the political institutions of the State and the social institutions of society had an organic structure. Disraeli has expressed this view in the words : [1]

> The phrase " the people " is sheer nonsense. It is not a political term. It is a phrase of natural history. A people is a species ; a civilized community is a nation. Now, a nation is a work of art and a work of time. A nation is gradually created by a variety of influences—the influence of original organization, of climate, soil, religion, laws, customs, manners, extraordinary accidents and incidents in their history and the individual character of their illustrious citizens. These influences create the nation—these form the national mind, and produce in the course of centuries a high degree of civilization. If you destroy the political institutions which these influences have called into force, and which are the machinery by which they constantly act, you destroy the nation. The nation in a state of anxiety and dissolution then becomes a people ; and after experiencing all the consequent misery, like a company of bees spoiled of their queen and rifled of their hive, they set to again and establish themselves into a society.

The idea that a nation or state forms a sort of spiritual organism has often been interpreted in a sense hostile to liberty, democracy and progress. But this is not the only possible interpretation. Great English thinkers such as Green, Bradley and Bosanquet have developed it in a different spirit.[2]

(b) The Nation as a Natural Organism

The rise and popularization of a naturalistic philosophy have favoured the interpretation of society in terms of a natural organism. In this view the social groups are the organs and the individuals the cells of the social organism. This theory is still more liable to be abused for an anti-liberal and anti-democratic policy. The aims or functions of a spiritual organism can be reason, right and love, while those of a natural organism can only be life, survival and power. Darwin's theory of the struggle for existence has been exploited by numerous writers for the defence of a policy of conquest, domination and oppression, though Darwin himself did not encourage such views. Curiously

---

[1] Disraeli, in " The Spirit of Whiggism ", 1836, reprinted in the collection of his writings, *Whigs and Whiggism*, 1913, p. 343.
[2] Cf. Robert Murray, *Studies in the English Social and Political Thinkers of the Nineteenth Century*, 1929, vol. ii, p. 274 f. For the arguments against the theory, cf. L. T. Hobhouse, *The Metaphysical Theory of the State*, 1918 ; H. Laski, *The State in Theory and Practice*, 1938 ; C. Joad, *Guide to the Philosophy of Morals and Politics*, 1938, p. 572.

enough, the analogy between natural and social organisms has been elaborated by Herbert Spencer, who was an extreme individualist.[1] His attitude, as does that of the English Hegelian school, shows that the practical interpretation of a philosophy largely depends on the national spirit. The same philosophy has been used in Germany for discarding individual rights and in England for stressing them.

In any case, the identification or comparison of a social organism with a natural body is a fallacy. Society is not composed of individuals like a body of cells; it is not a body but a movement or action. Its constituent parts are typical relations between individuals. A social community differs from an animated body in many respects, as in lacking a sharp demarcation, fixity, exclusiveness, specific unity and organic creation. The individuals constituting a nation are products of organic creation, but the nation is not such a product. It consists in national consciousness which is not inborn but a product of history. Very often arbitrary or accidental acts have decided which peoples and lands were to form a nation. A natural organism cannot be formed in this way. It is also possible to leave a nation, either collectively by forming a separate one, as the American colonists did in the Declaration of Independence, or individually by emigration or change of nationality. A cell cannot leave the organism to join another one except in the course of propagation, which is not open to a nation. An individual can also belong to various groups as to a nation, a State, a Church, a class, a party, etc., and perhaps even to more than one nation, while a cell cannot belong to various organisms. This fact is of special significance. A part of a natural organism has only a function within this body. But a human being does not exclusively belong to his nation, and is not even strictly bound to it. A man is also a member of a larger community, which implies human duties and rights, not merely national ones.

A nation, furthermore, does not grow old and decay in a biological sense as a natural organism does, though this is often asserted to be so. Lastly, the idea of natural selection through the struggle for survival cannot be simply transferred from natural science into sociology. Social evolution is determined by other factors than mere biological ones. While all human groups possess culture, no animal group possesses it.[2]

---

[1] Murray, *op. cit.*, vol. ii, pp. 25, 27. Before Spencer the theory has been worked out by Schaeffle.
[2] Cf. Charles Ellwood, *Cultural Evolution*, 1927.

The ideas of a social organism and of organic evolution are very useful instruments of scientific investigation and presentation. But they are liable to gross misinterpretation if they are used as political slogans, and become elements of a political ideology.

7. The Historical Origin of Nationality

Historians and political scientists have often discussed the question whether national consciousness and the idea of nationhood have existed in former ages. The prevailing opinion seems to be that they are of relatively recent origin, though there is great disagreement about the time when they first began to manifest themselves.[1] Attempts to locate the birth of nationality in a specific epoch, however, disregard the fact that national consciousness is composed of various aspirations, and is, moreover, inseparably connected with objective factors like the national language, territory, state and civilization. All these elements have undergone a long historical evolution, and the pace of progress was not the same in different fields. Elementary traits of nationality may be as old as humanity, or even older, as we find parallels in herds of animals. The more complicated phenomena have gradually arisen at different times. It is impossible, therefore, to state a definite time when nationality was born. The widespread view, however, that national sentiment was unknown at former ages is not merely historically wrong, but also misleading in regard to our political problems. It responds to the wishful thinking of politicians who are inclined to underestimate the power of nationalism; frequently because they believe in the possibility of securing peace by some form of international organization which is incompatible with the spirit of nationalism. They therefore declare that national sentiment is not deeply rooted in human nature since people had no idea of it in former times.

It is possible to discern certain phases and types in the development of nationality. Our modern type implies ideas which were more or less alien to former times such as the claim to unrestricted

---

[1] While August Thierry believed that the French national spirit was already awakening in the ninth century, Longnon attributed this process to the early twelfth, and Ranke to the thirteenth. Guizot, Michelet and many others stressed the importance of the Hundred Years War in the fourteenth and fifteenth centuries, the time of Jeanne d'Arc. Many historians assume that the achievement of political unification, great military triumphs and cultural splendour render the sixteenth and seventeenth centuries the decisive epoch. Lavisse and Aulard, however, think that it was the great revolution of the eighteenth century which awakened French patriotism and nationalism.

national sovereignty in a given territory, or to uniformity of laws, language and customs, and the idea of unlimited national solidarity, irrespective of differences in social status, local traditions and feudal rights. In the Middle Ages most people recognized their duty to fight for the Church, and their lord, or in defence of their small homeland, but they would not have understood the idea that national honour obliged them to make every sacrifice for people of kindred language and civilization, or subject to the same king, with whom they had hardly any contact. The idea, moreover, that nationality was the supreme value, and that national loyalty had precedence of all others, even religious duties, was absent. Even in quite recent times the idea of nationality has undergone great changes. In the era of Enlightenment and Liberalism the personal worth of the individual was very widely considered as much more important than his nationality, and an efficient foreigner was usually preferred to less efficient nationals. Monarchs and aristocrats frequently took a similar view and had no objection to employing foreigners, even of low rank. In 1862 the Tsar Alexander II asked Bismarck, then Prussian ambassador in Russia, whether he would not enter the Russian diplomatic service.[1] In our time the idea of such a change in loyalty would appear monstrous. Present national sentiment frequently implies that an individual must be born into a nationality if he is to be considered a full member of the nation, and that a foreigner must be admitted only in exceptional cases.

The historian, therefore, must be on his guard against the temptation to interpret facts according to his experience of modern nationality. He must not rashly conclude that the formation of a national territory or State or language was the outcome of the growth of national sentiment. Their development was largely due to the policy of kings and their helpers and they only later acquired national significance. This also applies to the interpretation of subjective facts. If a mediaeval writer praises the virtues or denounces the vices of his, or another, people he may have been more actuated by class feelings than by national sentiment. Loyalty to a cause may have been rooted in dynastic rather than in national feelings, and pride in gallant exploits in the mentality of knighthood. Prejudice and hatred of foreigners are not necessarily symptoms of national consciousness, but may be due to egoistic rivalry about posts or markets. Quasi-national prejudices also divide tribal or local sections of the same nation.

[1] Bismarck, *Gedanken und Erinnerungen*, 1898, vol. i, p. 309.

If certain facts are found to have been real symptoms of national sentiment, it must also be ascertained of which classes or sections of the people they were typical in order to form a view of their historical importance. How far professions of national solidarity are genuine can only be tested in a national emergency, and even then it is difficult to distinguish between real and faked enthusiasm, as the enigma of present Germany or Italy shows.

The development of nationality has not followed a straight line throughout the ages towards its present forms. National sentiment has undergone many ups and downs. It was much stronger in ancient Greece than in later times, and there were epochs when it was almost completely obliterated by other emotions. There are many parallels between national phenomena of our time and those of previous epochs. But each nation and each period also shows peculiar features and we should be very cautious in applying modern political terms to remote times and civilizations. The fundamental traits of human nature, of course, have always and everywhere been the same. Many writers, therefore, would deny that the mentality of various peoples and epochs shows any differences at all. This, however, is a complete misjudgement, both of human personality and of the relation between individual and social psychology. Even if the mental outfit of the individuals of different groups were exactly the same, the differences in the structure of the groups, and in their traditions, may effect great divergencies in social mentality. As regards nationality, the decisive question is not whether a certain national feeling existed at all at a given time, but how strong it was in relation to other forces. The historical analysis must not only be qualitative but also quantitative and structural, and the historian is often faced with the task of weighing elements which are imponderable.

The investigation of nationality in a certain epoch cannot be restricted to the collection of manifestations of national sentiment. We must also try to form a view of the whole mentality of the nation in that epoch, to gain insight into its social structure, the aspirations of the classes and their interrelations. National sentiment is not an isolated factor but an element in a national organism which can only be fully understood in connection with the social and historical structure of the nation. The nature of this national organism is expressed in a system of sentiments, ideas, and aspirations which form the national ideology. In this ideology the idea of the national character plays a particularly important rôle.

8. NATIONAL CONSCIOUSNESS AND NATIONALISM

It has already been mentioned that English usage identifies nationalism with national consciousness, which had often the consequence that in judging foreign nations the difference between peaceable and aggressive national sentiment was overlooked, obviously because the optimistic ideology of modern Britain was disposed to overlook it. Professor MacDougall, for example, says : " It is very necessary to insist strongly on the fact that to decry nationalism is to be an enemy of democracy." [1] This usage might perhaps even be criticized from a linguistic point of view.[2] About a hundred years ago Mazzini distinguished clearly between nationality, which he considered as sacred, and nationalism, which he called narrow, wretched, usurping, and so on.[3] The French and Germans, too, use nationalism in the sense of national aggressiveness.[4]

The Royal Institute of International Affairs has recently published an excellent report, worked out by a study group of scholars, and named " Nationalism ".[5] In an introductory note this definition of nationalism is put forward :

> Nationalism has been used in the report to denote a consciousness of the distinctive character of different nations, including the one of which the individual is a member, and a desire to increase the strength, liberty, and prosperity of nations. Its effect is not necessarily taken as being confined to the individual's own nation, although admittedly this is very often the case, nor is the nationalist necessarily conceived as making the interest of his own nation supremely important. In short, the term is used in such a sense that Mazzini, Gladstone, and Woodrow Wilson can be described as exponents of nationalism as well as Herr Hitler.

The use of the term " nationalism " in such a wide sense that both Gladstone and Hitler are included seems, in our view, to encourage the conclusion that the difference between the men-

---

[1] Cf. MacDougall, *The American Nation, its Problems and Psychology*, 1925, p. 70.
[2] The words ending in " ism " commonly denote a collective striving or a school of thought, characterized by a very strong, and usually one-sided, or militant, accentuation of a principle. Communal enterprises or welfare services are not the same as communism. Militarism means much more than a mere interest in military matters, and pacifism more than a pacific disposition.
[3] Mazzini, *Thoughts upon Democracy in Europe* (1847), in Works, vol. vi, p. 115, *Autobiography*, vol. iii, pp. 10, 12, 77.
[4] Cf. Carlton Hayes, *France, a Nation of Patriots*, 1930, pp. 2, 318. The German word *voelkisch*, which is a translation of " nationalist " means that form of nationalism which Hitler represents.
[5] Cf. *Nationalism*, Report by a Study Group of the Royal Institute of International Affairs, 1939. The chairman of the group was Professor E. H. Carr, and its secretary M. G. Balfour. The book is a most valuable contribution to the problem.

tality of these two men is only one of degree, and that Hitler has similar ideals as Gladstone had. Such an assumption would obviously be misleading. The vagueness about the meaning of nationalism is one of the greatest assets of nationalist propaganda abroad. It helps foreign nationalists to win the support of people who are quite opposed to wars and conquests by representing to them their aims in a harmless light.

The use of nationalism in the sense of national sentiment has also the consequence that national aggressiveness is designated by jingoism, imperialism [1] or chauvinism, and this seems to support the German and Italian thesis that it is only Britain and France who are aggressive, as other nations have not even a word for that disposition. The ambiguity about nationalism has, furthermore, helped to spread the belief that Hitler is the continuator of the cultural " nationalism " of Herder and Fichte.

If a nationalist in the continental sense is asked to define his creed he will say it consists in passionate devotion to the nation and in putting its interests higher than everything else. But further questioning will reveal that the interests for which he is prepared to sacrifice everything are quite specific ones. He does not think primarily of increasing political liberty, or of securing a better standard of living to the people, nor does he lay the main stress upon augmenting the spiritual treasures of the nation. What he first of all has in mind is national honour. By honour nationalists do not chiefly mean being esteemed for a high state of civilization, for moral or spiritual qualifications, nor does it mean to them a state of equality with other nations. Honour to nationalists denotes superiority, a higher rank among nations, prestige, domination. A policy of nationalism, therefore, demands a powerful state machine for the realization of its aims of prestige. All material and spiritual things are chiefly appreciated as instruments for increasing the independence, power, and prestige of the nation. Of course, even nationalists cannot live on power and prestige alone, nor could they hope to win a large following in the people if they neglected all its other interests. Economic, social and cultural aims also form part of their programme. The typical nationalist attitude, however, is to assume that national power and prestige are the best keys to all the treasures of the world, and that a strong State alone can solve the social problems and secure the best possible con-

[1] General Smuts in 1919 said in a speech : " Nationality overgrown became Imperialism and the Empire led a troubled existence on the ruin of the freedom of its constituent nations."

ditions for the development of national civilization. Moreover, if nationalists have to choose between prestige and other aims, they will certainly give preference to prestige. Finally a real cult of power develops, and nationalism becomes a sort of religion with prestige and power as the supreme gods.

The nature of nationalism is usually not clear to the majority of its followers. It requires a good deal of critical analysis to see through the ideological disguises of its real aims. It cannot be expected that the man in the street or the average politician should be able to form a far-seeing judgement of international affairs if one sees that even experts who had unusual opportunities of studying foreign nations often display rather primitive views of the mentality of foreign peoples and individual aliens. In an atmosphere of tension very few people seem to be able to judge other nations with common sense. The majority are apt to fall into one of the extremes of undue optimism or undue pessimism.

It must not be overlooked, however, that nationalism appears in other forms besides that of aggression against foreign nations. In many cases nationalist intolerance and oppression is mainly directed against internal " enemies ", either against national minorities or against other elements regarded as not sufficiently national, especially against the Jews, or against a racial section, especially coloured people. Furthermore, there is also a sort of sneaking nationalism which is not openly avowed and usually appears associated with economic egotism. It forms one of the motives of all sorts of economic protectionism such as high customs on imports, and of similar measures. National prejudice and animosity underlie also restrictions of immigration and a labour policy which denies the right to work, or better posts, to aliens or to coloured people. Economic protectionism easily assumes an aggressive form, and also racial, or national discrimination as regards immigration or employment often has an aggressive and provocative character, if it exceeds certain limits and seems to degrade the people affected to the position of an inferior race. Even democratic and liberal countries which are free from aggressiveness against foreign nations often follow a policy of racialism and anti-alienism.

The spirit of nationality has two aspects. Its positive and constructive side is the striving for national solidarity and freedom ; its negative and destructive side is the mental seclusion against other nations which often leads to mutual distrust and prejudice, and to a striving for superiority and domination. A certain vague and restricted disposition to national solidarity is widespread, but a high degree of it, implying the readiness for self-sacrifice, is rare. It is an ideal which inspires a small minority only, but the great majority usually puts egoistic interests, class-solidarity, and party loyalty much higher than the duty of self-sacrifice to the nation. The exclusive and invidious strain, which is manifested in nationalism, anti-alienism and racialism, is in many nations much more frequent than the beneficial variety of national solidarism. It is often very difficult, however, to estimate the strength of either variety in a reliable way, since their manifestations may to a very high degree be due to the pressure of the State and public opinion. It is often assumed that hostility against another nation is indispensable for internal national solidarity. Professor Pillsbury remarks that a common hate is one of the most frequently effective factors in making and uniting a nation,[1] and history, indeed, shows that almost all nations have been born out of great wars and through a long and violent antagonism to other nations.

9. The Idea of National Character

(a) Popular Views and Scientific Theories

The belief that every people has a specific character which persists through all time, and can be traced through its whole history, and in all branches of its civilization, is very widespread. It forms a powerful element in every national ideology, and commonly implies the glorification of one's own national character and the denigration of that of the national enemy. Even people otherwise trained in critical thinking cling to obvious prejudices of this kind without questioning them. Others realize the necessity of careful examination of such beliefs; they reject the grosser forms of national prejudice, but hold that the existence of a national character cannot be denied, though they cannot say what it really is. Leopold von Ranke, one of the greatest and most impartial historians of all times, came to the conclusion that the national spirit could only be felt but not understood; it was a "spiritual air", permeating everything.[2] Many other historians, however, did not share this reserved attitude. It would be easy to compile any number of facile and fallacious

[1] Cf. Pillsbury, p. 83.
[2] Cf. A. Gasparian, *Der Begriff der Nation in der deutschen Geschichtsschreibung des 19. Jahrhunderts*, 1918.

judgements on national characteristics by prominent men of many nations.[1] Most of these views imply the identification of a nation with a racial group. But the question of national character has also often been treated in a more detached spirit.[2] Ancient travellers, statesmen, and writers were struck by the diversity of laws, customs, habits, and temperaments among peoples, and pondered its causes. Mediaeval thinkers gave little attention to such diversities, but the humanists revived the interest in them, and took up the ancient explanations of their causes. Countless books have since been written about national characteristics, either merely describing them or attempting to trace their origin and causes.[2] In former times national peculiarities were chiefly explained by the influence of natural forces such as the stars, the climate, or the soil on the blood, the inner secretions and temperament of men. A classical source of all later theories on the influence of climate was a book attributed to Hippocrates. The astrological theory was put forward by Ptolemy and Galen. Some Greek writers, like Thucydides and Strabo, however, realized that it was less the direct influence of nature on the blood that formed the mind of a people than the action of many geographical factors on social conditions which then determined the mentality of the people. The first theory would have explained the character of peoples living in the desert by the direct action of sun radiation, while the second would point out that deserts caused nomadism, which produced a typical mentality. It was further more and more realized that the peculiar traits of peoples were moulded by the dynamics of history such as wars, migrations, traffic, social differentiation, discoveries, inventions, revolutions, cultural contact, and so on, and that these determined the physiognomy of a civilization. These historical movements were, of course, partly conditioned by nature. But it became clear that nature was on the whole a relative factor. The influence of a specific natural environment was not the same on all peoples and in all circumstances, but its effect depended on the constellation of numerous factors. Per-

---

[1] Numerous views of this kind are criticized by John M. Robertson, *The Saxon and the Celt*, 1897; J. M. Robertson, *The Germans*, 1916; John Oakesmith, *Race and Nationality*, 1919; F. Hertz, *Race and Civilization*, 1928; Hamilton Fyfe, *The Illusion of National Character*, 1940.

[2] I have surveyed many descriptions and explanations of national characteristics in several articles. Cf. my article on Greek theories in *Kölner Vierteljahrshefte für Soziologie*, 1923, and on these theories in later times in *Archiv für Sozialwissenschaften*, vol. 54, 1926, pp. 1–35, 657–715. Further literature is quoted in my article in the *Sociological Review*, vol. 26, 1934, p. 369. For a careful and illuminating discussion of the problem cf. M. Ginsberg, " National Character ", in the *British Journal of Psychology* (General Section), xxxii, 1942.

sonality, both individual and collective, was a very potent force in this constellation.

From the sixteenth to the eighteenth century the diversity of customs and laws, and their causes, formed a favourite subject of writers inspired by the ideas of Humanism and Enlightenment. The most influential books of this kind were written by Bodin, Huarte, Barclay and Montesquieu. In particular, Montesquieu brought together a wealth of important observations and stimulating ideas, and exerted the greatest influence on all succeeding thought on the subject. He exaggerated, however, the force of climate. Hume and Herder were among the first who deprecated the idea that climate was all-powerful.[1] While the writers of the eighteenth century often overstated the influence of natural forces, the Romanticists stressed organic, historical growth, and often indulged in the construction of a mystical national spirit, alleged to be traceable throughout the whole history of a people. Many historians, especially in Germany and France, tried to show that the whole history of their own nation proved the continuity of its national character, and frequently they interpreted its achievements as an outcome of the national genius, while the failures were ascribed to foreign influence. This view, however, has proved untenable, and has been abandoned by serious students.

The increase in geographical and historical knowledge, and the development of critical methods, has led to a more scientific and systematic treatment of the problems of national character. Eminent geographers like Karl Ritter, Friedrich Ratzel, Jean Brunhès, have worked out comprehensive systems, called anthropogeography or *géographie humaine*.[2] Many historians, sociologists, anthropologists and psychologists have also given great attention to the elucidation of national traits. It was especially valuable, moreover, that not merely the general issues were studied but also the conditions of specific nations, with particular emphasis on the development and rôle of their traditions, ideals and mental dispositions.[3] The geographical approach resulted

[1] Cf. David Hume, *Essays*, No. 21, " Of National Character," J. G. Herder, *Ideen zu einer Philosophie der Geschichte der Menschheit*, 1784 f.
[2] Cf. F. Ratzel, *Anthropogeographie*, 2 vols., 1882–91, new ed. ; *Politische Geographie* 3rd ed., 1923 ; Jean Brunhès, *Human Geography*, 1920. Ratzel's system has been expounded with many additions by E. Ch. Semple, *Influences of Geographic Environment*, 1911.
[3] Cf. particularly Alfred Fouillée, *Esquisse psychologique des peuples Européens*, 5th ed., 1914 ; P. Lacombe, *La psychologie des individus et des Sociétés chez Taine*, 1906 ; H. Th. Buckle, *Introduction to the History of Civilization in England*, 1857–61 ; John Mackinnon Robertson, *Buckle and His Critics*, 1895 ; Ernest Barker, *National Character and the Factors in its Formation*, 1927 ; E. Hurwicz, *Die Seelen der Volker*, 1920.

in broad generalizations illustrated by instances from many different peoples, and was most suggestive, though it also implied certain dangers. The study of the social structure of one people only against its natural and historical background, and with a view to the national mentality, as the outcome of social and historical forces, was better suited to avoid hasty generalizations. While formerly writers often started from a preconceived idea of the national character, and tried to show its manifestations in all events in the history of the people concerned, critical students now describe and analyse the institutions and the civilization of a people, and then search for general traits characteristic of this people. If they still employ the rather discredited term national character, they usually identify it with predominant tendencies of that civilization. This method too, however, raises some critical doubts. It can be disputed whether the same general tendencies rule in all the different fields comprised in a civilization, as well in politics and economics as in literature and art. It has even been doubted that a single field showed a close unity, and that one could speak, for example, of the spirit of English literature as a whole.[1] A national civilization, moreover, is not merely the expression of the national character. Every people has imported large parts of its civilization from abroad. Institutions have often been imposed upon a people without its assent. Christianity, for example, has often been introduced against the fierce resistance of a people, though it has later moulded its whole outlook. The same outward form, moreover, may have a different significance in various nations. Lastly, the comparative study of nations in the same phase of social evolution leads to the conclusion that no trait whatever is exclusively to be found in one nation or entirely lacking in the mind of any nation. Differences are only those of time, degree and combination. A certain feature may emerge earlier, or may be more frequent or more pronounced in one nation than in others, or it may be combined with other traits in a way peculiar to one nation.

The chief arguments against the idea of a national character are (1) the wide diversity of individual characters and cultural traits in each nation, (2) the absence of any very marked and decisive differences of individual characters and cultural traits between nations, provided that comparable social types only are compared, (3) the frequent and fundamental changes which have taken place in views held of the character of specific nations.

[1] Cf. F. Baldensperger, *La Littérature*, 1927, p. 287 ; L. M. Price, *English-German Literary Influences*, 1919, p. 120.

These arguments are certainly a cogent refutation of all those views which exaggerate the unity, persistence and peculiarity of national traits, as, in particular, all racial interpretations do. Racialism assumes that nations are fundamentally separated by their racial mentality which is homogeneous and unalterable. Such notions are certainly fallacious. Nevertheless, the idea of a uniform and unchangeable national character is very widely held, even by people who do not believe in race. To a certain extent this is due to a mistaken view of character in general. As mentioned already, even the individual character is neither strictly uniform nor absolutely unchangeable. It comprises antagonistic tendencies and within certain limits is liable to change. We may understand by character a constellation of forces tending towards a certain unity and fixity, under the influence of inherited tendencies, a central will and outward circumstances. It is clear that an individual as a rule will show greater unity and fixity of character than a group. The reason is that the will of an individual is a more centralized force than the so-called collective will, that a group comprises a wider variety of elements than the mind of an individual, and that the group lives longer, and, therefore, has more chances of developing and transforming itself. We may speak of a national character by analogy only, as we also speak of the character of a landscape which comprises many different things, and still forms a certain unity to the eye of the geologist, botanist, zoologist, geographer or artist. It would be desirable to replace the term " national character " by a less ambiguous one, and " national traditions " has been suggested as a substitute. But the mentality of a nation is not merely a matter of tradition, it is also conditioned by its social structure and by powerful individuals. " National Mentality " would be a correct term.

(b) *The Structure of National Character*

National character can only be defined as the totality of traditions, interests and ideals which are so widespread and influential in a nation that they mould its image, both in the mind of the nation concerned and in that of others. Its subjective significance for national consciousness has already been discussed in a previous chapter (p. 19), but we must also examine its objective significance. The beliefs which a nation holds concerning its own character and that of other nations are usually a mixture of some truth with a large amount of exaggeration and distortion. But even illusions are mental facts which may have a great share in producing national solidarity, national ambitions and national rivalries. The illusions, moreover, often have a background of natural and social conditions which may exercise a considerable influence on history. The dangerousness of national illusions and prejudices consists precisely in the fact that there is also a grain of truth in them. Opinions on national characteristics, furthermore, can often be traced back through centuries, and this too strengthens the belief in their truth and besides creates the impression of an inherited racial character. The persistency of national traits, however, is by no means an invariable rule. The history of most nations shows also sudden changes in the national mentality. In former ages it was the English who had the reputation of being an unruly, revolutionary, " fickle " people, while the French prided themselves on their loyalty to their kings and the stability of their institutions.

The question how far the mentality of a nation is changeable, if at all, is obviously of great importance both for the interpretation of history and for practical politics. Before discussing it a few further remarks on the structure of the national character must be made. The traditions, interests and ideals of which it is composed refer partly to the life of individuals, partly to that of the nation. Every nation has certain predilections as regards food, drink, housing, clothing and other ways of life, and also habits of thought and sentiment. The English interest in outdoor sports is very old. In the twelfth century William Fitzstephens, in his life of St. Thomas Becket, gave a vivid description of it. It has also influenced the national ideals. The phrase " This is not cricket " shows how sport and fairness are associated in the English mind. German nationalist writers often blamed the English for regarding even war under the aspect of sport.[1] This seemed to them a profanation of the " sacredness of war ", while the English idea was that also war should be waged with fairness. Sir Richard Acland may be exaggerating when he says that " as a nation we give ten thousand-fold more serious painstaking thought to the football match than to our foreign policy ",[2] but in any case football is an institution of significance for the English national character.

National differences in the habits of private life often give rise to prejudices. Almost every nation looks down upon others because of their predilection for certain foods and praises its own

[1] W. Sombart, *Händler und Helden*, 1915, p. 47.
[2] *Why I am a Democrat*, a Symposium edited by R. Acland, 1939, p. 14.

favourite dishes.[1] In former times the English people, for example, derided the French as " frog-eaters " and despised them for wearing wooden shoes, while they were proud of the " roast-beef of old England ". But also differences in thought and sentiment have often been pointed out as national traits. The French regard rationalism, strict logic and clarity of language as their special virtues, the English consider empiricism, common sense and dislike of abstract and systematic thought as their way of reasoning, while the Germans exalt German " profundity ", and their preference for a metaphysical " vision of the world " (*Weltanschauung*). A special group of beliefs are those referring to the noble origin, the " better blood ", the destiny and mission of a nation, which have already been discussed. Some of these beliefs have a direct connexion with national aspirations, while others have no direct bearing upon them, though it is difficult to draw a line of demarcation. The former may be called the national ideology proper.

Most ideas of national traits combine tradition, interest and ideals, though one or the other of these elements is usually predominant. Freedom is certainly cherished in Britain as a tradition going back to Magna Charta, but it is also an interest and an ideal. Traditions preserve their vitality mainly through their connexion with the interests and ideals of those classes which form the so-called " national will " and set the standard for the nation. Now these classes are subject to constant change, and new classes rise and obtain a share in political and social power. Such changes seem to be the main causes of the decay of traditions and the development of new ones. For centuries, for example, the maintenance of the Balance of Power was the cardinal principle of British foreign policy, but after the last war it was abandoned and replaced by that of Collective Security. This change in tradition was obviously a consequence of the transformation of the social and political structure of Britain and other nations.

Natural environment and social structure comprise many factors which partly favour the development of a certain unity of character, partly discourage it. A small people living in comparatively uniform natural and social conditions will be more homogeneous in its mentality than one stretching over wide territories with great climatic, economic and social diversities. This argument induced the ancient political thinkers to assume

[1] Cf. many examples in Robert Michels, *Der Patriotismus*, 1921, p. 74. This book is a very valuable contribution to the sociology of national sentiment and national ideology.

that a small people only could form a nation, a community united by a common outlook, and numerous modern writers have adopted the idea. But modern conditions have produced a great change. On the one hand social and cultural progress has made possible an extraordinary development of individual differences. On the other hand, technical inventions and the advance of political and social organization have produced numerous unifying factors such as elementary schools, the press, railways, post, telegraph, telephone, cinema, radio and the agglomeration of large masses in towns and industrial districts. The strongest of all factors, however, is the modern State, which concentrates in its hands means of moulding the mentality of its nation which were unknown in former ages. The degree of State influence is, of course, different in various nations. David Hume in his essay " Of National Characters " writes that in England the mixed government and the freedom enjoyed by all religions, classes and individuals work against the fixation of a national character. He even says that the English " of any people in the universe have the least of a national character, unless this very singularity may pass for such." But Hume overlooks in this observation that the political system is by no means the only factor determining the national character, and in other places he himself discusses other influences. English freedom has not hindered the development of traditions which are very widely accepted in all classes of the nation. Many foreign observers even found that the English people showed a greater mental homogeneity than others, a view which needs qualification. A certain uniformity of opinions, customs and habits in a nation is largely due to the facts that the ruling classes use their political, economic and social influence for spreading those which serve their interests, and that all classes more or less imitate the models established by the ruling classes or " good society ". In former times each rank had its separate mode of life, and it was even prohibited to adopt the costume or habits of a higher rank than one's own. The development of national unity, however, broke down these barriers, and each class began to imitate as far as possible the style of living of the next higher class. Since the traditions of the ruling classes were often very stable, the national character assumed thereby a certain stability. The difference in the national ethos of Germany and England is largely due to the fact that the German nobility to a great extent preserved the character of a warrior caste and that their example was largely followed by other classes, while in England the nobility adopted the mentality of wealthy landowners and capitalists and created a style of life which was widely imitated by other classes. It is significant for the relations between classes in England that the word " gentleman " which originally designated a social status has come to describe a pattern of behaviour for all classes. This was not the case with the French word *gentilhomme* and the German word *Edelmann*, which had the same origin. The French and the German even borrow the word " gentleman " from the English language for expressing a certain type of behaviour.[1]

(c) *The National Ideology*

Many elements of the national character are not necessarily connected with national aspirations proper, but are merely national in the sense that they are very widely held by individuals of all classes. The fact that English people as a rule love animals or are fond of sport has nothing to do with national sentiment, unless a football match with a foreign team arouses rivalry. But there are also traits which are directly and regularly connected with the striving for national personality. This striving is perhaps the strongest force working for a unification of the national character and leads to the development of a national ideology. A fully developed ideology comprises not only distinct political doctrines but also a particular interpretation of history and a specific philosophy. The substance of the national ideology consists in ideas on the character of the nation and that of other nations, on the past, present and future of the nation, on its mission in the world, on the tasks of the State and on the duties of the individuals towards the nation. The longing for independence of all foreign models often leads to the stressing of peculiarity as such, even if there be little reason to be proud of it. National vanity is stronger than common sense. Helvétius tells in his work *De l'esprit*, an Indian fable of a hump-backed people where a foreigner of normal growth is derided as a monster, and he addes : " Every nation admires its own faults and despises the opposite qualities. In order to have success in a country one must bear the hump of the nation."

The development of a national ideology often leads to a differentiation in the rules of conduct which implies almost two different characters in the same person, a private character in regard to private affairs and a national character in national

[1] Cf. A. Smythe Palmer, *The Ideal of a Gentleman*, 1908.

affairs.[1] Significant instances can be found in the memoirs of General von Moltke, the chief of the German General Staff at the beginning of the last great war.[2] His diary and letters to his wife show a friendly, kind-hearted man who speaks of wars with horror and with deep compassion for the sufferers. He doubts of Christianity because the doctrines of Christ's expiatory death and of predestination seem cruel to him. Yet the same man did much to bring about the outbreak of the war, arguing that the situation was so favourable for Germany that it ought to be used in any case. He refused to respect Belgium's neutrality even if England should promise to remain neutral.

This multiplicity of moral standards makes it clear why an individualist concept of the national character is quite inadequate. People may be peaceable and humanitarian in their private affairs and ruthlessly aggressive in national matters, especially in such as affect the so-called national interests and honour. It is not necessarily the real interests and true honour which are considered as vital by nations. Very frequently a point of honour is made of things which people not imbued with the specific national ideology cannot but regard as insignificant. The national ideology may be compared to a pair of coloured or distorting spectacles which only very few persons in the nation concerned are able to take off.

The development of two characters in the same person is not only expressed in different moral standards but even affects logical thinking. It is often impossible to argue with a convinced nationalist because he is unable to think logically if conclusions do not agree with the demands of national ideology. The enormous literature produced by German professors during the last war in defence of German policy offers most interesting illustrations. The German intellectual classes, especially many professors and teachers in higher schools, have become a mainstay of the philosophy of force underlying the German militaristic system. One of the greatest German scholars, Dubois-Reymond, declared in an academic speech with pride that the German professors were " the scientific crack regiment of the Hohenzollerns ". In no other country has such a vast literature on the national character been produced as in Germany, and its aim has mainly been to exalt the German race and mould the national character to a model purporting to be the only true German one.

[1] Lord Salisbury said in an address, on March 10, 1897, that he had often pondered on the curious contrast between the individual and the collective character, and he gave an interesting illustration concerning the English character.
[2] Cf. Helmuth von Moltke, *Erinnerungen, Briefe, Dokumente*, 1922.

Under the Hitler regime even a special sort of German physics and mathematics has been discovered which is alleged not to be accessible to scholars of non-Nordic blood. In the Western democracies, where a national State was attained much earlier and where national sentiment is more balanced, the aim of forming the national character by means of compulsory education, military service and scientific authority has never been tackled with the same thoroughness. The striving for national originality has prompted German nationalists to abandon rules of conduct which everywhere else are regarded as essential for civilization. Parliamentarism, democracy, human rights, Christianity are despised, not only because they are opposed to the militarist spirit but also because they are considered as of foreign origin and, therefore, incompatible with true German ideals. This, however, did not prevent the German nationalists from imitating certain methods of Italian fascists and Russian bolsheviks.

The national ideology tends to determine the private character, especially in countries where the individual is totally subordinated to the nation. Even the most private affairs, which to us seem to have no connexion with the national honour or greatness, such as relations between parents and children, or man and wife, are then regulated by the national ideology. A subject of Nazi Germany cannot marry the woman he loves if she has not sufficient " Aryan blood ", and a father is not sure whether his boy will not denounce him to the police for insufficient devotion to the Leader. Long before Hitler, however, Prussian militarism produced a tremendous change in the whole character and forms of behaviour of the German people. Nietzsche remarked that in his time quite a new and disagreeable way of pronouncing the German language penetrated the nation. It was the harsh and sharply accentuated North German tone of the Prussian officer commanding his men which superseded the former milder pronunciation. The Austrian or South German immediately recognizes a North German by his accent and finds it most irritating. Yet gradually also many South Germans became more and more infected by this way of speaking, especially the official and educated classes, which had the privilege of becoming officers in the reserve.

The function of a national ideology is to bind all classes firmly together, to unify their mentality, and to establish or strengthen the influence on policy of those classes which are the main seat of the national ideology. These aims often cannot be attained by preaching the same ideology to all classes. German militarism and nationalism, before the last war, produced several sets of ideas for winning the support of all classes for war. One was designed for the masses which were averse to aggressive wars, and was to prove that Germany was in constant danger of being attacked by England, France, and Russia, who wanted to annihilate Germany, and that, therefore, the gigantic German armaments were purely defensive. Much use was made of the argument that Britain was jealous of Germany's export trade and wanted to destroy it. Another ideology was inculcated into other sections of the nation which were less averse to war, such as the educated middle class, students and officials. According to it, Germany lacked " living space ". If her youth could not find good posts and trade was going badly, this was due only to the greed and rapacity of England and France. They had divided the world between them and left nothing for Germany. A war was justified for securing living space for the fatherland. A third ideology was reserved for the élite of convinced nationalists who did not need any justification of war. It represented international relations as a relentless and ruthless struggle for power. Every great nation had won its position by force, and now the day of the German was due. A fourth type was administered to more intellectual nationalists. Its purport was that the German and the English ideas of State and society were opposed to each other like heaven and hell. German culture was idealistic, English civilization materialistic. The former was striving for the most exalted ideals, the latter aimed at satisfying the lower instincts of man. Therefore German supremacy in the world meant the triumph of the higher principle over the lower one. Though single tenets of those different ideologies frequently contradict one another, they were very often simultaneously believed by many persons. National ideologies have such an authority and power over minds that inconsistencies are generally overlooked or wilfully ignored, just as convinced believers in the Bible will not be shaken in their creed by inconsistencies in the Bible.

(*d*) *The National Ideology and International Relations.*

In peaceable democratic States the ideas about international relations are formed according to the standards valid in home politics. Their national ideology includes the belief in the possibility of an international reign of law, of a parliament of nations and elimination of wars by compromise and arbitration. Militaristic nations, on the contrary, apply their view of international relations, which they regard as perpetual open or disguised war, also to internal politics. This tendency expresses itself even in the language. Mussolini invented the slogan of " the battle of the grain " in order to stimulate the production of grain, and the Nazis spoke of the " butter front " when discussing the measures of the government to regulate the butter supply. It has long been regarded as a principle of foreign policy that differences in internal systems must in no way influence relations between nations. If it were maintained that nations of different ideology may sometimes be able to co-operate usefully, and that sympathies and antipathies springing from similarities or dissimilarities of internal systems should not be a hindrance, one could assent. But a general veto against any consideration of internal policy of another nation in deciding the course of foreign policy may lead to disastrous consequences. That principle was true in a time when differences in the political ideology of nations were comparatively insignificant. But in our time it amounted to the resolution to close eyes and ears to reality and to be led by illusions. In fact, any pact or co-operation between nations of vastly different national ideology will always be of doubtful stability. The efficacy of every pact depends on its interpretation, and this depends on ideology.

Every great statesmen was fully aware of the importance of public feeling on policy. Grey once remarked to the German Ambassador that it was not policy or interests which determined a nation to enter a war, but sentiment. Salisbury said in 1897: " If you keep the unofficial people in order, I will promise you that the official people will never make war. . . . In our time the organized governments are distinctly losing force, and public opinion is distinctly gaining in power." Public opinion, indeed, is a great force. But it would be advisable to distinguish two factors which are usually comprised under this name. There is first the store of fundamental traditions which has developed over a long course of time and is little subject to change. This I should call the national spirit. In England the stressing of individual liberty and welfare as the supreme aim of the State is such a tradition. In Germany the authority and power of the State have mostly had precedence of individual rights and interests. Besides such traditions, we observe frequent movements on the surface of the political ocean which I should call public opinion. In every country public opinion is sometimes more Right or more Left, more peaceable or more warlike, and so on, but the groundwork of the national spirit does not change quickly.

Though statesmen have usually recognized that the mind of a people and its traditions are decisive factors in politics they have often made mistakes in estimating those forces.

Joseph Chamberlain, on November 30, 1899, made a famous speech at Leicester in which he pleaded for a new triple alliance between England, America and Germany, setting forth amongst other arguments that such an alliance was the natural one because the racial character of these three nations was almost the same. He obviously believed that nations of the same blood had a similar political character and that this would facilitate co-operation. This view, however, was not confirmed by subsequent events. German and British diplomatists were talking over the idea of an alliance for several years, though with interruptions. Many historians have since analysed their reports and have tried to find out which party was responsible for the complete failure of those negotiations. I believe it was inevitable because each side was standing on a national tradition which could hardly be reconciled with that of the other. In the British documents the matter ends with a retrospective letter by Baron Holstein, at that time the dominant influence in the German Foreign Office. Holstein quotes with approval a recent remark of President Roosevelt summing up his ideas about British policy. " It seems to me," said the President, " that there will have to be fundamental reform in the British character if Great Britain is to continue to stand in the front rank and to bear her burden of vast and widely extended Empire." The leaders of all three nations, therefore, believed in the significance of national character for foreign policy. They held that a similarity of character was necessary for close co-operation. But Chamberlain thought, or pretended to think, that common race was a guarantee of a common character, in which the two other statesmen rightly disagreed with him.

Transitory alliances against a common danger or for common profit can succeed without an ideological community, but lasting co-operation cannot be achieved between nations imbued with vastly different ideas. In this respect difficulties were less great before the development of modern nationalism. The Holy Alliance, formed after the fall of Napoleon, was based on a common ideology of the allied monarchs. They all wished to maintain the existing order, to prevent revolutions and wars, and they declared their intention to adhere to the principles of Christianity in international relations, though in this respect their sincerity was not beyond doubt. The later Concert of Europe was also founded on a certain similarity of ideas. It consisted of a small number of Great Powers which differed in their internal constitutions and external aims but still had much in common as regards the unwritten laws of international intercourse. Their rulers and governments could on the whole be trusted to observe treaties and engagements, they were used to behave as gentlemen and not as gangsters, they all desired peace and were in favour of economic co-operation and a large measure of economic freedom. The danger was the rising power of nationalism outside the governments. After the Great War the League of Nations was founded for international co-operation; but the rise of nationalism and the irruption of Bolshevism and Fascism frustrated the development of the ideological community, lacking which no fruitful activity of the League was possible.

CHAPTER II

NATIONALITY AND RACE

1. Differences and Parallels in the Ideas of Race and Nation

Nation is a term of social science, race one of natural science. The two concepts, therefore, refer to different sides of human existence, and a careful investigator will not use them indiscriminately. In popular thought, however, both ideas are closely associated and often identified. The reason obviously is that most people find it difficult to conceive a close social unity without a physical bond, and that they cannot think of common mentality without common blood. An intimate solidarity or fraternity between members of a nation seems to them to imply a real relationship as between members of a family. The nature of group consciousness, indeed, is such a complicated matter that even scientifically trained observers often go astray in its interpretation. The same holds good as regards the force of tradition which a mind not trained to a real understanding of historical forces will usually conceive as a transmission by heredity.

Most people are ignorant of the fact that each nation is composed of different racial elements and that its composition changes in the course of time. Hitler is certainly not of the same stock as Charlemagne was, and the fact that both were striving for world domination should not be interpreted as a proof for the innate disposition of a " German race " which does not exist. To a certain degree, of course, there is a racial community between many members of the same nation, and between different generations of a nation. Intermarriages between individuals belonging to the same national group being more frequent than marriages between members of different groups, there must be a certain consanguinity within a nation. In every nation, therefore, a tendency towards racial unification exists, which, however, is counteracted by other tendencies, namely, by the segregation of racial traits discovered by Mendel, by the social seclusion of sections of the nation from one another, and by the invasion, immigration or infiltration of foreign races.

Common usage does not sharply distinguish between race and nation. Crabb's well-known book on English synonyms even says that a nation is a people connected by birth, and that, therefore, the Americans and English, having distinct governments, are distinct peoples, but only one nation, because they have a common descent. The Oxford Dictionary, however, mentions common descent as one of the factors making a nation, and then says of the usage of the word nation that in early examples the racial idea is usually stronger than the political, while in recent use the notion of political unity and independence is more prominent. Thoughtful people have now become averse to mixing up the notions of race and nation because this seems to favour political racialism of the Nazi type. Nevertheless, the word race in the sense of nation is still frequently used in political rhetoric without a racialist tendency. When statesmen wish to give emphatic colour to the idea of the nation, they often speak, for instance, of " the British race ", though they do not mean it in a racial sense at all.[1] This shows that the word race carries associations of great emotional value.

2. National and Racial Sentiment

In any case, an investigation of national sentiment requires an inquiry into racial sentiment too. Between the two concepts many parallels exist, and it is sometimes not easy to keep them apart. In theory, of course, the distinction is clear. Racial sentiment consists in the belief in a deep, natural, hereditary diversity not changeable by education and assimilation, while national sentiment assumes merely historical and social differences which can be modified by society. In practice, however, few people seem to have a clear idea of this distinction. The great majority are not aware of it and constantly interpret national divergencies as racial ones. The power of racialism is so great that even highly educated people, who know that distinction and reject racial doctrines, often unconsciously lapse into racial sentiment and thinking. Likewise people may sincerely oppose class hatred and, nevertheless, in a practical case show symptoms of class prejudice themselves.

Racial arrogance, antipathy and prejudice are more intense and intolerant than parallel national feelings. National aversion is usually qualified and tempered by the admission of a certain community of moral and cultural standards between the

---

[1] Much more regrettable is it that the word race was used for nation in the Peace Treaties in 1919. An Austrian government has interpreted this ambiguous expression for purposes of an anti-Jewish policy which was quite opposed to the intention of the Peace Treaties.

rival nations. As a rule it is not denied that there is some good or some right on the other side. Those individuals of a national minority who adopt the nationality of the ruling nation are welcomed and enjoy equal rights and treatment. This is usually not the case, however, if either the skin colour is different or if a minority has been stigmatized as an inferior race by racial ideology and propaganda. In former persecutions of the Jews a Jew who adopted Christianity and consequently abandoned his special customs, language and separation, which constituted a quasi-nationality, was no more persecuted. But under Nazi rule this makes no difference at all, because the Jewish peculiarities are considered race characteristics which are indelible.

Racial contempt tends to deny that certain races have anything whatever in common, and either degrades the despised race to a sort of cattle or loathes them like noxious and repulsive animals. The violent belief in the superiority of one's own race is one of those creeds which have a tendency to become an obsession. Discrimination may first be practised against the black race, then it will be extended to the yellow race, then to South or Eastern Europeans and Jews, and finally the relations between the white elements of the country will also become strained. Racialism if not vigorously kept in bounds fosters the growth of injustice, inhumanity and fanaticism in general. It soon permeates the whole atmosphere and poisons all relations. The dominating race considers it a point of honour vigorously to insist on its racial prerogatives and to enlarge them, and every suggestion of a compromise is branded as national treason. The oppressed race becomes extremely irritated and susceptible to every slight and often suspects an offensive tendency even when it was not intended. National conflicts, therefore, become practically insoluble when they assume the character of a racial antagonism.

The main points of dispute in racial struggles are : (1) The right of intermarriage (connubium). The privileged race often puts a legal or social ban on intermarriage with the " inferior " race. The denial of connubium may also spring more from reasons of religion, caste or rank than from racial grounds. (2) A fair chance of social rising. Unequal opportunities of obtaining remunerative work, of acquiring a higher education, of rising to a better social position and of having a share in political rights do not necessarily arouse racial antagonism. But if the dominating race reserves all the good posts, all more advanced education and all the political influence to itself, and if the oppressed race seems doomed to live in miserable conditions for ever, without prospect of improvement, it is difficult not to conclude that it is treated with racial contempt. (3) The possibility of social intercourse. Even within each nation there is not much social intercourse between the higher and the lower classes. But the absence of any social intercourse between comparable classes of different races must stir up racial resentment and lead to complete estrangement between the two camps.

The national rivalry between two peoples living side by side is often aggravated by differences in wealth, education and political influence, and by the lack of opportunities of social intercourse, mutual understanding and assimilation. In such circumstances each side tends to segregate and to avoid any contact with the other. It is a matter of degree and of historical memories whether the estrangement assumes the character of racial antagonism. If this point is reached it becomes impossible to settle the conflict at all. Even a fair and reasonable compromise has then no chance of being accepted, because too much racial feeling has accumulated, and resentment for past wrongs, lack of faith in the good-will of the other side and other psychological obstacles form an insurmountable barrier.[1]

The modern alliance of nationalism and racialism has the strange effect of hindering the realization of fundamental aims of national aspirations. National sentiment strives for a close national community and solidarity, and this is incompatible with sharp distinctions of rank and a system of hereditary castes within the nation. Moreover, it tends to expand the influence and the prestige of the nation, either by a peaceful propagation of the national civilization or, in the phase of nationalism, by conquest and by forced assimilation of the conquered peoples. Racialism, however, counteracts these tendencies of expansion and assimilation. An inferior race cannot be assimilated, it can only be either exterminated or kept down by force. The cult of the noble blood inherent in racialism, moreover, leads to the setting up of caste barriers within a people dominated by the ideology of racialism, and it thus tends to destroy national unity and solidarity.

---

[1] The Irish obviously cannot forget that in a critical epoch they were treated with racial contempt by the English, and all later efforts of British policy to heal this sore were in vain. Burke declared that in Ireland the various descriptions of the people were as much kept apart as if they were not only separate nations, but separate species. Chesterfield said in 1764 that the poor people in Ireland were used worse than negroes by their masters. J. Morley, Burke, 1902, p. 35.

3. The Social Origin of Racial Sentiment and
Its Bearing on Nationality

Primitive society was largely based on groups of real or assumed blood-relationship, and neither national nòr racial sentiment played a rôle as a bond of the group. Seclusion or aversion from foreigners seems to have sprung mainly from religious or magical grounds. There is no evidence that racial aversion is a natural instinct, though group aversion against outsiders or intruders may have a root in instinct. Racial feeling seems to a large extent to have sprung from social differences and conflicts. In many cases it can be traced to the rise of powerful classes which regarded themselves, and were regarded by others, as of noble blood and as entitled to a privileged position which implied seclusion as a caste. In India the caste-system has developed in a unique way. Its origins were the seclusion of conquerors against the conquered people, and that of higher against lower functional groups and occupations. The prestige of the Brahmin class, which was credited with magical powers and hereditary sacredness, and the power of the warrior-class formed its main pillars. The growth and spread of the caste-spirit has resulted in the formation of countless castes, separated by social seclusion and mutual contempt. This system was mainly responsible for the fact that India has for the greater part of her history been dominated by foreign invaders. A French scholar, E. Sénart, says of former Indian conditions : " National feeling exists hardly at all ; life is much more narrowly focused. The community of the caste or the tribe is strong enough in its solidarity and tradition to fulfil all needs. This society constitutes the true fatherland." [1]

In mediaeval Europe tribalism and conquest aroused deep-rooted enmities and prejudices. The knightly warriors formed privileged ranks which usually became hereditary and exclusive. Nevertheless, the Occident has not developed real castes. Fierce traditional enmity sometimes assumed the character of racial antagonism. The German knights, e.g. often looked upon the heathen Slavs as hardly more than beasts, and enjoyed killing them like hunting wild boars or stags. The beginning of national States and conflicts led to early manifestations of an almost racial hatred.[2] On the whole, however, rank was decidedly more

---

[1] Cf. Emile Sénart, *Caste in India*, 1930, p. 16.
[2] Throughout the Middle Ages French and Scotch national hatred of the English relished the story that the English were tailed like animals, and it was also believed

NATIONALITY AND RACE 57

important than race. German, French or English knights regarded the Arab knights whom they met in the crusades as their equals. They did not object to intermarriage between nobles of different colour,[1] but they would as a rule have found it beneath their dignity to marry a person of inferior rank though of the same race. All over Europe the nobles believed themselves to descend from other ancestors than their serfs. The legends of chivalry traced the origin of the nobility to Trojan warriors who had fled to the West after the fall of Troy. The purpose of such fables was obviously to establish a relationship with the famous Romans who had first claimed descent from the Trojans.[2] The origin of the serfs was traced to Ham, who had been cursed by Noah for his impiety and condemned to eternal bondage. Yet the idea of a common descent of all mankind as taught by the Bible, the Christian doctrine of universal brotherhood, the political work of the Church and royalty and economic development lessened the inequalities of rank and thus prepared the ground for nationhood. England was ahead of all peoples in this process, and her early formation of a united and strong nationality was chiefly due to the fact that hereditary class distinctions were much less marked than in continental countries. The common law of the land knew no important privileges connected with birth among free men, and serfdom disappeared centuries earlier than on the Continent. In Germany the higher classes became widely imbued with extraordinary pride of rank and contemptuously looked down upon the lower. Intermarriage with people of inferior rank was proscribed. German history is partly characterized by a particularly fierce antagonism between the ranks and classes, and this has been a main obstacle to the rise of national solidarity and national consciousness. The same

in other countries. In some parts of England it was told of the people of other parts, and in the nineteenth century, Baring-Gould as a child heard from his Devonshire nurse that all Cornishmen were born with tails, which he believed till he had cross-examined a native of Cornwall on the subject. Cf. George Neilson, *Caudatus Anglicus*, 1896. This is a typical example of the credulity engendered by national aversion.

There were despised peoples, such as the mysterious " races maudites " in France, which were treated like pariahs or outcasts, though nobody knew why. Cf. Francisque Michel, *Histoire des races maudites*, 1847. In mediaeval Germany certain professions, chiefly rural ones, were widely regarded as infamous : as millers, shepherds, barber-surgeons, tanners, knackers, linen-weavers, perhaps because of their servile character. They and their offspring were not admitted to craft-guilds. Cf. H. Mascher, *Das deutsche Gewerbewesen*, 1866, p. 74 ; E. Otto, *Das deutsche Handwerk*, 1900, p. 43.

[1] In the thirteenth century Pierre Dubois proposed to marry well-educated French ladies to Oriental princes in order to convert them to Christianity and monogamy and to pave the way for French domination in the Orient.

[2] Geoffrey of Monmouth was a chief source of this fable, which, however, could be found already in the Chronicles known under the name of Fredegar (seventh century).

tendency existed in France, but it was counteracted by other developments.

In Spain the long struggle of the Christians with Mohammedans led to glorification of warlike virtues and to the cult of the " pure blood ", i.e. pure from contamination with Moorish and Jewish blood. After its victory the Spanish nation was imbued with the belief that service in the army only was an honourable profession, while trade, industry and intensive farming, which were mainly in the hands of the infidels and Jews, were despised. " In the sixteenth century ", says an English scholar, " zeal for the purity of the blood reached Nazi standards, and certificates issued by the Inquisition became an indispensable preliminary to almost any ambitious career." [1] The Moors and Jews were at last expelled, and this victory of racialism, with the concomitant contempt of most economic activities and the general mentality of militarism, have greatly contributed to the decline of Spain's power and prosperity.

The social origin of racial prejudice is also obvious in regard to relations between the Europeans and the coloured races. It has often been observed that the different European nations differ in their attitude towards coloured people. Professor Toynbee believes that the Germanic and Protestant nations have shown more prejudice than the Latin and Catholic ones, and he traces this to the influence of the Old Testament, which was especially appreciated by the Protestants, and which exhorted the Chosen People to exterminate the infidels inhabiting the promised country.[2] This may occasionally have had some influence, but it was certainly not the principal cause. Toynbee's observation, moreover, demands certain qualifications. On the Catholic side the Spaniards were very race-conscious towards Moors and Jews; but this was due to their long struggles with the Mohammedans for the possession of Spain, and to their military mentality, which held manual labour, trade and industry in contempt. Among Protestants the Dutch were racially tolerant towards the coloured people of their colonies. Many aristocratic Dutch families have coloured women among their ancestors. On the whole, however, it is true that the Catholic peoples were less given to race prejudice than the Protestant. The Catholic Church was the pioneer in missionary work and in protecting and uplifting the natives. The Protestants came later, but have also done admirable work. In our time the Catholic Church is making a firmer stand against

[1] Cf. R. Trevor Davies, *The Golden Century of Spain*, 1937, p. 16.
[2] Cf. A. Toynbee, *A Study of History*, vol. i, p. 211.

race prejudice than any Protestant communities. While these have separate churches for the Whites and the Coloured, the Catholic Church rejects segregation. A prominent Protestant expert, Mr. Oldham, Secretary of the International Missionary Council, states : " The Roman Catholic Church has in this matter been truer to the genius of Christianity than the Protestant bodies." [1] In Germany the Catholic Episcopates and other Catholic spokesmen have to a large extent shown great courage in denouncing the evils of racialism and of the Nazi system, while the Protestant Churches—with notable exceptions—seem to have offered less resistance to Hitlerism. Professor Hans Kohn ascribes the origin of racialism and nationalism, particularly in Germany, to the Protestant separation of religion and politics.[2] The true religious doctrine demands man's whole and undivided allegiance. But Luther's separation left the settlement of all non-religious questions to the State, which resulted in the growth of the cult of power and nationalism. This theory certainly explains one of the roots of nationalism, but it does not fit the case of racialism and ignores the fact that Calvin did not share Luther's attitude. Calvinism even tended to subject the State to the Church, and to subordinate the whole of life to the precepts of religion. The real cause of the difference in the attitude of the Churches to racial prejudice seems to be that the Catholic Church remained a supra-national institution in which the priest had a sacred character and a hierarchic authority independent of the community, while the Protestant Churches became national and either subject to the Government or to congregations, more or less dependent on public opinion, and therefore liable to infection by public prejudices.

That it was neither the Old Testament nor any other religious factor which created racial prejudice is shown by the fact that in former times, when religion was a much stronger force, prejudice was much weaker or absent. Even the Dutch in South Africa, who unlike the Dutch in Holland and the Dutch Indies, are very colour-conscious, had formerly no objection to legal marriage with coloured women.[3] The same holds true for the early English traders in India and other countries with a coloured population. In the days of long, wearisome and dangerous journeys round the Cape white women were scarce in the Tropics,

[1] Cf. J. H. Oldham, *Christianity and the Race Problem*, 1924, p. 263.
[2] Cf. H. Kohn, *Nationalism in the Soviet Union*, 1933, p. 123.
[3] About former conditions in South Africa cf. J. Hoge in *Zeitschrift für Rassenkunde*, 1938 ; about the Dutch East-Indies cf. E. Rodenwaldt in *Archiv für Rassen- und Gesellschaftsbiologie*, 1930 and 1938.

and the Europeans had more intercourse with the higher classes of the indigenous population than in later times. It is significant that in the eighteenth century Negroes and other coloured individuals of culture and special ability played a brilliant rôle at various European Courts, were treated as equals and married ladies of rank.[1] In questions of colour aristocratic society was often much less prejudiced than later on the bourgeois and the workers. Aristocratic privileges were not threatened by the recognition of a few individuals, and many aristocrats of the Age of Enlightenment were less imbued with the spirit of petty egoism and self-complacency than our age.

The rise of racial prejudice was largely due to slavery. The increasing use of Negroes as slaves in the plantations accustomed the whites to regard the black man as merely a beast of burden. The English were the chief slave-traders of the world, and, therefore, also showed this mentality. Later on, the Christian and humanitarian spirit asserted itself in England more than anywhere else and won the most glorious victory in the history of moral progress by emancipating the slaves, urging the suppression of slavery all over the world and promoting the cultural advance of the coloured races in many ways. This trend, however, was soon counteracted by several new tendencies. The invention of steam-boats and the construction of the Suez Canal facilitated the journey to India, increased the number of white women there, and made possible the formation of a white society which became more and more exclusive against the Indians. In North America and the Dominions the rising power of white Labour and the lower middle class led to rigorous measures against the immigration of coloured workers who were regarded as dangerous competitors. In an attempt at self-justification the egoistic motives of this policy were often disguised by its advocates as the necessary defence of white civilization against black and yellow barbarism and immorality.[2]

There is no doubt, therefore, that racial prejudice is pre-

---

[1] Under Tsar Peter I a Negro Hannibal rose to the position of an artillery general. The great poet Pushkin was his grandson. At the Court of Louis XVI the mulatto Chevalier de St. Georges was greatly in favour through his many talents, and was also a personal friend of the Prince of Wales, afterwards George IV. In Vienna the cultured Negro Angelo Soliman was much appreciated in high society. Shakespeare describes Othello as a black African, but he is treated with greatest respect by the Venetian aristocracy.

[2] Certain circumstances which cannot be discussed here may, of course, justify restriction of immigration. It may even be advisable to limit the entry of certain nationalities according to a quota system. Yet a complete ban on immigration of large racial groups cannot be justified on reasonable grounds and obviously springs from racial aversion.

dominantly due to social and economic causes. Partly it is the mentality of a ruling class which despises menial labour and tries to perpetuate practical slavery by declaring that the inferior race is destined by nature to serve the superior one. Partly it is the egoism of white workers and traders who wish to monopolize all good posts for themselves and, therefore, refuse to recognize the claim of the coloured races to equality or fair treatment. This attitude is often prejudicial to the economic and national interests of the whites themselves.

The social origin of racial prejudice is also proved by the fact that peoples which have never been slaves and which have shown a warlike spirit, like the Red Indians or the Maoris, are not regarded by the whites with racial contempt. North Americans who abhor even the slightest admixture of African blood consider a strain of Red Indian blood as not degrading and even as aristocratic.

4. The Rise of Modern Racial Ideology [1]

Modern nationhood depends on the overcoming of social divisions based on " better blood ". There can hardly be a genuine national community between people who are barred by law from mating or from social intercourse, or where people of lower rank have no chance of rising. Yet the tendency towards equal status has always met open or disguised resistance. In the eighteenth century, spokesmen of the French nobility put forward the view that the nobles were descended from the Frankish conquerors and the common people from the subdued Romans and Gauls, and they tried to base on this argument their claim to a ruling position. This was the starting-point of long controversies about the racial background of social structure and its bearing on French history and politics. The most famous French historians and many leading politicians and writers took part in this struggle, and many different theories were put forward.[2] The contention that the higher classes were of a more noble race than the lower aroused passionate opposition and did much to poison class relations and jeopardize national solidarity. In truth, the racial diversity of the classes had been completely obliterated by

[1] Cf. Comte de Boulainvilliers, *Histoire de l'ancien gouvernement de la France*, 3 tomes, 1727.
[2] Augustin Thierry has compiled and discussed these controversies in his *Recits de temps merovingiens* and *Considerations sur l'histoire de France*, and Ernest Seillière in the introduction to his book *Le Comte de Gobineau* has also surveyed them. Recently the subject has been treated by Jacques Barzun, *The French Race, Theories of its Origin and their Social and Political Implications Prior to the Revolution*, 1932.

mixture in the Middle Ages; but the diversity of traditions survived and created a sharp antagonism between the mentalities of the nobility and the middle class which rendered the national evolution of the French very different from that of the English. After the revolution of 1848 the Comte de Gobineau took up the old aristocratic argument and modernized it by identifying the noble and culturally productive elements of the nations with the Aryans or Teutons.[1] He confessed that he wanted by this theory to strike at the heart of liberalism, and as an admirer of feudalism he specially detested the idea of the Fatherland, which he called a Semitic monstrosity. Gobineau became the chief pioneer of modern racialism,[2] and through his friendship with Richard Wagner the doctrine was introduced into Germany, where it found many adherents. In France herself Gobineau had no success, and for a long time was almost forgotten till his popularity in Germany drew some attention to him again. Vacher de Lapouge and a few other writers propagated the theory that the upper classes had more noble Nordic blood than the masses. But France's national traditions were too deeply imbued with the spirit of equality and the Rights of Man and offered no favourable soil for racialism.

In Germany Gobineau's prestige was eclipsed by that of Houston Stewart Chamberlain,[3] who was an ardent disciple of Richard Wagner and married his daughter. He was of English origin but later became a fanatical Pan-German and hater of England. The Emperor William II was his enthusiastic friend and did much to spread his ideas in Germany.[4] In his old age Chamberlain hailed Hitler as the coming saviour of Germany. Hitler's racialism, indeed, is nothing but Chamberlainism served up for the mob.

Like his predecessors, the Pan-Germans, Hitler used racialism for the purposes of an anti-democratic and aggressive policy.

[1] Cf. Ernest Seillière, *Le Comte de Gobineau et L'Aryanisme historique*, 1903; Fritz Friedrich, *Studien über Gobineau*, 1906; L. Schemann, *Gobineau*.

[2] Disraeli, however, put forward racial ideas before Gobineau, though chiefly through the mouth of figures in his novels. Carl Koehne tried to show that Gobineau got the idea from Disraeli, which seems to me not sufficiently proved. Cf. Koehne, in *Archiv für Rassen- und Gesellschaftsbiologie*, 1926. Further forerunners of modern racialism are mentioned in L. Schemann, *Die Rasse in den Geisteswissenschaften*, 3 vols., 1928–30, and Th. Bieder, *Geschichte der Germanenforschung*, 2 vols., 1921.

[3] Cf. E. Seillière, *H. St. Chamberlain*, 1918, and Frederick Hertz, *Race and Civilization*, 1928. My book gives a detailed criticism of the doctrines of racialism, and of Chamberlain in particular.

[4] The German diplomatic documents and memoirs relating to the epoch of William II show that the Kaiser was actuated by strong race prejudices against the Russians and other Slavs, the Japanese, the Chinese and even the Latin nations. His uncle, King Edward VII, however, declared that the Japanese differed from the whites only in the colour of the skin.

The Nordic or Germanic race was represented as the élite of mankind, destined to rule and to exploit the inferior races. Of course, even the German racialists could not maintain that the Germans of to-day were of pure Nordic stock. All nations were shown by science to be mixtures of different races. But the racialists contended that the Nordic element in a nation was the only really creative one, and that the value of a nation and its claim to a place in the world depended on its share of Nordic blood. There is no evidence, however, that genius is restricted to one race only. Goethe and Beethoven, the two greatest geniuses of German civilization, were certainly not of Nordic type. Both were very dark, and many of their physical characteristics seem to prove their non-Teutonic origin. The greatest Russian poet, Pushkin, was the grandson of a negro; Dostoyewski, Tolstoi and Gorki showed marked Mongolian features. The two Dumas, both famous authors, were typical Frenchmen, though they were mulattoes by blood. The most striking refutation, however, of the racial explanation of the national character results from a comparison of English and German ideals. The two peoples are surely closely related in race, though not quite identical. Yet, as regards political ideology, philosophy, literary traditions and the spirit of the language, the development of the two nations was widely divergent.

5. The Social Background of German Racial Doctrines—Racial Antisemitism

The way for the extraordinary success of racialism in Germany was prepared by national traditions. In a large part of Germany the warrior-class has always been the strongest factor. In Prussia Frederick II made the Junkers a highly privileged caste, which became almost a ruling military race, despising all other classes. Bismarck gave Prussian militarism the domination over Germany, and made it national by winning through his victories and the foundation of a mighty Empire the support of the bourgeoisie and a large part of the Protestant middle classes. The modern German doctrine of Nordic race superiority was first directed less against other nations or the Jews than against the lower classes of the German people itself. The early German racialists like G. Klemm and Otto Ammon were chiefly concerned to prove that the lower classes in Germany were of less noble blood than the ruling classes. Their doctrine identified the upper strata with the Aryans and the lower ones with Mongolians, in order to justify the domination of the lower by the upper classes.

A special feature of present German racialism is the limitless denigration of the so-called Jewish race. Anti-Jewish sentiment has, of course, been strong in many ages and in many peoples and has sprung from various motives. It is racial antisemitism only with which we are concerned here. Anthropology has found that the Jews are not a homogeneous race but a mixture of different racial elements predominantly identical with the racial elements of south and east Europeans with an admixture of Nordic and Oriental stock. The Nazi views of Jewish racial mentality, their treatment of the Jews and the answer to their allegations need not be discussed here in detail.[1] The idea, however, that the Jewish success in trade was due to innate racial tendencies is not restricted to the Nazis or to Germany but very widespread in other countries too. In truth, the economic ascent of the Jews in the nineteenth century was due to special historical and social conditions and has nothing to do with race. A major reason was the wide dispersal of the Jews through persecutions, which provided them with many international experiences and contacts, knowledge of languages, and markets. In the period of capitalistic development this enabled the Jews to become to a large extent economic, financial and cultural mediators between different nations. Their success was particularly great in countries where the ruling classes were still imbued with a feudal and military spirit and found trade beneath their dignity, while no national trading middle class had developed, as in large parts of central and eastern Europe. The nobility in those countries frequently left the sale of the agricultural products and the industrial development of their landed estates to the Jews, whom they often also protected against the animosity of the nascent middle class. Many Jews thus had exceptional opportunities of acquiring wealth. Their sons or grandsons, however, soon tried to abandon the world of commerce and to join the medical or legal professions, or to become writers, scientists or officials. As a rule, the third generation of rich Jewish families showed little commercial interest or ability but

[1] Cf. for the facts G. Warburg, *Six Years under Hitler*, *The Jews under the Nazi Regime*, 1939; Cecil Roth, *The Jewish Contribution to Civilization*, 1938.
It is a complete mistake to assume that the old-established Jews in Germany were, before Hitler, regarded as an alien element by the majority of the Germans, except by extreme nationalists. A certain vague prejudice was widespread, but it was hardly more acute than the prejudice against Catholics or South Germans in certain Prussian circles, or the aversion of the Bavarians against the Prussians. Bismarck in his beginnings showed the anti-Jewish prejudice of the Junker class but soon got rid of it. He once said that mixed marriages of Germans with Jews seemed to produce a good blend, and that he did not know whether he would not advise his sons in this sense.

produced many intellectuals. This alone explodes the racial explanation of the Jewish economic success.

The conditions which prepared the ground for racialism in Germany have already been indicated. Hitler played upon the mob instincts, latent in large sections of various classes, which envied the wealthy Jews and wanted to rob them or to get rid of competitors. Moreover, the extraordinary achievements of numerous Jewish scholars, scientists, physicians, lawyers, authors, musicians, artists, technicians, economic and financial organizers, though credited by the world to the German account, aroused the violent resentment of those German rivals who saw themselves outdistanced. Hitler, furthermore, wanted a universal scapegoat which was to be made responsible for all social evils and the loss of the last war. The Germans, being of noble blood, could not be made mainly responsible without contradicting the fundamental thesis of racialism. The Jews, therefore, were a very handy object for symbolizing the forces of evil and for serving as a target for popular passions.[1] The main reason for Hitler's anti-Jewish fanaticism, however, was the fact that a large number of German Jews were the mainstay of opposition to a policy of ruthless aggression against other nations. Many German Jews were eager patriots, and some even nationalists, and many had no political interests at all. But there is no doubt that the majority of Jewish intellectuals and business men were strongly in favour of a policy of international conciliation and co-operation which coincided with all their traditions and interests. Many of them belonged to the most active advocates of this policy and as editors, journalists and writers had considerable influence on public opinion. Hitler, therefore, acted quite logically when he decided to crush and exterminate the Jews in order to clear the way for his conquest of the world.

Though Hitler named his movement Nationalsocialist Workers Party, it is clear that this appeal to socialist and democratic sentiment was only a disguise for a thoroughly oligarchic policy. Hitler himself, in his book *Mein Kampf*, did not conceal his contempt for the masses. Even the official commentary on the Nazi programme, moreover, contains two most contemptuous remarks about the " miserable race mixture " of the average German. The real aim of Nazi policy is to establish the rule of the most ruthless elements over the great majority under the pretext that

[1] Mussolini for years scoffed at racial antisemitism, but later discovered the usefulness of this device, and adopted it for his purposes. It has been remarked that the Japanese complained bitterly that they had no Jews who could be used as a scapegoat.

they are of superior Nordic blood. The masses are to be kept in subjection, partly by a most mendacious ideology and by constant intoxication, partly by an unparalleled system of spying and terror. This, obviously, does not conform to the ideal of a nation as a free, civilized, self-governing community. The German people is to forget its enslavement and degradation through the pride of belonging to the most noble race on earth.

6. RACIALISM IN BRITAIN

Racial and national prejudice was widespread in England too. In the Middle Ages and later, numerous foreign visitors to England noted the contempt and hatred of aliens shown by the English people, while the French were usually credited with friendliness towards strangers.[1] Much of this sentiment was either due to commercial rivalry or to jealousy of foreign workers. But the main cause was obviously the early development and wide diffusion of national pride which often bordered on racial arrogance. When William III was attacked by English adversaries for his foreign origin and entourage, Daniel Defoe wrote his brilliant *The True-born Englishman*, in which he ridiculed racial pride and animosity, pointing out what a mixed race the English were. In general, anti-alienism was strongest in the lower classes. When in 1753 a bill facilitating the naturalization of foreign Jews, proposed by the government and supported by the bishops, was passed in parliament, there was such an outburst of mob passion that it was soon repealed.[2]

In the nineteenth century Britain's record as the liberator of the slaves, the friend of freedom and peace in the whole world and the pioneer of social reform aroused general admiration. Whatever may be said about the seamy side of this picture, it cannot be disputed that Britain has made an enormous contribution to the progress of racial and social equality in all parts of the globe. She was not only the centre of the world's trade but also the centre of active interest and helpfulness on behalf of all oppressed races, peoples and other groups, and of movements for international peace, goodwill and co-operation. Every foreigner willing to do useful work, or seeking a refuge from persecution,

---

[1] Cf. many judgments of foreign visitors in R. Ehrenberg, *Hamburg und England im Zeitalter der Königin Elisabeth*, 1896, p. 15–19; Malcolm Letts, *As the Foreigner saw Us*, 1935, pp. 28, 49, 51. Cf. further the voices quoted by Robert Michels, *Der Patriotismus*, 1929, p. 121, and in *Ethos*, 1925, vol. ii, p. 197. Bulwer-Lytton, *England and the English 1833* (ed. 1874, p. 37).

[2] Cf. Gerald Hertz, *British Imperialism in the Eighteenth Century*, 1908.

found hospitable reception. The racial broad-mindedness of wide sections of the people has been evidenced by many facts. Several times English constituencies elected Indians as their representatives to the House of Commons, among them the prominent Indian Nationalist Dadabhai Naoroji. Men of Jewish origin have held the posts of Prime Minister, Ministers, Viceroy of India and Governor-General of Australia, besides many other prominent positions.

National prejudice, of course, was widespread too, but it was seldom expressed in such a violent form as in certain continental countries, except in war-time. Sometimes racial prejudice too made its appearance. It is interesting to note that it was prominent Liberals who taunted Disraeli with his Jewish race and discovered that his foreign policy was not English but "Oriental".[1] In truth, Disraeli's political principles were practically those of Bolingbroke and Burke, adapted to his time, while his foreign policy continued that of Palmerston, except that Disraeli was much less meddlesome and did not encourage revolutionary movements abroad. His stressing of the national character and national honour and his dazzling foreign policy were certainly of that type which moderate nationalists of all countries praise as "truly national". Yet the fact that he was of different "blood" had much greater weight in the eyes of his opponents than the spiritual relation between his political attitude and English national traditions.

Racial prejudice was most frequently manifested towards the Irish. Many writers and politicians declared that the Irish, owing to their Celtic blood, were unfit for self-government.[2] In particular, Carlyle and his disciples have shown racialist tendencies. Yet racial doctrines have, on the whole, found little encouragement on the part of English statesmen and scholars, and have been sharply rejected by eminent thinkers, such as J. S. Mill, E. T. Buckle, T. H. Huxley.

A moderate form of racialism has recently been represented by the well-known psychologist Professor William MacDougall. He has put forward the theory that the logical deductive tendency of the French intellect, and the empirical inductive of the English, were rooted in race, though tradition had accumulated and

[1] Cf. examples in *Encyclopedia Britannica*, article "Antisemitism" by L. Wolf. A distinguished historian, W. H. Dawson (*The German Empire and the Unity Movement*, 1919, vol. ii, p. 120) says: "A Jew of undiluted blood, this remarkable man typified at once the qualities and the defects of his race.—An Oriental in every fibre of his being, Disraeli sought to orientalize English political thought."

[2] Cf. numerous instances and criticism in John Mackinnon Robertson, *The Saxon and the Celt*, 1897.

accentuated such differences.[1] Such tendencies can, in fact, be observed, but a knowledge of history shows that they neither existed from the beginning, nor characterized the whole civilization of the two nations as implied in a racial interpretation of national character. In the field of political science, for instance, the antagonism between Rousseau and Burke seems, indeed, to confirm MacDougall's view.[2] But it is not in agreement with a great many other facts. The greatest French political thinkers, such as Bodin, Hotman, Montesquieu, Voltaire, Comte, Tocqueville, belonged to the historical-empirical school, while English political philosophers, such as Hobbes, Locke, Bentham, Austin and many others showed the abstract type of political thought.

It would be wrong to assume that racialist beliefs are quite negligible in Britain. Oakesmith says [3] that while no distinguished British writer has tried to vindicate the racial hypothesis, it has permeated with its influence much of British literature and politics. Even when it is not expressly asserted it is tacitly admitted as the premiss of important conclusions. Though, furthermore, government, parliament and the responsible press avoid, and sometimes disapprove, any racial discrimination, there surely exists a certain social racialism the extent of which is difficult to gauge. It has often been complained that even Indians, completely English in language, education and customs, were refused accommodation in some London hotels and boarding-houses. The social relations between races, of course, are of special importance in the Empire.

7. Racialism Outside Europe

British experts of great weight have drawn attention to the fact that certain sections of the British in India have adopted towards the Indians an attitude of aloofness which has created the impression of racial arrogance and has greatly aggravated

---

[1] Cf. W. MacDougall, *The Group Mind*, 1921, p. 112.—In fact, French civilization, like that of every other nation, shows a great variety of different types which cannot be summed up in brief formulas. Cf. A. Guérard, *French Civilisation from its Origins to the Close of the Middle Ages*, 1920, p. 58. MacDougall also expresses racialist views in his book *Is America Safe for Democracy?*, 1921 (published in England under the title *National Welfare and National Decay*). He rejects, however, extreme doctrines.

[2] Even Rousseau, however, was not exclusively an abstract thinker. In a large part of his writings his thought is empirical and pays great regard to historical conditions and national differences. Cf. C. E. Vaughan, *Political Writings of Rousseau*, 1915, vol. i, pp. 71, 78, 82.

[3] Cf. John Oakesmith, *Race and Nationality*, 1919, p. 39.

the tension between the races.[1] It would certainly be quite misleading to generalize such observations. Countless British in India have proved their sincere friendship and admiration for the Indian people by their life's work, and have particularly devoted their efforts to the promotion of equality. The government of India has tried hard to combat those tendencies. Nevertheless, certain fundamental facts of the British Raj in India and the unwritten laws of " good society " seem to have counteracted the endeavours of far-seeing statesmen and experts. The main reasons why there was not more sympathetic social contact between the two races were the small number of British residents in India, and the still smaller number of those who regarded India as their permanent home ; furthermore, on the British side certain traditions of society life and clubs from which Indians were excluded, on the Indian side caste-rules and the seclusion of women. However this may be, the example shows how easily the suspicion of racial arrogance is aroused if there is not wide and close contact between two races living in the same territory. Racial estrangement does not even presuppose any real racial difference. Many instances from Europe, America and Africa could be quoted, showing that nationalities of the same race, and living in the same country, hardly mix in society. They live side by side as if in two different worlds, and this goes far to explain why there is little understanding and sympathy between them and frequently an astounding amount of ill-will and friction.

All over the world the British Colonial administration, prompted by the missionaries and liberal opinion, has done admirable work in promoting the welfare of backward races and in opening the road towards racial equality. In Cape Colony the coloured people, who are the descendants of slaves and a mixture of various races, as early as 1852 received civic equality and the franchise, though subject to qualifications which a small part only possessed.[2] In West Africa and the West Indies a large measure of equality has been realized, and black Dominions seem to loom in the future. Where a large number of whites, however. are settled and wield political power the coloured peoples are usually denied any equality.[3]

[1] Cf. the statements of prominent experts in W. Hancock, *Survey of British Commonwealth Affairs*, vol. i ; *Problems of Nationality*, 1937, p. 171 ; Sir G. Schuster and G. Wint, *India and Democracy*, 1941, p. 63 ; C. Andrews and G. Mukerji, *The Rise and Growth of the Congress in India*, 1938, p. 81 ; K. Krishna, *The Problem of Minorities*, 1939, p. 42 ; S. Zimand, *Living India*, 1928, pp. 187, 212.
[2] Cf. W. Macmillan, *The Cape Coloured Question*, 1927.
[3] A very good brief survey of racial discrimination in different parts of the world is given by J. Oldham, *Christianity and the Race Problem*, 1924, p. 159.

It is interesting to compare the spirit of the British and the French Colonial administration in Africa and other parts of the world.[1] The French try to make the Africans French in language and civilization and to render them politically an integral part of the French nation. This implies the recognition of their full equality and a centralized government. In the older French colonies the black man, indeed, has the franchise and is represented in the parliament in Paris. In other colonies the franchise can be obtained by natives who have certain qualifications. Negroes have held posts as deputies, vice-president of the Chamber of Deputies, Under-Secretary of State for the Colonies, colonial governors, high officials, generals and admirals. In the colonies white and black soldiers, officials, clerks, workers, students and children live and work side by side on terms of complete understanding and equality. Many black families are already completely French in language and outlook. Besides, there are schools for more primitive tribes where the Africans are taught to develop along their own lines.

The British system does not aim at making the natives thoroughly British. It offers them either an English education or a training for the tasks of native life, and employs to a large extent the system of indirect rule in which the natives remain under the rule of their own chieftains but under British control. There is more scope for local autonomy in the British system than in the centralized French one. In the long run the British way seems to lead to national independence for the Africans. In spite of all benevolent efforts the British do not encourage full social equality for the Africans. There are no legal bars to intermarriage and social intercourse, but relations are restricted by custom. The British Army and Navy did not accept black men for service side by side with whites, though now a change seems to have taken place in this respect. In the Dutch empire there is no colour bar, the Javanese enjoying political rights and a wide autonomy. A consequence of the Dutch administration is that the numerous peoples with different languages and customs gradually acquire a sentiment of unity which may lead to common nationhood, probably in the form of a federation.

In the Dominions the antagonism against coloured races is outspoken. Its chief protagonists are the Boers of South Africa,

---

[1] Cf. three most informative books compiled by study groups of the Royal Institute, of International Affairs : *The Colonial Problem*, 1937, pp. 58, 114, 117, 121 ; *The British Empire* ; *The French Colonial Empire*. The British and French educational systems in Africa have been compared in a book by W. Bryant Mumford and G. Orde-Brown, *Africans Learn to be French*.

but sections of the English population, especially farmers and workers, share their attitude. The traditional Boer outlook is to regard natives as destined to be their serfs, though they are sometimes treated in a patriarchal way. The natives form almost three-quarters of the population of South Africa, 74 per cent of the agricultural workers, 89 per cent of the miners and 60 per cent of the industrial workers.[1] Nevertheless, the Boer ascendancy in the Union and the new attitude of white Labour denies them the claim to essential civic and political rights, and has even curtailed rights which the coloured people have enjoyed for generations. The schools for natives are completely inadequate, their wages, health and standard of life are very low, and consequently their productivity too. The enforcement of the principle of racial inequality, moreover, has a demoralizing influence on a large part of the white workers, who regard hard work as beneath their dignity, and insist on getting " white-collar " work from the government. Besides, a " colour bar " has been set up by the trade unions which practically reserves all better-paid work to white workers.[2] The conditions in the Union have encouraged the white settlers in other parts of Africa to press for similar treatment of the natives. It must be said, however, that many British and Dutch South Africans of high standing combat the policy of sharp racial discrimination, and strive to improve the status and living conditions of the black Africans.

Racialism also affects the Indians, of whom many have settled in South Africa for generations. Economic development brought about a great import of indentured workers from India who lived and worked in conditions of semi-slavery. Resentment in India was so strong that this emigration to South Africa was at last stopped. On the other hand, the South Africans wanted to prevent the Indians in their country from staying and rising to better positions, and a policy of racial discrimination set in which aroused great indignation in India. The Indian Government protested, and after a long struggle a compromise was reached in

[1] Cf. the most instructive books by Edgar Brookes, *The Colour Problems of South Africa*, 1934; Alfred Hoernlé, *South African Native Policy and the Liberal Spirit*, 1939, the work, *Coming of Age, Studies in South African Citizenship and Politics*, by various authors, 1930, especially the chapter on the poor white and the native, p. 129 and G. Calpin, *There are no South Africans*, 1941, p. 171.

[2] A biography of General Smuts explains this change in the attitude of the trade unions by stating that before the last war the South African Labour Movement was still under the influence of English leaders and traditions, and therefore did not advocate a policy of racial oppression. During the war, however, the English largely went to fight, and were replaced by young Backveld Boers who soon demanded the complete submergence of the black workers. Cf. S. G. Millin, *General Smuts*, vol. ii, p. 347.

1927.[1] Nevertheless, even now the Indians born in South Africa, and possessing citizenship, are excluded from the franchise, and practically from universities and schools frequented by whites. On the railways they have to travel in compartments for natives.[2] The racial policy of South Africa has given a great impetus to Indian nationalism. Gandhi was converted to his policy of non-co-operation through his experiences in South Africa. The British Government tried to induce South Africa to avoid words likely to give offence to India, but could achieve little in the essential questions, as any pressure would have aroused violent resentment in the Dominion.

The other Dominions have not gone as far as South Africa in racial discrimination, and on the whole their policy has not aroused the same resentment in India. But in regard to immigration they have all adopted many direct and indirect measures for keeping out Asiatics.[3] Everywhere, moreover, the restrictions have become increasingly rigorous, and have been extended to more and more peoples, even to Europeans. Professor Bailey of the University of Melbourne has observed that in the beginning the idea was that Australia should form an outpost of white civilization; following the Great War and the arrival in greater numbers of south-eastern European peoples, the concept was limited, and Australia was to be an outpost of the British race. Then followed a still narrower concept—Australia for the Australians.

A remarkable case, however, is the absence of marked racial prejudice towards the Maoris in New Zealand.[4] This people forms about 4·5 per cent of the population, and there is no colour bar in the Australian or South African sense. Many long-established white families are proud of the admixture of Maori blood among their ancestors, intermarriage has continued, and half-castes have played an important rôle as mediators between the races. Sir James Carroll was a half-caste and the most trusted Maori leader of his day, yet he represented a European

---

[1] Cf. Hancock, " India and the Race Equality " in his admirable *Survey of British Commonwealth Affairs*, p. 166.

[2] There are even separate counters for natives in post-offices and separate tramcars; they are not admitted to hotels nor in most cases to railway restaurants; they are not addressed as Mr. or Mrs. and so on. Chinese, who belong to an Allied nation, are treated as natives in South Africa, while Japanese, who belong to a hostile nation, are regarded as Whites.

[3] For details, cf. the very informative work, *The Legal Status of Aliens in Pacific Countries*, by various writers, edited by Norman MacKenzie, 1937. Cf. further, E. Gey van Pittius, *Nationality within the British Commonwealth of Nations*, 1930, pp. 163–76.—Further literature is quoted in the *Encyclopedia of Social Sciences*, vol. 7 (1932), p. 594.

[4] Cf. W. Morell, *New Zealand*, 1935, p. 299.

electorate. The Maoris have the franchise, and a Maori was Minister of Native Affairs. Though there is a certain social separation and discrimination, this is outweighed by a long tradition of mutual good-will and respect.[1]

In the United States racial discrimination, partly by law, partly by social pressure and intimidation, plays a considerable rôle. The descendants of Negro slaves, who number about 12 millions, are legally American citizens. They have become thoroughly Americanized, and, given the necessary educational and social conditions, their development has offered overwhelming evidence for the possibility of complete mental assimilation and for fundamental intellectual and moral equality.[2] Nevertheless, the coloured Americans are often subject to humiliating disabilities which vary in different parts of the Union.[3] A number of states prohibit intermarriage, and their legislation has been taken as a model by the Nazis in drafting the Nuremberg laws. This state of things is much criticized by liberal opinion and constant efforts are being made to improve it. Increasing restrictions were imposed on the immigration of Asiatics, and finally it was completely prohibited.[4] After the Great War the immigration of Europeans, too, was greatly restricted, especially for the peoples from eastern and southern Europe. The German racialist doctrines of the superiority of the Nordic race, represented in America by many writers, have had some influence in preparing the soil for this policy. The rigid restriction of immigration has had a far-reaching effect on the fate of the world, partly by fostering the rise of violent nationalism in Japan and other countries, partly by greatly aggravating social tension in Europe, thereby paving the way for Hitler.

The reasons given for the exclusion of Orientals from the countries settled by whites are alleged dangers to the level of wages and the general standard of living, and the necessity of

---

[1] " Though there are two races in New Zealand ", declared the Prime Minister in 1937, " we are but one people." Cf. Hancock, *Survey*, vol. ii, p. 70.

[2] Cf. the comprehensive survey on this much disputed subject in *The Physical and Mental Abilities of the American Negro*, ed. by the Department of Education, Howard University, Washington, D.C., 1934.

[3] The race problems in America have recently been excellently treated by a Dutch scholar, Dr. Schrieke, Professor at the University of Batavia and Secretary of Education for the Dutch East Indies. Cf. B. Schrieke, *Alien Americans. A Study of Race Relations*, 1936 (with bibliography). Cf. further, Oldham, pp. 164, 177.

[4] Professor W. MacDougall, himself a racialist, says that the anti-Asiatic policy of the Pacific States was first little appreciated in the Eastern States, and the differences of the views even seemed to threaten the unity of the nation, for " the Westerners were ready to fight and secede rather than submit to have their restrictive measures overruled and forbidden by the Federal Government ". But at last the nation accepted their point of view. W. MacDougall, *The American Nation*, 1925, p. 147.

protecting the white race and its civilization. It is doubtful, however, whether these objects could not also be secured by other measures (for example, by fixing quotas of immigrants and wage standards which must not be undercut), and whether they would be menaced at all under a system of reasonably regulated immigration. Some of the restricting countries are definitely underpopulated and would greatly profit by an increase of workers and consumers. As regards other forms of discrimination it is difficult to see how they could serve those purposes. White civilization is certainly not threatened if an Indian or Bantu sits in the same school or railway compartment as a white man who may be much less civilized than he. It is obvious that to a very large extent all those measures are merely due to racial prejudice.

If it were true, of course, that men in general, or white men in particular, are such pugnacious, envious and unreasonable beings that they cannot live side by side with men of a different skin colour without the gravest danger for social order, then the only escape would be to keep the races separated. The coloured peoples, who amount to the greater half of the world's population, would then also be entitled to exclude whites from their countries. It is not intended to examine whether that pessimistic view of human nature is true. If it were, it would strike at the root of the belief in democracy.

8. Racialism and Relations with Japan

The closing of almost all white countries to Asiatic immigration has aroused great bitterness in India, China and Japan. Large parts of these countries are either overpopulated or hindered by climatic and other reasons in their agricultural and industrial development. The density of population per arable square mile (average 1920–33) was calculated for Japan at 2,750, while it was only 229 in the United States, 172 in the Soviet Union, 476 in France and 819 in Italy.[1] In Great Britain it was 2,170, but this country does not depend on the products of its own soil and lives largely on industries and foreign trade. It is understandable that the problem of population pressure has aroused anxieties in Japan. To many the alternative seemed to be either peaceful emigration or colonization of countries to be conquered by the sword. Economists, however, have found that both colonization and emigration could have but a very limited effect.[2] Many

---

[1] Cf. Albert Hindmarsh, *The Basis of Japanese Foreign Policy*, 1936, p. 43.
[2] Cf. Hindmarsh, p. 99, Ryoichi Ishii, *Population Pressure and Economic Life in Japan*, 1937, pp. 194, 252.

Japanese are traditionally reluctant to leave their homeland. The door was more and more closed to Japanese by almost all suitable countries such as the United States, Mexico, many South American States, all British Dominions and the Soviet Union. In some countries discrimination was also imposed in regard to employment, business opportunities, right to own real property and so on. The Japanese greatly resented all these discriminations—not so much, as they often declared, because of the economic disadvantages as because of their humiliating tendency.[1] There were no substantial trade conflicts between Japan and the United States,[2] and each country was one of the best customers of the other. Neither was an inundation of America with cheap Japanese labour probable. Nevertheless, in 1906 a violent agitation against Japanese immigration was started in California, and Japanese children were excluded from the general schools. Their sitting at the same desk with white children was represented as a moral danger. The total number of Japanese children involved was but 93, and they were distributed over 23 schools! Japan obviated the agitation by concluding a so-called " gentleman's agreement " with the United States, in which she undertook to check the emigration of Japanese labourers to America completely. But in 1920 the agitation was revived. The great American Federation of Labour adopted a resolution requesting Congress " to have the gentleman's agreement revoked, and to have the Japanese and other Asiatic peoples altogether expelled from America." In fact, immigration was soon completely prohibited.

When the Covenant of the League of Nations was drafted, the Japanese asked for the insertion of a clause endorsing the principle of the equality of nations, and their right to equal and just treatment.[3] A minority of the Commission prevented its acceptance, and President Wilson ruled that, in the face of formal opposition, unanimity was required. Japan, France, Italy, Brazil, Czechoslovakia, China, Greece and Yugoslavia voted for the clause, while Britain, the United States, Poland, Portugal, and Roumania voted against it. Mr. Balfour remarked that " the proposition that all men are created equal was an eighteenth-century proposition which he did not believe was true ".

In 1902 Britain had concluded an alliance with Japan which was twice renewed and brought considerable advantages to both

[1] Cf. Hindmarsh, pp. 193, 215.
[2] Cf. Hindmarsh, p. 228.
[3] Cf. the particulars in Georg Schwarzenberger, *Power Politics. An Introduction to the Study of International Relations and Post-War Planning*, 1941, p. 312, and C. A. Macartney, *National States and National Minorities*, 1934, p. 220.

sides. In the Great War Japanese warships convoyed British transports. The alliance, however, was unpopular in the United States and in the Dominions, partly because Japan's militarism and expansionism aroused distrust, partly out of general racial antagonism. In 1921 the alliance was due to expire. Both the British Government and Japan were in favour of renewing it, but the influence of America and the Dominions succeeded in bringing about its end.[1] The Washington Conference led to the Four Power Pact for securing peace, and to several other pacts. But the friendship between Britain and Japan was not restored. The estrangement was largely due to the activities of the militarist party in Japan. Militarism and nationalism were always powerful in that country, but there were also strong counterforces. After the Great War the military party lost power, while the commercial and financial interests standing for a peaceful penetration in search of new markets gained influence.[2] A prominent American, President Schurmann, stated after a visit to Japan, that in his view she would in twenty years become one of the most democratic countries in the world. Other American experts also expressed optimistic views.[3] An American writer, Dr. Sidney Gulick, warned his country that the reviving anti-Japanese agitation in America was directly playing into the hands of the most dangerous and unscrupulous elements in Japan and gave Japanese militarism the most cogent arguments for promoting anti-American feeling in Japan.[4] In 1930 the struggle between the civil and the military power over the London Naval Treaty ended in an overwhelming victory of the civil government of Japan.[5] But the militarists staged an " incident " in China as an excuse for a policy of conquest which was to restore their prestige. The economic world crisis led to new discrimination against Japanese goods and enabled the militarists with the help of the distressed classes to defeat the Liberal Government. Japan left the League of Nations and denounced the Naval Treaties. In 1936 a Japanese naval officer published a book in which he came to the conclusion that a war with Britain was hardly avoidable. Hostile relations between the two countries, he declared, were " the natural result of the denunciation of the alliance ".[6] The rise of the power of militarism in Japan was primarily

[1] Cf. R. Jebb, *The Empire in Eclipse*, 1926, p. 40.
[2] Cf. E. Causton, *Militarism and Foreign Policy in Japan*, 1936, p. 130.
[3] Cf. Iichiro Tokutomi, *Japanese-American Relations*, 1922, p. 148.
[4] Cf. Sidney Gulick, *The American-Japanese Problem*, 1914 ; *Toward Understanding Japan*, 1935.
[5] Cf. Causton, p. 137.
[6] Cf. Lt.-Comdr. Tota Ishmaru, *Japan Must Fight Britain* (Engl. tr.), 1936, p. 55.

responsible for all the tragedies that followed. But one of the most potent factors which helped the militarists to seize power was undoubtedly the racial discrimination against Japan adopted by so many nations. Another factor was the experience of the weak attitude of the democratic powers towards the aggressions of Fascism.

The anti-Japanese movement in America was not due to fear of Japan's aggressiveness. The Chinese and other Asiatics who were certainly not aggressive nations were treated even worse. Professor Gulick, an expert in this problem and spokesman of a great organization of American Churches, wrote of the anti-Chinese riots of the eighties : " Scores of Chinese have been murdered, hundreds wounded, and thousands robbed, by anti-Asiatic mobs, with no protection for the victims and no punishment for the culprits." Chinese immigration was completely stopped by several laws though this was a direct breach of the American-Chinese treaties of 1868 and 1880, and the Supreme Court laid down that Congress was not bound by international treaties and could repeal or modify them at its pleasure.[1]

[1] Cf. S. Gulick, *Asia's Appeal to America*.

CHAPTER III
NATIONALITY AND LANGUAGE
1. Language as a Symbol of Personality

Language is not only a means for communicating with others. It also constitutes the most powerful implement for developing personality, both individual and collective. Every social differentiation gives rise to special forms of speech which then emphasize and enhance the social diversity. The linguists have found that almost every village and region, every trade and profession, every corporation and association and social class have their peculiarities of speech which are often regarded as a badge of that special community.[1] In primitive society sometimes different vocabularies are prescribed for men and women, the old and the young. There are many examples of the use of a special language for sacral purposes, for speaking to God, as Latin is still employed in the Catholic Church and Hebrew in the synagogues. In former times different languages, or dialects, were often used by the same persons for different forms of literature, either according to the social station of the readers or according to tradition.[2]

2. Nationality and Language in Antiquity and the Middle Ages

In our time, the national community has assumed paramount power, and all its local and social rivals have lost in prestige and influence. The national language has become one of the idols of a new religion. All nations regard it as a symbol of their independence and honour, as the supreme expression of their personality, and they esteem its exclusive domination within their national territory more highly than obvious spiritual and material advantages. Peoples, of course, have always clung to their language and were often inclined to look down on the foreigner, whose speech seemed to them barbarous.[3] Yet in ancient times there seem to have been no parallels for our idolization of the national language and intolerance towards other languages. In former ages rulers and peoples tolerated different tongues in their territory, or even adopted a foreign one, though they were not

---

[1] Cf. abundant examples in J. Vendryes, *Language, a Linguistic Introduction to History*, 1925, p. 240. On language and personality cf. K. Vossler, *The Spirit of Language in Civilization*, 1932, chap. ii.

[2] Cf. Vendryes, p. 272.

[3] The original meaning of barbaros probably was stammering, stuttering, babbling unintelligibly. Many other peoples had similar designations. The Slav word for German, for example, means dumb, mute. Cf. J. Juethner, *Hellenen und Barbaren, Aus der Geschichte des Nationalbewusstseins*, 1923, pp. 1, 4, 124.

devoid of national sentiment and pride. They may have laughed at the foreigner mangling their speech, but we hear nothing of coercion having been employed for imposing a national language upon minorities or aliens.

This attitude was the outcome of social conditions. In early times peoples were not yet firmly attached to the soil. Migrations, invasions, and infiltrations, the large number of foreign slaves, the transplanting and extermination of whole peoples, and the settlement of soldiers on the soil of the conquered, often brought about changes of language. The rulers of a conquered country were often of foreign stock. Kings and aristocracies were always favourably disposed towards foreigners who could be useful to them.

By about 1500 B.C. the Babylonian language and script was generally used by all the Oriental kings for their international correspondence, even by the Egyptians, who despised the " miserable Asiatics ".[1] The Babylonians made great use of the Sumerian language in inscriptions, in their cult and in legal documents. When there was no more a Sumerian people their language survived and played the same rôle as Latin did in our Middle Ages. Later on the Assyrians became politically predominant, but about the same time Aramaic widely replaced the languages of the Babylonians and Assyrians and became the lingua franca, the general tongue of intercourse, in the greater part of south-western Asia. The power of Babylon was for some time revived by an Aramaic dynasty. Then the Persian king Cyrus and his son Cambyses conquered all other empires. But they appreciated their title as Kings of Babylon more than their national one, and adopted Aramaic for their communications with their subjects in the west. After Cambyses' death the Persians revolted against the babylonizing, supra-national policy of the dynasty.[2] Even the Jews, in spite of their strong national consciousness after the captivity, abandoned Hebrew in everyday life for Aramaic to such an extent that the text of the Bible was no longer understood by the people and had to be translated into Aramaic at service in the synagogues.[3]

[1] Cf. H. Winckler, *Babylonische Geisteskultur*, 1919, p. 21 ; B. Meissner, *Kultur Babyloniens*, 1925, p. 11.
[2] Cf. Winckler, p. 27.
[3] Cf. W. Robertson Smith, *The Old Testament in the Jewish Church*, 1926, p. 35.—Most of the post-biblical, rabbinical literature, too, is in Aramaic.—The spread of this language was neither due to political power nor to cultural achievements. The commercial importance of the Arameans and the flexibility of their script seem to have been major causes. Cf. *Cambridge Ancient Hist.*, 1925, iii, pp. 248, 423 ; S. Schiffer, *Die Aramaeer*, 1911.

In the time of Hellenism the Greek language spread over wide areas of the East, though it was chiefly the tongue of the towns and of the educated classes, while the country and the common people retained their vernaculars. The expansion of Roman domination was quickly followed by that of the Latin language, though the Romans did not propagate it by means of coercion: the settlement of Roman veterans in the conquered countries and the attraction of Roman citizenship and civilization were sufficient. The language of large and civilized peoples like the Etruscans, Tartessians and Gauls, and many other tongues, disappeared completely, and it seems that there was no strong national resistance against Romanization. Neither is any particularism of these peoples traceable in the later Roman Empire. The Gauls and Spaniards soon became patriotic Romans and made a great contribution to Roman statesmanship and literature.[1] On the other hand, in the Roman Empire the educated classes largely used Greek for cultural purposes, while Latin remained the official language. The Teutons who established themselves on the soil of the decaying Empire soon became romanized, and abandoned their native language for Latin.

When the Arabs swept over the Mediterranean world they claimed a dominating position in all the conquered countries, but they did not aim at imposing their language upon the subdued peoples. On the contrary, Omar forbade the Christians to learn the Arabic language and the Mohammedans to use any foreign language. Soon, however, these barriers proved untenable, and Arabic spread enormously. Unlike the ancient religions Islam was a democratic creed, and even the lowest classes received instruction in order to read the Koran. Moreover, Islam also attracted many highly cultivated minds of many nations, especially Persians, Greeks, Syrians, Kopts, Berbers and Visigoths. All this furthered the expansion of the Arabic language.

The Normans had a dazzling career as conquerors and organizers of states. Yet nowhere did they show tenacity in maintaining their language. Most of them changed their language twice or thrice in the course of a few centuries. In Normandy they soon dropped their original Teutonic speech for French. In England they retained French for a longer time, but soon began to mix it with Anglo-Saxon elements and to evolve English. In Ireland the Anglo-Norman barons soon became celticized, and the Statute of Kilkenny of 1367 failed to prevent it.

[1] On the causes of the Romanization of Gaul, cf. Fustel de Coulanges, *Histoire des institutions politiques de l'ancienne France*, 1877, pp. 37, 55.

In Scotland, too, they adopted Celtic speech and were leaders of the Celts against English aggression. Later on English became more and more the language of Scotland. " Celtic kings ", says Professor Rait, " compelled the greater portion of Celtic Scotland to adopt English law and custom and, to a lesser degree, English speech." [1] It was northern English, however, which became the national speech, and its peculiarity served as a symbol of Scottish nationality.

From the eleventh to the thirteenth century A.D. the French language and civilization permeated wide territories in Europe and the Orient, while the German language and civilization spread in the east of Europe. Norman adventurers and French crusaders conquered numerous States and introduced their language and customs. Moreover, in the whole of Europe aristocratic society eagerly adopted French chivalrous civilization and learned French.[2] The German expansion was partly the work of conquering knights, as in the Baltic countries, and partly an achievement of German traders, miners, artisans and peasants who settled in central and eastern Europe among Slavs, Hungarians and Roumanians. Slav and Hungarian princes furthered this immigration, which stimulated economic and cultural progress. In the eleventh century King Stephen I of Hungary declared in a statute : A realm with one language and one kind of customs only is powerless and frail.[3] In Bohemia the great Czech King Ottakar II, like his predecessors, favoured the immigration of Germans ; he granted them great privileges, and he was blamed for it by fervent Czechs. The court of the Czech Kings was a centre of German poetry, the Czech aristocracy adopted German customs, language and civilization, and their castles had German names which also became the names of their families.[4] It would be wrong, however, to assume that kings and nobles had no national sentiment. Ottakar II, for example, vigorously defended the Czech language when it seemed necessary.[5]

3. THE ORIGIN OF MODERN NATIONAL LANGUAGES

In the Middle Ages State and society were split up by feudalism into countless fragments, and in some States the kings and

[1] Cf. R. Rait, *History of Scotland*, p. 14. James I in 1617 demanded that the Highland lairds should send their children to schools in the lowlands to learn English.
[2] L. Reynaud, *Histoire générale de l'influence Française en Allemagne*, 1914, p. 66 ; F. Kluge, *Deutsche Sprachgeschichte*, 1920, p. 274.
[3] Cf. Decr. Steph. lib. I, cap. VI, § 3.
[4] Cf. F. M. Mayer, *Geschichte Oesterreichs*, 1909, i, p. 266.
[5] Cf. F. Palacky, *Geschichte von Boehmen*, 1839, ii, 1, p. 294.

their helpers later on succeeded in building up larger units again which became the nucleus of new nations. Within these nascent national States, however, there was a considerable diversity of languages and dialects. In England, for example, this diversity was so marked that in the fourteenth century men of the North were unintelligible to men of the South in oral speech, and books written in one of these tongues had to be translated in order to be understood in other parts.[1] In Germany even Luther's Bible, though written in a middle language, was translated into Low-German,[2] and in France, Italy and other countries conditions were similar. Even when national consciousness had reached a certain stage of development, a national language was still lacking. National sentiment, therefore, was restricted to those classes which could communicate with one another, but its extension to all classes presupposed a wider linguistic unity. Where a central Government existed the formation of this unity was largely the work of the royal chancelleries, and that dialect became the groundwork of the national language which was spoken at the seat of government, where usually also trade, learning and literature had their centre.

Royalty furthered the formation of nations, though without aiming at it. Henry II was unconsciously the greatest promoter of English nationality. He spoke several languages but knew no English. What the kings wanted for overcoming feudal and tribal particularism was a language fitted for legal, administrative, and diplomatic use which was understood by the educated classes. For a long time Latin served this purpose best. Decisive progress in the formation of national languages was everywhere made in the fourteenth and fifteenth centuries which were also marked by great democratic, social, anti-ecclesiastical and national movements. Even at the Great Councils of the Church the members had been since 1274 divided into nations, as also the students at the universities, and there was much national rivalry and strife among them.[3] The great conflict between England and France, which extended over two centuries, contributed much to the development of national sentiment. When in 1295 Edward I appealed to the Model Parliament to defend England against aggressive designs of the French King he tried to arouse national

---

[1] G. McKnight, *Modern English in the Making*, 1928, p. 7.
[2] J. Nadler, *Literaturgeschichte der deutschen Staemme und Landschaften*, 1912, i, p. 234.
[3] At the Council of Constance in 1417 the French denied the English the right to form a separate nation, while the English pointed out that language was decisive, and that the English nation could even claim to form five nations as five quite different languages were spoken in England.

sentiment by accusing him of proposing to blot out the English tongue from the face of the earth. In 1362 English began to replace Anglo-Norman as the language of Parliament and the Courts. In France French was definitely declared the official language of the Courts in 1539, though the Provençals protested against the exclusion of their tongue.

The growth of national languages was closely connected with the rise of the middle and lower classes. Matthew of Westminster, referring to 1263, says that " whoever was unable to speak the English language was considered a vile and contemptible person by the common people ". In the fourteenth century Latin was used for learned books, French for writings for the upper classes, and English for literature designed for people of humble station. John Gower wrote books in all three languages. In Dante's youth four languages were used in Florence ; Latin for scholarly works, French for elegant didactic literature, Provençal for aristocratic love songs, and Italian for democratic bourgeois writings.[1] Dante, himself an aristocrat, immensely influenced the evolution of Italian, he wrote in defence of its use, but he also scoffed at human vanity which caused every people and every small town to regard its own tongue as the most beautiful and as the primeval language of mankind.

4. LANGUAGE, ARISTOCRACY AND ENLIGHTENMENT

The invention of printing and the spread of popular education, Humanism and the Reformation, have been decisive factors in the development, spread and enrichment of national languages. At the same time, however, the higher classes of many countries cultivated another language, attracted by the glamour of a refined, foreign civilization, and as a symbol of aristocratic separation. In the sixteenth century Italian was fashionable at the French Court, and in the seventeenth century Spanish took its place, largely through the influence of Italian and Spanish queens and their courtiers.[2] English high society at the time of the Restoration adopted French manners and taste. The Court of Vienna followed the Spanish model, the Russian Court first

[1] Cf. K. Vossler, *Frankreichs Kulturentwicklung im Spiegel seiner Sprachentwicklung*, 1913, p. 30.
[2] This was still resented in the time of the French Revolution, and Barrère in 1794 flayed in the Convention the " courtier who was not content to distinguish himself by his vices and his depredations but also wished to distinguish himself in his country by another language so that one could have said that there were two nations within a single one ".

the German, then the French. In the seventeenth century so many foreign words, especially French ones, had intruded into the German language through the influence of courts, nobles, soldiers and scholars that national sentiment revolted, and societies for the purification of the language were founded which, however, also imitated Italian and French academies. French was absolutely dominant in German high society in the eighteenth century. When Voltaire was in Berlin as a guest of Frederick II he wrote to his friends in Paris that he felt as though in France. French was spoken exclusively, and German " was only fit for the horses ". The King's brother advised a Prussian nobleman to learn French, since he surely could not want to be " a German beast ". Even a considerable time later Prussian and Austrian ministers preferred French for their official correspondence with their sovereigns and others.

It was not exclusively aristocratic caste feeling, however, which expressed itself in this custom. The cosmopolitan and liberal spirit of the Age of Enlightenment to a large extent reflected the mentality of cultured aristocrats, and many of the great enthusiasts for humanity who adorned that age belonged to the high ranks of society. The kings who laid the foundations of national States tried to make one language the official one for facilitating a centralized administration, but as a rule they did not care to impose it upon the masses of the people. It was sufficient if the officials and the educated classes understood it. National struggles were not unknown in those times, but it was religion rather than language which served as the symbol of nationality. Henry VIII, himself of Welsh descent, introduced English in the Courts of Wales, calling it "the national mother tongue used within this realm ". Yet, " his intention was not oppressive and did not constitute an attempt to eradicate Welsh nationality as such ".[1] For Ireland, however, in the reign of Henry VIII a statute was passed, entitled " An Act for the English Order, Habit and Language ", under which every clergyman was to be bound by oath to teach the English tongue to all in his cure, and to keep or cause to be kept a school for the teaching of English. This statute was confirmed under William III and was not repealed for a long time.

At the end of the eighteenth century Joseph II tried to make German the official language in all parts of the polyglot Austrian Empire, convinced that all peoples would immensely profit by it, and hoping that a common language would bind them together

[1] So C. A. Macartney, *National States and National Minorities*, 1934, p. 41.

by brotherly love and make them patriots. The effect was just the opposite and the attempt failed. The Emperor, however, was not a German nationalist at all. His letters were all in French, the only poets he read were Italians, and he did much to protect oppressed nationalities and to prepare their national revival.[1] The Age of Enlightenment saw in language an instrument for expressing and exchanging ideas, and the rank of a specific language depended on the treasures of civilization to which it opened the road.

The example of the ruling classes was often followed by all those who aspired to social promotion and a higher grade of civilization. The result was that in many countries with a mixture of nationalities the language of the upper classes obtained complete predominance and alone adapted itself to the needs of the new civilization. The tongue of the bulk of the people became a vernacular, spoken by unlettered people only, and therefore did not acquire the vocabulary and flexibility needed to express the thought and feelings of cultured people. In this way the intellectually active elements of many peoples abandoned their native speech for another language, for example, in Brittany Breton for French, in Flanders Flemish for French, in Ireland, Scotland, and Wales Celtic for English, in Bohemia Czech for German, in Slovakia Slovak for Hungarian, in Galicia Ruthenian for Polish, in Dalmatia Croatian for Italian, in Norway Norwegian for Danish, etc. Such changes were not primarily brought about by coercion but for practical reasons. People who had much to do with administration or with trade, or desired to mix with the upper classes, or had cultural interests, adopted that local language which was most suitable for their purposes. Many also acquired a knowledge of a language which served as a means of international communication. French was the language of the aristocratic world, German that of the traders and the professions in wide parts of central and eastern Europe, while Italian and Greek were used in other parts for international intercourse.

5. The Attitude of Democracy and Romanticism to Language

The great change in the appreciation of language which led to modern nationalism was effected by the progress of democracy and the rise of Romanticism. In the Age of Enlightenment and

[1] Cf. Jakubec und Novak, *Geschichte der tschechischen Literatur*, 1913, p. 125; Paul von Mitrofanov, *Joseph II*, 1910, i, p. 265.

early liberalism the educated classes only were regarded as the real nation, at least on the Continent. When the masses began to claim and to obtain a share in political power, their language naturally was regarded as an integral part of the national personality. Democracy, moreover, intensified the tendency towards centralization. In France, for example, the Monarchy was tolerant towards the languages and customs of minorities. On the eve of the Revolution this spirit still prevailed, and the memoranda of grievances and instructions, drawn up by the electoral assemblies, show almost no national intolerance.[1] In the course of the Revolution, however, national fanaticism developed, and leading Jacobins now wished to wipe out the non-French languages spoken in France, namely Breton, Basque, German and Italian. They saw in them instruments in the hands of royalist priests and aristocrats for the defence of the old regime. Barrère in his report to the Convention called them barbarous jargons and rude dialects which only served the purposes of fanatics and counter-revolutionaries. The Alsatians were accused of sympathizing with Germany and of being traitors. St. Just, Monet and other Jacobin leaders demanded the most ruthless measures against them, even mass deportation of all Alsatians who did not speak French and settlement of French revolutionaries in Alsace, who should also take possession of the wealth of the "traitors".[2] During the whole nineteenth century democratic and national strivings were in continuous alliance. Language became the symbol of national sovereignty, independence and prestige.

Romanticism originally was to a large extent a movement of middle-class intellectuals sympathizing with revolutionary ideas. They discovered that each language had a unique value, irrespective of the level of its civilization. The Romanticists believed that the natural goodness of man had only been preserved in peoples and classes unspoilt by civilization, and they praised the beauty and wisdom of neglected popular languages. Rousseau, Herder, Fichte and their disciples asserted that the whole soul of a people lived in its mother tongue, and that every people had

[1] Cf. Beatrice Fry Hyslop, *French Nationalism in 1789, according to the General Cahiers*, 1924.
[2] Cf. the speeches by Barrère and Gregoire, delivered on January 27 and June 4, 1794, on the propagation of the French language (*Choix de rapports, opinions et discours prononcés à la tribune nationale*, tome xv, p. 247). Cf. further, C. Hayes, *The Historical Development of Modern Nationalism*, 1931, p. 50; G. van Deusen, *Sieyès, His Life and His Nationalism*, 1932; E. Wittmann, *Past and Future of the Right of National Self-Determination*, 1919; about the Jacobin attitude towards the Alsatians, cf. J. Venedey, *Die deutschen Republikaner unter der Franzoesischen Republik*, 1870, pp. 70, 102, 193.

no more sacred heritage than its language. Though the theories of the Romanticists on language have largely proved untenable, they had a most stimulating influence on the study of languages and literature and on politics and education. In former times scholars had not taken much interest in the languages of other peoples, except for the study of the Bible and classical antiquity or for missionary purposes. Now the language of every people in the world, their history and literature, were carefully studied to the greatest possible profit of learning, taste and deeper understanding of the human mind. Romanticism aroused enthusiasm for a new cosmopolitanism which was more fruitful than the superficial variety cultivated by the elegant world of the eighteenth century. It seemed that the sympathetic interest in the spiritual life of all peoples would help to spread international goodwill and the feeling of human brotherhood. At the same time the Romanticists in all nations also awakened a strong interest in their national past, and contributed much to the rise of nationality and of nationalism.

6. Language in the Age of Nationalism

National consciousness sees in the national language the principal traditional bond of the community, the means for educating the people to solidarity, and a symbol of national personality. Nationalism, moreover, regards the absolute domination of the national language in its country as a matter of prestige and often claims the incorporation of all elements speaking the same language but living in other countries. In all States of an outspoken national character the national language has a privileged position. Nationalists, moreover, wish to purify their language from all foreign admixtures,[1] they are jealous of every other language spoken in their country, and even resent it if foreigners speak their own tongue aloud in public. The true interests of a civilization are not served by this attitude. Goethe remarked : " He who is ignorant of foreign languages knows nothing of his own."

[1] A striking criticism of nationalism in language is given in Logan Pearsall Smith, *The English Language*, 1934, p. 55. Another great authority comes to the same conclusions, and says, " we cannot reasonably deny that English has been immeasurably improved by the incorporation of alien elements ". Cf. H. Bradley, *The Making of English*, 1904, p. 110. The close affinity of nationalism and racialism has led to the belief that language is an outcome of racial disposition and that a people is mentally crippled if it loses its original tongue and adopts another one. This view, however, is completely refuted by countless historical experiences and linguistic research. A Negro or Chinese may speak English or French as well as any Englishman or Frenchman, provided he has had the same education and access to the same social circles. Cf. F. Hertz, *Race and Civilization*, 1928, p. 93 ; J. Vendryes, *Language*, 1925, p. 238.

Sometimes, however, the heralds of nationality were so imbued with longing for prestige that they were prepared to sacrifice the language peculiar to their own nation. The pioneers of the Slavic renaissance were dreaming of uniting all Slavonic peoples in one great Slav nation which would be the most numerous and powerful in the world. Some saw the best road to this aim in an amalgamation of all Slavonic languages in a common tongue, others believed that Russian would become this universal language of the Slavs.[1] The Slav languages, however, were too far distant from one another for a fusion, and many of those pioneers found it expedient to write their books in German in order to make them understood by other Slavs. Neither did the plan of adopting Russian as a common tongue appeal to the non-Russian Slavs. They clung to their particular languages and traditions, and showed no more inclination to sacrifice them to the glory of Russia than to the phantom of an artificial language.

A still more difficult problem would be the selection or creation of a common Indian language for the Indian peoples. More than 200 languages are spoken in India, and there are countless diversities of caste and religion. Suggestions for the creation of a single Indian language of communication, indeed, have been made, but hitherto with little result, mainly for the reason that the people interested in these questions can exchange their ideas in English.[2] If one of those languages, however, should be declared the national language, this would certainly arouse the resentment of peoples speaking another tongue.

States inhabited by peoples of different language are usually faced with fierce struggles between them about the legal position of their tongues in courts, administration, schools, etc. From a practical point of view it would usually not be difficult to work out a solution which would satisfy all real needs. Such proposals, however, have frequently been rejected by one or more of the peoples concerned. In most cases both the majority and the minorities regarded language not so much as an instrument of civilization but as a symbol of domination, and put the point of prestige higher than common sense. Before the last war Russia and Prussia denied to their minorities almost every right to an adequate use of their languages. In old Austria, where ten or more languages were spoken, there was no privileged "language of the State", though German was used as a means of communica-

[1] Cf. L. Leger, *Le panslavisme et l'interêt français*, 1917 ; A. Fischel, *Der Panslavismus bis zum Weltkriege*, 1919.
[2] Cf. Lord Meston, *Nationhood for India*, 1931, p. 45. There are, however, other widespread languages which also serve as a lingua franca.

tion between the Government and the officials and in the army. Nobody, however, was compelled to learn another language than his own, and everybody had a right to the use of his language in courts, the administration and schools.[1] In Hungary the minorities had many grievances, as the ruling nation, the Magyars, disregarded their legal right to a satisfactory position of their languages. In France the use of the Celtic Breton language in elementary schools was strictly prohibited, and also the army was used for suppressing it. A model of fairness was Switzerland.[2] The Constitution (Art. 116) declared the three chief languages, i.e. German, French and Italian, as national languages of the Confederation and in certain districts also Romansch is recognized.

After the last war a number of new national States were established which, however, also comprised considerable minorities. Their treatment of these minorities was to be controlled by the League of Nations, but this control was not very effective. As regards language rights some of the new States adopted a liberal policy, for example, Czechoslovakia,[3] while others were rather intolerant. Italy, which, as a Great Power, was not subject to the control of the League of Nations, grossly oppressed her new Slav and German minorities, while the Soviet Union accorded to all her numerous peoples equality and encouragement as regards their languages and education. The question of a just and fair treatment of national minorities, however, does not consist merely in the recognition of their right to their national language.

7. Ireland and Her National Language

In Art. 8 of the present Constitution of Ireland Irish is declared as the national language and the first official one, while English is recognized as the second official language but not as a national one. This creates the curious and even unique situation that a language is declared the national one which is only spoken by

[1] Cf. this book, p. 200. A detailed treatment of the legal position of the languages in old Austria is given in a collective work, *Das Nationalitätenrecht des alten Oesterreich*, edited by Hugelmann, 1934, and in A. Fischel, *Das österreichische Sprachenrecht*, 1910, and *Materialien zur Sprachenfrage in Oesterreich*, 1902.

[2] Cf. H. Weilenmann, *Die vielsprachige Schweiz*, 1925.

[3] Nevertheless, the Czech language was the "language of the State" and enjoyed a privileged position which was emphasized in many ways for reasons of prestige, though this aroused resentment. A typical instance, for example, was that the municipal administration of Prague strictly prohibited any German signboards or notices on hotels, banks, shops, etc., though Prague was the capital of a country numbering 3·4 million Germans, and though it was the seat of a German university, many daily papers in German, and other German institutions. In Vienna, both before and after the war, the Czechs were free to display any notices in Czech they wanted.

a small section of the people. The Irish Government, however, hopes to change this in the course of time, and has stated that the Gaelicization of the primary schools is the first aim of public education.[1]

The case of Ireland significantly illustrates the change in the attitude to the national language which has been mentioned already. The Anglo-Normans who settled in Ireland quickly adopted the Gaelic tongue and Irish customs. Since Henry VII, and especially since James I, however, this process was reversed.[2] The old Irish aristocracy became English-speaking, or emigrated to France, Spain and Austria, where they took up a military career. Many English and Scots were planted in Ireland, and the Irish people were grievously oppressed. Gradually a new Irish nationality developed out of the fusion of old and new elements. The upper and middle classes spoke English but were Irish in sentiment, while the mass of the peasants retained the Gaelic tongue. Henceforth Ireland had a sort of double nationality, and many writers assume that two Irish nations existed and still exist side by side.[3] All the protagonists of Irish nationality and freedom before Sinn Fein, such as Swift, Grattan, Flood, O'Connell, Parnell, Redmond and many others, belonged to the English-speaking Irish nation. Most of them showed little or no interest in a revival of Gaelic as the Irish national language. The greatest of all, O'Connell, was definitely opposed to it, though he spoke Irish from his childhood.[4] He was convinced that it was in the best interests of Ireland to employ the English language, which opened the road to the highest culture and to the world. At the beginning of the nineteenth century the great majority of the Irish still spoke Gaelic, and this lasted perhaps up to the middle of the century. In 1926 17·9 per cent spoke Irish and English, and 0·42 per cent Irish only. In the long epoch of national oppression the masses of the Irish people clung to the Gaelic language, but in the nineteenth century when the oppressive legislation was repealed, or made ineffective, they gave it up voluntarily. A change in the attitude of the Irish national movement, however, was initiated by the foundation of the Gaelic League in 1892, and Sinn Fein now lays great stress upon making the knowledge of Gaelic universal. Whether its endeavours will succeed is doubtful. The children learn Irish in school but speak

[1] *Irish Parliamentary Handbook*, 1939, p. 184.
[2] Cf. E. Curtis, *History of Ireland*, 1936, pp. 170, 222.
[3] Cf. W. F. Monnypenny, *The Two Irish Nations*, 1913.—The English speaking section was often called " the middle nation ".
[4] Cf. Stephen Gwynn, *Ireland*, 1924, p. 135.

English at home, and often forget Irish as soon as they leave school. From a practical point of view they would profit more if they learned one of the other widespread languages besides English. The cultural prestige of Ireland, too, would obviously suffer if Gaelic supplanted English. Many Irish poets, writers, politicians and scholars have become famous everywhere through the medium of the English language. Swift, Burke, Sheridan, Goldsmith, Berkeley, Moore, O'Connell, Shaw and other Irishmen have been highly appreciated all over the world. If they had written or spoken in Irish only they would not even have become known to the majority of the Irish. True, many Norwegian, Swedish and Danish writers have won international fame through translations, but this was largely due to special conditions which are not likely to obtain in the case of Ireland. A universal bilingualism would, of course, obviate the danger of cultural isolation. But in this case Irish would probably be a language for patriotic display only, while English would remain the language of everyday life, literature and science. Lastly, it is obvious that any attempt to discourage the use of English would greatly exacerbate relations with the English-speaking section of the Irish nation, and would be an insuperable obstacle to a union between northern and southern Ireland.

The Welsh have preserved their language more than the Irish, though they have not shown the same national fanaticism. While in 1926 the Irish-speaking population in Eire numbered 543,511 (of whom 531,051 also spoke English), the Welsh-speaking population in Wales was about 900,000 and it has hardly diminished in the last forty years. A Welshman, Mr. Lloyd George, as Prime Minister of Great Britain, has played a rôle in the history of the world and has added more prestige to the Welsh name than a statesman of a small independent nation could ever have done.[1]

8. The Jews and Language

In the Middle Ages the Jews were cruelly persecuted in Germany and Spain, and finally driven out. They found a refuge in Poland and Turkey, and they have preserved there the German and Spanish speech which they had adopted in Germany and Spain, though not without admixtures. In later times many of the Polish Jews re-emigrated to the West, and for some time

[1] An ardent Welshman, Mr. J. Vyrnwy Morgan, *A Study in Nationality*, 1911 pp. 324, 414, recognizes that his people has obtained great advantages through its union with the English people, and has prospered in a manner which would have been impossible under a system of Welsh independence.

retained certain peculiarities of speech. With the spread of Western education among them, however, these were more and more eliminated, and many Jewish writers and speakers are counted among the greatest masters of German, French and other Western languages. This too contradicts the alleged connexion between language and race, though the Jews, of course, are not a homogeneous race. In recent times, the rising tide of antisemitism and the growth of Zionism have induced numerous Jews of eastern and central Europe to emigrate to Palestine. Many of them were inspired by the ideal of forming a Jewish nation, and the question, therefore, arose which language should be adopted as the national one. One section advocated Hebrew, which had always retained a certain place in the religious instruction of the Jews, comparable to that of Greek and Latin in our civilization, though in modern western Europe few Jews could speak Hebrew. On the other hand, a large number of the emigrants spoke Yiddish, which is basically mediaeval German, with Hebrew and Slavic admixtures. A struggle developed between the advocates of the learned and of the popular tradition, which is still going on, and a large literature was produced in both languages.[1] Religious and historical sentiment spoke for Hebrew, while practical reasons and popular traditions told for Yiddish, which was a living language closely connected with the life and feelings of the masses of the Eastern Jews and was especially favoured by the women, who were not instructed in Hebrew.

9. CONFLICT OF LITERARY AND POPULAR LANGUAGE. GREECE AND NORWAY

In modern Greece, too, we find a difference between the attitude of the more highly educated classes and the lower classes towards the national language. The aim of national prestige induced the upper classes to adopt a language which greatly differs from the popular tongue. The philologist Adamantios Koraés tried to purify the popular tongue from all foreign admixtures with the aim of approximating the language as much as possible to ancient Greek. This artificial product became the language of Parliament, the laws, the Church, science, the schools, administration and most newspapers. Unfortunately, the people found it difficult to understand this language, and it was little suited to express the emotions and ideas of modern men. The

[1] Cf. S. W. Baron, *Social and Religious History of the Jews*, vol. ii, p. 333; vol. iii, pp. 126, 168, where much literature is quoted.

object in assimilating the language of modern Greece to the ancient language was the identification of the present people with the old Hellenes. This striving obviously sprang from the romantic belief that the soul of a people was bound up with its tongue, and that the restoration of the original language, free from all later admixtures, would restore the genius of ancient Greece in the modern nation. The translation of the old Greek classics and the Bible into the popular tongue provoked the nationalists to riots and bloodshed, and prohibitions against corruption of the language were inserted in the Constitution of 1911. The adverse influence of this treatment of the living language can be guessed if one imagines that modern English writers would have to conform to the grammar and vocabulary of Beowulf. In the course of time, however, modern forms were more and more used in poetry and fiction.[1]

The opposite course was advocated by a movement for the reform of the national language in Norway.[2] In this country the language of about two-thirds of the population, including the greater part of the educated and urban population, was a modified Danish known as the Riksmaal. It dated from the former long connexion with Denmark which was severed in 1814. A part of the peasantry, however, spoke several Norwegian dialects which were used by Ivar Aasen for elaborating a new language, called Landsmaal. The Norwegians had no resentment against the Danes, and in 1905 even elected a Danish prince for their king. Yet a great campaign developed aiming at the replacement of the foreign Riksmaal by the national Landsmaal. The greatest Norwegian writers from Björnson and Ibsen to Hamsun and Undset have all used the " foreign " tongue. It was also objected that an artificial language could not be a suitable instrument for higher literature, and that its adoption by a small people would lead to cultural isolation. After a very long struggle a bill was passed which sanctioned a compromise, namely, an amalgamation of both languages. The Conservatives had strongly protested against the " vulgarization " of the language as they called it, while the majority of the Left favoured the reform.

10. SCRIPT AND NATIONALITY

Besides language, script is also significant for nationality. Before the development of script, and for a considerable time

---

[1] Cf. P. Martin, *Greece of the Twentieth-Century*, 1913, K. Krumbacher, *Populaere Aufsaetze*, 1909 ; G. Deschamps, *La Grèce d'aujourd'hui*, 1905; p. 95.
[2] Cf. G. Gathorne-Hardy, *Norway*, 1925, p. 177.

after, the laws and traditions of a people were largely in the hands of the ruling classes, and their formulation in writing was an important step towards the emancipation of the middle and lower classes, and towards nationality founded on a broad popular basis. Every language would really need a special script, suited for its system of sounds. Moreover, a peculiar script was often appreciated as a symbol of national personality.[1] German nationalists regarded the Gothic as the true German script, which is not borne out by history, and they condemned the use of Roman script as un-German. The Serbs and Croats speak almost the same language. But the Serbs use the Slavonic script while the Croats use the Latin one, which corresponds to the diversity of their churches and traditions. In Turkey after the last war the Arabic script was replaced by the Latin one, not for practical reasons only, but also as a symbol of a new national spirit.

11. Script, Language and Nationality in China

In China the old classical script was retained, in spite of its extraordinary difficulty.[2] Chinese script contributes to national unity through its peculiar character. It is ideographic, every sign denoting not a certain sound but an idea. This makes it possible that people of different language can understand its meaning. There is a considerable diversity of languages and dialects among the Chinese. Educated people, as a rule, know classical Chinese. The greater part of the people, moreover, speak some form of Mandarin Chinese, a language used also by the central administration. This language is spreading over the whole of China and has become the national language. People who do not understand one another can communicate by means of the script. Everyone knows that a certain sign means " house," though the participants in a conversation may associate with it quite different words in speaking.[3] This system also enables the present Chinese to read their classical writings, for example, those of Confucius (sixth century before Christ), while a modern

---

[1] In the Cameroons a young king invented for his people a separate script, though he knew European and Arabic script, which he rejected out of national pride. Soon 600 of his subjects could read this script. Cf. *Anthropos*, iii, p. 83.

[2] James Yen developed a simplified script by selecting a thousand characters suited for the instruction of the people. Cf. H. Hodgkin, *Living Issues in China*, 1932.

[3] Cf. J. Escarra, *China Then and Now*, 1940, p. 68. It was a favourite idea of Leibnitz to invent an ideographic universal script which everyone would be able to understand, irrespective of his language. Cf. Kuno Fischer, *G. W. Leibnitz*, 1902, pp. 14, 37.

European will hardly understand writings in the mediaeval form of his tongue if he has not made a special study of it. This script, therefore, strengthens the hold of the old classics on modern Chinese thought. Classical Chinese is still the language used for poetry, history, philosophy, religious and administrative literature, while novels and plays are written in the vulgar tongue.

Professor Lancelot Forster of the University of Hong Kong says that the difficulty of the Chinese classical language was the chief factor in conserving and maintaining the old social and political order before the revolution. " Mastery of it, as the key to the knowledge necessary for taking part in the government, required such a long period of study, and such a power of concentration and memory, that it was quite impossible for the average individual to arrive at this position." Yet, he continues, it won for itself the general approval of the community, and the people had a profound respect for those who achieved what to them was quite impossible.[1] It can be said, therefore, that the peculiarity of the Chinese language and script has had a profound influence on the social and political structure of the people.

12. Language as a Criterion of Nationality

We have so far considered the significance of language for the status and structure of a nation. It has, furthermore, great importance for national demarcation. In common opinion a nation is simply a people with a separate language, and in cases of dispute about the nationality of a people most persons immediately pass judgement on the criterion of linguistic relationship. It appears to them as natural that peoples speaking the same, or almost the same, language form one nation. Cases which do not accord with this view are disposed of as exceptions. This identification of a nation with a language group is, however, untenable. It conflicts with both the legal and the sociological concept of a nation. The groups constituted by sentiment, citizenship and language very often do not coincide but overlap. In many cases, peoples of different tongues are citizens of the same State, and sometimes also regard one another as members of the same nation. On the other hand, many different nations in both senses speak the same language. Furthermore, demarcation according to language is occasionally made difficult by the fact that large parts of a population speak two languages, or a lan-

---

[1] Cf. L. Forster, *The New Culture in China*, 1936.

guage intermediate between two others, so that it is not easy to determine to which other nation they have the closest affinity.

The English, the North Americans and a large part of the population of the Dominions speak English. French is spoken also in parts of Switzerland, Belgium and Canada, German in a great many European countries, Swedish in Finland. In South and Central America Spanish is the national language in eighteen States. Yet the citizens of each State regard themselves as a separate nation, and between some of these nations considerable antagonism has developed. The Dutch and the Flemish languages, Czech and Slovak, Serbian and Croatian, Danish and Norwegian, are practically only dialects of the same languages. However, mere dialectal differences often contribute to national antagonism or are regarded as precious peculiarities. Germans and Austrians both speak German, but a north German will usually find it difficult to understand the Austrian dialect, and vice versa. The German Swiss dialect is almost unintelligible to other German-speaking people, and the Swiss lay great stress upon speaking it among themselves in order to demonstrate their national distinctiveness from the Germans.

It is clear, therefore, that language is in many cases not a sufficient criterion for determining nationality, though it is always an important factor. When the Peace Treaties of 1919 were framed it was generally assumed that people of approximately the same language wished to form a common nation, and that no further proofs of their common nationality were required. Thus the Czecho-Slovak nation was formed out of Czechs and Slovaks, and later on the hyphen was suppressed in order to emphasize the unity of the nation. Serbs, Croats and Slovenes were also united in one State, which was first called the " State of the Serbs, Croats and Slovenes ", and was later renamed Jugoslavia in order to express the unity of the nation. All these settlements met great opposition and resistance, not only by the minorities but also by nationalities which were included in the name of the state, and thereby recognized as a privileged part of the nation, like the Slovaks and the Croats. In some cases the Peace Treaties or later settlements made the decision dependent on plebiscites which were to manifest the will of the population as to which nation they wanted to belong to. It is significant that the result of these plebiscites usually contradicted the assumption that nationality was sufficiently indicated by language. Slavs such as the Masurians in East Prussia and many Slovenes in Carinthia voted against their inclusion in Slav States, and for joining the German-speaking populations of Germany or Austria. On the other hand, the people of Oedenburg (Sopron), who predominantly spoke German, decided to join Hungary. The population of Hultschin or Hlucin, of whom about 80 per cent speak a Czech dialect, were joined with Czechoslovakia by the Peace Treaty without a plebiscite. Yet they soon put up a strong opposition to the Czech regime, and about 80 per cent even voted for the Sudetendeutsche Partei which was German-nationalist.[1] The Allied Powers themselves, however, in other cases did not regard language as decisive. German-speaking populations like those of Austria, northern Bohemia and other minor districts were not permitted to join Germany.

The view that language is the criterion of nationality plays a particular rôle in the ideology of German nationalism, though it is not confined to it. Historical events have scattered German-speaking populations over a large part of central and eastern Europe which were separated from Germany in the course of time, or never belonged to it. The Pan-Germans and their successors, the Nazis, have always looked upon these people as parts of the German nation, and Hitler has many times proclaimed himself as their protector. German is the language of the Austrians, and of the majority in Switzerland. Moreover, there are, or were, German-speaking minorities in the Baltic States, Poland, Czechoslovakia, Rumania, Hungary, Jugoslavia, Russia, Italy, France, the U.S.A., Brazil, many other American states and the former German colonies. The Pan-Germans, moreover, count even the Dutch, Flemish and Danes among the Germans in a wider sense, and regard their languages merely as German dialects. This German view of nationality is not shared by most other nations. Otherwise the English would have to claim the incorporation of the North Americans in their Commonwealth, or vice versa, and the French would have to strive to incorporate the French-speaking Swiss and Belgians in France and to recover a part of Canada. The Spanish would have a title to most of South America and the Portuguese to Brazil. The Dutch could aim at extending their frontiers over a part of Belgium and annexing the Boers.

[1] Elizabeth Wiskemann, *Czechs and Germans*, 1938, p. 231. For significant details regarding the plebiscites cf. Edward H. Carr, *Conditions of Peace*, 1942, p. 45, and Sarah Wambaugh, *Plebiscites Since the World War*, 2 vols., ed. by the Carnegie Endowment for International Peace, 1933.

CHAPTER IV

RELIGION AND NATIONALITY

1. Religion as a Social Force

The term religion has been used for such different phenomena that one of the most competent scholars has come to the conclusion that it cannot be defined.[1] It is difficult, indeed, to say where it begins and where it ends, and to demarcate it in specific cases from ethics, philosophy, poetry, magic, superstition and politics. However this may be, it is obvious that it is in many respects closely correlated with nationality. Religion has been, and largely still is, a powerful bond between the individuals of a community; national unity and solidarity has to a great extent grown out of religious roots, and every national civilization has been moulded by religious forces. It must be emphasized that this enquiry is restricted to the national implications of religion; and no attempt is made to judge the truth or the general merits or demerits of religious systems. As the spirit of every nationality, however, can only be understood against the background of its civilization, we must also try to assess the influence of religions on civilizations.

Religion has played an enormous rôle as a symbol of nationality. The real motive behind many struggles which are commonly regarded as religious was nascent national sentiment, striving for expression in national personality. On the other hand, it was religion which to a large extent imparted to a people that close solidarity which is implied in the idea of a nation, and which decisively contributed to the rise of the conviction that devotion to the national cause, and self-sacrifice in its service, were duties, commanded by an authority, higher than any human government.

The social influence of a religion cannot be simply deduced from its dogmatic beliefs. Sometimes Churches closely akin to one another in their beliefs have developed quite divergent national mentalities, as is shown by the examples of the Greek Orthodox and the Roman Catholic Churches, or of Lutheranism and Calvinism. On the other hand, religions as widely separated as monotheism, polytheism and pantheism, have often produced very similar phenomena, for example the same moral standards.

[1] Cf. Clement Webb, *Group Theories of Religion and the Individual*, 1916, p. 59.

It must not be forgotten, moreover, that every great religion has in the course of time brought forth the most different forms of belief, sentiment and organization, and therefore has moulded social relations, and in particular nationality, in quite different ways. We often find that monotheism, through mystical contemplation or speculation, ran into pantheism, or through the intrusion of popular superstitions assumed a polytheistic colour, and vice versa. The interactions between religion and social forces are complicated, and frequently indirect and unconscious.

Sentiments and ideas more or less approaching modern nationality can be found in many peoples of all ages, and in a few cases the parallels are marked. Yet national aspirations first reached a comparatively high degree of realization and a very conscious form in Western Europe. It is obvious that the modern type of nationality is a product of our Western civilization, which has grown up on the soil of Western Christianity. The great Oriental peoples, and even Hellas and Rome, have not created our type of nationality and national State. Nor have they produced systems like our experimental science, our critical history, our technical and economic organization, and our fundamental social and political institutions which were so closely interwoven with the rise of modern nationality. The reason was by no means any difference in the mental equipment of those peoples.[1] Many inventions which have been fundamental for our modern civilization were made much earlier in Asia, for example, printing. But no great use was made of them because the social system had no need of them.

We have defined national aspirations as a striving for unity, liberty, individuality and prestige, or for personality. Our present task, therefore, is to examine how religion has influenced these aspirations. The most characteristic trait of our modern civilization is the high degree of intellectual, social and political freedom, which implies equalizing and unifying tendencies. The growth of this spirit has been decisively stimulated and fostered by Christianity. Before entering, however, into the investigation of this specific connexion, it is advisable to glance at certain general aspects of the problem.

[1] It must be emphasized most strongly that the spirit of a civilization is the product of most complex historical and social forces, and cannot be interpreted as the manifestation of the soul of a race. The unity of the human mind is not disproved by the diversity of civilizations. An Indian scholar says : " It is impossible to mention a single institution or ideal in the Occident for which a parallel or replica is not to be found in the Orient." Cf. Benoy Kumar Sarkar, *The Political Institutions and Theories of the Hindus*, 1922, and *The Futurism of Young Asia*, 1922, where ample parallels of this kind are given. Cf. also my book *Race and Civilization*, 1928.

The most important tenet of every religion is its idea of the Divine. In primitive societies religion is as a rule inextricably mixed up with magic, i.e. the attempt to compel supra-natural forces to obey our will and to fulfil our wishes.[1] Magic has always proved the greatest obstacle to spiritual freedom, to intellectual progress, technical and social improvements and personal initiative. The backwardness of certain peoples is usually the consequence of a particularly strong development of the belief in magic, and of magical rites.[2] Their whole life is petrified by magical prohibitions which not only obstruct any change in customs and traditions, but also foster specific habits of reasoning, which bar the road to a rational interpretation of their environment.[3] It is clear, furthermore, that polytheism is much more liable to magical implications than monotheism. The idea of one all-powerful God discountenances any attempt to force or bribe God by magical means to comply with our selfish wishes. Monotheism, furthermore, fosters the idea that there is one great law regulating the course of nature, and it encourages man to search for this law. The great pioneers of science and learning were actuated in their research by the desire to discover the divine order in nature and society. Ethical monotheism also emphasizes the unity of mankind, and overcomes the barriers of race, caste and class. The value of mere outward magical rites is disparaged or denied, while the purity of the will is declared essential.[4]

Polytheism was certainly no absolute hindrance to the attainment of a high moral level by individuals; but, in the main, it did not encourage a development towards high standards. The mythology of all polytheistic religions was full of stories of the doings of gods which appeared scandalous to refined moral sentiment, after their original sense had been forgotten. It was widely

---

[1] An important contribution to the distinction between magic and religion has been made by Karl Beth, *Religion und Magie*, 2nd ed., 1927. Though they are quite different types of behaviour, they spring from the same root of a wide feeling of community with the Universe, or some part of it.
[2] Cf. especially Raoul Allier, *Le Non-civilisé et Nous*, 1927 (Engl. tr.: *The Mind of the Savage*, 1929).
[3] This pre-logical mentality of the primitives has been described by L. Lévy-Bruhl, *Les fonctions mentales dans les sociétés inférieures*, 1922; *L'âme primitive*, 1927 (Engl. tr.: *Primitive Mentality*, 1923). His conclusions, however, exaggerate the divergency between primitive and civilized thought. Cf. the criticism of Allier and Webb, op. cit.
[4] True, great Christian thinkers have taught predestination which denies both moral freedom and human equality. But the ethical substance of the Bible prevailed over the dangerous implications of this belief. Both Luther and Calvin carried predestination to the length of saying that even the evil that man does, he does not merely by the permission or prescience, but by the power of God. He works his will in the devil and the wicked in accordance with his good pleasure. Many modern Calvinists, however, have abandoned the belief in predestination. Cf. James Mackinnon, *Calvin and the Reformation*, 1936, pp. 234, 291 f.

felt, therefore, that man need not much bother about moral laws which the gods themselves did not care to observe. The inadequacy of polytheism induced philosophers to transform the popular beliefs in the direction of monotheism or pantheism. But philosophy was never more than a field for a small intellectual élite and had little direct influence on wider circles. Pantheism, moreover, usually conceived the world as a mirage which could not be penetrated by empirical observation. Science, therefore, was smothered by metaphysical speculation, and could not develop freely. Pantheism, in general, easily leads to moral indifference : good and evil are equally conceived as Divine manifestations. The individual feels himself either to be a demigod, or a superman beyond the bounds of morality, or as a fleeting ripple in the immeasurable ocean of nature. Political liberty, too, is not furthered by polytheism or pantheism. Both foster the identification of right with might. The political dangers of pantheism are illustrated by Hegelianism and other German philosophies.

Ethical monotheism has been a decisive factor in developing our modern nationality and civilization, though many other forces have also contributed to it. Hellenic and Oriental polytheism and pantheism have certainly produced traits of extraordinary sublimity of thought and sentiment, and careful Christian scholars have come to the conclusion that frequently Oriental piety, charity and thought have surpassed the standards of European Christians.[1] Yet in spite of such achievements the main stream did not lead to freedom and nationality. One of the causes, perhaps, was that no Oriental civilization produced an organization comparable to the Christian Church.

2. JUDAISM

In ancient times many peoples displayed a close connexion between religion and nationality. A most momentous development towards both nationality and supra-national ideals took place in Judaism. Historic events crushed the national independence of the Jews ; they lost their own state, and a large part were torn from the native soil and settled in Babylonia. Though later on

---

[1] For comparisons of Christianity with other religions cf. D. A. Stewart, *The Place of Christianity among the Great Religions of the World*, 1920, and Sidney Cave, *Christianity and Some Living Religions of the East*, 1929. Parallels can be easily ascertained from texts concerning the great religions which have been compiled in *The Bible of the World*, edited by Robert Ballou and F. Spiegelberg, 1940, and *The Bible of Mankind*, edited by Mirza Ahmed Sohrab, 1939.

this national downfall was partly made good, the people had to suffer a new catastrophe under the Romans. The Jews were dispersed over all countries, their language had already been abandoned for Aramaic, and the upper classes had largely become Hellenized.[1] The first national disasters provoked the rise of great religious and ethical preachers, the prophets, who felt inspired by God to show the right way of life to their people. Their teachings show different trends and phases which need not be followed here in detail.[2] The principal result was the emergence of ethical monotheism, the gradual evolution of the idea of a single, all-powerful and most just God who had chosen the Jewish people for a great mission, provided they strictly obeyed his commands. At first it was expected only that he would restore their independence and make them a great people at the expense of some neighbours, or even would give them the first rank among nations. But this idea was then more and more sublimated to ethical universalism.[3] God was the spiritual father of all mankind, which formed one great family. He has created man in his own image, says Genesis, and the human soul is of divine origin. The Jews, in particular, ought by a strictly religious and moral life to give an example to all peoples; they would then be redeemed by the miraculous advent of a Messiah, and the whole of mankind would enjoy the blessings of peace, brotherhood, righteousness and love.

Further features of the greatest importance for the growth of modern civilization and nationality were the complete rejection of all attempts to force or influence God by means of magic, the condemnation of orgiastic rites, a tendency to belittle rites in general,[4] the exaltation of spiritual purity or holiness, the demand for social justice and equality, the idea of the collective responsibility of every individual for the whole community, together with the idea of individual redemption. The precept of love of every neighbour, including the alien, was emphasized, though segregation from foreigners was also inculcated as a means for preserving religious and moral purity. Philosophical speculation about God and the Universe was disparaged. The national

[1] It is significant that even Philo, the greatest representative of Judaism in the Hellenistic world, in spite of his intense piety and patriotism, hardly read the Bible in Hebrew. Cf. S. W. Baron, *Social and Religious History of the Jews*, 1937, i, p. 145.
[2] A masterly sociological analysis of Jewish religious development is given by Max Weber, *Gesammelte Aufsätze zur Religionssoziologie*, 1923, vol. iii
[3] Cf. Norman Bentwich, *The Religious Foundations of Internationalism*, 1933 ; Israel Zangwill, *Chosen Peoples : The Hebraic Ideal versus the Teutonic*, 1918.
[4] The sacrifices, too, more and more assumed a symbolic and spiritual significance, and at last disappeared. Cf. W. Robertson Smith, *The Old Testament in the Jewish Church*, 1926, p. 378, and Baron, i, pp. 100, 297

restoration under Ezra and Nehemiah, the rise of the Puritan sect of the Pharisees and of rabbinic Talmudism, as also later on the struggles with Christianity and Islam, strengthened this striving for segregation from the Gentiles, and the accentuation of numerous prescriptions which had to be scrupulously carried out, led to an exaggerated formalism though the universalist tendencies were never forgotten. Among the peoples of antiquity the Jews show perhaps most parallels with modern nationality and even nationalism. Yet there are also great differences. Even before the Assyrian conquest the Jews were divided into two states and peoples. The motives of the prophets were predominantly religious and often conflicted with what we should call the national point of view. Religion became the most powerful unifying factor among the later Jews; to many it was the substitute for nationality, but it also transcended the aims of merely national aspirations.

3. The Beginnings of Christianity

The tendency towards ethical universalism which had arisen in Judaism reached its climax in Christianity, essentially a supranational creed. All mankind were to Jesus children of God and brothers and sisters. Though some of his sayings imply his special mission to the Jews, many more reject their claim to be the chosen people, and stress the equality of Jews and Gentiles. The Kingdom of God which he was preaching was neither a Jewish national state nor any other political organization. No form of government and no political or social system can claim to be the specific Christian State or Society.[1] It is the spirit of the individual that matters, the spirit of love, truthfulness, humble service and prudence, not any external machinery working by compulsion, passion and deceit. Jesus advised submission to the temporal authority as far as it did not conflict with the duties towards God, but he disapproved of any violence, of war, revenge and punishment. The attitude of the early Christians towards the State was one of deep distrust and aversion. They refused to do homage to the image of the Emperor as a god, and many also opposed war and military service. The Christians regarded themselves as a separate nation, the people of God.[2] They with-

[1] Cf. Cecil J. Cadoux, *The Early Church and the World, History of the Christian Attitude to Pagan Society and the State Down to the Time of Constantinus*, 1925, and Ernst Troeltsch, *Die Soziallehren der christlichen Kirchen und Gruppen*, 1912 (Engl. edition: *The Social Teachings of the Christian Churches*, 2 vols., 1931).
[2] Cf. A. Harnack, *The Expansion of Christianity in the Three First Centuries*, 1904, i, p. 300. Marcianus Aristides says that four nations exist, namely barbarians, Greeks, Jews and Christians. He obviously regarded the non-Christian Romans as Greeks.

drew from active participation in the courts and in public life, and formed a separate community, based on non-compulsion and brotherly love, which to their enemies seemed to be a State within the State. They rejected the ideas of loyalty to a specific fatherland and this tradition can be traced through the whole history of Christianity. At the end of the second century the Letter to Diognetus, ascribed to Justinus, says that the Christians are like strangers in their own country and regard every foreign country as their fatherland. Their real home is heaven. More than a thousand years later Vincent of Beauvais, quoting Hugo of St. Victor, wrote : Who is fettered by the fatherland is still weak ; strong is he who regards every country as his fatherland ; perfect is he to whom the whole world is a place of exile.[1] This was also Thomas More's conviction.

The early Christians were also indifferent or hostile to the acquisition of wealth, to the pursuit of learned studies and the refinements of civilization. This attitude, however, was soon modified when ever more people from the higher and educated classes embraced the new faith. Many of the new leaders were deeply versed in Greek and Oriental thought, in Roman law and statecraft, and tried to bring them into agreement with Christianity. The Old Testament, too, which often breathed another spirit than that of Jesus, was inseparably linked with Christianity, and, moreover, was indispensable for filling gaps in Jesus' teachings. When the Church developed and rose to a powerful position in the Empire, she thereby assumed a character which was often much at variance with the spirit of the Gospel.

4. Christianity Fundamental to Modern Freedom and Nationality

Both the Gospel and the Church have had a paramount share in moulding our modern civilization and preparing modern nationality. To a large extent this result was neither intended nor foreseen, nor, indeed, welcomed by the leaders of Christianity and the Church. Yet it cannot be doubted that the spirit of Christ was the most powerful leaven in the development of ideals, and that the Church was the greatest organizing factor in history.

[1] From the sixth century onwards Ireland poured out hosts of monks who wandered from one country to the other, everywhere founding monasteries, or living as hermits, from Egypt to Iceland. Their motive was the deliberate renunciation of the fatherland as a means of asceticism. The Irish life of St. Columba says the perfect pilgrimage is that of the man who leaves his fatherland completely, in body and soul, and becomes an exile in the world. Cf. *The Church of Ireland*, ed. by Bell and Emerson, 1932, p. 75.

The belief in the unity and fraternity of mankind, furthermore, contained the germs of the modern ideas of freedom, equality and solidarity. Their growth, however, was to some extent slowed up by the teachings and practice of the Church. The Fathers taught that God had destined mankind for freedom and equality, but that the fall of Adam brought about a depravation of human nature which made necessary the introduction of coercion and inequality, the rise of governments, legal differences of rank and sex, war and bondage. It was the duty of the Church and a Christian Government to overcome these consequences of Adam's sin in the spirit of Christ. The State and the existing social order, therefore, were regarded both as a consequence of sin and as a remedy against it, and this dualism in the teachings of the Church sums up her whole history. The Church was forced to recognize existing powers and to use compulsion herself, but the conviction that this was fundamentally opposed to the spirit of Christianity was never quite absent. No demand was made for immediate abolition of inequalities, but much was done to mitigate them and their gradual disappearance was furthered. The position of women was decisively improved through the insistence upon monogamy and female rights. Infanticide and exposure, or sale, of children, which were so frequent with the Greeks, Romans and Teutons, were suppressed.[1] The Christian belief in the worth of every individual soul led to the idea of inviolable Rights of Man which no State must infringe as this would destroy its own moral foundations. The idea was familiar to some ancient philosophers, especially the Stoics. But in antiquity it never became the groundwork of the State. Neither the Sovereign People of Athens nor Roman Emperors scrupled to condemn citizens to death whose opinions they suspected or whose fortunes they coveted, even men like Socrates and Seneca. The idea of the Sovereignty of the People, too, found support in the Bible, and the Huguenot and Puritan enemies of absolutism drew many of their arguments from the Old Testament.

5. Christianity and National Diversities

Nationality, however, also implies a striving for individuality and prestige, which have no value, or may even be evils, from a Christian point of view. The biblical story of the Tower of Babel indicates that the diversity of languages and nationalities

---

[1] Pope Gregory VII asked Archbishop Lanfranc to repress the custom of the Scotch to sell their wives.

was a divine punishment. It is difficult, indeed, to combine the idea of ethical monotheism and a universal moral law, valid for every people, with the fact, that the different peoples had very different moral standards. This difficulty was also felt by non-Christians who had advanced in the direction of monotheism. The Emperor Julian in his polemic against the Christians, preserved in a refutation by Cyril of Alexandria, combats the Christian tendency to ignore or deprecate national peculiarities, and ridicules the myth of the Tower of Babel. He describes the widely different customs of the peoples, which are rooted in racial dispositions and symbolized by the character of their gods. The supreme God had placed each nation and each section of civilization under a separate protecting God. While the Teutons love freedom and independence, the Orientals voluntarily submit to every despot. The Greeks abhor incest, the Persians see nothing wrong in it. Julian also tries to idealize the hideous and obscene cult of the Phrygian mother of gods in a symbolic way. Polytheism, therefore, is defended on the ground of unalterable differences in national character due to different gods. The Emperor personally had a high religious and moral standard, hardly different from the Christian one.[1] But his justification of polytheism touches the fundamental point. Polytheism stands for racial inequality and for maintenance of every national peculiarity, however immoral, while ethical monotheism stands for the unity of mankind and the universality of moral law. Polytheism completely subordinates the individual to the national group, while ethical monotheism sees in the individual the higher value.

In spite of its indifference to national peculiarities, Christianity has done much to maintain and develop them because they were deeply rooted in the soul of the peoples, and because the propagation of the faith demanded the use of the vernacular and a certain adaptation to popular customs and traditions. The Church frequently tolerated or adopted pagan customs and tried to give them a new and Christian sense.[2] It was important that the Church brought the art of writing to the barbarians and thus opened the road for a higher civilization and the development of

[1] Some early Fathers, however, showed a belief rather similar to that of Julian. The distinctions of nationality were carried back to a divine distribution of the human race among guardian-angels who imparted various customs to the nations controlled by them. The angels then were largely seduced or overpowered by Satan, which explained the evil traits of national characters. Cf. C. J. Cadoux, *The Early Church and the World*, 1925, pp. 211, 295, 465, 510.
[2] Many instances are given by K. S. Latourette, *History of the Expansion of Christianity*, 1938, vol. ii, p. 413.

national characteristics. The literature of every modern language in Europe and far beyond begins with books written by monks. Beowulf, in spite of its heathenish subject, as well as the songs of Cædmon and Cynewulf, were written in monasteries. The fact that the Christian Churches themselves soon showed considerable national diversities was due partly to the influence of pre-Christian civilizations, partly to the circumstances in which the new faith spread and took root.[1] Far-sighted rulers of barbaric peoples often realized that the new religion and the civilization connected with it could advance their peoples and their own power. They, therefore, were the first to adopt it and then induced their peoples to accept it, frequently by force. This Christianization, of course, was superficial and thousands were often baptized without much religious instruction, though this followed later. In many cases pagan kings had Christian wives who persuaded them to become Christians. Women naturally were well disposed to a faith which gave them a more dignified position. In the East, with its old civilization, Christianity was faced with very different conditions. The new faith was often embraced here with intense religious devotion. On the other hand, however, the civilized peoples of the East were then in a period of national decline and ruin, and were largely imbued with despair of the world while the barbarians of the West were inspired with the naïve optimism of youth. This diversity accounts to some degree for the different influence of Christianity on national character in East and West.[2]

6. The National Churches of the East

One of the greatest differences, furthermore, was that the Eastern Churches assumed a national character, while the Western Church remained supra-national in spirit. The Roman Empire had everywhere destroyed national independence, and Greek language and thought had widely ousted national languages and civilizations. Many religious tendencies competed for predominance. Greek thought tried to combine polytheism and pantheism in Neo-Platonism, the Jews stressed the absolute unity and spirituality of God, the Persians assumed an antagonism between the principles of good and evil, which led to a dualistic religion. Thus the development of Christian theology took place in a whirlpool of conflicting ideas, and resulted in the formation

---

[1] For the history of the expansion of Christianity compare Harnack, Latourette, and Charles H. Robinson, *The Conversion of Europe*, 1917.
[2] Cf. R. Church, *On Some Influences of Christianity upon National Character*, 1873, p. 109.

of different Churches. The religious struggles often had a national and social background.[1] The spiritual conflicts sometimes reveal national animosities, as evidenced by the bitter anti-Jewish bias of the Greek Gnostics, or the challenge of the Syrian Tatian that the barbarians were better than the Greeks. Peoples having lost their national States and cultural heritage found a substitute in religion. It was to them a matter of national pride to possess the only true faith guaranteeing them the road to heaven. Thus religion served as a national badge, and struggles which are commonly regarded as purely religious were also a groping after nationality. Sometimes a national antagonism was aggravated by that between classes. In Egypt the Roman and Greek ruling classes regarded the Egyptians hardly as human beings in spite of their wonderful cultural achievements in the past.[2] The Egyptian language sank to a vernacular of illiterate peasants, and was revived only when Christianity began to speak to the poor and oppressed in their language. Many Eastern Churches have used a national language, in their service, for example, Greek, Syrian, Armenian, Coptic, Georgian, Slavonic, Arabic, Ethiopic.[3] Many Teutons adopted Arianism, a creed of Eastern origin, and used Gothic and other vernaculars in the liturgy. In Syria dogmatic and ecclesiastical divisions led to the development of different nationalities and languages. At all times the Eastern Churches have been bulwarks of nationality, and under Ottoman domination the millet system strengthened this yet more, giving the Churches a wide autonomy in civil, educational, fiscal and other affairs. These religious communities were almost nations, and a member who adopted another creed was regarded as a national renegade.

The national principle in the Churches, was not however, an unmixed blessing. The splitting up of Eastern Christianity into numerous groups, often in bitter conflict with one another, was a source of weakness, made the Churches dependent on the State and led to religious questions being often decided according to political interests. Byzantine Caesaropapism proved an unconquerable obstacle to the rise of freedom. In the Ottoman Empire the Orthodox Patriarch and the bishops were practically tax-collectors for the Government, and they used this for their

[1] Cf. E. Woodward, *Christianity and Nationalism in the Later Roman Empire*, 1916.
[2] Cf. W. Schubart, *Aegypten von Alexander d. Gr. bis auf Mohammed*, 1922, p. 330.
[3] As to the Oriental Churches compare three works by Adrian Fortescue, *The Orthodox Eastern Church*, 1907, *The Lesser Eastern Churches*, 1913, *The Uniate Eastern Churches*, 1923; further, B. Kidd, *The Churches of Eastern Christendom*, 1927, and Brockelmann, Finck, Leipoldt, Littmann, *Geschichte der christlichen Literaturen des Orients*, 1909.

own enrichment. Their offices were usually sold to the highest bidder. In later times the Orthodox Churches became deeply involved in the ruthless national struggles which the Balkan peoples waged against one another. Also the use of national languages in the Churches had unfortunate consequences. The languages as spoken by the common people were subject to constant transformation, wrought by migrations and by the change of habits and customs. The Eastern Churches, however, clung to the form of language sanctified by use in sacred books and liturgy, and also maintained its domination in learning, literature, and higher education. The consequence was that in many countries the educated classes long used a classical language, especially for literary purposes, which was unintelligible to the lower classes and out of touch with the sentiments and ideas of the age. The use of national languages in the liturgies, therefore, led to their ossification and was harmful to national unity and to the creative spirit in literature.

7. THE ATTITUDE OF THE GREEK AND ROMAN CHURCHES TO NATIONALITY AND THEIR INFLUENCE ON NATIONAL CHARACTER.—THE BYZANTINE EMPIRE.

The greatest of all Eastern Churches was the Greek Orthodox Church, the national Church of the East Roman or Byzantine Empire. It comprised also many non-Greek peoples and encouraged to some degree the use of their tongues in the liturgy, though it also tried to propagate the classical Greek language. The Orthodox Church was divided into many autonomous Patriarchates, Churches and other communities which all had the same faith, ritual and hierarchy, but were independent of each other, used different languages and often represented different nationalities.[1]

While the Eastern Churches were national, the Roman Church was in principle supra-national. The Orthodox Church, in particular, was directed by a Patriarchate which was a State department of the Byzantine Empire, and her religious questions were often decided by the Emperors, largely on political grounds. The Roman Popes, on the contrary, came to assert their independence, and for some time even their supremacy, in regard

[1] Fortescue enumerated in 1907 sixteen independent Churches which had in 1931 decreased to twelve. Cf. M. Constantinides, *The Orthodox Church*, 1931. To this number must be added numerous Oriental Churches which do not belong to the Orthodox creed, and many Uniate Churches which are Eastern in rites and language but Catholic in their allegiance to the Pope.

to the temporal powers. The liturgical and official language of the Roman Church was everywhere Latin, though the clergy was foremost in developing a literature in the vernaculars too.[1] The cause of this difference was that the Greek Church grew up on the soil of ancient civilizations and under a Government maintaining Roman traditions, while the Roman Church developed partly on the ruins of the old Roman world, partly among uncivilized peoples. The Roman Church, therefore, was absolutely indispensable to the temporal rulers for maintaining or building up an administration and civilization. This gave the Roman Church a unique authority, even in purely temporal matters. In the West the foundations of modern States and nations were everywhere laid by ecclesiastical statesmen, while in the East the administration was in the hands of a lay bureaucracy.

The Orthodox Church has enjoyed warm sympathies among Western anti-Roman theologians from Wycliffe and Luther to our time. She has been especially praised for her national tendency and alleged democratic character which was contrasted with the unnational despotism of the Pope.[2] In truth, however, this praise needs considerable qualification. The Orthodox Church has certainly brought forth great religious personalities and remarkable achievements. Yet her influence was much less favourable to freedom, progress and nationality than that of the Roman Church, though it would be going too far to say that their development in the West was chiefly due to deliberate encouragement on the part of Rome, or that the Orthodox Church was solely responsible for their suppression in the East. The Turks in the Balkans and the Mongols in Russia were certainly formidable obstacles to progress. Nevertheless, the difference in the spirit of the Eastern and the Western Church was an important factor in creating the cultural and political cleavage between the East and the West of Europe.

[1] In some countries, indeed, the Church showed national peculiarities, especially in Ireland. The old Irish Church tenaciously clung to its special rites which, obviously, had a certain national significance. But its language was Latin, and the authority of the Pope was never repudiated. Cf. *History of the Church of Ireland*, edited by W. Phillips, 1933, 3 vols. The only important case in which Rome conceded the use of language other than Latin was that of the Slavonic Churches, and this was brought about by the rivalry with the Orthodox Church and was soon revoked. Cf. M. Murko, *Geschichte der älteren sudslawischen Litteraturen*, 1908, p. 36.

[2] In England many prominent Churchmen have for centuries tried to bring about a rapprochement or even union of the English and Greek Churches, and some also wanted to include German protestantism. The idea also played a great rôle in the thought of Gladstone, and was associated with his pro-Russian and anti-Austrian attitude which became a tradition of considerable political weight among Liberal politicians. Cf. Bruno Bauer, *Einfluss des englischen Quakertums auf die deutsche Kultur und auf das englisch-russische Project einer Weltkirche*, 1878.

The estrangement of the two Churches was a gradual process, and the final break came in 1054. The differences in doctrine and rites were slight. Though the rivalry between Rome and Constantinople for pre-eminence was one of the motives, it was not the only one.[1] Out of many frictions grew a deep national aversion and jealousy. The Greeks regarded the Romans and their Teutonic protectors as uncultured boors, as barbarians, and the Romans looked upon the Greeks as provincial upstarts who had usurped the prerogatives of Rome, and, moreover, accused them of untruthfulness. Byzantine wealth aroused the envy of the Westerners, and many plans were made for conquest of their territories. A savage outbreak of mob passion against the foreign merchants in Constantinople was terribly revenged by Latin Crusaders. Thenceforth the gulf was unbridgeable. Several attempts at re-uniting the two Churches were made by Popes, Byzantine Emperors and high ecclesiastics of both sides, but they were foiled by the violent opposition of the greater part of the Greek clergy and people. The Emperor Manuel II remarked : " The pride of the Latins and the obstinacy of the Greeks will never agree." Constantinople was already in the greatest peril of being conquered by the Turks when the Emperor and the Orthodox Patriarch reached an agreement with the Pope about re-union which was a fair compromise and was accompanied by the Papal promise to call up Western Christianity for the defence of their Eastern brethren. Even in this critical hour, however, Greek national pride rejected this settlement, and the Grand Duke Lucas Notaras declared that he preferred the Sultan's turban to the Cardinal's hat. When, however, a few years later the Sultan actually conquered Constantinople, he had Notaras and his whole family executed.

The establishment of Turkish domination in Constantinople and over a large part of eastern Europe was one of the most disastrous events of history. Most of the national conflicts which have for centuries disturbed the peace of Europe, including the great European wars of our time, were chiefly due to conditions brought about by the rise and decay of the Ottoman Empire. East and West shared in the responsibility for this catastrophe but the reason was the same here and there, namely, the strength of national egotism and isolationism which rendered rulers and peoples blind to the common danger. In vain Aeneas Silvius, the principal Papal diplomat, endeavoured to arouse the Western

---

[1] Cf. Ch. Diehl, *Byzance, Grandeur et Décadence*, 1919, p. 241 ; N. Jorga, *Histoire de la vie byzantine*, 1934, vol. ii, p. 263.

rulers for a crusade against the Turks. Before the fall of Constantinople they replied that the danger was overstated, and after the fall they were prevented by mutual jealousy from uniting for a common expedition. Aeneas Silvius wrote in 1454 :

> Christendom has no head that all men will obey. . . . Pope and Emperor have become mere dignified but empty titles ; they are no more effective than two impotent pictures in a frame. . . . There are so very many different nations, and who could shepherd such a mixed flock ? Who has command of the multitude of tongues they speak, or is able to deal with men of such widely different manners and character ? Where is the mortal man that could bring England into accord with France, or Genoa with Aragon, or conciliate Germans, Hungarians and Bohemians in their disputes. . . .[1]

The nationalism of the Orthodox Church was not only an obstacle to co-operation with Western Christianity. It was also largely responsible for the lack of national solidarity within the Empire. True, the Byzantine Empire had constantly to struggle with powerful external and internal enemies ; but being the most efficiently organized and most civilized State of the Middle Ages it would have conquered and largely assimilated them, if its own people had been more united. In spite of the strong national consciousness and excessive pride of the Greek educated classes, however, it is doubtful how far there was a Byzantine nation. The population showed great differences in language and traditions. The Government followed a policy of paternalism protecting the poorer classes, and regulating everything in an almost socialist spirit.[2] Yet Byzantine history is filled with revolutions and civil wars in which frequently parties invoked the help of foreign invaders, without any regard for national interests.[3] The uprisings were largely due to the excessive burdens of bureaucratic centralization and to the violence of militarism, both inherited from the old Roman Empire, but also to the bitterness of theological and sectarian strife and partly to the rise of feudalism. The absence of political freedom induced large masses of the people to participate in dogmatic struggles which thereby assumed great fierceness. The mysticism and asceticism of the Orthodox Church was not favourable to intellectual freedom and individual initiative. It was chiefly cultivated in the monasteries, and the monks

---

[1] Cf. W. Boulting, *Aeneas Silvius*, 1908, p. 207. The Papacy itself was discredited at that time by the great schism which was largely brought about by the rise of national states. In spite of all Papal efforts the King of Hungary and Poland alone took up arms against the Turks but was defeated. Cf. G. Hertzberg, *Geschichte der Byzantiner und des Osmanischen Reiches*, 1883, p. 566. Many Popes made further efforts to organize a crusade, and contributed much to the final repulse of the Turks in 1683.
[2] Cf. Steven Runciman, *Byzantine Civilization*, 1933, pp. 102, 173.
[3] Cf. Diehl, pp. 137, 171.

wielded great influence both with the masses and the Emperors. Still more revered, however, were the hermits who lived in squalid caves and the ascetics who spent their life standing on pillars.[1]

The Orthodox monks were not pioneers of agriculture, arts and crafts and welfare work as were the Western monks. The world seemed to them not worth the while to improve it. They preferred to torture themselves in order to win a place in heaven.[2] We also frequently find monks as leaders of a fanatical mob, raging against the Government about some abstruse point of theology. Eastern Christendom has produced an abundance of subtle theological speculations, but no rational thought on philosophical, moral and political questions such as Western scholastics did. Worldly learning was largely disparaged as a temptation to intellectual pride, and the Church exalted instead the humility and charity of ignorant souls. Byzantine national pride emphasized descent from the old Hellenes and, therefore, tried in the most pedantic way to pin down language and literature to the old classical models, ignoring the living Greek vernacular and popular thought and feelings. This attitude was largely responsible for the lack of creative genius in literature,[3] for the failure to raise the people intellectually, and to hellenize the non-Greek elements. Slavery persisted much longer than in the West, though the Church discouraged it. The difference in the spirit of the two Churches and civilizations is also illustrated by the

[1] The Hesychists (Quietists) of Mount Athos believed that by fasting and intense contemplation of their navel they could discern the light which appeared to the Apostles at the transfiguration of Christ. Their doctrine was declared orthodox by the Council of Constantinople in 1341. Cf. A. Hore, *Eighteen Centuries of the Orthodox Greek Church*, 1899, p. 458.

[2] One of the greatest historians of the Church, Adolf von Harnack, in a comparative study of the spirit of the Oriental and the Occidental Churches, comes to the conclusion that there is a deep, unbridgeable gulf between Eastern and Western civilization, due to the influence of their Churches. The antagonism of the Orthodox Christians against Western Christianity was stronger than that against Turkish domination. Many Patriarchs and other leading Churchmen of the Orthodox Church have declared that Turkish domination was a Divine blessing because it safeguarded Eastern Christianity against the dissolving Western spirit. The Eastern Churches concentrated all their efforts on the eternal life beyond this world, and unlike the Roman Church neglected the moral improvement of men in this life. Theological thought made little progress after the sixth century. The spirit of the Eastern Church was quietistic, ascetic, meditative, opposed to progress and pessimistic in regard to this world. In the Orthodox Church survived the petrified civilization of late Hellenism and Orientalism. In politics this spirit wavered between the mild anarchism and pacifism of Tolstoi and revolutionary fanaticism. Harnack also shows that the antagonism between Eastern and Western civilization was not a product of racial diversities. Cf. A. von Harnack, *Aus der Friedens- und Kriegsarbeit*, 1916, pp. 101–40. This view is combated with special reference to Slavic (especially Russian) Christianity by Pawel Kopal, *Das Slawentum und der deutsche Geist*, 1914.

[3] The most important exception is a popular epic in the vernacular on the exploits of Digenis Akritas. Cf. on the sociological causes of the lack of creativeness, K. Dieterich, *Geschichte der byzantinischen und neugriechischen Litteratur*, 1909.

following comparison. The Byzantine Empire made extensive use of eunuchs in the highest positions, even as leading ministers, generals and heads of the Church.[1] The noblest families had their sons castrated to help their advancement, and the castrated official had precedence of the non-castrated one of the same rank. The underlying idea was that a eunuch was a more reliable servant of the State and the Church as he could not found a family, and had no interest in accumulating wealth or power for descendants. In the West the same idea furthered the introduction of celibacy in the Church which—as the leading statesmen were ecclesiastics—to a large extent also obtained in the civil service.[2] Yet what a difference! One understands that a society which for material reasons held a eunuch in higher esteem than a normal man could not produce great poetry.[3] After the fall of the Empire Russia became the heir of Byzantine Caesaropapism and Orthodox traditions, and her national traits have to a large extent been formed by these factors.

8. The Roman Church and the Origin of Nationality in the West

The Roman Church has often been described as the implacable enemy of nationality. Professor Masterman, for example, says:

> The two great enemies of nationality in history have been Imperialism and the Roman Catholic Church. And in both cases the hostility has sprung from the same cause—distrust of the value of freedom. The Roman Church has been in the past a magnificent foster-mother of nations in their infancy, but she has resented and resisted their efforts to grow into manhood.[4]

In spite of the admission about the past, however, this view needs considerable qualifications. In the Frankish Empire, and in other States too, the Church was at first quite dependent on the Government, while in Anglo-Saxon England State and Church were almost fused but under the practical guidance of the Church. In the course of development Church and State everywhere contended for predominance, and it was often doubtful which

[1] Cf. Runciman, pp. 92, 203.
[2] In England, however, it took a long time till celibacy prevailed.
[3] It may be mentioned, however, that castrated singers were employed in the Papal choir until modern times. It was Leo XIII who definitely banned them from the Sixtina in 1878.
[4] Cf. J. Masterman, *The Rights and Responsibilities of National Churches*, 1908. The author also quotes with approval F. D. Maurice who wrote: The Church " thought it could exist without distinct nations, that its calling was to overthrow the nations. Therefore, the great virtues which nations foster, distinct individual conscience, sense of personal responsibility, veracity, loyalty, were undermined by it; therefore it called good evil and evil good; therefore it mimicked the nations while it was trampling upon them; therefore it beca.ne more bloodthirsty than any nation had ever been ".

side defended the really national cause. The supra-national character of the Roman Church worked for the unity of Christendom and in particular of Christian Europe,[1] but it also fostered the formation of wider and firmer regional communities out of the chaos of tribal and feudal diversities and rivalries. These traditional differences seemed of minor importance to ecclesiastics who regarded Christianity as one great mystical organism. St. Thomas Aquinas wrote: " Though one distinguishes peoples according to diverse dioceses and states, it is obvious that as there is one Church there must also be one Christian people." It was the Church that first looked upon the English, French and German peoples as units, which combated the existence of different tribal laws in the same territory, each valid for members of a specific tribe only, and which in many ways furthered that spiritual, social and political unification that led to the ideal of nationhood.[2] To the Teutonic and feudal tendency of regarding Government as a profitable appurtenance of landed property,[3] she opposed the idea that it was primarily a responsibility to God. The Teutonic custom, therefore, of dividing a realm on the death of the king among his sons was combated. The feudal tendency of separating the classes to such an extent that the unity of the people was almost wiped out also met with the opposition of the Church. Many ecclesiastical writers such as John of Salisbury compared a people to a great organism in which each organ depended upon all the others, and which formed an indissoluble unit. After the Norman conquest of England the Church bridged the gulf between the ruling and the subdued people, and brought about their amalgamation.[4] In Italy, however, the Papacy was an obstacle to political unity since this would have threatened its position. Moreover, the Church greatly enhanced the authority

[1] An excellent survey is given by Christopher Dawson, *The Making of Europe, An Introduction to the History of European Unity*, 1932.
[2] Cf. William Stubbs, *Constitutional History of England*, vol. i, chap. v; Ch. Petit-Dutaillis, *The Feudal Monarchy in France and England*, 1936, p. 113; Alfred Rambaud, *Histoire de la civilisation française*, 1911, i, p. 149. The Anglo-Saxon Boniface and his helpers in their missionary work among the German tribes were the first to conceive them as a unit, and to call their language theodisca (= popular) which led to the formation of the word Deutsch by which the Germans name themselves to-day. Cf. especially two essays about the re-entry of the national principle into history and the development of the name German in Alfred Dove, *Ausgewählte Schriftchen*, 1898; F. Kluge, *Deutsche Sprachgeschichte*, 1920, p. 225.
[3] The same idea was also applied to the Church. The Germanic landowners regarded the Churches on their territory as their private property and as a profitable investment since they brought in fees for baptisms, marriages, funerals, etc. Cf. Ulrich Stutz, *Die Eigenkirche*, 1895; *Geschichte des kirchlichen Benefizialwesens*, 1895; Loening, *Geschichte des Deutschen Kirchenrechts*, 1878, ii, pp. 357, 375, 638.
[4] Cf. W. Stephens, *The English Church from the Norman Conquest to the Accession of Edward I*, 1909, pp. 47, 194. It may be noticed that this national conciliation was chiefly the work of ecclesiastics of foreign origin.

of the kings by the rite of coronation and consecration, giving them in this way a divine sanction, the position of a magistrate instituted by God. This too strengthened the forces making for unity. But the Church was far from thereby proclaiming the king an absolute ruler. According to ecclesiastical doctrine neither the king nor the people was sovereign in the sense of unlimited power, an idea also incompatible with that of an organism. Both were subject to divine and natural law, and the Church claimed to decide whether this law had been infringed, and, if necessary, to order redress.[1] At the coronation of every king the officiating bishop asked whether the people consented. The people present, of course, were the great nobles who were thought to represent the rest. Yet the principle was implied that the people was the source of royal power and that the will of God acted through the people.

The rise of the Papacy to monarchical power, and the development of Church law, administration and finance served as a model for the rulers of states. Most of their great ministers and advisers were ecclesiastics and many of them were foreigners or of low birth. These men created the institutions which became fundamental to the development of modern states and nations. They not only laid the foundations of monarchical power but also had a great share in preparing and developing parliamentary institutions. The origin of the English parliament, in particular, was to a very large extent due to the counsels of Churchmen, and in Simon de Montfort's parliament the lords spiritual had an extraordinary predominance over the lay lords.

The evolution of England and France towards nationhood was greatly furthered by the fact that their relations to the Papacy remained comparatively undisturbed by the great struggles between the Emperor and the Pope for supremacy which had such a fatal influence on Germany's national unity. In these struggles the Popes frequently supported or even aroused national and democratic aspirations of the peoples against the emperors. They, furthermore, claimed suzerainty over a large number of states, and this was not merely an outcome of their striving for domination but was also meant as an encouragement of forces striving for freedom. The Popes stood not merely for the enhancement of their own power, they also stressed the pre-eminence of the spirit over the sword ; and their combat against worldly

---

[1] Cf. especially the great work by R. and A. Carlyle, *History of Medieval Political Theory in the West*, 6 vols., 1903 f. ; Fritz Kern, *Gottesgnadentum und Widerstandsrecht im früheren Mittelalter*, 1915, and essays in a collective work edited by F. Hearnshaw, *The Social and Political Ideas of Some Great Medieval Thinkers*, 1923.

rulers was largely directed against their claim to use the Church like a profitable property in the interests of their dynasty, and their helpers, the feudal nobility. Gregory VII, the son of a peasant, wrote to a German bishop : " Who does not know that kings and princes descend from those who, disdaining God, and persuaded by Satan, the lord of this world, were striving with arrogance, malignity, murder and every sort of crime to domineer over human beings, their equals, driven by blind passion and unbearable presumption." The revolutionary pathos of these words reveals the theocratic origin of later democratic ideas. For centuries the political life of the Italian cities and States was dominated by the struggle between the Imperial and the Papal party, the Ghibellines and the Guelphs, in which the former usually consisted of the aristocratic class and the latter of the more democratic elements. John of Salisbury taught that a tyrant who violated the natural law might be deposed or even killed, and Aquinas seemed to approve this principle. Manegold of Lauterbach declared that the people had the right to chase away a bad king as a farmer had the right to turn out a bad swineherd. Later on many ecclesiastical writers proclaimed the sovereignty of the people though subject to eternal law.

9. THE NATIONALIZATION OF THE WESTERN CHURCH AND THE REFORMATION

While the Popes were the first to appeal to the peoples in their struggles with emperors and kings, these soon took their revenge by appealing to the peoples against the Popes. There has almost always been rivalry between the temporal and the spiritual power, between the warrior and the priest, and this antagonism was rooted both in the divergency of ideals and in the clash of interests. These struggles frequently assumed the character of a combat between the national and the supranational principle, especially when representatives of the nation, or the clergy of a country, took the side of the king against the Pope. Other issues, however, were often connected with the demand for nationalization of the Church like that of general Church reform, or the striving for influence over the Papacy. The movement for nationalization started in England,[1] and soon

[1] The aim of a national Church was brilliantly put forward about 1100 by an anonymous member of the circle of Archbishop Gerard of York. His religious ideas, moreover, showed many striking parallels with those of the Protestant Reformers. Cf. Heinrich Boehmer, *Kirche und Staat in England und der Normandie im 11. und 12. Jahrhundert*, 1899. Later on Wycliff advocated a national Church, and anticipated many teachings of the Reformation. Cf. Herbert Workman, *John Wyclif*, 1926, 2 vols.

made great progress in many countries. The grievances against the Papacy were financial, political and spiritual. The Popes tried to maintain the clergy as a separate body within the nascent nations, as a State within the State, dependent on their command and contributing exclusively to their treasury. Their international policy often conflicted with national aspirations. The corruption of the Church was notorious. Moreover, the greed of kings and nobles for appropriation of ecclesiastical wealth and power, and the commercial middle classes' jealousy of the Church caused by economic competition, were important factors. The Papacy suffered a crushing defeat at the hands of French royalty, and for a long time was degraded to an instrument of French policy. The movement culminated in the Great Schism and in the Councils of Constance and Basle. The Reform of the Church failed largely through the Anglo-French antagonism in the Hundred Years War. But the Popes made compromises with the rulers which gave them large powers over the Church in their states.[1] Many factors combined to foster the rise of national states, ambitions and rivalries, and to prepare for the advent of the Reformation.

The great reformers were not actuated by a conscious striving for nationality, but the aspirations of their political allies and the course of events gave the Reformation everywhere a strongly national character. Before the Reformation the Hussites were inspired by many of its ideas which Huss had learned from Wycliff, and they combined them with the national struggle of the Czechs against German domination. Through the Reformation religion became a symbol of nationality everywhere and provided the means for moulding and expressing national personality. The decision for or against the new faith fell in many cases more on political grounds than on religious ones, and dynastic interests mingled with national motives. In England its victory was largely due to the fact that Catholicism was abhorred as the faith of the national enemy, Spain; and in Scotland the adoption of Protestantism as the national religion by the Lords of the congregation in 1557 was closely linked with their revolt against French domination. The Hungarians in their long struggles with the Hapsburgs and the Jesuits for their national independence and religious freedom were imbued with the revolutionary, warlike spirit of Calvinism, which they called

---

[1] For the national factor in these struggles cf. J. Haller, *Papsttum und Kirchenreform*, 1903; A. Flick, *The Decline of the Mediaeval Church*, 1930, 2 vols.; A. Werminghoff, *Nationalkirchliche Bestrebungen im deutschen Mittelalter*, 1910.

the " Hungarian faith " in opposition both to Catholicism and Lutheranism. Catholicism, after many vicissitudes, remained the national religion of France because it was in the interests of national unity. The French Protestants favoured both regional particularism and a limitation of the Sovereign's power by aristocratic control. In Germany the principle *cuius regio illius religio* decided for particularism against national unity. The conflicts between nations were now often intensified by the combination of national and religious hatred. In the terrible civil wars of that time it often happened that both Protestants and Catholics sought or accepted foreign help, sometimes even from national enemies. In external and internal wars every party believed itself to fight for the true faith and in the service of God, but the attempts to ally all powers of the same religion against those of the other faith never succeeded. Political interests always proved stronger than religious ones.

The Hussites had already adopted the Old Testament as a canon of morality and politics, and the Reformation more or less followed this path. This fostered the rise of ideas connected with the national aspirations of the old Chosen People, in particular the revival of the republican and warlike spirit of their theocracy. Many English Puritans believed that the English were destined to become the new Chosen People. Frederick II of Prussia, though he ridiculed all Christian religions, still found it useful to pose as a defender of Protestantism, and the Prussians adopted the battle-cry : For God, King and Fatherland ! The Russian Slavophils believed that the Slavs were destined to save humanity from decay through their pure conception of Christianity, and identified Russian nationality with the Orthodox Faith.

The influence of religion on the formation of national personality is still an important factor, and sometimes even overrides the community of language. The Flemings of Belgium and the Dutch of Holland speak almost the same language but are largely separated by religion. Their union in a single state by the Congress of Vienna was soon broken up by the Belgian revolution. The Croats and the Serbs too have almost the same language. But the former are Catholics and the latter Orthodox, which implies cultural diversities too and was a major cause of their separation into two nationalities, and of considerable national antagonism between them. The Slovaks are very near the Czechs in language, and have the same religion, namely Catholicism. Nevertheless, the Slovaks claim to be a separate nationality though the founders of Czechoslovakia stressed the unity of the

Czechs and the Slovaks, and invented the term Czechoslovaks. The main difference seems to be in the attitude to the Church, the Slovaks being fervent Catholics while the Czechs cultivate the national tradition of Hussitism, though they are not Hussites in the religious sense.

10. THE CHURCHES AND THE RISE OF LIBERTY

The close connexion of the religious struggles initiated by the Reformation with political liberty need not be discussed here in detail. The Sovereignty of the People was invoked by Protestant and Catholic leaders,[1] and the long civil wars between them led to an intense longing for national unity, especially in France where royal absolutism utilized this yearning for establishing its power. In Germany the Thirty Years War likewise furthered the cause of absolutism and, in particular, prepared the rise of the Hohenzollerns and their militarism. The Popes followed a policy of the Balance of Power, which put their political before their religious interests, and directly favoured the rise of Protestantism.[2] It was essentially the same foreign policy as that followed by England; it was due to the same cause, namely, the lack of a strong army, and it led to the same result, namely, the safeguarding of small nations against the aggressions of powerful states. The Popes dreaded nothing more than the rise of a state to such power that the independence of the other states, and their own position, would be jeopardized. For this reason they made many efforts to curb the expansion of Catholic rulers who were the champions of Catholicism, such as Charles V, Philip II, Ferdinand II and Louis XIV, and even allied themselves with Protestants against them. When William III landed in England and took up arms against Louis XIV, the Pope was on his side and influenced the Catholic powers to support him. The rise of national and political liberty was largely due to the never-ending rivalry between the spiritual and the temporal powers.

Many prominent historians have attributed the rise of spiritual liberty, and, in particular, of the spirit of free critical research, to Protestantism, and there is certainly some truth in this contention. The Mediaeval Church, moreover, was frequently represented as

[1] R. H. Murray, *The Political Consequences of the Reformation, Studies in Sixteenth-Century Political Thought*, 1926 ; Pierre Mesnard, *L'essor de la philosophie politique au XVIe siècle*, 1936 ; G. P. Gooch, *English Democratic Ideas in the Seventeenth Century*, 2nd ed., 1927.
[2] Cf. Martin Philippson, *Westeuropa im Zeitalter von Philipp II, Elisabeth und Heinrich IV*, 1882, pp. 11, 86, 92, 112, 354, 368 ; Georg Winter, *Geschichte des dreissigjährigen Krieges*, 1893, pp. 76, 330 ; William Barry, *The Papacy and Modern Times*, 1911.

the enemy of intellectual freedom, and some historians even included Christianity itself in this charge.[1] Modern research, however, has proved that neither was the old Church so reactionary nor the new Churches so progressive as formerly assumed.[2] The truth was that on both sides there were forces working for intellectual liberty and toleration, and forces of obscurantism. Modern freedom owes more to Gregory VII, Francis of Assisi and Thomas Aquinas than to Luther, and if Catholicism has brought forth a Torquemada, and many others of his kind, it has also produced a Dante, Nicholas of Cusa, Erasmus, More, Fénelon and Lamennais. Some scholastics already harboured the idea that the diversity of religions was part of God's plan for the education of mankind.[3] Every religion, therefore, might contain some truth, different religions might supplement each other, and their very multitude might foster a beneficial rivalry. Christian Humanism encouraged toleration, but the struggles of the time of the Reformation and Counter-Reformation aroused new intolerance and fanaticism. It was Protestant Free Churches which first claimed freedom of conscience, especially in Holland, England and America.[4]

11. Modern Nationalism and Religion

Modern nationalism finds itself in a difficult position as regards religion. On the one hand it is hostile to the loyalty of its followers being divided between the nation and God. It tends to idolize the nation itself and to make nationalism a religion. Furthermore, the aims of aggressive nationalism are incompatible with Christianity, and racialism, moreover, takes exception to the Jewish origin of Jesus. Yet nationalists often do not dare to show their hostility too openly as this might hurt the feelings of many followers. Moreover, the traditionalist element in every national ideology demands recognition of the national rôle of religion in the past. A typical instance is the attitude of the Nazis, who waver between open contempt of religion and lip-service to it, between praise of Luther for his revolt against Rome, and opinions

---

[1] Cf., for example, the statement of Professor J. B. Bury, *History of Freedom of Thought*, 1913, p. 67 : " In the period then in which Christianity exercised its greatest influence reason was enchained in the prison which Christianity had built around the human mind."
[2] The historical judgement must be balanced between the exaggerated views put forward both by Protestant and Catholic writers. Cf. A. S. Turberville, *Mediaeval Heresy and the Inquisition*, 1920.
[3] Cf. Alois Dempf, *Sacrum Imperium*, 1929, pp. 202, 241.
[4] On the development of toleration compare the articles on toleration in the encyclopaedias *Die Religion in Geschichte und Gegenwart*, 1913, vol. v, p. 1271, and *Encyclopaedia of Religion and Ethics*, 1921, vol. xii, p. 360.

which are the very opposite of Luther's creed, between disparagement of "Jewish" Christianity, attempts to make Christ an "Aryan", and a revival of Teutonic mythology. Similar inconsistencies can be found in the ideology of the nationalism of other nations too. French nationalists like Charles Maurras, for instance, have little sympathy with Christianity for similar reasons as the German nationalists. But they emphasize the great rôle which the Catholic Church has played in building up French nationality and civilization. They, therefore, are against Christianity but for the Catholic Church. The Church, however, has refused to accept this curious loyalty. Many French nationalists tended to regard only a Catholic as a true Frenchman. German nationalists of the older type were convinced that only Protestants could be true Germans, and showed great distrust of and aversion to Catholicism. It also seems that not a few English people still think that a Catholic can hardly feel English.[1] Every nationality really wishes to have a religion of its own symbolizing its national spirit.

12. The Influence of Religion on the National Character

The adoption of a religion as a national symbol was frequently connected with struggles between nations, and was due to reasons of national power or prestige. A strong motive was the striving for national unity which did not seem safe except on the basis of religious unity. Most persecutions of a religious minority were really directed against a community which was considered dangerous to the political or social order. In England the cause of Protestantism was long identified with that of liberty, while in France and Spain Catholicism was regarded as the guarantee of monarchical absolutism. It is clear that this belief was founded less on the specific spirit of those religions than on their rôle in the history of the peoples concerned. True, the social and

[1] Dean Inge wrote: "It is impossible to converse long with a Catholic without being conscious of an unsurmountable barrier; and if we consider what this barrier is, we find that we cannot confidently appeal to those instincts and moral traditions which are the common heritage of all English people." Cf. William R. Inge, *England*, 1926, p. 68. H. G. Wells (*Guide to the New World*, 1941, p. 35) attacks Catholicism not because it is un-English but because it is incompatible with the foundations of social intercourse. "You can no more trust a devout Catholic in your household and in your confidence than you can risk frankness or association with a Nazi spy. Never will the devout Catholic be really frank with you. Always there will be a reservation; always the priest will be lurking in the background.... To marry a Catholic is only half a marriage, and your children will be only half your own. And manifestly if you do business with Catholic shops, if you subscribe to Catholic charities, if you entrust your children to Catholic teachers, you are helping to sustain a hostile campaign against the candid life." These views of Mr. Wells savour of the seventeenth century rather than the twentieth.

political implications of a religion are never insignificant, but their interpretation always depended on the specific historical traditions and aspirations of a nation. The rise of modern historicism increased attention to the importance of religion for national traditions. The development of nationalism, moreover, gave vogue to the idea that religion was an outcome of the racial soul of the nation. This thesis, however, is incompatible with history. Every great religion has brought forth such different concepts, ranging between the opposite poles of unity and plurality of the Divine, transcendence and immanence of God, free will and predestination, mystical self-effacement and magical self-assertion and so on, that it can never be interpreted as the expression of necessarily restricted racial dispositions. Neither can it be proved that certain concepts were favoured by specific races. The correlation of religious ideas with the national character in the sense of historic traditions, however, is more in accord with the facts. Every religion has to a certain degree been shaped by national experiences and aspirations, and has also moulded them. On the other hand every nation has seen its religious ideals in the light of its traditions and through the spectacles of its temperament.[1] It has already been pointed out that the Greek Church and the Roman Church have had a very different influence on the national character. The same holds true of the different creeds which existed after the Reformation. Most great peoples of Europe had just entered on a period of special spiritual and social plasticity and growth when the Reformation set in, and this explains why the traditions formed in those days have still a great hold on the mind of nations, even where religion itself has lost much of its power. We must restrict ourselves here to a few illustrations of the influence which some religions have had on social and political ideas, and on philosophy.[2]

13. THE SPIRIT OF CATHOLICISM AND ITS INFLUENCE ON NATIONAL CHARACTER IN ENGLAND, FRANCE AND GERMANY

The Church in the Middle Ages developed numerous systems of thought, comprised under the name of Scholasticism, in which

[1] " Every age, every nation has shown a pathetic eagerness to trace in Him the lineaments of its own ideal. . . . Is it disrespectful to say that the Christ of Renan is a Frenchman, the Christ of Seeley's Ecce Homo an Englishman, the Christ of some recent German biographers a German of the new type ? " W. R. Inge, *Personal Idealism and Mysticism*, 1907, p. 89. The various concepts of Jesus' personality against the background of the times are surveyed in Gustav Pfannmüller, *Jesus im Urteil der Jahrhunderte*, 1908.
[2] The social spirit of the Churches has been described by Ernst Troeltsch, *Die Soziallehren der christlichen Kirchen und Sekten*, 1912.

a Christian philosophy was elaborated that became the fundamental tradition of Catholicism. The general aim was to bring into agreement reason and revelation, human nature and the mysteries of faith. The scholastics, for this purpose, attempted to combine the Bible with Greek, Arabian and Jewish philosophy, while at the same time the canonists incorporated large parts of Roman Law in ecclesiastical statutes, and clerical statesmen in all countries constantly worked out compromises between the principles of Christianity and the necessities of time and place. The Roman Church, therefore, was animated by a strong intellectual activism, by faith in the power of human reason to understand the plans of God, and in the power of the human will to act accordingly. This faith, however, was not a boundless optimism. It was not the reason of every individual, without regard to his education, experience and morality, which was recognized as a guide, but the reason of the élite of the hierarchy, the great fathers, saints, thinkers, and dignitaries of the Church under the monarchical lead of the Pope. True, this rationalism was hemmed in by many factors, as by the sacrosanct character of every word of the Bible, the temptations of symbolic interpretation and mystical speculation, the authority of great teachers of the past, hierarchical and political interests, and the backwardness of scientific knowledge and criticism. Nevertheless, Scholasticism was a tremendous training in thought. It laid the foundations of modern natural and political science, it teemed with the germs of progressive ideas, and even its negative results had at least the effect of inviting a tolerant spirit in advanced thinkers.[1]

The comparatively compromising spirit of the old Church had its parallels in many Empires which endeavoured to create a wide spiritual unity. The danger implied, however, was that of religious and moral laxity, and the Reformation was largely a revolt against this laxity as evidenced in the practice of indulgences and gross corruption. The enormous importance of Protestantism for the growth of modern ideas was that it revived a spirit of uncompromising religious and moral earnestness. The Catholic Church too was greatly purified in the Counter-Reformation, and consequently became much more intransigent. On the

[1] The rise of mediaeval rationalism in its wider sense has been described by Hermann Reuter, *Geschichte der religiösen Aufklärung im Mittelalter*, 2 vols., 1875–7. The shortcomings and superstitions of mediaeval Catholicism have found an equally learned historian in G. G. Coulton, *Ten Mediaeval Studies*, 1930 ; *Five Centuries of Religion*, 1929. The contributions of the Church to civilization have been described from a catholic standpoint by Gustav Schnürer, *Kirche und Kultur im Mittelalter*, 3 vols., 1924–9, and by Georg Grupp, *Kulturgeschichte des Mittelalters*, 6 vols., 3rd and 4th ed., 1923–32. For the political and social theories, cf. Carlyle and Troeltsch.

other hand, however, the rejection of compromise led to radicalism in every field. The equalitarian implications of Christianity prepared for the advent of modern democracy and nationality, and the odium theologicum survived in the acrimonious quarrels of modern professors and intellectuals.

The English have embraced Christianity with greater fervour than any other Teutonic people.[1] Anglo-Saxon laws and institutions were more strongly influenced by the Church than Frankish ones. English missionaries won wide continental countries for Rome. When this spirit flagged the Normans came who were deeply stirred by the religious revival which emanated from the monastery of Cluny.[2] A further renewal of religious zeal was brought about by the coming of the friars, the Franciscans and Dominicans, who were received with greater enthusiasm, and exercised a stronger influence on kings, nobles and the people, and contributed more to the advance of charity, science and learning than anywhere else.[3] They also had a large share in preparing and founding parliament, and in the revolutionary movements of the later Middle Ages they were champions of the poor and even preachers of communism.[4] There was less heresy in England than anywhere else, and the inquisition was never introduced. The English Peter's Pence was the backbone of the Papal treasury, but the crusades evoked less enthusiasm than in France. King and parliament early and successfully resisted Papal encroachments, though the conflicts were never so bitter as in Germany and France. Wycliff taught the main tenets of the Reformation 150 years before Luther.[5]

English mediaeval thought developed chiefly the rational sub-

[1] This statement is substantiated by a detailed comparison of ecclesiastical influence on the institutions and traditions of various Teutonic peoples which I hope to be able to publish elsewhere, as space does not permit to summarize it here.

[2] Cf. T. Crutwell, *The Saxon Church and the Norman Conquest*, 1909. W. Stephens, *The English Church from the Norman Conquest to the Accession of Edward I*, 1909.

[3] Cf. the testimony of Albert of Pisa in Edward Hutton, *The Franciscans in England*, 1926, p. 112. Felder says : " The English nation has given to the Franciscan order a greater number of prominent scholars than all other nations together, and of the greatest authorities all were English, except St. Bonaventura." Hilarius Felder, *Geschichte der wissenschaftlichen Studien im Franziskanerorden bis um die Mitte des 13. Jahrhunderts*, 1904, p. 316.

[4] Many of them were hanged for their propaganda. Cf. Arthur Jennings, *The Mediaeval Church and the Papacy*, 1909, p. 207 f. ; Bede Jarrett, *The English Dominicans*, 1921, pp. 17, 149. As to the influence on parliament cf. E. Barker, *Dominican Order and Convocation*, 1913, but also the critical remarks by A. Pollard, *The Evolution of Parliament*, p. 137 ; Coulton, *Ten Mediaeval Studies*, 1930, p. 58, calls the Franciscans " the high ancestry of Puritanism ", and describes them as Puritans in the invidious sense of the word.

[5] Their spirit, however, was different. Luther was chiefly actuated by religious impulses. Wycliff, as Hearnshaw expresses it, was first and foremost a nationalist, Cf. F. Hearnshaw, *The Social and Political Ideas of Some Great Mediaeval Thinkers*, 1923, pp. 216 f.

stance of Christian philosophy. Roger Bacon's empiricism and William of Occam's nominalism show many parallels with characteristic tendencies of modern English thought.[1] On the other hand, England participated least of all nations in mediaeval mysticism. Particularly striking is the absence of mysticism in the English nunneries, which produced no personalities that can compare with the great German mystics.[2]

In France and Germany the Church owed her organization and education largely to the Anglo-Saxons Boniface and Alcuin.[3] After Charlemagne, however, the Church was devastated by the progress of feudalism, which also infected the spirit of the Church herself. The monastery of Cluny became the birthplace and centre of a movement for Church reform striving for liberation from the domination of worldly powers over the Church throughout the Christian world.[4] A peculiar achievement of the French Church was the taming of the warlike half-barbarian nobility, and the evolution of French chivalry with its refined code of honour and splendid civilization which was admired and imitated by the knights of all countries. This chivalry created ideals which for many centuries had a very strong influence in forming the national mind.[5] One of them was a quite new spiritualized concept of relations between the sexes, the rise of a romantic idea of love. The share of the Church in building the nation and preparing national unity was as decisive as in England. The strengthening of royal power was also here marked by sharp conflicts with the Papacy and by the striving for a national Church. The greatest pride of France was her scholastic learning, but the great teachers at the University of Paris were chiefly English, Italians and Germans. Nevertheless, the preference for rationalism which now dominates French civilization is partly a heritage of that time. But French anticlericalism too is very old. To a large extent, scholasticism ended in scepticism, and the spread of Arabic-Jewish pantheism undermined orthodoxy. In southern France heresies

[1] On national characteristics in mediaeval philosophy cf. Karl Werner, *Die Scholastik des späteren Mittelalters*, 1887, vol. iv, 1, p. 5 ; A. Dempf, *Sacrum Imperium*, 1929, p. 355.
[2] Eileen Power, *Mediaeval English Nunneries*, 1922, p. 239. The spiritual difference between English and German nunneries was in my view partly due to social conditions, partly to the fact that the English nunneries stood chiefly under the guidance of the Benedictines and Cistercians, who represented another and more feudal spirit than the Dominicans who had the guidance in Germany.
[3] Cf. Albert Hauck, *Kirchengeschichte Deutschlands*, 1900, vol. ii ; K. Werner, *Alkuin und sein Jahrhundert*, 1876.
[4] Cf. E. Sackur, *Die Cluniacenser* 2 vols., 1892.
[5] When in twentieth-century France even radical and socialist politicians used to fight out points of honour by sabre or pistol, they proved the strength of the traditions of chivalry.

of Oriental origin and anti-clericalism were rife before their barbarous extermination by the crusaders against the Albigenses. France has also produced great mystics, in particular those of the emotional type, though also some speculative mystics. In art religious sentiment culminated in Gothic architecture which spread from France over all countries.

In Germany the Saxon dynasty founded their power on the Church since the lay-vassals were quite unreliable. The Church received immense donations and privileges but was absolutely controlled by the Emperor. This led to the great conflict with the Papacy which was at last settled by the Concordat of Worms. In the beginning of the thirteenth century, however, the Emperors lost their influence, and the Church came entirely into the hands of the nobility. The bishops and abbots mostly rose to the rank of rulers of principalities, and the monasteries were little more than institutions for the maintenance or profit of nobles.[1] German ecclesiastical history shows many great and saintly churchmen, but the predominant type was for a long time the bishop who spent his life like a nobleman with feuds, hunting, wine and women. Many of these bishops were ruthless warriors who enjoyed warfare and committed the greatest horrors against the people. When Richard of Cornwall was elected Emperor and came to Germany he was struck by this peculiarity of the German Church. He wrote to his brother, King Henry III of England: " how fierce and warlike are these German archbishops "! According to Caesarius of Heisterbach a Frenchman remarked that he could believe a great deal; but he would never believe that a German bishop's soul could be saved.[2]

The most remarkable feature of German mediaeval thought was the extraordinary development of religious mysticism. It was chiefly cultivated in nunneries, under the spiritual direction of Dominicans, and was represented both by learned theologians and by many nuns of outstanding genius. Hegel and the Romanticists have regarded these mystics as the founders of German philosophy and as the characteristic expression of the German soul. This view has been repeated by countless authors,

[1] Cf. Aloys Schulte, *Der Adel und die deutsche Kirche im Mittelalter*, 1910; A. Werminghoff, *Verfassungsgeschichte der deutschen Kirche*, 1913, pp. 60, 69. In Scotland too the power of the nobility led to the corruption of the Church. The contribution of the Church to the building of the modern State, and the number of clerical Chancellors was much smaller than in England. " The condition of the Church, which was certainly much worse than in England, goes far to explain the vehemence and the violence of the Scottish Reformation." Cf. R. Rait, *History of Scotland*, pp. 124, 130.
[2] Caesarius of Heisterbach, *Dialogue on Miracles*, ii, chap. 27.

and has become a national dogma, aiming at exalting German profundity and spirituality at the expense of Western shallowness and materialism. Modern research, however, has shown that German mysticism was to a large extent determined by foreign models. Its speculative branch followed Neo-Platonism, its emotional one the road shown by Bernard of Clairvaux and Francis of Assisi.[1] In scholasticism, the more rational sort of Christian philosophy, Germany was behind France, England and Italy, though she counted Albertus Magnus among her sons. The reason was that universities which were the seats of scholasticism were founded much later in Germany than in those countries. Thought, therefore, was chiefly cultivated in monasteries which had escaped the demoralization of the Church. These, however, and still more nunneries, fostered mysticism. Moreover, the desperate political and ecclesiastical conditions of Germany induced many true Christians to withdraw from the world which seemed to be ruled by Satan, to seek a refuge in the innermost recesses of their soul, and to indulge in mystical contemplation and speculation. The ancient master of the greatest German mystics, Plotinus, had also belonged to an age of disintegration and national ruin. The mystical tradition became one of the strongest factors in the religious, philosophical and poetical evolution of Germany. Luther, the modern metaphysicians and the romanticists, have all been strongly influenced by mystical ideas.

14. Luther and the German Mind

Towards the end of the Middle Ages the German people had more grievances against the Church than the Western nations, England, France and Spain, which had already made great progress with the nationalization of their Churches, and which probably had less to suffer under the exactions of Popes and their own clergy than the Germans. Luther's motives in starting a revolution against Papacy and its creed were not national nor political but religious. His mind was as exclusively centred on the relation between God and the individual soul as that of a great mediaeval saint, and his whole outlook, indeed, was, to a very large extent, mediaeval.[2] But his extremely violent tempera-

[1] Cf. Martin Grabmann, *Die Kulturwerte der deutschen Mystik des Mittelalters*, 1923, pp. 5, 10, 23, 41, 62.
[2] Many eminent Protestant historians of the Church admit to-day the strength of the mediaeval element in Luther, though in important points he went back to Paul and in other respects he developed more modern concepts. In a great many things, however, especially in regard to political and social freedom, the people's rights, toleration, superstitions, trade, mediaeval scholastics have held much more progressive

ment and combative coarseness were the opposite of saintliness. His concept of human nature was deeply pessimistic. Reason he called " the devil's whore who can nothing but blaspheme and revile whatever God says and does ". Human will he regarded as utterly unfree, and unable to avoid sin except by God's grace. All human knowledge was but folly, the virtues of the ancients but shining vices. Erasmus's striving to show the agreement of Christianity with natural reason—which was also the aim of scholasticism—seemed to Luther a horror. Jesus has put love higher than anything else, and said that we should forgive the erring brother seventy times seven. Luther thundered : " Damned be love into the abyss of hell if it is maintained to the damage of faith."

Politics did not interest Luther. The Christian had simply to obey the orders of his government, however unjust and cruel it was. Every government was ordained by God, and wicked rulers were a divine punishment for the sins of their subjects. No right of resistance was admitted by Luther. " It is better," he declared, " that the tyrants should a hundred times do wrong to the people than that the people should once do wrong to the tyrants." The depravity of human nature could only be restrained by a rigorous government. Stern and pitiless justice was needed to maintain order and discipline. When the downtrodden peasants rose against their oppressors and claimed abolition of serfdom as a postulate of Christianity, Luther rejected their moderate demands with the greatest violence, and exhorted the princes and nobles in words of appalling cruelty to show no clemency. The revolt was quenched in streams of blood, and the nobles took horrifying revenge. Luther later said : " I, Martin Luther, have slain all the revolting peasants for I have advised that they should be slain—all their blood is on my head. But I attribute it to our Lord God, he has bidden me to speak thus."

It was Luther's gloomy view of human nature which made him distrust the people. The populace, he insisted, must be firmly

views than Luther. Cf. Troeltsch, *Soziallehren*, p. 427 ; A. v. Harnack, *Dogmengeschichte*, 1898, p. 380 ; " Die Reformation und ihre Voraussetzungen " (in *Erforschtes und Erlebtes*, 1923, pp. 72–140) ; H. Boehmer, *Luther im Lichte der neueren Forschung*, 1913, pp. 134, 149 ; K. Holl, *Gesammelte Aufsätze zur Kirchengeschichte*, vol. i, 1927 (against Troeltsch). Most important for the understanding of the German Reformation is the masterwork by Friedrich von Bezold, *Geschichte der deutschen Reformation*, 1890. Cf. further, L. von Ranke, *Deutsche Geschichte im Zeitalter der Reformation*, 6 vols. ; H. Grisar, *S. J. Luthers Leben und sein Werk*, 1927 ; R. Pascal, *The Social Basis of the German Reformation*, 1933 ; G. von Below, *Ursachen der Reformation in Hist. Ztschr.*, 1916 ; F. Meinecke, " Luther über christliches Gemeinwesen und christlichen Staat ", in *Hist. Ztschr.*, 1920.

kept in check, for " to the ass is due his fodder, burden and whip ". " The ass wants to be thrashed, and the mob wants to be governed with force." Melanchthon, his principal disciple and assistant, even found that serfdom was rather too mild " for such a wild and uncouth people as the Germans are " True, Luther wished for a paternal and peaceable government ; the prince was to rule like a father over his family. Many German rulers, indeed, have heeded this advice, and have governed their petty principalities in a more or less patriarchal way. Some have done much for education and for charitable institutions. The fatal influence of Luther's teachings on the German mind, however, was that they inculcated complete submissiveness to the Government, that they were absolutely anti-liberal and anti-democratic, and that they prepared the soil for later doctrines exalting ruthless force in the service of militarism and nationalism. Luther held no special brief for princes, but in practice he greatly furthered the rise of absolutism, partly through the fact that full power over the Church and the ecclesiastical estates came into the hands of the rulers.

Present German nationalists praise Luther as the greatest national hero, the truest expression of the German soul. The Reformer in his attacks against the Pope frequently incited national animosity for his purposes, but nationality and patriotism as such had no value in his eyes. The " German nation " he defines as the rulers into whose charge God has given the people. The idea of nationhood, therefore, was alien to him, and could not grow in the atmosphere of orthodox Lutheranism. The Hohenzollerns, who later laid the foundations of Prussian nationality, learned much from Calvinist Holland and Catholic France and became Calvinists themselves. The revolution which Luther started plunged Germany into terrible internal strife and external impotence. The Protestant princes pretended to defend " German liberty " against " Spanish tyranny ", but were always ready to sell the national interests to the King of France. The advance towards national unity and nationhood was frustrated ; for a long time Germany lagged behind the Western States in every respect, and through her internal struggles excluded herself from a share in the New World overseas. This later rankled deeply in the German mind, and led to the demand for " living space " and to the catastrophe of our time.

Most important of all was Luther's influence on German ethics. His practical moral and social teachings were largely drawn from the Old Testament, which did not hinder him from haranguing the Germans against the Jews with a violence which even Hitler has not surpassed. Luther's concept of faith and grace laid all stress on the subjective state of the soul while external works were declared valueless. This attitude gave direction to the whole evolution of German moral philosophy. Almost all German philosophers thenceforth stressed the subjective side of morality, and rejected any allowance for human happiness and social improvement which played such a rôle in English moral philosophy.

It would be easy to contrast sayings of Luther with those of Jesus, and to wonder how they could possibly be brought into agreement. Yet Luther sincerely believed that he was the mouthpiece of the Lord, as when he put the responsibility for the slaughter of the peasants on God. There is a parallel in the spirit of German nationalists who justify the most blatant aggression and the most ruthless barbarism as mere self-defence against the insidious plans of other nations, and as a service to " culture ". Many traits of the dominating German spirit, such as the preferring of mysticism to reason, of extremism to compromise, of heroism to common sense, and the belief in being inspired by God while behaving like Satan, can be traced back to the demonic personality of Luther, though other factors too have had a share in developing them. Even Nietzsche's superman is his legitimate offspring.[1] At the same time, there is also quite a different German, a good paterfamilias, an indefatigable, conscientious worker in every field, a dreamer longing for the stars, a thoughtful admirer of nature, an easy-going lover of " wine, women and song ". All these traditions too owe much to Luther. German civilization has been stimulated by him in many ways. The atmosphere of the pastor's home has bred countless German scholars. The mystical element in Luther's faith had great significance for the development of German philosophy, poetry and music. In particular, the ground was prepared for romanticism and pantheism which have inspired great poets and artists but which also had a great share in undermining Christian standards in modern Germany.[2] Hegel, Wagner, Nietzsche, Bismarck and Treitschke have carried on certain traditions of Lutheranism, and transformed them in a sense which Luther would have abhorred.

[1] This has been convincingly proved by a prominent theologian and ardent defender of Luther, Karl Holl, op. cit., p. 533.
[2] On the other hand, Luther has also influenced the forerunners of the Quakers and Wesley.

15. Calvinism and National Character

Luther's Protestantism was unable to defend itself against the striving of rulers and nobles to exploit religion for their selfish interests. The Church was threatened with becoming a mere instrument of the State like the Eastern Church. In this critical moment Calvin vigorously stressed the independence of the Church, and thus continued the policy of the great Popes who had contended with the temporal powers for freedom and, practically, for supremacy of the spiritual power.[1]

Though the fundamental theological doctrines of Calvin are about the same as those of Luther, the influence of Calvinism on the national character was very different from that of Lutheranism. To Luther God appeared as the loving father whose grace was extended to every fervent believer in him. Religion was primarily a matter of pious and humble feeling, and whoever sincerely trusted in God could be pretty sure of salvation. Calvin conceived God as the stern, majestic ruler who had arbitrarily selected some men for salvation and condemned others to hell for enhancing his own glory. To him God was primarily power and will, and energetic action in the service of God was the best proof of belonging to the elect. Luther wanted to save the souls of individuals and was not interested in communities. He preferred patient suffering to action, and left public affairs to the existing authorities. Calvin aimed at founding the perfect Theocracy, a community of saints, or a new Chosen People, on the model of the Old Testament, and stressed strictest moral discipline, and ascetic devotion to working and struggling as a means of self-discipline. There was no room for toleration in his community, he distrusted the people as much as Luther did, and rejected any right of revolution, though he approved the defence of existing rights by authorities instituted for this purpose such as assemblies of the Three Estates. Events, however, gave Calvinism a revolutionary tendency. In several countries it was taken up by the nobility in their fight against royal absolutism. In Scotland John Knox organized the Church on democratic and anti-hierarchical lines. His successor Andrew Melville once took King James VI by the sleeve, called him God's silly vassal, and added that there were two kings and kingdoms in Scotland, the commonwealth under King James, and the Church under Christ.[2] No wonder that in France, where the national cause

---

[1] Cf. Bernard Lord Manning, *The Making of Modern English Religion*, 1929, p. 94.
[2] This was exactly the theory of the mediaeval Church. Cf. O. Gierke, *Political Theories of the Middle Ages*, 1900, p. 104.

was widely identified with royalty, Calvinism appeared as a danger to national unity and this decided its fate. In economic matters Calvinism was less hostile to Capitalism than Lutheranism, and even to some extent stimulated its development, though not intentionally.[1]

16. THE BRITISH CHURCHES AND NATIONAL CHARACTER

The Church of England prides herself upon her traditional moderate and tolerant spirit and emphasizes that these traits correspond to the national character. Her doctrinal teachings and rites are not revolutionary innovations, but continue old Christian thought and practice, they keep the middle way between extremes, and her ministers and members enjoy a wide measure of freedom in their beliefs. True, the Church has not always been tolerant, and has in former times been severely criticized for subservience to the ruling powers. With certain qualifications, however, those claims are justified. The chief cause of the compromising spirit of the Anglican Church was the wish of the men who guided the course of the English Reformation to make the Church both national and supra-national, to give her national traits, and yet to maintain her position as a member of the universal Church under a General Council.[2] It was the idea of a world-confederacy, a sort of ecclesiastical League of Nations, which animated them. Further factors were the care of Henry VIII, Elizabeth and William III for national unity, the conservatism of the majority of the nation, the moderation of Cranmer, the broadmindedness of Hooker, and later the influence of the spirit of enlightenment.

The English character, furthermore, has been decisively moulded by the activity of the " Free Churches ", which in spite of divergent views agreed in the attempt to revive a truly Christian spirit. Puritan sects, such as the Independents, suffering under persecution, became the pioneers of toleration and democracy, and tried to realize the ideals of a Christian society in the wilderness of the New World. The Quakers saw the essential spirit of Christianity in the rejection of violence and self-sacrificing practice of brotherly love. The Unitarians tried to combine Christianity with enlightened and humanitarian thought. The

---

[1] On the much-debated question of the influence of Calvinism on the development of capitalism, cf. Max Weber, *Gesammelte Aufsätze zur Religionssoziologie*, 1922, vol. i, and the criticism by R. Tawney, *Religion and the Rise of Capitalism*, 1926, pp. 212, 226, 319, and by J. Kraus, S.J. *Scholastik, Puritanismus und Kapitalismus*, 1930.
[2] Cf. Professor H. Shuttleworth in *Religious Systems of the World*, 1903, p. 508.

Methodists brought Christianity near to the broad masses again, and had a large share in sharpening the social conscience.

If we investigate how far the ideals of modern nations agree with Christian standards we find that Britain probably heads the list, though it cannot be said that the motives which underlie the growth of her traditions and institutions were mainly religious. Peaceableness, for instance, is not only a Christian precept but also a rule of economic success and general common sense. Anyhow, the Christian background of British civilization is outspoken even in many features which are no more consciously connected with religion. German and other writers are accustomed to dismiss any reference of British politicians to Christianity as cant, but this only shows a lack of understanding rooted in their totally different national mentality.

It is neither possible nor necessary to investigate these problems here in detail. But it may be mentioned that one of the main causes of the comparatively efficacious christianization of British social life was the multitude of Churches in Britain which stimulated a beneficent rivalry in practical Christianity. The work of the British Churches recalls the vision of the great thinker and reformer, Cardinal Nicholas de Cusa, who taught that every religion showed some fragment of truth, that every faith and nation had their specific virtue, and that their diversity, therefore, was in the plans of God.[1]

17. Religion and the Supra-national Spirit

Great religions have in a certain phase of development transcended the boundaries of nationality, but have soon been faced by the open or disguised resistance of the national principle. They have been forced to make compromises with nationality or even to submit to its domination. Yet their supra-national spirit has never been eradicated. Aspirations of a cosmopolitan character have become real forces, but on the soil of religious sentiment irrespective of dogmas and Churches.[2] Merely economic, political, intellectual or artistic interests are no substitute for the bonds constituted by religion. Religious intolerance

---

[1] A fine appreciation of Cusa's ideas and personality is given by R. Stadelmann, *Vom Geist des ausgehenden Mittelalters*, 1929. Cf. also J. M. Düx, *Nicolaus von Cusa und die Kirche seiner Zeit*, 2 vols., 1847.

[2] Cf. Norman Bentwich, *The Religious Foundations of Internationalism*, 1933. The influence of religion in the development of the idea of humanity has been traced in the monumental work by F. Laurent, *Histoire de droit de gens et des rélations internationales, Etudes sur l'histoire de l'humanité*, 18 vols., 2nd ed., 1865–80.

has certainly often aggravated national antagonism. On the other hand, toleration too is essentially a religious idea.

In ancient Rome the Fetial priests kept strict watch over the observance of international law and had to prevent the declaration of wars for unjust causes.[1] In the Middle Ages the Church regarded all mankind as one community under the overlordship of the Pope though with autonomy of the different peoples.[2] The Popes claimed to be supreme arbiters in international disputes and frequently performed this function in a remarkable way. On the other hand, they also started the crusades against the Mohammedans. Their aim was not primarily the expansion of Christianity. Gregory VII first called up the Christians, not for the deliverance of the Holy Sepulchre, but for the liberation of Asia Minor and the salvation of Constantinople. His plan, however, did not materialize. The chief motive of the Popes was the striving to promote peace among the Christians by diverting the warlike passions of the feudal nobility from internal feuds to a great holy war against the infidels under their own supreme direction, which promised greatly to strengthen their position.[3] The failure of the Crusades, however, impaired the authority of the Papacy; the crusaders of different nations became increasingly aware of national diversities between the Christians, and the more thoughtful among them began to admire the Saracens for their gallantry, loyalty and other merits. Many princes, knights and chivalrous poets expressed their belief in human equality, in religious and national toleration,[4] frequently emphasizing the brotherhood of mankind as a Christian tenet. These feelings were shared by many Mohammedans.

The development of the ideas of international law, and of an international organization as an instrument for maintaining peace among the nations, was also initiated by religious thinkers. The scholastics already had given thought to these problems; then the Christian humanists, Erasmus, Vives, More, Grotius and others, revived the early Christian abhorrence of war and taught cosmopolitanism. Two Spanish theologians, the Dominican Franciscus a Victoria and the Jesuit Franciscus Suarez, may be

[1] Cf. Coleman Philipson, *The International Law and Custom of Ancient Greece and Rome*, 1911, vol. ii, p. 318.
[2] Cf. Gierke, p. 10.
[3] This policy of the Popes has later been paralleled by that of many statesmen who used a foreign war for bringing about internal peace and national consolidation.
[4] Many examples of the awakening of national consciousness and rivalries among the Christians, and of the spirit of toleration and comradeship in chivalry towards the Saracens are given in H. Prutz, *Kulturgeschichte der Kreuzzüge*, 1883.

considered the founders of international law, which was soon developed further by Gentili and Grotius. Franciscus a Victoria and many other theologians were also great defenders of the rights of the natives in the newly discovered world, and in England it was the Christian conscience which brought about the suppression of slavery. The Christian missionaries of many denominations were the first who studied the soul of the backward peoples and recognized them as brothers. The missions protected the natives against the greed and brutality of white traders and settlers, and led them on the road to a higher civilization. Moreover, the missionaries became the founders of the science of cultural anthropology which had an immense influence on modern views of history, psychology and sociology.

18. Religion and Nationality in India

The importance of the religious factor in developing Western civilization and nationality becomes particularly clear by a comparison with Indian conditions. In India thought and social life have been most powerfully moulded by religion. The numerous religious systems that have appeared in the course of history represent almost every possible form. The dominant factor in Indian life is Hinduism, a somewhat indeterminate agglomeration of customs and beliefs which comprises numerous and widely divergent varieties and has evolved as well profound religious philosophies as primitive cults of natural forces and demons. It has produced many saints and ascetics whose devotion to their religious ideas was unsurpassed, and its ethical teachings were often such as to command admiration. On the other hand, in the prevalent forms of Hinduism the whole of life is controlled by traditions and hedged in by rites which have magical significance, and which frequently appear to us as superstitious, cruel and immoral. Certain systems of Hinduism are inspired by a lofty spirit, and often show striking parallels with Christianity at its best. On the whole, however, Hinduism as a living force in social life did not stand for those ethical ideals which have paved the way for the idea of nationhood in Europe, namely the spiritual unity, liberty, equality and fraternity of mankind as taught by Hebrew prophets and Christ.

Hinduism is predominantly a national, or rather racial, creed which cannot be adopted by people not born as Hindus, though a few exceptions exist in certain parts of India. Its most conspicuous peculiarity is the division of society into a vast number of castes and sub-castes which are separated by countless barriers, forbidding or greatly hampering intermarriage and social intercourse and even casual contact. In many cases a caste is also connected with a specific profession which is hereditary. It has been much discussed whether the caste-system has developed more out of racial or out of professional divisions. But there is no doubt that the members of a caste regard themselves as a sort of racial unit superior to many other castes, and that each caste looks down upon the lower ones, and strives to avoid contact with them as this would contaminate its purity.[1] The so-called outcasts—who in reality belong to low castes—are treated with incredible contempt. Their mere approach is regarded as a pollution, and they are subject to the most humiliating and harmful restrictions. They are also known as the untouchables, and their number was estimated in 1930 at 43·6 millions, or nearly 30 per cent of the Hindu population.[2] Some specially rigid castes, however, even forbid intercourse with higher castes, and would not accept water or food from a Brahmin. In the estimation of orthodox Hindus Europeans are equally untouchable.[3] There is much fierce strife between castes. Conditions, however, greatly vary in different parts of India, and in many cases certain relations between castes are permitted. Though the caste-system is sanctioned by religion it is frequently not regarded as necessary that all members should belong to the same religion.

The caste-system certainly has its good sides too, but it is now widely recognized that it is the greatest obstacle to the development of national unity and solidarity in India. The caste is to the orthodox Hindu far more than the nation or the fatherland is to most Europeans. On the other hand, some features of this system are definitely baneful. Rabindranath Tagore has described it as " a gigantic system of cold-blooded repression ", and is of the opinion that the regeneration of the Indian people, directly and perhaps solely, depends upon its removal. European influence and Indian reformers are working in this direction. Under British rule the outcasts are legally treated as equals, and their position has been improved in many ways. Yet the opposition of Hinduism to any reform is very

---

[1] " All the castes, even the most despised, are animated by vanity and by a passion to be exclusive, which has strangely embittered these quarrels." Émile Sénart, *Caste in India*, 1930, p. 19.

[2] On their position compare especially chapter viii in L. O'Malley, *Indian Caste Customs*, 1932, p. 137.

[3] " British residents in India are not always aware that some of the Hindu gentlemen with whom they shake hands think it incumbent to remove the consequent contamination by bathing," O'Malley, p. 141.

strong, and often results in terrorism against those who recognize the untouchables as human beings and brothers. Even Gandhi was threatened with personal violence when he denounced untouchability as a disgrace, and urged its abolition. But Gandhi does not reject the caste-system as a whole, and would not personally agree to a marriage out of caste. It is significant that, while laxity as regards the rules of caste is gaining ground among highly educated Indians and the urban classes, who belong chiefly to the privileged castes, the great mass of the Indians who live in villages, and belong to low castes, tenaciously stick to the rigid precepts of the system. Even the untouchables, though anxious to remove the stigma of birth, rarely suggest the total abolition of caste.

Besides caste, other sacred institutions of Hinduism are hardly less incompatible with our idea of a nation as a community based on freedom, equality and self-government. In particular, the position of women according to orthodox Hinduism is still very far from freedom and equality. Yet women, especially the elder ones in the rural districts, are a mainstay of orthodoxy and conservatism. Lord Curzon is said to have made the remark that what India needs is a new grandmother. The European idea of nationhood, moreover, is that of an advanced, vigorous and progressive people. In India frequently magical prohibitions and prescriptions tend to paralyse individual initiative and to stifle cultural and economic progress.[1] Many rules and habits of Hinduism are also prejudicial to the health and vigour of the race, such as the marriage of children, and the rejection of modern hygiene, medicine and technical methods. The British administration has suppressed the most harmful manifestations of this spirit such as the burning of widows,[2] human sacrifices, infanticide, slavery, castration, co-habitation with wives under the age of 12, conditions fostering plague and famine, and so on. Most reforms have been fiercely opposed by defenders of orthodox Hinduism, and many British plague officers have been murdered by them for carrying out their duties. The British administration, moreover, has opened the road to the development of a national spirit by many positive reforms. In earlier times great rulers have

[1] Cf. Lord Meston, *Nationhood for India*, 1931, pp. 21, 57. A detailed analysis of Hinduism and its influence on social life is given by Max Weber, *Gesammelte Aufsätze zur Religionssoziologie*, 1923, vol. ii.

[2] When Bentinck prohibited the burning of widows in 1829 there was strong opposition in orthodox Hindu circles, and for a long time the custom was indulged in surreptitiously. The last known case was in 1937 near Agra. In the Punjab 10 wives and 300 concubines perished on one Sikh noble's pyre in 1844. Cf. R. Coupland, *Britain and India*, 1941, p. 26.

twice for short periods united almost the whole of India in an empire, but they did not found an Indian nation, and their empires were soon dissolved into numerous fragments. The religious and social system of Hinduism was an insurmountable obstacle to the formation of Indian nationhood. It was British rule, and the influence of Western civilization, which created the conditions for national unity and liberty through the maintenance of peace, security and the reign of law, the spread of education and modern ideas, the development of economic resources, and the gradual introduction of self-government. It has, moreover, also provoked a growing striving for independence among Indians, and the example of Western nationality and nationalism has been eagerly imitated. It seems inevitable, however, that this spirit must result in the rise of several nationalities instead of one Indian nation as the Congress patriots hope.

Many forerunners and pioneers of the modern Indian national movement were aware of the necessity of thoroughly reforming Hinduism in order to prepare the soil for the growth of nationhood.[1] While maintaining the fundamental traditions of Hinduism they also derived inspiration and stimulus from contact and controversies with Christian missionaries. Ram Mohan Roy and others tried to reconcile Eastern and Western traditions. With the rise of a political national movement, however, the new national consciousness began to repudiate everything foreign, irrespective of its value. Modern Indian "nationalism" to a large extent stresses Hinduism, and defends it as the symbol of Indian nationality, in spite of the incompatibility of some of its tenets with modern nationhood.[2]

19. Islam and Nationality

Mohammed received his religious and ethical inspiration largely from Judaism and Christianity, and the theologians and lawyers who later on supplemented his very incomplete and inconsistent teachings and developed a system of doctrines were also greatly influenced by Christian, Jewish, Hellenistic and Persian ideas, and by Roman law. Islam, therefore, shows an extraordinary number of parallels with mediaeval Christian

---

[1] Cf. C. Andrews and G. Mukerjee, *The Rise and Growth of the Congress in India*, 1938, pp. 13–53.
[2] Cf. Meston, pp. 24, 34, 65, 89. Lord Meston thinks that Indian nationalism is largely the revolt of a privileged class against modern influences, threatening its social predominance, and the struggle of an ancient civilization to stem the advance of Western ideas and liberty.

thought and practice which, however, were partly due also to the influence of Islamic civilization on the Christians.[1] The forces which prepared the soil for nationality in Christian Europe also existed in Islamic religion, civilization and politics, but they did not develop farther than was possible in a predominantly mediaeval atmosphere. All believers in the true faith were to be regarded as brothers and many precepts of Islam admirably served the purpose of welding all Moslems into a great fraternity.[2] Nevertheless, inequalities of sex and status were not abolished. Moslems could be slaves, and the position of women was far from equality with men, and often assumed a degrading character. The brotherhood of the believers transcended the boundaries of nationality, but Mohammed did not preach the brotherhood of all men. His teachings formed a creed for enthusiastic warriors; Jews and Christians were to be tolerated, but had to pay tributes and were later subjected to humiliating discriminations. Pagans were to be given the choice of conversion or death. The prophet's utterances about other peoples and creeds varied greatly under the changing impulses of his fiery, warlike temperament and his milder feelings. In the second surá, for instance, he rejects all coercion in matters of faith, and in the fifth he declares that God has given to every people a separate law and an open road to salvation, and that, therefore, all peoples should try to surpass one another in good works. Yet other utterances (for instance, surá nine) breathe a very different spirit. On the whole, however, Islamic rulers have in the past been more tolerant towards other religions than the powers of Christianity, though partly for reasons of policy.

Islam was not an offspring of Arabic traditions, but through the personality of its founder it became intimately connected with the Arabian people. The eruptive expansion of the Arabs over many countries was primarily actuated by their striving for wealth and power, not by religious motives. But the new faith gave the tribes a national cohesion, and intensified their fighting ardour to the highest degree. It was declared the duty of a Moslem ruler to reduce all non-Moslem states to subjection by force of arms. Death on the battlefield opened the road to paradise.

The Arab State, especially under the Omaiyad dynasty, can in some respects be called a national one. Each Arab tribe had

[1] Cf. especially C. H. Becker, *Islamstudien*, 1924, p. 386. For the general character of Islam, cf. D. Margoliouth, *The Early Development of Mohammedanism*, 1924; Horten in *Religion in Geschichte und Gegenwart*, vol. iii, 1912, under "Islam".

[2] Cf. T. W. Arnold, *The Preaching of Islam*, 3rd ed., 1935, p. 416.

a strong tribal consciousness and pride, which through common conquests and a common religion assumed sufficient compass and unity to approach national consciousness. On the other hand, however, the Arabs were at first more an army of occupation than a nation and they were even forbidden by Omar to possess landed property, in order to maintain their mobility. The subject peoples were not permitted to learn Arabic nor encouraged to become Moslem as this would have freed them from the tribute on which the victors wished to live. No common nationality, therefore, developed. Soon, however, fierce enmity revived among the Arabian tribes and did much to destroy the unity and power of the nation. The binding force of their religion proved insufficient to form a durable unified nationality. In the Christian world of that time, however, nationality was equally undeveloped. The Arabian conquerors were often welcomed by sections of the Christians, for example in Spain, Sicily, Naples and southern France or were even called in by them in order to obtain help against other Christians.

In the Arab World Empire, moreover, the subject peoples, especially the Persians and Syrians, were more highly civilized than the ruling Arabs, and indispensable for the growing tasks of administration. The victory of the Abbasid dynasty marks the ascendancy of the Persians over the Arabs. The Empire now looses its national traits and becomes a despotism, based on the military force of the ruler, not on the tacit consent of the ruled. The rulers more and more employ mercenary troops and these, like the Pretorian guards in the Roman Empire, undermine stability by frequent risings and arrogating to themselves decisive influence on political affairs. Failing a strong national bond between the subject peoples, religion was emphasized by the rulers as a uniting factor. All the later Mohammedan states were founded more on religion than on nationality. Religion, however, proved inadequate for this task. Theological strife, the rise of sects, often with a national background, frequent rivalries for the throne based on religious grounds (usually on alleged descent from the clan of the Prophet), and at last the decay of religion itself through its mixture with politics and worldly interests, were common features of the Islamic world. Islam has no real priesthood or Church, in the Christian sense. The unalterable rule of the Koran is maintained by a class which is halfway between theologians and lawyers. Though this class has produced great intellectual and ethical achievements, its influence has on the whole been unfavourable to the growth of nationality. The complete subordination of law and science to theology proved an insuperable obstacle to progress beyond the limitations of the mediaeval world. A special obstacle to individual initiative and progress was the spirit of fatalism produced by the doctrine of predestination. It must be remarked, however, that later Christian believers in predestination, such as the Calvinists, did not show this spirit, but were even stimulated by the idea of predestination to an extraordinary activism, both political and economic. The fatalism of the Moslem, therefore, was probably a joint product of religion and military despotism.

The Turkish conquest of the Islamic world and many other countries was prepared by the employment of Turkish bodyguards and mercenary troops by Arab rulers, as the ascent of the Teutons in the Roman world had been made possible by their rôle in the Roman army. The Ottoman Empire by the conquest of Constantinople became the successor to the Byzantine Empire and took over some of its institutions. Turkish, Islamic and Byzantine traditions co-operated in creating a despotic regime which in principle was not based on a common nationality but on a dominant religion.[1] The Turks were never more than a minority and resembled more an army of occupation than a nation. They had a semi-feudal organization, living on the spoils of incessant wars and the tributes of subject peoples. The most prominent part in the army and the administration, however, was played by soldiers and officials of non-Turkish origin who had embraced Islam, and were legally slaves of the Sultans. After the conquest of the Balkans most of the Grand Viziers and generals were converts of Slav, Albanian, etc., origin. All economic work and higher intellectual activities were left to the subject-peoples. They were organized in religious communities (millets) which enjoyed a wide autonomy and formed states within the state. The Turks used the millets as organs for fiscal exactions, and otherwise were glad not to have to deal with the internal affairs of the Christians. Foreign merchants, moreover, were granted great privileges (capitulations) which gave them a sort of extra-territorial position, and the Christians in later times stood under the protection of foreign rulers. This state of things was completely opposed to the principle of the Western national State, and has greatly contributed to the ruin of the Ottoman Empire. A still more potent factor in this process,

[1] Cf. A. Toynbee and K. Kirkwood, *Modern Turkey*, 1926; Sir Harry Luke, *The Making of Modern Turkey, from Byzantium to Angora*, 1936.

however, was the despotism of the Sultan. His arbitrary will was restricted only by the laws of Islam as interpreted by its great lawyer-theologians. Their doctrines contained also some ideas which we regard as essentially modern,[1] but their chief influence was opposed to freedom and progress. The religious character of the Empire implied a privileged position of the Moslem which was very grievous to the members of other religious communities, but it also saved them from extinction. When Sultan Selim planned a radical unification of the Empire by compulsory prescription of Islam as the religion and Arabic as the language for everybody, the clerical lawyers pronounced that this was contrary to the law of the Prophet, and the Sultan dropped his plan.

The Empire was distintegrated and finally ruined through its lack of national unity, its militarism, the lawlessness and corruption of its soldiers and officials, and the indifference and later the revolt of most of its peoples. The misrule of the rulers and the discontent of the ruled culminated under the long reign of the Sultan Abdul Hamid. He dreaded the spirit of nationality which was already everywhere undermining the Empire and emphasized its religious foundations. Panislamism seemed to him the remedy for the revolutionary principle of nationality. The liberal reforms which his predecessors had enacted under the pressure of England and France and the hopes for national unity were invalidated by the aggravation of despotism and mediaevalism, the religious fanaticism of the Turkish masses and the national fanaticism of the revolting Christian nationalities. The Young Turk Movement which overthrew despotism in 1908 aimed at the fusion of all the nationalities in a common Ottoman Nation, with Turkish as the language of communication. The Young Turks abandoned the idea of basing the Empire on Islam; they were hostile to the hierarchy of clerical lawyers and promised freedom and equality to all religions and nationalities. Yet they also tried to foster Turkish patriotism by an appeal to Turkish racial pride. For this purpose they encouraged Pan-Turanianism, cultivating the memory of the alleged Mongolian ancestors of the Turks [2] and the idea of solidarity and national unity of all peoples of Turanian stock, which implied the liberation of millions of

[1] Cf. Count Léon Ostrorog, *The Angora Reform*, 1927.
[2] In the seventies and eighties a French writer, Léon Cahun, in his books glorified the Mongol conquerors Jinghiz Chan and Timurlenk, who were the most terrible butchers in the history of the world, as supermen, and the Mongols as a racial aristocracy. The Turks, according to him, descended from the Mongols and were for superior as doughty warriors to the Arabs and Persians. The Arabs poisoned them

people living in the Russian Empire. A movement set in for purifying the Turkish language from Persian and Arabic words, and for adopting words and names derived from Turanian roots. The Turanian idea, however, was incompatible with that of an Ottoman Nation, based on equality of all races, and, in particular Young Turk policy led to the growth of estrangement between Turks and Arabs. The efforts to save the Empire were thwarted by wars which ended in its ruin. After the World War the Ottoman Empire was dismembered, and the peace terms of the Allies even menaced the integrity of Turkish territory and the whole national future of the Turks. General Mustapha Kemal Pasha organized victorious resistance to these claims, seized power, and then set out to create a national State on entirely new foundations.

This policy began with the ethnic unification of the State by expulsion of all elements considered as alien, and by the reception of kindred immigrants expelled from the Balkans.[1] It is significant, however, that the criterion of what was alien and kindred was still religion. Turkey expelled the Christians, even if speaking Turkish only, and the Balkan nations expelled the Moslem, even if speaking Slavic or Greek only. Soon, however, the Turkish reformers more and more discarded religious institutions and traditions from political life. The millets disappeared as also the Capitulations, the people was declared Sovereign, the self-determination of the Arabs was recognized, and Ankara became the capital instead of Constantinople. The Caliphate, which implied the duty of defending Islam and which still appealed to the feelings of millions of Moslems outside Turkey, especially in India, was abolished. In the mosques Turkish replaced the sacred Arabic language, the Koran was translated into Turkish, and the purification and Turanization of the language was continued. Arabic script gave way to Latin script, which meant a great saving of time in the learning of the art of reading and writing. The fez, which had become a symbol of religious conservatism, was abolished and the European custom of wearing hats introduced. Law was completely emancipated from religion, the Swiss civil code and other foreign

with their hypocritical Koran, denationalized and weakened them, and prevented in this way the building up of a great Turkish world empire, extending over the whole of Asia and Europe. His theories show an affinity to Nietzsche's praise of the ruthless warrior, the wonderful " blond beast " and his contempt of Christianity. Cahun's ideas mightily appealed to the Turkish intelligentsia and laid the foundations of Pan-Turanianism. Cf. Ostrorog, p. 56.

[1] Cf. C. Macartney, *National States and National Minorities*, 1934, p. 433, where the exchange of minorities after the last war is described and criticized.

laws were adopted *en bloc*, without any discussion of single clauses. The legal position of women was fundamentally altered by the abolition of all laws and customs encroaching upon their equality with men. Polygamy was doomed to extinction by prohibiting any further marriage with more than one wife. The sacred custom of women wearing a veil before their face was suppressed too. Education was taken out of clerical hands and reformed according to European standards. All these and other reforms were quite incompatible with Islamic precepts and traditions. They implied the recognition that modern nationality could only grow in an atmosphere permeated by Western ideas. In this respect the Turkish, like the Chinese, national revival differed from the national movement in India.

The connexion of modern ideas of nationality with Western civilization is also shown by the rise of Arabian national aspirations in the Ottoman Empire and after its fall. It is significant that the pioneers of the Arab national revival were chiefly Christian Arabs, educated in missionary schools, both Catholic and Protestant.[1] The missionaries and their pupils were the first who gave a modern education in Arabic, established printing presses for Arabic, published many important books and journals, and united the warring creeds among the Arabs by a common ideal. Egypt, however, detached herself from the Arab cause as national pride was aroused by the great civilization of ancient Egypt, which was much older than Arabian civilization.

[1] Cf. G. Antonius, *The Arab Awakening, the Story of the Arab National Movement*, 1938, pp. 43, 54, 79.

CHAPTER V

THE NATIONAL TERRITORY

1. The Significance of Territory for a Nation

By national territory is understood the country with which a nation by long tradition is so intimately connected that it regards it as the homeland and as an integral part of its whole existence. We can imagine a nation without a State of its own but hardly one without a more or less contiguous area which it inhabits, and in which it is rooted, both physically and spiritually. The close community and personality implied in the idea of a nation presupposes this connexion with a territory. A people scattered over many countries, and nowhere rooted in the soil, would as a rule soon lose its personality. It would decrease in number, become denationalized and at last disappear.

The relations between nations and territories are manifold and reciprocal. A nation is to a large extent the product of a natural territory. Soil, climate, and configuration produce a specific social structure which then creates the striving for a separate nationality and leads to the development of national characteristics. On the other hand, the territory is also a product of the nation. The nature of each country has been immensely transformed by the activities of the peoples which have lived in it throughout the ages. This interaction is particularly obvious in regard to the so-called natural frontiers. The germs of a nation have first grown in narrow confines under the protection of natural barriers, and later national aspirations were directed towards wider natural boundaries such as the sea, great rivers, and high mountains. The territory between these frontiers was regarded as the rightful living-space of the nascent nation, and its success or defeat has then had the greatest influence on the natural conditions of the country.

The national territory is not merely a place of residence which can easily be shared between different nations as a house between different families. Modern national consciousness differs from older forms in the claim to exclusive power over its territory.[1]

[1] In societies of a mediaeval, pre-national structure this was not the case. Many Oriental and European peoples had no objection to foreign traders, or colonists, settling their own affairs among themselves according to their own laws and under their own magistrates. This was the origin of the Capitulations which played such a rôle in Turkey, China, etc. When the Oriental peoples became nation-minded, they regarded this system as derogatory to their national dignity, and demanded its

The claim to national self-determination is primarily a claim to the domination of a specific territory. Very frequently, however, two or more peoples live in the same country, and it may be that none has the majority or a better right than the others, and that a partition is impracticable. This raises many momentous questions, for example, whether a territory can be a national home for more than one nation, whether the advantages of possessing a large country in partnership with another nation can induce a people to merge its national personality in a wider one, whether expansion by conquest has led to the formation of real nations, what causes lead to the creation of new nations or to the disruption of old ones, and so on. It may also be asked on what principles, if any, the right of a nation to a territory can be founded, and if every people has such a right, regardless of its capacity adequately to use the territory. The size of a country also greatly affects its political fate. Many peoples in the course of history have either not reached, or not maintained, nationhood because they were either too small or too large, and in any case the structure and character of a nation are largely determined by its size and geographical conditions.

2. Is a Territory essential for the Concept of a Nation?
The Case of the Jews

It has sometimes been contended that a territory is not absolutely essential for a nation, though, certainly, of great importance. There are, indeed, communities scattered over different countries which are widely regarded as nations such as the Jews, the Parsees and the Gypsies. In spite of certain parallels, however, they should not be called nations nowadays. The Jews have once been a nation, and their religion has in many of them kept alive the hope that their nationality will revive. Until modern times, moreover, the Jews were secluded from the Christians by a double religious barrier; they formed separate communities living in their ghettos, under their own magistrates,

abolition. In its beginning, however, it was the Orientals who did not wish to be bothered with the affairs of foreigners and were glad to leave this business to the heads of the foreign settlements. In Europe many kings up to comparatively recent times have favoured the settlement of foreigners in their realms who promised to introduce new trades and industries, and have even tried to attract them by the grant of the right to live under their own laws and in autonomous communities. The wide dispersal of national minorities over many countries of central and eastern Europe is due to this policy. In England the German traders, organized in their Hansa, almost formed a state within the state. All foreign merchants, however, were tried before courts in which half of the members were of their nationality.

laws and customs, and frequently spoke a language other than that spoken by the Christians. This explains why it was usual to call the Jews a nation before their emancipation.[1] The abolition of territorial and social segregation, however, soon led to increasing assimilation and mixture, and the great majority of the Jews who lived under conditions of civic equality abandoned all idea of forming a separate nation. They felt themselves British or American or French or German by nationality, and Jews by religion, and a very large number abandoned their traditional religion in order to facilitate assimilation. The rising tide of anti-Semitism, nationalism, and national sentiment in general has led to the development of Zionism, which postulates a Jewish nationality. Nevertheless, the recent evolution of the Jewish question shows clearly that national aspirations, without a strong historical connexion with a territory, do not constitute a nation. The Zionists, indeed, regard Palestine as the Jewish national territory, and wish to build there a Jewish national State and to make Hebrew the national language. Other Jews think of Palestine, or some other country, as a refuge for persecuted coreligionists without stressing national aspirations, or would be satisfied with sharing Palestine with the Arabs. Some Jewish thinkers would wish to create in Palestine merely a centre for the maintenance of the Jewish cultural heritage. Many orthodox Jews hope that their people will sometime return to the promised land under the Messiah, but they reject and combat the national ideas of the Zionists which conflict with their purely religious outlook. In eastern Europe very many Jews regard themselves as a separate nationality and wish to be legally recognized as a national minority, but most of them wish to stay in the country where they are living and oppose the idea of a general return to Palestine. In their eyes Yiddish is the national language, not Hebrew. This diversity of opinions shows that the Jews as a whole cannot be called a nation, though many are aiming at this goal. In the countries where they enjoy equal rights the vast majority share the national traditions and aspirations prevailing in those countries, and many are particularly patriotic citizens, obviously for the very reason that they have to face prejudice.

[1] Cf. S. Baron, *Social and Religious History of the Jews*, 1937, vol. ii, p. 262. Even in that time, however, the territorial dispersal of the Jews resulted in considerable diversities among them. Between the Sephardim (Spanish-Portuguese Jews) and the Ashkenazim (German- and Eastern-European Jews) an antagonism existed which sometimes amounted almost to a racial one. Its origin, however, was mainly social.

3. Home Feeling and National Feeling

The main significance of territory for nationality is its influence on national sentiment. It is often assumed that the national spirit is nothing else but attachment to the native soil. Yet national feeling and home feeling are not the same, and the national territory, that is that claimed by a nation as its country, is not identical with the home country in the narrower sense, that is the place where we have been born or which is nearest to our heart through long residence and many cherished memories.[1] This narrow territory has a psychological significance quite other than that of the fatherland. It means the remembrance of childhood and youth, of family life, relatives and early friends. Its woods and meadows, its valleys and rivers, its villages and historic monuments are much more familiar to us than those of other parts of the fatherland, many of which we have only seen as passing visitors, if at all. Our youthful dreams and hopes, the decisive phases of our own development, the image of our forefathers, are intimately connected with the natal soil. The fact that a certain, rather small, territory is so bound up with the growth of our personality explains why the barrenness and bleakness of a home country usually does not diminish our affection for it, nor are people necessarily more home-loving or patriotic if they have been born in a fertile or beautiful tract of land. The hold of the natal soil over minds is most movingly expressed in Negro songs of longing for the old Kentucky home, the land where they have been slaves and where they have been exposed to lynching.

Affection for the national territory is implanted in our mind by a common history, by the force of public opinion, by education, by means of literature, the press, national songs, monuments, and in many other ways.[2] Our feelings for the small territory are the

[1] The German word *Heimat* designates particularly this narrower territory, while the English word home country may also be used for the larger one. The Home Office is a Ministry for the whole of England and Wales, and Home Rule does not mean local autonomy but self-administration in a national territory. The word *Heimat* could not be used in this wider sense except in a metaphorical way. The English language, furthermore, has made little use of emotional words like *patria, patrie, Vaterland*, etc. True, the Oxford Dictionary shows several cases of the use of the word fatherland in the seventeenth century; but it cannot have sounded familiar to the English, as Temple in 1672 remarks that the Dutch say fatherland for our country. In our time fatherland means usually Germany, often with some irony. Shaftesbury complained that the English had no word for *patria*, though they certainly had a public spirit.

[2] An instructive study of the means employed for this purpose is Carlton Hayes, *France a Nation of Patriots*, 1930.

The teaching of history has a particular share in the development of national sentiment and nationalism. Cf. J. F. Scott, *The Menace of Nationalism in Education*,

products of many intimate personal experiences in a decisive epoch of our life. Home sentiment, therefore, has more the nature of an organic growth, while national sentiment is more artificial, though there are many connexions between them. Maurice Barrès has tried to centre his doctrine of nationalism in the cult of the soil and the dead, and the Nazis proclaim a gospel of blood and soil. The smaller a nation is, the more its territory has the character of the natal soil. This may be one of the reasons why the national sentiment of small nations is often particularly sensitive in regard to the integrity of what they look upon as their national territory. Home feeling, in any case, is only one of the factors creating national loyalty.

Modern national States, as a rule, strive to concentrate all sentiments of loyalty, pride and affection upon the national territory at the expense both of wider and of smaller territories. This implies, on the one hand, isolationism in regard to the fate of other nations, and, on the other, the suppression of particularism within the nation. The French Revolution abolished the historic provinces of France and introduced a new artificial division of the territory into departments. Italy after her unification followed this example. After the last war the national States formed out of the territories of Austria-Hungary abolished the provincial diets and similar institutions. Hitler too laid great stress on suppressing all institutions and traditions, helping the maintenance of patriotism to the historical territories of the Reich and of his conquests. He even wiped out the name of Austria, connected with such g orious pages in the history of civilization. As a substitute for the suppressed feelings towards the old territories, the nationalists encourage harmless manifestations of local sentiment such as folk-dances, popular songs, peasant-costumes, and so on.

The idea of the national territory is an important element of every modern national ideology. Every nation regards its country as an inalienable sacred heritage, and its independence, integrity, and homogeneity appear bound up with national

1926, and Ch. Altschul, *The American Revolution in our School Text Books, An Attempt to Trace the Influence of Early School Education on the Feelings towards England in the United States*, 1917.

After the last Great War there was a strong tendency among democratic educationists, especially in Austria, to foster local sentiment through the schools, and to replace in the teaching of history the record of wars by that of cultural progress as evidenced in local monuments and traditions. Text-books were written in this sense. The change was mainly advocated on grounds of pedagogical method as it was believed that local monuments and traditions would appeal more to the juvenile mind than the dry text of books. But one of the motives was also the wish to eliminate from instruction elements likely to foster the spirit of warlike nationalism.

security, independence and honour. This territory is often described as the body of the national organism and the language as its soul. In the ideology of almost every nation, therefore, its historical territory is looked upon almost as a living personality which cannot be partitioned without destroying it altogether.[1] The symbolic value of the historical territory constitutes the greatest of all difficulties for a fair settlement of national conflicts. Many territories are regarded by more than one nation as their national heritage on equally strong grounds, and as a rule the idea of a compromise seems to them as repulsive as the idea that a person should agree to lose a limb of his body for a material compensation.

4. Factors determining the Formation of Territories

Views on the historical development of the national territory vary according to the political ideology of the historian. Nationalists, tending to identify nation with race, believe that a community of blood and the concomitant common character and sympathy were fundamental in demarcating the territory. Conservatives stress the influence of dynastic policy and wars in bringing together and unifying nations. Liberal Democrats think that the community of language and civilization led to a spontaneous striving for unity and that unification was effected by self-determination. Socialists usually attribute the formation of large national territories to the influence of capitalism aiming at wide markets. All these views contain some truth, but the exclusive application of any of them to politics has often had dismal consequences.

A community of language and civilization and interests may certainly foster a common outlook in politics and thus influence the development of a national territory. But democrats have usually exaggerated the spontaneity of movements for national unity and liberty. History shows that for a very long time peoples have tenaciously stuck to their small homelands, and have never evinced a longing for merging their individuality into a large nation. In most cases large national territories and common institutions have been formed by kings and statesmen

---

[1] Lord Curzon in 1905 partitioned the immense province of Bengal into two halves in the interests of better administration. Cf. L. Fraser, *India under Curzon*, 1911, p. 385. This measure was felt by Indian nationalists as an outrage to Indian nationality, and aroused an enormous storm of indignation, followed by a campaign of terrorism, boycott, and other revolutionary acts. The measure, though in itself beneficial, had to be modified.

against the will of the peoples. If a plebiscite had been taken, it would have gone against unification, particularly in such towns or territories as had already developed a democratic spirit and, therefore, possessed a national character rooted in the people. Many nations, furthermore, have been formed by separation from larger territories, either through the disintegration of empires or through revolt against a rule considered as foreign domination. In these cases, too, the initiative was usually with small minorities which gradually imposed their will upon the masses, by terrorizing opponents and arousing the fighting instinct and national pride, by appealing to material and ideal interests, and most of all by acquiring overwhelming prestige through successful wars against the national enemy.

The student of history is often faced with the astounding stability of fundamental state traditions which seem to override all differences of parties and classes. Both the Jacobins and the Bolsheviks in certain respects continued the traditions of the regimes which they had set out to exterminate. Uncritical minds are apt to interpret this stability as a proof of racial dispositions. In truth, it was the product of several factors, and among them the national territory has played an important rôle. The nation-building kings have tried to win for their realms favourable national frontiers; they have chosen a site as their permanent residence, and marked out certain regions for further expansion. All these facts and traditions have then been incorporated in the national ideology, and have irresistibly influenced the policy of every following regime. It was not merely kings, however, who have fixed national traditions. In many cases the development of a separate nationality was due to geographical causes which led to the growth of a distinct social structure. If we look at the map of Europe, we find that most of the present small nations are situated on the sea-coast, on great rivers or on international cross-roads. In former times there were more nations of this kind, as, for example, Venice, Genoa, Ragusa, the Hansa towns the city republics of the Low Countries. This indicates that the impulse to the development of a separate national individuality was given by social factors. A town which became the seat of international trade, or a territory which produced goods for export, developed a social structure and interests other than that of the large rural, feudal and military inland-states. They, therefore, tried to make themselves independent, and often succeeded.

The significance of social differentiation for the development of national individuality can be traced in most struggles for liberation from foreign domination, for instance, in the revolt of the Netherlands against Spanish rule in the sixteenth century. The cause of this revolt was not primarily oppression of the people, as the Low Countries enjoyed a very wide autonomy and the Spanish sovereignty was exercised in a very cautious way. The origin of the conflict was due to many causes, but the decisive factor was probably the incompatibility of the national character of the two peoples. The Spaniard, as an English scholar says,[1] despised everything the Netherlander was, his commercial outlook, his inclination towards heavy drinking and eating, his lack of religious fanaticism, and his whole civilian mentality. The Netherlander, on the other hand, mocked at many Spanish traits, and hated the haughty Spanish soldiers who regarded themselves as the aristocracy of mankind.[2] The revolt, however, was started by the high nobility of the Low Countries, who largely pursued their own interests. In the course of the struggle other classes and issues were implicated, and both sides committed atrocities which made the gulf unbridgeable.

5. Empires as Cradles and Graves of Nations

The development of nations is closely connected with the history of multi-national empires.[3] Modern national and democratic opinion is apt to judge Empires severely as destroyers and oppressors of free, peaceable nations, actuated by lust of power. Nevertheless, it cannot be ignored that it was the empire-builders who probably first created territorial states [4] and political institutions which became the cradles of nations. The groundwork was laid by aggressive nomadic tribes which, owing to their social organization, possessed a strong sense of solidarity and military efficiency, and were able to subjugate the unwarlike populations of fertile countries. The descendants of the conquerors mixed

[1] Cf. R. Trevor Davies, *The Golden Century of Spain*, 1937, p. 153.
[2] Cf. F. von Bezold, *Geschichte der deutschen Reformation*, 1890, p. 318.
[3] The word empire implies a misleading ambiguity. Originally *imperium* meant the commanding power of the supreme Roman magistrate, his power over life and death, as symbolized in his terrifying retinue of twelve lictors carrying sticks and axes. Later the imperator was the victorious Roman general who soon became a practical dictator and emperor. Empire always had the connotations of conquest, domination, dictatorship and ruthless exploitation. The designation British Empire, therefore, was an unfortunate one, as it suggested the parallel with the Roman Empire which was entirely different. Here the word Empire is merely used for a large state or group of states under the same ruler, and comprising several peoples.
[4] Primitive government was mainly founded not on territory but on kinship, as Morgan and Maine have shown, though there were associations which can be considered as germs of a state. Cf. Robert Lowie, *Primitive Society*, 1920, p. 390.

with the subject-people, adopted their language and customs, and fused with them into a wider national unity. It was everywhere the warrior-class, the nobility, which, though partly of foreign stock, first developed a sense of nationality ; and the kings, in their struggle with the nobility, also tried to win the people by becoming national in outlook. The kings who laid the foundations of modern national states did so largely with a view to using the expected increase in power for creating an empire. In fact, the great national states of to-day are former empires which have been successful in welding different peoples together into a nation. On the other hand, history shows that whenever a nation had risen to power it almost immediately began to strive for expansion and to aim at the formation of an empire. The disintegration of empires, too, led to the emergence of nations. Many of the present nations of Europe have their origin in provinces of the Roman Empire. Another way of forming new peoples was common conquest. The Germanic peoples of the Frankish epoch, for example, were compounds of former tribes, welded together by the great migrations. Many small nations have in the course of time been swallowed by large ones, but the rivalry of the Great Powers has also helped to create and preserve small nations, such as Switzerland and the Low Countries, since the attempts of one power to annex them were opposed by the others. The small states, moreover, understood how to play off the large powers against one another, and they became in this way the originators of diplomacy and the Balance of Power. The Italian principalities and Venice were leaders in this respect.[1] Then England adopted the principle of the Balance of Power, and has helped many small nations to win or maintain their independence. The small states were regarded as buffers between the great powers, and some of them, especially Holland and Switzerland, have played a most beneficial rôle as cultural bridges between them.

The size of a territory has a bearing on its social and political structure, and in many ways determines the national character. The Greeks believed that only a small city state could form a fatherland, a national community. History, indeed, shows many examples which seem to confirm this view. A widely extended state has usually been brought together by force, and must be maintained by it. As a rule it comprises different peoples and

---

[1] Cf. E. Kaeber, *Die Idee des europäischen Gleichgewichts in der publizistischen Literatur vom 16. bis zur Mitte des 18. Jahrhunderts*, 1907 ; Charles Dupuis, *Le principe d'équilibre et le Concert Européen de la paix Westphalie 2 l'act d'Algeçiras*, 1909.

various regions with divergent traditions and interests which easily give rise to the growth of different social types and nationalities. Large territories have many enemies and are often difficult to defend. This frequently compels their rulers to follow a policy of expansion in order to acquire strategical frontiers. A large state confronted with powerful enemies must have a strong army, and this often leads to the predominance of the military class in politics. The consequence is that either the growth of democracy is stifled or that an established democratic regime is destroyed. Democratic peoples, moreover, are apt to concentrate all their political interest on internal questions and very frequently neglect defence and foreign affairs.[1] Democracy prospers most where the problems of government are simple and directly related to the welfare of the people, as in the administration of small states or cities. The issues of power are usually alien and antipathetic to democratic politicians and therefore liable to be ignored or treated in a perfunctory way. The political development of other nations either receives little attention, or is viewed in an unrealistic light which encourages a passive attitude. Experience, furthermore, shows that democracies find it very difficult to practise active solidarity towards their friends abroad when these have to struggle for their existence. The development of nationality and democracy in a large state, therefore, often implies the danger of disintegration, partly through military unpreparedness or inefficiency, partly through obstinate isolationism, and blindness towards the most imminent dangers.

Many political theorists have discussed the relations between the size of states and their political structure. Montesquieu came to the conclusion that a large state could only be governed despotically.[2] A large republic, in his view, was liable to decay through internal troubles, while a small one was easily destroyed by external enemies. The only way out of this dilemma and the sole possibility of combining strength with freedom seemed to him a federation of small republics. Since his time the develop-

[1] A Canadian delegate to the Commonwealth Relations Conference at Toronto (1933) said in a speech : " One of the hard facts of this world is that each of the British Nations is a democracy, and that it has a parliament, and that back of this parliament there are parties, and that parties are made up of politicians, and that one of the prime purposes of political parties is to turn governments out of office, and that there is no issue so useful for turning a government out of office as a suggestion that it is giving more consideration to external than to domestic interests " (*British Commonwealth Relations*, ed. by Toynbee, 1934, p. 172).

[2] Montesquieu, *Esprit des Lois*, vol. viii, 16–20 ; vol. ix, 1–6. The liberal and democratic writers of the Age of Enlightenment, in general, believed that it would be the best for humanity if the large empires would fall asunder into small states, which then would live in peace and concord with one another. Cf. E. Sieber, *Die Idee des Kleinstaates bei den Denkern des 18. und 19. Jahrhunderts*, 1920.

ment of means of rapid communication, popular education, the press, the cinema, etc., have diminished the disintegrating influence of distances and of local diversities. On the other hand, however, the rise of national consciousness has increased national separatism and isolationism, and democratic nations have hitherto shown little disposition to join forces by way of federation. The dissolution of the unions between Belgium and Holland (1830) and between Norway and Sweden (1905), the formation of numerous small national States on the territory of former Austria-Hungary and Russia (1919), and many other facts of this kind,[1] have shown that the striving for full national independence was stronger than obvious interests of security and prosperity. The splitting up of larger units into tiny nations, and the destruction of the Balance of Power through the last Peace Treaties, have paved the way for Hitler's triumphs, and all those small nations have paid for their spell of full independence with the total loss of freedom. If Ireland has survived her practical separation from Britain she owes this exclusively to the British Navy, though her policy shows no appreciation of this fact and does not contribute to the defence of national freedom.

6. The Thousand-Year Struggle over the Heritage of Charlemagne

Mediaeval political thought was completely under the spell of the idea of Empire. On the authority of the book of Daniel it was believed that the history of mankind showed a succession of world empires, and that the last one was the Roman Empire, which would exist till the end of time. Charlemagne revived the idea of the Roman Empire and identified it with his own realm. It was a loose structure, and after Charlemagne's death it soon disintegrated. Nevertheless, its tradition has for a thousand years kindled the ambitions of princes and aroused national passions. The Empire was divided among Charlemagne's grandsons into three parts without regard to the nationality of the peoples. Each of these parts was really an empire, consisting of many different peoples. The western part later became France, the eastern one Germany. The middle part was for a short time known as Lotharingia after Lothar II, and was connected with the imperial title. It was composed of the Low

[1] We may also mention the separation of Iceland from Denmark (1918), though under the same king, the separatist movements among the Catalans, the Slovaks, the Croats, etc. As to the problem of the small state in our age cf. E. H. Carr, *Conditions of Peace*, 1942, p. 37.

Countries, the Rhinelands, Lorraine (which name is derived from Lotharingia), Alsace, western Switzerland, Burgundy, Provence, and the whole of Italy. Its territory comprised the great valleys of the Rhine, the Meuse, the Rhone and the Po, destined to bring forth numerous industrial towns, and in general the most fertile and civilized parts of Europe. A very important fact, moreover, was that these regions soon formed the bridge between the great civilizations, and stood in close cultural and economic relations with France and Germany, with Italy, Spain and the Levant. This was a great stimulus to progress and developed a wider outlook than prevailed in large parts of Europe. Already in the eleventh century a priest of St. Lambert at Liége wrote: "We are looked upon as the last of the Gauls or the first of the Germans. We are neither Gauls nor Germans; we belong at once to both of them." [1] In this middle zone between East and West the soil was prepared for a supra-national spirit which later on found its greatest expression in Erasmus.

The greater part of the Middle Empire, in particular the Low Countries, Burgundy and Italy, and the Imperial Crown were soon joined with Germany, and the empire in which Germany formed the central and dominating part was known as the Holy Roman Empire. In theory, the German kings, after their election by the principal German princes, and after their coronation by the Pope, were regarded as successors of the Roman world emperors, all kings being subordinated to their authority. But only some emperors tried to assert their supremacy or to pursue a very ambitious policy of expansion. The authority of most emperors was more theoretical than practical, and towards the end of the Middle Ages most non-German countries had become almost completely independent,[2] and the power of the emperor was at a very low ebb. Yet the claim to world supremacy was never abandoned and went far to arouse tremendous pride.[3]

[1] Cf. H. Van der Linden, *Belgium, the Making of a Nation*, 1920, p. 43.
[2] At that time the name "The Holy Roman Empire" was supplemented by the words "of the German nation", which originally meant that part of the Empire which was of German nationality. Later on it was interpreted as meaning that the Empire was subject to the German nation. Cf. F. Hartung, *Deutsche Verfassungsgeschichte*, 1922, and A. Werminghoff in *Histor. Vierteljahrsschrift*, xi, 1908. J. Bryce, *The Holy Roman Empire*, 8th ed., 1899, is still a classic.
[3] When Henry VI, the most ruthless representative of the striving for world domination, died in 1197 the Annals of the monastery of St. Blasien in the Black Forest commented upon his death in the words: "The German people shall lament his death for eternity, for he has made it glorious through the riches of other countries, he has made all peoples tremble before its warlike valour, and it would obviously in future have become superior to all nations, if death had not prematurely seized him." The influence of mediaeval Imperialism on German national pride can be gathered from many examples in F. Schultheiss, *Geschichte des deutschen Nationalgefühls*, vol. i, 1893 (till the thirteenth century).

Though the Empire was called Roman, it was in fact German, and the German princes, bishops and knights drew great profit from it. The Church maintained that the Pope had transferred the Empire to the Germans, while the Germans liked to emphasize that they had won it by the sword.

In other countries the German claim to world supremacy aroused widespread resentment and jealousy, and has greatly contributed to the development of national sentiment and ideology. Anglo-Saxon kings already used the imperial title, or similar ones, for emphasizing their independence and equal rank, and many later kings and queens of England, and also rulers of other countries, have occasionally claimed to be emperors in their realms.[1] Most of all, however, it was the French who opposed the German claim, asserting that they had a much better title to the heritage of Charlemagne, who was represented as a Frenchman. Many French kings aimed at being elected emperors by the German princes, and hoped thus to restore the empire of Charlemagne. Moreover, French policy constantly tried to acquire parts of the former Middle Empire, which to a large extent had a French-speaking population. In the late Middle Ages, however, the idea of the Middle Empire was revived by the Dukes of Burgundy, whose dominions also comprised the wealthy towns of the Low Countries. They began a policy of expansion, mainly at the expense of France, and even threatened the foundations of the French realm in alliance with England. The English had been foremost in the development towards a national State, and the policy of conquering France which had sprung from feudal and dynastic motives soon became a national venture. In the same way, the evolution of France towards national unity and power was soon followed by a policy of conquest in Italy. It aroused the jealousy of Spain and Austria, and for centuries led to the subjection of Italy to foreign invasions, intrigues and domination.

7. The Supra-National Empire of Charles V

In the fifteenth century the Burgundian lands and aspirations went by heritage to the Habsburgs, and Charles V united the Low Countries with Spain and his Austrian possessions and the Imperial Crown, though he soon ceded Austria to his brother

---

[1] Cf. E. A. Freeman, *History of the Norman Conquest*, 1877, vol. i, pp. 117-47, 548-65. Cf. also Ch. Firth, *Oliver Cromwell and the Rule of the Puritans*, 1923, p. 422. Several English kings, however, such as Richard I, Henry II, and Edward III, have recognized the supremacy of the Emperor. Henry VIII hoped to induce the German princes to elect him Emperor.

Ferdinand.[1] Charles called himself king of twenty-five realms, and the ruler of the East and West Indies and all isles and continents in the Ocean. Dante's longing for an emperor as guardian of peace and justice in the world no longer appeared an unpractical dream. Charles V, the admirer of Erasmus, though proud and ambitious, did not strive for the bloody laurels of a Caesar. He laughed at the idea of a universal empire, attributed to him by his enemies, and asserted that it had never entered his conception however possible it might have been. Though his reign was full of wars, this was not mainly his fault.[2] The Emperor owed his Empire chiefly to the Habsburg policy of concluding dynastic marriages and family compacts which has provoked the verse : " Bela gerant alii, Tu felix Austria nube ! Nam quae Mars aliis, dat tibi regna Venus." [3] Charles continued this policy, which formed an important feature of his system. Almost all kings and many other important rulers were closely related to him by family ties.[4] This often helped to settle conflicts, especially by uniting two rival dynasties through a marriage and giving the disputed territory to the offspring. It also prepared for future acquisitions of lands by heritage, and, on the other hand, facilitated the cession of territories, as they remained in the wider family and did not pass into the hands of an implacable enemy.[5] This system, in principle, implied more possibilities of a peaceful settlement of territorial conflicts than one centred on the absolute integrity of a certain territory. In

[1] Cf. Edward Armstrong, *The Emperor Charles V*, 2 vols., 1902. Karl Brandi, *Kaiser Karl V*, 1937 ; Martin Hume, *Spain, Its Greatness and Decay*, 1925 ; R. Trevor Davies, *The Golden Century of Spain*, 1937 ; Leopold von Ranke, *Deutsche Geschichte im Zeitalter der Reformation*, 6 vols., 1925 ; H. Pirenne, *Histoire de Belgique*, vol. iii, 1912.

[2] The judgement of one of the most competent historians is : " The wars of Charles were, in fact, all defensive " (Armstrong, vol. ii, p. 370).

[3] " May others make war, you, fortunate Austria, marry ! For the kingdoms others owe to Mars, you get from Venus." The verse has been attributed to Mathias Corvinus, King of Hungary (fifteenth century).

[4] As regards England, for example, Queen Catherine was the Emperor's aunt. He himself was promised the hand of his niece Mary, the daughter of Henry VIII, and when this failed, Mary was married to his son Philip, who, until her death, was King of Spain, King of England and ruler of the Netherlands. The personal union of England and Spain, however, was not intended to be permanent. It was agreed that the eldest son of Philip and Mary should have England, the Netherlands and the Free County of Burgundy. If Mary had had a son, a third Habsburg dynasty would have been established in England, besides the two other ones in Spain and Austria. Cf. Ranke, vol. v, p. 313.

[5] In the beginning of his reign Charles, reared in Burgundian traditions, attached the greatest importance to the recovery of all Burgundian lands, which was quite unacceptable to France, though she was to receive Milan for Burgundy. Soon, however, Charles was ready to waive this claim, and to settle the conflict between the two dynasties by a marriage of one of his female relatives with a French prince. This new dynasty should either get the Netherlands and the Free County of Burgundy, or the Duchy of Milan. Had one of these plans been realized, Spain, France and Europe might have been saved immeasurable calamities. Cf. Hume, pp. 72, 75.

spite of its essentially monarchical character, moreover, it was not incompatible with national sentiment. The Emperor himself did not belong exclusively to any nationality of his Empire, though he certainly had sympathy and understanding for many of them.[1] The statesmen who were his principal advisers were chosen from all nations. His most important minister was an Italian, the Grand-Chancellor Gattinara. Though Spain became more and more the centre of the Empire, and Spanish interests determined the main course of policy, the Spaniards did not rule the rest. Among the eight Councillors of State only two were Spaniards. In all countries there was much jealousy of foreign advisers of the Emperor, and he had to give elaborate guarantees in order to appease national distrust and animosity among the peoples of his Empire. Particularism, however, was still so strong that everywhere an official from a neighbouring province was opposed as a foreigner. To the Hollander a Fleming was a foreigner, and to the Castilian an Arragonese. The Emperor's policy did much to overcome this narrow particularism and to foster national unity. He would probably also have influenced Germany and Italy in the same sense but for overwhelming odds against him.[2]

The Empire of Charles V, therefore, was not kept together through the domination of its peoples by one ruling nation. It was practically a loose confederation of autonomous states, a sort of League of Nations in a feudal-monarchical form. Each state retained its traditional privileges and institutions. Both in the Netherlands and in Spain the Estates, composed of delegates of the clergy, nobles and towns played a prominent rôle, and often refused demands of the Emperor.[3] In the Low Countries during

[1] Charles was born at Ghent in Belgium and was brought up in the French language and civilization of the Burgundian court. Later on he also learned Spanish, German and Flemish. He regarded Flanders as his homeland. In later life he became more Spanish, but occasionally he professed to be " a good Italian " or gave the Germans similar assurances.

[2] The great contribution of the Emperor to the growth of nationhood in the Low Countries is described by Armstrong, vol. ii, pp. 310, 325 f., 344, and Pirenne, vol. iii, pp. 186, 206. Charles also showed remarkable understanding of national sentiment in realizing that it was apt to lead to the desire for a separate sovereignty. He, therefore, planned to create a Burgundian kingdom, comprising mainly the Low Countries, and independent of Spain, under a second son whom he expected but who was not born. This would have forestalled the revolt of the Netherlands which broke out under his successor Philip II, who had become a Spanish national king and thereby had alienated the hearts of the Low Countries. In Germany the Emperor proposed a thoroughgoing administrative reform which would have restored internal unity, but this was rejected by the princes.

[3] The view that Charles broke the power of the Estates in Spain is wrong. Cf. Trevor Davies, p. 59. There was, however, an increase in the power of the Crown as the lesser nobility, the hidalgos, rallied to the side of the king, after a revolutionary movement had assumed the character of a social war.

Charles's reign the Estates assembled more than fifty times. The power of the Estates often hampered warfare, and the Emperor could not rely on the participation of all his countries in a war against aggression. In France, during the long reign of Francis I, who was Charles's rival, the Estates were not assembled on a single occasion. Besides enjoying their autonomy, the peoples of the Empire had also economic advantages through their adhesion to the Empire. Charles was in favour of freer trade within the Empire, and of giving all its members access to the Spanish dominions beyond the Ocean. This, however, was strongly opposed by the Spaniards. Nevertheless, both Belgian and German trade profited much in this respect. An important guarantee of the unity of the Empire, furthermore, was seen in the unity of religion. Charles made great efforts to prevent the disruption of religious unity by a reform of the Church and by bringing about a compromise between the contending parties. This was frustrated by the intransigence of both sides, and largely also through the fact that the Popes feared the political predominance of a Catholic Emperor much more than the danger to the Church of Protestantism. The Popes, therefore, were often allied with all the enemies of the Emperor, even with the Protestants and the Turks.

The most implacable enemy of the Empire, however, was the French king Francis I who had attempted to become Emperor himself and had failed. The French king and his statesmen regarded the power of the Emperor as an intolerable barrier to French expansion in Italy and the Low Countries, and even as a threat to their security as France, indeed, was encircled by the dominions of the Emperor. The countries of Lothar's Middle Empire, the Burgundian and Italian lands, became for centuries the battlefield for the rivalry of France, Spain and Austria, and England too became involved in these wars.

Louis XIV shared the view that the Crown of Charlemagne rightfully belonged to the French dynasty and this ambition was the backbone of French national ideology.[1] He seemed destined to found a French Empire dominating the whole of Europe and much more powerful than that of Charles V. In this he failed through the joint resistance of England and Austria, and the long struggle over the Spanish Succession ended in a partition of the Spanish Empire between the Bourbon and Habsburg dynasties.

[1] Cf. Louis XIV, *Œuvres*, 1806, vol. i, p. 71 f. After the acquisition of the Spanish Crown Louis XIV declared that the French and the Spaniards were now united to such a degree that henceforward they formed but one nation.

8. Napoleon's National Empire and the Rise of Modern Nationalism

Napoleon succeeded in establishing his direct or indirect rule over the greater part of the Continent. He laid great stress upon appearing as the true successor of Charlemagne. His public declarations and political correspondence often repeated this claim, or alluded to it, and he even tried to obtain the old crown and insignia for his coronation but had to put up with imitations. His Empire, however, was totally different from those of Charlemagne and Charles V. Its spirit was that of Diocletian, as Napoleon himself once said. It was a French Empire in which all conquered countries were ruled according to the dictates of the Emperor and ruthlessly exploited for his personal ambitions. Both the annexed countries and the vassal states had to pay enormous contributions, and to place at his disposal large contingents of troops which were used as cannon fodder. The conquered peoples were thus forced to make great sacrifices in blood and wealth for further conquests. This enabled him to spare the French people the greater part of the burdens of war, and thereby to maintain his popularity.[1] The " liberated " peoples of Italy, Holland, etc., had, moreover, to hand over to their liberator their most precious art-treasures and historic relics. All subject-peoples had to introduce French laws and administration. They were controlled by French ministers and had to employ French as an official language besides their own. Their frontiers, constitutions and rulers were often arbitrarily changed by the dictator without regard to their wishes. To a large extent they had to admit French products freely to their markets while their manufactures were excluded from France by high tariffs, and they had to join in the blockade against England to their own great loss.

The introduction of French laws which had been moulded by the equalizing influence of the Revolution implied also many advantages, such as the abolition of privileges of rank, of serfdom and other remnants of feudal times ; the establishment of religious equality, the removal of trade obstacles, and the improvement of communications. On the other hand, all institutions limiting absolutism, such as territorial diets, municipal self-government, ecclesiastical independence, and the spirit of freedom in research,

[1] H. A. Fisher, *Napoleon*, 1932, p. 155.

education, literature and the press, were suppressed wherever they had grown up.[1]

The ultimate aim of the Napoleonic system was the destruction of the nationality of the subject peoples. Napoleon sometimes posed as the champion of oppressed peoples, or aroused national hopes. But this was mere propaganda, and it can be proved by many acts and words of the Emperor himself that he never took such declarations seriously.[2] Napoleon, says Taine, " following the example of Rome which Latinized the entire Mediterranean coast, wanted to render all Western Europe French ".[3] " Spain must be French," said Napoleon, " the country must be French and the government must be French." In Germany, too, according to his own confession, he aimed at denationalizing the people. For the reorganization of Holland he nominated a commission which, as Driault, an enthusiastic admirer of Napoleon, says, " soon left nothing in Holland which was Dutch ". Belgium, like Holland, was to be " entirely assimilated and incorporated in the French fatherland ".[4] In the same way Italy was organized completely on the French model and merged in the French Empire.[5]

Napoleon's belief that so many great peoples with proud national traditions could be denationalized and converted into Frenchmen seems almost unintelligible to our mind, considering that otherwise he possessed an amazing psychological understanding. But he shared in this respect the view, widespread in his epoch, that nationality, like religion, was hardly more than a prejudice which the enlightened ruler could either use or suppress according to his purposes. Moreover, he was essentially a militarist and, therefore, believed that a powerful government could achieve almost everything. Lastly, we must not forget the fact that cosmopolitanism and French civilization were common to the educated classes in many countries of Europe, and most of all in Germany. A large section of the German intellectuals were imbued with the greatest admiration for the

[1] Cf. Edouard Driault, *Napoléon et l'Europe, le grand Empire*, 1924, p. 162 ; H. A. L. Fisher, *Studies in Napoleonic Statesmanship in Germany*, 1903.
[2] Napoleon often assured the Italians of his sincere wish for their liberty and greatness while at the same moment, in confidential documents, he spoke of them in terms of the greatest contempt, qualifying them as absolutely unfit for liberty. Cf. A. Fournier, *Napoléon I*, 1913, vol. i, pp. 127, 135. His attitude to Polish national aspirations was characterized by the same duplicity, cf. Fournier, vol. ii, pp. 159, 188, 313 ; vol. iii, p. 87 ; and H. A. Fisher, *Bonapartism*, 1908, p. 53.
[3] Cf. H. Taine, *Les origines de la France Contemporaine* (Engl. tr. : *The Modern Regime*), 1891, vol. i, p. 149.
[4] Cf. H. Van der Linden, *Belgium, The Making of a Nation*, 1920, p. 215.
[5] The idea that Napoleon's final aim was the creation of a unified and free Italy is quite improbable. It has been refuted by Driault, pp. 219, 265.

Emperor who had destroyed the Holy Empire and degraded Germany to a French colony.

The Napoleonic domination of Europe was at last broken by the rising tide of national revolt. The French Revolution had already given proof of the vast energy which could be made available by arousing the masses. The Austrian Government in 1794 wanted to resort to the general armament of the people, in order to repel the French invader.[1] But the military caste-spirit of Prussia opposed the introduction of a principle regarded as revolutionary. Nevertheless, Austria at times appealed to her peoples, and the rising of the Tyrolese under Andreas Hofer was enthusiastically greeted by all friends of freedom. England's war against the French Caesar was a national struggle, at least at sea. The Spaniards showed in their long struggle a fierce national spirit that startled the world and aroused new hopes. The same spirit was soon surging in Russia and Germany too, and it led to the final downfall of Napoleon's despotism.

The national sentiment aroused in those struggles, however, remained alive, and reached a strength dominating all peoples. The French Revolution had paved the way for the gigantic wave of national feeling and nationalism which now flooded the world. Its gospel has in many ways stimulated the sense of nationality. Napoleon thus unconsciously furthered the spread of this sentiment over the whole of Europe. A powerful factor in this process was also his policy of suppressing the independence of countless small states with their separate individualities and loyalties, and merging them in larger territories. History shows that all the national movements of the nineteenth century, in particular those of the Italians, the Germans, the Poles, the southern Slavs and the Greeks, have been decisively though unintentionally stimulated by revolutionary France and Napoleon.[2] Both Pan-Germanism and Panslavism have their roots in these traditions.

We have traced here only one main stream of Imperial ambition and its influence on nationality. It was the tradition of the Roman Empire as revived by Charlemagne. A parallel tradition, however, emanated from the eastern part of the Roman Empire which, through Byzantium, led to the formation of the

[1] Cf. Langwerth von Simmern, *Oesterreich und das Reich im Kampf mit der französischen Revolution*, 1880, vol. i, pp. 18, 24, 314, 395, 515. It is a mistake, common to most English historians if H. A. Fisher (*Napoleon*, 1932, p. 176) says that Austria was merely a bundle of states swayed by no common passion and obeying the control of a government which found neither source nor sanction in the popular will.

[2] Switzerland too became a national unity through Napoleon's interference in her independence. Cf. I. Schollenberger, *Geschichte der Schweizerischen Politik*, 1908, vol. ii, pp. 7 f.

Turkish and the Russian Empires. Both claimed to be true successors of the Eastern Roman Empire. Their rivalry for the domination of the Balkans recalls the rivalry of the great Western Powers for the possession of the Middle Empire.[1] There was furthermore the Austrian Empire, which united vital traditions of the West and the East, and took part in the struggles in both parts of Europe. This policy seemed to be symbolized in the double-headed eagle of the Austrian Empire which it took over from Byzantium. Lastly, still another type of Empire developed in the great colonial dominions of European nations, among which the British Empire and its American offshoot stand in the front line.

Before looking at some further examples of imperial and supra-national organization, we have first to discuss the process of national unification, that is the fusion of small national individualities into large nations. If we use the term " particularism " for the loyalty to a small territory, we must not ignore the fact that this loyalty was often a national one, and only appears as particularism retrospectively.

9. The National Unification of France

A classic example of successful dynastic expansion and centralization is the history of French national unity. In the Middle Ages already the royal legists began to proclaim that France was the rightful successor to old Gaul, and therefore could claim the frontiers of Gaul, as described by Caesar, namely, the Rhine, the Alps and the Pyrenees.[2] This doctrine became a tradition of French foreign policy and has involved Europe in many great wars. Within the territory of present France there were many different nationalities, and the forces of particularism were very strong.[3] Besides considerable Breton, Basque, German and Flemish elements it comprised the Provençals, who spoke

[1] Space forbids to describe this rivalry and its influence on nationality. But I refer to the treatment of the subject in my book *Nationalgeist und Politik*, vol. i, 1937, chaps. 6, 9 and 12.
[2] On the evolution and influence of this idea, cf. Albert Sorel, *L'Europe et la revolution française*, vol. i, pp. 30, 244, 324 ; Fritz Kern, *Die Anfänge der französischen Ausdehnungspolitik bis zum Jahr 1308*, 1910, pp. 14, 27, 323. On the evolution of national sentiment, cf. D. Kirkland, *Growth of National Sentiment in France before the Fifteenth Century in History*, 1938 ; A. Jacquet, *Sentiment national au 16. siècle in Revue des questions historiques*, 1895 ; M. Aulard, *Le patriotisme Français de la Renaissance à la Revolution*, 1921.
[3] The name of France originally designated the country near Paris, delimitated by five rivers, and, therefore, called Isle de France. At the universities, for example, the students from the territory now called France were divided into several " nations "—in Bologna into eight—of which one only was the French nation. The States-General of 1484 were divided into six nations.

a separate language, nearer to Catalan than to French, and who had developed a high civilization. Their country was conquered by French crusaders from the north with abominable cruelties. In the Hundred Years War the people of the south-west, especially of Guyenne and Gascony, were on the English side, while the nobles often supported the French, though not for national reasons.[1] When the war was over the burgesses of Bordeaux did not rejoice over the victory of the national cause, but looked sadly back to the golden days of English rule. In 1457 the King of France wrote to the King of Scotland: "The people of Guyenne are at heart entirely inclined to the English party."[2] In the later part of the war many towns of the north supported the Duke of Burgundy, who was allied with England, against the national unification under the Crown of France. On the whole those French towns where the democratic party was in power were for Burgundy, while the nobility and the patrician party in the towns were for France. The industrial free towns of the Low Countries were the backbone of the Burgundian party.[3] Many French towns were more attracted by the proud position of the Belgian towns than by the ideal of French national unity under a king in alliance with feudalism. If Burgundy and England had won, several independent nations would have developed on the territory now forming France, in particular a Great Belgium in the north and a Provençal nation in the south.

The sense of independence was strong in other parts of France, too. When Louis XIV and his successors tried to win large French-speaking countries it was success alone which decided whether that policy appears to-day as national unification or as an attempt at annexation. The attacks upon Belgium are regarded as unjustified aggressions, while the incorporation of Lorraine and the Franche Comté to-day seems justified by the principle of national unity. In reality, however, neither the people of Lorraine nor that of the Franche Comté wished any more to become French than the Belgians did. The Lorrainers fought desperately against the French, a large part were killed, and the French Government thought of deporting the rest to Canada.[4] Lorraine was definitely united with France only as late as 1766. Maurice Barrès, the most prominent representative of nationalist thought in recent

[1] Froissart relates (iii, 43) that the Gascon nobles in the great wars between France and England often changed from one side to the other, but that they loved the English more because the war against the French was more profitable, especially as they had more opportunity of plundering French traders.
[2] Cf. Eleanor Lodge, *Gascony under English Rule*, 1926, p. 130.
[3] F. Funck-Brentano, *National History of France*, 1922, vol. i, p. 437.
[4] Cf. H. Derichsweiler, *Geschichte Lothringens*, 1905, pp. 107, 111.

times, a native of Lorraine, remarks that the people of Lorraine were only won for France by the benefits offered by the Revolution and by the fraternity in combat and glory, created by the wars of the Republic and Napoleon. The Franche Comté was ceded to France in 1674; but thirty-five years later the peace conference which prepared the Peace of Utrecht received a petition from the people of the Franche Comté, asking to be liberated from French slavery and to be permitted to return to the Empire.[1] On the eve of the Revolution some districts of France still wished to be recognized as separate nations.[2] In the case of Alsace, however, the French succeeded in winning the people in spite of their German language and character, and the above-mentioned petition even says that the inhabitants of Alsace had already become more French than the Parisians.

Though France has for centuries been subject to a centralizing regime, the memory of former national independence has not vanished in some of her territories. In the nineteenth century movements for cultural particularism and political autonomy developed in many parts of France, and were supported by prominent writers, though they nowhere acquired considerable political influence.[3]

The policy of expansion, followed by the French kings and their successors, corresponded to the ambitions and interests of influential sections of the French which then were alone regarded as the nation. It satisfied their longing for glory and supremacy among nations, and sometimes diverted national passions from internal strife to external wars. The doctrine of natural frontiers was so deeply rooted in French ideology that even the heralds of national liberty and self-determination took it over from the old regime. Rousseau wrote:

> The mountains, seas and rivers form the frontiers for the nations living in Europe, and it is clear that nature itself has determined the number and greatness of nations. The political order of this continent is the work of nature. The Alps, the Rhine, the sea and the Pyrenees are not insurmountable obstacles to expansion; but other factors increase their strength, and restore these boundaries if they have temporarily been transgressed by violence.

The leaders of the Revolution proclaimed the right of every people to determine its fate; they repudiated any policy of conquest, and declared that they only made war against the

---

[1] Cf. B. Erdmannsdörffer, *Deutsche Geschichte 1648–1740*, vol. ii, p. 257.
[2] Cf. B. Fry Hyslop, *French Nationalism in 1789*, 1934, p. 185.
[3] Cf. the interesting survey in Alphonse Roche, *Les idées traditionalistes en France*, 1937, pp. 110–37.

tyrants in self-defence, for the liberation of oppressed peoples, in order to end war and to establish perpetual peace among the liberated peoples. Soon, however, all these good intentions were thrown to the winds, Belgium and other territories were invaded, ruthlessly plundered and exploited, and annexed according to the French national tradition of natural frontiers. In Italy this principle could not be applied, but this did not hinder Bonaparte from extending the same treatment to her.

10. THE NATIONAL UNIFICATION OF GERMANY

The classical example of extreme particularism was Germany.[1] In olden times there was much hereditary enmity between the German tribes, especially between Saxons and Franks. North and South Germans hardly understood each other, and had to resort to Latin if they wanted to communicate. Numerous nobles rose to the rank of territorial rulers, and made their separate policy and their separate wars without any regard to common national aims. This policy of particularism was primarily dynastic, but it also found strong support among the Free Towns and among the people. The old Empire was not a national State but a loose federation which in the eighteenth century comprised 1,800 rulers. Some were kings, dukes, margraves, counts, archbishops, abbots, and so on, but 1,475 of them were merely free knights who were subordinated to nobody but the Emperor and who ruled altogether 200 square miles.[2] There were also 51 Free Cities and even some Free Villages. Many princes ruled not only German but also foreign states, for instance, Great Britain, Russia,[3] Sweden, Denmark, Poland, Holland, Belgium, Bohemia, Hungary and territories in France, Italy and Switzerland. Even tiny states claimed to be separate nations. In 1794, for example, the Diet of Calenberg petitioned their ruler, King George III of Great Britain, to declare the neutrality of the " Calenberg nation " in the war against France.[4] The army of Calenberg consisted of 22 cavalry and 140 infantry.[5] These conditions, of course, were in many respects harmful and grotesque. Some writers complained of the lack of unity and strength, but there

---

[1] Cf. on German national sentiment and the movement for unity, P. Joachimsen, *Vom deutschen Volk zum deutschen Staat*, 1920, F. Meinecke, *Weltbürgertum und Nationalstaat*, 7th ed., 1928.
[2] Cf. Max von Boehn, *Deutschland im 18. Jahrhundert*, 1921, vol. i, pp. 4, 22.
[3] The Duke of Holstein-Gottorp became, in 1762, Tsar of Russia, but only ruled a short time.
[4] A. Ward, *Great Britain and Hanover*, 1899, p. 18.
[5] H. Berghaus, *Deutschland vor hundert Jahren*, 1860, vol. ii, p. 136.

was no national movement, and on the whole the Germans were not discontented with their political constitution.

A complete change, however, was effected by the French Revolution and Napoleon. Most of the small principalities were wiped out by Napoleon, and the humiliations, exactions and oppressions inflicted by him upon Germany, and the ideas of the Revolution and of romanticism, aroused the longing for a united and strong nation. Yet particularism was strongly rooted in the German mind. At the Congress of Vienna Bavaria and Württemberg protested against a proposal on the ground that " it would create out of different peoples such as Prussians and Bavarians so to say a single nation ".[1]

The extraordinary strength of particularism has caused much misery and humiliation to Germany. On the other hand, it had also its good side. It led to a rivalry among many rulers, nobles and citizens in founding all sorts of cultural institutions, and people persecuted for their creed or views in one state usually found a refuge in a more tolerant one near by. The outward attachment to the soil fostered the inward freedom of the spirit, and the citizen of a small country without power and wealth found it easy to be a good citizen of the world.[2] The marvellous development of learning and thought, of education and industries, was largely due to the decentralization of Germany. In spite of all the shortcomings of particularism Bismarck's unification by Prussianization was not in accordance with the real wishes of the majority of the German people outside Prussia,[3] though this policy was approved by influential sections. It appealed to their longing for power and prestige, and Bismarck skilfully used wars to arouse national passions, and the introduction of manhood suffrage to win the support of democratic sentiment.

The idea is now often ventilated whether, after Hitler's downfall, German particularism should not be encouraged. There is no doubt that the old particularist structure of the Reich furthered the maintenance of European peace. The multitude of rulers and the rivalry between them, their close connexions with almost all dynasties of Europe, the cosmopolitan spirit of the intellectuals,

[1] G. Gervinus, *Geschichte des 19. Jahrhunderts*, 1855, vol. i, p. 282.
[2] It is significant that the two greatest German poets, Goethe and Schiller, created their immortal works in Weimar which then was a mere village. They travelled little, and only once in their life visited Berlin (*ca.* 130 miles from Weimar) for a few days on special business. They never saw Vienna, then the greatest German city, nor Paris or London. Immanuel Kant spent his whole long life at or near Königsberg. He never crossed the frontiers of his native province.
[3] For the unpopularity of Prussia among the other German states, and the opposition to Bismarck's " unification ", cf. W. H. Dawson, *The German Empire, 1867–1914, and the Unity Movement*, 1919, vol. i, pp. 54, 271–8, 282, 371.

the inability of the small states to make war—these and other factors were checks to an aggressive policy. Yet it must be said that the spirit of our time is not favourable to intense feelings of local patriotism and loyalty to patriarchal rulers.

11. The National Unification of Italy

Italy's frontiers were well marked by natural boundaries, historical traditions and language. The struggle between Pope and Emperor hindered the unification of Italy under one rule, and the early development of flourishing towns, proud of their republican independence, had the same effect. Ferocious strife reigned between many towns.[1] Salimbene says that between the citizens of Pisa and Genoa a natural loathing existed as between different kinds of animals, and that each people tried to exterminate the other, actuated by mere rivalry and vanity.[2] Humanism strengthened national pride by extolling the greatness of old Rome, regarded as the ancestor of the Italian race, and by stressing the superiority of Italian civilization in comparison with all other peoples which were contemptuously designated as barbarians. From the end of the Middle Ages Italy became the battleground of France, Spain and Austria, which all competed for the possession of Italian territories. In vain Machiavelli longed for the liberation of Italy from the foreigners.

In the eighteenth century the War of the Spanish Succession established Austrian rule and hegemony in Italy and the Austrian administration then was enlightened, progressive and popular. There was practically no movement for national liberation and unification as particularism was deeply rooted in the mind of the peoples. But the French Revolution aroused the longing for national liberty and the temporary unification of Italy under Napoleon's rule greatly strengthened the sentiment of unity. After Napoleon's fall Austrian predominance was restored; but was soon faced with the rising tide of the national movement. The antagonism to foreign rule was aggravated by the illiberal character of the Metternich system, and the Italian national move-

---

[1] The fact that the Emperor Frederick I razed Milan to the ground arouses Italian national feelings to the present day. But Milan had treated other Italian towns in exactly the same way, and the Emperor left the destruction of Milan to her enemies, the citizens of Lodi, Como, Pavia, Cremona and Novara, who relished their revenge to the full. Cf. H. Prutz, *Staatengeschichte des Abendlandes im Mittelalter*, 1885, vol. i, p. 492.

[2] Quoted by G. Coulton, "Nationalism in the Middle Ages", in *Cambridge Historical Journal*, 1935, where further interesting facts about mediaeval nationalism are given.

ment strove not only for independence but also for political freedom. It was only natural that the national aspirations were not satisfied with the efficient administration and the material advantages of a rule which was stamped as foreign, though most of the officials were Italians, and which was associated with particularism.[1]

Nevertheless, particularism had still a strong hold on the people of the various Italian states. When Genoa was united with the kingdom of Sardinia and Savoy by the Congress of Vienna, this could be regarded as a step towards unity. But the people of Genoa bitterly resented their subjection to the dynasty of Savoy and longed for their old republican independence. Rome, Milan, Venice, Florence, Naples, too, were proud of their glorious past, and were for a long time unwilling to sacrifice their independence to the idea of national unity. The national movement at first embraced a small minority only, in which former officers and officials of Napoleon's Italian realms were conspicuous. Then the students and many of the nobility and the middle classes joined the movement. The Liberals advocated a federation of the historical Italian states,[2] with the King of Sardinia or the Pope as president, while the radicals under Mazzini stood for complete unification in a democratic republic on the French model. The broad masses were long loyal to their traditional rulers, or indifferent, and frequently even fought against the propagandists of national revolution.[3] With growing success, however, the movement became increasingly popular, and it obtained the powerful support of Napoleon III, who hoped to use it for the aggrandisement of his own power, but was outwitted by Cavour's diplomacy.

After the defeat of Austria by the French and Italian armies the union of the Italian states under the King of Sardinia, as well as the union of Savoy and Nice with France which formed

[1] Some historians believe that an early grant of autonomy or of political rights would have reconciled the Italians to Austrian overlordship. Cf. Bolton King, *History of Italian Unity*, 1899, vol. i, p. 52 ; vol. ii, p. 281. This seems to me quite improbable. About the Austrian administration, Bolton King (vol. i, p. 51) says that the Neapolitans, Romans and Piedmontese might well envy the institutions under which the inhabitants of Lombardy-Venetia lived, and he gives many proofs for this statement. Also Tuscany and Parma, which were under Austrian influence, had a good government. An effective local government with a wide franchise existed in the Austrian provinces only, and they had even a sort of representative assembly which, however, had no legislative functions and was denied development by absolutist distrust. Cf. Bolton King, pp. 56, 109.

[2] Austria too was in favour of an Italian federation, but her suggestion was rejected by Sardinia because the participation of Austria would have implied Austrian hegemony.

[3] Cf. G. Berkeley, *Italy in the Making, 1815 to 1846*, 1932, vol. i, pp. 19, 38, 92, 94, 125.

the price for Napoleon's help, were submitted to plebiscites and were everywhere accepted almost unanimously. The unification was realized in the form of complete union. Italy wiped out every trace of particularism, and the latent opposition to the rule of Italy by the Savoy dynasty, therefore, later on swelled the ranks of anti-dynastic radicalism, especially in the south.

12. THE DEVELOPMENT OF BRITISH NATIONAL UNITY

The English attained to a certain national unity earlier than other European nations, and the disintegrating forces of particularism had never the same power as on the Continent. It was obviously the Danish menace which furthered the unification both in England and in Scotland. The successors of Alfred, building on the foundations laid by him, established the supremacy of Wessex over all other states, English, Danish and Celtic, and even acquired a nominal suzerainty over Scotland and Wales. This unity was weakened under Canute and Edward through the rise of great earls, and England seemed to fall asunder again. The Norman Conquest, however, welded the country together and prevented a feudal decomposition such as took place on the Continent. Since that time particularism has never played a great political rôle in England.[1] The history of the world might have taken another course if the Angevin Empire had been maintained and the Kings had conquered France for good. They would then probably have regarded France as their principal realm, and the forces of internal disruption would perhaps have gained the upper hand in England, as they did in Germany through the domination of Italy by the Emperors, and especially through the acquisition of Sicily.

England, moreover, succeeded in integrating her nationality into a higher, British, one by taking the Welsh and the Scots into partnership and establishing with them a common State. Wales was conquered by Edward I and remained subject to the English Crown after a transitory restoration of independence. Edward I excluded the Welsh from any participation in the administration of their country, but Welsh mercenaries in English service played a great rôle in the wars with France, which may have strengthened Welsh loyalty to England. In the fifteenth century, however,

[1] There were, however, traditional enmities between different parts of England as the long and bitter quarrels among the Oxford Students show. These fights between the Northerners and the Southerners also had a political background, and in the thirteenth century were widely regarded as forerunners of civil strife. Mathew Paris gives examples of the animosity between the knights from the North and the South. Cf. A. Pollard, *Evolutions of Parliament*, 1934, p. 136.

Wales was in a state of anarchy. It was from Wales that Henry Tudor drew the bulk of the troops which won the Battle of Bosworth, and the King himself was the descendant of Welsh kings and national heroes. His son Henry VIII introduced into Wales English administration, law and language, and gave the Welsh a share in their local government and representation in the English Parliament. The Welsh gentry, the natural leaders of the people, welcomed Anglicization, which opened to them wide opportunities in England and this policy was not resisted by the Welsh people. Wales always remained loyal and the union with England was never unpopular.[1] Both the Welsh and the English derived the greatest benefit from this co-operation, and the Welsh were also able to maintain and develop their national individuality and a remarkable national civilization.

Scotland was originally peopled by various elements which were merged in a common Scottish nationality by the menace of Scandinavian and English domination. For a certain time Scotland was under English overlordship, but in the fourteenth century she regained her independence and then for three centuries was almost continually at war with England, often in alliance with France. Yet Scotland had already to a large extent adopted the English language, laws and institutions, not under any English compulsion, but through the influence of Celtic kings, Scottish magnates of Anglo-Norman descent and English settlers and traders.[2] This did not prevent the Scots from developing a very strong national consciousness and from regarding the English as their hereditary enemies.

The union of Scotland and England was prepared by the advent of the Scottish dynasty of the Stuarts to the English throne in 1603. James I in vain tried to bring about " a perpetual marriage between the two nations ". The English Parliament was only willing to accept a union under conditions which the Scots rejected. Cromwell for a short time united the nations by force, and gave the Scots a share in Parliament, but Charles II restored Scotland to her former status and this enabled him to re-establish his absolutism in Scotland. The definite and lasting union was brought about under Queen Anne. Relations between the English and the Scots at that time were very strained, national prejudice and hatred were strong on both sides, and the Scots, in particular, felt that the dynastic union with England placed them

---

[1] Cf. W. Llewelyn Williams, *The Making of Modern Wales, Studies in the Tudor Settlement of Wales*, 1919, pp. 8, 23 ; J. B. Rees, *Tudor Policy in Wales*, 1935.
[2] Cf. Robert Rait, *History of Scotland*, 1914, pp. 14, 28.

in a subordinate position. Their foreign policy was really controlled by England, and Scottish trade was excluded both from the English and the colonial market. England was engaged in her great struggle with Louis XIV, and the possibility of an independent Scotland, perhaps under a Stuart and in alliance with France, was a grave menace. When negotiations about a union were already being carried on, both countries adopted such hostile measures against each other that they seemed to be on the point of war.[1] At last, however, in 1707 the Union was accepted by both parliaments, though in Scotland only with a small majority, many members abstaining from voting, and a flood of angry protests and rioting showing how unpopular the Union was. " There is no doubt ", says Ramsay Muir, " that if a plebiscite of the nation had been taken at this moment, there would have been a large majority against the Union." [2] Lecky says that the majority of the nation was certainly against the Union. It was chiefly the nobility and the wealthier classes which were in favour of the Union or, at least, accepted it as the lesser evil. Scotland lost her separate parliament which, however, was never so near to the heart of the people as the General Assembly of the Church, which survived. Scotland received representation in Westminster, though only by 45 members, while according to population she could have claimed 85 members, and according to taxation 13. The chief price paid by England was the guarantee of Scotland's ecclesiastical independence and the admission of the Scotch to the English and colonial markets. The Union was a unique act in creating by legislation a new nation out of two peoples. England and Scotland henceforth constituted the Kingdom of Great Britain. A secure basis was laid for the ascent of a new Great Power to political and intellectual leadership in Europe. The Scots had a very large share in this process. An independent Scotland would have had a very precarious existence. She could hardly have maintained her independence, she would have been torn by internal strife and hampered in her progress by religious orthodoxy and extreme poverty. The Union opened out a wide field to Scottish energy and talent. Thenceforward they played an enormous rôle in the economic, political and cultural development of the British nation. Particularly great also was their share in building up the Empire. It need

[1] Cf. G. M. Trevelyan, *England under Queen Anne, Ramillies and the Union with Scotland*, 1932, p. 247. Trevelyan also gives many proofs of the deep national aversion between the two nations. Cf. Lecky, *History of England in the Eighteenth Century*, chap. vi.
[2] Ramsay Muir, *Short History of the British Commonwealth*, 1920, p. 585.

not be said what England owed to the Union. The advantages were immeasurable on both sides.

The success of the Union had a very great influence on Anglo-Irish relations. It was constantly adduced as a proof of the desirability of the Union of Ireland with England. This Union, indeed, took place in 1800 but it did not meet with the same success, and after more than a century full of bitter strife had to be repealed. The causes of this divergence between the Irish and the Scottish attitudes have often been discussed by historians. The difference of religion obviously was not decisive, for Scottish presbyterianism in former times was hardly less opposed to the Church of England than Catholicism was. The main reason was that the Irish had a much more bitter heritage of experience from the time when English ascendancy in Ireland was established. The Scots have never been driven from large parts of their own country or ruthlessly oppressed as the Irish were at the time of Cromwell and later, nor subjected to the rule of a foreign aristocracy. It was probably also a misfortune that the Irish aristocracy largely emigrated in the seventeenth and eighteenth centuries, and took service in foreign armies. Neither was there a wealthy Irish middle class. The Irish people thus lacked just those classes which in Scotland were decisive for the acceptance of the Union. True, the English Protestant gentry settled in Ireland had a large share in the early Irish national movement, and also later prominent Irish leaders came from this class.[1] Nevertheless, events showed that this class could not maintain its leadership. Irish politics have been poisoned by the mixture of national and social hatred on the Irish side, and by the development of a sentiment of racial superiority on the English side. The Irish national movement has often resorted to extreme violence, to acts of terrorism and parliamentary obstruction, and this has fostered the growth of a spirit of intransigence and fanaticism that has had disastrous consequences for Ireland herself, as evidenced by the alienation of Ulster from the Irish cause. England has certainly done much to make good old wrongs. All this, however, has not prevented Eire from declaring herself neutral in a struggle in which England defends the existence of Christian civilization against the worst barbarism of all times.

[1] In Swift's mouth " nation " meant the Irish Protestants, not the Catholics. Cf. Stephen Gwynn, *Ireland*, 1924, p. 34, and Edmund Curtis, *History of Ireland*, 1936, pp. 282, 300, 306.

13. NATIONAL PROBLEMS OF THE BRITISH EMPIRE

The British Empire has primarily sprung from private commercial enterprise and colonization of territories, inhabited by primitive tribes, though national rivalry with France and other reasons led to further expansion by conquest.[1] Some of the early prophets and pioneers of colonial expansion looked upon it from a national point of view.[2] In 1589, the year after the defeat of the Armada, Richard Hakluyt published his great work, *The Principal Navigations, Voyages and Discoveries of the English Nation*, in which he recommended colonization as a remedy for unemployment, misery and crime at home. He was inspired by the ardent wish to advance his country among the nations and he had a great and noble vision of the position which England would reach through colonization in the new world. But the course of events brought it about that the old colonial Empire was mainly a private commercial venture, and not primarily a national enterprise. The purpose of the ruling classes in England was to enjoy a commercial monopoly without being burdened with the responsibilities of government.[3] As regards the colonists, they mainly migrated to the new world to improve their living conditions or to escape religious persecution and to live according to their conscience. Unlike the settlers of other nations who devoted themselves mainly to trading, to fur hunting or to exploiting the natives, a large part of the settlers in English colonies became farmers who governed themselves, and this enabled them to become the fathers of new nations.

The American Revolution, and other events, discouraged further expansion. The opinion became predominant that every colony inhabited by white settlers would in the course of time strive for independence and nationhood, and that any attempt to prevent the achievement of this aim was futile. The ideas about the Empire were fundamentally changed by the tremendous expansion of world trade and British economic supremacy, and by the growing strength of Christian humanitarianism and political liberalism.[4] The combined influence of these forces

---

[1] The great authoritative history of this development is the *Cambridge History of the British Empire*, 8 vols. For a shorter treatment of the subject, cf. Ramsay Muir, *Short History of the British Commonwealth*, 2 vols.

[2] Cf. Bacon, Essays " Of the True Greatness of Kingdoms and Estates ", and " Of Plantations " ; further, the first projects of Raleigh, and his disciples, cf. Sidney Lee on Sir Walter Raleigh in his *Great English Men of the Sixteenth Century*, 1907 ; on Harrington, cf. H. Russell Smith, *Harrington and his Oceana*, 1914.

[3] Gerald Hertz, *British Imperialism in the Eighteenth Century*, 1908, p. 38.

[4] A brilliant exposition of the history of these ideals has recently been given by W. K. Hancock, *Survey of British Commonwealth Affairs*, vol. ii, *Problems of Economic Policy*, 2 parts, 1940–2.

tended to transform the Empire from a monopolistic business enterprise into a free association of advanced nations, a trusteeship on behalf of the backward peoples aiming at their education for nationhood, and an open field for the peaceful competition and emigration of all nations. The development of the Empire along these lines, in spite of many shortcomings and hardships, has brought immeasurable advantages not merely to its peoples but to the whole world. The Empire tended to become a real League of Nations, the mainstay of the world's peace, and the most potent agency for universal prosperity, progress and civilization. On the other hand, its expansion aroused the intense jealousy and rivalry of other nations, which in the second half of the nineteenth century resulted in a general scramble for the partition of the last available territories not constituted as modern states and, therefore, not considered entitled to national self-determination. This rivalry and internal issues, have, moreover, led to the emergence of a new Imperialism.[1]

Many Victorians were convinced that the great white colonies would develop into separate nations, and that there would be no other bonds between them, if any, than sentiment and interests. The new Imperialists, however, hoped that they would form essentially one nation, though in a federal form. This idea underlies Seeley's famous book, *The Expansion of England* (1883), which can be regarded as a manifestation of the new interest in Imperial unity. His idea of Imperialism is certainly not tinged with lust of expansion or prestige. He ridicules the " bombastic " glorification of a state merely because it is large, and the view that the maintenance of the Empire is a point of honour or sentiment, or that the dependencies of England are a sort of property belonging to her. But he also rejects the " pessimistic " school of thought which sees in the Empire only a product of aggression and rapacity, a useless and burdensome acquisition which exposes England to wars and quarrels in every part of the globe. Though Seeley mentions the federal system as one of the means for maintaining a large state he does not lay much stress on it. The emphasis is on national unity. He further says : " Our Empire is not an Empire at all in the ordinary sense of the word. It does not consist of a congeries of nations held together by force, but in the main of one nation, as much as if

[1] On the ideology of modern British Imperialism, compare the surveys and the bibliographies in William Langer, *The Diplomacy of Imperialism*, 1935, vol. i, pp. 67–99 ; Esmé Wingfield Stratford, *History of English Patriotism*, 2 vols. ; Jacques Bardoux, *Essai d'une psychologie de l'Angleterre contemporaine, les crises belliqueuses*, 1906 ; Friedrich Brie, *Imperialistische Strömungen in der englischen Literatur in Anglia*, vol. 40, 1916.

it were no Empire but an ordinary state." With the exception of India, which is an Empire herself, the Empire appears to him as " a vast English nation ", as " a very large state " with " a population which is English throughout ". The fact that it was not entirely homogeneous was not overlooked by Seeley ; but he regarded the existence of " a good many French and Dutch, Caffres and Maoris " in the Empire as mere exceptions which did not refute his general proposition. However, Seeley's view of the Empire forming merely a vast English state and one nation has not been confirmed by the subsequent development.

The advocates of Imperial Federation were faced with two tasks, that of uniting the dispersed settlements in each of the main natural regions of the Empire in a regional union, and that of federating these unions in the wider Empire. In both respects the advantages of co-operation were obvious. Many ingenious plans have been devised, and great efforts have been made for realizing that double federalism, and to create both adequate institutions and the right spirit for working them.[1] The result was that regional unions have been formed in three continents, which gradually became independent sovereign states within the Empire or, as it was later and more appropriately styled, the British Commonwealth of Nations.[2] The plans for developing common Imperial institutions, however, had little success.[3]

Even regional unity, however, was in certain parts only achieved after long struggles. In Canada the French population, separated from the British by language, religion, traditions and territory, did not merge with them into a single nation, and there were also other considerable minorities. Less than half of the people of Canada look upon the present United Kingdom as their mother country. For a long time bitter strife reigned between the French and the British elements, and several rebellions took place, the last in 1885. This spirit is now a matter of the past, and both nationalities have learned to co-operate, though the statistics show that there is still little intermarriage. Side by side with the sentiment of a common Canadian nation-

[1] Cf. J. Tyler, *The Struggle for Imperial Unity (1868–1895)*, 1938.
[2] An excellent survey is the book *The British Empire, a Report on its Structure and Problems by a Study Group of Members of the Royal Institute of International Affairs*, 1937 (quoted as *Rep. R.I.I.A.*). Cf. further, Arthur Berriedale Keith, *The Governments of the British Empire*, 1935 ; *The British Commonwealth of Nations*, 1940 ; E. Barker, *Ideas and Ideals of the British Empire*, 1941.
[3] For the development since the last war, cf. Richard Jebb, *The Empire in Eclipse*, 1926.

ality, provincial feeling is still strong,[1] and the two main nationalities have their sentimental loyalties to their ancestral countries and traditions which sometimes lead to divergent political attitudes.[2] The loyalty to the Empire has a rival in the strong feeling that Canada is primarily an American nation, and that relations with the United States are of paramount importance. Some categories of Canadian citizens are debarred from the franchise for racial reasons, especially those of Oriental descent, but also some others. The question, therefore, whether the Canadians form a united nation is difficult to answer.[3]

In South Africa the conflict between the Afrikanders and the British culminated in the great Boer War. A few years after the war Britain gave South Africa political unity and liberty, though the claims of the coloured population which forms the great majority were largely disregarded. That policy has certainly done much to heal the wounds of the past. Nevertheless it is perhaps premature to think of the South Africans as a single nation.[4]

In Australia there were no warring nationalities, but territorial particularism, partly rooted in economic interests, was strong and even now has not died out. The dissatisfaction of Western Australia with the Union in 1933 led to a plebiscite in which nearly two-thirds of the electorate expressed themselves in favour of secession. The State legislature sent a petition to the British Parliament, praying for severance from the Australian Commonwealth, but it was refused on legal grounds.[5] New Zealand has always shown a particularly strong loyalty to British traditions and to the Empire. Imperial Federation was for a long time popular in New Zealand, and she was very reluctant to accept the new Dominion independence, declaring that she was quite content with her position in the Empire.[6]

[1] It has been remarked that the federation would probably have been rejected if it had been submitted to plebiscites of the single parts. Newfoundland actually refused to join but was financially unable to maintain its independence as a Dominion.

[2] The French were always strongly for isolation, which, however, was also professed by many others. Many isolationists would have preferred secession from the Empire to participation in a war for it.

[3] R. A. Falconer, " The Quality of Canadian Life " (in *The Federation of Canada, 1867-1917*, published by the University of Toronto, 1917, p. 112), says : " It would be a counsel of despair to abandon faith in the possibility of a unified Canadian nation." But later on he assumes that there is one Canadian nation. Cf. further, R. MacKay and E. Rogers, *Canada looks Abroad*, 1938, and J. Dafoe, *Canada, an American Nation*, 1935.

[4] Cf. the recent pessimistic statement in G. Calpin, *There are no South Africans*, 1941. On South African nationality, compare the very instructive book *Coming of Age, Studies in South African Citizenship nad Politics*, by a group of writers, 1930, especially the chapter by Currey and Haarhoff.

[5] Cf. *Rep. R.I.I.A.*, p. 45. Cf. further, W. Hancock, *Australia*, 1931, pp. 76, 104, 124.

[6] *Rep. R.I.I.A.*, p. 51.

A completely different attitude was taken by the Irish Free State, which has gone much farther in cutting the ties with the Empire than any other State.

In each Dominion the development of a separate nationality has been determined by particular factors.[1] In some countries most immigrants belonged to the lower classes and many of them were non-British. They comprised also many Irish, Germans and Slavs. Their specific ideology often implied a distrust of British politics, which were regarded as mainly actuated by capitalistic and imperialistic motives. The outspoken democratic character of the new countries also manifested itself in the attitude to defence. Military preparations were almost completely left to Britain, in particular to the British Navy. On the other hand, most Dominions were suspicious as regards the possibility of entanglements in Empire conflicts,[2] and liked to emphasize their aloofness. The longing for prestige led them to resent even the slightest legal or practical dependence on Britain or the Empire. A very strong motive, furthermore, was protectionism, which was believed to serve the purpose of economic emancipation and the raising of wages and the standard of life. Another point in which the Dominions took a different line from the mother country was the attitude to Asiatic races.

The divergencies in the traditions and the general outlook of Great Britain and the Dominions were the main obstacle to the success of federation. The Dominions were preponderantly loyal to the Empire, and whenever it was threatened they made great sacrifices in blood and wealth for its defence. In peace time, too, they showed their feelings in many ways. For a long time they granted Britain one-sided preferential tariffs which were meant as some return for the protection by her navy. But the Dominions have never been willing to accept constitutional limitations of their independence in favour of federal institutions. The loyalty towards the Empire, therefore, is not equivalent to a national solidarity. The Commonwealth is neither a federation, nor an alliance which also implies fixed obligations. It is based

---

[1] Cf. Richard Jebb, *Studies in Colonial Nationalism*, 1905; Hancock, *Australia*, pp. 51, 60–8.

[2] The fear of such entanglements, however, did not always prevent Australia from increasing the friction between Britain and other European powers by her claim to exclude these powers from founding colonies in the Pacific, which she regarded as an Australian preserve. Many times Australian statesmen have put great pressure on the British Government to make no concessions to France or Germany in Pacific questions. Hancock, *Australia*, p. 65, speaks of Australia's " aggressive imperialism " and gives significant instances. In 1899 the Samoa question, in which Australia took the same attitude, almost led to the breaking off of diplomatic relations between Britain and Germany, though Kaiser William must mainly be blamed for this tension.

merely on sentiment and interest, and in this way agrees more with the forecast of Victorian Liberals than with the expectations of the Imperialists. Anyhow, it is such a unique historical growth that its definition in terms of law or political science is almost impossible. The Empire also comprises several members which are semi-independent and will probably reach Dominion status, and the national aspirations of its numerous peoples present to the student of nationality most interesting phenomena.[1]

Nations which are hostile or biased against Britain seem unable to understand the nature of the British Empire. In their ideology Britain dominates and exploits her enormous Empire, and in this way deprives other nations of " living space ". This view springs from their jealousy and envy and is furthered by the word Empire, which conveys the idea of domination. In reality the Dominions often had more influence on Imperial and even on British affairs than Britain had on their policy, and they were in some respects more strongly represented in the League of Nations than Great Britain. In vital questions of international policy Britain had—against her own inclinations—to yield to the opinion of the Dominions.[2] Though these accorded to Britain lower tariffs than to other states, British trade was most hit by Dominion protection because it was much larger and fell more under the tariffs. American goods pay on the average less duty in Canada than British goods. The economic nationalism of the Dominions has more and more compelled Britain to abandon her system of Free Trade, which formerly was regarded as the very cornerstone of British prosperity and as the strongest guarantee of the world's peace.[3]

The policy of Britain towards other nations has for centuries

[1] Many of these problems have been brilliantly treated by W. K. Hancock, *Survey of British Commonwealth Affairs*, vol. i, *Problems of Nationality, 1918–36*, 1937.

[2] The fact, for example, that the racial policy of the Dominions embarrasses the United Kingdom in her international policy is often acknowledged by writers in the Dominions. Nevertheless, it has become there a gospel with the peoples, as T. Mackenzie (*Nationalism and Education in Australia*, 1935, p. 37), says. For a defence of Australia's racial policy, cf. Hancock, *Australia*, p. 77. The book *Canada Looks Abroad* (1938), published under the auspices of the Canadian Institute of International Affairs, says of the policy of racial discrimination of America and the Dominions that " there can be little doubt that the policy tends to provoke the ill-will of Oriental peoples and that it may be laying up trouble for the future—trouble not alone for Canada and other Anglo-Saxon countries of the Pacific, but perhaps for the British Commonwealth as well. Indian peoples, no less than Canadians, are subjects of the King ; but Canada treats them as undesirable aliens." Nevertheless, it is further said, this policy was perhaps necessary in order to maintain friendly relations with the United States, and Canada was more likely to follow in this matter the lead of the U.S. than that of Great Britain.

[3] For a criticism of the results of the Ottawa Conference, cf. Hancock, *Survey II*, pp. 198–267 ; *Rep. R.I.I.A.*, p. 279. Ramsay Muir, *The Expansion of Europe*, 1935, p. 305.

been determined by the principle of the Balance of Power. After the last war this principle was replaced by that of Collective Security through the League of Nations. There was only the choice between these two policies if Britain wanted to have a foreign policy at all and not let the affairs on which her fate depended simply drift. The Dominions, however, were neither for the one nor for the other of these alternatives. It was psychologically understandable that they rejected any policy of a European Balance of Power, but they also refused to back an effective policy of Collective Security which might involve them in a war. The Canadian Prime Minister, Mr. Mackenzie King, in 1937 declared in Parliament that he doubted very much if the British Government would ever send another expeditionary force to Europe, and that it was extremely doubtful if any of the British Dominions would do so. Such declarations unintentionally encouraged the aggressive powers. This attitude too was understandable. It was shared by all other democracies of the whole world, and therefore must be interpreted as the expression of fundamental tendencies. Britain herself did not realize in time the full implications of Fascism and Naziism. In the days of Munich the influence of the Dominions was strongly for the policy of appeasement. Canada and Australia declared that they could not support Britain in a war.[1]

A full discussion of all these issues is beyond the scope of our investigations.[2] We had to mention them, however, because they may be significant for the general problem of Empire and Liberty mooted by Montesquieu. The solution by means of a federation suggested by him has been rejected by the democracies of the Commonwealth. A substitute has been found in the strength of traditions, interests and ideals. When the war came the Dominions—with the exception of Eire and a minority in South Africa—realized that their own fate was bound up with that of Britain, and they proved by their exertions that the British Commonwealth of Nations was really a living force in the hearts and minds of millions of citizens all over the world.

14. The Origin of American Nationality

The development of the national individuality of most European nations to a large extent took place in times when historians

[1] Cf. John Kennedy, *Why Britain Slept*, 1940, p. 201.
[2] Cf. the most instructive survey in British Commonwealth Relations (*Proceedings of the Toronto Conference*, 1933), ed. by A. Toynbee, 1934.

gave little, if any, attention to collective psychology. The origin of the United States of America, however, belongs to modern history, and the historical sources, therefore, give us much information about the driving forces in the formation of the American nation. The legend that the revolution was brought about by English tyranny is now abandoned by critical American historians. English colonial policy at that time certainly was corrupt, shortsighted and narrow-minded but not oppressive. The colonies were prosperous and there was no general, deeply felt grievance. American historians now judge that the colonists had far more liberty than the English at home, and that they revolted just because they were the freest of all peoples.[1]

The distance between England and America estranged the two peoples, the vast and empty continent filled the Americans with the vision of a great future, and the rough frontier life created a spirit of sturdy individualism rejecting any State interference and any dependence. Many settlers were the descendants of men who had left England for political or religious reasons, a considerable section of the population, moreover, was of Irish, Scotch, German or Dutch descent, and many of them had a traditional dislike of England. The majority of the people belonged to the poorer classes and looked upon England as the embodiment of the spirit of aristocratic and capitalistic class rule. The ideology of democratic radicalism was one of the main driving forces in the antagonism to England. The rank and file of the rebels were small farmers, frontiermen, labourers and colonists of non-English stock.[2] The great leaders, however, came mostly from the more highly educated and wealthier English element. In the beginning very few wished for independence, and it is probable that for some time the great majority was not for a break with England.[3] The energetic propaganda of the Radicals, however, often supported by tarring and feathering of Conservative opponents, the blunders of English policy, and the war turned the tide. The American war was also a civil

---

[1] James Truslow Adams, *Revolutionary New England, 1691–1776*, 1923, pp. 14 f.; Claude van Tyne, *The Causes of the War of Independence*, 1922, p. 456. Nicholas Murray Butler, *Building the American Nation*, 1923, p. 36, says that it made no difference what policy England might follow towards the colonies. They had all the elements for a separate nation, and their revolution, therefore, was only a matter of time.

[2] While the old and wealthy settlements on the coast were largely English, the pioneer farmers in the back-country were very generally of non-English origin. Cf. Frederick J. Turner, *The Frontier in American History*, 1921, pp. 23, 206.

[3] J. T. Adams, pp. 385, 407; Lecky, *History of England in the Eighteenth Century*, chaps. 12, 14, 15 *passim*.

war in which over a hundred thousand opponents of revolution, the Loyalists, were driven out of the country or killed.[1]

This social background shows many parallels with other national and revolutionary movements. The building of the American nation, however, is not adequately explained by social forces alone. This was also the work of great leaders inspired by enthusiasm for freedom and noble ambition, some of them men of outstanding genius. Their wish was to break away from " the pernicious labyrinth of European politics ", to found a new and better world, and thus " to vindicate the honour of the human race ". The idea of a great mission was one of the strongest motives of these men, and it was often expressed in exuberant words.[2] These leaders steered America through the waves of popular passions which threatened her with anarchy and disruption, and they became the founders of a great nation.

The unity of the American nation, however, was not yet definitely secured. The question whether the United States comprised one people or as many peoples as States was for a long time the object of sharp disputes. The greatest factors making for unity were the vast uncolonized territory which could only be developed by common efforts and was in the hands of the Federal Government, the dangerous neighbourhood of colonies of several great European powers, the immigration of millions without loyalty to any particular American State, but looking upon America as a whole as the home of freedom. Nevertheless, also the forces of disintegration were powerful. Almost every State, both in the North and the South, and both great parties, have occasionally followed a policy of extreme particularism, and it was a group of prominent Northern States which first threatened to dissolve the Union and to found a separate nation, possibly in alliance with England.[3]

As in all nations the spirit of national unity was decisively furthered and spread through war. The war of 1812 against England was largely an aggressive war, undertaken by America

---

[1] Cf. Claude van Tyne, *The Royalists in the American Revolution*, 1902. Lewis Einstein, *Divided Loyalties, Americans in England during the War of Independence*, 1933.

[2] John Adams wrote as early as 1768 that he considered " the settlement of America with reverence, as the opening of a grand scene and design in Providence for the illumination of the ignorant and the emancipation of the slavish part of mankind all over the world ". In 1813 he wrote to Thomas Jefferson : " Our pure, virtuous, public-spirited federative republic will last for ever, govern the globe, and introduce the perfection of man." Cf. Charles Sumner, *Prophetic Voices Concerning America*, 1874, pp. 54, 62.

[3] Cf. Kendric Ch. Babcock, *The Rise of American Nationality, 1811–1819*, 1906, pp. 16, 160–6, 195 ; James Truslow Adams, *America's Tragedy*, 1934, pp. 44, 48 ; Nicolas Murray Butler, *Building the American Nation*, 1923, p. 161.

for the purpose of conquering Canada, and thus expelling England from the American continent, and for uniting the whole nation through a common effort and common feelings of hatred and pride. " The consciousness of nationality ", says Babcock, " which came out of the second war with Great Britain was the chief political result, the one most far-reaching in its effects." The war gave the people " a new, almost intoxicating sense of self-respect ".[1] Another important effect was the awakening of the striving for economic emancipation from England through protectionism. During the war the exclusion of English competition fostered the springing up of industries in America, and after the war high tariffs were introduced in order to protect them and to encourage further industrialization. The arguments put forward were the same which have since played such a decisive rôle in all national aspirations, namely, national independence and preparedness for war.[2] This protectionism became known as the " American system ", and had a great share in spreading economic nationalism in Europe too.

In spite of this progress of the spirit of unity it was not yet certain, however, that the Union would prevail over antagonistic forces. Tocqueville in his classic book on America (1835) discussed the question whether the Union would last, and weighed many arguments for and against its duration.[3] " The Union ", he said, " is a vast body which presents no definite object to patriotic feeling. Patriotism is still directed to the State and is not excited by the Union." One of the strongest factors for its preservation was the extraordinary similarity of opinions and feelings among the peoples of the twenty-four sovereign states which really made one people out of them. This unity was, furthermore, strengthened by common separation from the rest of mankind. " For the last 50 years no pains have been spared to convince the people of the United States that they constituted the only religious, enlightened and free people, and they have an overweening opinion of their superiority, and are not very remote from behaving themselves as belonging to a distinct race of mankind." Slavery, however, Tocqueville says, creates a striking difference of character between the North and the South, and may induce the South to secede from the Union. Tocqueville even finds that the laws of human nature render the duration of

[1] An interesting feature was the enthusiasm for successful generals. Babcock says (p. 198) : " The American people, while essentially peace-loving and unmilitary by temperament, have shown a curious hero-worship of the successful military leader."
[2] Cf. Babcock, p. 231.
[3] Cf. Alexis de Tocqueville, *Democracy in America, 1835-40*, vol. ii, pp. 364-423.

the Union extremely improbable, though in other places he seems to be less sure about this point.

The antagonism between the South and the North aroused by the issues of slavery and protection steadily grew. The South had an extraordinary share in providing the Union with statesmen, owing to the greater political training of its ruling class, and this was resented by the North. The Southern planters felt as an aristocracy, and even cherished the belief that they were of the superior Norman race while the North was peopled by descendants of Celtic and Saxon serfs.[1] This romantic racialism was suggested by the novels of Walter Scott, and, moreover, the Southerners made use of the fantastic Aryanism of Count Gobineau which suited them well for combating the demand for emancipation of their slaves. Gradually the social antagonism attained to such a degree that the North and the South were like two hostile nations which represented totally incompatible social ideals and civilizations.

This time the South invoked the right of secession, and the North denied it on the ground that there was only one American nation, and that the Southerners, forming merely a part of this nation, had no claim to national self-determination. Their declaration of independence was branded as rebellion. The constitutional arguments for this thesis need not be examined here. Even Motley, who in a famous letter to *The Times* (1861) denied the right of secession, recognized that British and American history was full of rebellions and revolutions which superseded the letter of the law. Opinion in Britain was predominantly on the side of the South.[2] Prejudice against American democracy and economic egoism had a great share in this attitude. But even Gladstone, who had no sympathy for the Southern slave-owners, and who believed that all the interests of England were bound up with the preservation of the Union, held the view that the Southerners formed a nation, and that the war was sure to end in their favour.[3] England was at that time very near recognizing the independence of the South and gliding into a war with the North. The break was to a large extent prevented by the Queen, who acted on the advice of the Prince Consort given a few days before his death.

[1] Cf. J. T. Adams, pp. 95, 118.
[2] Cf. Ephraim Douglass Adams, *Great Britain and the American Civil War*, 2 vols., 1925.
[3] Gladstone expressed rashly his views in a speech at Newcastle which he later deplored as an error. His different utterances on the war show the multitude of arguments speaking for and against secession.

Everybody to-day will regard the preservation of the Union as a blessing for America and the world. If the right of self-determination had been granted to the South, this might have led to further secessions and to the total dismemberment of the Union. Could the great interior States, it was asked, allow those possessing the seaports to cut off their direct access to the sea, and perhaps to throttle their import and export trade? Would not rivalries have broken out in regard to the settlement of the great unoccupied territories of the West which might have ended in the devastation of America by constant wars? More than half a century after the end of the war an American President proclaimed the right of self-determination as the clue to the lasting appeasement of Europe. The consequences of this idealistic approach have now become so patent that nobody would wish that America should have had to go through a similar ordeal.

The Civil War too had a considerable influence in strengthening the idea of unity in wide parts of the Union. The antagonism between the North and the South smouldered on for at least twenty years, but at last died down. The unity of the American nation was never seriously menaced again. It only shows how long old half-conscious traditions may linger, if even in our generation an ecclesiastical conference took exception to the proposal to introduce a prayer for the American nation because this savoured too much of unity. It was resolved instead to pray for the United States.[1]

The development of national unity in the North American federation seemed to confirm Montesquieu's hopes that in a large territory unity and liberty could be combined by federation. Very frequently Americans have asked why Europe could not follow their example. It is clear, however, that the case of America can in no way be compared with the conditions of Europe. The number of the states which originally federated was much smaller than the present one. They were all weak, and had necessarily to join hands, if they wanted to hold their own against England and other powers which then had large colonies near by. Most states developed later in the empty land held by the Union, and in this way they were really created by the federation. There were lastly no old rivalries and animosities between the states such as poisoned relations between European nations. With the exception of the War of Secession the Continent could develop in peace, and this was probably the factor which decided the success of federation.

[1] Cf. James Bryce, *The American Commonwealth*, vol. i, p. 2.

15. NATIONAL PROBLEMS OF INDIA

The Indian nationalists [1] of to-day claim the whole of India as the Indian national territory to be ruled by the one and indivisible Indian nation. The moderates more or less recognize that this unity is largely due to British rule and influence, while the radicals contend that it is a spontaneous outcome of Indian history, and that the British have but delayed and hindered its growth by withholding political freedom, by economic exploitation, and by stirring up dissensions among the Indians. Their opponents argue that India is not suitable to form one single national state because her population consists of many peoples different in language, race, religion, customs and traditions.[2] She is not a country but a continent like Europe, which could never be united in one single state. Moreover, they used to say, the present unity of India is more or less the product of British rule and could not subsist without this bond, especially without the support of the British army and navy, and of the British administration as an umpire between contending parties. Lastly, they allege that the economic and cultural backwardness of the great majority of the Indian peoples precludes for the time being their full independence.

The idealizing picture of India's past, drawn by certain Indian historians in order to support the charges against the British, is greatly disputed.[3] Great conquerors have for short periods united almost the whole of India under their mainly nominal overlordship, but they have not attempted to weld the different parts together to a national unity, nor has their rule unintentionally had this effect. There were some great and beneficent rulers but quite predominantly the history of India alternated between unlimited despotism and complete anarchy, and frequently the people were in a state of boundless misery. In particular, the conditions which prevailed in the time of

---

[1] We designate the Indian national movement as "Nationalist" because this is the generally accepted name, though we feel great reluctance in describing Gandhi's political attitude by the same name as Hitler's.

[2] The linguistic survey of India states that there were 179 languages and 544 dialects. The diversity is mitigated, however, by the widespread use of languages of communication such as Urdu, Hindi, Tamil and English. Urdu is a mixture of Hindi with Persian and Arabic elements and the Moslems regard it as their common language, while the Hindus prefer Hindi. Tamil, the lingua franca of south India, belongs to a quite different group. Among the educated classes English is generally used, and even Congress, the nationalist organization, predominantly used it for their assemblies until quite recent times.

[3] Cf. Guy Wint in Sir G. Schuster and G. Wint, *India and Democracy*, 1941, p. 17, and *Modern India and the West*, edited by L. O'Malley, 1941, chap. i.

the dissolution of the Moghul Empire, immediately preceding the establishment of British rule, abounded in indescribable horrors. The decisive difference between Indian and European developments was that the forces making for political liberty and social equality, and, therefore, for national unity were much weaker than in our continent. There cannot be the slightest doubt that British rule has immensely strengthened these forces by establishing peace and introducing a reign of law and Western civilization. Indian national pride need not be offended by this view, considering that Western civilization was not merely a product of the Western mind but was largely built on the foundations laid by the ancient Orient and that it has also received great contributions from India.

The present idea of Indian Unity is certainly of recent origin. It has been pointed out that there was no word for India or Indian in any vernacular tongue, and that it was the British who first spoke of Indians.[1] Likewise Roman missionaries first spoke of the English as a unit and Anglo-Saxon missionaries of the Germans. It was British rule too which created the national movement, partly by spreading Western ideas, partly by direct encouragement,[2] and most of all by uniting the most diverse elements in common opposition. This too has many parallels in European history. The great question, however, is whether this unity is merely a negative one or also a positive factor which would survive the withdrawal of the British from India. It cannot be ignored that the possibility of Hindu domination has aroused the fiercest opposition of the great majority of Moslems who demand the establishment of a separate Moslem state. There is danger that India in the event of a Hindu government would be ravaged by civil war. This has even been admitted by Gandhi, though he expressed the view that a civil war would not last long as the Indians were not trained in arms.[3] But the Mohammedans have a martial tradition and they are strong enough to hold their own, and even to found an independent Moslem state. Besides the 80 million Moslems there are other peoples which with the progress of education and political interest might develop and assert a separate national consciousness. There are, furthermore, 60 million of untouchables who are looked upon by most Hindus

[1] Cf. Sir R. Craddock, *The Dilemma in India*, 1929, p. 1.
[2] The founder of Congress was Allan Hume, and he was encouraged in his plan by the Viceroy Lord Dufferin. Cf. C. Andrews and G. Mukerji, *The Rise and Growth of the Congress in India*, 1938, pp. 121, 123, 146. Sir W. Wedderburn, *A. O. Hume*, 1913. Moreover, the national movement has been greatly furthered by British friends and the Congress has frequently been presided over by them.
[3] Cf. Schuster and Wint, p. 346.

very much as are the Jews by the Nazi, and who might also become a problem for a purely Hindu state. The British administration has introduced a system, designed to afford to important minorities a fair representation in elected councils and in official appointments which is called " communal representation ".[1]

The British Government in 1917 defined its policy as that of increasing the association of Indians in every branch of the administration, and the gradual development of self-government in India as an integral part of the British Empire. The great constitutional reform of 1935 constituted a most important step towards this goal. In the territory under direct British rule no less than 36 millions were enfranchised, and it is the Indian peasantry which has thereby been invested with the political power. The full realization of Indian nationhood was made dependent on the solution of the questions of federation and of the minorities. The British Government, moreover, has by its attitude towards Ireland given ample proof of its readiness to respect the principle of national self-determination even at the expense of the national security of Britain. In both cases the nationalists on the other side have for years not facilitated the task of combining liberty with unity.[2]

Summing up, it must be said that the Right of Self-determination cannot be denied to the Indians, if it is not to lose all its authority, and that Britain has recognized this and is willing to act accordingly. The realization of the principle, however, proves difficult for several reasons. First, it is not clear at all which organized groups are entitled to be regarded as forming one nation and how their national territory is to be demarcated. Secondly, there may be latent nations which sooner or later may also claim self-determination, and it would certainly be in the interest of all to provide for this possibility beforehand. Thirdly, the maintenance of some unity between the parts of India and of some connexion of India with the British Commonwealth of Nations would surely be of such paramount importance for India,

[1] Congress accepted the principle in the Lucknow pact of 1916. Cf. Andrews and Mukerji, p. 253. Many nationalists, however, are opposed to communal representation, e.g. K. Krishna in his book, *The Problem of Minorities or Communal Representation in India*, 1939. The author attributes all evils to British Imperialism which has made the Indians "slaves in their own land". The British, according to him, have invented the minorities in order to sow dissensions. The minorities are backward elements, painting their imaginary grievances in lurid colours, and only out to get posts from the Government.

[2] G. Wint says that both Gandhi and de Valera have really fostered disunity in their countries, Gandhi by arousing intense Moslem opposition to the Hindu national aims, and de Valera by deepening the gulf between Eire and Ulster. Cf. T. Chinna Durai, *The Choice before India*, 1941, p. 169, for an Indian criticism of Congress.

the other nations concerned and the whole world, that every friend of India and the world's peace and prosperity should hesitate to sacrifice it to mere feelings of resentment for past injustice and to a sort of inferiority complex. If India were inhabited by a purely European population, equipped with the highest standard of general and political education hitherto reached in the most advanced European countries, but in addition perpetuating the present historical diversities between the peoples of India, there would hardly be a doubt that India would soon fall to pieces and become a new Balkan on a gigantic scale.[1] At present three factors hinder this development: British influence, colour-feeling, which gives the Indians a certain solidarity against the Europeans, and the low standard of education of wide sections, which is an obstacle to the awakening of the national-consciousness latent in many peoples. A total break with the British Commonwealth would possibly lessen the influence of colour-feeling and an increase in popular education would probably lead to the development of new aspirations to form separate nations. It might be said that the experience formed from a study of European history does not apply to India. But this argument is hardly confirmed by the lessons of India's past and would imply a belief in a radical diversity in the mentality of races which is not compatible with the results of scientific research.

16. Nationality in the Russian Empire and the Soviet Union

In old Russia many factors led to the development of a system of unlimited absolutism which for a long time showed few national traits. In the eighteenth century and even later the dynasty, the court, and the higher officers and bureaucrats were often more German than Russian, while the nobility adopted the French language and French manners. The higher circles had a cosmopolitan outlook, and the lower classes had hardly any national consciousness except a strong attachment to the Orthodox Creed which served as a substitute for nationality. After the overthrow of Napoleon the Tsar Alexander under the influence of liberal and Christian ideas granted a certain autonomy to the

---

[1] A well-known friend of India, Professor Harold Laski, says in his *Grammar of Politics*, 1926, p. 220: "The disappearance of England from India will almost certainly, if it comes within some near period, result in anarchy for a time; yet there are thousands of Indians to whom the idea of an Indian-created anarchy is preferable to a British-created peace".

Poles and the Finns, but under his successors this policy was abandoned, mainly as a consequence of the Polish insurrections, which were cruelly stamped out. The rise of the middle class fostered the growth of national aspirations and nationalism among the Russians and some of the more advanced peoples of the Empire. This soon led to a policy of ruthless Russification of the numerous national minorities. Though the Russians proper formed only 43 per cent. of the population their language was made the exclusive language of the administration. With a few exceptions the minorities had no government schools and no cultural institutions in their own tongue. Every means was used to exterminate the non-Russian languages, especially among the Ukrainians and other Slavs, who officially were counted as Russians.[1] The Jews who in Russia showed certain traits of a nationality were persecuted with particular brutality. The revolution of 1905 brought some alleviations but conditions soon deteriorated again.

The Bolsheviks adopted an entirely different policy.[2] Each of the large nationalities was constituted as a separate Republic in which the minorities were granted autonomy, and which, therefore, had a federal character. All the federal Republics then formed the Federation of Soviet Republics. The old name of a Russian Empire was abandoned for that supra-national name. Each nationality, moreover, was even declared free to leave the federation, though this was never a practical possibility.

According to the Census of 1926 the Soviet Union was inhabited by 185 peoples speaking 147 languages. There were, however, only five widely spoken languages. These peoples were organized in eleven federal Soviet Republics, comprising twenty-two autonomous republics, five territories, thirty-four departments, nine autonomous regions, and a few national districts of minor importance. The administrative division follows partly national, partly natural and economic lines of demarcation. Supreme power is vested in the Supreme Soviet, composed of two Chambers, the Soviet of the Union, and the Soviet of Nation-

[1] On the treatment of nationalities cf. *Russen über Ruszland, ein Sammelwerk, herausgegeben von J. Melnik*, 1906, pp. 538–670. On Russian Nationalism compare the chapter by S. O. Yakobson p. 57, in the book *Nationalism, A Report of a Study Group of the R.I.I.A.*, 1940, and my book, *Nationalgeist und Politik*, 1937, p. 309.

[2] Cf. Hans Kohn, *Nationalism in the Soviet Union*, 1933 ; the chapter on nationalities in Sir John Maynard, *The Russian Peasant and other Studies*, 1942, p. 377 ; S. and B. Webb, *Soviet Communism*, 1937 ; Ewald Ammende, *Human Life in Russia*, 1936 ; Marc Slonim, *Les onze republiques Sovietiques*, 1937 ; *Russia, U.S.S.R.*, a complete handbook edited by P. Malevsky-Malevitch, 1936 (contains a chapter on nationalities by C. Tcheidze) ; Chimnaz Aslanova, *The National Question Solved*, 1939 ; Yanka Kupala, *Cultural Progress among Non-Russian Nationalities of the U.S.S.R.*, 1939.

alities. The two chambers enjoy equal rights. Each of the principal Republics, irrespective of the size of its population, sends 25 deputies to the Soviet of Nationalities, and each of the smaller autonomous units also sends the same number. In this way the smaller nationalities have a further protection against the preponderance of the larger. The Central Soviet has very wide powers, while the territorial Soviets are chiefly concerned with local affairs.

All nationalities have been granted full freedom and equality in regard to the use of their languages in representative bodies, courts, the administration and schools. Great efforts have been made to organize education in all languages and to raise the economic and cultural level of backward nationalities. The Soviets have founded universities, schools, libraries, scientific institutes, museums, theatres, cinemas and wireless stations for all peoples, have encouraged their literature, developed new alphabets and compiled dictionaries. The Russian language is no more a privileged tongue, though it develops into a lingua franca for the whole Union.[1] The new alphabets are not based on Russian but on Latin script. The Turco-Tartars have abandoned their Arabic script and the Germans their Gothic script for Latin letters, while the Russians and Ukrainians have retained their Slavonic script.

The achievements in furthering national languages and cultural institutions are doubtless very considerable, and constitute an enormous progress if compared with conditions in the former Empire. The Soviets naturally use the results of this policy for propaganda abroad, where they spread the view that under the Bolshevik system alone have national freedom and equality been realized. It seems that this contention has made a great impression, especially in India. This allegation, however, requires considerable qualifications. National self-determination, according to the usual democratic view, does not consist merely in the right to use the national language but implies also the right to determine the whole policy affecting the nation and to develop its culture in accordance with national traditions. The peoples of the Soviet Union, however, are not free to adopt any policy which suits them best. They must accept Marxism and its practical interpretation by the Communist headquarters in Moscow as the supreme law. The Central Soviet has full powers to lay down general rules in all important matters. A great expert,

[1] In 1938 Russian was made a compulsory second language in non-Russian schools.

very sympathetic to the Soviets, Sir John Maynard, comes to the conclusion that " the political system is one of intense centralization " and that " the constitution gives little or nothing in the way of actual power to the constituent bodies which are parties to the federation ". In particular the right to secede from the Union, embodied in the Constitution, is a right on paper only. If any of the federated Republics should dare to declare its independence or to make laws inconsistent with Bolshevik ideas or the directions of the Communist Party, this attempt would be suppressed with the utmost rigour.[1]

The Bolsheviks recognize the principle of self-determination, but subordinate it to the interests of Bolshevism or that of the proletariat. They accord equal rights to all, irrespective of nationality, which includes the right to the use and development of one's vernacular. But they do not share the view that nationality is a value by itself and that, therefore, every nationality, however small and backward, has a right to unlimited development of its cultural and political personality with the final aim of independence. This view, indeed, is the outcome of liberalism and romanticism; it smacks of individualism and anarchism. Neither do the Bolsheviks believe that every nation has a mission. They believe in the mission of a class, the proletariat, and Stalin has declared that the world-wide triumph of Communism would finally bring one common culture and language to all peoples. Bolshevik policy, therefore, does not envisage the permanent existence of many national languages or cultures, but finds it opportune to favour their development for some time as a means for strengthening a system of social equality which is closely bound up with national equality, though social equality takes precedence. Stalin himself is like a symbol of national equality. He is a Georgian, and the conquest of Georgia was largely his work. On the other hand, his paramount position in the Soviet Union flatters the national pride of the

[1] The invasion and incorporation of the Republic of Georgia in 1921 seems to be a striking example. The problem of Georgia, however, is a very complicated one. There is no doubt that the Socialist Government which was backed by the majority of the people was overthrown by Soviet troops and the resistance of the people broken. Cf. K. Kautsky, *Georgia, A Social-Democratic Peasant Republic*, 1921. In 1924 a rising of the people took place and was also suppressed. The British Trade Union Delegates to Russia and Caucasia in their Report (published 1925) come to conclusions favourable to the Soviet Union. They recognize that a very large majority of the Georgians were in favour of the former Socialist Government (p. 212) but find that this regime was a failure, both financially and economically, while the Bolsheviks were a success (p. 208). This judgement implies that economic and administrative efficiency may override the right of self-determination. Revelations about the attitude of the Powers were made in Zourab Avalishvili, *The Independence of Georgia in International Politics*, 1940.

Georgians and may have contributed to make them acquiesce in the loss of their independence.

The Soviet policy regarding the nationalities has been made possible by specific conditions which have no parallel in other countries. The Russian nationality alone is more numerous than all others together, and next to it come the Ukrainians, who number about 40 per cent of the Russians. All the other nationalities are so small that they appear like pygmies assembled around two giants.[1] Three nationalities, the Russians, Ukrainians and White Russians, moreover, are so closely related to each other, that they are often regarded as three branches of one people, and together they number 80 per cent of the total population of the Soviet Union. Most of the small nationalities, furthermore, were exceedingly backward in cultural development and had not yet reached the stage of an articulate national consciousness. Many of them had neither a literature, nor historical traditions fostering national pride, nor an intelligentsia, which is indispensable for the development of national sentiment. In more advanced peoples where a middle-class intelligentsia had already developed, it was crushed by the Bolsheviks for the very reason that it was, or threatened to become, the champion of national independence. All the tiny and backward nationalities had hardly a chance of standing on their own feet, and they could certainly not have maintained separate States surrounded by a hostile Soviet Union. Many of the nationalities neither liked Communism, nor its anti-religious propaganda, nor the prospect of a Russian hegemony. On the other hand, the advantages of belonging to a vast empire, of living under its mighty protection and enjoying its financial, economic and cultural assistance, were enormous. If the small nationalities did not like Bolshevism it was open to them to form separate federations on a democratic basis. This, however, proved impossible. Democratic republics could neither overcome the national and tribal hatred which separated many of those peoples, nor could they cope with the military, financial and economic difficulties of the anarchic time after the war. All these problems could only be solved by a strong government, able to impose great sacrifices upon the people. But how could a government dependent on the will of a people totally untrained in politics adopt such a policy?

[1] Cf. Apart from the Russians and Ukrainians there were only three nationalities numbering between 3 and 5 million, eight between 1 and 3 million, and seven between ½ and 1 million. No others reached even half a million, most of them not even 100,000.

Overwhelming arguments, therefore, spoke for the union of all the nationalities under Soviet leadership. Nevertheless, this union was not achieved without compulsion. A considerable section of the nationalities would probably not have joined the Soviet Union if they had not been forced to do so. Neither did the establishment of Soviet power and the inauguration of the policy of equal rights for all nationalities put an end to aspirations aiming either at separation from the Union or at a much more widely extended autonomy. This is proved by a number of risings, disturbances and plots which were all suppressed with great energy.[1]

17. THE AUSTRIAN EMPIRE

The Austrian Empire was constituted in 1804 and after 1867 was named the Austro-Hungarian Monarchy.[2] Its real origin, however, dates back to the year 1526, when King Ludwig II of Hungary and Bohemia was utterly defeated by the Turks and lost his life on the battlefield. The Ottoman Empire at that time was the most formidable military power and its aggressiveness threatened the whole of Europe. This was the reason why Bohemia, Croatia and a part of Hungary elected as their king the Archduke Ferdinand of Austria, who later succeeded his brother Charles V as Emperor. It took a long time, however, before the numerous countries of the Austrian Habsburgs assumed the character of a united Empire. The most important step towards unification was the Pragmatic Sanction of 1713. Yet the Austrian Empire never became a strict unity, and always showed more or less the features of a federation. The diets or estates of its different territories and the spirit of particularism often limited the power of the Crown, and compelled the dynasty to pursue a policy of caution and to rely more on diplomacy and compromise than on war. The history of the Empire, nevertheless, was full of wars with the Turks, the French, the Swedes, and German rulers, especially Prussia. The Empire existed for about four centuries, of which only a third was a time of peace. The unruly nobility of Austria, Bohemia and Hungary often rebelled against the authority of the Crown, and as a rule associated their striving for power with the cause of Protestantism and

---

[1] Cf. Maynard, pp. 388, 398 ; E. Ammende, *Human Life in Russia*, 1936.
[2] Cf. Franz M. Mayer, *Geschichte Oesterreichs*, 2 vols., 1909. On the national struggles cf. my book *Nationalgeist und Politik*, 1 vol., 1937, pp. 335–438 where relevant literature is quoted.

nationality. The dynasty could only maintain itself, and the nascent Empire too, by combating the aspirations of the nobility and by curbing their power through a centralizing policy. It is significant that the Crown always pressed for centralization when the existence of the Empire was at stake, as in the Thirty Years War, and in the struggle against Prussian aggression.

When the great revolts of the nobility in the seventeenth century were crushed by the Emperors, this was followed by ruthless Catholization and by the spread of the German language by the Imperial bureaucracy, though not at all for national reasons. That time has left very bitter memories in the minds of the Czech and Hungarian nations and every believer in religious toleration and the rights of man will feel repelled by the measures of Ferdinand II and Leopold I against the defeated Protestants. They exhibited the same spirit as Louis XIV's persecution of the Huguenots, though they did not equal in ruthlessness the oppression of the Irish by Cromwell. The ways of history, however, are so strange that one may wonder whether the treatment meted out to the Bohemian and Hungarian rebels by the victorious Habsburgs was not really to the lasting profit of the Czech and Hungarian nations. It was sixty-three years after the battle of the White Mountain that a powerful Turkish army besieged Vienna, and was only defeated by the greatest exertions of Austria, the Empire, Poland, and the Pope.[1] If the Austrian, Bohemian and Hungarian nobility had won in their struggle with the Habsburgs, the nascent Empire would have been split up into many small states, which would never have been able to withstand the Turkish onslaught. Europe would probably have become Turkish up to the Rhine, and the whole of western Europe would have become a French Empire, which, having the navies of France, the Netherlands and Spain at its disposal, would probably also have swallowed England. If Louis XIV failed in his efforts to dominate Europe, this was primarily due to the combined strength of Austria and England which secured the maintenance of the Balance of Power. If Austria had been destroyed through a victory of the Protestant nobility, there would have been no longer any obstacle to the expansion of the two great military despotisms, France and the Ottoman Empire, which were constant allies in the struggle against the Habsburgs. The German princes were to a large extent already in the pay of the

---

[1] The Turkish army before Vienna amounted to 230,000, while 23,000 Austrians defended the city, and the rescue army consisted of 86,000, of whom 27,000 were Poles. The Pope had a large share in the victory by his diplomatic and financial aid.

French king, especially Brandenburg-Prussia—and they neither would nor could have resisted him effectively.

The powerful position of the two allied Habsburg dynasties was founded on the fact that between them they still ruled the bulk of the Empire of Charles V. Moreover, the head of the Austrian dynasty was always now elected Emperor, and in this capacity had still a considerable influence on the German princes. The connexion of the Austrian lands with Spain, Italy and Belgium, and with the hegemony in Germany, involved the Habsburgs in endless struggles, exhausted their resources and prevented them from consolidating their most important realm, the Danubian countries. For a long time they had a good chance of liberating the Balkan peoples from the Turkish yoke, and of extending their rule as far as the Black Sea and the Aegean Sea. But this was frustrated by the constant necessity of waging wars all over Europe for the possession of the countries of the Burgundian and Spanish heritage. Many Austrian statesmen were well aware of the fact that the possession of far-distant countries was a heavy burden, and ought to be abandoned for the purpose of concentrating all forces on nearer tasks. But attempts to act accordingly, for instance, to exchange Belgium for Bavaria, failed, and the Austrian dynasty, like all dynasties and states, was too firmly bound to the maintenance of traditional positions to be able to liquidate the fatal heritage of the past. Only when the Habsburgs were forced by Bismarck, Cavour and Napoleon III to give up their hold on Germany and Italy could they at last devote themselves freely to the fundamental problem of the real Austrian Empire.

This problem consisted in the organization of ten or more small nationalities for common defence, economic co-operation and cultural development. A certain unity was indispensable, as all these peoples were too weak to secure their freedom and their progress in isolation. Unity implied sufficiently strong central institutions, and it was naturally the main concern of the Crown and its officials to maintain unity and strength. On the other hand, each of the nationalities naturally demanded national rights which easily came into conflict with the unity of the Empire, and with the demands and rights of other nationalities.

The history of modern national struggles in Austria-Hungary starts with the revolution of 1848, and the defeat of the revolution was followed by a time of absolutism and centralization. This regime, however, collapsed as a result of the wars of 1859 and

1866, and Austria-Hungary now entered a period of great reforms in the spirit of liberalism. The Emperor Francis Joseph, moreover, realized the necessity of winning the loyalty of all his peoples by meeting their national aspirations as far as was compatible with the existence and strength of the Empire. Fundamental to the whole further development was the Austro-Hungarian Compromise of 1867 which restored the old position of Hungary as a kingdom independent of Austria. Only foreign affairs and the army became common institutions, though both Austria and Hungary had besides the common army also their own national armies. Economic conditions were regulated by agreements which were revised every ten years. There was internal free trade and a common currency in the whole Monarchy. The settlement with Hungary was followed by the grant of a very wide autonomy to Croatia and by a law securing the rights of minorities in Hungary. This legislation was for its time a model of liberalism, and it was hailed by the Liberals of all nations as a victory of the cause of freedom and nationality. Unfortunately the law on the rights of the national minorities soon became a dead letter through the growth of Hungarian nationalism, and nationalism in general. Important provisions, for instance, regarding secondary schools for the minorities, were not carried out, and the Hungarians began a policy of oppression and vexation towards the nationalities which aimed at their denationalization. This policy had little success but made very bad blood.

The Austro-Hungarian Compromise divided the Empire into two totally different halves, a Hungarian and an Austrian one. Hungary was, in theory, a national State; that is one nationality, the Magyars or Hungarians, dominated the others, though they did not quite form the majority of the population. The victory of the Magyars greatly stimulated the aspirations of other peoples of the Empire for a similar position. On the other hand, the Magyars used their influence for preventing the fulfilment of these aspirations as this would naturally have diminished their power. The Emperor Francis Joseph has often been blamed for having conceded such a position to the Magyars. But it must be considered that these won this triumph through centuries of rebellions, vigorous opposition and co-operation with foreign enemies, and that they would never have been satisfied with less. Towards the end of his reign the Emperor made efforts to curb the power of the Magyar nationalists and demanded the introduction of the general franchise. This would have greatly improved the position of the other nationalities, but the outbreak of the War of 1914 made it impossible to continue this policy.

The other half of the Empire, usually called Austria, was not a national State. It was not dominated by one nationality, but guaranteed equal rights to all its ten peoples, though, of course, there were great *de facto* inequalities of wealth, education and political power which were gradually levelled up by the development of the more backward peoples. Austria was a group of seventeen autonomous countries of which each had its separate local Parliament and its separate administration. Moreover, there was the central parliament and the central administration in Vienna. This State had not even a name. Officially it was not called Austria, but " The Kingdoms and Countries represented in the Imperial Parliament ". In each of the territorial diets the majority was in the hands of the nationality which formed the majority in that country, and each territorial diet elected a governor who was the head of the autonomous administration. There was also an Imperial governor who administered affairs common to all the countries. It is significant that after the dissolution of Austria and the formation of national States these territorial diets and administrations were suppressed.

After the settlement with Hungary and Croatia a very wide autonomy was accorded to the Poles in Galicia, and the Poles thenceforward were always loyal to the Austrian connexion. Their loyalty was so outspoken that they were often called the only Austrian patriots. Many Poles, however, hoped that Austria would one day be able to liberate the Poles in Russia, where they were grievously oppressed, and to unite them with the rest. The powerful position of the Poles in Galicia had the unfortunate consequence that the Ruthenes or Ukrainians in that country were in many respects oppressed by the ruling Poles. Nevertheless, the Ruthenes made great economic and cultural progress and always were predominantly loyal to Austria, where they enjoyed incomparably more national freedom than did their kinsmen in Russia. After the dissolution of Austria they were handed over to Poland and their position as a nationality greatly deteriorated.

The examples of the Magyars and the Poles show that an increase in freedom for one of the nationalities always implied a practical diminution in freedom for another nationality which formed the minority in a specific country. The crucial point of the national problems in Austria-Hungary, as in other countries of the world, was that in mixed territories the nationality which was the strongest was never prepared to be satisfied with a position of real equality in regard to the minority. Any nationality having attained a certain level of civilization and political development claimed the right to a ruling position in its national territory and to domination over the minorities. In Austria, moreover, the aggressive and oppressive tendencies of the nationalists were furthered by the wide scope of territorial and local autonomy which everywhere enabled the nationality which dominated the diet or town council to abuse its power for discriminating against the others. The Crown often vetoed, and the central government and the supreme administrative Court often cancelled, measures of local bodies offensive to another nationality. This policy of protecting minorities, of course, aroused the anger of the nationalists of all nations and the Austrian Government was as much accused by the Germans as by the Slavs of helping their enemies.

After having satisfied the Magyars and the Poles the Emperor tried to win the Czechs too by offering them in 1871 a wide autonomy. This scheme was accepted by the Czech leaders and hailed as fulfilling their national aspirations. But it aroused the violent resistance of the Germans, who feared that the Czechs would use their power to their detriment, and the Magyars supported the Germans. As these two nationalities together were more than three times as numerous as the Czechs, the Emperor had to drop his scheme, but soon resumed his policy in another form. In 1879 Count Taaffe was appointed Prime Minister and formed a government in which some of the most important posts were held by Polish and Czech ministers and which was supported by all the Slavs and the small party of German Conservatives, while the great majority of the Germans formed the opposition. This government lasted fourteen years. It brought the Slavs substantial national advantages, enhanced their political and economic power and greatly furthered their progress towards real equality.

This long reign of a government, backed by the Slavs and constantly enlarging their rights, aroused bitter resentment among the Germans. A Pan-German movement developed which violently accused the Government of striving to make Austria a Slav state and made propaganda for the annexation of Austria by Germany. The extension of the franchise to the lower middle class furthered the growth of a demagogic nationalism among all the nations. In 1893 the Prime Minister Count Taaffe, tried to counteract the growth of this radical and irresponsible nationalism by a bill introducing manhood suffrage for the central parliament. He hoped that the opening of parliament to the representatives of the broad masses would divert politics from sterile nationalist strife to fruitful social reforms. It was the Minister of Finance, Steinbach, a great administrator, of Jewish origin, who persuaded the Emperor to appeal to the broad masses against the blind nationalism of the ruling parties. Taaffe's bold policy, however, failed, for the great majority of Parliament turned against him and forced him to resign.

The subsequent twenty years were filled with violent struggles between the warring nationalities. The Pan-Germans surpassed all the others in aggressiveness and created the ideology which determined Hitler's mentality. The Government made many efforts to bring about a reasonable settlement of the various national conflicts, and also achieved some success, though the parties could not be induced to accept a wider compromise. In 1906, moreover, the Prime Minister, Baron Beck, succeeded in carrying through a great electoral reform which introduced manhood franchise. This fundamental reform was largely put through by the Emperor Francis Joseph, who used all his influence to break the resistance of the Conservative parties and of the House of Lords against the democratization of Austria. The hopes set on this measure seemed to come true. The elections resulted in a big decrease of the Nationalist votes and an increase in the strength of the Socialist, Christian Social and Agrarian parties. A large part of the peoples were sick of the Nationalist slogans and wanted social progress.

It seems now to be generally held that Austria was a moribund state which was bound to fall to pieces on the death of the Emperor. This view, however, is very disputable. One of the greatest authorities on the history of Central Europe was Louis Eisenmann, Professor in the University of Paris. *The Cambridge Modern History*, vol. xii (first published 1910, reprinted 1920), contains a chapter by him on Austrian history before the Great War. He sums up his survey by saying that the apprehensions about Austria-Hungary's future have much decreased in the last ten years.

> The acute crisis has been dispelled solely by the internal forces of the Monarchy. The external dangers, that is to say, Pangermanism and Panslavism, appear much less serious to-day than at that time. Pangermanism has been swept aside by universal suffrage

and the Panslavonic feeling is growing weaker. There is still a violent struggle between the nationalities, but the inevitable solution is in sight. It seems as though all the Austrian, Hungarian and Austro-Hungarian questions could be settled from within.

He attributes a large share in this achievement to the Emperor, but also emphasizes that the peoples have come to realize the common interest which keeps them united in the Empire. " The Monarchy no longer rests on the power of the dynastic tie alone but also on the conscious desire for union. This is the great, the enormous result of the reign of Francis Joseph."

Another great expert, Professor Seton-Watson, wrote, in his book *The Future of Austria-Hungary* (1907), that the view that the Monarchy would soon collapse was entirely superficial and that he disbelieved not merely in the probability but even in the possibility of a break-up of Austria-Hungary. In any case, he continued, France and Great Britain should make every effort to preserve the Dual Monarchy as a political and economic unit. In his book on the Southern Slav Question (1911, 2nd ed., 1913), Seton-Watson calls the view that Austria-Hungary was a weak, decadent state, ripe for partition, a senseless myth. In the same book he describes the attitude of Professor Masaryk in the words : " too liberal to be a Pan-Slav in the Russian sense, he believes in Austria's mission and in a great future for the Slavs under Habsburg rule ".[1]

Another writer who had carefully studied the problems, Mr. Wickham Steed, then correspondent of *The Times* in Vienna, wrote in his book *The Hapsburg Monarchy*, 1913,

> I have been unable to perceive during ten years of constant observation and experience—years, moreover, filled with struggle and crisis—any sufficient reason why, with moderate foresight on the part of the dynasty, the Hapsburg Monarchy should not retain its rightful place in the European community. Its internal crises are often crises of growth rather than of decay.

It may be interesting to add the judgement of the most prominent leader of the Czechs in the pre-war time, Dr. Karel Kramar, who was strongly anti-German and an outspoken Pan-Slav in sympathy. He wrote in 1906 :

> Nobody will deny the clear and obvious fact that our people has comparatively the best possible conditions for its cultural, political and economic development in Austria. There is no other way : the position of our people in the heart of Europe and the

---

[1] Cf. R. W. Seton-Watson, *The Southern Slav Question and the Habsburg Monarchy*, 1911, p. 252.

existing conditions of international policy compel us more than ever to see the best guarantees for the future of our people in a strong and internally healthy Austria.

Dr. Eduard Beneš, later the co-founder and President of Czechoslovakia, published a book in 1908 in which he proposed a federalization of Austria.[1] His proposals were not at all revolutionary and had certainly a chance of being realized within the old Empire. Beneš comes to the conclusion :

> People have often spoken of a dismemberment of Austria. I don't believe in it at all. The historical and economic bonds between the Austrian nations are too powerful to make such a dismemberment possible. The introduction of the general franchise and the democratization of Austria, especially of Bohemia, prepare the soil for national appeasement.

The book ends with the statement that the Austrian question is on the way to its solution.

A few statistics may illustrate the position of the Czechs in the last years of old Austria. Their share in the population was 23 per cent, in the members of Parliament 21 per cent, in Cabinet Ministers (1900–14) 19 per cent, in officials 24·9 per cent, in teachers 24·9 per cent; of the elementary schools 24·5 per cent were Czechs, of secondary schools 23·3 per cent, of students in universities and technical colleges 19 per cent. Among all the nationalities of Austria the Czechs had the smallest percentage of illiterates, namely, 2·4 per cent, while the Germans came next with 3·1 per cent. The Czechs also possessed a highly developed agriculture and industry, and, besides a large share in the banks without any national colour, they also had their own national banks with assets of more than 200 million pounds sterling. These figures illustrate how well-informed was a famous British statesman when he said in a speech after the Great War the Czechs had been so oppressed by Austria that they could only become coalminers.

Internal and external peace, however, was threatened by the growth of irredentist movements among parts of the Southern Slavs, the Roumanians and the Italians. The overwhelming majority of the peoples living in the Austrian countries had certainly no wish to break away from the Empire. In the countries under the Crown of Hungary irredentism was stronger, partly owing to the policy of the Hungarian Government which, actuated by short-sighted nationalism, encroached upon the rights of the minorities, neglected their cultural interests and

[1] Cf. Eduard Beneš, *Le problème Autrichien et la question Tchèque*, 1908, p. 307.

combated their national aspirations in an arbitrary way. Apart from such reasons, however, the Southern Slav movement was also rooted in the longing for national unification. The Southern Slavs in the Empire were not a national unit, but were divided into three nationalities, the Croats, Serbs and Slovenes. Among them existed considerable diversities of tradition, religion and language, and, moreover, they lived not under one government, but under several central and provincial administrations. This state of things was certainly very unsatisfactory, and it was difficult to find a practicable solution. The idea of uniting all Southern Slavs of the Monarchy in one independent state, but under the same Crown as the Hungarian and Austrian countries, was widely discussed, and the Archduke Franz Ferdinand, the heir to the Throne, was credited with plans of this sort. Whether such a scheme could have been carried out is a matter of speculation and we need not enter here into its discussion. It must be said, however, that the difficulties were not merely the resistance of the Magyars, Germans and Austrian Slavs, but also the difficulty of appeasing the old antagonism among the Southern Slavs themselves. It was temporarily softened down by common opposition to Magyar domination, and by resentment against the Crown which had for a long time left it a free hand. But when after the Great War all the Southern Slavs were united in Yugoslavia, a bitter struggle immediately broke out between the Croats and the Serbs which menaced the foundations of the State.

Before the war the idea gained ground among the Southern Slav intelligentsia, and particularly among the youth, that Serbia was destined to liberate and unite all the Southern Slavs with the help of Russia. Secret revolutionary and terrorist organizations were formed, in which high-placed officers of the Serbian General Staff took part. This movement played into the hands of a group of high officers in the Austro-Hungarian General Staff, headed by its chief, General Conrad von Hoetzendorff. For years he urged a preventive war against the foreign enemies of the Empire, either against Italy or against Serbia and Russia. The endless strife between the nationalities encouraged, indeed, all the external and internal enemies of Austria-Hungary, and gave them the impression that it would be easy to break up the Empire. The wish to counteract this view and to restore the prestige of the Empire inspired the hazardous foreign policy of Aehrenthal. When the Bosnian crisis was peacefully settled, Conrad continued his propaganda for war. The Emperor was opposed to a war, and dismissed him in disgrace. Unfortunately he was soon reinstated in his former office and the assassination of the Archduke Franz Ferdinand by Serbian fanatics gave him the opportunity of achieving his purpose, with the powerful backing of the German war party.

The outbreak of the war naturally wrecked all the hopes for national appeasement in Austria-Hungary. The war which the Austro-Hungarian war party had planned as a means for strengthening the Empire, could not but destroy its moral foundations, even if the war had not ended in defeat and collapse. It is impossible to deny that the different nationalities, after the cruel experience of the war, were fully entitled to dissolve the Empire, and to constitute their independent national states. It is quite a different question, however, whether the dismemberment of the Empire, and in particular the way it was done, were really in the interest of the nations concerned, and whether it would not have been preferable to preserve unity among some of the nations in the form of a democratic federation. The opinion is now very widespread that the dissolution of Austria-Hungary was an immeasurable disaster for all its nationalities, for Europe and for the world.

CHAPTER VI

THE NATIONAL STATE AND THE NATIONAL WILL AND CHARACTER

1. Feudalism and Nationality

The modern national State has to a great extent arisen in opposition to the Teutonic and feudal ideas of government, though some of its institutions and traditions have developed from feudal germs. To the old Teutons the tribe was the nation; they had no idea of a wider unity, and they possessed only a minimum of government. It has even been disputed whether their communities could be called States.[1] The great migrations, contact with the Romans, and the establishment of Germanic domination on the soil of the Empire were accompanied by the growth of royal power and the formation of larger peoples by fusion of different tribes. The kings then began to build states with the help of Roman officials and the Church; but soon feudalism gained the upper hand, and when not curbed by a strong kingship, resulted in the splitting up of State and society into countless fragments. The feudal fiefs tended to assume the character of patrimonial states or of private estates in which the rights of government and property were inextricably mixed up.

The effect of the unchecked growth of feudal power was that there was neither national territory, national citizenship nor much of national solidarity. In the same village some men, or some dues, or some rights of government might belong to one lord, and others to another. A noble might for different fiefs be a vassal of different kings and owe them loyalty, which in case of conflicts between them led to a conflict of loyalties as well. Feudal relations were often so complicated that it became impossible to say where the frontiers of a state were. In feudal society, moreover, community of rank usually implied a stronger mutual loyalty than common nationality. The solidarity between the nobles, or between the towns, of different countries was often stronger than that between the nobles and the towns of the same country. On the battlefield, for instance, knights from different countries spared one anothers' lives and tried only to take prisoners, who as a rule were well treated and released for a ransom. In battles between warriors of different rank, even if of the same

[1] Cf. on this controversy G. von Below, *der deutsche Staat des Mittelalters*, 1914, vol. i; F. Keutgen, *der deutsche Staat des Mittelalters*, 1918.

country, no such clemency was shown. True, knights also showed national pride or contempt; but the positive side of nationality, the feeling of an obligation towards men of the same country or language was very little developed. Nevertheless, feudalism has made a great contribution to the development of modern nationhood: Parliament has grown out of the institutions of feudal society. Feudalism, moreover, fostered the ideals of liberty and martial honour which have become incorporated in the traditions of modern nations. It is remarkable that countries such as India, China and Turkey, where no feudal nobility of our type has existed, have developed neither Parliaments nor a modern national consciousness. On the other hand, Japan, where the feudal nobility showed many parallels with Western conditions, was foremost in adopting Western political institutions, civilization and nationalism.

2. THE BUILDING OF NATIONAL STATES

The national State has to a very large extent been created by kings and their supporters, who hardly had much vision of the results of their policy. The aim of the kings was mainly the enhancement of their own power, partly for the better fulfilment of their royal duties, and partly for the expansion of their dominions. It is significant that those kings who took the decisive steps towards unity were rulers who were inspired by the ambition to form large Empires, such as Henry II in England and Philip II Augustus in France, both of whom dreamt of world-domination. In England and France however the kings began a policy of expansion on a large scale only after they had consolidated their power at home, whereas in Germany the Emperors neglected or failed to achieve this before seeking to increase their dominion abroad. This policy resulted in catastrophe and in the frustration of national unity for many centuries. The great divergency between the political traditions and aspirations of the Germans and the Western nations is largely due to this difference in their evolution.

The efforts of the kings necessarily conflicted with feudal interests. It was most important therefore that the Church, though itself the greatest feudal landowner, usually took the side of royalty, and fostered the growth of unity. The nobility often did their utmost to resist any increase in the power of the king, and sometimes frustrated internal appeasement. In England, however, the nobility soon began to prefer collective action in

Parliament to isolated insurrections and individual violence, which attitude was largely due to the sense of unity engendered by the royal policy.

The main instrument of the rulers in building the framework of the national State, and often the real driving power behind them, was a new class of legally trained officials, the forerunners of modern bureaucracy. At first these officials were mostly ecclesiastics, but later these were largely replaced by laymen. This class was chiefly recruited from the middle class and the lesser nobility and in many countries the royal service also attracted ambitious men from abroad. The kings everywhere liked to employ foreigners and people of humble birth who were free from feudal and local traditions and who depended exclusively upon their favour.[1] Another mainstay of royal power consisted in mercenary troops, also predominantly foreign. The possession of an army gave the kings the opportunity of gaining a portion of the nobility by employing them as officers. Of great importance, furthermore, was the contribution of the urban middle class to national unification. This class provided the kings with able advisers and helpers and, though reluctantly, with money. It would be going too far, however, to credit the middle class with national initiative, a keen sense of nationality, or much vision of the economic potentialities of national unity.[2] The burgesses served the royal cause, and the kings bestowed their favour upon them so far as their common interests against the nobility or clergy went. The burgesses themselves were not at all free from the spirit of feudalism and particularism. The town was their fatherland, and they were often as unwilling to make concessions to wider national interests as were the nobles.

---

[1] The great struggle of the barons against the foreign favourites of Henry III is well known. Joinville relates that King Louis IX made a non-Frenchman his *connétable* and advised his son to win the people's love; otherwise it were better that a foreigner should justly rule the country. The famous legists of Philip IV, men like Philip Flot, Guillaume de Nogaret, Pierre Dubois, came from southern France or Normandy, and were regarded as foreigners. Philip de Comines, the adviser of Louis XI, was a native of Flanders. Later the Italian Mazarin belonged to the builders of the French national State. The Stuarts and William III, the Habsburgs, Hohenzollerns and Romanovs too made great use of foreigners in their service. Italian towns often entrusted foreign officials, the *podestas*, with the administration, in order to end violent struggles between the parties and classes, and to secure impartial government.

[2] In France, for example, many customs barriers were created between the provinces at the end of the fourteenth century, just at the time of the growing power of the bourgeoisie in the Estates. The reasons were financial ones. The Estates, however, soon advocated a policy of internal free trade, but the barriers were not abolished before the second half of the eighteenth century. The king made at several States-General great efforts to unify weights, measures and currency, but the deputies of the towns rejected these proposals as contrary to the interests of the common people. The reason was that the nobles would have had to be indemnified. The unity of weights and measures was not reached before the Revolution.

In countries, moreover, where the towns were not controlled by a strong kingship they became the scene of bitter social and political struggle which endangered national unity.

The building up of the national State comprised countless small steps; the detailed description of this process must be left to constitutional, administrative and social history and only a few general lines of approach to the national State can be indicated here. The development of a unified and strong State depended on a settlement of rights of succession which should obviate struggles for power on the death of a king, and it was furthered if a dynasty lasted long, which implied the accumulation of power and experience in the hands of royalty. In the Middle Ages France enjoyed great dynastic continuity, whereas in Germany the princes who elected the Emperor often tried to change the dynasty, so as to prevent the growth of its power. It is also a remarkable fact that in France no king was deposed before the Revolution of 1789, while in England during the Middle Ages five kings were deposed or killed, and later two more, and yet others were in danger of a similar fate. This was probably the reason why the English in the Middle Ages had the reputation of being " fickle ". In reality these depositions were a symptom of the power of the nobility. Territorial unity was secured when once the idea prevailed that the Realm was indivisible and inalienable. Further steps towards a united nation were the advance of social, economic and cultural factors, the development of a common law, a common administration and a common language, the mitigation and abolition of slavery, serfdom and excessive class privileges, the unification of weights, measures, currency, tariffs and the establishment of internal free trade. The Middle Ages could only achieve a part of these tasks. The idea of the State also underwent a great transformation. The feudal idea of loyalty to the person of the king was superseded by the idea of the impersonal, never dying Crown, the " corporation sole " of English law. The Germanic and feudal idea of the competence of the State, moreover, was that it had merely to uphold existing rights, and that its principal aims, therefore, consisted in defence and justice. It was in the mediaeval city-republics that it was first considered a responsibility of the State to care also for the welfare of the people, and this contributed to the development of the ideal of a close solidarity between the citizens which is implied in our idea of a nation.

While all these developments primarily furthered the growth of national unity, other tendencies brought about great changes in the idea of national liberty. Of decisive importance for nationhood and national character was the creation of organs for forming the national will.

3. The Influence of Parliament on National Unity in England, France and Germany

Parliaments developed during the Middle Ages in many countries from two roots. The one was the feudal court of a king or prince which was composed of his principal vassals and some clerks who advised and assisted him in his judicial, administrative and political affairs. The other was an extraordinary assembly, consisting of a large number of influential or wealthy persons who were summoned by the king in times of stress, especially of impending war, for the purpose of securing the support of the whole Realm. This council was often designated as the Community of the Realm. When such assemblies became regular institutions and represented a large section of the nascent nation, they approached the character of a Parliament in our sense. For a long time, however, the regular council was often more a court for judicial cases than an assembly concerned with legislation.[1]

In the first phase of parliamentary development the initiative everywhere lay with royalty. Parliaments on a wider basis were formed by kings for the purposes of their government. The two fundamental principles of modern democracy and nationality, namely, representation and majority, were usually due to royal insistence. The middle class of the towns in all countries were little pleased with the demand that they should send delegates to an assembly for voting taxes for the king, and with incurring expenses of travelling and living. Many towns petitioned, therefore, that they should be relieved from the burden of sending a delegate. Moreover, the particularism of the towns, and the Teutonic and feudal principle of unanimity were strongly opposed to the ideas that a delegate should have power to bind his electors by his vote, and that the consent of a majority should be binding on the minority.[2]

[1] This was particularly the case in England. Cf. Charles H. McIlwain, *The High Court of Parliament and Its Supremacy*, 1910; A. F. Pollard, *The Evolution of Parliament*, 2nd ed., 1934. The view, however, has recently been revived that the English Parliament had in early times already the purpose of discussing all matters affecting the nation at large. Cf. B. Wilkinson, *Studies in the Constitutional History of the Thirteenth and Fourteenth Centuries*, 1937, p. 263.
[2] On the evolution of the principle of majority. Cf. Pollock and Maitland, *History of English Law*, vol. ii, p. 621; Josef Redlich, *Recht und Technik des englischen Parlamentarismus*, 1905, p. 536.

Among all classes it was the nobility, first the barons and later the knights, who showed most aptitude for converting Parliament from an instrument of royalty into one for their liberty, if often a rather feudal liberty. Even the nobility, however, did not at first insist upon a regular share in the governance of the Realm. This claim was only raised in exceptional circumstances if the nobles had serious grievances against the king. It was a long time before the stage was reached when the representatives of the nation in Parliament claimed wide and permanent power to control its destiny.

Similar institutions existed in most countries and frequently they played a considerable rôle. Yet, nowhere has Parliament had such a share in forming national unity and national consciousness as in England. Professor A. F. Pollard says:

> Parliament, indeed, has been the means of making the English nation and the English State. It is really coeval with them both. There was, it is true, an England centuries before there was a Parliament, but that England was little more than a geographical expression. It was hardly a nation, still less a State; and Edward I was the first English king of an English people that could be described as even partially united and conscious of its unity.

The principal value of Parliament in the Middle Ages was that it bridged over local, provincial and social barriers, and that it produced a public opinion and a common sentiment. " Parliament has thus been the peculiar means through which the English people achieved their unity and nationality."

The nations of the Continent have received their national unity, consciousness and traditions to a greater extent through royal absolutism, military triumphs, religion and civilization than through their parliamentary institutions. The reason why Parliament was a much greater success in England than on the Continent lay in the fact that in critical epochs royalty there was strong enough to ensure internal peace, together with a measure of national unity, while the nobility, backed by the middle classes, were strong enough to prevent the king from becoming too powerful. On the Continent this development was checked by frequent external and civil wars which provided the rulers with a strong army, by the particularism and isolationism of the provinces and towns and by the acute antagonism between the classes. This antagonism gave the king the chance to play off one class against another and often induced large sections of the people to welcome royal absolutism as the restorer of internal peace and order.

The national significance of the English mediaeval Parliament consisted in the early development of the idea of a national representation as a standing institution, in the absence of a sharp division into Estates, and in its broad groundwork of local self-government.[1] A peculiar feature was the extraordinary over-representation of the boroughs as compared with the counties. But it was not the spirit of the urban middle class which developed or dominated Parliament. The boroughs usually elected knights, and for a long time the parliamentary seats of numerous boroughs were completely at the disposal of either the king or of aristocratic families. The franchise in the counties and in at least some towns was rather wide, but after the close of the Middle Ages the power of royalty and oligarchic tendencies were on the increase. Nevertheless, the old English Parliament was always recognized as the mouthpiece of the nation, and this was mainly due to the rôle of the lesser nobility or gentry which formed a class of great political energy, training and ability. This class was not predominantly a warrior caste, enjoying high privileges, like the knights on the Continent. It stood nearer to the people, formed a link between all classes, and provided the nation with an experienced and comparatively progressive leadership. In England as elsewhere kings have tried to ally themselves with the lower classes against the upper ones, but it was perhaps the salient point in the evolution of English characteristics that the upper classes at last got the better of royalty through the support of large sections of the other classes. After the revolution of the seventeenth century England became more aristocratic than before. She practically became an oligarchic republic, in a monarchical form, ruled by a small number of aristocratic families. This system, in spite of all its defects, was the only one which was able to develop the Cabinet system that forms the backbone of parliamentary democracy to-day. At that time also the industrial revolution set in and prepared the soil for the evolution of democracy. It is doubtful whether England would have become a great industrial Power under a reign of absolutism or democracy.

In France the States-General showed many parallels to the English Parliament.[2] At several assemblies, particularly in 1357 and 1413, principles were laid down which if they had been carried out would have converted France into a national parliamentary State. The spirit of parliamentary liberty, however,

[1] Cf. F. W. Maitland, *Constitutional History of England*, 1911; Julius Hatschek, *Englische Verfassungsgeschichte*, 1913.
[2] Cf. Paul Viollet, *Histoire des institutions politiques et administratives de la France*, 1903, 3 vols.; Georges Picot, *Histoire des États Généraux de 1355 à 1614*, 4 vols., 1872.

did not prevail against the rising tide of absolutism. There were several reasons for the divergent development of England and France. While in England there was one Parliament only, we find in France numerous provincial and local assemblies; and when the king failed to obtain from the States-General what he had asked for he applied to the provinces or towns separately or to assemblies of selected notables, and he usually succeeded in getting what he wanted. This procedure was furthered by the strength of particularism and the unwillingness of the towns to give representative powers to their delegates. The franchise became in France more democratic than in England. The great feudal principalities, however, were represented by their princes only. In the course of time they escheated to the Crown, and the whole country was for the first time represented by elected deputies in 1560. In England the whole country from the very beginning sent representatives to Parliament. Moreover, in England the nation appeared in Parliament to a larger degree united than in France.[1] In France the Three Estates, the clergy, nobility and middle class, formed separate bodies, and no resolution was valid but by the agreement of all three Estates. The greatest weakness of the French States-General was that they never became a permanent institution but were only summoned by the king from time to time.

The States-General were rivalled by the High Courts of Paris and some other cities which were called Parliaments. The Parliament of Paris aspired to the position of a supreme Senate, and regarded itself as the guardian of the unwritten constitution of the Realm, even against the king. Its members formed a hereditary aristocracy of lawyers, mainly of bourgeois descent, though ennobled. The influence and prestige of the Parliaments was great, and a seat in the Parliament of Paris was much more coveted than a seat in the short-lived States-General. The States-General, furthermore, lacked the broad foundation and political training school which the English Parliament possessed in local self-government. In mediaeval France a number of towns enjoyed an autonomy which made them almost independent republics. They were often unwilling to subordinate their interests to those of the whole nation. But they could not maintain this position, and the whole administration of the country became ever more controlled by royal officials.

[1] The peerage and the casual use of the words "three estates", in reference to Parliament, do not contradict this statement, as Pollard shows (pp. 61, 81). The clergy had their separate Convocations, but they did not split the unity of the nation.

Finally one of the main reasons why the French parliamentary movement did not achieve the same results as in England lay in the mutual distrust and jealousy of the classes. The disintegration of society through feudalism had gone much farther in France than it ever did in England, and the nobility had to a much greater degree preserved its character of a privileged warrior class. Many of them despised the middle and lower classes, and were hated by these for their arrogance and ruthlessness. While in England the towns had bought their charters from the Crown, French and German communal liberty had largely been won through fighting the feudal nobility, and the citizens preserved their hatred against their former foes. The nobles, moreover, deeply resented the fact that the kings often employed men of low birth in high offices and gave them titles of nobility.[1] The distrust of the third Estate went so far that they often refused even to appoint delegates for negotiation with the privileged Estates.[2] These, on the whole, were superior in political understanding and interest to the bourgeois, but they too put their class interest first. The kings, therefore, had no difficulty in playing off the classes against one another. In the Hundred Years War great military defeats and civil strife discredited the nobility and gave the middle class of Paris decisive power in the Estates (1357, 1413). This development led to revolutionary movements of the masses, to dictatorship and terrorism, and to the danger of a general social conflagration. The result was that large circles which had sympathized with democracy were frightened and put their trust in royalty.[3] The king alone, moreover, was able to free the country from the English invaders and the still more terrible exactions of the mercenaries fighting for France. The Hundred Years War greatly furthered the rise of royal power. In 1439 the king laid the foundations of a standing army, and obtained from the Estates for this purpose the grant of a tax which he interpreted as perpetual. The consequence was that for a long time there was no further need for the king to convoke the Estates.

After the victorious end of the war a rapprochement took

[1] The mentality of the French nobility is characteristically expressed in a document given by Matthew Paris, *English History*, tr. Giles, 1853, p. 202. The nobles claim to be the chief men of the kingdom " considering that the kingdom was not acquired by written law, nor by the arrogance of the clerks but by the sweat of war ". They accuse the clerks of having with foxy cunning " so engrossed the jurisdiction of secular princes, that the sons of slaves judge freemen according to their own laws, although they ought rather to be judged by us according to the laws of their former conquerors ".
[2] Cf. G. Picot, *Histoire des États Généraux*, vol. iv, pp. 209, 290.
[3] F. Perrens, *La democratie en France au moyen age*, 2 vols., 1875.

place between the different Estates. At the Estates of Tours (1484) the deputies were no longer separated according to rank, though they were divided into six sections, called " nations ". Even the peasants were represented. Philip Pot, Sire de la Roche, a deputy of the nobility of Burgundy, declared that the sovereignty rested with the people, which comprised all inhabitants of the Realm, and that royalty was an office, and depended on the people. The speech of this prominent statesman was not an isolated symptom. Democratic and national convictions were widespread in France. The unity of the classes, however, was of very short duration, The French invasion of Italy in 1494 initiated a period of wars which greatly enhanced the warlike and domineering spirit of the nobility, and their contempt for the middle class. The Reformation gave the nobles a new banner for their struggle against royalty and for their own power, while the broad masses of the people were ardent partisans of the Catholic cause. The fanaticism of the religious wars at last induced all moderates to desire the establishment of a powerful monarchy in order to save France from anarchy.

At the States-General of 1614—the last held before the great revolution—the changed spirit of the nobility manifested itself in a striking manner. After acrimonious bickerings the speaker of the third Estate, the President de Mesmes, said that the Estates were like three brothers, children of their common mother, France. He admitted that the nobility was of higher rank, but begged that the nobles should not despise the third Estate which comprised so many prominent judges and officials, and should recognize them as brothers. This appeal aroused the greatest indignation among the noblemen. Some of them exclaimed that there could be no fraternity between the third Estate and themselves, as they were not of the same blood and virtue, that they did not wish that the sons of cobblers or soapboilers should call them brothers, and that the difference between the two Estates was that of masters and servants. A deputation of noblemen was sent to the king, and the speaker, Baron de Senecey, said he was ashamed to report that the third Estate had dared to compare the State to a family composed of three brothers, and that this was an insult to the nobility.[1]

When the great revolution broke out the attempt was made to revive the States-General, but it was bound to fail. They had not met for 175 years, and they had left no traditions and sentiments which could satisfy the needs of the time. The monarchy

[1] Cf. A. Thibaudeau, *Histoire des États Généraux*, 1844, vol. iii, p. 121.

had fostered national pride in the unity, power and splendour of France. But this was no substitute for a parliamentary training and, in particular, for the education of the citizens in national solidarity through Parliament. The striving for the creation of a new and higher sort of national patriotism could only start from general principles and an ideal view of human nature and society. This approach did not lead to the goal of a united nation. The revolution soon turned into a ferocious struggle between the classes and parties and ended in anarchy and in the establishment of a military despotism, followed by a series of triumphs and defeats, revolutions and counter-revolutions. The causes of this development had their roots far back in the past.

The German Empire possessed no central Parliament, for the Imperial Diet did not deserve this name. It was chiefly an assembly of princes and almost the whole power was in the hands of a few rulers. The knights of the Empire ceased to attend after the downfall of the Staufer dynasty. On the other hand, a number of free towns began to take part in the thirteenth century, but they were long denied the right to vote by the princes, and they had never much say. Moreover, the towns themselves were so imbued with the spirit of feudal particularism that they were very reluctant to make any sacrifices to general national interests. In the separate States, however, of which Germany was composed, Diets developed which often had the character of Parliaments. They contributed to the growth of a territorial loyalty which was largely an obstacle to the rise of the idea of a common German nationality. In many cases these Diets served mainly the egotistical interests of the privileged classes, and they were at last suppressed or silenced when the rulers attained to absolute power.[1]

4. The Influence of War on the Formation of Nation and of Fundamental National Traditions

The modern large nations have been mainly formed by wars partly by conquest, partly by fusion under the menace of conquest. Every nation, furthermore, has developed its personality in great wars and everywhere the national ideology and character have been deeply influenced by them. Territory and language, religion and civilization, ideas of national interest and honour, the

[1] Cf. F. Hartung, *Deutsche Verfassungsgeschichte*, 1922, pp. 34, 54. Cf. G. von Below. *Territorium und Staat*, 1900 ; M. Spangenberg, *Vom Lehenstaat zum Ständestaat*, 1912, and F. W. Unger, *Geschichte der deutschen Landstände*, 1844.

organization of the State and the structure of society were always to a large extent the product of wars.[1]

A war against external enemies has at all times been regarded by powerful classes as the best remedy against internal strife. Countless wars, indeed, have been waged in order to suppress or avoid the danger of internal disintegration, or in order to weld different elements into a larger national unit by evoking a common hatred and common pride. War, therefore, could be called the greatest instrument of national unification but for the fact that it also fosters the growth of forces which often imply a new menace to national unity. A typical instance was the Hundred Years War between England and France. It has decisively furthered national unity on both sides, and also developed fundamental national traditions. Later on, however, the English knights and soldiers who returned from the war had a large share in the peasants' revolt and the internal Wars of the Roses. In both countries it required the strong hand of a powerful royalty to restore unity and peace.

Great wars in which vital interests of the country are at stake usually lead to the concentration of power in the hands of the rulers and to the predominance of the military over the civil element. The consequence is a restriction of freedom, especially freedom of speech, the demand for blind obedience and the rise of a dictatorial rule. On the other hand, great wars also compel the Governments to appeal to the help of wider circles, or even to the people as a whole, and this tends to lead to an increase in popular rights and social equality. Wars therefore imply both a democratic and an anti-democratic tendency.

In many countries war has to a great extent moulded the mentality of the ruling and politically active classes who represented the nation and determined its destiny. The most important difference between English and continental conditions was that the English nobility much earlier and to a greater degree ceased to be a privileged warrior caste. Anglo-Saxon feudalism already showed a less warlike character than feudalism in the Frankish Empire.[2] The Normans conquered England largely through

[1] Aristotle already emphasized the relations between military, social and political organization, cf. *Politics*, iv, 3, 10 ; v, 3 ; vi, 4, etc. The influence of warfare on the structure of politics is especially stressed in the great work by Hans Delbrück, *Geschichte der Kriegskunst im Rahmen der politischen Geschichte*, 6 vols., and in that of his disciple, Emil Daniels, *Geschichte des Kriegswesens*.

[2] The Frankish knights were professional soldiers, specially trained for expeditions to distant countries. There were many differences between Frankish and Saxon feudalism. Cf. W. Stubbs, *Constitutional History*, vol. i, chap. vi, p. 65 ; chap. ix, p. 93 ; Paul Vinogradoff, *English Society in the Eleventh Century*, 1908 ; in many places, S. M.

their superior military organization and many maintained their warrior spirit for centuries. On the other hand, they seem also to have brought traditions with them which helped the kings to lay the foundations of the modern State. The kings revived the old national militia and promoted the demilitarization of the nobles by the prohibition of feuds and fortified castles, and by converting feudal services into contributions of money which they used for hiring mercenaries. The nobles, however, were always apprehensive of the danger which a strong royal army would imply to their power and for this reason tried to prevent its development, and especially opposed the employment of foreign mercenaries. Many of the English nobility seem soon to have had more interest in the management of their estates and in politics than in war.[1] The knighthood of England took less part in the Crusades than that of France and Germany.[2] Edward I gave a great impetus to the rise of national sentiment both by his organization of a representative Parliament and by his great wars of conquest in which a new military technique was used. Edward III continued both lines of policy with astonishing success. Petrarca wrote in his letters: " When I was young the English were considered the most timid of the barbarians and now they have defeated the most warlike French."[3] This remark shows that the English before the French wars were regarded as a comparatively non-military people. They waged the French wars not with a feudal army as did the French, but with troops recruited from all ranks. In later English history factors gained considerable force which in the long run tended to discourage militarism, namely, Parliament, the commercial interests and the Christian and liberal spirit. Parliament has sometimes been more warlike than the king, but on the whole

Stenton, *The First Century of English Feudalism*, 1932 ; F. Liebermann, *Gesetze der Angelsachsen*, 1903, vol. ii (Glossar) ; in many places, Helen Cam, *Local Government in Francia and England*, 1912 ; H. Delbrück, *Geschichte der Kriegskunst*, 1907, vol. iii.

[1] England was far ahead of all countries (except Arabic Spain) in progressive agriculture, as evidenced by the treatises on farming by Fleta, Walter of Henley, Grosseteste and Fitzherbert. Walter of Henley's *Husbandry* (edited by E. Lamond and W. Cunningham, 1890) shows that already in the beginning of the thirteenth century there were lords who were interested in good methods of production and book-keeping, and did not leave the management of their estates entirely to their bailiffs. The continental nations began much later to produce comparable books and even then at first used mainly the precepts of the ancient Greeks and Romans as compiled by monks and humanists or preserved by Byzantine writers. German and French treatises of greater importance begin in the sixteenth century but were mainly concerned with rules for breeding and healing war-horses. Cf. C. Fraas, *Geschichte der Landbau- und Forstwissenschaft*, 1865, pp. 31, 42, 45. Among the French writers Olivier de Serres marked a great progress with his *Theatre d'agriculture* (1600). Cf. A. Rambaud, *Histoire de la civilisation française*, 1911, vol. i, p. 494.

[2] H. W. C. Davis, *England under the Normans and Angevins*, p. 103.
[3] Davis, p. 223.

it was strongly opposed to the formation of a big army because it saw in this a possible danger to its predominance.

In France and Germany the nobility preserved their character as a warrior caste much more than was the case in England. In both countries the warlike spirit was maintained not merely by great wars against foreign enemies but also through incessant internal wars and feuds. Many attempts to restrict the feuds were made by the Church and the kings but for a long time with little success. In Germany the breakdown of the imperial power in Italy after the death of Frederick II and its consequences deprived the knights of their employment in imperial service, impoverished them and forced them to become robbers, in which capacity for centuries they committed the greatest atrocities against the German people. This had the consequence that the knights and the middle class became extremely hostile to one another, that a spirit of violence permeated all classes, and that the social tension between the upper and lower classes became more acute than in any other country. A main reason why no central Parliament could develop in Germany was the long degradation of the knights to a robber class, which unfitted them for political leadership. The German episcopate which was mainly in the hands of the nobility was deeply infected by its warlike and ruthless spirit and the lack of a strong central authority led to constant class struggles and to revolutions. In the towns the patricians overturned the rule of the bishops and nobles and subsequently their reign was overturned by the artisans. The peasants often rose against their lords and were defeated and cruelly punished. The fierce antagonism between the classes was later partly aggravated and partly replaced by the hatred between Catholics and Protestants. This mentality was the chief reason why Germany lagged so far behind other nations on the road to national unity and liberty. In France, national unity was at last restored and enlarged by the progress of royal absolutism, though at the expense of liberty. In Germany it was mainly the absolute power of the territorial princes which gradually succeeded in putting down anarchy, and in restoring a reign of law, though at the expense of unity and liberty.

The national differences in the position and mentality of classes and their influence on the national character did not escape the attention of mediaeval writers. John of Salisbury (twelfth century) complains of the inefficiency and sluggishness of English military leaders in struggles with the savage Welsh, who were devastating English territory, and he praises the former warlike valour of the English which could be restored by training and discipline.[1] He quotes Pope Eugenius III's opinion that the English were by nature better fitted than anyone for any enterprise they might choose if it were not for their levity. It was not military power, indeed, on which the English prided themselves, but their freedom, wealth and merriness. Henry of Huntingdon's famous praise of England as a free, merry, wealthy and generous country was repeated by numerous other English writers, and this view was also accepted by foreigners.[2]

The interests of the lower classes were better protected in England by the Royal Courts than in countries where the central authority was weak. This was particularly noticeable in the French possessions and explains the popularity of English rule. An angry Count of Armagnac wrote to Henry III that under the rule of no other power did burgesses and rustics so domineer over nobles as in the territory subject to the king. Froissart says that the English nobles were chivalrous and loyal while the artisans and common people were cruel, dangerous, proud and disloyal, and that the nobles were anxious to keep on good terms with them. They only demanded from the people what was reasonable and dared not to take an egg or hen without payment. In the fifteenth century Philippe de Comines, the adviser of Louis XI, admired the English Parliament, and pointed out that in no other country were public affairs better conducted and less violence committed on the people. Sir John Fortescue drew his proud picture of the constitutional monarchy in England which he contrasted with French despotism. While in France the people were terribly oppressed by the soldiery and by arbitrary acts of the Government, the English people lived in security and were better fed and clothed than any other people.

The German and the French knights vied with each other in boasting of their pre-eminence in warlike virtues. Nevertheless,

[1] In the French wars great stress was laid, indeed, on military training of the whole people. In 1377 and 1477 all sports were forbidden except archery which, moreover, was made an obligatory exercise. Henry VIII continued this policy. Cf. G. Coulton, *Social Life in Britain from the Conquest to the Reformation*, 1919, p. 397.

[2] Cf. George Ascoli, *La Grande-Bretagne devant l'opinion Française depuis la guerre de Cent Ans jusqu' a la fin du 16. siecle*, 1927, p. 31. Ascoli has also collected many other interesting French views of the English, held in the later Middle Ages. Froissart, who knew England well, speaks of their custom of enjoying themselves in a gloomy way, which he ascribes to their dreamy, imaginative temperament. Pierre de Celle explains this by the influence of the water that surrounds them. The English were also described as great drinkers of ale, fond of swearing, naïve, laconic, and awkward, but also as rich, liberal, and despising all other nations. After their invasion of France the French recognized their great gallantry, though it was combined with cruelty. Anyhow, they treated their prisoners correctly but had more interest in plunder than in knightly exploits. Some of these traits are significant for the popular nationalism of the English army.

the Germans appeared to the other nations as particularly ruthless warriors. John of Salisbury comments bitterly on German arrogance and calls the Emperor Frederick I a "Teutonic tyrant".[1] He also refers to King Louis VII of France, who was despised by the Germans resident in Paris because he lived like a citizen among his people, and did not appear in public guarded by an escort of soldiers like a tyrant going in fear of his life. Walter Map tells a story in which the English king is characterized by his wealth, the German Emperor by his military might, and the French by their enjoyment of life. An interesting tract, named *Noticia Saeculi* (1288), written by a German, probably Alexander of Roes or Jordanus of Osnabrück,[2] discusses the diversity of national characters. The author finds that the Italians are ruled by the economic instinct, the Germans by the lust of domination, and the French by their thirst for knowledge. This leads to the predominance of the people in Italy, of the warriors in Germany, and of the clergy or the scholars in France. Each nation shows many good and bad traits corresponding to its fundamental tendency and the ethos of its ruling class. The author describes these traits in great detail and some of his observations still agree with views widely held to-day.

Towards the end of the Middle Ages the German knights, according to Froissart, had a very evil reputation for ruthlessness towards their enemies and for neglecting the code of chivalry. Philippe de Comines describes the extraordinary number and violence of the robber-knights in Germany who have little to fear from the princes, as these need their military services in their wars. In 1519 Erasmus wrote to a friend that he had discovered such brutes among Christians as he could not have believed to exist. The disorder in Germany was partly due to the natural fierceness of the race, partly to the division into so many separate States, and partly to the tendency of the people to serve as mercenaries.[3] This tendency maintained itself for several centuries longer.

The internal wars and insecurity that reigned in France and in Germany in the Middle Ages led to the foundation of numerous fortified points of refuge which later developed into towns, and also other reasons fostered the growth of towns. The feudal disintegration of the central government, furthermore, gave many towns the opportunity of winning an almost republican indepen-

[1] Cf. Clement Webb, *John of Salisbury*, 1932, p. 127.
[2] Cf. F. Wilhelm in *Mitteilungen des Instituts für österreichische Geschichtsforschung*, xix, 1898.
[3] T. A. Froude, *Life and Letters of Erasmus*, 1895, p. 260.

dence. This movement went farthest in Germany, where the reign of violence and the weakness of the Government were particularly pronounced, while in France the rise of royal power increasingly restored peace and restricted municipal autonomy. In England, where conditions were more peaceful, urban development was much slower than in Germany, except in London, and the English towns were always firmly under the control of the central government. Some of the German town-republics achieved a remarkable development of wealth and civilization which aroused the greatest admiration of such foreign observers as Aeneas Silvius, Machiavelli and Bodin. The German merchants for some time played a paramount rôle in English trade and finance, and Edward III even pawned the Crown of England to them for a loan. Many German towns, moreover, became great seats of industry and the Germans excelled in many crafts and manufactures. The fundamental differences in the social structure of the nations also expressed themselves in the sphere of industrial evolution. In Germany the great demand for armour, swords and other implements of war, together with natural conditions,[1] stimulated the rise of the iron and metal industries, of mining, and of machinery for these productions. The Free City of Nuremberg became the foremost place in Europe for mechanical products. In England natural and social conditions fostered the rise of sheep farming and later of the cloth industry. In France the ascent of royalty to power was connected with the development of artillery for the royal army, and of such luxury industries for the Court and the aristocracy as silk, glass and porcelain. The national peculiarities in the field of industry which developed many centuries ago to some extent still characterize the economic life of the nations at the present day.

5. The Development of Modern Militarism

One of the most important factors which fostered the rise of modern nationalism was militarism. This term is commonly used in as vague and misleading a way as nationalism. The two concepts are sometimes almost identified, and sometimes entirely dissociated, for instance, when Gandhi is called a nationalist, though he is certainly quite opposed to any sort of

[1] In the old times the most important materials were for smelting charcoal and wood, and for hammering hydraulic power. Germany was much richer than England both in forests and in water-power, and this too accounts for her early development of the mechanical industries.

militarism. From a sociological point of view militarism is not simply nationalism, nor the maintenance of a strong army, nor even a policy which might lead to war. Militarism in our terminology designates a specific body of ideas and sentiment relating to politics and social life.[1] One of its historical roots was the old warrior-spirit, as embodied in the traditions and ideals of a privileged warrior-caste. This spirit implied a specific code of honour, centred on the prestige of the warrior, the cult of warlike heroism, of noble blood, and of symbols such as the flag and the sword, later also uniform, duelling, etc., the belief in war as the profession most worthy of a nobleman, the contempt for manual labour and trade, the claim to a privileged position, and the rejection of the " bourgeois ethos " and of equalitarian and democratic tendencies. This spirit has been modified by the development of military technique and political organization. Whereas the old way of fighting consisted in individual combats between knights, the new way became that of disciplined mass-action. The mailed knight was replaced by the officer. It was no longer so much personal courage and strength which were the decisive factors but tactics and strategy, technical means of warfare and the art of swaying public opinion. A new mentality arose which esteemed qualities and methods quite alien to the spirit of knighthood, such as unity of command, strict subordination, mechanical obedience, cunning stratagems, political propaganda, the principles of *raison d'état* and of a double morality. Modern militarism consists of a mixture of the warrior-ethos with the new technical mentality, and their application to politics. Moreover, militarism has in recent times become allied with nationalism, and both have gained immense power through this alliance.

In former times militarism was mainly a professional ethos restricted to professional soldiers. The knights who took service for wages, the condottieri, lansquenets, and other military adventurers had neither a dynastic nor a national loyalty, though they had their typical mentality and code of honour. Kings later created a dynastic militarism which often also possessed some national traits, in so far as the king and the nobility represented the nation. It took a long time, however, until in certain nations militarism became fully national. In the Hundred Years War the national English army proved superior to the feudal French army. The French nobility showed the greatest contempt for

[1] The most comprehensive and instructive book on the subject is Alfred Vagts, *History of Militarism*, 1938.

the non-noble auxiliaries of the king and they always opposed the arming of the common people as this was regarded as a menace to their own position. In the fifteenth century the Swiss developed new infantry-tactics which were superior to those of all other States. For some time there was even an aggressive Swiss militarism, though the Swiss fought predominantly as the mercenaries of foreign kings. In the sixteenth century the Spaniards were foremost in the art of war and also in militarism, and later on the Dutch contributed much to military technique. In the seventeenth century the French gained supremacy in both fields. Louis le Grand paved the road for Frederick the Great. England outdistanced all rivals in the development of maritime power.

The decisive event in the history of militarism was the rise of Brandenburg-Prussia in the seventeenth and eighteenth centuries.[1] In the Middle Ages the Teutonic knights founded in Prussia a State with a highly organized administration and army, and its memory may have contributed to the spirit of later Prussia. In the seventeenth century the " Great Elector " Frederick William began an ambitious and unscrupulous policy of expansion with the organization of military power for his aims. He and his successors, in particular the Kings Frederick William I and Frederick II, succeeded in building up a highly organized military machine and a civil administration and financial system which was exclusively focused on the increase of military power. The most significant feature in this system was the position of the King as supreme military leader and unlimited dictator. Before Frederick II the greatest incarnation of the striving for military glory and power was Louis XIV. But the King himself did not regularly lead his armies, and he was much less of an all-powerful dictator than Frederick. In Prussia the King was a soldier first, the army was the foundation of the State and the officer was regarded as far superior to any civilian. Frederick II became the most perfect representative of a completely unscrupulous policy of *raison d'état* or Machiavellism. In his two Political Testaments of 1752 and 1768 Frederick gave an account of his principles for his successors. " The best way of concealing one's secret ambitions is to profess peaceable intentions till the favourable moment comes for putting the cards on the table." All religions, declares the King, are but absurd fables and Christianity is an Oriental fairy-tale which only idiots believe. Two incentives govern men : fear of punishment and hope of reward. The common soldier

[1] Cf. for details and literature, F. Hertz, *Nationalgeist und Politik*, 1937, vol. i, p. 64.

must mainly be directed by fear. He must fear his officers more than all the dangers of the battle. The officers, however, must be actuated by ambition. The nobility alone has a sense of honour and must, therefore, form the groundwork of the State. Nationality was quite alien to the King. His policy was even frankly anti-national, and he envisaged the carving up of Germany. He hardly considered the middle class as belonging to the nation. The only class he trusted was that of the officers, and only a nobleman could become an officer. This class was granted extraordinary privileges while the common soldier was treated with brutality and contempt.

The concentration of all power in the hands of the King enabled him to realize also some beneficial reforms, though many achievements ascribed to him by his admirers are mere legends. Frederick's profession of " enlightened " views and his intercourse with Voltaire and other French wits have won him the praise of numerous intellectuals, though many of the great German writers of that time regarded him with aversion or mixed feelings. When the King died, Mirabeau found to his surprise that nobody in Berlin mourned for him. Not a word of regret or praise was to be heard. Everybody was utterly sick of the King. In his last years republican convictions had made great headway among the educated classes of Prussia. Though Frederick had no interest in German nationality he later on became the idol of German nationalism and his name was never pronounced in modern Germany without affixing " the Great ".

The fact that Prussian militarism had not yet become national was one of the reasons for the catastrophe in the struggle of Prussia with Napoleon. The French dictator was certainly a pronounced militarist too, and has made characteristic confessions in this regard. But he had gone through the school of the Revolution and had learnt to make use of the principle of equality for his purposes. Those of humble birth had the same chance under the Emperor as the nobles, and the civil service had a more dignified position under him than under Frederick. Napoleon's militarism therefore was national. He intoxicated large masses of the French people with the sense of being " la grande nation ". After his death the Napoleonic legend represented him as the friend of the people, of liberty and nationality, and with great success.

The defeat of Prussia in her struggle with Napoleon (1806) greatly discredited the militaristic system and led to a thorough reorganization of the State in a Liberal spirit, in which the Baron von Stein had a large share.[1] Prussia was thereby enabled to win wide sympathies among progressive elements in all parts of Germany, and later on to take the lead in the establishment of a strong national unity. Prussian militarism also gradually became national, though there was great resistance to be overcome. The King and the Junker class for a long time were against arming the whole people because of possible dangers to their power, and the Liberals rejected conscription as hostile to civilization. It was Gneisenau who advocated " an alliance of the Government with the nation ", and a rising of the people against French domination. The King first objected that a revolutionary, popular war was possible only in a nation that was endowed with intelligence but not in Germany where it would lead to chaos.[2] Gneisenau and Clausewitz were also brilliant exponents of the philosophy of militarism which was centred in the dogma that from time to time war was indispensable for moral regeneration. Militarism recovered its full power over Prussia and then over Germany only through its victory over the revolution of 1848, and through the successful wars which Bismarck waged for national unification. Bismarck's policy led to an immense increase in German aggressive nationalism which went far beyond his own aims and views.[3]

6. The Development of Totalitarian War and its Influence on Politics

In former times war was by no means regarded as the concern of the whole people, nor was the State willing and able to make use of all its forces for war. If wars frequently inflicted horrible sufferings on the masses, this was mainly due to the fact that the rulers had no power to control the soldiery, and were compelled to tolerate their excesses. With the growth of military discipline individual violence was more and more repressed, but the Governments themselves systematically organized the exploitation of all the forces of the nation for warfare. War became national and totalitarian, and this greatly contributed to

---

[1] Cf. J. R. Seeley, *Life and Times of Stein*, 3 vols., 1880, and M. Lehmann, *Freiherr vom Stein*, 3 vols., 1902–5.

[2] Cf. A. Herrmann on the King's share in the reform of the army in *Historische Vierteljahrsschrift*, 1908. The long opposition of all Liberals and Democrats against conscription is described by Hans W. Pinkow, *Der Kampf gegen die Institution des stehenden Heeres in Deutschland (1815–1848)*, 1912. On Gneisenau and the other military reformers Max Lehmann has published many important papers; cf, for example, *Historische Zeitschrift*, vol. 126, 1922.

[3] On the spirit of Bismarck's foreign policy compare my book *Nationalgeist und Politik*, 1937, vol. i, p. 113, and the literature quoted there.

preparing the ground for the totalitarian State of our time, though specific historical circumstances were required to bring it to life.

In the age of feudalism it was in principle the feudal classes only which had to wage war. An old French verse says : " The clerk's duty is to pray to God, the noble's duty is to fight, the peasant has to provide the bread." The nobles regarded war as a chivalrous sport and as their privilege. Their object was by no means to kill their noble enemies but to capture them and to get a high ransom for their release.[1] They detested and condemned the use of unchivalrous weapons such as the long-bow, the cross-bow, or the gun, which enabled a low-born man to kill the most valorous knight from a distance.[2] The common people who lived in the territory where war was waged were often treated with the greatest cruelty without distinction of friend or foe, though the Church made many efforts to protect the people against violence. Towards the end of the Middle Ages the Welsh and English archers and the Swiss pikemen proved superior to the knights in warfare. They did not observe the feudal code of honour, they aimed at killing the enemy, and the Swiss rustics were notorious for refusing quarter even when a ransom was offered.

In the era of royal absolutism war was the occupation of mercenaries recruited from the scum of the earth, and the civil population often had to suffer terribly at their hands. The civilians were not liable for the defence of their country. Recruitment and training of the soldiers was expensive and the kings had little money. Strategy, therefore, was anxious to economize in shedding blood. In many cases large numbers of prisoners of war were enlisted in the army of their former enemy where they were usually quite willing to serve. Armies were small and in autumn and winter fighting was stopped. The officers who came predominantly from noble families to some extent preserved chivalrous traditions. At the battle of Fontenoy (1745) the English and French officers commanding the ranks confronting each other exchanged polite salutes before beginning to fight, though modern research has discounted Voltaire's story that each side carried courtesy so far as to leave it to the other to shoot first.[3]

[1] This custom was still widely observed in the eighteenth century. Cf. A. Babeau, *La vie militaire sous l'ancien régime*, 1889, vol. i, p. 290 ; vol. ii, p. 263.
[2] Montaigne remarks that in his youth the French nobility regarded the reputation of being good at fencing as injurious and abstained from learning the art of fencing because subtle feints were derogatory to true and ingenuous virtue. Cf. Montaigne, *Essays*, ii, 27.
[3] Cf. F. H. Skrine, *Fontenoy and Great Britain's Share in the War of the Austrian Succession*, 1906, p. 172.

The French infantry had the tradition of charging first with the bayonet, and not even answering the fire of the enemy.[1]

The growth of the power of governments and of discipline and the spread of the ideas of Enlightenment in the eighteenth century resulted in warfare becoming steadily milder. Barbarities against the civil population were no longer tolerated, though wholesale devastation of a country was sometimes resorted to for strategical reasons. Even the practice of Frederick II seems mild when compared with that of Napoleon. " There are several striking examples in the eighteenth century of the way in which the Austrian armies in particular forfeited success through their extreme scrupulousness in abstaining from any demand on the civil population ", as a great English authority says.[2] The American and French Revolutions inaugurated a new era of warfare, and the revolutionary methods were then perfected by Napoleon and by the Prussian strategists who organized the war of liberation against him. Popular mass levies began to replace the small professional armies, the principle of general compulsory service was introduced, the soldiers were inspired by democratic and national enthusiasm and able to fight in open order instead of in close formation. The mass armies could no longer be fed by supplies carried in trains or stored in magazines but were obliged to live on the country. The Americans employed war methods and tricks which the English condemned as ungentlemanly,[3] and the French revolutionary armies also increased the fierceness of fighting. As regards relations between invading armies and the population the French revolutionary armies undoubtedly had a lower standard than the old royal armies.[4] Robespierre and the Convention decreed that no quarter should be given to English, Hanoverian and Spanish troops, and though the army was reluctant to carry this out, in 1795 some eight to nine thousand Spaniards were massacred. Napoleon in general adopted the Jacobin principle of terror in war, and he often applied methods of warfare which his enemies did not consider compatible with honour. Military aims, however, were usually not served by wholesale destruction, and in point of fact Napoleon used terroristic methods but sparingly. A characteristic instance

[1] Cf. on this tradition Henri Martin, *Histoire de France*, tome xv, 1860, p. 282. In the Austrian cavalry even in the last Great War it was regarded as unfair to encounter a cavalry attack of the enemy otherwise than on horseback, though it would have been more advantageous to receive it with machine-gun fire.
[2] Sir G. Butler and S. Maccoby, *The Development of International Law*, 1928, p. 145.
[3] Cf. Vagts, pp. 99, 101, about the French, pp. 120 f.
[4] Cf. Butler and Maccoby, p. 137.

occurred in the French-Austrian war of 1809.[1] The Archduke Charles defeated Napoleon in the Battle of Aspern, but when it was suggested to him to pursue the retreating French he refused, saying that enough blood had been shed. A few days later Napoleon defeated him at Wagram by concentrating an unusually large number of guns and smashing the Austrian troops by artillery-fire instead of using the bayonet. Napoleon, though quite free from humanitarian qualms, excused himself for this new technique in a talk with General Bubna in the words: " What should I have done? My best infantry is in Spain." But he also realized that the new method which cost him more blood than the old one implied a great risk, and this induced him as it had the Archduke in the same situation to prefer diplomacy to war.

In the course of the nineteenth century it was typical of the policy of reaction that general compulsory service was abolished, or greatly restricted, because the monarchs and the ruling classes were afraid of arming the masses and of admitting large numbers of non-nobles to the officer-corps. On the other hand, in every revolution the principle of a popular army was proclaimed by democrats who saw in it an instrument for securing liberty against reactionary powers with their professional armies. The final outcome was an extraordinary expansion in the size of armies, and the subjection of the whole life of the nations to military regimentation. This development, which took place only gradually, was due to two factors, namely, to the application of new technical measures in warfare and the rise of nationalism. Moltke was the first great master to make use of railways and telegraphs for moving and directing a mass army of up to 500,000 men, an operation which before would have been considered impossible. Bismarck's knowledge of human nature and German efficiency in thoroughgoing organization of administration and popular education succeeded in rendering the German people a reliable tool in the hands of the militarists. The mass army which the democrats had planned for establishing a reign of justice and equality within and among nations became in reality the best instrument for imbuing large masses with a longing for national power and prestige, and with blind obedience towards their military leaders.

In the nineteenth century political liberalism, though in principle opposed to war and violence, fostered the rise of nationality, and thus involuntarily contributed to the outbreak of many wars

---

[1] August Fournier, *Napoleon I*, 1913, tome 2, p. 292.

which were caused by the conflict of national aspirations and which were fought out with national fanaticism. On the other hand, economic liberalism tried to prevent war from embracing the whole economic and social life of the peoples. In the Crimean War Russia continued to pay interest on her loans to British bondholders and even raised a loan in the City for this purpose,[1] and Russian raw materials were imported by Britain via Prussia. In the Franco-German War of 1870–1 business relations between the two belligerents were not interrupted. Business men in Berlin received letters from their correspondents in Paris, which was besieged by the German army, by way of balloon-mail. If business men did not take part in the wars of the Governments, the latter did not regard it as their task to defend business-interests abroad by military means. According to the Liberal principle of non-interference the British Government and British organs of public opinion often declared that if British investors had lent their money to foreign creditors who did not pay, it was not a matter for the Government to intervene to enforce payment.[2] Apparent departures from this principle are mainly to be explained by reasons of high policy. The most notable exception was Britain's intervention in Egypt. The real cause, however, was not care for the interests of the bond-holders but the wish to protect the road to India which the decay of Turkey exposed to danger.

A step towards what is called to-day " total war " was made in the Civil War in America.[3] It became an aim of warfare to wreck the morale of the civilian population by destroying the resources of their country. The democratic North took the lead in this new type of warfare while the aristocratic South clung more to the old idea of war as a knightly duel, a " gentleman's war ". In the Franco-German War of 1870–1 the American General Sheridan visited Bismarck and stayed with him behind the German lines for some time. Once when the question of humanity in war was being discussed, and a high Prussian official was advocating humane methods, Sheridan dissented and said it was advisable to treat the population with the utmost vigour. It was an aim of strategy to cause the inhabitants so much suffering that they must long for peace and force their Government to demand it. The people, Sheridan remarked, must be left nothing but their eyes to weep with. This observation pleased Bismarck.[4]

[1] Cf. E. L. Woodward, *War and Peace in Europe, 1815–1870*, 1931, p. 88.
[2] Examples are given by Woodward, pp. 95 f., 104.
[3] Cf. James Truslow Adams, *America's Tragedy*, 1934, p. 338.
[4] Cf Moritz Busch, *Bismarck, Some Secret Pages of His History*, 1898, vol. i, pp. 171, 223.

The wars which Bismarck made for establishing Prussia's hegemony in Germany opened an era of great armaments for which the progress of technology furnished quite new means. In many states great efforts were made to render all resources available for war. Nevertheless, belief in the reign of law was still so widespread and potent that serious attempts were made to bring about disarmament and to mitigate warfare. In 1898 Tsar Nicholas II of Russia issued a manifesto which deplored the intolerable burden of armaments and the horrors of war and which proposed international agreements for restricting them. The Tsar was doubtless actuated by a genuine love of peace, though Russia had also financial and military reasons for limiting an increase of armaments in which she could not keep pace with other Powers.[1] The result was the first Conference at The Hague in which all Great Powers and most other States took part. The Russian main proposals were a standstill in armaments and compulsory arbitration. The majority of the Governments represented there were more or less favourably disposed, but Germany wrecked the whole plan by her sharp opposition. The German diplomatic documents reveal that the Emperor Wilhelm II was furious and spoke in the rudest and most contemptuous way of his cousin Nicholas. The Dutch Government moved to discuss also the inviolability of private property at sea. Opinions, however, were much divided and the discussion was postponed for the next Conference. The British naval expert, Admiral Sir John Fisher, showed himself a militarist *pur-sang* if only behind the scenes. A second Conference was held at The Hague in 1907, which was followed in 1909 by a Conference in London. The Liberal Government in Great Britain took a keen interest in peace and the mitigation of war and was ready for substantial concessions as regards naval warfare. We need not enter here into details of international law, and only wish to emphasize how strong the forces working for an international reign of law were in many States. Even in Germany the Foreign Office opposed the intransigent militarism of the Admiralty and the Kaiser.

The outbreak of the war in 1914 smashed all hopes of a peaceful development by international co-operation. The invasion of neutralized Belgium and other acts struck at the heart of international law : confidence in the pledged word of a State.

---

[1] The Tsar had read several pacifist books such as that by Bertha von Suttner and the great work on war in which J. de Bloch, a banker of Jewish origin, described war as a scourge of humanity and a menace to social order.

Germany's conduct of the war, moreover, showed for the first time the picture of a totalitarian war with all the means of modern technique and on the greatest scale.[1] This sort of war completely obliterated the distinction between the soldier and the civilian. The whole population, even women and children, were employed in the service of the gigantic military machine in which the individual and his rights were reduced to total insignificance. Ludendorff's practical dictatorship already foreboded that of his later companion, Hitler, though in many respects it by no means attained to the same degree of bestiality. After the war the League of Nations attempted to build an international reign of law. It is not intended here to discuss the relations between the League and the problems of nationality, and this subject must be left for another occasion.

7. THE NATIONAL WILL

Certain ideas connected with nationality such as the national personality and character, national sovereignty and self-determination, the national mission and responsibility play a paramount part in modern politics. They all imply the existence of a national will, but there is the greatest possible divergency of views about what this means. Both the word " nation " and the word " will " can be understood in different ways, and it is difficult to grasp how a great multitude of people widely differing in interests, opinions and insight can form anything like a common will at all, especially if we understand by " will " not a fleeting impulse caused by blind emotions, but a reasonable will formed on careful consideration of all circumstances and in accordance with the true interests of the people, the will corresponding to what the people really wants. Even individuals of mature character and trained in judgement are often not immune from illusions, prejudices and passions which may hinder them from forming a reasonable will, and the great majority of individuals are still more dominated by irrational factors. If they, nevertheless, succeed in managing their private affairs in a fairly reasonable way, this is due to the fact that in most cases they are told how to act, or not to act, by laws, public opinion, their technical training and experience and the advice of experts, and if they act contrary to these rules they are either punished by the State or suffer certain losses. In national affairs the risks implied in a misjudgement are immensely greater. On the one hand, these

[1] Cf. James Garner, *International Law and the World War*, 2 vols.

affairs are much more complicated than private affairs and the consequences of a mistake may be ruinous for a whole nation. On the other hand, the overwhelming majority of the people have no special training in judging such affairs, they are to a great extent swayed by prejudice and illusions, and international law is lacking in effective sanctions.

The problem of the national will forms the crux of modern political science.[1] It arose with the growth of national consciousness and of the idea that the nation was Sovereign. Public law formerly often distinguished different sections of the population by special names indicating their political status. In countries with rigid barriers between the social ranks the upper and ruling classes were often designated as the " nation ", while the lower strata were the " people ". In England, however, this distinction never became a practice, though the classes were certainly very different in political influence. An Elizabethan statesman, Sir Thomas Smith, in his book on the Commonwealth of England (1565), defines a commonwealth or nation as a society of free men united by a common accord. Slaves or bondmen form no part of it. In Parliament every Englishman from the King to the lowest is assumed to be either present or represented. Smith particularly praises the classes of gentlemen and yeomen, who in his description appear as the core of the nation. The humblest class which the Romans called proletarians have no vote, though they have some share in local administration. In England at that time serfdom had already practically disappeared, while it still existed on the Continent.

In German documents of the fifteenth century " German nation " stands for the princes and the Free Cities, who formed the Imperial Diet. Luther in his appeal to the Christian nobility says that " the German nation, i.e. the bishops and princes, should act as Christians and protect the people given into their charge ". Nation is clearly distinguished here from people. In Hungarian constitutional law, compiled by Verboeczy, the nobility was designated as " populus ", and the lower classes, who were without political rights, as " plebs ".[2] Aulard says that in the eighteenth century " nation " in France meant the rich and lettered classes. In 1758 a spokesman of the third Estate, the bourgeoisie, called it an indignity that lawyers, authors, artists, merchants and financiers were counted among the people ; they

[1] Cf. Harold Laski, *Grammar of Politics* ; *Foundations of Sovereignty*, 1921, p. 209 ; T. Bryce, *Modern Democracies*, 2 vols., 1929 ; Hans Delbrück, *Regierung und Volkswille*, 1914.
[2] Cf. A. von Timon, *Ungarische Verfassungs- und Rechtsgeschichte*, 1904, p. 581.

really belonged to the higher classes of the nation. The German historian Archenholtz, a great admirer of English liberty, wrote in 1793 : " By nation I understand the upper classes of the people only. The lower classes, i.e. the artisans and peasants, are on the whole everywhere semi-human beings." The conception of the upper and middle classes as alone forming the nation was maintained in Germany far into the nineteenth century. The difference was elaborated with further arguments by a French writer, Fievée, who in 1802 wrote : [1]

" Rousseau made a mistake and misled all minds with a single word, the word 'people'. Whenever you meet in the Contrat Social the word 'people', replace it by the word 'nation', and you will be greatly surprised to find that what impressed you before has lost its sense. The reason is simple. I am not saying that in France and in almost all countries the word 'people' represents the idea of that part of the nation which by its poverty and lack of education is naturally excluded from the discussion of great interests of the State. I am going much farther and wish to point out that the French people is not equivalent to the French nation. The nation implies the citizens, the Government, the laws, and even the habits, while in the word 'people' in its widest sense, the Government may not be comprised, which leads to all the errors of the Contrat Social."

Fievée further tries to show that the people cannot have a will because they are not a unity. But a nation can have a will because it comprises a people constituted under a government.

The difficulty of conceiving how a plurality of divergent wills can be united into one single, rational will has often been put forward by defenders of Monarchy arguing that this system alone was able to guarantee the unity of the national will. Bismarck, however, pointed out in his memoirs that in an absolute Monarchy the decision of the Sovereign frequently was the result of the most various influences by irresponsible persons,[2] and history shows that in autocratically governed States policy was often extremely vacillating, according to the change of influence of rival groups and individuals.

The forming of a reasonable collective will implies two tasks, that of forming a plan likely to further the true interests of the community and that of inducing its members to accept it. The prospect of solving these tasks increases and decreases with the difficulty of the social and political problems concerned and with the number of people who have a share in determining policy. Now in modern society the nations are faced with problems

---

[1] Cf. J. Fievée, *Lettres sur l'Angleterre et réflexions sur la philosophie du XVIIIe siècle*, 1802, p. 15.
[2] Cf. Bismarck, *Gedanken und Erinnerungen*, 1898, vol. i, p. 278 ; cf. also p. 15.

immensely more numerous and complicated than ever before. The activities of governments have greatly increased and many problems have arisen which are exceedingly difficult to judge, for example, those of international policy. On the other hand, many more people are taking part in politics to-day than in former times and very few only have the time and ability for careful political thinking. In such circumstances it is hopeless to expect that the people as such could form one single reasonable national will, and this holds good for the highly educated intellectual classes even more than for the masses. It is the function of parties to form a uniform will at least in a section of the people, or rather to win the confidence of a section and to obtain a tacit mandate to form a will for the members of the party which is not necessarily in full accordance with what these members really desire. Nevertheless an investigation of the political psychology of various classes and groups would lead to the result that the political mentality of the great majority still shows a large amount of vague, wishful, inco-ordinate and inconsistent ideas, the propensity to think in analogies and symbols, and a strong influence of prejudices and illusions.[1]

The idea of the national will as that of the whole nation has hardly ever been realized. In its stead the idea has been adopted that the will of the majority stands for that of the whole nation, which is obviously a fiction. Certain cases, moreover, are excepted from the rule that the majority decides; for example, the rights of national minorities, and in general the principle of majority tacitly implies the condition that it is not used in an oppressive way. Even in democratic countries, moreover, large sections of the nation were often excluded from the franchise,[2] for example, women, and sometimes the mode of voting resulted in giving the majority of seats in Parliament to the minority of voters.

In the United States the Presidents have several times been elected by the minority, mainly owing to the system of indirect voting. The most momentous election in American history was that of Abraham Lincoln in 1860. Lincoln was elected with 1,866,452 votes, while his rivals received 2,787,780, or almost a million more. In 1876 Hayes and in 1880 Harrison were elected by minorities. In 1913 Woodrow Wilson became President with

[1] Cf. Graham Wallas, *Human Nature in Politics*, 1910 ; J. Bryce, *Modern Democracies*, 1929, vol. ii, p. 601.
[2] Even Rousseau was of the opinion that a democracy must not necessarily comprise the whole people. It could also be restricted to the half of it. In France women have never obtained the right to vote.

6,157,800 votes, while the other candidates polled 8,139,000 votes, and 3 millions did not vote at all. If the national will, therefore, means the will of the total electorate, he represented only about a third of it. If the adult population over 21, both male and female, exclusive of aliens, are regarded as the nation, then Wilson represented only 12 per cent of it.

The greatest instrument for the formation of a national will to-day is the Cabinet system which developed under the Whig ascendancy in the eighteenth century. But whether this momentous evolution was at that time desired by the nation at large is very doubtful. If the Whig aristocracy had not disposed of such a large number of more or less rotten boroughs, the majority would have fallen to the Tories, who probably had the great majority of the people behind them.[1] The Tories would hardly have asserted the power of Parliament by the development of Cabinet-rule. They believed, moreover, that " trade would be the ruin of the English nation ", and opposed " turning England into a mercantile republic like Holland ".[2]

Bryce in his monumental work on democracy comes to the conclusion that " Free Government cannot but be, and has in reality always been, an Oligarchy within a Democracy "—not an oligarchy of class but one based on natural talent. The functions of the people consist mainly in control and are more negative than positive, i.e. " the people can more readily reject a course proposed to them than themselves propose a better course ". In spite of these limitations modern Democracy has a proud record, especially in regard to the social and cultural progress of the people. The widespread view that the rule of Democracy hinders the rise of great personalities to leadership is contradicted by countless examples of outstanding democratic statesmen. True, Democracy alone is not enough ; many historical, social and moral forces must co-operate in order to secure a successful development. Most of all the rivalry between classes must not go so far as to exclude a certain solidarity and confidence between them. The longing for internal unity and harmony has inspired many thinkers and leaders to work out the idea of a nation as a close solidarity with one single will. This ideal cannot be realized, unless in exceptional cases, but it can be replaced by the spirit of compromise and toleration. The idea of a uniform national will has even done much harm, especially in judging

[1] Cf. Lecky, *History of England in the Eighteenth Century*, chaps. 1 and 2. On the electoral structure of England cf. L. B. Namier, *The Structure of Politics at the Accession of George III*, 1929, vol. i, p. 79.
[2] Cf. George Macaulay Trevelyan, *England under the Stuarts*, 1906, p. 477.

other nations and interpreting their actions as the outcome of an invariable national character.

The idea of a nation comprises both the political organization of the State and the economic and cultural organization of society, and the national will is assumed to be a function of both. There are several types of the concept of a nation, each implying a specific view of the national will. Before the rise of nationality the State was conceived as a Divine institution in which the only real Sovereign was God. When the nation came to be regarded as Sovereign, it took over from royalty its mystical, sacred character and philosophers ascribed to the nation a Divine character, mission and authority.

The conservative theories of the State see in it an historical personality composed of various ranks with separate functions. The national will is identified by them with the national traditions, the wisdom of the forefathers, and their interpretation is entrusted to the Monarch and the aristocracy. Society is in these theories hardly separated from the State. Church and State, public and private rights are in many ways intertwined. Liberalism identifies the State with a society for the maintenance of the Reign of Law, the Rights of Man, inherent in human reason. Nationality is assumed to be subordinated to reason and morality and means hardly more than voluntary membership in a society for mutual defence. Society is to the Liberal much more important than the State. The spokesmen of the nation are the enlightened middle class, the intellectual professions and the wealthy bourgeoisie, but many Liberals expected that the diffusion of wealth and education would lead to the extension of the franchise. The ideology of Democracy regards all inhabitants of a State as the nation and rejects the idea of a leading class, though in democratic States citizens of a different skin, colour or language have often hardly been recognized as true nationals. Society is regarded as subordinate to the State and this leads to the transformation of Democracy into Socialism. Now the nation was again identified with a class endowed with a mission. Marx declared in his " Communist Manifesto " : " The workers have no fatherland. The proletariat has first to seize political domination, elevate itself to the position of the national class, and constitute itself as the nation, thereby still remaining national, though not in the bourgeois sense ". But Marx predicts that the abolition of internal class divisions through the victory of the proletariat will lead to the disappearance of antagonism between nations. Modern nationalism, lastly, sees the essence of a nation in its honour and power and bases nationality on race. Its theory of State is strictly authoritarian and society is completely subordinated to the State. In this respect and in others too nationalism differs from conservative authoritarianism. It is not the Monarch and the historic aristocracy who embody the spirit of the nation and are entitled to represent it, but a racial aristocracy composed of elements of various classes. But the real driving power of nationalism has everywhere been a section of the intelligentsia, and the military caste with auxiliaries from other classes.

In the ideology of every nation various concepts of a nation are more or less combined. As has been said before, a nation is held together partly by tradition, partly by interests, partly by ideals. The Conservative concept stresses tradition, its adherents feel as members of a nation mainly because they are proud of its glorious past, and if a State abandons this legacy, this seems to them to amount almost to the end of the nation. The democratic concept accentuates interests, and inclines towards the view that there is hardly a nation as long as the great mass of the people has no adequate share in the national wealth and civilization.[1] The Liberal concept emphasizes the ideal of right. In this view there is no nation if the Reign of Law has ceased to exist. Many Liberals, moreover, attributed to the nation the mission to propagate certain ideals in the world, namely, the ideal of national self-determination, and that of an international order for securing peace and goodwill. The firmest national solidarity is achieved if all three concepts are adequately used in the building of the national ideology.

The national will is the work of a leading élite composed of various factors such as a dynasty and its servants, a Church, a ruling class, or a party. In order to deserve the designation "national" this will must be accepted, or at least tolerated, by a considerable section of the nation which must have the ability and power to make this will prevail within the nation. It must, moreover, be consistent with the existence of the nation, for it cannot be assumed to have the will to commit suicide. These conditions imply that there is a certain community of aspirations between the different parties and classes of the nation overriding their antagonisms. Where no common ground exists between them there is neither a national will nor a nation.

[1] Cf. Otto Bauer, *Die Nationalitaetenfrage und die Sozialdemokratie*, 1907.

8. NATIONAL SELF-DETERMINATION

National self-determination has become a principal dogma in modern politics. Almost all nations and parties recognize this, at least in theory, but they put the most varied interpretations upon the principle. Self-determination means that the nation itself is the ultimate authority in the determination of its affairs without foreign intervention, and, as a territory is inseparably linked with the idea of a nation, this implies the right to make use of a specific territory. Self-determination in this general sense appears so natural to common sense that it can hardly be disputed, except by those who claim a divine mission, or the right of racial superiority, or simply the right of Might, to impose their will upon other people. In fact, the principle that a people has a right to its fatherland, has always been admitted though not always practised.[1] The modern concept is merely a new interpretation of an old principle.

The demand for national self-determination is usually represented as one for liberty. Nevertheless national self-determination is by no means identical with political liberty. It does not necessarily imply a democratic regime, but merely freedom from foreign interference, The Irish did not lack political freedom when they were still united with England, Scotland and Wales. As a matter of fact, they possessed more seats in the British House of Commons than corresponded to their share in the population,[2] and their political influence was still enhanced by the fact that they often held the balance between the two great parties. Their national and social interests were by no means neglected in modern times, as the British Government made great efforts to win the Irish by meeting their demands for social improvements. What the Irish wanted, however, was not good government but a national government.[3]

The idea of self-determination implies three questions:
(1) The criteria for determining nationality.
(2) The means of forming and expressing the national will.
(3) The purposes and limits of the national will.

---

[1] Matthew Paris, who was rather hostile to the Welsh, nevertheless says in his *English History* (tr. Giles, vol. iii, p. 238) that in their struggle against English oppression their cause appeared even to their enemies to be just, and what chiefly supported and encouraged them was the thought that like the Trojans, from whom they were descended, they were struggling with a firmness worthy of their descent for their ancestral laws and liberties.

[2] In 1884 one M.P. corresponded to a population of 49,500 in Ireland, of 53,200 in England, and of 62,100 in Scotland. In 1885 the ratio for Scotland was improved. Cf. S. Buxton, *Handbook of Political Questions of the Day*, 1903, p. 5.

[3] Cf. N. Mansergh, *Ireland in the Age of Reform and Revolution*, 1910.

The demarcation of a nation can be founded on either the territorial or the ethnic principle. It can either identify the nation with the inhabitants of a given territory, or with a group irrespective of territory, but showing certain ethnic characteristics. Both principles have many varieties. Territory can mean an historical state or province, or a region forming a natural unit independent of historical frontiers. An ethnic group can be characterized by race, language, religion, civilization, or occupation; and either the present state of things can be taken as a starting-point, or that of a former age. Now, the outcome of any consultation of the national will, whether by means of a plebiscite or otherwise, obviously depends on the demarcation of the group considered as the nation.

The most frequent usage has been to start from historical territories, though great conquerors like Napoleon have frequently used their power for creating quite new frontiers on strategical, political, administrative or economic grounds. If these territories should also be ethnically homogeneous this was often regarded as an additional asset, though sometimes it seemed more desirable to join in one State different peoples who could then be played off against each other. With the growing strength of democratic and national sentiment, however, the demand arose that national self-determination should be exercised independently of territories. The existing States or provinces were to be partitioned according to ethnic criteria, and each of the new units was then to have freedom to join the nation to which it felt akin. Unfortunately, in practice it often proved impossible to find any criterion which would be generally acceptable. The classical example of an irreconcilable conflict of views on this point was Macedonia.[1] In the last decades before the Great War six nations claimed the Macedonians, or sections of them, as their nationals and fought their rivals with every weapon they possessed. The question as to which nationality the Macedonians really belonged to was the despair of ethnologists and the nightmare of all the European Cabinets. The oldest claim was that of the Greeks, who had for long dominated the Church and the schools and still possessed a strong position in both fields. The greater number of the Macedonians did not speak Greek, but Greek propagandists pointed out that their civilization was Greek. The Bulgarians argued that the majority were Bulgarian both in speech and in sympathy. This was contested by the Serbians, who claimed that certain features of Macedonian dialects, as well as their folklore,

[1] Cf. N. Brailsford, *Macedonia, its Races and their Future*, 1924.

were rather Serbian than Bulgarian. The Albanians maintained that the essential thing was race. The Macedonians, they said, were of the hardy Albanian race, and not effeminate Greeks. The Roumanians maintained that a certain section of the population was related to them in language and civilization. Finally, their rulers, the Turks, also had some relatives and followers among the population. Their chief argument, however, was that only they could provide a government not partial to one of the struggling nationalities. All the nationalities carried on an incessant propaganda of the utmost unscrupulousness and violence. Terrorism and bribery were used on a large scale and sometimes with great success. Frequently a whole village would change over from one side to the other so as to avoid being murdered, or more frequently for material profit. Of course, ideal motives also played a rôle. But it was clear that a large part of the population did not possess a firm national consciousness determining their nationality. Many, obviously, had no idea of the nature of nationality; their village was to them the nation. Others spoke more than one language or had other affinities with several nations in different respects.

The multitude of conflicting criteria for determining nationality was often further increased by the claim that not the present share of a nationality in the population should count, but that which existed before a country came under the influence of a foreign domination. All those, it is contended, who came after that date were intruders who must either be expelled or subjected to confiscatory measures and in any case were to be excluded from taking part in a plebiscite. In cases, however, where foreign rule had lasted for a considerable time it was almost impossible to carry out this *restitutio in integrum* without a great deal of arbitrariness and injustice.

A further difficulty in fixing the territorial basis of a nation according to ethnic principles is the fact that frequently different nationalities are living so mixed up with one another that it is impossible to form large territories without including considerable minorities. Theoretically it would, or course, be possible to accord self-determination to enclaves too. In practice, however, this would lead to impossible conditions. A modern State and society cannot be built up in a tiny territory surrounded by hostile neighbours. Small States had a better chance of surviving at the time when the European equipoise and free trade were still in force. After the last war their prospects deteriorated through the destruction of the Balance of Power and the rise of an aggressive economic nationalism. In general, moreover, it must be emphasized that national self-determination is intended for nations and not for fragments of nations. It would certainly be absurd to allow every province or town of a State to claim the right of secession. This would lead to a paralysing instability in everything and to political and social desintegration. This limitation of the right of self-determination, however, presupposes the clear and undisputed determination of nationality. We cannot state what is merely a fragment if we have no settled idea of what is the whole.

The Irish nationalists claim that the whole of Ireland forms a natural territory which cannot be divided. According to their view the people of Ulster—of whom two-thirds are opposed to incorporation in the present Irish Free State—form a part of the indivisible Irish nation and therefore cannot exercise a right of self-determination which is open to the whole nation only. It is also argued that the people of Ulster are descendants of Scots and English intruders who settled in Ireland in the time of oppression. Ulster, of course, rejects these interpretations of self-determination and claims that the principle of ethnic personality should be applied. The standpoint of Sinn Fein is not unlike the claim of the German nationalists to Alsace. This country has always been predominantly German in language, and it was also German in sentiment before Louis XIV annexed it against the will of the people. But the majority later became French in sentiment without being directly coerced. In our time, therefore, the Germans maintained that besides language the popular will at the time before the annexation by France was decisive, while the French contended that the later will of the population should decide. The Boer War arose from the claims of foreign newcomers to political rights in the Transvaal—claims backed by the British Government. In the case of Palestine, however, the British Government wishes to prevent the immigration of large numbers of Jews which might jeopardize the Arab majority. The Jews also claim Palestine on historical grounds, while the Arabs reject this argument. The Czech claim to the dominating position not only in Bohemia and Moravia, where they form the majority, but also in Silesia, where they are a small minority,[1] was based on the ground of the historical and natural unity of all countries of the Bohemian Crown, and on the argument that the Germans were settled there in the Middle Ages or later while the

[1] In the former Austrian province of Silesia the Czechs formed 24 per cent, the Poles 32 per cent and the Germans 44 per cent of the population.

claim to Slovakia was based on the opposite ethnic principle. In the former Kingdom of Hungary the Serb minority descended from refugees who found asylum in Hungary when the Turks conquered Serbia. In this case the historical and natural unity of Hungary was not recognized by the Peace Treaty, but the non-Magyar populations were united with their kinsmen according to the ethnic principle, together with large Magyar minorities.

The realization of self-determination, moreover, depends on the method of forming and expressing the national will. In former times this will was largely identified with that of the historical Estates, that is the ruling classes. Even to-day the national ideology of many democratic nations assumes that in the struggles of former ages the nobility fought primarily for the national cause. The revolt of the English barons against Henry III because of his favouring foreigners in his service appears to our time as a national struggle, though the barons themselves were largely descendants of foreign conquerors, and their leader Simon de Montfort was attacked by his enemies because he was a foreigner and still wanted to hold the sovereignty of the whole Kingdom in his hands, as Matthew Paris says. The struggle for Irish independence was formerly mainly one of the Anglo-Irish upper classes. In the revolt of the Bohemian nobility against Habsburg rule in 1618 some of the most prominent leaders of the rebellion were Germans, for instance Thurn and Vels, while the leaders of the Imperial Party were the Czechs Zdenek Lobkowitz, Martinitz and Slavata.[1]

With the rise of democracy the method of a plebiscite appeared more and more as the right way of realizing self-determination. Nevertheless, after the last war plebiscites were only granted in a few cases. As a rule it was not considered necessary to hold a plebiscite in order to ascertain the will of the people and the Allies made use of other evidence. President Wilson even thought that the whole of Upper Silesia should be given to Poland without a plebiscite ; but Lloyd George insisted on taking a ballot, which resulted in 60 per cent. of the votes being cast for Germany. The country was partitioned between Germany and Poland as far as possible according to ethnic frontiers, though this engendered great economic difficulties. In this case great care was taken to safeguard the freedom of voting and to mitigate untoward consequences of the partition. In general, however, plebiscites have seldom proved a reliable method of ascertaining the genuine will of the people. History shows that they were mainly used by

[1] Cf. Adam Wolf, *Geschichtliche Bilder aus Oesterreich*, 1878, i, p. 309.

dictators for securing a popular assent to their seizure of power or to annexations. The two Napoleons were very successful in managing plebiscites, which always resulted in overwhelming majorities in their favour, and Hitler has further " improved " upon their methods. Terrorism, of course, played a great rôle in Hitler's plebiscites, but the hypnotizing of the masses by an extraordinary technique of suggestion was also most effective. Exciting speeches and articles full of intoxicating slogans, clever allurements, sinister intimidations, the radio howling at every street corner, gigantic posters and symbols, propaganda by cinema, the fascination exercised by masses marching, shouting and singing, the din of big drums and martial music, the flood of flags, dazzling illumination, the roar of bombers in the air and the clattering of tanks and guns in the street, and the feeling of being surrounded by spying eyes every moment, day and night : all this creates an atmosphere to resist which would require a combination of considerable critical intelligence, extraordinary energy and willingness to sacrifice everything.

True self-determination obviously presupposes conditions which enable a people to form a judgement free from pressure, terror, suggestion, prejudices and ignorance. In normal times there is no terrorism and political misjudgements can as a rule be made good without too much damage ; but issues of national self-determination always arouse passions to a high degree, the calculation of consequences is often extremely difficult, and errors in judgement can seldom be made good in a peaceful way.

The third question implied in the problem of national self-determination is that of its legitimate objects and its limits. A nation cannot interpret this right in the sense of unlimited power to do as it likes, at least not without incurring the risk of self-destruction. International law has in this regard developed many rules, and we need not enter here into the details. The reconstruction of an international reign of law after this war will be faced with the urgent necessity of restricting national Sovereignty much more than hitherto. The bitter experience of recent history leaves no doubt that the idea of unlimited Sovereignty which was disguised as national self-determination has had disastrous consequences. When Hitler militarized the Rhinelands contrary to International Law democratic public opinion in certain countries regarded this as justified by the principle of self-determination. Now everybody realizes that this act was the first step towards Hitler's aim of world-enslavement. Before the last war the mighty Russian Empire never repudiated its obligation under the Treaty of Paris to abstain from any fortification of the Aaland Islands and France respected the neutrality of Haute-Savoie laid down by the Congress of Vienna. The idea of a reign of law implies that nobody is entitled to exercise his rights in a way damaging vital interests of others. Nobody is permitted to set fire to his house with the possibility of destroying adjacent houses.

Denials of self-determination, indeed, have frequently been defended on the ground that otherwise vital interests of another nation would be menaced, and this argument has very often been misused for purposes of aggrandisement or domination. The most frequent cases were the demands for strategical frontiers, for access to the sea and for the possession of natural resources. The invention of aircraft, tanks and submarines, however, has greatly decreased the value of strategical frontiers, and effective defence now depends primarily on industrial potential and man-power. Small nations will only be able to resist a powerful aggressor by combining their forces and forming federations and by the establishment of an international reign of law. Access to the sea and to raw materials can also be achieved by means other than the annexation of territories and the denial of self-determination.

Self-determination, furthermore, has often been denied on the ground that another nation has either in the past opened the country to civilization or is the best suited to do so in the future. The weight of this argument depends on many circumstances. If Mussolini claims extensive non-Italian countries for Italy because the Romans once introduced civilization there, or if Hitler likes to justify his annexations by the civilizing rôle which the Germans have performed in those territories in past centuries, these arguments obviously are nothing else but paltry pretexts for conquest. But nations like Britain, France, Holland and Belgium have certainly a good record as trustees of less developed peoples, and it is clear that their rule is not opposed to self-determination, but rather a preparation for it. A suspension of self-determination may also be justified when a nation is temporarily unable to form a sound national will. This will be the case with Germany and some other States after this war. Hitler has gone far in exterminating those elements among his opponents which were indispensable for the formation of a national will and it will certainly take time till this loss has been made good. A true national will cannot be formed by an amorphous mass, it **depends** on a highly complicated national structure which cannot be reconstructed at once when it has been destroyed.

9. The Rights of National Minorities

There are few countries in the world which possess a population of homogeneous nationality. Many have active national minorities and others have latent ones. In Europe the Western nations are on the whole more homogeneous than those of the East,[1] which is due partly to the fact that Eastern Europe in the past was often invaded by warlike peoples from Asia and was exposed to great movements and mixtures of races, and partly to the fact that the national State developed much earlier in the West and succeeded in amalgamating numerous small peoples into large national units. When later the Eastern nations tried to follow the example of the West by assimilating their minorities, they failed, owing to the facts that in the meantime every people had developed an intense national consciousness and that the rise of Liberal principles had rendered any large absorption of minorities by official pressure almost impossible.

The Peace Treaties of 1919–20 formed a number of new national States, and, since these comprised large national minorities, also imposed upon them certain obligations designed to protect these minorities against denationalization. These obligations were embodied in a number of treaties and declarations, and the League of Nations was entrusted with the supreme control of their execution. Some agreements, furthermore, were concluded between different States with the object of safeguarding the position of certain minorities. The League of Nations, indeed, made great efforts to protect minority rights and its influence was certainly beneficial.[2] If its rôle, nevertheless, was widely criticized and found ineffective, this was not due to a lack of zeal or efficiency on the part of the League but to the enormous difficulties inherent in the problem.

The minority rights guaranteed by the Peace Treaties were very restricted in scope and there is, for instance, no doubt that the actual measure of protection which minorities enjoyed in the former Austrian State was greater than that afforded by the

---

[1] Cf. especially the excellent survey on these conditions given by C. A. Macartney, *National States and National Minorities*, 1934.
[2] The practice and achievements of the League of Nations have been described in Lucie P. Mair, *The Protection of Minorities*, 1928. The procedure has been discussed in detail in Julius Stone, *International Guarantees of Minority Rights*, 1932. Cf. further W. O'Sullivan Molony, *Nationality and the Peace Treaties*, 1934.

Treaties, though certain of the Succession-States granted their minorities somewhat more extensive rights than the minimum prescribed by the Treaties. Most Succession-States, however, resented the restriction of their Sovereignty implied in the minority treaties, and some of them strongly opposed their subjection to any international control as incompatible with their national independence, and consequently tried to evade their obligations. Poland even openly repudiated her obligations under the treaty. The Succession-States particularly resented the fact that no similar obligations in the interests of minorities were imposed upon the Great Powers. Italy indeed committed the worst acts of oppression against the German-Austrian and Slovene minorities annexed by her after the war. Germany also was free from such restrictions, except in Upper Silesia, and subsequently the Nazis could treat minorities with the greatest brutality. Finally, the general policy of the League was characterized by timidity and weakness in reprimanding and correcting arbitrary acts of member-States. This was the inevitable consequence of the constitution of the League itself and of its lack of any real power.

The clauses of the treaties which promised minorities equal civil rights, " facilities " for the use of their language in the law courts and in their primary (though not in the secondary) schools and so on, although valuable, merely touched the fringe of the problem. Even where special agreements granted minorities more than minimum rights, their actual position in many cases remained unsatisfactory. They complained that they had no adequate share in the civil service, especially in the higher posts, that their special economic and cultural interests were neglected or violated, that they had no political influence, that the conduct of foreign policy was opposed to their national sentiments and that many officials showed great partiality and animosity in dealing with their requests. Many of these grievances were certainly justified while many others were grossly exaggerated. The relations of nations are so vitiated by distrust and jealousy and by open or veiled striving for superiority and domination that contending nations see every question in a wholly different light. The difficulties of minority protection consist in the facts that the State to-day has power to control almost the whole life of the citizens and thereby possesses countless possibilities of discriminating, and that any special protection of minorities under international control implies a limitation both of national Sovereignty and of the principle of majority which is considered essential for democracy. The solution of the problem, therefore, would require that both the majority and the minority were imbued with respect for human rights and with sympathetic understanding for each other which unfortunately is very rarely the case. In theory democracy is internationally-minded, but in practice even nations with a great democratic and humanitarian tradition are often unable to overcome national prejudices and animosities. This is particularly apparent from their treatment of racial elements which differ in the colour of their skin, or are supposed to possess different " blood ". Another instance is the attitude of many modern democracies to aliens who do not constitute national minorities but who wish to settle in a country as individuals, to earn their living by honest work, to become citizens and to be recognized as nationals. The attitude of large and influential sections to these problems was often characterized by extraordinary narrowmindedness which was a combination of economic jealousy and national arrogance. Other sections of the same nation at the same time have often exhibited a totally different spirit and have done everything in their power to combat racial and national prejudices, and to give the foreigner a fair chance.

Individuals who have sprung from a national minority or who have lived among a foreign nation have made a particularly great contribution to the rise of nationalism. In Germany before the last war the spread of Pan-German sentiment and the growth of hostility towards Russia and the Slavs were to a great extent the work of Germans from the Baltic provinces of the Russian Empire. The Baltic Germans formed an intellectually very active and energetic group with an aristocratic tradition, and for a long time they had provided the Tsars with many excellent officers, administrators, scholars and industrialists. The growth of Russian nationalism considerably restricted their rôle, and led to oppressive measures against the German minorities. Many of them emigrated to Germany where they had family contacts with the nobility and obtained influential posts in the army, in the civil service and in intellectual life. Their share in stimulating German nationalism was very great. A similar rôle was played by German intellectuals from the mixed territories of Austria-Hungary, who harboured the memories of countless local frictions with Slavs or Magyars and were imbued with bitter animosity against them. Adolf Hitler can only be rightly understood as the product of the mentality of this group as adapted to the level of the lower semi-intelligentsia. The " Auslands-

Deutschen" (Germans living abroad), or at least large sections of them, were also particularly ardent nationalists, and besides Hitler many of his closest collaborators such as Rosenberg, Hess and Darré, belong to this class. The phenomenon, however, is not exclusively a German one. In other nations too it is exhibited by individuals who have returned to their home country after long residence abroad where they had often enjoyed a privileged position, and had had to face national animosities and the rising tide of another people which they had come to look upon as inferior. Many retired colonial officials or officers of various nations are said to possess a special contempt of coloured races.

CHAPTER VII

THE SOCIAL BACKGROUND OF MODERN NATIONALISM

1. Opinions on the Causes of the Rise of Nationalism
   The Influence of Ruling Classes

Opinions on the causes of the rise of aggressive nationalism in our age are widely divergent owing to differences in political ideology, or in the sociological or philosophical outlook. Political parties are compelled to oversimplify the explanation of social facts, and to look at them from a one-sided point of view. Abstract thinkers, too, often incline to overstating one single factor. The recent rise of nationalism, however, cannot be traced to one cause only, and an objective investigation must take account of many forces.

Liberals and democrats ascribe the phenomenon to the ambitions of kings, the aristocracy and professional soldiers; they see in the rise of aggressiveness a relapse into the spirit of the past, and also stress the influence of economic distress and the lack of political education. Conservatives point out that the rise of nationalism coincided with the decline of monarchies and religion and that it was precisely certain modern achievements like our technique of production and propaganda which have made possible the fury of present national enmities and national wars. Socialists burden capitalism with the responsibility, they interpret international rivalries as the conflict of the striving of the capitalists of different nations to monopolize markets, and they regard the slogans of national honour or unity merely as pretexts for breaking the power of the working class. The nationalists, on the other hand, like to describe their policy as aiming at the political and economic freedom of their nation.

In discussing these allegations it will be found that they all mix truth with untruth, and that they all oversimplify the problem. As regards the warlike propensities of rulers and ruling classes, history, indeed, offers many striking instances. In former ages the aristocracy was primarily a warrior-class, and the king often had to wage war in order to employ them abroad and to prevent them from devastating his own realm and thereby destroying national unity. Sometimes, however, a king was even more warlike than the privileged classes. On the whole, a new dynasty and especially a usurper, had more need of wars for stabilizing and increasing their prestige than old-established dynasties. Napoleon said in 1812 to the Austrian ambassador Prince Schwarzenberg, who offered mediation, that he would never accept a humiliating peace as it would overthrow him. He was a usurper and dependent on public opinion. The French had a lively imagination, they liked glory and excitement, and were of a nervous temper. The real cause of the overthrow of the Bourbons by the French Revolution was the defeat of Rossbach.[1] The unpopularity of the Stuarts which led to the English Revolution was partly due to the peaceable policy of James I and the military reverses of Charles I. The downfall of Louis Philippe in 1848 was largely caused by the discontent of the Left with the peace-policy of the government. Bismarck says in his memoirs [2] that among European peoples on the whole those kings were the most popular and beloved who had been the most warlike, for instance, Charles XII of Sweden, Louis XIV and Napoleon. There is no example, he says, in the history of European peoples, that sincere and conscientious attention to their peaceful welfare had ever satisfied their emotions as much as the glory of war, victorious battles and the conquest of foreign territories.

The spirit of the aristocratic warrior-class has in the course of time undergone great changes, and in countries like Britain or France it has been assimilated to the general mentality. More or less this has also been the case as regards the professional soldiers and the view of many pacifists that aggressiveness is inherent in every army and navy and that, therefore, all nations which have not disarmed are equally militaristic cannot be taken seriously. A soldier is naturally disposed to look on politics from a military point of view which easily leads to militarism; but it is obvious that in countries like Britain and France the counterforces in public opinion for a long time have been so powerful that even the mentality of many soldiers has been deeply affected by them. Even in Germany the warlike traditions of the Prussian Junkers were not at all shared by the whole aristocracy. The huge collections of diplomatic correspondence on the origins of the last Great War show that the great majority of aristocratic diplomatists were sincere friends of peace who did their best to prevent war. This holds good even for the leading representatives of Germany in Britain such as Hatzfeld, Eckardstein, Wolf-Metternich, and Lichnowsky.

[1] Cf. John Holland Rose, *Napoleon I*, vol. ii, chap. 33.
[2] Bismarck, *Gedanken und Erinnerungen*, iii, 1919, p. 123.

Nevertheless, monarchs and their advisers have even in modern times occasionally had a great share in aggravating national tensions and the making of wars. No careful student of the diplomatic documents relating to the last Great War can deny that the Emperor William II is burdened with the overwhelming responsibility for the deep antagonism between the Germans and other nations, and the great conflagration. He was, of course, not the only guilty man in Germany, and one can dispute that he really wanted a war. Yet his rôle in making it unavoidable was decisive. The deeper causes of his policy must be sought in his excessive vanity, and neuropathic disposition, in the sway of nationalist and militarist ideas over his mind, and in his wish to check the rapid progress of the democratic spirit in Germany by a dazzling policy of expansion and military glory. It is interesting to compare this attitude of the Kaiser with that of his cousin Tsar Nicholas II who was also afraid of the growth of the democratic forces in his Empire. Nicholas was much less intelligent than William; yet he realized that a war might greatly strengthen the revolutionary movement and he did his best to avoid it. Events showed that he had had a clearer vision of the consequences of war than the Kaiser.

The view that the progress of violent nationalism was due to certain much praised achievements of our civilization contains some truth which, however, must not be exaggerated. There is hardly any cultural achievement which has not been misused for war or other sinister purposes. Yet there is no alternative. We can only state that the danger exists and try to avoid it, but nobody in his senses would suggest we should destroy all chemical factories because they might be misused for making poison gas.

2. THE INFLUENCE OF CAPITALISM. WAR AND CAPITALISM

The view is very popular to-day that aggressive nationalism is nothing else but an ideological screen for the selfish interests of capitalists. It is capitalism, according to this view, which necessarily leads to wars, and since nobody would fight merely for increasing the profits of Big Business the money-magnates must employ slogans that appeal to the masses such as national security, national interests, or national honour. This theory is not only preached by Communists and Socialists, it has also found acceptance in wide circles of the middle class who are not outspoken Socialists, especially among intellectuals and pacifists, and the nationalists also like to play on the general antipathy against capitalists. Hitler and Mussolini denounce the Western democracies as " pluto-democracies " or as the instruments of capitalistic Jewish warmongers. As to the question, however, what is to be understood by capitalism and for what reasons and how capitalism brings about war, opinions greatly differ.

The most obvious connexion between the interests of certain capitalists and war seems to be the case of the armament industries.[1] It seems clear to most people that manufacturers of guns must have the greatest interest in increasing the demand for guns and that propaganda for war is the best investment for them. Another group of theories does not restrict responsibility to this special industry, but tries to prove that it is the capitalistic system as such which engenders war. Some of these explanations are based on the under-consumption theory which has been put forward in various forms by economists. The gist of this theory is that capitalism reduces the wages of the workers to a minimum and thereby diminishes their buying-power too. The consequence is that they cannot buy sufficient goods from industrial and agricultural producers, and that economic crises and unemployment break out. The industrialists who cannot sell all their products to the under-paid working classes of their own countries are forced to seek markets abroad, and this kindles rivalries between the industrial nations for the appropriation of territories which culminate in wars. The most influential representative of this theory in the English-speaking countries was J. A. Hobson.[2] Some economists, however, have used this argument merely for explaining unemployment without going so far as to assert that under-consumption leads to a scramble for expansion and to wars.

Hilferding and Lenin have put forward another theory which attributes the responsibility for war not to the exporters of goods but to the exporters of capital, to finance-capital, or the big banks. They maintain that the concentration of production and capital results in the formation of big concerns which try to secure a monopolistic position by developing the production of vital materials in all parts of the world, and concentrating them in their hands. This striving results in a clashing of rival groups and finally in wars for the possession of territories rich

---

[1] The thesis that armament industries are the cause of war has been treated in a careful and interesting way by Philip Noel-Baker, *The Private Manufacture of Armaments*, vol. i, 1936.

[2] Cf. J. A. Hobson, *Imperialism*, 3rd (e. rely revised) ed., 1938.

in resources and industries. Still another theory lays the main stress on the striving of capitalists for the suppression of the Labour Movement at home. It is the fear of socialism and the trade unions which induces them to give financial support to movements which promise to divert the masses from their real interests, and which aim at the elimination of class-war by arousing national hatred and wars against other nations and by establishing a dictatorship.

The armament-industries, indeed, in order to sell their products must keep in close touch with high military circles, and to a certain extent they will be likely to share their outlook and support their policy. It is also true that many wars were a source of great enrichment not only to manufacturers of armaments but also to other suppliers of goods necessary for warfare and to financiers.[1] In our time conditions have greatly changed, partly through experience gathered from former wars, and partly through the rise of democracy. The war-industries proper form but a small part of the industries of a country, and what they gain through a war is by far outweighed by the loss of other industries through war-conditions. Most armaments, moreover, are produced by firms which manufacture also goods that only sell well in peace-times. Their interest therefore is divided, and it may be that they lose much more through the reduction of civilian consumption and of new investments for this purpose, such as motor cars, building materials or railway-carriages, than they could ever gain by increasing the output of armaments. The time of great war-profits on supplies for the army has passed. They were possible at a time when the governments had little experience in safe-guarding their financial interests, and were unable or unwilling to go far in controlling industries. The reaction of public opinion to the scandal of war-profiteering and the political evolution after the last war have radically changed the situation. In the democratic countries severe measures have been taken to restrict war-profits to a minimum, by means of excess-profit taxes, fixing of prices, suppression of credits for speculative purposes, prevention of inflation, and so on. The most striking proof that capitalists in general do not believe in wars as a means of increasing their profits is the fact that in recent times the mere prospect of becoming involved in a war, and still more its outbreak, have regularly led to a great fall of

---

[1] The historical relations between capitalism and war have been described in great detail by Werner Sombart first in his book *Krieg and Kapitalismus*, 1912, and then in his work *Der moderne Kapitalismus*, 3 (in 6) vols., several editions.

the prices of industrial shares on the stock-markets, even of the prices of armament industries and often to a long period of low quotations.

Manufacturers of armaments may sometimes have aggravated tension by making use of the distrust between certain nations for inducing them to buy more guns or other implements of war. But an examination of the available evidence leads to the conclusion that their influence on the outbreak of wars has been grossly overestimated. It would not have made the slightest difference if the armament works had been owned by the State. The idea that it is mainly the increase of armaments which is the source of war springs from an ideology which misunderstands the real motives of aggressive nationalism.

Neither does historical research confirm the view that modern wars are mainly a struggle for the possession of markets or natural resources. In the age of Mercantilism such motives, indeed, played a great rôle in causing wars ; but the fundamental conditions of trade have completely changed since that time, as will shortly be shown. In particular, the different versions of the under-consumption theory are either refuted by accurate economic analysis [1] or do not bear out the charge against capitalism but only incriminate the monetary system. Secondly, the historical investigation of the origin of modern wars shows that in the great majority of cases they had nothing or very little to do with a struggle for markets. Professor Robbins in his excellent book, quoted below, gives many instances which make this absolutely clear, and it would be easy to multiply them. After the last Great War, and also after other wars, all the diplomatic dispatches and numerous memoirs relating to the events have been published in the countries concerned in order to clear up the question of war-guilt. Their careful study is absolutely indispensable for forming an adequate judgement on the causes of these wars. Yet these documents furnish no proofs of a large share of industrial or financial influence in bringing about the outbreak of war. True, governments sometimes put forward the necessity of protecting the export trade as an argument for armaments or for a warlike policy ; but in most cases this was mere propaganda for winning the support of sections of the people who had no interest in a policy of prestige and power. In cases of great colonial enterprises it was frequently the governments which first induced the banks or industries to embark on

---

[1] Cf. Lionel Robbins, *The Economic Causes of War*, 1939, and Hellmut Gottschalk, *Die Kaufkraftlehre*, 1932.

these ventures, which they often did only reluctantly. The real motives of certain governments was the increase of national power and prestige, and the alleged economic interests were merely a pretext. The financiers and industrialists of different nations were usually eager to co-operate with one another, and to share the risks in developing the resources of backward countries, and it was the governments which often vetoed this for political reasons. The documents further show that leading financiers and heads of great enterprises such as the Rothschilds,[1] Cassel, Ballin, Schwabach, Siemens, Gwinner, Wiegand, Caillaux, had a horror of a policy which might lead to war, and did their best to smooth down international tensions and to secure peace.

A special case was that of the great German iron-magnates of Rhineland-Westfalia and of other German industrialists who supported the Pan-German League, which stood for a policy of aggressive nationalism. The brothers Mannesmann tried with the help of the League to induce the German Government to defend their claims to mining rights in Morocco against the French Government, and this could, indeed, have led to a serious conflict. But the Government denied its support and the Chancellor Bethmann-Hollweg sharply reprimanded the League for its propaganda, and even refused to accept its protest. It is interesting to note that Hugo Stinnes, who was the most prominent Pan-German industrialist, entirely took the side of the Chancellor, and condemned the attacks of the League on him. The Chairman and leader of the League, Heinrich Class, relates in his memoirs that Stinnes told him frankly that his whole policy of stressing political power was wrong. Economic power, Stinnes said, was much more important, and he was constantly buying up mines and industries all over Europe. Only a few years' peace and Germany would quietly acquire economic predominance in Europe. The noisy propaganda of the League for a German share in the resources of Morocco was a nuisance. The brothers Mannesmann had proceeded in a clumsy and brutal way. If the League had not stirred up public opinion abroad about the rich resources of Morocco, he could have quietly secured the ore deposits together with large tracts of land.[2] Class, of course, was greatly upset by this rebuke, and remarks that this attitude revealed that one could be the greatest

[1] Cf. H. Frh. v. Eckardstein, *Lebenserinnerungen*, 1919, vol. i, p. 268.
[2] Cf. Heinrich Class, *Wider den Strom. Vom Werden und Wachsen der nationalen Opposition im alten Reich*, 1932, p. 217.

merchant and the most successful industrialist in Germany, far superior to all others, and yet in politics lack every instinct and judgement. The incident was very significant indeed, though in another sense than Class meant. Stinnes was a Pan-German and during the war supported plans of annexation. But he was still more an industrial organizer of great experience, and for this reason he had quite a different mentality from that of the average nationalists who believed that the only method of furthering national interests was to bang the mailed fist on the table. The bankers who were much less infected with Pan-Germanism showed this spirit to a still greater degree. A German Secretary for Foreign Affairs remarked : " As soon as you mention Morocco, the banks all go on strike."

The belief that wars are mainly caused by the conflicting interests of capitalists has been particularly propagated by many enemies of Great Britain who wanted to mask their own greed for conquest by putting the responsibility on the other side. The two classical arguments which were used innumerable times were the alleged commercial envy of England of her competitors and the Boer War. Before the last Great War it was the German nationalists who made the most unscrupulous use of these arguments, though they were not the only ones. The capitalistic origin of the Boer War, furthermore, has been stressed also by English politicians who combated the policy of Chamberlain. Yet the movement against the Kruger oligarchy was not primarily the work of capitalists. The leaders came at first from the working class and attacked the capitalists, who kept aloof. This changed later on through the intervention of Cecil Rhodes, who induced some of the mine-owners to support the movement, while others remained neutral or even hostile. To describe Rhodes as actuated mainly by capitalistic motives is nonsense. In reality, the war was a clash between two nationalist movements, both striving for predominance.[1] The legend of British commercial envy as the cause of the German-English conflict is still more unfounded. I have dealt with this at length in another book,[2] and have shown that it is in complete disagreement with the facts. After the last war even the German historians abandoned this myth.

There is more truth in the argument that employers have

[1] Cf. for proofs Edward Cook, *Rights and Wrongs of the Transvaal War*, 1901, p. 250, and also my book F. Hertz, *Recht und Unrecht im Boerenkriege*, 1902, in which I combated the Pan-German distortion of the causes of the war which aimed at preparing the German people for a conflict with Great Britain.
[2] Cf. F. Hertz, *Nationalgeist und Politik*, 1937, vol. i, p. 262.

subsidized Fascist movements in order to break the power of organized labour which, however, does not prove that they wanted to bring about war. It is probably the most widespread view of the causes of Nazism that Hitler merely was the tool of the capitalists, who financed him for their own economic purposes. Yet this view is entirely misleading; it obscures the real nature of that movement, and tends to result in a political attitude which weakens the combat against nationalism and Fascism. Though Hitler was always eager for contacts with wealthy people whom he tapped for money,[1] he was never their pawn nor was his party mainly financed by them. The bulk of the funds which were required for his colossal propaganda were raised from the rank and file by his power as a stump-orator and political organiser. In 1931 the party possessed 800,000 registered members, of whom each paid at least 12 marks a year, and further vast amounts flowed in from the sale of books, newspapers, tickets to his meetings, etc. Nevertheless, in 1932 the party was faced with bankruptcy; its debts were estimated at 12 million marks. In these straits Hitler made a supreme effort to win the big industrialists for financial help on a large scale. His middle-man was Otto Dietrich, who had family-connexions with the iron and coal magnates and had already introduced him to some of them. Dietrich has given us a vivid description of how Hitler won over the industrialists.[2] As he says, the great majority of them before 1932 refused to have faith in Hitler and firmly clung to the system of the Weimar Republic. On January 27, 1932, the Industrial Club at Duesseldorf held a meeting which was addressed by Hitler. Most of the members had only come from curiosity, in a spirit of scepticism, and at the beginning the " vast majority bore an air of superiority and cool reserve ". Hitler received a " chilly reception "; but the meeting later warmed up. Hitler contrasted the unselfish idealism of the German youth and his working-class followers with the lack of comprehension and materialism of the wealthy bourgeoisie. At last Hitler, Dietrich says, " succeeded in piercing the armour of the West German industrial magnates " and the result was the same in the subsequent meetings at other places. Heiden, however, asserts on good authority that only a third of the audience applauded and that the majority remained lukewarm or negative.[3] Anyhow, Hitler from this time received considerable contributions from

[1] Cf. Konrad Heiden, *Hitler* (Engl. ed.), 1936, pp. 100, 232–41.
[2] Cf. Otto Dietrich, *With Hitler on the Road to Power*, 1934.
[3] Konrad Heiden, *Geburt des Dritten Reichs*, 1934, p. 41.

the organizations of employers. Fritz Thyssen, the greatest iron magnate and richest man of Germany, who at that time was his enthusiastic follower, gave him over several years altogether 1 million marks ; but few other industrialists gave him great amounts.[1] The associations of employers made contributions to a fund collected by Hugenberg, who placed about a fifth at the disposal of Hitler. All in all, the amounts given by heavy industry to the Nazis according to Thyssen amounted to 2 million marks a year, apart from subscriptions for special purposes.

Hitler satisfied the expectations of certain industrialists that he would smash the trade unions and the socialists and his economic policy increased the share of profits in the national income while the share of wages remained practically constant.[2] It was mainly the armament industries, however, which profited, while the production of consumption goods lagged far behind. In the long run, Hitler's economic policy greatly disappointed the industrialists. Thyssen fled to France and in his Memoirs violently attacks the Nazi system. He comes to the conclusion that this regime has ruined German industry (p. 188) and gives ample proofs for this opinion.

Historical facts, therefore, prove that Hitler received large subsidies from rich industrialists who thereby saved him from great financial troubles and strengthened his striking power. But these subsidies were given when his movement was already the greatest political party in Germany, as was demonstrated by the elections of 1932. Many of the industrialists obviously thought it good business to put their money on the winning horse. Most of the money which enabled Hitler to win the race for power came from the masses. Konrad Heiden, who has written the most valuable history of Hitler's rise, shows [3] that it was a mighty wave of anti-capitalistic and socialist sentiment which carried him to power. Hitler cleverly exploited both the forces of socialism and of capitalism ; but he never became the captive of either. One could say that he double-crossed both the capitalists and the socialists among his followers and led them on a road which they had not expected or desired, though subsequently large numbers of both sections were intoxicated and carried away by his unprecedented triumphs.

Cool-headed and far-seeing businessmen have usually realized

---

[1] Cf. Fritz Thyssen, *I Paid Hitler*, 1941, p. 133.
[2] Cf. C. Guillebaud, *The Economic Recovery of Germany*, 1939, p. 244.
[3] K. Heiden, *Geburt des Dritten Reichs*, pp. 38, 48, 88, 233.

that nothing was more dangerous to their interests than a warlike policy. Under the conditions of our time profits from war are transient and fictitious and every war, moreover, implies the possibility that a victory must be paid for by concessions to the working classes and that a defeat may lead to a social revolution.[1] These prospects have in the last years before this war determined the conservative and capitalistic classes of Great Britain and America to support a policy of appeasement and isolationism at almost any price and until the last possible moment. Hitler knew very well that he could rely on the horror of war which inspired both the capitalists and the working classes in the democratic countries. There are also many examples of great capitalists like Carnegie, Rockefeller, Nobel, Rhodes, Nuffield, Rosenwald, who were convinced that a peaceful world order was the first necessity for progress and civilization, and who generously endowed foundations or assisted activities directed at that aim. The Society of Friends which professes radical pacifism also comprises a large number of very wealthy industrialists. These different categories of peace-loving capitalists certainly by far outweigh the number of warlike ones.

Quite another question is whether the present economic system, which is only partly capitalistic, indirectly and unintentionally fosters the development of forces menacing peace. The excessive protectionism of our time, for instance, certainly contributes to social frictions, and mass-unemployment which have paved the way for Hitler. It is by no means sure, however, that these phenomena were mainly due to capitalism and they were not exclusively to be found in " capitalist " countries. The Soviet Union restricts imports and migrations even more than these, and is not free from unemployment, though in disguise.

The view that aggressive nationalism and wars were exclusively due to capitalism has made many people blind to the forces which really make for war. Many socialists, for instance, disbelieved in the danger of nationalism infecting the working classes, they were so sure that these were immune against its slogans, that they did not consider it necessary to take sufficient precautions.

[1] The German Foreign Secretary Kiderlen-Wächter said in 1910 in a confidential conversation one of the reasons why he was absolutely against a war was that a victory was always the work of the people which had to be paid for by enlargement of its rights. Germany had had to pay for the victory of 1870 by granting the general vote, and a new victory would bring parliamentary government which he would regard as an irretrievable misfortune. Cf. Kiderlen-Wächter, *Briefwechsel und Nachlass hsg. von E. Jäckh*, 1924, p. 234.

3. THE RELATIONS OF NATIONALISM TO LIBERALISM, DEMOCRACY
AND SOCIALISM

The spirit of liberalism, democracy and socialism has in the course of time undergone great changes. In the ancient world democracy was not liberal, cosmopolitan and peaceable, but intolerant, nationalistic and aggressive. The socialism of Plato and other philosophers was aristocratic. The ancient forerunner of liberalism was Stoicism; it was cosmopolitan and set its hopes on the enlightened spirit of absolute rulers of great Empires. The main causes of these differences in comparison with our time were that the Greeks and Romans never had anything comparable to modern industrialism and world trade, and the spirit of their religion. The peaceableness of modern democracy and its recognition of the inviolable Rights of Man are mainly due to Christianity and to modern economic development. Before the French Revolution liberalism showed an aristocratic and cosmopolitan character, but later it became a middle-class movement with democratic tendencies and indulged in the cult of the nation and the romantic praise of national individuality. In the nineteenth century liberal, democratic and national movements were closely interconnected.[1] Their alliance was founded in the fact that they had a common enemy in autocratic Empires ruling over various nationalities and in the necessity of overcoming the dissolving forces of political individualism which threatened to lead to anarchy. The old monarchies reposed on dynastic loyalties sanctioned by religion, but with the decline of these forces another loyalty was needed. Nationality became a religion. Liberals and democrats believed that every nation liberated from foreign domination and constituted in its own national State would be peaceable and tolerant, and that the triumph of the principle of nationality would inaugurate the era of Liberty, Equality and Fraternity. The rise of socialism implied a new change in ideology. In principle, class solidarity took precedence of national solidarity; but in practical politics democratic socialism to a great extent continued the traditions of liberal democracy in regard to nationality.

Modern democracy, though opposed to aggression and conquest, approved of war for the defence of democracy or for national liberation. The French Revolution, moreover, resorted to war in order to prevent the revolutionary spirit from slackening. The Jacobins wanted war as an instrument of propaganda and stimu-

[1] Cf. G. Weill, *L'Europe du XIX siècle et l'idée de nationalité*, 1938.

lation, but their wars of liberation soon became wars of conquest. The Jacobin tradition for a long time dominated the thought of democrats in France and elsewhere. Typical was the thought of Louis Blanc, one of the outstanding socialists of the Revolution of 1848, who advocated not only wars for revolutionizing Europe but also for large-scale conquest. The peaceableness of Louis Philippe and the bourgeois politicians was sharply criticized by him, and his instigations to war sound like the phrases of a rabid chauvinist, though he uses democratic and socialist arguments.[1]

The founders of German Socialism, Marx, Engels, Lassalle, Liebknecht and others, have all set their hope on great wars which would lead to the military defeat of Russia and other reactionary powers, and would give them an opportunity of starting revolutions. Their whole ideas of international policy aimed at bringing about such wars. Marx did not recognize the right of every nation to self-determination; his judgement of specific nations depended exclusively on their aptness to further the world-revolution. As most Slav nations of the Austrian Empire seemed to him to be supporters of conservatism and reaction, he spoke of them with greatest contempt and denied them the right to national self-determination. Both Marx and Lassalle have sometimes put forward ideas which greatly resemble those of Pan-Germanism though their motives were different. Also Italian and Slav radicals have often combined in their creed democratic, socialist and nationalist ideas, and preached wars of aggression and expansion. In the wars of the United States with Britain (1812) and with Spain (1898) it was certainly the American democracy which was the aggressor.

In spite of the fact that modern democracy is inspired by the wish for peace, and in spite of its belief in the equality of nations, it has nevertheless in many ways contributed to the rise of aggressive nationalism. The two principal dogmas of democracy are the sovereignty of the people and equality, and both principles have led to the doctrine of State-omnipotence which favours the rise of nationalism.[2] A claim to freedom from State-interference often appears to democrats and socialists as a claim to a privileged position and, therefore, as contrary both to the sovereignty of the people and to equality. The striving for equality, furthermore,

---

[1] The attitude of Democrats and Socialists to war and to nationality is carefully surveyed and discussed in the important books by Karl Kautsky, *Krieg und Demokratie*, 1932; *Sozialisten und Krieg*, 1937.
[2] Cf. on the incompatibility of the dogma of sovereignty with democracy, H. Laski, *Foundations of Sovereignty*, 1921, p. 129.

often went so far that its results appeared to its opponents as a new sort of inequality, namely, as the attempt of ignoring inequalities assumed to be rooted in the rights of individuality and in the functional structure of society. Levelling tendencies often led to fierce struggles between the classes and to the disintegration of national unity, and this usually enabled an ambitious ruler or general or demagogue to rise to supreme power, and to become a dictator, by arousing national passion against foreign nations, and by using wars as an instrument for restoring national unity.

Democracy and socialism demand the equality of individuals in a given society, but usually they shrink from extending this demand to international relations, or confine themselves to suggestions which are either ineffective or impossible of realization. Considerable inequalities, indeed, exist between nations, and to a great extent they have originated either through conquest or through economic development in a capitalistic form. It is not merely the upper classes of the possessing nations which profit from these inequalities, but it is the nations as a whole which are affected by the fact that some of them have abundance of land, capital and natural resources and others very little, that some are advanced in civilization and others backward, that some are creditors and others debtors. In the age of liberalism these inequalities were not regarded as onerous by the public opinion of most nations. Liberals did not grudge a nation its greater wealth or more advanced civilization or at least did not regard them as legitimate grounds for a policy of aggression. Many countries, moreover, were more or less open to foreigners who wanted to sell their goods or find employment. These conditions had the result that Britain, who then far surpassed all other countries in wealth and territorial extent and in freedom of trade, was on the whole looked upon with friendly feelings, though in some countries a sentiment of rivalry was not absent. This sentiment gradually increased with the rise of nationalism both in foreign nations and within the British Empire, and it was also furthered by the attitude of socialists to English capitalism. Marx and Engels, for example, often represented England as a capitalist nation exploiting all other nations which were depressed by her to the status of proletarians.[1] They also pointed out that the English working class profited from this position and, therefore, was for the time being not interested in socialism, though this would change when

---

[1] Cf. the statements by Marx and Engels quoted in Heinrich Cunow, *Die Marxsche Geschichts-, Gesellschafts- und Staatstheorie*, 1920–1, vol. ii, p. 25. This book gives also a good survey of the ideas on nationality held by Marx and prominent Marxists.

the English workers would also be depressed to a low level by the further development of capitalism. Marx and Engels, however, did not attribute this to England's possession of colonies and showed no interest in a redistribution of these. In their view it was due to the fact that England was the most capitalistic country of the world. Neither Marx nor the German Social Democrats have ever advocated the use of force for liberating the proletarian nations from English " exploitation ". This argument was later employed by German and other nationalists who refused to be satisfied with the economic opportunities offered by Britain's policy of the " open door " and who denounced the British Empire as an oppressive monopoly. The Fascists described their struggle against Britain in terms of a social conflict, as a rise of proletarian " have-nots " against the capitalistic " haves ". In fact, of course, this argument was merely a propaganda slogan, though a very effective one. If it is taken for granted that inequality in wealth justifies the expropriation of the rich, irrespective of how they have acquired their wealth or what use they make of it, then many people would find it difficult to understand that this principle must not be applied to relations between nations.[1] Well-meaning people have put forward the idea of internationalizing the colonies and thereby guaranteeing equal opportunities to all nations. But in an age of nationalism this plan has not the slightest chance of realization; it would neither work nor satisfy the nationalists, and it would prejudice the claim of the native populations to self-government. The inequality in the possession of colonies is only one of the grievances of nationalists, and in many cases of conflict plays no part at all. In many national struggles, for instance in those of the Irish, the Indians and various nations of central and eastern Europe, one nation accuses another that it is a capitalistic exploiter and that it has acquired this position by conquest and oppression. In India the Hindus use this argument against the British; but the Moslems who combat the Hindu claim to predominance in the whole of India and who want a separate Moslem State, charge the Hindus of being capitalistic usurers, sponging upon the poor Moslem peasants.[2]

[1] T. H. Huxley has put forward this argument in a witty form. Cf. Murray, vol. ii, p. 263.
[2] Antisemitism which is so typical of all movement of violent nationalism is also often defended with arguments of social liberty and equality. The Social Democratic Party of Germany at the Congress of Cologne of 1893 declared that Antisemitism sprang from a revolt against capitalism, which, however, went in the wrong direction, and a prominent Socialist leader at another occasion said that Antisemitism was the socialism of the simpletons.

In recent times democratic and socialist movements have as a rule become averse to revolutionary wars. This was partly due to the fact that the development of political liberty had made great progress towards democratic equality which discarded the motives for revolution. On the other hand, a great change has taken place in leadership. In former times the leaders of democracy and socialism were intellectuals who were mostly disciples of Rousseau, Fichte and Hegel, and their revolutionary inclinations were due to their cultural and social background. Among the founders of modern socialism, in particular, were hardly any proletarians, they mostly came from the upper classes. In later times the trade unions and other working-class organizations developed and a large number of workers or former workers rose to leading positions in the Labour Movement. This new class of leaders was honest, well-trained, and efficient, and had no interest in revolutionary activities though they often did some lip-service to Marxist doctrines. Above all they were thoroughly peaceable and professed pacifism and internationalism. Their weakness was that they had not sufficient understanding for questions of international politics and especially for the psychological forces underlying nationalism and power politics. They hated militarism and nationalism but regarded them as a mere disguise of capitalist or aristocratic interests which could never conquer great masses and could not compete with the forces of democracy. When a war threatened, they were convinced, the workers of the countries concerned would go on strike and make it impossible. The lack of realism in these views was revealed in 1914 when German militarism suddenly used the Austro-Serbian conflict for plunging Europe into war. On July 25 the Social Democratic Party protested in a manifesto in the most vigorous way against the war policy of the Austro-Hungarian Government which they branded as frivolous, brutal, provocative and criminal. They demanded that the German Government should use all their influence for peace, and if this shameful war should break out, abstain from any participation in it. This attitude was quite sincere. Nevertheless on August 4th the Social Democrats in Parliament voted almost unanimously for the war credits.[1] Several factors were responsible for this sudden change. The principal cause was that the Government with great skill convinced the people that Russia had suddenly and treacherously attacked Germany. This was a lie ; but it had full success. The result

[1] Cf. for the causes of this sudden change K. Kautsky, *Sozialisten und Krieg*, pp. 438 f., and K. Grünberg, *Die Internationale und der Weltkrieg. Materialien*, 1916, vol. i.

was an enormous outburst of popular emotions and passions which completely carried away the socialists in Parliament. They saw in their minds their country overrun and their homes and families threatened by a ruthless enemy who was hateful to all democrats for his tyranny. The main fault of the leaders, therefore, was that they did not resist the impact of mass-hysteria. On the other hand, it is understandable that the great mass of the people was quite unable to find out the truth and act accordingly in that critical hour. The enormous majority had never bothered in the least about international affairs, and had not the slightest idea of the real situation. Even most of the democratic leaders were rather ignorant in this respect, and a few of them were infected by nationalism themselves. The average democratic politician, moreover, had grown up in the belief that the people was always right, and that his duty was simply to do what the people wanted. In normal times this illusion was not so dangerous because errors of popular opinion could be criticized by all the means of public discussion, and saner views could be spread before it was too late. At this moment this was out of the question as the Government had the power to suppress all criticism. Particularly condemnable, however, was the attitude of the greatest German scholars, writers and artists who vied in expressions of the most violent nationalism, vicious vituperations of the enemies and the most absurd national self-praise.[1]

The tragic helplessness of great democratic parties in a most critical time was again demonstrated after the war. In 1930 the central government of Germany was still dominated by the Social Democrats. The economic crisis compelled the Government to work out a bill regarding unemployment insurance which would have burdened the workers with a sacrifice equivalent to a reduction of wages by 2 per cent. All the socialist ministers, except the Minister of Labour, consented to the bill; but the opposition of the Trade Unions forced the socialists to resign. They thereby abdicated voluntarily and for good, and thus paved the way for the enemies of democracy.[2] In Prussia for some time

[1] Many proofs can be found in the work of a scholar who opposed the war mentality of the great majority of his colleagues. Cf. Georg Fr. Nicolai, *Biologie des Krieges*, 1919, vol. i, pp. 7, 311.
[2] Otto Braun, the principal leader of the socialists, blames the doctrinaire obstinacy of those trade unionists who wanted to shirk the responsibilities of government from fear of the Communists. Cf. Otto Braun, *Von Weimar zu Hitler*, 1940, p. 292. In post-war Austria there was at first a coalition between the two great parties, the Social Democrats and the Christian Socials, and the Social Democrats played the leading part. Soon, however, they left the government and went into opposition, mainly under pressure of their own left wing, and though some time later they seemed disposed to form a new coalition, this failed mainly owing to the

there was still a Social Democratic Government, but Papen deposed it and the socialist ministers knew no more effective way of resistance than an appeal to the Supreme Court to declare this act of violence illegal. This helplessness, however, was not only shown by the German democrats. For years to come the world had ample opportunity of forming a view of Hitler's aims and methods. Nevertheless the statesmen and nations of the great Western democracies clung to the illusion that Hitler was peaceable and could be trusted and that the tiger of Nazi-bestialism could be appeased by kind words and lumps of sugar. Even after Hitler's real aims could hardly be doubted any longer, many democratic nations, great and small, still believed in the wisdom of the ostrich policy of isolationism.

A still more potent factor in preparing the road for Fascism and Hitlerism, however, was Bolshevism. In czarist Russia the development of a democratic Labour Movement, and of a class of leaders from the rank and file was very backward. Russian socialism was completely dominated by the old type of revolutionary intellectual. As Alexander Kerensky, a prominent leader of the Social Democrats, says in his memoirs,[1] Russian socialism was not a class movement of proletarians but an idealist, ethical movement. The foremost leaders came all from the upper classes, there were practically no workers or peasants among them. The military power of Russia broke down in the war with Germany and Austria, a government was formed by Kerensky and a Constituent Assembly was elected by universal franchise in which the Bolsheviks formed only about a fifth. Lenin who in 1917 had come to Russia with the help of the German General Staff soon seized power by force, deserted the Allies who had entered the war and had made enormous sacrifices in order to help Russia, and initiated the Bolshevik regime with terrorism on an unprecedented scale. The Bolsheviks developed the whole technique of terrorism which was later imitated by the Fascists and Nazis. It is beyond the scope of this book to narrate the history of Bolshevism or to discuss the merits or demerits of this system.[2] It is merely the influence of Bolshevism on the rise

resistance of the Christian Social leader, Dr. Seipel. In 1931, however, Seipel wanted the Socialists to rejoin the government; but now they refused. The lack of co-operation between the parties encouraged the rise of a Fascist movement which, backed by Italy, became so powerful that at last democracy was suppressed by force.

[1] Cf. A. T. Kerensky, *The Crucifixion of Liberty*, 1934.
[2] Cf. however, Colin Clark, *Critique of Russian Statistics*, 1939, and *The Conditions of Economic Progress*, 1940, p. 86. Dr. Ewald Ammende, *Human Life in Russia*, 1936; William H. Chamberlain, *A False Utopia*, 1937; Sir Walter Citrine, *I search for Truth in Russia*, rev. ed., 1938; Sir John Maynard, *The Russian Peasant and Other Studies*, 1942.

of aggressive nationalism which has to be pointed out here. This influence manifested itself in various ways. Bolshevism split the socialist movements of many countries into different sections which owing to the fanaticism of the communists fiercely combated one another. In Germany the communists directed their main attack against the Social Democrats and against the democratic Republic. They did everything to ruin democracy and worked into the hands of the Nazis. In order to form a majority in Parliament and to prevent chaos, the Social Democrats were forced to co-operate with nationalists and reactionaries and this paralysed the defence of democracy. In many countries large sections of the people which formerly were more or less friendly to democracy, or at least not hostile, were driven into the camp of reactionary parties, especially the peasantry and sections of the middle class and the intellectuals. The Bolsheviks, furthermore, showed how a small minority by ruthlessness and rude propaganda could rule an enormous country without granting any political liberty. The idea of a Reign of Law, independent of class and party, which even the most reactionary statesman had not dared openly to deny, was declared rubbish. The Fascists have learned this lesson from the Bolsheviks, and the proletarians Mussolini and Hitler became the disciples of the intellectuals Lenin and Trotsky. After the rise of Fascism in many countries sections of the nation began to sympathize with the dictators and democracy was faced with the menace of secret internal enemies of great power.

The defeat of democracy in certain countries has had the consequence that in other countries many people either formed a very unfavourable opinion of the vanquished democratic parties and even charged them of never having taken democracy serious or laid all blame on democracy itself. Both views are incorrect and misleading. There is no doubt that the achievements of democracy in many fields far outweigh its shortcomings, and that even these were mainly due to causes which do not justify depreciation of democracy as such. But it would also be wrong to assume that the democratic parties which were destroyed by their enemies did nothing in defence of democracy. In reality many serious and well-planned attempts were made, though also here the retrospective critic may sum up his conclusions in the words : Too late and too little ! Apart from this historical question, however, the survey of democratic politics all over the world suggests that the ideology and political machinery of democracy need considerable reforms. The democrats of various countries ought to drop the illusions of political and economic isolationism, abandon racial and social prejudice and adopt a more realistic view of human nature and of the complexity of political and economic problems, especially of the psychology of other nations.

4. RATIONAL AND IRRATIONAL FORCES IN NATIONALISM

Modern nationalism exhibits a puzzling combination of irrational and rational elements, and its very strength reposes in the union of mental primitiveness with all the instruments offered by the progress of science and technique. In all national movements the leading rôle was played by the intellectual classes, by professors, students, lawyers, officials, doctors, teachers, writers and journalists and sections of them also were the moving power in aggressive nationalism while the uneducated masses were tools in their hands. In spite of the intellectual character of the leading élite its doctrines as a rule denounced reason and exalted emotions and instincts. Yet nationalism cannot merely be the outcome of instincts since in this case it would be equally strong at all times and in all members of the species. There must be social factors which account for its variations according to time, nation and class. Many writers see in nationalism a survival of primeval barbarism while others explain it as the product of modern society, surfeited with intellectualism and disgusted with its results.

A typical representative of the survival-school is H. Hankins, who in a scholarly book defines nationalism as self-assertion of that redoubtable being " the cave-man within us ".[1] In his view the mentality of nationalism has developed in response to the conditions of an early time and has been preserved in the " communal mind " which exists " independently of the individual mind ", and " outside the nervous system and body of the individual ". The author attempts to substantiate this thesis by parellels taken from the customs and habits of primitive tribes and the behaviour of animals. A representative of the other school is Caroline Playne, who in several important books [2] has interpreted nationalism and the war-spirit as " a social neurosis caused by the stress and strain of modern life ". The explanation of the primitive, fanatical tendencies of to-day as a return to barbarism, an atavistic upheaval, appears to her far too simple. The neurosis from which war springs is due to " the wear and

[1] Cf. E. Hanbury Hankins, *Nationalism and the Communal Mind*, 1937, pp. 151; 183, 187, 193.
[2] Caroline E. Playne, *The Neuroses of the Nations, the Neuroses of Germany and France before the War*, 1925; *The Pre-War Mind in Britain*, 1928; *Society at War*, 1930.

tear to men's nervous make-up caused by the increased pressure, complication and the fullness of life generally ". This thesis is elaborated in detail by an analysis of the psychological effects of social changes. Karl Mannheim in a profound study of modern mass-society has traced the growth of aggressiveness to social disintegration.[1]

The view that bellicosity is correlated with social factors has been expressed also by statesmen. Sir Edward Grey believed that modern war, the ultimate horror to him, was the logical outcome of the machine mind.[2] He was, moreover, convinced that every nation from time to time wanted a war for the sake of fighting. In 1906 he wrote in a letter to President Roosevelt : " We should detest war anywhere. This is not because we have grown weak or cowardly, but because we have had enough war for one generation. Before the Boer War we were spoiling for a fight.—Any government, during the last ten years of the last century, could have had war by lifting a finger. The people would have shouted for it. They had a craving for excitement and a rush of blood to the head. Now this generation has had enough excitement and has lost a little blood, and is sane and normal."

Many arguments could be put forward in support of either of the two schools. There are many parallels, indeed, between modern nationalism and the behaviour of primitive tribes, such as the strength of irrational forces, emotions and traditions, the belief in mysticism, and collectivism. Many primitives consider their names or their shadows as sacred ; they believe these to suffer damage if somebody treads upon their shadow or maliciously pronounces their names. Primitives intensify the communal feelings and bonds by ceremonies, dances, the use of narcotics, producing a high grade of nervous excitement and motoric intoxication. This resembles the technique of nationalism, brought to perfection by Hitler, of arousing the passions of the masses, and whipping them up into ecstasy by symbols, uniforms, music, dances, drumming, constant repetition of slogans, mass marching, and so on. Such means do not merely appeal to the common herd. Many great German philosophers, writers, and public men, of the highest culture have, time and again, praised war as the promoter of a mystical rapture, making the individuals conscious of their national integration.

Modern nationalism and racialism are always ready to reject

---

[1] Cf. Karl Mannheim, *Man and Society in an Age of Reconstruction*, 1940, pp. 126 f.
[2] George Macaulay Trevelyan, *Grey of Fallodon*, 1937, p. 53 ; for the subsequent passages cf. pp. 115, 155.

arguments of reason and experience and to exalt the call of the mystic mass soul, the urge of instinct, the voice of the blood. Both primitives and modern nationalists to some extent agree in the rejection of innovations, considered as foreign or opposed to old traditions. The Nazis, for instance, denounce democracy as a Jewish-English-French invention, entirely alien to the old Teutonic genius. In many primitive tribes secret societies play a great rôle; they are often composed of young men who perform mystical dances, exercise themselves in cruel acts, in shedding of blood and enduring pain, terrorize and plunder those who are weaker, and try to secure to themselves a privileged position. They show many likenesses with certain nationalist youth organizations, especially in Germany.

Yet modern nationalism cannot be merely explained as a harking back to primitive barbarism. It contains also much of misused intellectualism and utilizes the results of intellectual progress. The speculations of many great thinkers, the progress of science and the expansion of knowledge have all been misused for the elaboration of nationalist ideologies. Biological factors too seem to have contributed to the advance of nationalism. Young people are generally more easily inflamed by nationalism than older, more sedate ones, owing to exuberance of juvenile temperament, lack of experience, and their inclination for simple, forceful methods. Boys are fond of fighting without any special cause, simply as an expression of temperament. The time of puberty seems especially favourable for infection by nationalism. The ascent of Hitler began by capturing a large part of the youth. The main strength of the Nazis at first consisted in schoolboys and other youngsters. The mass of the older people were conquered much later, to a large extent through the action of the juveniles. Another factor of great importance in bringing Hitler to power, was the vote and influence of women, especially single ones. Female emotionalism was kindled by Hitler's hysterical demagogy and by boisterous young louts strutting about with daggers and revolvers and posing as heroes. Nazi writers themselves have often boasted that the followers of Hitler almost formed a separate race, an élite of dashing, courageous fellows, unfettered by any inhibitions. It is certain that Hitler's appeal to the instincts of the mob, to the bestiality hidden beneath the varnish of civilization resulted in the selection of specially brutal and unscrupulous elements from all classes of society. The fists were ranged against the brains. Certain groups, containing a high percentage of such types, naturally furnished more recruits than others. But as a whole it cannot be said that the true followers of Hitler were chiefly drawn from one class or the other. They came from all classes, thus contraverting the theory that class was the only decisive factor in politics. But the selection seems largely to have been made according to the afore-mentioned biological criteria. Hitler's advanced guard formed a band of adventurous, unintellectual, brutal, unscrupulous elements, but also of emotional youngsters and women, carried away by the torrents of his oratory and his appeal to heroism. This most varied medley of people was further joined by others who had no principles at all. They said : " Let's try this movement for once." The statistics show that at the elections which enabled Hitler to seize power (though he never obtained a majority of the votes) his gains were not at the expense of the great well-disciplined Socialist and Catholic parties. His increase of votes came either from other nationalist parties and only meant a radicalization of nationalists, or from people who had voted previously for small parties of muddle-heads, or not at all.

Certain classes of intellectuals, furthermore, form an important element in many nationalist movements. Nations, however, differ in this respect. While in Germany the universities and a large section of the classes which have enjoyed a higher education were the hotbeds of nationalism, this cannot be said of England at all. Even in Germany it was more a conservative nationalism that was widespread among academic people than the more vulgar form of Hitlerism. This sort of nationalism of the German intellectual classes was largely a symptom of class mentality and snobbishness. It meant opposition to democratic, liberal, socialist and internationalist tendencies which were considered as incompatible with social respectability. Yet, the disposition of the intellectual classes for nationalism has also deeper roots.

Social and intellectual development are coupled with an increasing longing for individuality. In bygone times the whole life of a group was regulated by traditions. Parents determined whom the son or daughter should marry and which occupation they were to enter. Modern youth would not accept such interference, they object to the rule of traditions and conformity, even if they would be to their advantage, and want to " live their own life ". The acquisition of knowledge, the influence of newspapers, democracy and many other factors increase people's estimate of their own importance and their longing for recognition. Yet, the conditions of modern life make it very difficult for most individuals to become more than a very small part in an enormous machine. Though modern democracies try to enable their citizens to develop their personality and to make the cultural treasures of the nation accessible to all, the striving for the loftier ideals of personality is often frustrated by social reasons.

This frustration of the increased longing for individual personality is partly made good by the stressing of collective personality, especially that of the nation or of the party. The personality and prestige that the individual cannot attain in his own name, may be accessible to him in form of collective personality in which he has a share. Individuals who have developed a rich cultural personality of their own and have won thereby ample recognition, usually lay little stress on participating in the prestige of a group. Most people, however, feel compelled to emphasize their belonging to some larger group for winning recognition.

Certain currents of thought also played a large rôle in making the intellectuals disposed towards nationalism, by shattering the belief in Christianity, and in reason, progress, humanity, natural rights of man and solidarity of all nations which form the groundwork of liberalism. Many intellectuals were disappointed with the fruits of civilization and particularly with the result of their own efforts. Even such as had given much time and thought to the search for truth, often felt that they had failed. Reason seemed to them unable to solve the riddles of the world and to bring about a satisfactory state of society, it seemed to have only succeeded in destroying all beliefs without offering a substitute. Intellectualism appeared to result in interminable quarrels and uncertainties, and many intellectuals ended in moral nihilism and despair. They often began to yearn for the return of primitiveness, they believed they would find a new religion in the sensations of mass enthusiasm, a new morality in submitting to the iron discipline of a sort of pan-militarism, and a substitute for science in the intoxicating myth of race. This mentality, moreover, was fostered by the increase in the sense of power and in the appreciation of belonging to a mass, inherent in our age.

The disposition for nationalism is largely a product of the spirit of the time and, therefore, more or less permeates all classes, but it depends on the particular conditions of a nation how far this disposition is actualized. The wide diffusion of potential nationalism is a factor of special significance which is often underestimated. Before the rise of the dictators the number of extreme nationalists was not very great in their countries and their extremism gave good arguments into the hands of their opponents. But there were large masses of people whose nationalism was so vague that it was difficult to argue against it or who had no clear political opinions and for this reason were apt to become an easy prey of demagogues who possessed the gift of arousing their latent passions. In other countries also experience has proved that a certain form of moderate nationalism is more difficult to combat than a more extreme type. This applies also to the types of internal nationalism such as oppression of minorities, anti-Semitism and anti-alienism. The dangerous anti-Semites, for instance, are not those who denounce the Jews as ritual-murderers, but certain sneaking ones who are much more effective in poisoning the atmosphere and preparing the soil for Hitlerism.

The triumphs of extreme nationalism and racialism in our time, furthermore, were facilitated by the attitude of many statesmen and politicians who were not in sympathy with their aims, but either believed that it was too dangerous for their own position and that of their parties to take energetic measures against them, or even considered them as necessary evils. Politics, indeed, comprise many factors which are evils, but which cannot be eliminated without incurring the risk of still greater evils. Many statesmen dislike the ways of nationalism, but think that it, nevertheless, is the lesser evil. Another habit inherent in modern politics is the tendency to over-simplify complicated issues. Most great political questions of to-day are very complex ; they show an inextricable mixture of rights and wrongs, pros and cons, and incalculable risks. On the other hand, they must be made understandable to all those who have influence on politics and the solutions proposed must appeal to the mentality of the voters. This makes it necessary to present them in a very simple form. It is not merely the masses which are unable to afford any interest in complicated plans not directly touching their own vital interests. Even highly educated people are often very reluctant to give much thinking to political problems, especially those of other nations, and prefer to believe what agrees with their own wishes.[1]

5. The Economics of Nationalism

Both liberalism and socialism regard economic activity as a means for providing the people by peaceful work and co-operation

---

[1] Cf. the acute analysis of the mentality which was largely responsible for the failure of the democratic nations to maintain peace in Edward H. Carr, *The Twenty Years' Crisis, 1919–1939*, 1939.

with the greatest possible amount of the goods in demand, while nationalism looks upon it primarily as a means of increasing power and prestige of the nation. The production of wealth merely for the purpose of improving living conditions appears to extreme nationalists even as a mean occupation and in their ideology economic activity assumes the character of a struggle for domination and exploitation by force. The creed of liberalism is that all those engaged in the production and exchange of useful goods profit thereby and that an increase in the wealth of one nation is an advantage for all others too because the prosperous nation will be able to buy more from them. Liberalism, moreover, assumes that the expansion of world trade is the greatest guarantee for peace because it makes all nations ever more dependent on one another. Nationalism, on the other hand, harks back to the doctrine of mercantilism that a nation can only grow rich at the expense of another, and that what one nation wins, another must lose. Mercantilism primarily aimed at the increase of the power of the State. Within the nascent national State it fulfilled the function of economic unification by the destruction of internal barriers and local monopolies, but between States it fostered the struggle for monopolizing markets and often contributed to the outbreak of war.

In the course of the eighteenth century many writers attacked mercantilism, and Adam Smith proved that freedom was more productive than regulation by the State, that competition was more beneficial than monopoly, and that there was a great solidarity between the economic interests of all nations which would all prosper by exchanging their goods freely. In the nineteenth century the economic isolation of the nations gave way to freer trade and intercourse. Free Trade won its greatest triumph in Britain, and many other states also adopted a liberal trade policy. A new wave of protectionism, however, set in after the American war of secession and after the Franco-German war of 1870–1. The latter war inaugurated an epoch of rapidly rising armaments and it was argued for the increase in tariffs that their returns would help to pay for the armaments and that national security demanded that vital goods should be produced at home. Nevertheless, the growth of protectionism was moderated by the strength of liberal opinion. To a large extent every nation produced the goods for which its conditions were most favourable, and all profited by the exchange of their products. The whole world formed a vast economic system, in which all nations were closely co-operating for their mutual benefit. Goods, labour and capital could flow freely from one country to the other. Everybody could go to almost any country without even requiring a passport and could earn his living there by honest work. This system of a liberal world economy brought about a great rise of the national income, and especially of wages.[1]

No country has profited more under this system than Germany. Her goods could enter Great Britain and her colonies (though not the Dominions) without paying any customs, while English goods imported into Germany had to pay duties. German trade made stupendous progress in all the markets of the world. Everywhere Germans owned flourishing industries, banks, shipping lines, mines and other businesses. German clerks and employees found well-paid posts in all countries. The liberal world economy, therefore, secured a very wide living-space to the German people and its economic rise was not detrimental to other nations as these too were prospering. Nevertheless, the German nationalists violently attacked world economy and international division of labour as a menace to Germany because she was dependent on the import of foreign goods which might be stopped in a war. They obviously did not appreciate the economic and social benefits which the German people enjoyed under that system. What they wanted was power, the foremost rank in the world, by dint of the sword, and they were convinced that this was also the key to the world's riches.

The pre-war system of protectionism often led to the abuse of protective tariffs for aggressive purposes. High tariffs enabled producers to keep prices in the home market high, particularly by means of cartels, and to use their profits for underselling their competitors in the world markets by so-called " dumping ". Their losses abroad were more than counterbalanced by gains at home, and the conquest of world markets enabled them to produce on a much bigger scale and at much lower cost. The big iron industries of Germany have largely attained their tremendous strength through such methods which, of course, were regarded as very unfair by the producers in the other countries affected. They complained that German protectionism not only closed the German market to them but also helped the German industrialists to push them back on their own markets. It was not Germany alone, however, where economic nationalism gained ground. In the mentality of the nationalists of all nations jealousy of wealthier nations always played a dominant rôle. Backward nations were

[1] Cf. A. Carr-Saunders and D. Caradog Jones, *Survey of the Social Structure of England*, 2nd ed., 1937, p. 101.

apt to attribute their low standard of life exclusively to exploitation and oppression by richer nations, and believed that they would become free and prosperous only when they had destroyed the economic position of these " capitalist-nations ".

The encouragement of new industries by means of tariffs may achieve its aim in certain conditions which we cannot discuss here. But the good effects of tariffs are strictly limited in time and degree. It is characteristic of economic nationalism that it rejects these limitations and strives for the permanent exclusion of foreign goods and for the greatest possible self-sufficiency or autarchy. Economists find it easy to show that this way does not lead to a higher national income or to better real wages. But their arguments are ineffective because nationalists do not attach primary importance to economic aims. Partly they estimate power more highly than wealth, partly it is to them a matter of national prestige to produce everything at home, irrespective of cost. Their most common argument is : Why should we not make every commodity ourselves instead of buying it from foreigners ? Is it not humiliating that people believe we cannot produce what we need ?[1] Besides, would it not create employment and raise wages ? From an economic point of view this argument is primitive but it nevertheless appears to be irresistible.

The reasons why the arguments of protectionists are much more effective than those of free traders is that they appeal more to a mind untrained in economic thought, and that they are backed by the selfishness of powerful individuals and groups and by nationalist sentiment. Economic theory investigates the effects of economic policy on the welfare of the people as a whole ; but this is too difficult a problem for the average man. The spread of protectionism, moreover, is greatly furthered by the real or alleged necessity of retaliation. Protectionism is a most infectious disease. If one trade is protected all others want to enjoy similar treatment, and usually get it, though every spread of protectionism to further trades must diminish the profits of those already protected, and though universal protection largely cancels out all individual gains. Likewise, if one nation increases its tariffs or other restrictions, usually all others follow suit. Even if the economic grounds given for this imitation are not convincing,

[1] As early as in the fifteen century Florence introduced very high tariffs on foreign goods, defending this with the argument " what damage would be done to the honour and reputation of Florentine industries if it were said that in a city like Florence there is not sufficient spirit of enterprise for manufacturing cloth in the manner of Perpignan though it is made almost everywhere in Italy ".

the psychological urge is overwhelming. Lastly, experience shows that it is almost impossible to reverse the trend and to abolish protection once afforded, because too many vested interests have been created. Though the advantages of protection may often be quite illusory, the favoured classes cling to it most tenaciously and are much more vocal than those suffering under its effects. To sum up : the alliance of individual and national egotisms starts a movement of progressive exclusion of all against all. It goes on automatically, increasing continually in extent and intensity.

After the last war protectionism and nationalism were greatly stimulated by the consequences of the war and the Peace Treaties, and the great economic crisis which broke out in 1929. A particular factor which contributed to this development was the creation of numerous small states which all wanted to secure and emphasize their national independence by following a policy of exclusion.[1]

The increase in the strength of the Labour Movement led to restrictions on the immigration of foreign workers, and to the exclusion of aliens from employment. This policy was in principle the same as the protectionism of industrial and agricultural employers, and it was based on equally specious grounds. The system of giving every class a monopolistic or highly privileged position thereby became universal, and it played a decisive part in bringing about the world crisis of 1929, which devastated the world for years. The gravest feature of this crisis was mass-unemployment on an unprecedented scale, which paved the way for Hitler and for the present war. It was the most tragic proof of the mental blindness produced by nationalism that, nevertheless, the remedy for the crisis was largely sought in further increase of protectionism and monopolism, and this in spite of countless warnings on the part of the greatest economic authorities.

A fatal aftermath of the Great War was inflation, which was due partly to the economic disorganization caused by the war, partly to political causes. In many countries inflation had great social and political consequences favouring the growth of radical nationalism. Depreciation of currency sometimes amounted to involuntary bankruptcy, forced upon a people by overwhelming necessity, but in the age of nationalism it was frequently due to a laxness of economic morality and could rightly be called fraudulent bankruptcy. Inflation was like a dangerous drug,

[1] Cf. Leo Pasvolsky, *Economic Nationalism of the Danubian States*, 1928.

first speeding up circulation and creating the impression of a flourishing business, but later heading for the abyss and complete chaos. Its results were the annihilation of a large section of the middle classes and the spread of extreme doctrines among the youth. Both paved the way for the advent of dictators, whose followers differed in the colour of their shirts, but were all inspired by absolute ruthlessness and contempt for every moral obligation.

One of the worst consequences of economic nationalism after the war was the extension of insecurity in all countries. Production and trade can only prosper where law reigns and rules of elementary morality are recognized. These fundamental conditions were increasingly attacked, undermined and destroyed by the policy of extreme nationalism. The effect was that in many countries new investments were exposed to abnormal risks, owing to the fact that the investor could not rely on being protected by the existing laws, on the impartiality of the administration, and on the good faith of the State. This general state of insecurity and the ensuing lack of new investments were a further cause of unemployment. Another cause was the wasting of large parts of the national income and capital on uneconomic expenditure, on gigantic armaments, on production without economic justification, on colossal public buildings for mere purposes of propaganda and prestige. True, the nationalist dictators boasted of having suppressed unemployment by these very means, and their assertions were even believed and repeated by democratic politicians. Yet that claim was obviously fallacious. Unemployment was not suppressed by such means, but only concealed, disguised or shifted to other shoulders. If a disproportionate part of the national labour is spent on unproductive work, the supply of consumption goods will be diminished. If the policy of putting military independence first leads to the production of expensive substitute-materials instead of importing cheap foreign goods, this too reduces supplies. Under normal circumstances this will cause unemployment. But the dictators had the power of concealing it by employing workers in all sorts of sham jobs and by distributing the reduced employment and supplies over the total of workers. It is very easy to " abolish unemployment " if the Government has the power to force every worker to accept any employment, in any place, at any wages, and under any conditions. Many of such workers seemed to be employed without really being so in an economic sense. Whether a man is paid for doing uneconomic work or for doing nothing at all, makes no difference. Unemployment was concealed in the dictator-states behind a screen of uneconomic occupations though at the price of reducing the standard of life of the people. The decrease of their consumption then reacted on other countries which hitherto were used to deliver supplies. Imports shrank, and the consequence was that those countries also were affected by unemployment. The evil results of this system were for some time hidden by various measures such as the spoliation of helpless classes, like the Jews, or of foreign creditors through defaulting on loans, or by means that implied the eating up of the national capital, and lastly by the invasion of weaker countries. In the last resort nationalism led to the wholesale destruction of wealth, and of all the moral foundations necessary for producing wealth, namely peace, the reign of law, good faith and security. Our modern economic system was the product of free creativeness, initiative and labour. With the rise of the modern totalitarian slave-States world economy became more and more a welter of ruins. Most States were forced to transform themselves into fortresses equipped for a perpetual siege and sudden attacks by land, sea and air.

A factor which has also contributed to the setting up of barriers between States, and to the destruction of international co-operation was the growth of State-industries and rigid State-regulation of industries at the expense of individual enterprise. It is not possible to enter here into a discussion of the controversy whether central or individual planning is economically more productive and socially more advantageous. The most competent economists agree to-day that both systems have their merits and demerits and that some combination of them is desirable or inevitable. It is only the implications in regard to nationalism which are to be considered here. Now it is not doubtful that a far-reaching influence of the State on production tends to decrease international exchanges of goods, capital and labour. In many branches State-production cannot compete with private initiative on a free market, and, therefore, leads to measures designed to exclude foreign goods from the home market, or to dump exports on foreign markets at a loss, which naturally provokes the States afflicted to protect themselves against this unfair competition. The mere fact of a foreign State entering into competition with nationals, moreover, arouses much more national jealousy than competition by private foreign merchants. As a rule it is immediately interpreted as a political move with sinister intentions. A private merchant is as ready to sell as to buy on any market where it is profitable, while an exporting State-monopoly usually is very reluctant to take an adequate amount of foreign goods in exchange for its exports. The well-meant plans of " barter " between States have hitherto seldom had good results.

A further consequence of the increase of State activities in production and in the regulation of production is the multiplication of officials who in many countries form a class particularly susceptible to nationalism. The psychology of State officials often implies the predominance of a sense of power and many of them naturally incline towards exhibiting their function as the wielders of power. The smaller and less educated officials are usually even more apt to do so than those with greater responsibilities.[1] Now our social development leads to a rapid increase in the number of individuals who possess a certain measure of education and who may be called semi-intellectuals. This spread of education is in many respects a most welcome fact, and it is to be hoped that it may assume even larger proportions. But it must not be overlooked that it also results in the increase of people with the ambition of obtaining a position of influence and power. In many cases the situation of the class of semi-intellectuals lacking adequate chances of satisfying their ambitions has become a major social problem. An economic system which affords a certain scope for private initiative offers many of them an opportunity of a career in business, and of becoming the Caesar of a department store or a factory as far as Parliament and the Trade Unions permit. The concentration of more and more economic activities in the hands of the State, however, narrows this field, and must divert ambitions to politics and State Service which may imply an intensification of nationalism and struggles for power. Whether full communism is compatible with any form of democracy is most doubtful The magnitude and complexity of the problem of regulating the whole life of a people is bound to give rise to countless diversities of opinions and frictions and the clash of interests and ambitions would become too intense to be overcome without a dictatorship.

---

[1] Long observations in various countries of central and eastern Europe have convinced me that no class comprises such a proportion of rabid nationalists as that of the subordinate State officials. All the national struggles of those regions have mainly sprung from the rivalry of the semi-intelligentsia for posts in the service of the State.

CHAPTER VIII

POLITICAL THOUGHT AND NATIONAL IDEOLOGY

1. The Influence of Thought on Politics

Philosophers and historians have evolved many different views on the relations between thought and life, and on the rôle of ideas in determining politics.[1] In former times they often over-estimated the share of individuals in shaping the destiny of nations, and this led to the view that history was mainly a result of individual deliberation and planning. In modern times the influence of collective social forces on history was ever more realized and this implied the recognition of the power of emotions and interests. Modern sociologists have shown that not only programmes of parties but also the theories of great thinkers were largely determined by their social environment,[2] and by specific historical situations. Rational and irrational forces, indeed, are as a rule so intertwined that they can hardly be separated. The true scholar endeavours to put truth above his dearest ideals and his vital interests, but even he does not always entirely succeed in eliminating bias. The propagandist, however, uses thought and knowledge merely as instruments for the defence of his preconceived aims. His type of thought is usually called an ideology to-day in order to distinguish it from disinterested scientific thought. In many cases, however, the difference is one of degree, and the borderline is difficult to draw.

The driving force and leaders in the striving for nationality have always been the intellectual classes, and it is obvious that these classes were particularly liable to the influence of doctrines, created by thinkers and dreamers, and heralded by great writers, orators and artists. The enthusiasm of the intelligentsia kindled by philosophers frequently carried away the masses though these knew little, if anything, of the philosophical background of their creed. The original ideas of political thinkers on the aims and significance of nationality, however, were usually so altered in the

[1] Cf. Ernst Troeltsch, *Der Historismus und seine Probleme*, 1922 ; Friedrich Meineche, *Die Entstehung des Historismus*, 2 vols., 1936 ; J. Goldfriedrich, *Die historische Ideenlehre in Deutschland*, 1902. The paramount significance of ideas has been emphasized in many profound reflexions by Lord Acton which have been compiled and interpreted by Ulrich Noack, *Geschichtswissenschaft und Wahrheit*, 1935. In particular the question whether the philosophers of Enlightenment were responsible for the French Revolution has been answered in many different ways, cf. Kingsley Martin, *French Liberal Thought in the Eighteenth Century*, 1929, p. 66.

[2] For the social background of thought cf. Karl Mannheim, *Ideology and Utopia*, 1936 (with bibliography) ; Ernst Grünwald, *Das Problem der Soziologie des Wissens*, 1934.

course of their realization that the result was totally different from, and even antagonistic to, what they had expected. It is necessary, therefore, in trying to gauge the influence of specific doctrines on the mentality of peoples, not merely to investigate the theories of philosophers but also their distortions in the ideologies of classes and of peoples.

It has often been asserted that each national character was expressed in a specific system of philosophy, but in reality the philosophical development of every nation shows many different types of thought. Nevertheless, it is true that in each nation a certain type has obtained the preponderance which was mainly effected by the strength of certain political and social factors and that each nation to-day regards a certain type as characteristic of its nationality, in regard both to civilization and to politics. The English regard empiricism and aversion to abstract theories as their national characteristics, and connect them with their preference for compromise, liberalism and democracy. The French pride themselves on their great tradition of Rationalism and the dominant position of clear reason in their politics. The Germans are equally proud of their great metaphysical philosophers, of the idealistic, mystical and romantic elements in their thought, and they also assert a close connexion between their national philosophy and their politics.

The correlation between philosophy and politics, however, has not only been pointed out by writers who were inspired by national pride. It has often been stressed with the intention of making another nation responsible for the evil features of its national evolution. In the last Great War, in particular, many famous German scholars accused the English and the French of having developed systems of thought favourable to the growth of a public spirit and of political doctrines which brought about the war. On the other hand, prominent French and English scholars asserted that it was precisely German philosophical thought which had moulded the political mentality from which the Great War sprang. Both sides, therefore, tried to show that the war was not merely an accident, brought about by the blunders of statesmen and diplomatists, but that it was deeply rooted in the antagonism of the whole ideals and beliefs of the peoples concerned.[1] This argument has been particularly

---

[1] On the German side some books of this kind, all by prominent scholars and writers, were Wilhelm Wundt, *Die Nationen und ihre Philosophie*, 1915 ; Max Scheler, *Der Genius des Krieges und der deutsche Krieg*, 1915 (cf. the post-war book by Scheler, *Nation und Weltanschauung*, 1923) ; Werner Sombart, *Händler und Helden*, 1915. On the French side the political mentality of the Germans was traced to their philosophy

stressed in Germany, and the view has found wide acceptance among the intellectuals that the war in the last resort was a clash between two irreconcilable mentalities, which were often described as German Idealism and Western Materialism.[1]

All these controversies between representatives of hostile nations were, of course, inspired by political passions and prejudice. Nevertheless, a certain connexion between philosophical thought and political ideologies cannot be denied. It is true that certain philosophies have contributed more to the rise of aggressive nationalism than others. On the other hand, it is a mistake to assume that it is only one type of philosophical thought which has furthered that evolution. It is a curious fact that of a great number of currents of thought, sentiment and interest each one has partly contributed to the rise of nationalism, and partly counteracted it. Idealism and Materialism, Determinism and Indeterminism, Rationalism and Irrationalism, Optimism and Pessimism, Individualism and Collectivism, religion and irreligion —they have all partly furthered and partly opposed the increase in national aggressiveness and self-adulation. Every school of thought implied divergent trends of development, and frequently a great thinker has awakened ideas which were later interpreted by his followers in a sense absolutely contrary to his own intentions.

The object of the following observations does not consist in tracing the correlations between certain philosophies and all aspects of the national character. This task would require a separate book for every single thinker. Our aim is merely to investigate the ideas of leading philosophers on some principal problems of nationality. The national character, furthermore, has also been moulded by thought in the form of religion, poetry and art, and the influence of such factors has usually been much more powerful than that of philosophy proper. The rôle of religion has been discussed in a separate chapter ; but that of poetry and art cannot be treated here, unless in occasional remarks.

---

by Léon Duguit, " Rousseau, Kant et Hegel ", published in the *Harvard Law Review*, 1917, and in the *Revue du droit publique et de la science politique*, 1918. Louis Bertrand has even discovered German imperialism in Goethe, cf. *Revue des Deux Mondes*, 1915. E. Boutroux (*Philosophy and War*, 1916) denies that the German philosophers taught the doctrines of present nationalism, but points out that their thought contained germs capable of being developed in that direction. Cf. especially Victor Basch, *Les doctrines politiques des philosophes classiques de L'Allemagne*, 1927.

[1] One of the most fanatical advocates of this thesis was Houston Stewart Chamberlain in different writings published during the war, and in his correspondence with the Kaiser William (published 1928).

2. Mediaeval Thought on Nationality, the State, Peace and War

It is often assumed to-day that the Middle Ages knew no nationality, though it would be more correct to say that the mediaeval notion of it differed from the present one. Peoples certainly felt affection for the native soil, for their clan, tribe and old customs; they showed pride in their small fatherland and its prestige, hatred and prejudice against enemies; but there was little solidarity between the different ranks of a people, and no idea of an unlimited loyalty to a national cause. Religion was definitely regarded as superior to national sentiment, at least in principle, though in the later Middle Ages there was a widespread national movement against the abuses of Papacy. Aggressive striving for expansion and domination was frequent, but it had seldom an outspoken national tendency, and the aim was not to impose the nationality of the conqueror on the vanquished people. Neither was there much intolerance towards peaceful foreigners merely because of their language or customs [1] and they were often permitted to live in a separate community which formed almost a state within the State. The language of the State, the Church and the Universities was Latin. What national sentiment existed was probably more spontaneous and sincere than many manifestations of modern nationalism which to a large extent is the product of artificial stimulation by propaganda.

Political thought was primarily determined by the teachings of the Church, and its fundamental attitude was expressed in the words which in 1095 Pope Urban used in his great oration exhorting the Christians to undertake a crusade: " Let no attachment to your native soil be an impediment : because, in different points of view, all the world is exile to the Christian, and all the world his country." [2]

This attitude implied two principles : the unity of Christianity took precedence of the national differences, and the spiritual power of the Church was assumed to be superior to the temporal power of governments. The true fatherland of the Christian was

---

[1] Though commercial or financial causes sometimes led to fierce conflicts.

[2] William of Malmesbury, *Chronicle*, tr. Giles, 1911, p. 363. The chronicler emphasizes that the text was taken from reliable sources. His own view probably was not very different. In another place (p. 285) he tells how Edgar, an Anglo-Saxon of royal blood, who had escaped to the Continent, after unsuccessful resistance to William the Conqueror, and was welcomed there with great honours, yet returned to England " For truly, the love of their country deceives some men to such a degree, that nothing seems pleasant to them, unless they can breathe their native air." The chronicler says that Edgar " was deluded by this silly desire ".

Heaven, and the terrestrial fatherland, therefore, was of only secondary importance. The mediaeval mind, furthermore, was deeply impressed by St. Augustine's vision of the two States on earth : the Community of God and the Community of the Devil. Though Augustine did not identify these two communities with the Church and the State, he assumed a certain affinity between them. The first State was founded by a murderer of his brother, namely Cain, and all further States were besmirched with blood and actuated by the lust for power, glory and domination, and by rapacity. In spite of its wickedness the State had, through the fall of Adam, become a necessary instrument of punishment and served the inscrutable plans of God.

It has already been shown that the struggle between the spiritual and the temporal power was of the greatest importance in the development of the national State. Popes, Emperors and Kings alternately endeavoured to win the support of the peoples against their rivals and thereby—much against their will—furthered the growth of the ideas of national independence, liberty and sovereignty. The unity of Christianity required a universal Emperor who had to defend this unity with the sword when it was threatened. But this did not imply world-domination in the modern sense, but rather an authority as supreme arbiter between the Christian rulers, and supremacy of honour, though some Emperors pursued more ambitious aims. The idea of sovereignty in the sense of unlimited power and the craving for uniformity which dominate the ideology of modern nationality were alien to mediaeval thought. Society was regarded as composed of numerous communities, each possessing particular rights, as sacred as those of the Government. The authority of all worldly rulers was closely restricted by folk law, by old customs, by feudal privileges, and most of all by the Divine and natural law which alone could be regarded as sovereign.[1] Popes, indeed, have claimed unlimited power, from Gregory VII onwards ; but they acted as God's representatives, they were naturally restrained by the tenets of Christianity and the fundamental laws of the Church, and neither their claim nor the rival ones which imperial jurists put forward on behalf of the Emperor, and with reference to Roman law, found general recognition.

The federal structure of mediaeval society was incompatible with the modern idea of a unitary and sovereign nation. Never-

[1] Cf. R. and A. Carlyle, *History of Mediaeval Political Theory in the West*, vol. iv, 1922, pp. 36, 68, 85. Otto v. Gierke, *Political Theories of the Middle Age*, tr., with an introduction by F. W. Maitland, 1900, p. 73. Cf. also several essays by various writers in *The Social and Political Ideas of some Great Mediaeval Thinkers*, ed. by F. Hearnshaw, 1923.

theless, the principle of popular sovereignty was not unknown. It had its roots in Roman and Germanic law, and could be substantiated with biblical and classical examples. The king was regarded as elected by the people, represented by the magnates, and if he violated his duties he could be deposed.

Gregory VII laid down that the spiritual power of the Pope was superior to all temporal government, and his famous letter to the Bishop of Metz described the rule of the kings in terrible words as of satanic origin and nature, practically indentifying the State with Augustine's City of the Devil. John of Salisbury worked out Gregory's principal thesis in a more moderate and practical spirit, and described the good State as an organism in which the priesthood is the soul, and the ruler the head which must be governed by the soul.[1] The various organs of State and society are compared to other parts of the body. This analogy was taken from a spurious ancient source, Pseudo-Plutarch's Institutio Trajani, and numerous writers followed the model of John of Salisbury. The aim of the State according to him is to enable every individual to achieve his salvation by a truly Christian life in his particular station. His State, therefore, is a Theocracy and has nothing in common with the modern national State; he hardly knows a nation, and in any case subordinated its Government to the supra-national power of the priesthood. Though John in many respects was a true Englishman, he later lived abroad, as Bishop of Chartres near Paris. When in 1285 the nationalist barons led by Montfort and Bigod expelled the foreign prelates from England, they justified this in a letter to the Pope by quoting John of Salisbury, that the State should be an organic unity and that harmony should reign between the members of a body.[2]

Mediaeval political thought was deeply stirred and greatly

[1] Cf. on John of Salisbury, Carlyle, vol. iv, p. 330, the essay by E. F. Jacob in Hearnshaw, op. cit., and Paul Gennrich, *Die Staats- und Kirchenlehre Johanns von Salisbury*, 1894.

[2] The struggle against the foreigners under Henry III fills a large part of Matthew Paris' *English History* (tr. Giles, 3 vols., 1854). This work shows the greatest possible animosity against all foreigners whether Poitevin or Gascon nobles, or Italian prelates and bankers, or German merchants. The Spaniards are described as " the scum of mankind, ugly in face, contemptible in behaviour, and detestable in their morals ". The chronicler constantly deplores the enslavement of England by the foreigners who carry all the money out of the country. He condemns marriage with foreign ladies, and even states that the foreigners had made a plot for poisoning the English, especially the nobles, and that many really died. The poison, a blue liquor, he asserts, was mixed in the house, and with the consent of Elias Bishop, a Jew of London, who saved his life by becoming a Christian (vol. ii, pp. 296, 314). Matthew Paris (vol. ii, p. 248) also relates that he was sent by the King of France to Haco, the King of Norway, offering him the command of the whole of the French fleet on a crusade, and that Haco declined this honour because the Norwegians and the French were by nature so disposed that any strife would lead to irreparable injury. Matthew Paris alone suffices to contravert the myth that national hatred was unknown in the Middle Ages.

furthered when Aristotle's *Politics* became more widely known in the original text and in translation. St. Thomas Aquinas (1226-74) tried to combine Augustine's supra-naturalism and Aristotle's naturalism. His social ethos was also influenced by the spirit of the Italian city-republics, the Old Testament, and Arabian-Jewish philosophy.[1] All Christians primarily form one people, their division into States is only secondary, and all Christian States form a family. It is a sin to take part in an ordinary war, though one cannot blame those who fight for God. Society is an organic hierarchy of functional ranks, the best form of government is an elective monarchy. The thought of Aquinas still forms the doctrine of the Catholic Church. It is inspired by aversion to the unitary, powerful State, centred on domination and prestige and the preference for peaceable small communities, living by the work of their brains and hands, and for autonomous guilds under the guidance of the Church. Aegidius of Rome, though a staunch defender of Papal supremacy, emphasizes the advantages of large, hereditary monarchies and he also adopts Aristotle's principle of the sovereignty of the people which was soon to be proclaimed in a more radical form by Marsilius of Padua and Nicholas Oresmius.[2] The developing national State already proved more powerful than the Universal Empire of the Pope and the Emperor. Dante once more pleaded for the World Monarchy of the Emperor which alone could safeguard peace and concord among the peoples. He deplores that mankind is torn asunder by incessant fratricidal strife. The man who looks on his native country and mother-tongue as superior to all others is silly. Dante says that his love of Florence had brought him unjust banishment, and from the point of view of his personal well-being he would rather live at Florence than anywhere else, but he regarded the world as his fatherland and was convinced that many peoples had a more noble and lovely country or a more beautiful and useful language than he.

Rivalry, pride, prejudice and contempt between peoples were frequent in the Middle Ages, though they usually referred to smaller units than our present nations.[3] Also ideologies for

[1] Cf. especially E. Troeltsch, *Die Soziallehren der Christlichen Kirchen*, 1912, p. 256 (also Engl. tr.) ; O. Schilling, *Die Staats- und Soziallehre des hlg. Thomas von Aquin*, 1923.
[2] Cf. on the political writers in the latest period of the Middle Ages, *Carlyle*, vol. v ; Hearnshaw, op. cit. ; Paul Janet, *Histoire de la science politique*, 5th ed., vol. i, p. 417 ; R. Scholz, *Die Publizistik zur Zeit Philipp des Schönen*, 1902.
[3] At great universities like Paris and Oxford, where students from many countries and different parts of the same country mixed, fierce struggles took place between students of different origin. At the University of Paris the students attributed particular vices to each nation which have been recorded by Jacobus de Vitriaco, cf. A. Budinsky, *Die Universität Paris und die Fremden an derselben im Mittelalter*, 1876, p. 46.

justifying them were not lacking, in particular the idea of a national mission. The fact that the Roman Empire was now in the hands of the Germans filled these with great pride and gave rise to various theories about their title to world-dominion. German writers declared that the Empire was given to the Germans, the supreme Priesthood to the Italians and leadership in learning to the French. This mission alone, however, did not satisfy the ambitions of those Frenchmen who were inspired by the idea of a great and powerful France. A typical representative of this party was the royal legist Pierre Dubois.[1] He was a pupil of Thomas Aquinas and it is perhaps the influence of his master which appears in his emphasis on peace as the highest good, and in his plans for a federation of all Christian rulers and an international Court for the maintenance of peace, and for a common crusade against the Turks. But he widely diverges from St. Thomas by his attempt to vindicate world domination, or at least supremacy in Europe, for the King of France, and by his suggestion of a great aggrandisement of French domination at the expense of the Pope, Germany and Spain.

The problem of the national character also aroused the attention of mediaeval writers. In the thirteenth century the English Minorite Bartholomew, a distinguished scholar, was for some time a professor in Germany and in France, and described the character of many European peoples.[2] The Germans seemed to him particularly fierce and warlike, though he excepts the peoples of the Rhinelands, the Low Lands and Misnia, the present Saxony, who were civilized. Roger Bacon was struck by the differences in national character which obtained even between neighbouring peoples such as the Picards, French, Normans, Flemings and English. He came to the conclusion that the diversity was due to the constellation of the stars.[3] Towards the close of the Middle Ages humanism and the rise of national sentiment greatly stimulated the interest in these problems.

The mediaeval view that the whole of Christianity formed one people was often contradicted by fierce struggles; but it was not entirely without influence on the relations between the peoples. The scholastics and publicists treated problems of international

[1] Cf. on Dubois Eileen Power in Hearnshaw, op. cit,, p. 139, Jacob ter Meulen, *Der Gedanke der internationalen Organisation in seiner Entwicklung*, 1300–1500, 1917, and Christian Lange, *Histoire de l'internationalisme*, 1919, vol. i.
[2] Cf. *Mediaeval Lore, Gleanings from the Encyclopedia of Bartholomew Anglicus*, by Robert Steele, 1893; Anton Schönbach, in *Mitteilungen des Instituts für österreichische Geschichtsforschung*, 1906.
[3] Cf. Roger Bacon, *Opus Majus*, ed. by I. H. Bridges, 1897, vol. i, pp. 138, 250, 254, 379, 393; vol. ii, p. 366.

law, and international arbitration played a considerable rôle. Novacovitch, who has made a special study of this subject, discusses in his work more than 150 treaties and cases of arbitration which took place between 1147 and 1475, and his list is not complete.[1] The main reason certainly was that there were not yet any large national Powers. The States were small and ruled by princes, more or less imbued with feudal traditions. The idea of solidarity between all Christian States, especially in face of the Turkish menace, was often invoked. A further plan of a federative organization of Europe was put forward by the King of Bohemia, George of Podiebrady, who submitted it to Louis XI, King of France.[2] Shortly after the end of the Middle Ages the principle of a permanent federation was even laid down in an important official document, the " Universal Peace ", concluded in London in 1518, on the initiative of Pope Leo X and of Cardinal Wolsey, between King Henry VIII of England and King Francis I of France, joined by King Charles I of Spain (later the Emperor Charles V) and the Pope. In this treaty the kings concluded a perpetual peace and an alliance not merely against the Turks but against any aggressor. If one of them should be attacked by another Power, it is laid down the other allies would first make diplomatic representations, and if these should fail they would immediately send military help to the attacked party. All other States could join the Alliance. This pact of " collective security ", however, was in force for a very short time only. It was wrecked by the death of the Emperor Maximilian I and the outbreak of a long struggle for power between France and Spain.

The peaceableness of kings was never a very reliable factor in international politics, not merely because at all times some of the kings were striving for expansion of their power by war, but also because they had to resort to war if they wanted to have peace at home. King Louis IX (Saint Louis) often complained that the pride of the French, and especially of the great nobles, threatened peaceful international relations. The building of national States required internal peace, and it was necessary to drain warlike passions into wars abroad which, moreover, also helped to create and enhance national unity by arousing national passions against a common enemy. Besides the doubtful peace-

[1] Cf. Novacovitch, *Les compromis et les arbitrages internationaux du 12. au 15. siècle*, 1905 (quoted by Lange, p. 123).
[2] Cf. Lange, p. 108, and ter Meulen, p. 108. The project was worked out by Antonius Marini, a French industrialist, who was an adviser of the Bohemian King. The King, however, had very ambitious plans which he tried to further by his move. The project was foiled by the Papal party at the French Court. About the Universal Peace of 1518 cf. Lange, p. 118.

ableness of the Kings, however, there was a sincere and ardent longing for peace and human brotherhood in religious and humanist circles. Christian thought had always pondered the problem of war, and tried to find a solution in the spirit of Christ. In the second century Marcion rejected the whole Old Testament because of its warlike spirit, while Origen tried to save it by explaining these wars as allegories, meaning the struggles of the believer with the temptations and sins of the world. In the Middle Ages Christian pacifism and anti-militarism were professed and practised by many sects, such as the Cathares, the Waldenses, a section of the Hussites and the Moravian Brethren, the Anabaptists, and the Lollards. Wyclif taught that according to the Gospel bloodshed was incompatible with the spirit of Christ,[1] and his teachings inspired the Lollards and had a great influence on Huss. In England the first conscientious objector, William Whyte, examined in 1428 by the Bishop of Norwich, declared that the law of Christ prohibited any killing of human beings, even of condemned criminals, and that it was not permitted to fight even for one's own heritage or fatherland. Another source of opposition to wars and violence was the humanist belief in the dignity of man and in the necessity of peace for the development of his spiritual faculties.

3. Nationalism and Cosmopolitanism in the Time of Humanism

The period around 1500 marks a most important phase in the development of national states and national aspirations. In many countries the kings strengthened national unity, and engaged in great international rivalries for power and prestige, making use of momentous innovations in military technique. The discovery of a new world overseas initiated a new epoch in trade and colonization which implied further motives of rivalry between the nations. Science and learning progressed rapidly, the invention of the printing press offered to reformers and writers an instrument of revolutionary power, and the civilization of the Renaissance attained to its greatest splendour. The Renaissance was not merely a revival of classical studies, but it was inspired by the longing for a rebirth of mankind.[2] A new class of intellectuals developed who professed humanism, which

---

[1] On mediaeval pacifism cf. Lange, p. 59. It is interesting to compare Wyclif's attitude with that of Luther, which was exceedingly wavering and confused. Cf. on Luther, Hans Prutz, *Die Friedensidee*, 1917, p. 73 ; Lange, p. 221.

[2] Cf. K. Burdach, *Reformation, Renaissance, Humanismus*, 1918.

word designates the philosophical and literary aspects of the Renaissance. Humanism emphasized human nature as the source of values instead of supra-natural revelation. The Church and the philosophy of the Middle Ages had to a large extent preached distrust of human nature, they had tried to shackle reason, emotions and will by a rigid discipline, and humanism was an intellectual revolt against this suppression of human nature, stimulated by enthusiasm for ancient thought and life.

The search of humanism for a new philosophy of life instead of the arid syllogisms of scholasticism raised the question of how to interpret human nature. Was man essentially a rational or an irrational being? Was there a specific " dignity of man " which distinguished him from all other creatures, and was a spark of Divine reason glowing in his soul, or was man merely a higher animal actuated by sensual appetites, by blind instincts or by lust of power? Humanism branched out in various philosophies with very different cultural and political implications. Certain interests, however, remained common to the majority of humanists, especially the interest in the comparative study of human individuality, of various types of men, and of the diversities of nations. A large literature on national character began to develop, which partly described the customs and habits of peoples, partly attempted to explain their origin and partly also expressed judgements on the merits or demerits of nations.[1]

Humanism itself, moreover, was influenced both by national diversities, and by national aspirations. The patriotism of the Greeks and Romans was everywhere praised and held up as a model, but also their cosmopolitanism was admired and imitated. The ancient views of the character of peoples contributed to the formation of national ideologies. The Italians were identified with the Romans, the French with the Gauls, and the Teutons with the Germans, and everywhere writers admonished their people to live up to the virtues of their alleged ancestors, and to mould their character according to their example. In each country social structure and cultural traditions gave to humanism a special colour.

The ranks of the humanists and their patrons comprised popes, emperors, and kings, statesmen and officials, historians, and other scholars, orators and poets. In Italy all courts, palaces,

[1] Cf. my survey on the history of these theories in *Archiv für Sozialwissenschaften*, 1926.

town-halls, and universities swarmed with them. Many humanists were indefatigable in flattering rulers and nobles, and in soliciting their favours, promising them to make their name immortal in their writings. Aeneas Silvius reproached the German princes for their lack of interest in immortality. They are only interested in their horses and dogs, he said, and like horses and dogs, they will be forgotten by posterity. Many humanists, moreover, were the heralds of the longing for national prestige. Italian humanists proclaimed that their people descended from the Romans and, therefore, were superior to all other peoples, whom they taunted as barbarians and judged with the greatest animosity and contempt. This aroused the indignation of the humanists of other countries, who hastened to rebut these insults and to assert the excellency of their nations.[1]

In Germany the Emperor Maximilian was a great patron of the humanists, and employed many of them for his political and cultural ambitions. The writings of this circle breathe a spirit of intense national pride.[2] Shortly before an Italian humanist had discovered in a German monastery the only extant copy of Tacitus' *Germania*, which describes the life and customs of the old Germans in an idealizing way, and in obvious contrast to the corruption of Roman society. The *Germania* aroused enormous enthusiasm among the German humanists, who soon wrote many books exalting the old Teutonic virtues, and proclaiming the superiority of the German nation over all others, in a spirit which recalls that of modern Pan-Germanism. Beatus Rhenanus in a letter of 1531 actually mentions a society of humanists at Augsburg which he calls " Pan-Germanic ".[3] German humanism also found some followers among the nobility and the patricians, but on the whole it remained restricted to the circles of scholars, some of whom like Sebastian Franck were outspoken cosmopolitans.[4] But Luther was intensely hostile to the spirit of humanism, and it was soon smothered in Germany by the storms

[1] On the national sentiment and the national animosity of many humanists cf. G. Voigt, *Wiederbelebung des klassischen Altertums oder das erste Jahrhundert des Humanismus*, 3rd ed., 1893, vol. ii, p. 309, and many places ; Jacob Burckhardt, *Cultur der Renaissance in Italien*, 8th ed., 1901, pp. 136, 329.
[2] Cf. J. Knepper, *Nationaler Gedanke und Kaiseridee bei den elsässischen Humanisten*, 1898 ; Paul Joachimsen, *Geschichtsauffassung und Geschichtsschreibung in Deutschland unter dem Einfluss des Humanismus*, 1910. For descriptions of national character cf. Erich Schmidt, *Deutsche Volkskunde im Zeitalter des Humanismus und der Reformation*, 1904 ; Hans Liebmann, *Deutsches Land und Volk nach italienischen Berichterstattern der Reformationszeit*, 1910.
[3] Cf. Theobald Bieder, *Geschichte der Germanenforschung*, vol. i, p. 11.
[4] Cf. Wilhelm Dilthey, *Weltanschauung und Analyse des Menschen seit Renaissance und Reformation*, 1914, p. 81. This book gives a profound analysis of Humanism and its historical development.

of the Reformation and Counter-Reformation. Only a sort of classical learning could survive which kept aloof from all questions obnoxious to orthodoxy and the ruling powers. In Italy too the free-thinking humanists were expelled or silenced. Advanced Christian humanism, however, found a favourable soil in England, the Netherlands and in Poland, and was also adopted by the Swiss reformer Zwingli. Before discussing the national significance of humanism in France and England, we must focus attention on two thinkers who represent opposite types of humanistic thought on the problems of nationality.

4. Machiavelli and Erasmus

Niccolo Machiavelli (1469-1527) witnessed the invasion of Italy by the French, which made this country the victim of endless struggles between the Great Powers. His most ardent longing was to see his city of Florence and the whole of Italy free and respected again, but he realized that the situation was almost hopeless and that perhaps the greatest obstacle lay in the national character of the Italians. The glory of old Rome filled his soul with admiring pride, and the contrast between her rôle in the world and that of Italy was depressing. The Romans owed their immortality to their " virtue ", a word by which he understood political energy, great ambition, boldness, sagacity, cunning in the pursuit of great designs, fitness for domination, heroism, self-sacrificing devotion to the fatherland. The most essential qualification among its various elements was a proper religion, as the example of the old Romans proved. Yet Italy was lacking in this force above all. The Church was utterly corrupted through the Papacy, and the policy of the Popes was also chiefly responsible for the lack of national unity in Italy. Christianity, moreover, was not at all the right religion for fostering patriotic heroism. Paganism had made gods of men who had won temporal glory like generals and statesmen. Christianity crowned the humble and contemplative virtues rather than the active ones; it esteemed humility and contempt of earthly things, and not a great mind, bodily force and all the qualities which make men feared, and which were honoured by ancient paganism. The Christian religion, he thought, had enervated the people and had rendered them prone to become victims of the wicked. History and politics appeared to Machiavelli merely as a play of natural forces which did not allow for the action of a moral law, though a ruler might find it opportune to make use of this fiction for political purposes.

A fatal weakness of Italian politics was also the bitter class war raging in the city republics between the rich and the poor. Machiavelli, however, regarded this as an almost inevitable natural process which even had the merit of stimulating a people to an expansive and aggressive policy as the example of the Romans proved.

A corrupt people cannot be regenerated by moral means. The only salvation in Machiavelli's view was a great prince who would transform their character by imbuing it with the virtue of the Romans. Every means was justified for this aim. The prince might employ every lie, perfidy, cruelty: he might use terrorism and treachery, provided that it served the great aim. Most of all he ought to make the nation warlike and train it in arms. Italy's weakness was mainly due to the habit of leaving warfare to mercenaries. Machiavelli therefore longed for a great leader or dictator who would liberate and unite Italy, possibly in the form of a federation, who would make the Italians a nation, and who would give them the power and prestige of their Roman ancestors. The deep antagonism between his nationalism and Christian standards is obvious. Mussolini has claimed the great Florentine as one of the precursors of Fascism. This, however, is only partly true. Machiavelli regarded the dictatorship of the prince as a temporary device only. In his heart he was a republican, though he had no illusions about the people. He detested Caesar as the murderer of Roman liberty, while Mussolini glorifies him as the summit of Rome's greatness.

The concept of human nature underlying this doctrine is that man is mainly an irrational being, actuated primarily by the lust of power and prestige. This involves all States in a constant rivalry, and no State can withdraw from it without risking destruction. Machiavelli's doctrine was soon called that of the *Raison d'État*, and countless writers have attacked, defended or modified it.[1] It contained the germ of the fundamental theory of nationalism which conceives the State as an organism that cannot be judged according to the ordinary standards of individuals, but possesses a standard and morality of its own, superior to that of the individual.

Erasmus of Rotterdam (1465–1536) was the greatest representative of Christian humanism, and the foremost scholar of his

---

[1] The development of the idea of *raison d'État* from Machiavelli to the modern nationalists has been admirably described by Friedrich Meinecke, *Die Idee der Staatsraison in der neueren Geschichte*, 1924. Professor Meinecke tries in this book also to trace the origins of the diversity in political thought between the Western nations and the Germans.

age.[1] He was the sharpest critic of all the abuses which distorted the Church and religion, such as superstitious beliefs, mechanical rites, squabbles about insoluble questions, instigations to war, financial greed and lust of power on the part of the Popes, prelates and monks. Peace and concord were to him the sum of religion and a life in the spirit of Christ seemed to him more important than all theological questions. The greatest thinkers of antiquity had exhibited a truly Christian spirit and were perhaps Saints without official recognition by the Church. When Pope Julius II wanted to drive the foreign invaders out of Italy by a great war, he commissioned Erasmus to write a book in support of his policy. Instead Erasmus wrote a book strongly deprecating war, which greatly displeased the Pope. The horror of war inspires most of Erasmus's writings. War seemed to him the worst scourge of humanity. It fosters violence and tyranny abroad and at home. The abolition of war depends on the overcoming of national antagonism by the spirit of Christ and international solidarity. The Rhine separates French and Germans, but it does not separate Christian from Christian. Princes should not have the right of declaring war without the consent of the whole nation. Erasmus suggests the setting up of a court of international arbitration and the mobilization of all the moral forces of society for the maintenance of peace. The teaching of history in schools which aroused national passions ought to be controlled. His political ideal is an enlightened monarch, imbued with justice, piety, tolerance and devotion to his duties, advised by the wisest councillors, and respecting the rights of peoples and local parliaments.

The influence of Erasmus on political thought was considerable, though he formulated no doctrines and founded no school. But his spirit kindled and guided numerous thinkers and reformers who longed for the reign of justice, peace and goodwill, among human beings, who believed in the solidarity of mankind, and worked for the realization of these ideals. It is remarkable that Erasmus's extremely frank and scathing criticism of ecclesiastical corruption and his condemnation of war did not prevent the rulers of the Church and of States from admiring and protecting him. Pope Leo X and the Emperor Charles V were especially well disposed towards him. Erasmus could have become a high dignitary of the Church; but he refused. Popes, emperors, kings and statesmen of many nations vied in asking his advice and in trying to win him for their causes. Erasmus was thoroughly

[1] J. A. Froude, *Life and Letters of Erasmus*, 1895; S. Hess, *Erasmus von Rotterdam*, 2 vols., 1790; Pierre Mesnard, *L'Essor de la philosophie politique au XWI^e siècle*, 1936.

cosmopolitan, and it would be difficult to say, to what nation, if any, he belonged. He loved England most, though he also found many good points in other nations ; but he spoke neither English, nor Italian, French or German. In his writings he makes many remarks on national characteristics, and is never influenced by prejudice. Nevertheless, he did not escape the charge of national animosity. When he criticized the exaggerated veneration and imitation of Cicero, this aroused a storm of indignation in France and Italy, and Étienne Dolet, called him an enemy of the French nation. Erasmus' remark that the Italians were seldom warlike, induced Peter Cursius to attack him as an enemy of the Italian nation. In reply Erasmus expressed his greatest admiration for the cultural achievements of the Italians.

5. HUMANISM AND NATIONALITY IN FRANCE. BODIN, POSTEL
MONTAIGNE

While in Italy the rulers, nobles, rich bourgeois and scholars were imbued with the spirit of the Renaissance and they all more or less participated in the cultural achievements of that period, France was backward in comparison with most other great nations. The Court and the nobility at first showed little interest in humanism, and even maintained that the French were a military race and had no vocation for studies and literature for which the Italians were much better suited.[1] The University clung to scholaticism, and was intensely hostile to humanism. As late as 1527 the Sorbonne condemned the theses of Erasmus, including his views of war, as pestilential heresies, in 1529 they burned Louis de Berquin, a learned royal councillor, at the stake because he had translated some of Erasmus' and Luther's writings into French, and in 1530 they prohibited the interpretation of the Greek and Hebrew text of the Bible.[2] The rising power of royalty discouraged cultural initiative which was suspected as subversive ; King Francis I knew no Latin, and in 1535 he prohibited the printing of any book whatsoever under capital punishment, though this was mitigated through the intervention of the Parliament of Paris.[3]

Nevertheless, humanism soon made headway by associating

[1] Cf. Louis Delaruelle, G. Budé, *Études sur l'humanisme français*, 1907, pp. 160-3.
[2] S. Hess, *Erasmus*, 1790, vol. i, p. 417 ; Ch. Nisard, *Le triumvirat littéraire au XVI*ᵉ *siècle* (J. Lipse, J. Scaliger, I. Casaubon), 1852, p. 11.
[3] Cf. A. Rambaud, *Histoire de la civilisation française*, 1911, vol. i, p. 482.

itself with the royal policy of national unification, expansion and prestige, and with national aspirations in general.[1] The Christian humanism of a Gaguin, Levèfre d'Etaples, Budé and others who deprecated the pagan longing for glory was more and more replaced by a humanism actuated primarily by national ambitions, especially by the wish to prove that the French genius was not inferior to other nations in learning and poetry, by the striving to develop the French language and to oust Italian from its dominating position in high society, and by the ideal of French cultural and political hegemony in the world. French became the exclusive language of the Law Courts, and humanism triumphed over the Sorbonne through the foundation of the Collège de France. France soon surpassed all other countries in classical scholarship and this had the greatest influence on the whole of French civilization. The language was much enriched by the introduction of numerous adapted Latin words, for instance, " patrie ", and was made more flexible by translations of ancient authors. Some humanists even wanted to approximate French as much as possible to Latin, and the idea was widespread that the French were destined to become the new Romans. In 1759 Henri Étienne published a book attempting to prove that French was superior to Italian and to all living languages.[2]

The Reformation did less damage to humanism in France than in Germany. Calvin himself was in his youth a humanist, he wrote a commentary on Seneca, and his mentality was strongly influenced by Roman law. Moreover, Calvinism, which became associated with the policy of a large section of the nobility, thereby threatened national unity, and appeared to the majority of the nation as anti-national, while humanism to a great extent served the cause of royalty and national unity.

Among the humanists of the sixteenth century various types can be distinguished which have all played a great rôle in the development of French national individuality. At that time France surpassed all nations in the study of Roman law and mathematics, as previously in scholasticism, and this fostered the propensity to acute and abstract thought which prepared the rise of French rationalism in the seventeenth century. Nevertheless, various forms of irrationalism were also represented : such as

[1] Cf. K. Vossler, *Frankreichs Kulturim Spiegel seiner Spachentwicklung*, 1913, pp. 219, 249. On national sentiment cf. Delaruelle, pp. 34, 90, 132 ; A. Renaudet, *Préréforme et humanisme à Paris pendant les premières guerres d'Italie*, 1916, p. 259 ; A. Jacquet, *Le sentiment national au 16ᵉ siècle in Revue des questions historiques*, 1895 (mainly on Seyssel).

[2] H. Etienne, *La précellence du langage François*, new edition by E. Huguet, 1896, p. xv.

mysticism, the appreciation of irrational forces in history and sensualism.

Jean Bodin (1530–96) was a scholar who mastered the whole of the learning of his time, and he was also a statesman and a thinker.[1] In the history of political science he is famous for his theory of sovereignty which he conceived as the supreme and indivisible legislative power, indispensable for national unity and harmony. But sovereignty was to him not an arbitrary power; he believed in a monarchy limited by religious and moral obligations, by the natural law and by the fundamental traditions of France. The central idea of his thought is the reign of law, and he strongly combats Machiavelli's attitude towards law and morality. The King is practically the first servant of the State, and Bodin conceives the State as a large family which aims at peace, piety, justice, fortitude and prudence. He had a strong sense of the organic structure and historical individuality of nations, and developed a theory on national character as a product of natural and social forces which had great influence on Montesquieu and other founders of modern sociology. Bodin was proud of French civilization, but also admired and loved that of other nations, and foretold that the unprecedented rise of the world's trade and the discovery of America would lead to universal peace and concord. The whole world would form a single great republic in which each nation would have its function according to its particular aptitudes.

Guillaume Postel (1510–81) was a learned mathematician, professor of Oriental languages, mystic, astrologer and political writer.[2] He hoped to bring about peace and concord between all nations of the world by the propagation of a universal religion, law and language. It was the mission of the Gallic or French race to lead the world to that goal, he called himself a " Gallic Cosmopolitan " and set his hopes on the expansion of French power. The King of France was entitled to world domination and those who resisted were to be forced or even exterminated. The King, however, took no interest in the project. The mystical belief in a mission of France to achieve world-unity by spreading her language and civilization and the connexion of this mission with a policy of political expansion was shared by many later French writers.

The interest in human nature and individuality which

[1] Cf. Roger Chauviré. *J. Bodin*, 1914; F. Renz, *J. Bodin*, 1905; Beatrice Reynolds, *Proponents of Limited Monarchy in the Sixteenth Century*, 1931.
[2] Cf. Pierre Mesnard, *L'essor de la philosophie politique au XVI* siècle*, 1936, p. 432.

humanism had kindled also inspired the *Essays* of Michel de Montaigne (1533-92). He was a Gascon, sprung from an ennobled bourgeois family, which had relations in England ; his mother was a converted Spanish Jewess. Montaigne's father engaged a learned German who knew not a word of French as tutor for his son and the young Montaigne spoke Latin much earlier than French. Among his other tutors were several famous scholars of different nationalities, and the guiding principle was education through gentleness and love. Montaigne was sceptical of all the high principles for which men fanatically combat and persecute each other, he regarded man as a being of ridiculous vanity and great fickleness ; and his rule of life was Epicureanism—the " cultivation of one's own garden " which also Voltaire and Anatole France cherished and which—in a less spiritual way—is the ideal of a large section of the French people. Life appeared to Montaigne as a dream, and a large part of it as a nightmare.[1] Most of all Montaigne hated war and all violence and cruelty, and he felt warm sympathy for the common people and for all those who were oppressed or wronged. The life and customs of the savages were an object of his keenest interest, and he came to the conclusion that the civilized nations were more barbarous than the so-called savages. National vanity is in his essays relentlessly castigated, and held up to ridicule. The French language, says Montaigne, is a poorer language than Spanish, and he confesses that he was a Frenchman exclusively on account of Paris which he loved with all his heart. He quotes a remark of the great Chancellor Olivier de Leuville, who compared the French to monkeys which climb up a tree, jump from branch to branch, and do not rest till they have reached the top, from where they then proudly display their buttocks. Montaigne was very fond of travelling in foreign countries, where he studied the character of their peoples. He judges other nations with great fairness and sympathy and professes himself a whole-hearted citizen of the world.

In the seventeenth century Descartes created a system of rationalism which decisively moulded French thought, and which in combination with the humanistic imitation of ancient poetry and art led to the rise of a great national style, called

[1] This idea has also been expressed by Shakespeare in *Hamlet* and the *Tempest*. John M. Robertson (*Montaigne and Shakespeare*, 1897) has given convincing proofs for his thesis that the French writer has greatly moulded Shakespeare's thought. Cf. Elizabeth Robbins Hooker, *The Relation of Shakespeare to Montaigne* (Publications of the Modern Language Association of America, vol. xvii, 1902). Hooker comes to the conclusion that Robertson overestimated Montaigne's influence ; but she herself seems to exaggerate what Robertson really said.

classicism. The supremacy of reason, clear logic and inviolable rules, the bias for abstract types, the ideal of majestic dignity and the horror of everything vulgar, popular, irregular and mysterious determined judgement in regard to language, poetry, art, love, religion, society and politics. The background of this style of classicism was the all-powerful monarchy which Richelieu had finally established.

6. Humanism and Nationality in England. Bacon, Shakespeare

In England humanism had early found powerful patrons among the enlightened nobility and high ecclesiastics, and became a fashion at the court of Henry VIII and Elizabeth. Erasmus admired the high scholarship of the English humanists, to whom he owed much of his Greek and who kindled in him the spirit of Christian humanism, he was impressed by the galaxy of distinguished men around the Throne, and declared that no land in the world could be compared to England. While on the Continent the rise of absolute monarchy and of Protestant and Catholic fanaticism set limits to the free development of thought and art, in England humanism could freely unfold itself and in the course of time this led to the evolution of the spirit both of enlightenment and of romanticism.

Henry VIII closely corresponded to the model of a prince described by Machiavelli. His system implied the essential thesis of the totalitarian State, namely the idea that the State itself was the highest aim and that its interests were far superior to the morality and welfare of individuals, that it embodied the national will, and that this will was laid down by a dictator. The King, indeed, was a dictator,[1] but he so skilfully manipulated Parliament and public opinion that his dictatorship appeared as leadership, and was generally accepted and even popular. The means which he employed to this end were the appeal to national pride and the furthering of material prosperity, especially that of the gentry and the wealthy commercial middle class. Elizabeth followed the same line of policy. The great humanists of the Tudor age were mostly inspired by Christian and Stoic cosmopolitanism; but also Machiavelli's humanistic nationalism found adherents who believed that the English were destined to become the new Romans.[2]

[1] Cf. A. F. Pollard, *Henry VIII*, 1919, pp. 262, 435.
[2] Cf. for expressions of national sentiment, Esmé Wingfield-Stratford, *History of English Patriotism*, vol. i.

Francis Bacon, a great admirer of Machiavelli, says that the principal point of greatness in any state is to have a race of military men. England is much superior to France in military strength because the middle people, especially the yeomanry, make good soldiers, while the peasants of France do not. Above all, he continues, it is most important for empire and greatness that a nation should profess arms as their principal honour, study and occupation. Nations that pretend to greatness should be sensible of wrongs and should not sit too long upon a provocation. Nobody can be healthful without exercise, and to a kingdom or State a just and honourable war is the true exercise. Bacon professes in these words views which have become the essential tenets of modern nationalism. Yet, he was not a full-fledged nationalist. He argued that a man's own country had some special claims on him more than the rest of the world, he approved of enlarging the power and empire of one's own country over mankind, but more sound and more noble seemed to him the enlargement of the empire of mankind in general over the universe through the progress of knowledge and science. In practical politics he did not advocate a policy of aggression. At the end of his life he deplored that he had wasted his time in writing books in English instead of Latin, which he regarded as the universal language. English books could never, he said, be citizens of the world.

Shakespeare has not only expressed the traits of the English character and contributed to its further development; his psychological intuition embraced the fullness of human nature and his artistic humanism has been a most powerful factor in the moulding of the modern spirit. His national sentiment was mainly exhibited in the historical plays. The dying John of Gaunt's praise of England, the Bastard Faulconbridge's challenge " come the three corners of the world in arms . . ." and King Henry V's address before the day of Agincourt belong to the greatest examples of patriotic poetry in the literature of the world. But Shakespeare, like all great poets and thinkers, believed in the fundamental unity of mankind and was free from national vanity and aggressiveness. When introducing foreigners he often characterizes them by peculiar national traits,[1] and sometimes repeats current English prejudices. In his early play *Henry VI* he even brutally defames the personality of Joan of Arc, though it is possible that those scenes were written by a col-

[1] Cf. Cumberland Clark, *Shakespeare and National Character*, 1932, and *Shakespeare and Psychology*, p. 94.

laborator. On the other hand, he frequently censures English foibles and in *Hamlet* makes a gravedigger remark that Hamlet was sent to England because the men there were as mad as he.

The poet has often been accused of aristocratic bias, and he naturally could not quite evade the limitations of his environment and of his time.[1] But as a rule he far transcends the level of politics, and interprets human nature with a sympathetic understanding for all its aspects. He pictures the dynamics of passion and the ravages of ambition, the futility of social prejudices and the grotesque meanness of man's animal appetites, the narrow egotism and overweening self-conceit of all classes and parties, and their ideological disguise by the great words of honour, liberty and equality, the self-destructiveness both of the exaggerated individualism of a Richard III and a Coriolanus, and of the collective mentality of a human crowd excited by a demagogue such as Jack Cade or Antonius. In *The Tempest* the old Gonzalo anticipates Rousseau in imagining an ideal society where men live in an innocent state of nature, uncorrupted by civilization, property and government. Complete equality, however, was not Shakespeare's ideal. In *Coriolanus* the jovial patrician Menenius Agrippa tells the rebellious plebs his famous story in which social inequalities are compared with the functional differences between the organs of a body, and speaks for compromise. In *Troilus and Cressida* Ulysses explains that the whole world depends on well-ordered inequality, on degree, priority, place, proportion, season, form, office and custom. If these were destroyed chaos would ensue. Later Ulysses speaks of the art of government and says :

> There is a mystery with whom relation
> Durst never meddle, in the soul of state ;
> Which hath an operation more divine
> Than breath or pen can give expressure to.

Shakespeare did not think of formulating political doctrines. Yet the wealth of his observations on human character must have stimulated political thought too. His general view of mankind and society spoke against abstract simplifications and illusions of every kind. Good and evil, right and wrong are in every cause inextricably intertwined. This excludes the realizations of an ideal Utopia on earth, but it also enables us to feel a certain sympathy for our political opponent, and encourages us rather

[1] Cf. on this controversy, H. B. Charlton, *Shakespeare's Politics and Politicians*, 1929 ; Albert Tolman, *Is Shakespeare Aristocratic ?* in Publications of the Modern Language Association of America, 1914 ; and F. Tupper, *The Shakespearean Mob* (in the same publications), 1912.

to make a compromise with him than to attempt to impose our will by force.

7. Puritanism, Mercantilism and Nationalism in the Seventeenth Century

The revolutionary movements which led to the establishment of the English Commonwealth were not the outcome of social distress or economic interests, nor did they imply a struggle between classes. Economic and social factors, of course, played a certain part, but they were by no means decisive.[1] Among the factors which brought about the Revolution Puritanism was foremost. Puritanism comprised many widely different forms which had in common a certain measure of religious individualism, a strong sentiment of responsibility to God and distrust of human nature. Most Puritans were more influenced by the spirit of the Old Testament than by that of Jesus, more by holy combativeness than by love, and like Judaism they laid great stress on everybody's responsibility for the salvation of the community by strict observance of God's laws, not merely on the salvation of one's own soul. This concentration on supra-natural aims, which was the opposite of humanism, seemed to depreciate nationality; but in practice Puritanism was in many ways related to national aspirations. Many people were Puritans, mainly because it was the symbol of national independence of Rome, and of fierce antagonism to the Catholic powers of Spain and France which were both national enemies and rivals in the struggle for maritime and colonial domination. The Stuarts were unpopular because of their foreign, Scottish, origin, because of their striving for religious and international appeasement, and for their lack of success in the wars which they were compelled to undertake, in order to satisfy national sentiment.

The Hebrew, national element, in Puritanism expressed itself in the belief that the English nation was the new " Chosen people " and in the manifold attempts at the building of a Biblical Commonwealth, or a " new Jerusalem " which had such a large share in the foundation of Puritan settlements in America.[2] The Christian, supra-national element, which was also of Hebrew origin, led to the idea of England's mission to become the leader

[1] Cf. Godfrey Davies, *The Early Stuarts*, 1937, pp. 127, 260, 267, 280; J. Deane Jones, *The English Revolution*, 1931, p. 70; Charles Firth, *Oliver Cromwell and the Rule of the Puritans*, 1923, p. 70.

[2] The correlation of Puritan Hebraism with nationality is stressed by Ernest Barker, *Cromwell and the English People*, 1937, pp. 24, 82, 104.

and protector of all Protestant nations. On the other hand, Christian individualism and the Calvinist doctrine of predestination also stimulated the belief that only God's elect, the "Saints", had that mission and, therefore, represented the nation. The idea of a national mission, however, was not exclusively due to Puritanism; it was also fostered by humanistic admiration for Rome and for her imperial mission. Both Puritan and humanistic elements, furthermore, contributed to the rise of republican, democratic and liberal ideas which became powerful currents in English political thought, and were widely incorporated in the idea of the national mission. The opposition to the Divine Right of Kings tended to convert England into a parliamentary republic, the democratic aspirations aimed at making the whole people, or wide sections of it, the real Sovereign, and the demand for toleration and the Rights of Men implied that national sovereignty was limited by the Law of Nature, and laid the foundation of liberal thought.[1]

A third factor of great importance was mercantilism, which consisted in economic nationalism of a monopolistic and often aggressive disposition. The development of national States had everywhere been accompanied by mercantilism, and in England the history of both goes back very far.[2] The seventeenth century, however, formed the peak in this evolution; at that time international policy was more strongly influenced by mercantilist motives than ever before, and many writers worked out a theory of mercantilism. The core of mercantilist policy was that trade was primarily a means for increasing the power of the State and the greatness of the nation, not one for the profit of individual merchants or for supplying the people with the goods needed in the best possible way.[3] The supreme aim both of trade regulations and colonial policy was to render the State independent of other countries and to increase its military, naval and financial strength.[4] Though certain sections of trade profited from this system, trade as a whole was certainly adversely affected by it, especially by the outbreak of wars to which mercantilism contributed. In particular the woollen trade which formed by far the most important branch of English commerce had grievously to suffer under the wars with Spain which Elizabeth and Crom-

[1] G. P. Gooch, *English Democratic Ideas in the Seventeenth Century*, 1927; *Political thought in England from Bacon to Halifax*, 1914–5.
[2] Cf. J. W. Horrocks, *Short History of Mercantilism*, 1925; E. Heckscher, *Mercantilism*, 1935.
[3] Cf. the quotations from Cunningham and others in Heckscher, p. 28.
[4] On the aim of power in colonial mercantilism cf. G. L. Beer, *The Origins of the British Colonial System*, 1908, pp. 6, 53, 70, 400.

well waged for political reasons, and the merchants, therefore, often protested against a warlike policy.[1] Sir Thomas Roe laid down the rule for the East India Company to avoid the use of force for extorting trade concessions, as war and trade were incompatible, and many writers expressed the same view. But the cult of national power and prestige which constitutes nationalism found strong support in men of all classes. One of its main principles was the old claim to the sovereignty of the sea which was stressed by the Stuarts and the Commonwealth. It first referred to the narrow seas around England, but was soon extended much farther,[2] and was often enforced in a highly provocative way. At the time of the Restoration Molloy proclaimed that sea power was world power and that England followed in this the example of the Romans, who founded their Empire on commerce and the navy.

Cromwell's policy combined religious, political and commercial motives to such a degree that the historians widely differ in their views as to the predominance of one or the other motive. In any case, however, he may be called a nationalist. True, he himself declared that the Christian interest took precedence of the national; but his religion was imbued with the belief in the great mission of his nation, to use its power for spreading the true faith in the world and for shielding it everywhere. He wanted to make England the leader of a federation of all Protestant States against the House of Habsburg; he claimed the right to protect the Protestants in France and other countries; but also allied with Catholic France against Spain. Dunkirk was occupied as a " bridle to the Dutch and a door into the Continent " and French and Spanish colonies were attacked and seized in spite of peace with these countries. The first Dutch war had brought England the possession of a powerful navy, largely captured from the Dutch, and Cromwell deliberated with his council whether the ships should be laid up, or employed in some advantageous design, and in this case whether against France or Spain, Cromwell pointed out that the design would cost little more than laying up the ships, that there was a chance of immense profit; and that surely the fact of this naval power being in the hands of England was a leading of Providence.[3] To disarm the Spanish King's suspicion, aroused by the despatch of the fleet to

---

[1] Cf. Jean McLachlan, *Trade and Peace with Old Spain from 1667 to 1750*, 1940, p. 19; Horrocks, p. 94; Pollard, *Henry VIII*, pp. 137, 250; James Williamson, *The Age of Drake*, 1938, pp. 13, 49; Firth, *Cromwell*, p. 387.
[2] Cf. Sir Butler and S. Maccoby, *The Development of International Law*, 1928, p. 40.
[3] John Morley, *Cromwell*, 1900, p. 458.

the Mediterranean, Cromwell assured him that this implied no ill intent and that the English Government counted him among their friends. Cromwell's foreign policy was designed to realize his favourite boast that he wanted to make the name of an Englishman as dreaded in the world as formerly that of a Roman was. His success in raising the power and prestige of England increased national pride. Edmund Waller in his panegyric praised him for having made England a glorious State, the seat of Empire, and for having forced all nations to greet each vessel of the English Fleet. Heaven has destined England " to give laws, to balance Europe and its states to awe ". The oppressed from all countries will henceforth resort to England, to crave justice, and the Lord Protector shall then be known as the world's protector.

Milton's idea of England's mission was that she should disseminate the blessings of freedom and civilization among citizens, kingdoms and nations. He saw in his mind " a noble and puissant nation rousing herself like a strong man after sleep, and shaking her invincible locks ". England appeared to him as another Rome in the West. Yet he devoted admiring words to the national character of the Germans, French, Spaniards and Italians too. The duty of a free Commonwealth, wrote Harrington in 1656, was to relieve oppressed peoples, and to spread liberty and true religion in other lands. " She is not made for herself only ", but should be " a minister of God upon the earth, to the intent that the whole world may be governed by righteousness ". A stationary State, he further argued, was doomed to weakness. The policy of the Republic must aim at increase and not merely at preservation. If it was to be lasting, it must lay great bases for eternity. If it was to be strong, it must have room to grow. " You cannot plant an oak in a flower-pot she must have earth for her roots, and heaven for her branches." [1] Firth says that Harrington in these words expressed the views of his contemporaries. He seems to have been the first writer who put forward the theory of " living space " for a nation entrusted with a great mission. Nicholas Barbon in 1690 wrote that England by means of her navy and the fighting spirit of her free and prosperous people was best fitted for founding a world Empire. He proposed that an act should be passed granting naturalization to all foreigners who purchased land in England. This would induce large numbers of foreign people who were oppressed and

[1] Ch. Firth, *Cromwell*, pp. 389, 393. Cf. further, James Harrington, *The Oceana and other Works*, new ed., 1737, p. 194 ; H. F. Russell Smith, *Harrington and his Oceana*, 1914.

enslaved by their rulers to migrate to England, and the strength of this country would thereby so increase that an Empire would result no less glorious and much larger than those of Alexander and Caesar.[1]

The idea of England's world mission can be traced also in many other writers of this and later times and was sometimes associated with nationalism and sometimes with cosmopolitanism.[2] The expansion of world trade soon tended to stimulate criticism of economic nationalism, and far-seeing merchants began to suggest the liberation of trade from the fetters of mercantilism. Sir Dudley North in 1691 wrote " that the whole world as to trade is but as one nation or people and therein nations are as persons ".[3]

Thomas Hobbes's views of human nature resembled that of Machiavelli, and was largely moulded by the experience of the endless religious and civil wars which ravaged Europe during his long lifetime. Man appeared to him as egotistic, vainglorious, aggressive and swayed by his craving for power and prestige. He believed that only an all-powerful State could guarantee security and order. But this State is not a super-organism, its aim is not the enhancement of its own prestige or domination, nor the universal regulation of all affairs. The State only exists for the promotion of the interests of the individuals, it should meddle as little as possible in the affairs of the citizens, and should not indulge in aggressive wars. Hobbes, therefore, does not agree with Machiavelli's idea of the aims of the State.

8. The Growth of Pacifism and International Law

The religious revolution, furthermore, also evoked many movements which abhorred war and every violence as utterly incompatible with the spirit of Christ. The Anabaptists in Germany, the Mennonites in Holland, the Polish Brethren and Socinians in Poland, the Moravian Brethren in the Bohemian countries, and the Quakers in England were the most important sects which were inspired by this conviction. Some sects not only rejected military service but also the paying of taxes which were used for maintaining soldiers, or even all government based on compulsion, and every social inequality. Fausto Sozzini denied that the Christian should prefer his fatherland to other

[1] Cf. Nicholas Barbon, *Discourse of Trade*, 1690 (new ed., 1905, p. 31).
[2] Cf. F. Brie, " Imperialistische Stroemungen in der englischen Literatur " in the periodical *Anglia*, vol. 40, 1916.
[3] Sir Dudley North, *Discourses on Trade*, 1691 (new ed., 1907), p. 13.

countries, if these were in some way better. His real fatherland, he declared, was heaven.[1]

Devastating wars and the growth of the longing for peace also led to the development of the idea of an international law. The pioneers of this spirit were Spanish scholars, especially the Dominican Franciscus a Victoria and the Jesuit Franciscus Suarez. Their work was continued and carried farther by the Italian Alberico Gentilis, who taught at Oxford, and by the Dutchman Hugo Grotius, who became the first classic of the Law of Nations. They all have been strongly influenced by the traditions of Erasmus.[2] Other reformers went still farther, putting forward plans for the organization of an international tribunal, a League of Nations or a federation of Christian States. Pope Leo X's proposal of a universal federation of Christian princes, for securing peace among themselves, has already been mentioned. In the sixteenth and eighteenth century many similar plans have been proposed, mainly by Catholic scholars like Campanella, Cruce, Postel, St. Pierre, but also by Protestants like Grotius, Penn, Bellers and others.[3]

9. Nationality and Enlightenment in England. Locke, Shaftesbury, Bolingbroke

In the sixteenth and seventeenth centuries the fierce struggles between the religious and political parties, and between nations, were accompanied by the silent growth of philosophy and science. In all nations great thinkers pondered the origin and nature of society and government. Society was either conceived as a contract between the citizens, and between them and the king, or it was compared to an organism. Both views could be interpreted either in a monarchical or in a republican sense, though the contract theory seemed to favour the cause of the people, which practically meant the upper classes. The notion was not lacking, however, that society had something of both a contract and an organism, that it implied both voluntary submission and the recognition of functional necessity. Both views had great influence on the ideas of national sovereignty.

This principle triumphed in the second English revolution,

[1] Cf. Christian Lange, *Histoire de l'internationalisme*, 1919, pp. 230–52, describes the growth and ideas of the pacifist sects.
[2] Cf. Lange, p. 262 ; P. Mesnard, *l'Essor de la philosophie politique au 16ᵉ siècle*, 1936, pp. 454, 617.
[3] Cf. Lange, p. 372 ; T. ter Meulen, *Der Gedanke der internationalen Organisation in seiner Entwicklung*, 1917, p. 128 ; Veit Valentin, *Geschichte des Voelkerbundgedankens in Deutschland*, 1920.

and the consequences startled the world. England seemed to have found the solution of the antinomies between national liberty and national unity, and between liberty and power. In the course of the eighteenth century she developed parliamentary government, became a World Power, gained enormous wealth, produced a brilliant civilization, and opened out vast new fields to thought. True, her development had another side too. National liberty meant not the rule of the nation at large, but that of a small oligarchy ; national unity was often threatened by violent and unscrupulous party strife, and later on by the deep cleavage which the economic revolution created between the classes. England's continental policy, colonial expansion and economic monopolism aroused national passions and enmities. Nevertheless, the positive achievements far surpassed the weaknesses. Everywhere England was admired and envied as the paragon of a united, free and proud nation. When the French complained that they were no nation, and indulged in endless longings for *la patrie*, they had the example of England in their mind.

The greatest of all achievements, however, was England's contribution to the rise of the spirit of enlightenment which appeared to all civilized men as a new gospel, and which rapidly began to transform the opinions and beliefs of all nations. Enlightenment continued the general outlook of humanism, its trust in human nature, and like humanism engendered many widely divergent philosophies. It was not a single doctrine, but a movement for liberation from the power of obsolete traditions and institutions. The thinkers who belonged to it differed on many points, but they agreed in their trust in the power of reason to realize the truth ; and this reason was that of the individual, not any collective reason embodied in old laws and beliefs. No law or belief was deemed too sacred to be examined by critical thought. The spirit of enlightenment, furthermore, implied the belief in laws of nature and society which could be studied by empirical methods, and the hope that the reign of reason would result in the furthering of progress and happiness. Most, though not all, of the philosophers of enlightenment had an optimistic outlook, and all stood for toleration and practical humanity.[1]

The enemies of enlightenment have represented it as an exaggerated intellectualism, in the sense of cold calculation, and have charged it with the neglect of the irrational forces of emotion

---

[1] Cf. the profound interpretation of the spirit of enlightenment given by Ernst Cassirer, *Die Philosophie der Aufklärung*, 1932.

and imagination. They have praised romanticism for having overcome the narrow utilitarianism and one-sided concept of human nature which they ascribed to the philosophy of enlightenment. In truth, however, the great representatives of this philosophy did not correspond to that distorted image. Many of them were well aware of the irrational forces in man, and appealed to them no less than to reason. Both rationalism and irrationalism were strivings for liberation of the individual from antiquated fetters. The time of enlightenment witnessed also the origin and growth of those irrationalist strivings which later were named romanticism ; but they were not yet conceived as being hostile to the rule of reason, if kept in their proper place and within the right limits.

Locke formulated the fundamental doctrines of liberalism. His idea of a nation implies the reign of law, the natural rights of man, government by consent, the separation of powers and subordination of national interests to those of humanity. By the law of nature, he says, all mankind forms one community, and, were it not for the corruption and viciousness of degenerate men, there would be no need for any other, no necessity that men should separate from this great and natural community and combine into smaller and divided associations.

The philosophy of Shaftesbury was a mighty fountain of irrationalism, tempered by enlightenment. Like Leibnitz, Spinoza and Herder he combined fundamental tenets of enlightenment with ideas which later on became the gospel of the romanticists. He was educated by Locke, and strove with him for religious liberty and toleration. Yet he disagrees with many rigid intellectualists in emphasizing the importance of emotions, affections and imagination. Virtue is to him not a result of reasonable considerations, but the same as beauty, a harmony of the soul, a noble enthusiasm. Man is not chiefly induced to social life by a calculation of his interests, but by his inborn social instincts, and he possesses a moral sense that makes him feel right and wrong without much reasoning. Nature, human personality and society appear to Shaftesbury as living units inspired by a creative, divine spirit, or, as we should say, as organisms, not mechanisms. Society is not based on contract. Even animals live in society.

Shaftesbury sees the essential quality of a nation in a public spirit, or " sense of public good " which he, in brief, calls " a publick ", and which we could define as a spiritual patriotism. A community, that is a " national brotherhood ", unites men for each other's happiness and support, and for the highest of all happinesses and enjoyments, " the intercourse of minds, the free use of our reason, and the exercise of mutual love and friendship ". Good government and public spirit are closely connected with morality. There is no real love of virtue without the knowledge of public good. Of all human affections, says Shaftesbury, the noblest is that of love of one's country. Yet this does not refer to the place where we live. It is an affection for something moral and social, for " a naturally civil and political state of mankind, called a People ". " A multitude held together by force is not properly united, nor does such a body make a people. It is the social League, confederacy and mutual consent, founded in some common good or interests, which joins the members of a community and makes a people one. Absolute power annuls the Public (spirit), and where there is no Public, or Constitution, there is in reality no mother country, or Nation." Shaftesbury complains that the English language has no word like patria, though he is proud that England has a public spirit, and, therefore, is a nation, thanks to her constitution with its happy Balance of Power between prince and people. Absolutism is ruinous to morality, religion and the public weal.

Yet Shaftesbury is opposed to every overweening national vanity and to national egotism.[1]

> What is knavery but narrowness ? Myself, that is to say, my purse against the public purse, my family against the public family, and what difference between this, and my nation or commonwealth against the world ? My country's laws against the universal laws ? My fancy against the universal decree ?
> The contests about trade, precedency, honour, the flag. England, mistress of the world ! Giving laws to the world ! But go now and tell us of justice, faith, honesty, the public.
> Thou wouldst serve thy country. Right. But consider withal and ask thyself : wouldst thou willingly be perjured, wouldst thou be false, wouldst thou lie, flatter, be debauched and dissolute to serve it ? Certainly I would not. But if I think to serve it as am now bid, all this will necessarily follow. For I must prostitute my mind. I must grow corrupt, interested, false, and where will then be the service I shall render to ?

Shaftesbury declares great empires unnatural since in them all power must lie with a few, and this must destroy the public spirit. The Roman Empire is a striking instance.

Bolingbroke in his *Letters on the Study and Use of History* points out that one of the main advantages to be derived from a study

[1] Cf. *The Life, Unpublished Letters and Philosophical Regimen of Anthony, Earl of Shaftesbury*, ed. by B. Rand, 1900, p. 103, 115. Shaftesbury, *Characteristicks*, 1732, vol. I, p. 106, vol. iii, p. 143.

of history consists in the fact that " history serves to purge the mind of those national partialities and prejudices, that we are apt to contract in our education, and that experience for the most part rather confirms than removes."

> There is scarce any folly or vice more epidemical among the sons of men, than that ridiculous and hurtful vanity, by which the people of each country are apt to prefer themselves to those of every other ; and to make their own customs, and manners, and opinions the standards of right and wrong, of true and false. . . . Now nothing can contribute more to prevent us from being tainted with this vanity, than to accustom ourselves early to contemplate the different nations of the Earth, in that vast map which history spreads before us, in their rise and fall, in their barbarous and civilized states, in the likeness and unlikeness of them all to one another, and of each to itself. By frequently renewing this prospect of the mind, the Mexican with his cap and coat of feathers, sacrificing a human victim to his god, will not appear more savage to our eyes, than the Spaniard with a hat on his head, and a gonilla round his neck, sacrificing whole nations to his ambition, his avarice, and even the wantonness of his cruelty.

But the study of history, he continues, not only contributes extremely to keep our mind free from a ridiculous partiality in favour of our own country ; it also creates in our mind a preference of affection to our own country. This sentiment is not an instinct, but is created by education and habit, obligation and interest, and it is indispensable for the prosperity of all societies, and the grandeur of some.[1]

10. NATIONALITY AND ENLIGHTENMENT IN FRANCE. LOUIS XIV, MONTESQUIEU, VOLTAIRE

In France the words nation and patrie became slogans of the opposition to royal absolutism. Nation meant a free and sovereign people and the word, therefore, was odious to the defenders of absolutism. Louis XIV emphasized that he alone was invested with the power implied in the word " nation ", saying : " La nation ne fait pas corps en France ; elle reside tout entière dans la personne du roi." In his instructions to his son he says that in a body the head only has to deliberate and to decide, and all other members have merely the function of carrying out its orders.[2] According to this view the King actually constitutes the

---

[1] Henry St. John, Viscount Bolingbroke, *Works*, 1809, vol. iii, p. 332.
[2] Cf. *Œuvres de Louis XIV*, 1806, vol. ii, p. 26. This was also Bossuet's doctrine, cf. Kingsley Martin, *French Liberal Thought in the Eighteenth Century*, 1929, p. 26.

nation or the State. Louis XIV even regarded it as an indecency, as Bolingbroke says, if the word " State " was frequently used in his presence. In his memoirs he sometimes speaks of foreign peoples as nations. But the French are regularly called " my peoples " and France " my States ". Even this representative of strict centralization, therefore, was averse to a word implying national unity which might endanger his power. In 1754 the Marquis d'Argenson wrote : " Never before have the words nation and State been repeated so often as now. These two words were never pronounced under Louis XIV, and no one had even an idea of them."

The revocation of the Edict of Nantes in which Henry IV had granted toleration to the Protestants, and the subsequent persecution of the Huguenots, caused 400,000 of them to flee abroad. Most of them found a refuge in England, Holland, Switzerland and Prussia, where they introduced many new industries. Among them, moreover, were numerous intellectuals who were enthusiastic admirers of England, who appeared to them as the country of liberty, humanity and toleration. They became indefatigable propagandists for England and the ideas of English enlightenment, which they contrasted with French despotism and obscurantism.[1] The Huguenot refugees flooded the whole of Europe with their books and periodicals, and with translations of English literature. France, in particular, was soon permeated with pro-English sentiment, and even Anglomania. The greatest French writers, such as Voltaire, Diderot, Rousseau, Montesquieu, followed the road shown by the Huguenots. Even when England and France were involved in great wars, in which France suffered humiliating defeats, the French intellectuals were largely imbued with enthusiasm for English institutions, ideas and civilization.

The French thinkers and writers of that time tried to combine patriotism and cosmopolitanism.[2] Their image of a nation was

[1] Cf. especially Joseph Texte, *Rousseau et les origines du cosmopolitisme litteraire*, 1895. Ch. Bastide, *Anglais et Français du XVIIe Siècle*, 1912, p. 167. The London Huguenots had their centre in the Rain Bow Coffee-House. The views of the age on English history and politics have been decisively moulded by the *Histoire de l'Angleterre* by the Huguenot refugee Rapin de Thoyras. Cf. E. Fueter, *Geschichte der neueren Historiographie*, 1911, p. 320.

[2] The most instructive analysis of French eighteenth-century thought on nationality is given in the book by Eva Hoffman-Linke, *Zwischen Nationalismus und Demokratie, Gestalten der franzoesischen Vorrevolution*, 1927. Cf. further A. Aulard, *Le patriotisme français de la renaissance a la révolution*, 1921, and H. Stewart and P. Desjardins, *French Patriotism in the Nineteenth Century* (1814-33), 1923, which has an interesting survey on the ideas of the eighteenth century too. A characteristic example of the modern tendency of condemning the most brilliant epoch of the French spirit is the thesis of a great French scholar, Émile Faguet, that the eighteenth century was lacking in patriotism and was alien to French nationality. Cf. Émile Faguet, *Dix-huitième siècle, études littéraires*, 1890.

that of a free, enlightened and harmoniously united people, and they believed that nobody had a fatherland under a despotic system. They were proud of the brilliant achievements of France, and wanted to maintain her cultural hegemony, but they abhorred war, conquest and national prejudice. Many of them were aristocrats and believed in the mission of the educated classes to lead the people. They had the deepest pity for the suffering lower classes, and many were willing to sacrifice their privileges in order to help them.

The most brilliant exponent of liberal thought was Montesquieu.[1] He showed the world that freedom was the moving principle of progress in every field, and that freedom depended on a balance of power, both in internal and external affairs. The English constitution was to him the most striking example of this rule. His interpretation of English politics came as a revelation even to the English, and was enthusiastically greeted by their greatest scholars and politicians. Montesquieu had learned much from England and also exercised a most stimulating influence on English thought and politics.[2] He had studied the institutions of many nations in a comparative spirit, and he confessed that he felt the same warm sympathy for every people among whom he had travelled. In spite of his admiration for England he did not believe that one single political system was good for all nations, but thought that a constitution had to conform to the spirit of the people, and that the legislator could change customs and traditions, only slowly and with great caution. Bodin and other writers had also taught this, and they had tried to explain national characteristics by the influence of natural surroundings, especially by that of the climate, on the human temperament. Montesquieu accepted this theory, and it forms one of the weakest points of his theories. But he also initiated the development of another view of great importance, by emphasizing more than his predecessors had done the action of social institutions and historical traditions on the spirit of nations. States and societies were not founded and moulded by contract, but were largely conditioned by circumstances beyond the control of individuals: they were maintained by organic solidarity, and each political system had its particular mentality. Each individual was working for the common good while thinking to work for himself. The exaggeration of climatic and other factors hindered Montesquieu from

[1] Cf. A. Sorel, *Montesquieu*.
[2] J. Dédieu, *Montesquieu et la tradition politique Anglaise*, 1909, has shown what Montesquieu owed to England, while F. Fletcher, *Montesquieu and English Politics*, 1939, tells what England owed to him.

realizing the full bearing of the organic view. But he was the pioneer of a deeper understanding of politics and history.

Voltaire has often been compared with Erasmus for his universal learning, his sparkling wit and irony, and his relations to powerful rulers. Yet he lacked the deep religious belief of Erasmus, he was an agnostic and sceptic. He neither exalted the power of reason, nor believed in the goodness of human nature, though he showed much practical sympathy for the suffering and oppressed. Moreover, he disliked fanatics and radicals, distrusted the people, and regarded the rule of an enlightened and tolerant king as the best one. Unfortunately most kings loved war and glory, and he had a horror of war. He wrote bitter words about the warlike ambitions of kings, and about the stupidity of men in admiring conquerors. The philosopher, he thought, did not belong to any fatherland or party. Nevertheless, he was proud of France's hegemony in civilization, and occasionally wars elicited his wish for France's success or pride in French victories. His longing for peace was sincere and sometimes bordered on radical pacifism. Yet he was sceptical of all plans for perpetual peace, and thought that disarmament and belief in the law of nations would result in the ruin of a State.[1]

Voltaire has put forward his view of patriotism in an article in his *Dictionnaire Philosophique*.

> Who has really a fatherland? [he asks]. Is it the Jew who is burned at the stake? Or the murderers in uniform who sell themselves to any prince whomsoever? Or the young labourer who does not possess anything of the natal soil, nor has any chance to acquire anything? The voluptuous Parisian who only loves his life for pleasure? Perhaps it is the financier who cordially loves his fatherland? Or the officer and the soldiers who would ruin the peasant on whom they are billeted if they were not hindered? . . . Euripides was the first who wrote: Fatherland is every soil which nourishes thee. However, the greater the fatherland is the less can one love it. Affection decreases with expansion. A too numerous family whose members one hardly knows cannot arouse our warm love. Patriotism, moreover, often leads to becoming the enemy of all other men. A country obviously can only win at the expense of another one. To wish for the greatness of one's own country means to wish for the misfortune of his neighbours. He only who has a share in the natal soil or other property under secure protection of the laws, and a share in political rights, forms a member of the community, and he only has a fatherland.

Voltaire, therefore, thinks that only people with some pro-

[1] Cf. Paul Sackmann, *Voltaires Geistesart und Gedankenwelt*. 1910; Georg Brandes, *Voltaire*.

perty, security and liberty can feel patriotism and that they form the nation. Occasionally he identifies the nation with the third Estate.

11. ROUSSEAU AND NATIONALITY

Among the political writers of all ages Jean-Jacques Rousseau (1712-78) has probably exercised the greatest influence on his and indirectly on all subsequent times.[1] His influence on the ideology of modern democracy, socialism and nationality was tremendous, though he would have repudiated some of the consequences. His doctrine also implies most of the essential ideas of the political philosophy of Fichte, Hegel, Mazzini and the socialists. Moreover, he was the most trenchant critic of enlightenment and the founder of romanticism which was associated with the growth of modern ideas on nationality. Like most great thinkers, Rousseau has not worked out an entirely consistent doctrine; his philosophy comprises different strands which reflect the conflicting tendencies in his own character and human nature in general. His thought was not guided by systematic study, but owed most to his immense sensitiveness and intuition, and to the experiences of his strange life. In many respects he typifies a section of modern intellectuals which has often had extraordinary influence on the public mind.

Before Rousseau began to write, the spirit of enlightenment had brought forth several views of State and society. Hobbes had formulated the theory of enlightened despotism, based on a very pessimistic concept of human nature. The terror of power alone could prevent man from killing and robbing one another. His State is, as G. Gooch remarks, " simply a policeman of superhuman size with a truncheon in his hand ".[2] Locke's view of human nature was the opposite: he believed in the essential peaceableness and reasonableness of man, and his State was mainly there to protect property, and could be compared to an insurance company with very limited powers; it corresponded to the Whig ideal of government. Montesquieu had developed a theory of relativism, in his view men were neither bad nor good,

[1] Cf. *The Political Writings of J. J. Rousseau* with Introductions and Notes by C. E. Vaughan, 2 vols., 1915; J. Morley, *Rousseau*, 2 vols.; Émile Faguet, *Rousseau penseur*, 1910; Paul Janet, *Histoire de la science politique*, vol. ii; G. Lanson, *Histoire de la littérature française*, 10th ed., 1908; Harald Hoeffding, *Rousseau*, 1897; Franz Haymann, *Rousseau's Sozialphilosophie*, 1898; Ernest Seillière, *Philosophie de l'Impérialisme*, vol. i.

[2] G. Gooch, " Hobbes and the Absolute State " (in *Studies in Diplomacy and Statecraft*, 1942, p. 359).

but their character depended on their environment; the spirit of the nations was the product of climate, geography and history. All these views had their merits, but none of them encouraged active patriotism and national sentiment. Neither Hobbes' nor Locke's idea of a State had any bearing on nationality. Neither the policeman nor the insurance company formed a personality whom one could love, of whom one could be proud and for whom one could be expected to sacrifice everything. Montesquieu, indeed, had made ample allowance for national diversities, but he looked upon them mainly as a sociologist, trying to explain their causes without taking sides, and his theory implied no justification of national sentiment; it rather encouraged cosmopolitanism.

Rousseau's whole being thirsted for love and enthusiasm, he hated the calculations of cold reason and revolted against the heartless superficiality and tyranny of society. The fashionable philosophers of his time distrusted and ridiculed enthusiasm and exalted reason, they believed that the progress of civilization would render mankind wise and happy. Now Rousseau flung in their face that the cult of reason and the development of civilization were a curse for humanity. Nature had made man good, peaceable, equal, free and happy, but society and civilization had made him bad, egotistic, vainglorious, unequal, unfree and unhappy. The main causes of the deep corruption of man were social inequality, especially the introduction of private property, and intellectualism. The development of class divisions between rich and poor, rulers and ruled, educated and uneducated, and the rise of government, ranks, war, agriculture, industries and trade, science, philosophy, arts, luxuries, town life had destroyed the original innocence of natural life and has made man increasingly unhappy and perverse. Only the savages, the peasants, the children still showed something of the original goodness of man.[1]

So far Rousseau's emotional individualism would seem to lead to anarchy; but he suddenly turns round and proclaims that only the merging of all private individuality in the collective organism of a national State can save man. Plutarch had kindled in him the enthusiasm for the heroic patriotism of the ancient world which he saw in a romantic light. The citizens, he demands, must completely subordinate their private interests to the common weal. In doing so they, nevertheless, are free because they obey a law which they themselves have made, which repre-

---

[1] Faguet remarks that Rousseau unconsciously adopted the biblical story of Adam's fall. Man, lured on by a demon with the promise that knowledge would make him like God, loses the innocence and happiness of life in paradise.

sents their true will. Government must be determined by the general will, which means both the will of all and the will towards the general, collective interest. This, however, is not always the will of the majority, which may be misled by passion and ignorance. The government by Parliament which was developing in England, and the idea of an internal Balance of Power were rejected by him, and he seems to have regarded direct legislation by the people—as in some Swiss cantons—as the ideal form of government. Political and social equality were the supreme aims in the organization of the State, and the community had the mission to educate all their members to citizenship, morality and nationality. Rousseau anticipated Hegel in his views that freedom meant moral freedom, that the State had the right to force the citizens to be truly free by forming their will towards morality, that there was no morality outside the State, and that the competence of the State was practically unlimited. Sometimes he even went farther than Hegel. In his project of a constitution for Corsica he says that he desired that the property of the State should be as large and as strong, and that of the individual as small and as weak as possible, which implies the principle of socialism, though it is a matter of dispute how far he may be called a socialist. He probably wanted merely equal distribution of property among all members of the State, not nationalization of production. Like Hegel in his youth Rousseau believed that Christianity was not compatible with ardent patriotism. It regarded heaven as the true fatherland, and preached meekness, justice, peaceableness and universal fraternity which was good for humanity in general, but threatened to enervate the State and disintegrate society. He, therefore, wished that the State should prescribe a minimum of civic religion and else grant tolerance to all beliefs, except Catholicism, atheism and agnosticism. Rousseau hated Catholicism because it tended to form a State within the State.

The spirit of enlightenment was inclined to regard the State merely as a necessary evil and national sentiment as a prejudice. Rousseau, on the contrary, saw in them the greatest value. He returned to Plato's theory in which the State appeared as a moral organism, the fountain of all morality, and to the view of Aristotle who looked upon the State as prior to the individual and the indispensable guarantor of a good life. His individualism in every respect transformed itself into a rigid collectivism.

Patriotism is a great and heroic virtue. It is the only effective love of humanity, for it is not possible to embrace the whole world in love. One must concentrate one's affection on the narrower field of the fatherland. In a primitive society man had a fatherland in the tribe. Liberty, equality and fraternity reigned, and this constituted the fatherland. But the introduction of private property in land aroused rapacity and led to wars, to the development of a warrior caste and to the annihilation of national liberties and citizenship. At last nobody had any more the slightest interest in the fatherland. To subjects it was the same whether they were oppressed by a native or a foreign tyrant. The fatherland had ceased to exist. Only liberty and equality can evoke true patriotism.

Rousseau specially admired the Sparta of Lycurgus with her iron discipline, her passionate patriotism and self-sacrificing heroism, Sparta who banished arts and science, stood on a higher level than Athens and later Rome who cultivated them, and forgot their military discipline, frugality and patriotism. Lycurgus showed his people the fatherland at every moment, in the laws, in games and festivals, in private affairs, even in love. He did not leave them a moment of rest to belong to themselves alone, and out of this continual coercion grew a glowing love of the fatherland which was the strongest, or rather the only passion of the Spartans and made them superhuman beings. In his enthusiasm for Sparta Rousseau closes his eyes to the fact that Sparta was certainly not founded on liberty and equality of the masses. It was ruled by a warrior-caste ruthlessly oppressing the subject population which was perhaps twenty times as numerous as their lords.

Rousseau, furthermore, emphasizes the necessity of national traditions as a means of cementing and intensifying the solidarity of the citizens. He rejects the fashionable cosmopolitanism which only serves as an excuse for shirking duties towards one's nation, and in particular the pernicious habit prevailing in the whole of Europe of aping French customs. Patriots are necessarily prejudiced, unjust and harsh towards foreigners, and this is excusable, as it is a consequence of their ardent love of their own nation. National institutions and traditions, customs and habits form the character of a people, and its pecularity is a mainstay of patriotism. When the Poles asked him for advice how to frame their constitution he laid great stress upon giving them a national physiognomy which was to distinguish them from all other peoples. A Pole of 20 years should be a Pole and nothing else. A child, when opening his eyes, should see the fatherland, and till his death nothing else. In other writings, however, Rousseau strikes in many respects a milder tune. He is not opposed to supra-national aims altogether, and admits that the weal of humanity is superior to that of any particular nation. In general, Rousseau much mitigates his theoretical intransigence when he comes to discuss concrete problems. He then pays regard to existing diversities and inequalities between and within peoples and sets his hopes in gradual improvement. His practical ideal was not the mode of life of primitive man, but probably a free community of peasants without social exploitation and vainglorious ambitions, living in happy frugality. " It is the country people ", he says, " who form the nation." Life in a city demoralizes man. Nevertheless, the *Discourse on the Origins of Inequality*, which contains the onslaught on civilization which made Rousseau famous, was dedicated to the city of Geneva, and in a lengthy epistle dedicatory he exuberantly praises her constitution as the nearest approximation to his ideal society, though Geneva at that time was a capitalist oligarchy.

In spite of Rousseau's praise of national prejudice and exclusiveness he was entirely opposed to the essential principle of modern nationalism, the worship of prestige and power. Both his Swiss origin and his enthusiasm for the ancient city republics made him a firm believer in the small State which alone could realize freedom and equality. He was convinced that a large State could only be despotic and would always be warlike and aggressive. Rousseau abhorred war and oppression, and he would have welcomed the partition of large States into small ones. which then would form a federation for the maintenance of peace.

Rousseau's passionate criticism of society, his plea for social equality, and particularly his ideas on education, stimulated the conscience and thought of men which led to most beneficial reforms. On the other hand, his influence also fostered antagonistic tendencies which have contributed to the tragic weakness of modern democracy in the conflict with its deadly enemies. His thought implied both an extreme individualism and an extreme collectivism and his disciples, therefore, were landed either in a doctrine of anarchy, or in the cult of the all-powerful State. His belief in the natural peaceableness and goodness of human nature made him underestimate the quarrelsome, pugnacious forces in it, he did not sufficiently realize that the demand for full social equality might lead to a bitter class war and to the total loss of national liberty and unity, nor did he foresee the danger implied in the onesided stimulation of national sentiment and the increase of the power of the State. Some remarks of his, however, show that he was not quite unaware of these dangers. In the face of death he confessed that " since infancy he was severed by many circumstances from the real world and lifted to ethereal regions where he formed romantic and false views of men and society, which all disastrous experiences could never cure completely ".

12. The French Revolution and Nationality

Rousseau's gospel is summarized in the motto of the French Revolution : " Liberty, Equality, Fraternity ". His teachings inspired the leaders of the Revolution. They believed that wars, oppression and domination were only caused by despots and privileged classes, and that all nations, having obtained their freedom, would realize the reign of equality and fraternity, both among each nation and between nations. This hope was shared by the intellectuals of many other countries.

At the beginning of the Revolution the Abbé Sieyès published his famous pamphlet : *What is the Third Estate?* In theory this word designated the middle class, urban and rural, though practically it meant the intellectuals and the wealthier bourgeoisie. The pamphlet is a terrible indictment of the two privileged classes, the aristocracy and the clergy. He describes the glaring injustices, oppression and misery, due to their privileges, and he emphasizes that the middle class is the only sound and valuable element in the State. The aristocracy, according to their own boasts, consists of the descendants of foreign invaders who ought to be driven out. The privileged classes are a poison in the national organism. The idea of a constitution after the model of England, with its two Houses of Parliament, is rejected. The time for compromise has passed. The third Estate alone is the nation, and must form the National Assembly. The nation is sovereign, its powers are unlimited, and its decisions are infallible.

Soon after the third Estate constituted itself as the National Assembly. Mirabeau proposed that it should choose the name " representation of the French people ", but the vanity of the bourgeois was offended by the word " peuple " which smelled too much of the mob in the language of the time. Mirabeau retorted that the English and Americans always employed people in a nobler sense. Just because this word was not sufficiently esteemed in France, it should be chosen and ennobled. His speech, however, aroused an uproar among the delegates. At the bottom of the controversy was the divergency of views on the meaning of " Nation ". There was general agreement that the nation was the sovereign. But which classes formed the nation? And how was the national will, Rousseau's general will, to be ascertained? The idea of a nation, underlying the English parliamentary system of that time, was obviously different from that of the Revolutionists.

Sieyès had referred to the claim put forward by some spokesmen of the aristocracy, that it descended from the Frankish invaders, and therefore was the real nation, entitled to rule the conquered race.[1] When the Revolution broke out, however, a considerable part of the aristocracy and the clergy sympathized with its aims, and some of the most prominent politicians and writers on the side of the revolutionists came from their ranks. Moreover, the two privileged estates soon joined the National Assembly. Yet, the idea of a racial difference between the aristocracy and the middle class, and its implications for the idea of the nation, continued to play a baleful rôle in French political discussions for a large part of the nineteenth century.

The disciples of Rousseau hoped to achieve the ideal of a close spiritual unity and general fraternity by two means. The first was the immediate enforcement of equality by suppression of every privilege. The bourgeois middle class used this policy for discarding the influence of the aristocracy. In this it had the support of the lower classes, the nascent proletariate. Soon, however, these classes found leaders who began to attack the new privileged class, the bourgeois. The poor, exclaims Marat, have no fatherland, they are condemned to servitude and suppressed by the possessing classes. The demand for equality was now directed against the bourgeoisie, and ultimately led to the rise of the idea of communism. The principle of equality became paramount in the ideology of the Revolution. But it did not lead to liberty, unity and fraternity; it soon resulted in the outbreak of class war, and anarchy and in the rise of a new military despotism.

The second means of the realization of national unity, recommended by Rousseau himself, was the fostering of a proud love of traditions, the exclusion of foreign models and the abandonment of cosmopolitanism. The revolutionists professed cosmopolitanism, they proclaimed the principle of self-determination, and they appealed to all nations to shake off the yoke of their tyrants. Yet a strain of national intolerance and aggressiveness was soon discernible in their words and actions. It has already been described how they tried to denationalize the minorities living in France, which the old regime had never attempted to do.[2] It

[1] Cf. this book, p. 67.   [2] Cf. this book, p. 86.

was their policy which brought about the war against the monarchies. Jean Jaurès in his masterwork on the revolution has again proved that it was the Girondins, the party of the wealthy bourgeoisie and intelligentsia, which did everything in their power to start the war, while their opponents, the foreign monarchical powers, were very averse to a warlike policy.[1] The aim of the Girondins was to give a new impetus to the flagging spirit of revolutionary enthusiasm, and to strengthen their hold on the nation. For this purpose they excited national vanity and the passion for prestige and power, they pretended that the nation was threatened by its enemies, and they proclaimed that the war would lead to the liberation of all peoples. Jaurès says :

> In this way the Gironde wished to use the war as a formidable manœuvre of internal policy. What a terrible reponsibility ! If we think of the unprecedented ordeal which France had to undergo, if we consider that the transport of a moment had to be paid for by twenty years of sanguinary Cæsarism, and that then, from 1815 to 1848, and even from 1815 to 1870, France had less freedom than under the Constitution of 1791, if one realizes that the armed propaganda of revolutionary principles has excited against us the national sentiment of other peoples and has created the terrible military burdens under which all nations labour, one asks whether the Gironde had the right to play that extraordinary game of dice.

In the course of the war all the good intentions of according self-determination to the liberated nations were soon discarded, and the policy of the French Republic towards Belgium and Italy became frankly nationalistic and oppressive.

13. BURKE AND THE IDEA OF NATIONALITY

The principles of the French Revolution and the political philosophy of Rousseau were subjected to severe criticism and condemned by Edmund Burke.[2] His famous *Reflections on the French Revolution* (1790) were written at a time when the Revolution had not yet degenerated into a reign of terror and into wars of conquest, and this proves that they were not merely inspired by outraged sentiment or disillusionment as the writings of many subsequent critics were. Burke's rejection of the great experiment which then was regarded with sympathy by almost all liberal-minded people sprang from a totally different system of

[1] Cf. Jean Jaurès, " La Legislative " (*Histoire Socialiste*, tome ii), pp. 791–958. A share in the responsibility, however, fell on a group around the King which hoped that a war would lead to the restoration of royal authority, and on the King who accepted their advice.
[2] Cf. John Morley, *Burke*, 1888 (repr. 1902) ; John MacCunn, *The Political Philosophy of Burke*, 1913 ; Alfred Cobban, *E. Burke and the Revolt against the Eighteenth Century*, 1929 ; Harold Laski, *Burke*.

political thought which may be described as a revolt against the rationalism and optimism of the eighteenth century, its belief in the omnipotence of individual reason, the goodness of human nature and the possibility of rapid progress by breaking all fetters of the past. Montesquieu had already initiated the abandonment of the abstract method in political thought and he had emphasized the historical and social relativity of all principles, the organic growth of society, and the power of the national character in determining constitutions and legislation. His doctrine had been enthusiastically received in England and Burke had become his ardent disciple.[1]

A people or a nation in Burke's view is not merely a multitude of human beings living together, but an historical personality with a specific political and social structure, united by a sort of tacit consent and guided by a small class trained in politics and public service and embodying the national traditions. Using Locke's terminology familiar to the Whigs he describes society as a contract and even compares it to a limited company in which the rights are fixed by the original pact and are proportionate to the holdings of shares. But Locke's State is limited to the protection of security and property and its members are the living generation of citizens who are free to do what they like with the State. Burke's concept of the State is that of a partnership in all spiritual and moral pursuits, binding together those living, the ancestors and the yet unborn generation. The State is as sacred to him as to Hegel. It is subject to eternal moral laws and its members are not at liberty to dissolve the State or fundamentally to alter its constitution, which incorporates the experience and wisdom of many generations. The most essential element in a nation is a natural aristocracy, possessing all the qualities necessary for leadership. It forms the soul of the nation and without it there is no nation. When in the French Revolution many aristocrats fled to Germany and established their headquarters at Coblenz, Burke actually stated that the French nation was there. That leading class included the peers, the leading landed gentlemen, the opulent merchants and manufacturers and the substantial yeomanry. The natural aristocracy of birth, wealth and talent was invested with the trusteeship on behalf of the people which it had to exercise according to its own discernment, not bound by instructions of its electorate. Burke steadfastly opposed any popularization of the franchise and would even have preferred to decrease the number of voters. The British constitution appeared

[1] Cf. F. Fletcher, *Montesquieu and English Politics*, 1939.

to him as a most happy blend of forces and principles, immensely superior to any constitution drafted according to abstract doctrines. He particularly appreciated in the character of the English people " their awe of kings and priests ", " their sullen resistance of innovation " and " their unalterable perseverance in the wisdom of prejudice ".

In our present terminology Burke's view of a nation would be defined as that of a spiritual organism, the product of long organic growth. But he was well aware of the danger of comparing it to a natural organism which implies that the parts of the whole have no independent will and that the whole has no other aim than its own existence. In his view at least the natural aristocracy had an independent will and the object of the State was the welfare of its citizens. His view of English institutions being the product of organic growth was essentially right, though he exaggerated this point. England too had passed through revolutions and dictatorships, had deposed or killed a number of her kings and had no less expropriated the estates of the Church than the French Revolution. True, Burke's horror of revolutions referred only to those which threatened to become social revolutions, while he expressly approved of several revolutions which had been made under the leadership of the aristocracy.

The spirit of enlightenment tended to regard every belief indemonstrable by clear logic or in disagreement with the standards of " common sense " as a prejudice or a superstition. Hume in his essay *On Moral Prejudices* criticizes " that grave philosophic endeavour after perfection, which, under pretext of reforming prejudices and errors, strikes at all the most endearing sentiments of the heart, and all the most useful biases and instincts which can govern a human creature ". Even many advocates of enlightenment, however, were not for enlightening the lower classes which, as they believed, needed certain prejudices for their own happiness and for remaining governable. This was the soil on which romanticism developed. Burke strongly defended prejudices provided they were sanctioned by long usage and had stood the test of time. He showed many parallels with Rousseau though he combated him as the arch-enemy. Like Rousseau, he emphasized sentiment and prejudice as bonds of society, appreciated nationality,[1] tended towards an organic view of the State and believed that real freedom was only possible through the State. While Rousseau praised the noble savage, Burke exalted mediaeval chivalry. But Rousseau pleads for equality and denounces pro-

[1] Cf. for details, Cobban, p. 97.

perty while Burke sees in inequality a God-ordained order and regards it like property as an indispensable guarantee of a well-poised and healthy society. Burke was mainly a traditionalist who revered the collective wisdom of the past and distrusted that of individuals, while Rousseau was a romanticist who believed in the essential goodness of human nature· and assumed that the common people, unspoilt by civilization, had preserved that original goodness best. Rousseau, moreover, was an inconsistent romanticist who largely indulged in abstract speculations and expected that an all-powerful State would make the citizens free, virtuous and happy.

Burke did everything to incite England to war with revolutionary France, but he was not a nationalist of the aggressive sort. His attitude in the questions of the American revolution and of justice for India show that national prestige and power were to him not paramount aims. He had a clearer view of the nature of national feelings than Rousseau and was well aware of the fact that the longing for superiority and domination could be found in all classes.[1] " The desire of having some one below them, descends to those who are the very lowest of all." As a young man he published his *Vindication of Natural Society*, in which he says that the mere division of mankind into separate societies was a perpetual source in itself of hatred and dissensions among them. History shows that far the greater parts of the quarrels between several nations had scarcely any other occasion than that these nations were different combinations of people and called by different names. To an Englishman the name of a Frenchman, a Spaniard, an Italian raises, of course, ideas of hatred and contempt. Yet the simple name of man, applied properly, never fails to work a salutary effect.

It is generally recognized to-day that Burke's attacks against the principles of the French Revolution were inspired by such fanaticism that he widely overshot the mark. Nevertheless, it must be said that the English tradition which Burke followed in his definition of a nation has in the long run proved more conducive to national unity, solidarity and freedom than the tradition of the French Revolution, though it must not be overlooked that this latter tradition had a great influence on England, too. When Friedrich Gentz, a great admirer of Burke, came in 1802 to England he was overwhelmed by the impression of her national organism. In his letters he praises the English as a perfect whole, as the only real nation that exists, with an entirely definite char-

[1] Cf. Morley, p. 113.

acter and a constitution that was all-embracing and interwoven with everything. If England should ever go down, he exclaims, the exalting spectacle of such a national greatness and happiness would never be realized anywhere on earth again.

Burke has for a long time made a deeper impression on the political thinkers of the Continent than on those of Britain.[1] The German romanticists and French traditionalists saw in his writings their gospel, and Hegel's political philosophy is to a very great extent identical with that of Burke, though Hegel combines it with certain traditions of the Revolution and Napoleon.

14. German Thought on the Eve of the French Revolution and After

In the course of the eighteenth century the ideas of enlightenment and early romanticism, as expressed in the writings of English and French philosophers, poets and novelists, permeated the upper and middle classes in Germany and the neighbouring countries, and were received with enthusiasm. Soon an extraordinary revival took place in every field of German thought and literature. The German writers were to a large extent inspired by foreign models, but many of them did not remain mere imitators, but showed great originality. Germany entered her classical age both in philosophy and in literature.

The general sentiment of the educated classes was cosmopolitan and completely alien to any political nationalism. The excessive particularism, the rivalry between the greater German States, and even between many small ones,[2] dynastic connexions between Germany and foreign territories, and other factors, excluded all possibility of an aggressive policy. Some writers complained of the lack of unity among the German peoples, the absence of an adequate central authority, and the intervention of foreign Powers in German affairs, but there was hardly a trace of political nationalism in the sense of a striving for national power. Neither was there any cultural nationalism in the sense of prejudice against foreign civilization or of excessive self-praise. The upper classes even preferred everything French, and when Frederick II founded the Academy at Berlin he made French

[1] Cf. Frieda Braune, *Burke in Deutschland*, 1915; Morley, p. 312.
[2] Even in the eighteenth century there were many petty wars between small princes. A Baron Fleming declared war to the Duchess of Sachsen-Weissenfels because she had had a stag shot on his territory, and in 1747 a war broke out between Sachsen-Gotha and Sachsen-Meiningen caused by a quarrel between two noblewomen about the right of precedence at court. Cf. many such instances in Max von Boehn, *Deutschland im 18. Jahrhundert, Das heilige roemische Reich*, p. 13.

its official language and a Frenchman its secretary. In 1783 the Academy offered a prize for an essay on the reasons of the universal diffusion of the French language, and the prize was awarded to Antoine Rivarol,[1] who attributed the fact that the French language was universally used by the educated classes to its superior qualities, especially to its clarity and logic, in which it surpassed all other languages. Rivarol received high honours from the King and the Academy for his essay. The dominating position of the French language and literature, however, soon induced writers to emphasize the merits of their own tongue, and one could interpret Fichte's exuberant praise of the German language as a belated counterblast to Rivarol.

Before the French Revolution liberal and republican sentiment and ideas were already widespread among the upper and middle classes of the Empire, though there was little scope for political activity in representative bodies. In 1790 the Emperor Leopold II set forth his political creed in great detail in a letter to his sister Maria Christina.[2] It was a programme of liberal constitutionalism. The Emperor regarded himself as a delegate or official of the people, bound to the scrupulous observation of the fundamental contract in which the people had invested him with authority, and liable to be removed in case of any infringement of that contract. The ruler has the executive power, he declared, but the legislative power and control over the executive belong to the people and its representatives. Leopold, however, reigned for hardly two years; he died suddenly, just before revolutionary France declared the war which he had made every effort to avoid. Liberal and republican views were also rife in Prussia and other parts of Germany, and were often put forward with astounding frankness, in spite of the censorship.[3] The multitude of separate States furthered a certain freedom of expression. Some rulers permitted the publication of very pro-

[1] Cf. A. Rivarol, *Œuvres choisies*, 1880, vol. i. The knowledge of other languages was also more widely spread in Germany than in any other country. An official report prepared for Napoleon in 1810 said: " There is scarcely an educated German who cannot read French, Italian, and English, as well as Latin." Cf. H. A. L. Fisher, *Studies in Napoleonic Statesmanship in Germany*, 1903, p. 5. This book gives many interesting facts on German conditions before and after the Revolution.

[2] Cf. A. Wolf, *Leopold II. und Marie Christine, ihr Briefwechsel*, p. 80, and A. Wolf und H. v. Zwiedineck-Südenhorst, *Oesterreich unter Maria Theresia, Josef II. und Leopold II.*, 1884, p. 325. It is significant that the high bureaucracy of the Austrian Government was largely in favour of giving representation in the diets to the middle class, and even to the peasants. Cf. Wolf-Zwiedineck, p. 367. Even the Archduke Franz—who later on as Emperor became the paragon of reaction—then leaned towards the " democratic party ".

[3] Cf. numerous voices in Woldemar Wenck, *Deutschland vor 100 Jahren, Politische Meinungen und Stimmungen bein Anbruch der Revolutionszeit*, 1887, vol. i, pp. 18, 47, 61, 69, 205, 232; vol. ii, pp. 10, 15, 57, 82, etc.

gressive views, partly from enlightenment, partly in order to annoy neighbouring princes, into whose lands the books were smuggled.

Johann Gottfried Herder (1744-1803) was a great pioneer of romanticism though, like Rousseau, he also remained true to the essential moral principles of enlightenment.[1] He inaugurated the enthusiastic appreciation of the " people's spirit " as manifested in its language, poetry, art and traditions. In particular he venerated the great cultural legacy of Germany's past, and ardently wished for a revival of her glory in the field of literature, art and learning. The political side of nationality did not much appeal to him. He regarded the State as an artificial creation, brought together by war and conquest which he abhorred. His heart was in the nation, in which he saw a natural growth like the family and which he regarded as a fundamentally peaceable community. Herder's whole philosophy of history centred in the idea of humanity, and his interest in nationality was predominantly cultural. Every people, he was convinced, however small and backward, possessed the divine spark of beauty and goodness, and in primitive peoples it was even less suppressed than in the conventional civilization of the advanced nations. The Slavs had up to that time been regarded by other nations as little more than barbarians, destined to eternal serfdom. But he discovered in them the most lovable qualities, especially peaceableness, and he predicted a great future for them. Thus he became the herald of Slav national resurrection, and he had a very strong influence on the ideas of the cultural revival of the Slav nations.

The German classical writers had little, if any, interest in the political implications of nationality, and in this they reflected the spirit of their time.[2] Wieland wrote in 1793 that in his youth he had never heard of any duty to be a German patriot, and that German in a political sense was an unknown word. Lessing wrote in a letter in 1758 : " I have no idea of love of the fatherland and at the best it seems to me an heroic weakness which I am very glad to lack." Schiller declared that the cultivated soul

[1] F. R. Haym, *Herder*, 1880/5 ; E. Kühnemann, *Herder*, 1912.
[2] On the political, national and cosmopolitan ideas of the classical poets cf. Karl Berger, *Schiller*, 1911, vol. ii, p. 574 ; G. Falter, *Staatsideale unserer Klassiker*, 1911 ; Otto Günther, *Schiller über Volk, Staat und Gesellschaft* ; A. Ruhe, *Schillers Einfluss auf die Entwicklung des deutschen Nationalgefuehls*, 1887-92 ; Friedrich Gundolf, *Goethe*, 1916, pp. 400, 536, 681 ; Albert Bielschowsky, *Goethe*, 30th ed., 1917, vol. i, p. 323 ; vol. ii, pp. 251, 326. Heinrich Schmidt, *Goethe-Lexikon*, sub " Internationalismus " ; F. G. Winter, *Goethes deutsche Gesinnung*, 1880 ; Reinhold Aris, *History of Political Thought in Germany from 1789 to 1915*, 1936, p. 166 ; Kuno Franke, *History of German Literature as determined by Social Forces*, 10th ed., 1916.

of the individual was of more value than the greatest society or State as such. The interest in the fatherland, he wrote in 1789, was important for immature nations only, for the youth of the world. The modern man had higher aims. It was a poor and petty ideal to write for one nation only. Even the most important nation was merely a changeable, fortuitous and arbitrary fragment of humanity, and the philosophic mind could take interest in it only so far as it served the progress of humanity. When in 1795 victorious French armies invaded and occupied the German Rhinelands, Schiller was not deeply perturbed. He wrote in a letter : " We must in body remain citizens of our own time as we have no other choice. But in spirit it is the prerogative and the duty of the philosopher and the poet to belong to no people and to no time, and to be in the proper sense of the word the contemporary of all times." In the following years the victories of Napoleon threatened the political structure of Germany with dissolution : in a short time the Empire came to an end, and Germany was completely under Napoleon's heel. At that time Schiller planned to write a poem on Germany's destiny, but abandoned the idea ; an unfinished draft was found among his papers many years after his death. The poet tries to reconcile the Germans to their fate by pointing out that German honour and greatness were not bound up with their State, but with the culture and character of the nation. The Germans may be proud of their moral and spiritual achievements, of their initiative in starting the Reformation, of their enthusiasm for ideal values such as intellectual freedom, of their philosophy, and especially of their language which in future will dominate the world. He who excels in cultivating the spirit will in the end attain to predominance. The Germans should not follow the example of other nations in serving the idols of material wealth and external splendour ; their mission is to adopt all great cultural achievements of other nations and to integrate them into a whole, " to unite all the rays of light in one beautiful image of humanity ". It is hardly necessary to say that there is not a trace of political nationalism in this vision.

Goethe has often expressed his cosmopolitan outlook, his warm appreciation of the achievements of other nations, and his disapproval of national prejudice. Towards the end of his life he declared that national hatred was strongest and most violent upon the lowest levels of culture, and that it vanished altogether upon a certain higher level. One then stands above nationality and feels the good or bad fortune of a neighbour nation in the same way as if it had happened to one's own. This, he said, was congenial to him.[1] Many other statements also make clear that Goethe felt primarily as a citizen of the world, as a member of the great spiritual community formed by the art, the thought, the higher aspirations of all nations. This does not mean that he was indifferent to Germany, but his idea of patriotism was solicitude for the culture and welfare of one's compatriots, and not hostility to other nations. Even the fact that Napoleon subdued Germany did not disturb him, and he remained an ardent admirer of the Emperor and a friend of France. When the war of liberation broke out, he did not share the national feelings against the French rulers; he kept aloof and forbade his son to enlist in the army. When the war was practically won he explained in a conversation with Professor Luden, that he could not see what was the good of it all. True, Germany had been liberated from one foreign yoke, but did this secure liberty from all foreign domination? The French had disappeared, but in their place were now Russian, Austrian and Prussian troops. Goethe had become imbued with a deep dislike of Prussia. He also told Luden that he understood the feeling of pride in belonging to a great, strong, esteemed and feared nation, and that he believed in Germany's great future. But this was probably meant as a sop to the professor who was an ardent nationalist. Fifteen years later, in 1828, Goethe discussed with Eckermann the unity of Germany and said that it would certainly be brought about through the improvement of roads and the future construction of railways. May the Germans love one another, and hold together against foreign enemies! It was further desirable to have a common currency, common weights and measures, and many similar things. It would be a great advantage if his luggage could pass the frontiers of all thirty-six German States without being opened, and if the passport of a citizen of Weimar would be accepted as valid within the whole of Germany. But he was entirely against any political centralization. The decentralization of Germany, he firmly believed, was the principal cause of the very wide diffusion of education and civilization. Every ruler had endeavoured to found cultural institutions such as universities, libraries, museums, theatres, technical schools and schools for the people. These and other utterances show that Goethe welcomed national unification only so far as it was in the interest of security, commerce and traffic, but that he had no wish at all for political centralization and an increase of power.

[1] J. P. Eckermann, *Gespraeche mit Goethe* (March 14, 1830).

Immanuel Kant (1724-1804), whose grandfather was a Scot, opened a new chapter in the history of philosophy.[1] His political ideas which he expounded only in his old age, have on some points been interpreted in various ways, and he probably had reasons to express himself about certain matters with reserve. There is no doubt, however, that Kant's principal aim in politics was the Reign of Law, by which he understood the greatest liberty of the individual compatible with the liberty of all others. Kant, therefore, was a liberal and his philosophy later became the gospel of German liberalism. Nothing could be more absurd than the view which has sometimes been put forward that he was a forerunner of modern Pan-Germanism, or that his " Categorical Imperative " was identical with the spirit of the Prussian military State.[2] Kant hailed the American and French Revolutions, and though he later was disgusted with Jacobin terrorism, and in his lectures deprecated any revolt, his intimate friends knew that he still believed in the essential right of the French Revolution, and hoped that it would further progress towards his ideals. He ardently wished for an enduring peace and elaborated a project for bringing it about, in which he says that only republics can be really peaceable, He recognized, however, that war too produced many noble qualities in men, and could be an instrument of progress. Like all the great German thinkers and poets of the time he was a convinced citizen of the world, and hostile to all forms of nationalism. In his interesting description of national characters he points out as a good side of the German character that the Germans have no national pride and are cosmopolitan.[3] Nevertheless, he assumed that Providence had created national pride and prejudice in order to separate mankind into different nations. Every nation cherishes the illusion that it is in some respect superior to others, and governments favour such illusions. Such blind instincts, however, which work on the animal side of our nature, must be superseded by reason. " This national mania (*Nationalwahn*), therefore, must be exterminated and

[1] His greatest predecessor was Leibniz, who must be mentioned here as the founder of a powerful trend of thought which distinguished German philosophy from that of England and France, and also for his defence of German nationality against French plans of universal domination. Most of Leibniz' books, however, are written in French and Latin. Cf. Kuno Fischer, *Leibniz*, 1902 ; V. Basch, *Les doctrines politiques des philosophes classiques de l'Allemagne*, 1927 ; Wilhelm Metzger, *Gesellschaft, Recht und Staat in der Ethik des deutschen Idealismus*, 1917 ; K. Fischer, *Kant*, 2 vols., 1898 ; Aris, op. cit. ; Rudolf Kress, *Die soziologischen Gedanken Kants*, 1929.

[2] His concept of duty is entirely different from the machine-like discipline enforced by Prussianism. Cf. A. O. Meyer, *Kants Ethik und der preussische Staat in der Festschrift für Erich Marks*. " Vom staatlichen Werden und Wesen ", 1921.

[3] These descriptions are collected in K. Vorländer, *Kants Weltanschauung aus seinen Werken*, 1919, pp. 257-68.

replaced by patriotism and cosmopolitanism." Kant's view is that national instincts and conflicts may be necessary for progress in a primitive stage of development, but that with the evolution of civilization reason must take the lead.

Liberalism was also the creed of Wilhelm von Humboldt (1767–1835), a profound thinker, a great scholar and a distinguished Prussian statesman.[1] In his book on " the limits of the State " he professes extreme distrust of every extension of State activity beyond the maintenance of security and justice. The aim of life was to him the harmonious development of all the forces of the individual. After the fall of Napoleon he realized that Germany needed some power both for defence and for satisfying her self-consciousness, but he did not wish to make her too unitary and powerful because this would imply the risk of rendering her a conquering State " which no true German could desire " and which would endanger the intellectual and scientific development of the German nation.[2]

When the French Revolution broke out, it aroused enthusiasm in Germany.[3] Many years later Hegel, who had since become the glorifier of the Prussian monarchy and of the powerful State, recalled the impression of the Revolution on his youthful mind in the words : " The idea of Right asserted itself, and the old fabric of injustice broke down. It was a glorious sunrise. All thinking beings celebrated that event. A noble emotion reigned in that epoch, the world was thrilled with spiritual enthusiasm as if the Divine had now become reality in the world."

Friedrich Gentz, too, who later became a pillar of Metternich's policy of reaction, belonged to these ardent admirers of the Revolution, but was converted to the spirit of the English constitution through the influence of Burke. Gentz was in the Prussian Civil Service but left Prussia mainly because the revolutionary spirit seemed to him to have gained too much ground in high places. He asserted that not only were some of the most influential statesmen, like Beyme and Lombard, friends and supporters of the Revolution, but that at least nine-tenths of the Civil Service were outspoken revolutionaries, besides countless other people, among them scholars and members of the high nobility and of the army.[4]

[1] Cf. O. Harnack, *W. von Humboldt*, 1913.
[2] Cf. F. Meinecke, *Weltbürgertum und Nationalstaat*, 1912, p. 195.
[3] Cf. G. P. Gooch, *Germany and the French Revolution*, 1920.
[4] Cf. Frieda Braune, *Burke in Deutschland*, 1915, p. 168. This book gives a most interesting picture of the influence of Burke on German opinion in regard to the Revolution, and on the development of German political ideas in general. Burke's

The growing violence of the Revolution and the outbreak of a reign of terror disillusioned many of the enthusiasts for the revolutionary principles. Nevertheless, a large number did not despair even when French policy became increasingly one of conquest, spoliation and national oppression. Even Napoleon's rise to power and his undisguised despotism, did not cause an immediate outburst of national revolt. For years a large part of the German upper and middle classes submitted willingly to French domination and indulged in unlimited admiration of Napoleon as a superman. The idea was widespread among the intellectuals that the French, the " new Romans ", would dominate the world while the Germans would enjoy the benefits of peace and order, and would excel in civilization as once the Greeks in the Roman Empire did. It was a long time before the national reaction against foreign domination and oppression became an irresistible force, but when the war of liberation broke out, national hatred spread rapidly and rose to a high pitch.

15. Fichte and Nationality

The philosopher Johann Gottlieb Fichte (1762–1814) is widely regarded to-day as the most important early pioneer of present German nationalism. The German nationalists celebrate him as their prophet, and a very active organ of their propaganda is called the Fichte League. This view, however, is not shared by scholars who have made a close study of his life and thought. Professor Victor Basch, a French scholar of special competence, concludes that all ideas of present Pan-Germanism were alien to him, and that he has rejected and combated all of them.[1] Another French scholar, Xavier Léon, whose great work on Fichte and his time is the standard book,[2] declares that " since his youth until his death Fichte was and remained in Germany the disciple and fervent apostle of the ideal proclaimed by the French Revolution ".

Fichte sprang from the lower ranks of society and as a boy had

influence on German reactionary romanticism was immense. It is significant, however, that most of his followers and admirers found that his attacks on the Revolution went too far and were too violent.

[1] Cf. Victor Basch, *Les doctrines politiques des philosophes classiques de l'Allemagne*, 1927, pp. 97–102.

[2] Cf. Xavier Léon, *Fichte et son temps*, 2 (in 3) vols., 1922–7. A similar view is expressed by H. Engelbrecht, *Fichte, a Study of his Political Writings with special Reference to his Nationalism*, 1933. Cf. further, F. Meinecke, *Weltbürgertum und Nationalstaat* (many editions) ; W. Metzger, *Gesellschaft, Recht und Staat in der Ethik des deutschen Idealismus*, 1917 ; Franz Haymann, *Weltbürgertum und Vaterlandsliebe in der Staatslehre Rousseaus und Fichtes*, 1924 ; Kuno Fischer, *Fichtes Leben, Werke und Lehre*, 1900.

to watch the geese. A benevolent nobleman, struck by the boy's oratorical gift, enabled him to become a student, and he developed Kant's doctrines of human liberty, creativeness and moral energy to extremes. His character was forceful, courageous and impetuous, and his thought was inspired by intransigent idealism. The philosopher, moreover, was a passionate orator which must be allowed for when his ideas are examined. When the French Revolution broke out he was full of enthusiasm. He defended it against its German enemies and had soon the reputation of a dangerous Jacobin. When the French invaded Germany he hoped for their overwhelming victory and expressed complete indifference as to the fate of Alsace. Newly found letters even show that he ardently wished to become a French citizen and to devote his life to the service of the Revolution.[1] He wished to be a Professor in a university under French rule where he could educate German students to become good French citizens and to work for a Revolution in Germany. The ideals of the French Revolution, and hatred of princes, privileged classes, soldiers, and economic inequality actuated him throughout life. Like Rousseau—with whom he showed many parallels—he inclined towards socialism, in the sense of economic equality by means of State regulation.

In 1800 Fichte published a book on the perfect State in which he proposed a system of strict social equality, self-sufficiency and State-control over economic life.[2] Work and living was to be secured to all. The nation was to be isolated and secluded from other nations in order to eliminate commercial competition which he regarded as a source of war. Like Plato, he believed that trade corrupts morals, creates social inequality, and undermines the community. For this reason he demanded a State monopoly of trade and an isolated currency. His plan, he believed, would further unity and spirituality and create a high degree of morality and national character. The aim of self-sufficiency was not military independence and strength, as in the present nationalist and militarist States, but a purely moral goal.

Nevertheless, Fichte also suggests that the State, before secluding itself should occupy a sufficient territory within natural frontiers, and should then give solemn assurance to all governments that it would henceforth strive for no further expansion and take no part in any war or foreign affairs. This idea has

[1] Cf. *Léon*, vol. ii, 2, p. 287 and Fichte's *Briefwechsel herausgegeben von H. Schulz*, 2 vols., 1925, and Supplement.
[2] Xavier Léon shows that Fichte was strongly influenced in his socialist ideas by the French socialist Babeuf and by the legislation of the Revolution.

been interpreted by R. Butler [1] as the recipe of Hitler's policy of securing " living space " by sudden treacherous invasion. Fichte, however, was fundamentally opposed to a policy of conquest and prestige, and condemned it often in the most violent words. If he seems to deviate from this principle in this case, and puts the principle of natural frontiers higher than that of self-determination this is consistent with the doctrine of Rousseau and the leaders of the Revolution, and is a consequence of State socialism. The revolutionists proclaimed that France had a sacred right to her natural frontiers, which included the German Rhineland, and Fichte agreed with this idea and even thought of settling himself in the Rhineland under French rule. It is clear, moreover, that a socialist State must seclude itself against free world trade, and monopolize external and internal trade. Yet self-sufficiency and universal State control cannot be achieved except on a territory of some extent and forming a certain natural unit. Germany at that time was split up into about 1,800 " States ", of which the large majority consisted of a few villages only, and hardly differed from a private estate. Even most of the larger States, however, formed to a great extent an agglomeration of unconnected possessions with many foreign enclaves and frontiers inconsistent with the requirements of a modern administration. Most of the populations had no real national sentiment. That socialism in former times could hardly be imagined without periodical expansion is also shown by Thomas More's Utopia, which probably inspired Fichte. The people of Utopia, in spite of their aversion to war, regard it as legitimate to conquer living space for settling their surplus population in backward countries.[2] More, however, suggests this policy as periodical, according to the increase of population, while Fichte proposes to renounce any further expansion after the necessary territory has been secured.

In different writings of that period Fichte set forth various other plans such as the formation of a League of Nations and even that of a single World State. He also declared it impossible that a free nation would ever attack another one for mere spoliation. It would not even pay. It is a small number of oppressors only who make wars. Up to now he had looked upon the State as a necessary evil, and envisaged its gradual effacement with the growing liberty of the individual. In later writings, however, he

---
[1] Cf. R. Butler, *The Roots of National-Socialism*, 1941, p. 43.
[2] Hermann Oncken in his introduction to a German edition of the Utopia (tr. by Gerhard Ritter, 1922) believes that Morus had to do with a project of settling English colonists in Ireland which was put before the Government as some passages in the Utopia show parallels with a memorandum concerning that project.

emphasized that it is the individual who is destined to subordinate and even to sacrifice himself to the community. This did not mean that the nation or the State were in irreconcilable conflict with humanity. The value of nationality in his eyes was exclusively determined by the striving for moral aims common to all nations. In 1804 he proclaimed that the fatherland of every really civilized European was Europe, in particular that State which was most advanced in civilization, and he spoke with contempt of a patriotism that sticks to the soil. Two years later he defined the relations of cosmopolitanism and patriotism. The idea of humanity is supreme, but we can only serve it in our fatherland. Patriotism, therefore, strives to achieve the good first in one's own nation, then to spread it over the whole of mankind when patriotism is called cosmopolitanism. He also set the clear and cosmopolitan patriotism of Athens above the dull and narrow patriotism of the military state of Sparta.

Meanwhile Napoleon achieved his meteoric ascent in Europe. Austria, Britain and Russia strongly resisted his ambitions and again and again took up arms against him. Prussia, however, followed a policy of neutrality and made every effort to maintain good relations with the dictator, hoping to profit through his favour and to win Hanover and other territories as the reward. Frederick William III and most of his ministers hated war and believed in a policy of peace at almost any price ; they neglected the maintenance of military strength and security, and had strong pro-French sympathies.[1] Thus Prussia looked quietly on while Napoleon conquered one country after the other, and brought a great part of Germany under his domination. At last he went so far as to march troops through Prussian territory, and when the King protested he demanded the disarmament of Prussia, invaded her, and smashed her army at Jena (1806). The Peace of Tilsit reduced her to half of her former size, subjected her to enormous financial exactions and led to a long occupation of the country.

Fichte felt deeply the fate of his adopted country, and it caused his thought to take a remarkable turn. Till then he had envisaged the State merely as an institution for upholding the reign of law and educating the citizens to morality, and that State, irrespective of nationality, seemed to him the best which performed this task most efficiently. If a progressive State had the political misfortune to go down, this was no irretrievable loss, for another one would soon replace it. Prussia's and

[1] Cf. Hans Prutz, *Preussische Geschichte*, 1901, vol. iii, pp. 352–6.

Germany's catastrophe, however, taught him that a State also needed power and could not escape the necessity of power-politics. He now studied Machiavelli's writings, which greatly impressed him. The parallel between the situation of Machiavelli's Italy and Fichte's Germany was obvious. In 1807 he published a paper containing translated passages from Machiavelli, and his comments on them were designed to be a lesson in statecraft for the King of Prussia.[1]

In this paper Fichte accepted Machiavelli's views that between States there was no secure reign of law but continual open or latent war. "Every nation wishes to spread the good traits peculiar to it as widely as it can, and to incorporate in itself the whole of mankind as far as this is feasible." This is a striving planted by God in human nature, and it determines the community of nations, their frictions and their progress. This striving renders conflicts about spheres of influence inevitable, even if the purest spirits reign, in spite of their excellent intentions and though each nation is sincerely convinced of its right. States, therefore, are forced constantly to maintain and extend their power if they wish to escape ruin. They cannot simply wait till an enemy attacks their frontiers but must be careful to safeguard their general power and prestige. Neither can they rely on mere promises of other States, and trust in their good faith, or try to conciliate them by subservience. The Balance of Power between strong States is the best guarantee of peace. Between States the Right of Force only is decisive, and a ruler is not subject to the precepts of the morality of individuals. Yet Fichte does not wish at all for perpetual war between civilized nations. The European youth should maintain its ability for war in struggles with barbarians in other continents who in any case are destined to be incorporated in our civilization, while peace shall reign in the common fatherland, Europe. This description of international relations was in full accordance with the historical reality of his time. Napoleon and his republican predecessors had pursued an absolutely unscrupulous policy of conquest, not to speak of the dynastic wars of the eighteenth century. This paper was intended to be an appeal to action in a critical hour, not an exhaustive scientific treatment of international relations. He, moreover, did not continue this line of thought, and his later writings moved in another direction.

In 1807–8 Fichte delivered his famous Discourses to the

[1] Cf. Fichte, *Machiavell*, edited by H. Schulz, 1918, and H. Freyer, on this paper in *Verhandlungen der sächsischen Akademie der Wissenschaften*, 1936.

German Nation. The terrible catastrophe of Germany was ascribed to the degeneration of the German character, especially to the egoism of the upper classes and the unprogressiveness of the older people.[1] Like Rousseau he put all his hopes in the comparatively uncorrupted lower classes and the youth. It was not only the rehabilitation of the German nation, however, which he has in mind. The whole world, indeed, had been corrupted by selfishness. The German people had a great spiritual and moral mission to fulfil for the benefit of mankind. It alone was fitted to carry out this task because of the fact that it had preserved its original tongue while the French and the English, who also came from German stock, had abandoned their old languages for mixed and partly foreign ones. Only Germans, Fichte says, have a living, popular and creative language, while the other nations are cramped in religious and philosophical thought and in poetry by their language. Their civilization is restricted to the upper classes, while the people is excluded from education through a language which is alien to its thought and feelings. The Germans themselves have been infected by the belief that foreign language and civilization were superior to their own. The higher educated classes secluded themselves from the people by using a foreign language (French) from snobbishness, and the people were despised as a mob.

The view of the superior creativeness of an original language was rooted in the romantic idea of an intimate connexion between language and the soul of the people. The philosophy of enlightenment addressed itself mainly to the higher educated classes, fostered a cosmopolitan spirit among them, and preferred a world language to the vernaculars. When the romanticists began to extol the common people, nationality and the language of the people, they naturally ascribed a special value to every vernacular, asserting that it alone could express the people's soul. Fichte's praise of the German language, therefore, had both a national and a social significance. He probably got his ideas of the superiority of the German language and the world mission of the German people from A. W. Schlegel, the leader of German romanticism. But he was strongly opposed to the romanticists in most other respects, especially to their dream of reviving the mediaeval world empire, their neo-catholicism, their mixture of mysticism and sensualism, their belief in the

---

[1] In another writing Fichte regards already the people over thirty years as old, and says " that it were best for their own reputation and for the whole world if they would die ", cf. K. Fischer, p. 615.

mission of the great genius, the man of destiny, and to their predilection for monarchy and aristocracy.

The most valuable peculiarity of the German spirit in Fichte's views is the moral and religious earnestness which expressed themselves in the Reformation and German idealism. Germany alone moreover, has solved the problem of a good republican constitution, namely, in the old city republics, the work of the pious, honest, modest, unselfish spirit of the burghers.

Fichte then discusses the nature of patriotism and national character. A people is a people only if it has a national character, i.e. the belief in a specific task or mission which is a manifestation of the Divine. " The German only—i.e. the original man not strangled by arbitrary rules—has a true people, while the foreigner has none. Only the German spirit, therefore, is capable of true love of its people and of true patriotism." The individual, by merging in the people's spirit or national character, perpetuates his life and attains to eternal life in this world. Patriotism is a religious sentiment. But love of one's own people is not opposed to love of humanity. Fichte regards the German people as destined to bring about the religious, philosophical and moral regeneration of mankind, and this alone constitutes its special value. He has no interest in conventional patriotism or national pride which have no connexion with the spiritual mission of his people.

The salvation of the German nation, and of mankind at large, was to be achieved through universal education, centred on the formation of a pure, unselfish will through clear thought, making use of Pestalozzi's pedagogical ideas and organized by the State. The Swiss educationist Pestalozzi, for whom Fichte had the greatest admiration, wanted to help the poor by education on modern realistic lines following Rousseau's suggestions, and he laid stress on the educational value of personal observation and manual labour. Fichte wished to organize the schools as self-supporting, autonomous communities in which the pupils were to be formed to unselfishness and self-sacrifice for humanity. His educational plans are thoroughly democratic. He utterly rejects a monarchical and centralized regime in Germany, not because of any affection for dynastic or traditional particularism, but because only the federal structure of a " Republic of German Peoples " allows free development to all tendencies of the people.

Fichte repeats his warnings against the political illusions which seem to him most odious and incompatible with the German character, i.e. power-politics, disguised as maintenance of the

Balance of Power, participation in world trade, which fosters egoism and war, and the striving for world domination. Nothing, he declares, is more repugnant to the German spirit than a universal Empire which would destroy spiritual life and defeat its own aims, for it could only be brought together by rapacity, barbaric brutality and ruthless egotism. In this way it may be possible to plunder and devastate the world, and to crush it to a sullen chaos, but it will never be possible to create a well-ordered universal monarchy. He also deprecates the widespread habit of admiring the "great genius" in power, i.e. Napoleon: it implies a measure of greatness which is un-German. The German measure is enthusiasm for ideas beneficial to the peoples.

In 1813 the war of liberation broke out for which Fichte had yearned. But he was not carried away by the enthusiasm of the patriots; he did not glorify war or excite the passions against the enemy. He pondered the question whether the war was really national or merely dynastic. A nation presupposed a representative system, founded on liberty, civil equality and mutual trust, while an aristocratic system implied slavery, oppression and exploitation of the people. The King of Prussia, he hoped, would unify Germany, but after his death a republic without princes and nobility would be set up. Prussia, the most enlightened State of the time, would after the war be peaceable, content with having recovered her ancient territories. In the same draft he also said that it was not merely the future of Germany which was at stake. If only German interests were to be considered it would matter little whether a part of Germany was governed by a French General like Bernadotte, who at least had once experienced in his mind the inspiring vision of liberty, rather than by a German nobleman, inflated by pride, uncivilized, and full of shameful brutality and arrogance. In another work of 1813 he stated that the final aim of political development was an era of universal justice. The warlike spirit would be overcome by love of peace. The reign of law and reason would be the first step to the advent of the kingdom of Christ.

Fichte intended to take part in the war as a preacher of his principles, and also trained in the Home Guard, though he felt that the use of arms was alien to him. Soon, however, he became the victim of an epidemic and died.

Like all great thinkers, Fichte has stimulated very different currents of thought, and his own thought was not free from inconsistencies and excentricities. Some of his ideas have been misused by later nationalists.[1] But his fundamental ideals were quite opposed to the mentality of the present nationalism of power and prestige. Among all the later heralds of nationality Mazzini had most in common with Fichte, and was, indeed, deeply influenced by him. But Fichte was not a politician; in particular he would never have made certain concessions which a politician can hardly escape. He was primarily a prophet of a new creed who believed in the power of a pure, heroic will and clear reason to transform mankind and to realize the ideals of humanity. The fact that his views were grossly distorted by disciples was a fate which he shared with many prophets.

16. HEGEL'S DOCTRINE OF THE STATE AND HIS ATTITUDE TO NATIONALITY

Georg Wilhelm Friedrich Hegel (1770–1831) was a native of Württemberg in southern Germany. The peculiar structure of his thought, the combination of rationalism and irrationalism, of radicalism and conservatism show an affinity to the culture of his Swabian homeland with its mixture of rational humanism, orthodoxy and mystical pietism, belief in progress and love of the past. The political and religious circumstances of his country early provoked Hegel's critical thought. Württemberg was ruled by a duke, but its parliament had a large share in the government. It was composed of representatives of the towns and the Protestant clergy, while the nobles had no representation.[2] The great Whig Charles James Fox compared the constitution to that of England. In fact the constitution, though much more bourgeois than the English one, was at least as oligarchic.

Hegel studied Protestant theology and philosophy and became

---

[1] The Nazi literature, for example, represents Fichte as a Jew-hater. In one of his early writings, indeed, he violently denounced the Jews, the officers and the nobility for their separatism which made them States within the State. Later, however, he changed his views on the Jews. When the University of Berlin was founded he became the first elected Rector. In this capacity he vigorously intervened against the anti-Semitism of a section of the students who brutally maltreated a Jewish student and he came into sharp conflict with the Senate which tried to palliate their behaviour and wanted to punish it but mildly. Cf. Max Lenz, *Geschicht der Universität Berlin*, 1910–18, and J. Levy, *Fichte und die Juden*.

Throughout his whole academic life Fichte unrelentingly combated the uncouth and brutal habits of the German students, their drinking and duelling, their terrorism, etc. This brought him into great trouble with the students and their protectors. Nevertheless, also in this respect his teachings produced effects which he had not intended. Treitschke says that Fichte had some responsibility for the "noble barbarism" of the German Burschenschaft. Cf. Treitschke, *Historische und Politische Aufsätze*, 1865, p. 149.

[2] Cf. K. Weller, *Wuerttembergische Geschichte*, 1909, p. 127.

deeply imbued with admiration for Hellenic culture and public life, with the rationalism of enlightenment, Kant's philosophy and enthusiasm for the French Revolution.[1] Among his comrades he was one of the most ardent speakers demanding liberty and equality. The modern State appeared to him as a tyranny suppressing the individual whereas in the Greek City-State the citizens had freely subordinated themselves to the community. All those influences inspired him with a critical attitude towards orthodox Christianity and its whole idea of life; and his opposition increased when he became acquainted with Spinoza's pantheism. The teachings of Jesus, he pondered, had been corrupted by Judaism and by the Church which had grafted Oriental ideas upon the mind of European peoples and had thereby denationalized them. The Christian dogmas were the product of a decadent age which had sought to escape from this world into a life beyond. Ancient religion was a creed for free peoples, which personified their moral ideas in their gods; it was enthusiasm for the fatherland, while Christianity was the outcome of the decay of freedom and nationality, and perhaps incompatible with the State. Similar ideas were held by many thinkers of the Age of Enlightenment, and Hegel was specially influenced by Gibbon. Montesquieu and Herder further stimulated his historical sense, Rousseau, Schiller and Fichte kindled in him the will to work for a new social and political order, founded on belief in the dignity, goodness and creativeness of man. Its heart was to be a new religion and morality, free from antiquated dogmas and in accordance with the life of Jesus, the glorious example of Greece, and the teachings of Spinoza, Shaftesbury and Kant.

In this way Hegel early adopted the mystical pantheism or panlogism which formed the fundamental idea of his philosophy. The whole world appeared to him as a manifestation of the spirit, as a developing organism in which the ideas inherent in the spirit unfolded themselves in a dialectic movement: every idea was bound to give birth to its opposite, and to be united with it again in a higher idea. On this basis Hegel built up a grandiose and fascinating architecture of concepts, which dialectically combined enlightenment and romanticism, and aimed at the

[1] Cf. Wilhelm Dilthey, *Die Jugendgeschichte Hegels*, 1906. On Hegel in general cf. Kuno Fischer, *Hegels Leben, Werke und Lehre*, 2 cols, 1901; Hermann Glockner, *Hegel*, 2 vols., 1929; K. Rosenkranz, *Hegel als deutscher Nationalphilosoph*, 1870, and in particular the criticism in Rudolf Haym, *Hegel und seine Zeit*, 1857. The political writings are in *Hegels Schriften zur Politik und Rechtsphilosophie*, ed. by G. Lasson, 1913; on Hegel's political views cf. Franz Rosenzweig, *Hegel und der Staat*, 2 vols., 1920.

harmonious reign of the spirit of reason and love in the world.[1]

A philosophy which sees in everything a manifestation of the Divine naturally inclines to denying the usual concept of morality, and, in particular, the applicability of common moral standards to historical evolution. Most metaphysicians of pantheism, moreover, have little interest in history. Hegel, however, was a great student of history and politics; he had a very wide knowledge of their facts, and the deepest understanding for their problems. The reign of terror in France soon destroyed his youthful enthusiasm for revolution. But he did not, like most romanticists, react by glorifying the past and praising the powers which the Revolution had overthrown. His personal observations in Germany and Switzerland, and his studies, convinced him that both monarchical absolutism and feudal oligarchy were untenable systems, and that democracy could not be realized in nations which had never been educated for it.

At this time out of the chaos in which the Revolution ended rose the dazzling star of Napoleon Bonaparte. His triumphs shattered the whole structure of Europe and the Holy Roman Empire broke down under his blows. Hegel meditated on its impending ruin in an important essay (1802). Germany, he says, is no longer a State. The political constitution of Germany was characterized by countless historical absurdities, complete disorganization and extreme weakness. In the last resort the cause was the indomitable German striving for liberty, and the inability to subordinate particular interests to the common weal. It had converted public affairs into a maze of private rights, which later on gave rise to numerous small sovereign principalities. A State could not exist without the power to defend its own. But Hegel did not admire the powerful State as such. Over-centralized States like republican France or absolutist Prussia seemed to him mere machines where the police regulated everything and left no freedom to the individual. Hegel wished the citizen to enjoy a wide self-government in all affairs not affecting public security, since their direct participation in the government as in the Greek City-States, was not possible in the large modern States. The Germanic representative system was indispensable for liberty.

Like Fichte, Hegel was deeply impressed by Machiavelli's argument that the political disintegration and demoralization of a nation could only be healed by a strong dictator. German

[1] On love cf. Haym, pp. 98, 101.

unity could only be expected from the rise of either Prussia or Austria to supreme power. Hegel preferred Austria, mainly because she had preserved her old provincial diets, was less dangerous to the smaller States, granted rights to the people and opened to everybody the road to the highest positions. Prussia had suppressed representative assemblies, and had by a separate peace with France abandoned all other Germans and aroused the deepest resentment in them. Hegel did not publish this essay because it was soon superseded by events.

Rousseau had taught Hegel that morality and freedom existed in and through the State only and that they were identical with the general will. Freedom consisted in voluntary submission to this general will, which included the real will of the individual, free from deception by passions and egotism. The Revolution had failed in the attempt to realize this general will, and had led to anarchy. Now Napoleon appeared as the saviour of society, the heir of the great principles of the Revolution, and the incarnation of reason and the general will. True, his policy did not comply with the ordinary rules of private morality; but the State obviously was free from these rules, it was the self-expression of the great intellect which inspired the world and had its agents in the great men of destiny.

When Napoleon in 1806 smashed Prussia in the battle of Jena Hegel was in Jena, and the French soldiers looted all his money. He saw the Emperor riding through the town and he was overwhelmed, as he wrote in a letter, to see the world soul on horseback. "As I already did before", he added, "everybody now wishes the French army good luck, and considering the immense difference which separates their leaders and soldiers from their enemies this cannot fail. Our place, therefore, will soon be freed from this crowd." The French victory, he wrote later, "was the convincing proof that civilization defeats crudeness, and the spirit vanquishes pedantry and pettifoggery". Other letters too prove his sympathies for the French invaders.

From 1807 to 1816 Hegel lived in Bavaria, first as the editor of a daily paper, and then in the service of the Government as headmaster of a school. Bavaria had been much enlarged and made into a kingdom by Napoleon, and was one of his most faithful vassals. The theory was officially spread at that time that the Bavarians were not of Germanic but of Celtic origin, and therefore kinsmen of the French. As an editor Hegel mainly reprinted the news and the propaganda articles published in the

Paris *Moniteur*, Napoleon's official organ, with all their glorification of the Emperor. Hegel himself derided the German opposition to Napoleon as " North Germanic patriotism ". There is no doubt that his loyalty to the Napoleonic system was quite sincere. In his eyes it preserved and developed what was reasonable in the ideas of the French Revolution, in particular the Rights of Man and equal opportunities for every citizen according to his merits. He eagerly wished for the introduction of the Code Napoléon in Germany, and advocated a wide publicity in all affairs of the State, as in France and England, for educating the people to patriotism. Moreover, he ardently desired that the people should be granted a sort of parliamentary representation on the model of the constitutions given by Napoleon in France, Italy, Westphalia, etc.[1] These assemblies were composed of representatives of the land-owners, the merchants, industrialists, and the intellectual professions, and they absolutely depended on the government. The Governments of Bavaria and Württemberg, indeed, introduced many reforms which aroused the stubborn resistance of the privileged classes. They raised the slogans that the liberty, the traditions and the religion of the people were threatened. In both countries the broad masses of the people violently took the side of the privileged classes, though the proposed reforms were surely in their interest. Hegel in these struggles defended the cause of the governments, which in his view stood for real progress.

The triumph of Napoleon coincided with the time when Hegel definitely formulated the fundamental doctrines of his philosophy. The deep impression made by Napoleon on Hegel's mind formed the background of his thought, and particularly of his philosophy of history and politics. Hegel—like Goethe—never altered his fundamental attitude. When in 1813 Napoleon's star was descending, Hegel absolutely disbelieved in the possibility of his defeat. He spoke ironically of the " liberation " for which the German people took up arms, and tried to dissuade his young friends from joining the colours.[2] When the Emperor was definitely vanquished Hegel was deeply discomfited, and interpreted his fall partly as the self-destruction of the great man, who had fulfilled his mission, partly as the victory of the mediocre multitude over the genius.

After the breakdown of Prussia, great reformers like Stein,

---

[1] The constitution of the Kingdom of Westphalia was considered the most perfect work of Napoleonic statesmanship, cf. H. A. L. Fisher, *Studies in Napoleonic Statesmanship in Germany*, 1903, p. 224.

[2] Cf. Rosenzweig, vol. ii, p. 27.

Hardenberg, Altenstein, Humboldt, laid the foundations of a new Prussia, inspired by progressive ideas and largely influenced by English and French models. Prussia seemed to become the most enlightened State in Germany, and there was hope that she would also adopt parliamentary institutions. But the forces of reaction were powerful too, and finally got the upper hand. In 1817 Hegel was appointed professor in the University of Berlin and soon reached the summit of his fame. He now believed in the mission of Prussia to realize the political ideas which he had formulated in the preceding epoch.

Nationality had not in Hegel's thought the same significance as in Fichte's. It was the State which embodied reason and objective morality. The philosopher, however, was fully aware that the spirit of a State was determined by national individuality, and its phase of development. The aim of the State was the realization of reason as determined by natural factors, history and social structure, not as an abstract idea of reason. It was not the text of a constitution or of the laws that guaranteed the realization of reason, but the whole spirit of the people. The idea of unlimited arbitrary state-interference, or an ambitious policy of power and prestige were alien to Hegel's mind. In a civilized state, he taught, legislation can only consist in further developing the existing laws, and so-called new laws should only settle details and particular cases which substantially had already been prepared or provisionally decided by the practice of the Courts. The State needed power for its purposes, but Hegel did not regard power as a value in itself. He had no special interest in a close political unity or in the power of Germany. But he believed that it was the mission of the German people to lead the world in philosophy.

The State was in Hegel's thought a spiritual organism, a manifestation of the World Intellect, and, therefore, had Divine authority and majesty. It was not bound to the rules of ordinary bourgeois morality, but its aim was to materialize the ethical spirit, the freedom and the substantial will of the individuals. The purpose of the individual is to live a universal life, that is to live in organic communion with his neighbours. True, many States do not realize this aim perfectly, and their activity is disfigured by error and historical accidents. Only when the universal aim of the State is allied to the full liberty and the well-being of the individuals can the State be considered truly organized. A State which suppresses the freedom and interests of its citizens is a castle built in the air. Mere external power can effect nothing in the long run.[1] The will of the majority of the people is not necessarily the real general will. A people without the organization of the State is a formless mass and unable to express its true will. This is the task of its representatives who must be the wisest men. The Representative Assembly should be composed of delegates of organized social classes and should have a share in the formation of the national will, though only by public discussion and criticism. The unity of will is personified in the monarch, who has absolute power. As a rule, however, the king was only to dot the *i*. The principal organ for ascertaining and formulating the general will was in Hegel's view the Civil Service, composed of carefully selected men who had a great sense of duty and responsibility and extensive scientific and practical qualifications. It was a modernized version of Plato's vision of a rule of wise men.

This sort of government seemed to Hegel much better suited to realize the common weal than the English parliamentary system which in his view only led to the overgrowth of private economic interests and the overstressing of the rights of property. In an essay on the Reform Bill he described the injustice and corruption which at that time marred England's political and social image. He admitted that the proposed reform of the franchise would improve conditions, but on the other hand it implied the danger of democratization, which could easily lead to revolution.

The absolute sovereignty of the State has also a decisive influence on the relations between different States. There is no stable basis for international law and war is the only means for settling grave disputes between States. Hegel, moreover, attributed to war the function of reviving the objective morality and the patriotism of the citizens which were jeopardized by a long spell of peace and the predominance of private egoistical interests. He referred to Gibbon's account of the effect of the Antonine Age on the Roman character. Gibbon said that it was doubtless the most happy and prosperous period in the history of mankind, but that the long peace and the uniform government also introduced a slow and secret poison into the vitals of the Empire, and enervated the character of the people. The idea that the bands

---

[1] Cf. *The Ethics of Hegel, Translated Selections from his Rechtsphilosophie* by J. Macbride Sterret, 1893, pp. 189, 194 f., 214. This translation has also been used in other places. Cf. further, Hugh Reyburn, *The Ethical Theory of Hegel*, 1921, pp. 220, 228, on Hegel's attitude to fundamental rights of man. It must not be overlooked that Hegel understands by freedom that of the spirit, not freedom for passions and an arbitrary, irrational will.

of society would break or weaken without war was also put forward by Adam Ferguson, whose *Essay on the History of Civil Society* was studied by Hegel.

Though Hegel recognized the utility of war for arousing or strengthening patriotism and manliness, he was by no means an enthusiast for war or for glory and conquest. His idea of patriotism was not of the heroic type. He defines patriotism as activity in harmony with the customs and institutions of the State, and as confidence in the State, which may attain to a more or less cultured insight. We ought not to understand by patriotism, he continues, only extraordinary actions and sacrifices. It is essentially the fulfilment of the every-day duties of the citizen. But as men, he continues, find it easier to be magnanimous than just, so they easily convince themselves that they possess heroic patriotism, in order to save themselves the trouble of having every-day patriotism.

A fruit of Hegel's work in Berlin was his philosophy of history, which, of all his works, probably had the greatest influence on his own time and posterity. History, in his view, consists in the evolution of the world-spirit to ever-increasing consciousness of freedom, namely spiritual freedom. The evolution of the world shows a steady progress from the reign of obscure instincts to that of clear reason. This process takes place in a logical order, but is largely actuated by irrational forces. The World-Spirit, so to say, makes use of the human passions for an ever-increasing rational organization of the world. This paradox, of course, is merely a new version of the old idea that God permits the existence of evil for the realization of His plans. In particular, it is the great heroes like Napoleon who, driven by their ambitions, unconsciously are the agents of the World-Spirit and also realize the true will of their peoples. Every people has its peculiar spirit which permeates its whole civilization and is the product of climate, soil, race, religion, political and social organization. In each epoch, moreover, a particular people eclipses the others through the realization of a higher stage of reason, and appears as the representative of the World-Spirit for its age. The other peoples have no right against this leading people, which dominates the world, but after having accomplished its mission sinks and is replaced in world-leadership by another people. Since the end of the ancient world the Germanic peoples which comprise most modern nations stand in the front rank, and among them the Protestant nations, and in particular Prussia, are foremost. This did not imply, however, a claim to political world-domination. Hegel's reflections on many historical events, especially on the rise and fall of the Roman Empire, leave no doubt that he considered a policy of expansion on a large scale as self-destructive. The Romans began as a robber-state, and this determined the ethos of their whole State, which produced that abstract spirit which Hegel described as a fateful legacy of the Romans in the modern world, especially in French civilization.

This philosophy of history contains many profound ideas and brilliant formulations. Its main theses, however, are not confirmed by the arguments which Hegel puts forward, and these frequently are even little more than a sophistic jugglery with words. Nevertheless for some time it fascinated many philosophers, scholars and writers all over Europe.

Though Hegel was not a nationalist, some of his teachings have contributed to the rise of ideas which form the core of nationalism, such as the divinization of the State, the doctrine of its higher morality, and of the effacement of individual reason, morality and interests, the praise of war and the superman, the idea of nations with a Divine mission. On the other hand, Hegel's philosophy was incompatible with the fundamental beliefs of nationalism. He judged a nation according to the degree of reason which its State and civilization represented, he was alien to the German national aspirations of his time, and sharply rejected political romanticism. The higher bureaucracy, which appeared to him as the organ of the national will, was at that time not likely to further aggressive nationalism and even combated the German national movement. Hegel fully approved this attitude.

The thought of the philosopher comprised germs which developed in quite divergent directions; it combined conservative and liberal elements and its core was the belief in a slow, continuous, organic growth of reasonable customs and institutions. Even in his old age Hegel preserved the habit of celebrating every year the day of the storming of the Bastille with a bottle of good wine; and his comments on the outbreak of the Revolution in his *Philosophy of History* show deep emotion.

Among the disciples of Hegel were Conservatives, Liberals and Radicals, and each regarded himself as the true interpreter of his master's teachings. Soon, however, the Radicals got the upper hand and influenced public opinion much more strongly than the rest. Among them were eminent scholars who attacked the historical foundations of Christianity, while others criticized Christian ethics and their political implications. Pantheism obliterated the distinction between right and wrong.[1] Many German intellectuals became either extreme individualists, like Stirner and Nietzsche, and devoted themselves to the cult of the superman, or they became extreme collectivists and made a god of race, nation or class. The fascination of Hegel's system vanished through the rise of natural science and other forces and the ruin of his all-embracing idealistic doctrine was followed by the general contempt for idealism and philosophy, by the cult of success, and by the race for financial or military power. Karl Marx, a disciple of Hegel, made use of the dialectical conjurer's wand of his master and transformed his idealistic interpretation of history into a materialistic one.

17. Romanticism and Politics

In the age of enlightenment romantic thought on art and life developed first as an undercurrent below the surface of rationalism and eventually revolted against its domination.[2] While the rationalists demanded the liberation of the reason of the individual from the rusty shackles of the past, the romanticists longed for freedom of fancy, emotions and passions. Their striving was first devoted to the reform of poetry but then also was directed against the conventions of society, and lastly extended to politics. Rousseau became the herald of political romanticism.

From a social point of view romanticism comprised both a revolt of youth against old age, and a reaction of intellectuals against the artificiality of conventions underlying society and civilization, a yearning for the lost paradise of the natural man, though many romanticists were not so naïve as to believe that it had ever really existed. Nevertheless, they loved the illusion of it, or, as their modern descendants say, the mythos. The tragedy of the French Revolution greatly discouraged the belief in the natural goodness of man and in the ability of nations to realize their own good. Napoleon's conquests and domination soon aroused the sense of nationality and nationalist ambitions all over Europe.

Romanticism which had begun as a revolutionary creed now to a large extent became a conservative and even reactionary force, at least in politics. Superficial observers have often

[1] Cf. Acton's criticism of Hegelianism in Ulrich Noack, *Geschichtswissenschaft und Wahrheit, nach den Schriften von John Dalberg-Acton*, 1935, pp. 70–3, 107, 143, 158, 181.
[2] Cf. on the origin of romanticism, Paul van Tieghem, *Le Preromantisme*, 1924; *Le movement Romantique*, 1923; J. R. Robertson, *Studies in the Genesis of Romantic Theory in the Eighteenth Century*, 1923.

identified romanticism with this later form only. Others have tried to find some system of doctrines characteristic of it, but no definition in terms of a specific doctrine fits all the phenomena going under this name. Romanticism is obviously merely a psychological type that combines the passionate striving for emotional freedom with disillusionment in regard to human reason, and the effort to overcome the anarchic and pessimistic consequences of these experiences. This mentality of the intelligentsia surfeited with intellect, and in desperate search of a creed, can adopt almost any political programme.[1] The romanticists, therefore, usually show a mixture of quite inconsistent tendencies and sudden changes of ideology, and they also reflect the differences in the predominant tendencies of the national ideologies.

Most romanticists were not practical politicians or serious students of political science. They were mainly poets, literary critics or philosophers, or intellectuals of some other profession who incidentally wrote on politics. In literature the romantic movement started as a protest against the rigid rules of classicism, and against an arid rationalism which suppressed the free play of fancy and emotions. Still more the romanticists hated sophisticated society and the bourgeois ideas of a happy and virtuous life. What they longed for was the extraordinary, the mysterious, the irrational, the fantastic, and they hoped to find it in exotic countries and primitive peoples, in unspoiled nature and man, among children, the youth, the uncorrupted peasants and the outcasts of society, the proletariate, in the Middle Ages, in old ballads, fairy-tales and other folk-lore, in an utopian golden age of the past or the future, in emancipated women, in unconventional eroticism, in mysticism, and in sentimentalism mixed with irony and self-derision. The rationalists ascribed value only to eternal ideas which were the same in all nations and at all times. The romanticists stressed historical, personal or national individuality, the peculiar features of a unique personality. While the analysing intellect tended to conceive nature and society as machines, the romanticists liked to describe them as organisms. The mentality and morality of the average man appeared to the romanticist as dull. They praised enthusiasm and heroism, and the inborn genius of the superman who stood above the obligations of ordinary morality. Many famous romanticists were in their youth absolute libertines and debauchees, while many others who personally were timid weaklings glorified war, cruelty and freedom from any moral restraint. Pantheism, the adoration of

[1] This has been pointed out by Carl Schmitt, *Politische Romantik*, 1925.

the Divine force of nature, offered them a convenient cloak. Their development frequently ended in almost complete nihilism and utter despair; they then suddenly turned round, forsook and condemned every form of individualism, and plunged their personality into collectivism, seeking a haven of refuge either in the discipline of the Church, in religious mysticism, the cult of the State, or the religion of nationalism.

Romanticists have been revolutionaries and reactionaries, believers in the majesty of the people or in the majesty of kings, glorifiers of feudal patriarchalism, and heralds of a new socialist order, advocates of nationality and of world-brotherhood. The political creed least congenial to them was liberalism, and especially a liberal democracy. This latter system is in principle based on reason, compromise and moderation, and to most romanticists it seemed to represent the reign of calculating commercialism.

18 Romanticism and Nationality in Germany

In the recent national ideology of Germany it has become a sort of dogma that romanticism is the true expression of the German soul. Many writers have tried to prove that the Germans throughout all their history have always shown romantic tendencies and that these, therefore, must correspond to their innate character. In reality the growth of mysticism which is to some extent related to romanticism has, in certain epochs, been favoured by the political and social conditions of Germany, and has had some influence on Lutheranism. But modern romanticism came rather late to Germany.[1] It was at first imported from abroad, mainly from England, and was regarded with suspicion by the authorities. In 1725 the ecclesiastical censorship of Zurich decided that the printing of Bodmer's translation of *Paradise Lost* could not be permitted since it treated the sacred subject in too romantic a fashion.[2] The official distrust was not quite unfounded, for the romantic claim for emotional liberty in

---

[1] Cf. on German romanticism, Rudolf Haym, *Die romantische Schule*, 4th ed., 1920; Oskar Walzel, *Deutsche Romantik*, 5th ed., 1923; Julius Petersen, *Die Wesensbestimmung der deutschen Romantik*, 1926; Kuno Francke, *History of German Literature as determined by Social Forces*, 10th ed., 1916, p. 399; Friedrich Meinecke, *Weltbürgertum und Nationalstaat*, 2nd ed., 1911; Marie Joachimi, *Die Weltanschauung der deutschen Romantik*, 1905; Wilhelm Metzger, *Gesellschaft, Recht und Staat in der Ethik des deutschen Idealismus*, 1917; Jakob Baxa, *Gesellschaft und Staat im Spiegel deutscher Romantik*, 1924; Hanns Thimme, *Deutscher Volksgeist in der Zeit des Idealismus und der Romantik*, 1925; Otto Brandt, *A. W. Schlegel, der Romantiker und die Politik*, 1919.

[2] Cf. G. Jenny, *Miltons Verlorenes Paradies in der Deutschen Litteratur des 18. Jahrhunderts*, 1890, p. 21.

literature was to many young intellectuals a substitute for the claim to political liberty which could not yet be pressed. Rationalism in thought and classicism in art were the closely associated doctrines of the ruling powers, the kings and the aristocracy. Romantic tendencies were in the eighteenth century usually the cloak of a passionate striving for literary, artistic and social liberty. Sometimes they led to quite a new interest in the past of Germany, though it was less mediaeval feudalism that attracted the youth than old Teutonic heroes like Hermann who were regarded as protagonists of national and political liberty.

Most German romanticists, of course, shared the enthusiasm for the French Revolution and the general cosmopolitanism of the time. Under Napoleon's domination they became more national, and in the war of liberation against the Emperor many romanticists, such as Arndt, Kleist, Koerner, Arnim and Goerres, wrote poems or pamphlets breathing fierce hatred of the French and extolling the German virtues. The main contribution of romantic thought to the national ideology, however, was the stressing of the idea of national individuality, and the attempt to describe and compare the individuality of the Germans with those of other nations. A survey of their ideas would take much more space than is available here.[1] Romanticism was not a clear-cut system but a spirit of restless longing and fermentation which expressed itself in the most various and often inconsistent ways. Its followers seldom systematically worked out their political ideas, they rather adumbrated them incidentally in irridescent aphorisms, in poems, novels or critical essays. The philosophers among them realized that romantic emotionalism was not sufficient for a philosophy, and tried to amalgamate in their thought rational and irrational elements. It is often difficult, therefore, if not impossible, to indicate where romanticism begins and where it ends, and who belonged to it.[2]

The most important romantic thinkers, such as the brothers August Wilhelm and Friedrich Schlegel, always retained a large measure of cosmopolitanism. A. W. Schlegel wrote in 1803:

> Is the lack of national pride really a great defect? Is it not clear that in other nations it often rests on onesidedness, narrowmindedness and even mere illusions? Where the highest interest of human nature, the development of its most noble forces, is con-

---

[1] I have surveyed the ideas of some romanticists on the national character in my studies published in the *Archiv für Sozialwissenschaft*, vol. 54, 1926, pp. 670–715.

[2] Kuno Francke in his excellent chapters on romanticism says: "The formation of an international league for the suppression of the terms both of Romanticism and Classicism would seem to me a truly philanthropic undertaking" (p. 401).

cerned, for example, in art and learning, I should think it would be more German not to ask whether something was German or foreign, but merely whether it was genuine, great and excellent, and not to worry whether liberal recognition of foreign achievements would not dim the glory of the home-bred. Universalism, Cosmopolitanism is the true German characteristic.

Novalis said : " Germans exist everywhere, Germanity as Romanism, Grecism, Britainism is not restricted to a specific State. They are general human types. Germanity is true popularity and, therefore, an ideal." " Germanity is Cosmopolitanism combined with vigorous individuality." Numerous romanticists and other idealistic thinkers pointed out that the Germans were destined to develop the universality or totality of human nature, to adopt and develop the highest cultural values of all peoples and to dominate not through the sword but through the spirit. The hope was frequently expressed that the Germans would lead all peoples to the highest humanity and that German would become the cultural world language.

Friedrich Schlegel has in many of his writings put forward his ideas on national individuality of which I have given a summary elsewhere. His views are based on wide historical studies and show great psychological and sociological understanding. He did not see a high value in an historical national character as such. Germanity was not merely a product of the past but an ideal lying in the future. " It is said that the Germans are the first people in the world as regards the sense for art and science. True, but there are very few Germans." " It is not Hermann and Wotan who are the national Gods of the Germans, but art and science." Friedrich Schlegel first put art much higher than politics. But later he sharply disapproved of the aesthetic dream-world and of the " unmanly pantheistic fraud ", which had dominated the finest German spirits almost without exception for the last fifty years, and which he traced to the suppression of political life. Once he said that the slumbering German lion would perhaps wake up one day and future history be full of German exploits.

Friedrich Schlegel was the most brilliant thinker among the romanticists and began as an outspoken republican. Later he became Catholic and conservative like many others of the same school, and entered the Austrian diplomatic service. His brother August Wilhelm translated Shakespeare and other foreign poets into German, and was for a long time associated with Madame de Staël, on whose famous book on Germany he seems to have had some influence. He eventually became a professor in Prussia.

The great controversy whether Austria or Prussia should realize Germany's unity also split the ranks of the romanticists. Many hoped that the old Holy Roman Empire of the Germanic nation, and the spirit of mediaeval universalism and feudalism, would revive under the hegemony of Austria, while others put their faith in the national mission of Prussia. The pro-Austrian section was conservative, supra-national and Catholic, while the adherents of Prussia were, on the whole, more liberal, national and Protestant. Among the writers of the latter section must be mentioned the theological Schleiermacher, who at the time of the war of liberation stressed national individuality. But soon after he declared that the philosopher could only be a cosmopolitan, that nationality was merely a phase of evolution, and that it was certain that national differences would gradually vanish.[1]

The most important exponent of romantic political and economic theory was Adam Müller.[2] He was born in Berlin, the son of a Prussian official, and studied at the University of Göttingen, where he became acquainted with the doctrines of Adam Smith, Montesquieu and Burke. For some time he was a great admirer of Smith and opposed in his spirit Fichte's idea of a self-sufficient, semi-socialist State. Later, however, he grew ever more hostile to Smith's economic liberalism, and in politics Burke became his idol. He praised him as the greatest statesman of the last three centuries, and in his lectures exhorted his audience to read him again and again, and even to learn his works by heart. Adam Müller took over from his master his opposition to the principles of the French Revolution,[3] the concept of the State and nation as a spiritual organism, the admiration of feudal institutions, and the veneration of old national traditions. England appeared to him, as to his close friend Gentz, to be the most perfect organic nation, while he often criticized with great aversion the Prussian " machine-state " as created by Frederick II, whom he detested. He also, after Prussia's defeat, opposed her reorganization in a liberal spirit, and associated with the re-

[1] Cf. Metzger, pp. 216, 289, 291. Cf. Theodor Kappstein, *Schleiermachers Weltbild und Lebensanschauung*, 1921, pp. 149, 298.

[2] Adam Müller was long almost forgotten, and has in recent time been unearthed and represented as the greatest exponent of German political philosophy, especially by Othmar Spann and his school. An abridged edition of his most important writings has been published by Friedrich Bülow, under the title *Adam Müller, Vom Geiste der Gemeinschaft*, 1931. Cf. further the summary of his theories in my paper in the *Archiv für Sozialwissenschaft*, 1926, p. 696.

[3] On Burke's influence cf. Frieda Braune, *E. Burke in Deutschland*, 1917, p. 183. Müller, however, judged the French Revolution with more moderation and in a fairer spirit than Burke.

actionary Junkers who resisted Hardenberg's reforms. This prevented his employment in the Prussian civil service, and in 1815 he entered the Austrian diplomatic service in which he became a tool of Metternich's policy. Already ten years before he had become a convert to Catholicism, and his political ideas assumed an ever increasing mystical tinge.

Adam Müller had a very high idea of nationality, which he conceived as a Divine harmony and mutual interaction of all private and personal interests, and as a link between the individual and humanity. National peculiarity is to a nation its highest value, and it has an expansive tendency. War is an indispensable means for national unification, consolidation, education and development. The State is an organism that embraces all the forces of the nation, and for it the individual must sacrifice everything. In his lectures of 1810 he criticized Prussia especially because her government regarded the army merely as a necessary evil and as a means to ward off war. But he believed that a national State was possible only in a territory of moderate size. Too large a State cannot attain to true national unity. Müller, furthermore, wished for a great federation of European peoples under German leadership. Feudalism, federalism, and agrarianism appear to him as the realization of Mosaic and Germanic principles, while the Reformation, enlightenment, the centralized machine-state, the striving for world domination, industrialism, capitalism and the French Revolution were all consequences of the dismal Roman spirit as embodied in the Roman Empire and the Roman Law. How these views can be reconciled with his admiration for England, which was certainly Protestant, liberal, centralized, a world-power, and capitalistic, is difficult to say. He also elaborated an economic system which was strictly antiindividualistic, and centred in the interests of the national State and culture, which seemed to him largely to coincide with the landed interest, in opposition to industrialism. A main point of his theory was a national paper currency as opposed to the international gold currency.

The romanticists were not the leaders of the rising national movement, nor had they great influence on public opinion in political matters. They formed a small intellectual élite and partly preferred art and literature to politics, partly supported the system of Metternich and the other reactionary governments of the Germanic Federation which tried to suppress the national movement. Nevertheless, they contributed to the formation of an ideology which later became the foundation of German nationalism. The school of historical jurisprudence, and many great scholars in the field of history and German philology, helped to develop the ideas of the organic individuality of the nation, to kindle enthusiasm for the national traditions of Germany, and to work for the spiritual and political unification of the German people.

The romantic mood flagged when the national movement put the demand for political liberty in the forefront. But the defeat of the Revolution of 1848 made many intellectuals despair again of reason and furthered the rise of pessimism which, however, had other causes too. Schopenhauer now became the most popular philosopher, and no other philosophical writer has ever found so many readers in Germany. He had nothing but contempt for German metaphysicians and romanticists, though he himself must be regarded as one of their kin.[1] The world seemed to him a ghastly nightmare, ruled not by reason but by blind, rude, greedy instincts, called the will to live. The only escape from this hell lies in compassion with all living beings and in creative art, especially music. The conviction that human character is radically evil was also held by Luther, and naturally leads to the rejection of political liberty. Schopenhauer violently combats the ideas of God, Christianity, educability, progress and democracy. Hegel's praise of the State as the embodiment of morality and his defence of war are pronounced to be absolute nonsense. Schopenhauer hated war and scorned national pride, which he regarded as typical of a miserable simpleton who had nothing else to be proud of. Of all nations he had most sympathies for the English except for their Church and their religious cant. The Germans were very unfavourably judged, and he declared in a paper found after his death that he despised them because of their excessive stupidity, and was ashamed of belonging to them. In other writings, however, he admitted, that there were at least a few things to their credit, namely their language, their lack of national pride, which was a proof of sincerity, and the fact that there were more atheists amongst them than in any other people.

Another unwilling heir to the romantic spirit was Nietzsche. He too believed that the world was not actuated by reason but by will, which he defined as the will to power. This idea had dawned upon him in the war of 1870 when he saw German troops hurrying to the battlefield. Though he admired warlike heroism

[1] Schopenhauer's and Nietzsche's romanticism have been well pointed out by Karl Joel, *Nietzsche und die Romantik*, 1905.

from an aesthetic point of view, and appreciated military discipline, he was doubtful of the alleged ennobling influence of war. The German spirit in any case had been degraded through the victory over France. He despised German metaphysics and romanticism and rejected the cult of the State, patriotism and nationality, as foolish, and as obstacles to the development of individuality and true culture. Though he thoroughly disliked democracy he occasionally found a few good points in it, especially so far as it opened the road to strong individualities. The spirit of militarism is a hateful symptom of a barbaric society, and Nietzsche dreamed of a people which at the summit of power voluntarily breaks its own sword. The greatest disease of the time is nationalism, and he especially abhorred German racial self-admiration. He professes to be a good European and wishes for the suppression of national differences. Every great genius was supra-national in his merits and national in his demerits. French cultural achievements are greater than the German. He despised English utilitarianism and democracy. Man does not strive for happiness but for power and he loves cruelty. Christianity and Christian morality, too, are but veiled strivings for power in the interest of the weak and of the priesthood. It is his main purpose to destroy the belief in Christian ethics.

Nietzsche's thought is full of real and apparent contradictions, and one can put the most different interpretations upon his philosophy. It is beyond doubt that some of his principal views have greatly stimulated the contempt for human reason and happiness and the revolt against all moral inhibitions which has become typical of German nationalism. It is a tragic irony that he has in this way fostered the mentality of German nationalism which he despised and hated more than anything else.

Richard Wagner and Nietzsche were once close friends. Later Nietzsche attacked Wagner vehemently and saw in his music and ideas the most dangerous expression of German nationalism and the romantic fraud. Nietzsche was right in regard to the general influence of Wagner on the German mind, though it was hardly his music which contained the germs of evil. Wagner himself was inspired by Schopenhauer's philosophy, which was certainly not nationalistic but centred in compassion. Yet Wagner was also a believer in racialism, and both Gobineau and Houston Stewart Chamberlain obtained their pernicious influence on the German people through their connexion with Wagner and the circle around him. Long after his death Hitler became the favourite of Wagner's family and disciples, and owed a great deal to their patronage.

Both Schopenhauer and Nietzsche represent a type of romanticism which was modified by modern naturalism. The philosophy of idealism and romanticism was based on the belief in the higher spiritual nature of man which expressed itself either in the reason of the individual or in collective reason. In the philosophy of romantic naturalism, however, man appears as a highly developed animal actuated by instincts. Nietzsche revels in admiration of the wonderful human beast of prey. Ideas of modern biology, especially that of the relentless "struggle for existence" and the power of heredity as instruments of racial vigour and progress, have played a great rôle in developing the ideology of modern nationalism. After the last war Oswald Spengler published his *Decline of the West* which, together with other writings of the author, preached the idea of a national and militaristic dictatorship on the basis of a naturalistic and romantic philosophy. His books had a great influence on the German intellectuals. Many books of the same spirit by other authors also served the cause of anti-democratic nationalism,[1] and contributed to that poisoning of the German youth which enabled Hitler to seize power. The romantic spirit was in its beginnings the temper of an intellectual élite of idealists. Finally it produced slogans of vulgar demagogy for the intoxication of a youth devoid of reverence for the spirit, and destined to become the instruments of the most powerful and anti-intellectual slave-holder in history.

19. INDIVIDUALISM, ROMANTICISM AND NATIONALITY IN BRITAIN

The middle of the eighteenth century marked the beginning of movements for great reforms, initiated by the revival of Christian humanitarianism and the rise of Utilitarianism. Both were more or less reactions against the one-sided rationalism of many exponents of enlightenment. Romanticism, the revolt of sentiment against reason and against a sophisticated civilization, also developed at the same time, often in close alliance with traditionalism. All these spiritual forces implied a better understanding of certain aspects of nationality, sympathy with nationalities striving for liberty, a wish for the strengthening of unity between the classes within a nation and for the improvement of relations between nations. Moreover, they had a great influence

[1] Cf. Rohan Butler, *The Roots of National Socialism*, 1941, and S. D. Stirk, *The Prussian Spirit*, 1941.

in moulding the individuality of the nation. In the ensuing century the national character of Britain was mainly marked by three traits which were much more pronounced than in other nations : Utilitarianism, Christian humanitarianism and traditionalism.

Hume, in his essay " Of National Characters ", remarks that national characteristics often change very quickly and he gives as an illustration the fact that the English in the seventeenth century were " inflamed with the most furious enthusiasm, and are now settled into the most cool indifference, with regard to religious matters, that is to be found in any nation of the world ". At that time, however, a great revival of religious enthusiasm was already preparing itself, namely the work of John and Charles Wesley, Whitefield and their disciples. The Methodists and the Quakers had the main share in an awakening of the Christian conscience which resulted in a moral revolution as momentous as the industrial revolution of that time.[1]

John Wesley was distrustful of governments, of the ruling powers, and of " that many-headed beast " the people, as a political factor. In his view the moral regeneration of man was immensely more important than political reforms. But his great achievements in arousing a sense of brotherhood and moral energy prepared the ground for a wider and nobler idea of a nation, and helped to save Britain from the poisonous doctrines of class war and revolution.

The " greatest happiness " principle was put forward by many British thinkers of the eighteenth century.[2] But its true prophet was Jeremy Bentham (1748–1832), whose influence was dominant in a large part of the nineteenth century.[3] It was he and his disciples who made Utilitarianism a national characteristic of modern British thought and politics. Starting from conservative views, Bentham became more and more hostile to all obsolete traditions and worked out a large part of the ideology of later liberals and democrats. Utilitarianism, however, is not merely liberalism. The happiness-principle inspired also many benevo-

---

[1] Cf. W. Warner, *The Wesleyan Movement in the Industrial Revolution*, 1930 ; Robert Wearmouth, *Methodism and the Working-Class Movements in England, 1800–1850*, 1937.

[2] For the history of English political thought cf. especially the admirable work by Robert Murray, *Studies in the English Social and Political Thinkers of the 19th Century*, 2 vols., 1929. On patriotism cf. Esmé Wingfield-Stratford, *History of English Patriotism*, 1913, vol. ii. In a later book, *The Foundations of British Patriotism*, 1939, Wingfield-Stratford states that he has revised his standpoint. But his first work is still the most valuable survey of ideas on patriotism and nationality in England.

[3] Dicey calls the time from 1825 to 1870 the period of Benthamism or individualism, cf. A. V. Dicey, *Lectures on the Relation between Law and Public Opinion in England*, 1905, p. 63.

lent autocrats and to-day forms the background of socialism. Nor did Bentham share the fundamental creed of liberalism, the belief in natural rights and the supreme value of liberty [1] ; and not until the closing years of his life did he advocate the extension of the franchise. He had strong cosmopolitan sympathies, and wished to be the servant of all progressive nations. The French National Assembly offered him the honorary citizenship of France, which he accepted, reserving his loyalty to his native country. Though he professed to be more of an American than an Englishman, and preferred the constitution of the United States to that of Britain, he was proud of English ideals and of the English language.[2] He defended national self-determination and stood for the emancipation of colonies. Nations, he maintained, were to be ruled by moral principles and he was the first to use the term " international law ", though he pointed out that it was only called law by metaphor because it did not possess the same force as national law. His views on war, disarmament, collective security, secret diplomacy, and a " European fraternity " of nations were those of modern internationalism. Bentham objected to expressions such as " My country right or wrong " as evidencing " a malevolence exercised on a wide scale " which " sometimes takes the name of *esprit de corps*, of nationality : sometimes the higher name of patriotism ".

The final defeat of Napoleon in 1815 ended a struggle between Britain and France which had extended over 126 years, of which more than half were years of open warfare. During this epoch Britain had acquired a vast empire and had become the first great industrial Power. In the course of the century the changes in social structure brought about a fundamental transformation of the political structure of many countries. In Britain alone were these changes effected without revolution, proving that her national unity was more firmly founded than that of other nations. Her fortunate history spared her many problems which in other nations caused endless speculations. Her frontiers, formed by the sea, secured her against invasion ; no Britons lived anywhere under foreign domination ; and apart from Ireland she had no grave difficulties with national or religious minorities. Political thinkers in Britain were not compelled to ponder the claims of conflicting loyalties, as in Germany and Italy, where particularism was struggling with the rising sentiment of national unity ; nor

---

[1] Cf. Atkinson, *Jeremy Bentham, His Life and Work*, 1905, pp. 104–8.
[2] Cf. Elmer L. Kayser, *The Grand Social Enterprise, a Study of Bentham in his Relation to Liberal Nationalism*, 1932, p. 32.

had they to devote much thought to the problem of how to appease violent civic discord, as in France. The British people, unlike other nations, did not much indulge in speculations about their national character and mission.[1] Their position in the world would have made such speculations seem gratuitous. Certain fundamental views of the national character were almost universally accepted. In opposition to French rationalism and German metaphysics the British emphasized the facts that they were empirical in their national way of thought, were averse to abstract principles and believed in common sense and compromise. Their utilitarian principle of the " greatest happiness ", however, was by no means less abstract and vague than the French revolutionary doctrines of liberty and equality, and the Christian conscience underlying British humanitarianism was no less rooted in metaphysical suppositions than were the German ethical systems. Though both Tories and Whigs were much afraid of democracy,[2] and did their best to prevent its progress, the transformation of the aristocratic system into the reign of the middle class, and later the advance of democracy were achieved with surprising smoothness. The growth of wealth and the progress of democracy resulted in convincing the whole nation that its paramount interest was peace. The unprecedented increase in wealth, however, was accompanied by the growth of an industrial proletariate which lived in appalling conditions. Robert Owen's efforts were inspired by a socialist interpretation of the utilitarian principle. But its predominant interpretation was imbued with the spirit of a self-complacent capitalism which had great influence on the prevailing views of the British national character. Bentham's man, says Leslie Stephen, was " the respectable citizen with the policeman round the corner. Such a man may well hold that honesty is the best policy ; he has enough sympathy to be kind to his old mother, and help a friend in distress ; but

[1] In 1833 Bulwer-Lytton (later Lord Lytton) published a book on the English national character (*England and the English*) which was brilliantly written and contained many shrewd psychological observations. Immediately after its appearance it ran into a second edition, but then was not reprinted for forty-one years. " In his own mind," he says, " the Englishman is the pivot of all things—the centre of the solar system." " In some countries Pleasure is the idol, in others Glory, and the prouder desires of the world ; but with us Money is the mightiest of all deities." " In other countries poverty is a misfortune—with us it is a crime." Respectability which includes a decent sufficiency of wealth is the supreme virtue. The author makes interesting comments on the enormous hold of the aristocracy on the mind of the nation and on its influence on the character of all classes.
[2] Even Macaulay, the herald of liberty in the Whig sense, wrote that he had not the smallest doubt that a democratic government in England, as in any other country, would only lead to the poor plundering the rich and to the destruction of liberty and civilization. Cf. Arthur Bryant, *Macaulay*, 1932, p. 144.

the need of romantic and elevated conduct rarely occurs to him; and the heroic, if he meets it, appears to him as an exception, not far removed from the silly." [1] In particular, most Utilitarians were convinced that all government was in itself one vast evil. This was the mentality which was violently attacked by the Romanticists.

Wordsworth, Coleridge and Southey all began as enthusiasts for the French Revolution and Wordsworth even wanted to become a French citizen and to be elected a Deputy to the French National Convention.[2] When war with France broke out their sympathies were on the side of France, but their mood changed when the policy of the Jacobins and that of Napoleon became increasingly aggressive and oppressive. The war in Spain and the rising tide of national revolt against French domination made clear the significance of nationality as a force working for liberation. Wordsworth wished for the rebuilding of Europe on the principle of nationality and in particular for the national unification of Germany and Italy. " The smaller States must disappear, and merge in the large nations and wide-spread languages." At that time he associated nationality with liberty, but in the period of reaction after the war the poet abandoned these ideas and became opposed to all reform. Southey and Coleridge too became staunch Tory. Coleridge was strongly influenced by German mysticism and metaphysics and was a Germanophile. Now industrialism, Utilitarianism, liberalism and democracy were detested by the Romanticists and they praised the old feudal times, the landed aristocracy and the simple country-people. Southey and Coleridge were deeply moved by the sufferings of the industrial workers and contributed to the awakening of the social conscience. The colonization of the Empire by the unemployed workers of Britain seemed to them an urgent task, and in this way they also helped to prepare the ground for a new Imperialism. As early as 1812 Southey had the vision of a British Commonwealth of Nations. Burke's idea of the State and the nation as an organic whole had great influence on their thought. The whole development of this school shows a close parallel with that of German Romanticism. But other English writers like Byron and Shelley remained true to the original revolutionary spirit of Romanticism.

[1] Cf. Leslie Stephen, *The English Utilitarians*, 1900, vol. i, p. 314.
[2] On the Romanticists cf. Crane Brinton, *The Political Ideas of the English Romanticists*, 1926; Alfred Cobban, *Burke and the Revolt against the 18th Century, a Study of the Political and Social Thinking of Burke, Wordsworth, Coleridge and Southey*, 1929, Murray, i, p. 161; George Brandes, *Main Currents in 19th Century Literature*, 1901.

In Thomas Carlyle's personality Romantic thought attained its greatest power and splendour. Many of his social and political tendencies were common to most Romanticists, such as the hatred of materialism and Utilitarianism, the bitter criticism of modern achievements and sympathy with the past. Carlyle conceived society as an organism, but nevertheless remained an individualist, at least in regard to the great men, the born leaders, while he had a very poor opinion of the masses. At various times he laid down the doctrine that Might is Right.[1] He was the first great modern writer to praise the hero, the super-man, and his works on Hero-Worship, on Cromwell and Frederick the Great, illustrated his doctrine. The masses, he believed, were craving for a great leader; but he could never be selected by the vote of a majority. Liberty, parliamentarism and democracy were objects of his scorn, and when Disraeli in 1867 enfranchised the industrial workers this bold step appeared to him like "shooting Niagara". In 1850 he demanded that an executive cabinet composed of the wisest among the British people should be formed under the leadership of a dictator, who, if necessary, would brush aside parliament and deal drastically with national problems, especially unemployment and emigration. Sir Robert Peel seemed to him the right man for dictatorship, but he died just at that moment and this plunged Carlyle in the greatest despair. Shortly afterwards he expressed his hope that the future kings of Britain would be of the type of Frederick the Great, who was an absolute autocrat.[2] Carlyle was keenly aware of the terrible social evils of his time and demanded the intervention of the State for improving the lot of the workers, mainly through organized emigration to undeveloped parts of the Empire. But like Wordsworth he detested that humanitarianism which had liberated the slaves and promoted the reform of criminal law and prisons. Slaves, he maintained, ought to be lashed and kept down with an iron hand and he would even have subjected the liberated slaves to a new bondage. The mutinous negroes of Jamaica, the Hindoos and the Irish people were all described by him with greatest contempt, and the Czechs whom he met on a tour in Bohemia seemed to him even worse than the Irish. The Italian movement for liberty and unity too aroused only his scorn, though he liked Mazzini as a man. The cry of "oppressed nationalities" was to him mere cant. Those who have allowed themselves to be subjugated deserved their fate. Nature had destined them for

---

[1] Cf. John Nichol, *Carlyle*, 1892, p. 199; John M. Robertson, *Modern Humanists*, 1895, p. 19.   [2] Emery Neff, *Carlyle*, 1932, pp. 232, 242.

servitude. He had much sympathy for the autocratic government of Russia which cruelly oppressed the Poles and other nationalities, and its policy seemed to him the right way of governing barbarians. Carlyle was an enthusiast for German literature and philosophy and indulged in glorification of the Teutonic race which he regarded as far superior to the Celtic. When in 1870 a feeling of sympathy for defeated France spread in England, Carlyle ardently defended Germany's cause and Bismarck's policy. But Carlyle, in spite of his admiration for warlike heroes, hated war ; he condemned the British policy which led to the Crimean War and expressed his full approval of the London Peace Congress of 1851.[1] It may be noted, however, that, in spite of his grim public denunciations of humanitarian movements he performed many acts of private charity. His adoration of strength, his harsh judgments upon most great men of his time and other eccentricities were probably to a great extent due to his neurotic temperament, to chronic dyspepsia, and that oversensibility which is typical of many Romanticists.

Carlyle was no nationalist, though he had strong national and racial prejudices ; but his philosophy has certainly helped to weaken the liberal and humanitarian spirit and to spread the longing for the dictatorship of forceful heroes. In Britain the national traditions and the development of democracy barred the road to the growth of these tendencies ; but in other nations Carlyle's teachings were used by the nationalists for the working out of their ideology.[2]

The development of thought on Britain's mission in the world and on international relations in general must be studied against the background of foreign policy which for a long time was dominated by the ideas of Canning and Palmerston. The aim of this policy was the maintenance, through the traditional principle of the Balance of Power, of Britain's security and of her position as the paramount nation. This involved Britain in constant antagonism to the great European autocracies and led to a policy designed to check the expansion of these Powers and to emancipate the smaller nations from their domination or pressure. In this respect Palmerston's policy was to some extent in agreement with

---

[1] The attitude of Carlyle and many other English writers to the question of war and national prestige are summarized in Jacques Bardoux, *Essai d'une Psychologie de l'Angleterre contemporaine, Les crises belliqueuses*, 1906, pp. 179, 211. The influence of German Romanticists on Carlyle is shown in detail by Leon Kellner, *Die englische Literatur der neuesten Zeit*, 1921, p. 83.

[2] At the time when the Fascists and Nazis were preparing for their seizure of power there was a great revival of interest in Carlyle in Italy and Germany. Cf. Neff, p. 269.

the Liberalism of his time and the aspirations of peoples striving for nationhood, and it was hailed by the Liberals of many countries. Palmerston's aim, however, was not primarily the promotion of nationality and liberty abroad, but the enhancement of British prestige. His policy, therefore, implied a strong element of nationalism, though it did not aim at territorial aggrandisement or military glory. It resulted in the Crimean War, it often involved Britain in grave international tensions and brought her to the brink of war with France, Prussia and America. The most outspoken opponents of this policy were Cobden and Bright.

Richard Cobden's ideas and work have been so disparaged by protectionists, nationalists and socialists that our generation seems to a great extent to interpret them as an obsolete ideology designed to serve the interests of the British capitalists of his time.[1] But though Cobden shared the prevailing opinions of the liberal school of economists that the interests of all classes were in harmony and that any interference in the natural play of supply and demand was wrong, he was not mainly actuated by sympathy for capitalism. He was primarily neither a capitalist nor a political economist, nor did he, like Burke and Marx, advocate the rule of a class ; he was in the first place an ardent internationalist, an enthusiast for peace and goodwill among nations which in his view could only be achieved by means of Free Trade.[2] Cobden considered himself in his own words more a Christian and Cosmopolitan than a Briton, though he was certainly not indifferent to his own nation.[3] His writings and correspondence contain many strictures on his own nation, and he even wrote that in foreign wars it has been " the most aggressive, quarrelsome, warlike and bloody nation under the sun ". Like every true Liberal, he had a deep distrust of the State as such. A State meant the accumulation of excessive power in the hands of a few implying the unescapable temptation to misuse this power for oppressing, misleading and corrupting individuals, squandering their lives and money, and embroiling nations in wars and continual jealousies and hatred. For this reason he laid down the rule : " As little intercourse as possible between the Governments ; as much connection as possible between the nations of the world."

[1] Marx, in a speech on Free Trade made at Brussels in 1849, said that the people considered the protagonists of Free Trade " its greatest enemies and the most impudent hypocrites ".
[2] This is conclusively shown in the excellent book by J. A. Hobson, *R. Cobden, the International Man*, 1919. Cf. also J. Morley, *Life of Cobden* (quoted 10th ed., 1903).
[3] The American habit of extravagant national self-praise, for example, aroused his " British blood " and impelled him to a spirited defence of British achievements. Morley, p. 33.

In 1859 he wrote: " I utterly despair of finding peace and harmony in the efforts of Governments and diplomatists. The people of the two nations (Britain and France) must be brought into mutual dependence by the supply of each other's wants. There is no other way of counteracting the antagonism of language and race. It is God's own method of producing an *entente cordiale*, and no other plan is worth a farthing." This was the motive which induced him to initiate and carry through the commercial treaty with France of 1860 which did, indeed, have a most beneficial effect on the relations between the two nations.

In spite of his belief in the inestimable value of peace Cobden was not a " peace at any price " man. Not only wars undertaken for self-defence seemed to him justifiable, but in rare cases even a war for the protection of another weaker nation or the liberation of an oppressed people. But he strongly opposed the popular tendency to espouse the cause of every oppressed nation and to endanger peace by hurling insults at their adversaries or to encourage national agitations and revolutions. Still more he condemned Palmerston's policy of the Balance of Power and national prestige disguised as the protection of nationalities struggling for freedom. He sometimes went so far as to express surprise that the common people should prefer a bad government by members of their own race to a better government by foreigners. " Patriotism ", he wrote, " or nationality, is an instinctive virtue, that sometimes burns the brightest in the rudest and least reasoning minds ; and its manifestation bears no proportion to the value of possessions defended, and the object to be gained."

In Cobden's view Britain ought to care first of all for making the peoples of her own Empire free and contented. He wished " to give Ireland to the Irish " by breaking up the large estates in the hands of English owners and transferring the land to small farmers.[1] Canada was to decide herself whether to remain in the Empire or to join the United States. The bombardment of Canton and the war with China aroused Cobden's greatest indignation, and he declared that the mercantile interest was responsible for it. British rule in India seemed to him unnatural, oppressive and destined to end in failure. He was afraid that it was bound to corrupt the national character just as the Romans had been corrupted and ruined by their conquest and domination of a world Empire.

Cobden's ultimate standard in politics was, indeed, a moral one. He judged every measure primarily according to whether

[1] On Cobden's attitude to Ireland, cf. Morley, p. 488 f., 552.

it was likely to arouse or to subdue the instincts of aggression, oppression and brutality in human nature. At first he believed that it was mainly the aristocracy which " has converted the combativeness of the English race to its own sinister ends " and that its members " parade their sympathies for the grievances of foreigners instead of doing the work of liberty at home ". But the Crimean War showed him that the war fever could get hold of the whole people.[1] All classes, and particularly those called middle and respectable, were in a frenzy and in a " devilish paroxysm ". In 1857 the second war with China and the Indian mutiny broke out. When Cobden carried a vote of censure in the Commons in regard to the policy of the Government towards China, Palmerston appealed to the electorate. At the polls Cobden and his friends suffered a crushing defeat. It was a plebiscite for Palmerston, who was the most popular man in the country because, as a modern writer remarked, he could impersonate the British lion. Even Manchester, the centre of the Free Trade interest, abandoned Cobden in his efforts for a policy of peace. Birmingham, the home of the rising mid-Victorian radicalism, showed itself truer to democratic principles. Cobden found that this was due to the fact that the hardware industry " was carried on by small manufacturers and artisans whilst the great capitalists of Manchester formed an aristocracy " imbued with " aristocratic snobbery " and anti-democratic prejudice (p. 194). Cobden's conviction of the desirable supremacy of the middle class, says Hobson (p. 394), " became sensibly modified in his later years, partly by disappointment with the warlike and imperialistic sentiments displayed by so many of his Free Trade adherents, partly by a growing recognition of the rightness and efficacy of the wider franchise to which his friend Bright devoted so much of his energy ". He now put more hope in the peaceable common sense of the working class than in that of the other

---

[1] Kingsley Martin has shown conclusively that the outbreak of the Crimean War was not primarily due to the Governments of Britain and Russia which made great efforts to avoid it, nor to any irreconcilable conflict of interests, but to the pressure of public opinion which was incensed against the Tsar because of his anti-democratic and oppressive policy in general. The Balance of Power, of course, played also a part, and Palmerston exploited the trend of public opinion for his personal glory and in opposition to the very pacific mood of the Prime Minister Lord Aberdeen and his colleagues. But the decisive fact was the surge of the violent indignation of the people against the Russian oppressor of liberty and of sympathy with the " gallant Turk ", whose treatment of the subject peoples was certainly no less oppressive than that of the Tsar. When the war had broken out famous writers like Tennyson and Kingsley and many Churchmen glorified war as a blessing, as the reviver of a heroic spirit, the saviour from enervation by a sordid commercialism, the remedy against " the long, long canker of peace ". Cf. Kingsley Martin, *The Triumph of Lord Palmerston*, 1924.

sections of the people. In 1861 he even wrote : " I wonder the working people are so quiet under the taunts and insults offered to them. Have they no Spartacus among them to lead a revolt of the slave class against their political tormentors ? "

In the American War of Secession Cobden, after short hesitation, took the side of the North which stood for the abolition of slavery, though the economic interest of the British cotton trade, the cause of Free Trade and the principle of self-determination, would have spoken for the South. This shows again that moral, not economic, standards were decisive in Cobden's thought. In this war he strenuously opposed the anti-American sentiment which was so prevalent in the upper and middle classes and worked for arbitration and the reform of the maritime law of nations.

Cobden's thought is the most typical specimen of consistent Liberalism. His attitude to international policy was that of non-interference or isolationism, disarmament and development of international law and arbitration. It must not be ignored, however, that a policy of isolation was more justifiable at that time than in our days. Britain's security was not yet threatened by submarines and airplanes, and by the rise of aggressive nationalist and totalitarian States. Liberalism was in the ascendant everywhere and it was possible to hope that all nations would gradually become imbued with goodwill towards one another. The spirit of Cobden and Bright not only helped to mould the policy of the Liberal Party and pave the way for the achievements of Gladstone but it influenced the other parties also, and thus contributed to the development of opinions and aspirations common to the whole nation.

Gladstone and Disraeli have both been elevated to the rank of national idols by their admirers, and this attitude of reverence has been sanctioned by great sections of the nation. Their ideas, therefore, may be taken as representative of the national mentality of their time. In spite of the great differences between their personalities and between their philosophies there was no great antagonism between the basic principles of their practical policies.[1] In Gladstone's thought the essential standards of Christianity were supreme. He believed, like Milton, in England's noble mission and often put human brotherhood and justice above con-

---

[1] Cf. the parallel between the lives of the two statesmen by D. Somervell, *Disraeli and Gladstone*, 1925. In international politics they both were most anxious to preserve peace, though they differed somewhat in their methods. Cf. Gladstone's statements of his views in J. Morley, *Life of Gladstone* (ed. 1905), p. i, p. 950, ii, p. 187, and Disraeli's views in H. E. Egerton, *British Foreign Policy in Europe*, 1918, p. 278, and in Walter Sichel, *Disraeli*, 1904, pp. 199, 209 f., 222 f.

siderations of power and prestige, particularly in his attempt to make good the old wrongs which Ireland had suffered. Disraeli was more of a Traditionalist, but nevertheless it was he who enfranchised the urban working-class and gave them substantial social rights which aimed at making one nation out of the two which he had described in one of his novels. The Romantic strain in him contributed to his conviction that imagination governed mankind, not cold reason. As a novelist he showed many Romantic traits,[1] but as a politician he was too shrewd a realist to indulge much in Romantic experiments. In some respects Gladstone too showed great power of imagination, though in a different way from Disraeli. He was always apt to be kindled by a holy passion for the cause of oppressed nationalities. Disraeli was more aware of the dangerous implications of nationality, and in 1845 he spoke scornfully of " this modern, newfangled, sentimental principle of nationality ". Since the Reformation he thought the salient point in English national psychology was the accumulation of wealth, of which industry is the instrument. Liberty and the reign of law were mainly valued by the English people as the conditions most favourable to the acquisition of wealth—a view which was certainly not romantic.

The extreme Individualism professed by most Utilitarians proved untenable both in social questions and in regard to the Empire. It was more and more modified by the rise of two new tendencies, those of Socialism and Imperialism. Their bearing on the problems of nationality has already been touched upon in other places. Imperialism, however, is a most ambiguous term. Its aggressive form is not represented among prominent English thinkers. Modern Britain has not produced any philosophy of militarism or nationalism, which can be considered as having influenced the national ideology. The Imperialism of Disraeli, Dilke, Seeley, Froude and many others was merely a striving to cement and develop the Empire. The Imperialism of Rhodes and Chamberlain did imply expansion, but its underlying ideas could only be discussed against the background of the whole policy of these statesmen, which is beyond the scope of this chapter.[2]

[1] Among them was the unfortunate tendency to stress the importance of race, especially that of the Jewish race, which has led to the belief that Disraeli was a racialist. But Wingfield-Stratford rightly says (ii, 545) that he meant by race primarily a spiritual bond.
[2] Cf., however, the survey given in my book *Nationalgeist und Politik*, 1937, vol. i, pp. 30, 240 f., and p. 176 of this book.

20. The Development of French National Ideology since the Revolution

In France, throughout the nineteenth century and after, the question was constantly discussed how far the aims implied in the idea of a nation had been realized by the Revolution and later political developments.[1] In the ideology of the Revolution a nation was a close community within natural frontiers, based on liberty, equality and fraternity, inspired by strong solidarity, and endowed with the mission of propagating those ideals in the world. A free nation, it was firmly believed, would be able to form a true general will, representing the will of all citizens and guaranteeing their happiness and morality. The course of events disillusioned many partisans of the Revolution. L. Carnot, the Jacobin patriot, in 1814 declared that in France there was no national spirit such as in England, no willingness to sacrifice one's own interest to the general interest. The defenders of the old regime went still further and rejected the revolutionary idea of a nation altogether. Count Joseph de Maistre taught that there was a " national reason " far superior to the reason of individuals, and that it consisted in " national dogmas ", in " useful prejudices ". Human reason is unable to invent good political institutions. The only effective and durable factors are the ancient rights and customs revealed by God through inspired heroes, prophets, kings and legislators and planted in the character of the people. France has misused her mission to teach Europe by demoralizing her and was punished for this crime through the Revolution which was to bring her back to her old traditions. It is a favourite idea of the author that God uses the evil for creating the good, and he even highly praises the executioner as the instrument of divine justice. The revolutionary constitutions were devised for man in general, but the abstract man does not exist. Man is always a member of a specific nation and the true constitution of a nation is determined by its traditions, which are mainly embodied in the aristocracy. The author even says : " What is a nation ? It is the ruler and the nobility."

One of the most brilliant exponents of liberal thought was

[1] Cf. for the whole following chapter, E. Faguet, *Politiques et Moralistes au 19ᵉ siècle*, 3 vols. ; Henry Michel, *L'idée de l'état essai critique sur l'histoire des théories sociales et politiques en France depuis la Révolution*, 1896 ; Roger Soltau, *French Political Thought in the Nineteenth Century*, 1931. On the traditionalists cf. Alphonse Roche, *Les idées traditionalistes en France de Rivarol à Maurras*, published by the University of Illinois, 1937 ; G. Brandes, *Main Currents in Nineteenth-Century Literature*, 1901 ; Harold Laski, *Authority in the Modern State*, 1919.

Madame de Staël.[1] Her great contribution to the problem of nationality was not in the field of theory, but in that of psychology. Many of her writings contain fine observations on national characteristics and she wished thereby to further the development of a supra-national, European spirit. Her best known work is her book on Germany which was first published in 1813. She gave in it an idealized picture of German civilization which then was in its golden age and contrasts it with the French spirit anticipating Taine's theory of the " classical spirit ". The most ardent wish of Madame de Staël was that the French and the German nations should appreciate the good points in one another's character and that French clarity, taste, order and knowledge of the world should amalgamate with German profundity, sincerity and enthusiasm.

In the hundred years after the fall of Napoleon the constitution of France went through five fundamental and violent changes, a cycle of revolutions and restorations of a monarchy, and, moreover, several times the country seemed on the brink of a revolution or a dictatorship. Between these events bitter civil strife hindered the consolidation of any regime and often led to a great instability of governments. All these revolutions were the work of small minorities. The great majority of the people, especially the peasantry which had profited most from the achievements of the great Revolution showed a very conservative mentality. When in 1871 the Third Republic was established the Monarchists possessed a majority in the National Assembly, but they were divided into Bonapartists, the adherents of the Bourbon dynasty and those who wanted a king from the Orleans family. The Republicans were also split into several parties. At subsequent elections the Republicans soon obtained the majority of the votes cast, though probably only because a large part of the electorate did not vote and women had no vote. The Republican parties first polled the majority of the electorate in 1893, and the Left first obtained a majority of seats in Parliament in 1902.

In international affairs France for a long time clung to the traditional cult of military power and glory. After the defeat of Napoleon the Allies took the greatest care to avoid in the Peace settlement anything which might hurt French national sentiment.[2] Nevertheless, and in spite of what the people had suffered under Napoleon, his name did not lose its magic power over the mind of

[1] Cf. Albert Sorel, *Mme de Staël*, 1890; Faguet and Brandes, op. cit.
[2] Cf. C. K. Webster, *The Foreign Policy of Castlereagh*, 1925.

a wide section of the people. The Napoleonic legend representing the Emperor as the true friend of the common people gained considerable popularity.[1] The Republicans continued the Jacobin traditions of the natural frontiers, of France's mission to liberate other nations from their tyrants, and of enmity against England, Russia and Austria. Their ideology showed a curious mixture of democratic praise of peace and civilization with warlike nationalism in the disguise of a national mission to exercise the overlordship of the world.[2] Thiers pointed out to Nassau Senior in 1853 the " innate French need for excitement, manifesting itself right through French history from the Italian wars to those of Louis XIV and Napoleon, content at times with the expression of conflict in ideas but usually needing ultimate expression in actual war ", adding that the superseding of parliamentary warfare by the absolutism of the Second Empire had now made a fresh war a necessity. Guizot in another conversation with Senior not only confirmed Thiers' diagnosis but declared that " while other nations hated war, France actually liked it. It is an amusement she is sometimes forced to refuse herself, but it is always with regret. She submits to peace with the reluctance with which you (the English) submit to war. Peaceful policy is called—and in one sense *is*—anti-national ".

The time of the " Bourgeois-Monarchy " and the Second Empire, however, was also marked by the rise of forces working for peace. The opposition to Napoleon III gained much ground, influential politicians severely criticized the Emperor's foreign policy and militarism, and great historians attacked the Napoleonic legend and tried to show that Napoleon I had ruined France by his aggressive policy. The greatest French scholars and writers were full of enthusiasm for German scholarship and poetry and ardently wished for close friendship between the French and the German peoples.[3] Economic development was soaring, the country entered a period of unprecedented prosperity and the industrial and commercial middle class wanted peace for making money and enjoying life. Socialism and pacifism were spreading. Proudhon, the most original thinker among French socialists, opposed the general enthusiasm for the liberation and unification of Italy, Poland and other nations, he saw in the principle of nationality nothing but a means of perpetuating and

---

[1] Cf. Albert Guérard, *Reflections on the Napoleonic Legend*, 1924, and Jules Deschamps, *Sur la légende de Napoléon*, 1931.
[2] Cf. Soltau, pp. xxv, 97, 108, 121, 126 ; H. Stewart and P. Desjardins, *French Patriotism in the Nineteenth Century (1814-1833)*, 1923, p. 254.
[3] For details compare my book *Nationalgeist und Politik*, 1937, vol. i, p. 276.

aggravating the power of militarism and the germ of endless wars. He hated the all-powerful centralized state and scorned Rousseau and Jacobinism, his ideal was Switzerland and he was one of the pioneers of syndicalism. The French nation, in his view, was made up of at least twenty distinct nations with clearly marked characteristics, and was held together only by force. He wanted France to be divided into twelve independent States and Europe to be constituted as a federation of federations. Proudhon detested war, but in his book on *War and Peace* (1861) he pointed out that war was one of the strongest factors making for the progress of civilization, and that the instinct of the masses regarding war as legitimate, was wiser than individual reason rejecting it. A nation was a collective being with the will to expand and recognizing no judicial authority above itself. He hoped, however, that a just organization of society would make the causes of war disappear and replace violence by labour. August Comte also wished for the division of the great nations into a great number of independent republics, each of about 300,000 families and only united by spiritual bonds. France was to be divided into seventeen republics; she was also to suppress her army and restore Algiers to the Arabs.

Like every national mentality that of France at that time comprised inconsistent tendencies; on the one hand the sincere wish for peace and on the other an ideal of national prestige which implied the risk of war. In 1870 it was Bismarck who brought about the war which he wanted for uniting Germany under Prussian domination. But French national vanity and excitability contributed considerably to its outbreak. It was France who declared war without making sufficient efforts to avoid it. Bismarck had cunningly dangled a red rag before the bull of French nationalism and thereby incited him to rush headlong into the trap.

The defeat of France gave rise to a strong longing for *revanche*, for the recovery of the lost territory and the restoration of the prestige of French arms. For a long time violent nationalism in alliance with all reactionary powers was a constant menace to the republican system and it was only after the Dreyfus crisis that the danger was definitely overcome.[1] The conflict with Germany over Morocco then caused a certain revival of nationalism but it seldom obtained decisive power again. The advance of the

---

[1] Cf. for a detailed treatment of these questions G. Gooch, " Franco-German Relations, 1870–1914 ", in his *Studies in Diplomacy and Statecraft*, 1942, and my book, *Nationalgeist und Politik*, 1937, pp. 272 f.

democratic spirit, of socialism and internationalism barred the road to the forces of militarism and nationalism.

The time of the Third Republic was not only marked by extraordinary cultural and economic achievements but also by a great expansion of France's colonial Empire and by the recovery of a powerful and respected position among nations. Nevertheless, the public spirit was always characterized by intense restlessness and civil discord. An English student of French politics, J. Bodley, in a penetrating analysis of modern France,[1] came to the conclusion : " It is to the French that Frenchmen display animosity more savage, more incessant, and more inequitable than to people of any other race." He traces this spirit to the time of the Revolution which proclaimed the principle of Fraternity as the highest aim. " French people then acquired the habit, never since lost, of regarding all political controversy as a desperate struggle between irreconcilable elements, in which every lethal weapon was lawful to use, and all ties of racial kinship were to be ignored." The result is, as Bodley says, that an air of pessimism hangs over the nation and that the great majority is indifferent in all matters political.

The extraordinary fierceness of internal conflicts can be traced back through many centuries of French history. For a long time the principal cause was the mentality of the aristocracy which regarded a peaceful life as beneath the dignity of a nobleman and strongly stressed that they were of better blood than the other classes. In the eighteenth century and later, spokesmen of the aristocracy still defended their privileges and claims with their alleged descent from the Frankish conquerors and thereby aroused violent protests on the part of the bourgeoisie.[2] This gave rise to a long controversy in which many famous historians and political writers discussed the question whether the French people was composed of two races or nations, that of the conquerors and that of the conquered. After the revolution of 1848 Count Gobineau and others transformed the old aristocratic thesis into a general theory of race, identifying the upper classes with the noble Aryans and the lower classes with inferior, pre-Aryan elements. This theory, however, was never widely accepted in France.

The traditions dominating the mentality of a section of the aristocracy, however, were not the only cause of the bitterness of party strife. After the great Revolution many writers saw the main cause in the effects of the revolutionary spirit, especially in the exaggeration of the principle of equality and the belief in

[1] Cf. John E. C. Bodley, *France*, revised ed., 1899.   [2] Cf. p. 61 of this book.

radical solutions by means of violence. Every further revolution or political catastrophe again induced great thinkers to investigate the fundamental national traditions. Ernest Renan in 1859 came to the conclusion that " the revolutionary philosophy, great and liberating as it was, contained a hidden poison : a belief in violence, an idea of justice based on a materialistic conception of property, a neglect of personal rights, all of which carry germs of destruction, herald the reign of mediocrity, the disappearance of initiative, all this for the sake of an apparent physical comfort, the conditions of which are really self-destructive ". After the defeat of 1871 he pondered its causes in his book *La reforme intellectuelle et morale* and came to similar conclusions. Taine soon began to publish his great work on *The Origins of Modern France* (6 vols., 1876-94), and countless other writers followed, discussing the influence of France's history, and particularly of the Revolution on her political mentality. In Taine's view the source of all the misfortunes of France was the " classical spirit " and, in particular, its specific form : the spirit of Jacobinism.[1] His arguments were much criticized, but his ideas made a deep impression. Seippel traced in all great events of French history two types, the authoritarian and the revolutionary spirit, which he regarded as varieties of the same " Roman mentality ", the spiritual heritage of the Roman Empire, grafted by the Church upon the French national spirit.[2] Both types were intolerant, dogmatic and anti-liberal.

The critics of French national traditions often contrasted them with those of England. Why was England spared the constant change between anarchy and despotism, the bitterness of party strife, the humiliation of defeat ? Why could England outstrip France in the growth of wealth, in the building of a world Empire and in international prestige ? The great historian and statesman, Guizot, made the English and American revolutions the subject of long and profound study which resulted in some of his greatest works and in the publication of a vast collection of historical sources. The English revolution, he found, widely differed from the French through its religious spirit, its respect for the past, its emphasis on the reign of law and the absence of a bitter struggle between the social classes.[3] When the republic of 1848 broke down many republicans found an asylum in England and had an opportunity of comparing English and French politics. The

[1] Cf. G. Gooch, *History and Historians in the Nineteenth Century*, 1920, pp. 238, 258 ; E. Fueter, *Geschichte der neueren Historiographie*, 1911, p. 582.
[2] Cf. Paul Seippel, *Les deux Frances et leurs origines historiques*, 1905.
[3] Cf. Gooch, p. 187 ; M. Bardoux, *Guizot*, 1894, pp. 119, 122, 135.

prominent democratic leader, Ledru-Rollin, wrote a book [1] describing England's social and political conditions in the most lurid colours. England was ruled by aristocrats and capitalists exploiting and oppressing the whole world and her system was marked by extreme inequality, while France was inspired by the ideals of equality, justice and humanity. Ledru-Rollin predicted the impending ruin of England's power and wealth. Louis Blanc, the leader of the Socialists, also published his impressions which were much more detached and friendly to England.[2] Taine in several of his works undertook to analyse English civilization and to ascertain its characteristic features.[3] He was a great admirer of England and was strongly influenced in his views on national character by Burke and Hegel. Towards the end of the century the opinion was widespread in France that England had outdistanced her in economic and political progress and that this was due to a fundamental difference in their national character. Demolins, a disciple of Le Play, discussed this question in a book which was very widely read.[4] He ascribed the superiority of the Anglo-Saxons mainly to their system of education, their home-life and political traditions, which all fostered the spirit of sturdy individualism and initiative, while the French expected everything from the State. The author also investigates the composition of the French and British Parliaments according to professions and finds that in France about two-thirds of the deputies consisted of members of the liberal professions, among whom lawyers, journalists and ex-officials were especially numerous, while in England the great majority of the M.P.s came from agriculture, industry and commerce. French political life, therefore was dominated by intellectuals, among whom representatives of the Left were conspicuous. The difference in the composition of the French and the British Parliaments was significant for the difference in spirit. Many other writers also investigated British institutions and traditions, comparing them with French ones and trying to trace national characteristics.[5]

[1] Cf. Ledru-Rollin, *De la décadence de l'Angleterre*, 2 vols., 1850.
[2] Cf. Louis Blanc, *Lettres sur l'Angleterre*, 2 vols., 1866.
[3] Cf. H. Taine, *Histoire de la littérature Anglaise*, 1863 ; *Notes sur l'Angleterre*, 1872.
[4] Cf. Edmond Demolins, *A quoi tient la superiorité des Anglo-Saxons* (Engl. tr. from the 10th French edition, 1899). Another book by a writer of the school of Le Play discussing the origin of fundamental differences in the psychology of England, France and other nations is Henri de Tourville, *Histoire de la formation particulariste, l'origine des grands peuples actuels*.
[5] Cf. Max Leclerc, *L'éducation des classes moyennes et dirigeantes en Angleterre*, 1901 ; *Les professions et la société en Angleterre*, 1901. Émile Boutmy, *Essai d'une psychologie politique du peuple Anglais au XIXe siècle*, 1903 ; Jacques Bardoux, *Essai d'une psychologie de l'Angleterre contemporaine*, 2 vols., 1906–7.

Alfred Fouillée, a distinguished scholar, devoted several books to the problem of national character and in particular to that of France.[1] He assumes a strong influence of temperament and climate on the national character, a view which has maintained its credit in France much more than in other countries. The author comes to the conclusion " that it is the France of 1789 which, in spite of her errors, faults and reverses will finally prove right ". Gustave Le Bon, on the contrary, has developed a theory of mass-psychology which is decidedly anti-democratic and he has also emphasized the importance of race.[2] His very pessimistic description of mass-mentality was obviously moulded by certain epochs of the French Revolution.

The most important representatives of modern French nationalism were Maurice Barrès and Charles Maurras. Barrès was a brilliant novelist and also took part in politics.[3] He began his career as a cosmopolitan, aestheticist and extreme individualist, and was deeply influenced by German philosophy and art. The Boulanger crisis and the rise of nationalism in Germany wakened his latent national sentiment and he tried to elaborate a doctrine of nationalism which should serve as a creed for a movement aiming at the establishment of a dictatorship. His later writings are marked by hatred of parliamentarism and democracy, dislike of Germany, foreigners, Jews and Protestants, longing for the re-incorporation of Alsace-Lorraine and a refined chauvinism in general. The motto of his nationalism was : The dead and the soil. Barrès' thought owed much to the German romanticists and was mainly of the romantic type, though he declared classicism as the true French tradition. His idol was Napoleon and he exalted France's great military traditions, but did not advocate a policy of aggression. Before the last war he had some influence on the younger generation of intellectuals. But his romantic aestheticism had no appeal to the masses and his nationalism was mainly an attempt to escape the menace of anarchy and nihilism implied in his own extreme subjectivism.

Charles Maurras developed a doctrine which he called " integral nationalism " and which became the programme of

[1] Cf. Alfred Fouilée, *Psychologie du peuple Français*, 1898 ; *L'idée moderne du droit en France, en Angleterre et en Allemagne* ; *La France au point de vue moral* ; *Psychologie des peuples Européens*.

[2] As to Le Bon, cf. p. 16 of this book.

[3] Cf. a more detailed exposition of Barrès's views in my book *Nationalgeist und Politik*, p. 295 ; M. Barres, *Scènes et doctrines du nationalisme*, 2 vols. ; Sylvia King, *M. Barrès*, 1933 ; E. Curtius, *Barrès*, 1921. For a criticism of Barrès, Maurras and other nationalists cf. D. Parodi, *Traditionalisme et démocratie*, 1909 ; Georges Guy-Grand, *La philosophie nationaliste*, 1911.

a movement, named Action Française.[1] He sees the source of all evils which disfigure the political and social life of modern France in an excessive individualism, leading to anarchy. This individualism appears in various forms such as romanticism, German philosophy, the revolutionary tradition, freemasonry, protestantism, Christianism and Judaism. The true tradition of France is classicism as embodied in the great achievements of the old monarchy, the French Church, the literature and art of the seventeenth century. The French are the spiritual successors of the old Greeks and Romans and therefore opposed to the Hebrew spirit of Christianity and to the German and English spirit of the Reformation and romanticism. Maurras particularly detests Rousseau, the father of romanticism and of the Revolution. The aim of the Action Française was a dictatorship which should prepare the return to the monarchy alone congenial to the French spirit. But this movement had no success at all. The view that Rousseau was mainly responsible for romanticism, democracy and national disintegration was also put forward by other writers.[2]

The traditions of the French Republic were not only attacked by writers of the Right, but also by such of the extreme Left. Georges Sorel in his books expressed unlimited contempt for Parliamentarism, and the belief in reason and compromise. Liberalism and democracy appeared to him as products of the timid bourgeois class and their dupes, the moderate socialists.[3] Sorel was an intellectual and had embraced the programme of revolutionary syndicalism. He demanded that the trade unions should stop the whole of economic life by proclaiming a general strike and should use the ensuing chaos for seizing power by force, and for establishing a dictatorship by means of terrorism. The proletariate would never be able to win power by peaceful methods nor merely by arguments of reason. It could only hope to realize socialism by violence and under the impulse of an intoxicating belief or vision which Sorel called a *mythos*. His thought was mainly moulded by Marx and Nietzsche, and he also adopted some ideas from Hegel, Proudhon and Bergson. The socialists refused to accept Sorel's ideas, but the extreme Right showed a keen interest in them. Towards the end of his

[1] Cf. Ch. Maurras, *Romantisme et révolution*, 1925 ; M. de Roux, *Maurras et le nationalisme de l'Action Française*, 1927.
[2] Cf. Ernest Seilliere, *Le péril mystique dans l'inspiration des démocraties contemporaines*, *Philosophie de l'imperialisme*, 3 vols. ; and other books ; Pierre Lasserre, *Le romantisme français*.
[3] Cf. Georges Sorel, *Reflexions sur la violence*, 1908 ; Pierre Lasserre, *Sorel théoricien de l'imperialisme*, 1928 ; Soltau, p. 442.

life Sorel declared his admiration for Bolshevism. His most ardent disciple, however, was Mussolini, who owes almost his whole political ideology to Sorel and to Pareto.

All the enemies of the republican system, whether right or left, denounced Parliament as the main source of instability, corruption, and disorganization. Their arguments, of course, were gross exaggerations,[1] but the problem remains why the public spirit showed so much party animosity and unwillingness to co-operate, and also so much scepticism, pessimism and indifferentism in regard to politics in general. Some observers saw the causes in alleged dispositions of the French temperament and mind, others emphasized the power of traditions or of social conflicts. An extraordinary factor was the rôle of the Church. Throughout the whole century a large part of the political struggles raged between the defenders and the enemies of the Church for which there was no parallel in contemporaneous English or German history.[2] Rousseau had planned to supersede Catholicism by a new civic religion which was to secure national unity and harmony and Robespierre had tried to carry out this plan. The intransigence of political struggles was partly due to the fact that they were conflicts between two creeds, that of Catholicism and that of Jacobinism. Some thinkers, however, came to the conclusion that the old religion had been destroyed in the hearts of the people without giving them a real new belief and that the absence of any religious spirit was the deepest cause of the prevailing moral nihilism and political chaos. Comte proclaimed that history consisted in the replacement of religious and metaphysical thought by science, but he ended as the prophet of a new religion. Maurras, though no believer in Christianity, which he disliked as a "Jewish invention", wanted to re-establish the power of the Catholic Church which he considered indispensable for national unity, discipline and greatness. The preponderance of lawyers, journalists and other intellectuals in Parliament certainly also furthered the tendencies of exacerbation and ambitious intrigues. Many intellectuals were for various reasons indifferent or hostile to democracy. The Académie Française, that august assemblage of the most distinguished scholars and writers, was for a long time the bulwark of a refined nationalism and militarism and many of its members longed for the dictatorship of a general. In the course of time, however, the number of prominent intellectuals who espoused the cause

---

[1] Cf. J. Bryce, *Modern Democracies*, 1921, vol. i, on French democracy.
[2] Except the *Kulturkampf* under Bismarck which, however, lasted only a short time.

of democratic and social progress and of internationalism increased. In the field of thought Charles Renouvier was perhaps the most remarkable figure [1] and in the field of action the greatest representative of the new spirit was the mighty personality of Jean Jaurès. After the last war the rise of Bolshevism and Fascism in the world deteriorated the political atmosphere again. The tragic downfall of France in our days was largely due to certain traditions of her political life.

After the last war André Siegfried gave an interesting description of French mentality.[2] He emphasizes that France is still mainly a country of small peasant proprietors and artisans, though in recent time large-scale industries have considerably increased. The national character is to a large extent moulded by the mentality of the peasants and small tradesmen and is very different from the picture formed by most foreigners of the French character from their impressions of life in Paris. The great majority is not frivolous, fickle and revolutionary, but imbued with a strong sense of family and property, the bourgeois longing for social distinction " for the sake of the children ", political scepticism and individualism, and complete indifference to foreign affairs, foreign markets and the colonies. The French people, as Seignobos says, has a horror of war but not the slightest knowledge how to avoid it. Professor A. Siegfried further says that principles and ideals are heart and soul of French politics, especially as subjects of eloquence, but the voters cast their votes for one of the numerous parties because they like or dislike a certain mode of life and principally because they loathe any distinction in dress, occupation and ideas. Political radicalism is often combined with social conservativism. The Frenchman wears his heart on the left side, and his purse on the right, and practically every Frenchman has a purse.

21. Mazzini

Many thinkers have prepared the soil for the unification of Italy, among them Rosmini and Gioberti, both Catholic theologians who worked for an Italian Confederation with the Pope as Honorary President. Gioberti's work on *The Moral and Civil Primacy of the Italians* (1843) proclaimed the mission of the Italian

---

[1] Cf. on Renouvier's vigorous criticism of nationalism, Soltau, op. cit., pp. 306, 316-19.
[2] André Siegfried, *France, a Study in Nationality*, 1930. Another very instructive study is Carlton Hayes, *France, a Nation of Patriots*, 1930, which describes mainly the methods by which French patriotism is formed and stimulated.

nation to be the spiritual leader of the world towards unity and harmony, and visualized a League of Nations under the presidency of the Pope.

Giuseppe Mazzini (1805–72) was one of the most fascinating figures of the *Risorgimento*.[1] His whole life was devoted to the liberation and unification of Italy which, he hoped, would lead to the liberation of all oppressed peoples and to the unification of mankind in the form of an association of free nations under Italian leadership. For this purpose he was constantly engaged in planning and organizing secret societies, conspiracies, and revolutions, not only in Italy but also in other countries, and in 1849 he was the soul of the Roman Republic. The greater part of his life, however, he had to live as an exile, mainly in England, and even after the liberation of Italy was achieved he formally remained an exile and could only visit Italy disguised as an Englishman.

Nationality was to Mazzini a religion. It was the fundamental thought of his doctrine that no real community and no important progress was possible without a strong religious belief. Neither the doctrine of the rights of the individual, proclaimed by the French Revolution, nor the principle of the greatest happiness, taught by Bentham, nor the materialism of the socialists could form the philosophical basis of a well-ordered society in which men could develop all their faculties. If the liberty and happiness of the individual were the supreme aims, how could it be demanded that the individuals should subordinate their interests to those of the community and should sacrifice themselves to its welfare? The duties of men to society were prior to their rights, and the idea of duty implied a supra-natural, religious sanction. Men existed not for being happy or doing what they liked but for fulfilling a mission in the service of humanity. Liberty was the faculty of choosing among the various modes of fulfilling duty those most in harmony with our own tendencies.

Mazzini's religion, however, was not that of the Churches which in his view had outlived themselves. He hated papacy and regarded it as doomed, and he criticized Christianity for being too individualistic and lacking in patriotism, and in political and social interest in general. The French Revolution with its Rights of Man was an off-shoot of Christianity, and it had soon led to materialism. Both individualism and materialism

[1] Cf. his autobiography in *Life and Writings of Joseph Mazzini* (in English), 6 vols., 1864–70; *Mazzini's Letters to an English Family*, ed. by E. F. Richards, 3 vols., 1920–2; Bolton King, *Mazzini*, 1902; Gwylim Griffith, *Mazzini, Prophet of Modern Europe*, 1932.

were incompatible with democracy. They led either to anarchy or to despotism. Mazzini constantly struggled with the task of working out a new religion, in which humanity and nationality were to be in full harmony. The progress of humanity appeared to him as the highest aim, and nationality was the God-ordained instrument for this purpose, and, therefore, sacred. His striving for a new religion did not, however, lead to definite and clear views, but resulted in a wavering attitude between Christianity and pantheism. The progress of humanity was the self-manifestation of the Divine in various nationalities, each with a separate mission.

There is an obvious affinity between Mazzini's philosophy and German metaphysics, especially the systems of Fichte and Hegel.[1] Mazzini, indeed, made efforts to study some of their works and also imbibed Hegelianism through Cousin. His mystical enthusiasm for humanity was kindled by Herder and Vico. German and French romanticism too had great influence in moulding his thought. Like all idealists Mazzini preferred abstract reasoning to empirical study of concrete historical and social facts, and like all Romanticists he was apt to set intuition and imagination above cold reason, and believed that genius and the common sense of the people were able to discover truth without much study. He himself was widely read and a very acute political thinker.

The idea of a nation which Mazzini had in mind was that of a close community of equals co-operating among themselves and with other nations for the moral and spiritual elevation of mankind A nation was constituted by the will of the people to form a nation, and by a specific moral mission. The nation, therefore, was not an arbitrary product of the State, it was rooted in geographical and historical conditions, and in the traditions formed by them. The first necessity for a nation was unity, both in the political sense of uniting all people of the same language and traditions in one State, and in the moral sense of transforming them into an homogeneous whole by the unity of principles. Unity seemed to Mazzini the most important aim, and he vigorously combated the plans of uniting Italy in the form of a federation. A federated Italy, he thought, would always be weak, be subject to pressure by strong neighbours and unable to perform her mission. The nation, furthermore, had to be independent of foreign rule and influence, and free in its internal constitution which could only be democratic.

[1] Cf. Otto Vossler, *Mazzini's politisches Denken und Wollen*, 1927.

Mazzini drew a sharp line between nationality and nationalism. Nationality meant equality, peace and brotherly co-operation between all nations. Every free nation had the duty to help oppressed nations to win their liberty. He bitterly criticized England's policy of isolation and non-interference as materialistic, egotistic, short-sighted and tending to degrade her to a third-class power. The rivalries and wars between nations were merely due to the ambitions of kings and aristocracies. Once all nations were free, they would live in perfect peace, form great regional federations and a League of Nations. The striving for national power and domination at the expense of other nations was hateful to Mazzini. He called this perversion of nationality a narrow, wretched nationalism. This " savage, hostile, quarrelsome nationality " which the kings and their helpers had created was now a matter of the past. The peoples had been infected by it too, but " the nationalism of the peoples was rapidly dying out ". In another place Mazzini says : " The nationality of the peoples has never existed as yet—it is a thing of the future. We find no nationality in the past, save that defined by kings . . ."

In all his writings Mazzini showed a jealousy of France which appeared to him as opposition to her materialism, lust of power and domination and national vanity. This attempt at a justification was certainly quite sincere and to some extent correct. Nevertheless, its background was surely also envy of the great historical position of France and the wish to secure at least spiritual hegemony for Italy. Mazzini believed that it was Italy's function to give moral unity to Europe and the whole of mankind. The parliament of Nations would have its seat in Rome, the eternal, majestic city. After the first Rome of the Caesars and the second Rome of the Popes, he envisaged a third Rome, that of the Italian People which would also be the " soul of the world ", " God's word in the midst of the Nations ", the centre of a new religion of humanity.

When Mazzini founded his secret society " Young Italy " he defined the aim of the rising which he wished to bring about in the words : " What is it we want ? We demand to exist. We demand a name. We desire to make our country powerful and respected, free and happy." Unity he demanded because it implied superior force and he declared that the power of the nation was unlimited. The State was to be powerful and Mazzini rejected the liberal idea of denying power to the State by the establishment of an internal balance of power, by checks and counterpoises which should prevent the concentration of power in one hand.

True, Mazzini's wish for a strong State did not aim at conquest or domination. He only wanted to secure the national independence and the use of the power of the State for improving the lot of the great masses of the people. He had a passionate sympathy for all the oppressed, especially for the disinherited of society, he realized the necessity of great social reforms and foresaw the rise of Labour to political power. To some extent he also advocated socialism, though he did not wish for absolute communism. But he strongly opposed the materialistic outlook of Marxism and other socialist creeds, and the idea of class war. The French Revolution too had appealed to men's selfish and personal interests, and had promised them rights and happiness which led to its failure. The Italian Revolution was to aim at much higher ideals.

Mazzini did not sacrifice individual morality to a higher collective morality as Hegel did. Both private and public life were to be ruled by the same moral law, which not even the will of the people could overrule. The will of the people was sacred only as far as it was in accordance with the fundamental liberties of man. Mazzini was aware of the danger of a misguided will of the people. He pointed to the warning example of the Second French Republic where the artisans had sold their political rights to Louis Napoleon for the promise of social advantages, for a few drops of socialism. The greatest task of the State, therefore, was education. Democracy did not consist in free institutions alone but in the spirit of the people which could only be created by a great educational policy. This required far-reaching social reforms and the abolition of all political and social privilege.

Like most romanticists, Mazzini set all his hopes on the youth and the people. The League " Young Italy " which he founded for his propaganda excluded from membership all who were over forty years.

> Place the young [he wrote] at the head of the insurgent masses; you do not know what strength is latent in those young bands, what magic influence the voices of the young have on the crowd; you will find them a host of apostles for the new religion. But youth lives on movement, grows great in enthusiasm and faith. Consecrate them with a lofty mission; inflame them with emulation and praise; spread through their ranks the word of fire, the word of inspiration; speak to them of country, of glory, of power, of great memories.

The people too, Mazzini believed, often had a great collective intuition which grasped truth better than the reason of the individual. Trust in the people and in the youth implied trust in emotions, passions, enthusiasm, radicalism, activism, heroism. Cautious diplomacy, sober calculation of all circumstances were the way of the old and few. The masses could not be roused by carefully balanced arguments. Action must be roused by action, energy by energy. Avoid compromises, Mazzini taught, they are almost always immoral.

The first necessity for the realization of Mazzini's plans was national independence, and this made a war with Austria unavoidable. Mazzini yearned for this war and he hoped it would be the signal for risings in all countries where the peoples were oppressed by monarchs and aristocracies. He was always impatient to excite the peoples to rise, and wanted to plunge Italy in a war with Austria without carefully calculating the military forces on both sides or securing the aid of powerful allies. The Italian people was to achieve its liberation by its own strength without the help of a foreign power or an Italian king. As the means for achieving this aim he proposed a guerrilla war, if necessary with " daggers against cannons ". In its course the people would be able to seize stores of arms, the soldiers in the Austrian army who were largely Slavs, Hungarians, and Italians would desert, and soon the oppressed peoples would rise everywhere and shatter the Empire. War was not only the indispensable instrument of liberation but also the means for moral regeneration. It would give Italy again her national self-respect and her claim to the esteem of other peoples. Mazzini scorned the pacifism of the Cobdenites. The methods advocated by Mazzini for the war of liberation aroused much criticism, even among his friends. According to his instructions, which are printed in his *Collected Works*, the guerrilla bands were to fight without a uniform or any distinctive mark, visible at a distance, at least in the first period of war. Moreover, the war was to be opened by a sudden assault on unsuspecting officers and men of the enemy who were to be killed, following the example of the Sicilian Vespers of 1282. Orsini prints in his memoirs Mazzini's instructions of 1854 for suddenly murdering all leading Austrian officers in Lombardy as the prelude for a revolution.[1] This failed, but a number of soldiers were stabbed by civilians, and this provoked reprisals. In 1856 the great national hero, Daniele Manin, publicly condemned

---

[1] Cf. Felice Orsini, *Memoirs and Adventures* (Engl. tr.), 1857, p. 131. On Mazzini's attitude to political assassination in general cf. his Writings, vol. i, p. 221 ; vol. vi, p. 266, and Bolton King, *History of Italian Unity*, and *Mazzini*, p. 164. It is inter-

the " theory of the dagger " which he called " the great enemy of Italy ". Mazzini protested against this criticism and tried to show that he disapproved of political murder, unless in quite exceptional cases, and that the attacks against Austrian soldiers constituted a legitimate though irregular warfare. He was personally a most tender-hearted man, and had to give up the study of medicine because he fainted in the dissecting-room. In later years he confessed that he abhorred bloodshed and every species of terrorism, erected into a system such as the ideas of vengeance and expiation in a penal code. But he failed to realize the difference between the killing of a cruel lawless tyrant which has even been approved or tolerated by great ecclesiastical writers of the past, and attacks on individuals who were only the exponents of a political system. It must be emphasized, however, that Mazzini wanted to restrict such acts to the bare minimum, and that he rejected murder merely for vengeance, though he admitted in his memoirs that local groups of his followers might have exceeded his instructions. The Italian Risorgimento was not much blemished by acts of violence. The ideas, however, that the cause of national liberation justified every means, and that it was the mission of the youth to arouse the masses by heroic actions, assumed great power later on in many national movements and had an immense influence on the fate of humanity. In 1914 a Serb, aged nineteen, shot the heir to the throne of Austria-Hungary and his wife—after many other assassinations or attempts committed mainly by students—thereby causing the outbreak of the Great War which cost the lives of ten or eleven million soldiers,[1] not to speak of all the other sufferings, and indirectly the outbreak of the present war which sprung out of the first.

The frequent neglect of reality had the consequence that Mazzini held many views on concrete political questions which seem to be in glaring contradiction with his ideals. As mentioned already, he thought that each nation had its special task and mission. This idea probably came from Herder, Fichte and Hegel. But these thinkers did not teach that a nation without a mission had no right to exist, though Hegel at least thought that the nation, which in a certain epoch expressed the Divine Will,

esting to compare Mazzini's Milan plot with Fichte's attitude in a similar situation. When Fichte, whose thought and work showed so many parallels to those of Mazzini in 1813 discovered that German patriots planned to fall upon the French garrison in Berlin and to massacre it, he immediately informed the police and foiled the plan, taking care that the conspirators had not to suffer for it.

[1] Cf. S. Dumas and K. Vedel-Petersen, *Losses of Life caused by War* (publ. by the Carnegie Endowment), 1923, p. 380.

could claim leadership. Mazzini's ideas about the specific missions of nations were rather vague. England's mission was " industry and colonies ", Russia's " the colonization of Asia ", Poland's " the Slav initiative ". The specific function of Germany was " thought ", that of France " action ", and that of Italy " thought in unison with action ". Mazzini, furthermore, had a preference for the formation of large nations which he regarded as more perfect than smaller ones. He denied to the Irish people the right to form a separate nation because it had in his view no specific moral idea to represent, no historic mission.[1] It is obvious that this principle opens the road to the most arbitrary decisions on the right to nationhood, and that it could be used for justifying almost every denial of self-determination.

Mazzini thought that most small nations of Europe would either be merged in, or federated with, other nations, and that Europe would be composed of a small number of large federations. Italy and Germany, then divided in numerous small States, were each to form a nation. The Slavs too appeared to him as a unit though he later on assumed that there were four main branches of the Slavonic family, the Poles, the Russians, the Czechs, and the southern Slavs, which were destined to become nations, and then to join a vast Slav confederation. Numerous Slav peoples like the Ukrainians, Croats, Serbs, Slovenians, Bulgarians, Slovaks, therefore, were to sacrifice their separate nationality to a larger one. The Hungarians and the Roumanians were expected to join the southern Slavs. The Baltic peoples such as the Finns, Latvians, Esthonians, were not mentioned. But the Lithuanians formed part of Poland. The three Scandinavian peoples would unite in a common Scandinavian nation. Belgium had no future as a nation though Mazzini says nothing of what should become of her. Probably she was to be divided between Holland and France. Spaniards and Portuguese would become one nation. The Catalans and Basques were ignored. The Greeks should unite with them all the Greek-speaking peoples of the Ottoman Empire, conquer Constantinople, and then form a federation with the southern Slavs. Switzerland would be the nucleus of an Alpine federation, comprising also German Tyrol and French Savoy. This Alpine federation was to form a barrier against the adjoining Great Powers, which is hardly compatible with the idea that these too would become free and peaceable

[1] Cf. B. King, *Mazzini*, p. 107. Nicholas Mansergh, *Ireland in the Age of Reform and Revolution*, 1940, pp. 46, 55, shows that the protagonists of Italian nationality usually opposed the Irish claim for nationhood, mainly because of their anti-papal and pro-English feelings. Cavour, too, called the Irish aspirations an illusion.

nations through the rise of democracy. In general, Mazzini believed that the small nationalities would be a barrier to the aggressiveness of big States. This idea has been tested in the Peace Treaties of 1919, but it was not a success. The Austrian and Ottoman Empires were to be destroyed. In the American Civil War Mazzini espoused the cause of the North, though it was opposed to the principle of self-determination. In strange inconsistency, however, he also thought that America was wide enough for two or three confederations. That the peoples of Asia or Africa could also claim nationhood seems never to have entered his mind. His view obviously was that Asia was to be colonized by the Europeans, mainly by the English and the Russians.

When Italian unity was realized by Cavour's statecraft Mazzini refused to recognize the new state of things. In his view it was " the phantom, the mockery of Italy ". He even opposed the union of Rome with the Kingdom of Italy because he refused to sacrifice his ideal of a Republican Rome and her world mission to national unity with a king. In the Franco-German War of 1870 Mazzini took the side of Prussia. For several years already he had intrigued with Bismarck, whom he greatly admired, against the King of Italy, whom he suspected of Pro-French inclinations, and he was ready if Bismarck would send him arms and money to arouse a revolution against the King and to start a civil war. The new Italy, he complained, had found her inspiration not in Dante but in Machiavelli. He scorned a policy centred on economic prosperity to which in his view the ideal world-mission of Italy had been sacrificed. " It is my lot, he wrote, to consume my last days in the grief, supreme to one who really loves, to see the thing, one loves most, inferior to its mission."

22. GERMAN NATIONALISM IN THE NINETEENTH CENTURY

Napoleon's domination and the war of liberation against him led to a movement for establishing a united and strong Germany. This plan, however, was faced with great difficulties. The Germans lived in numerous States and not merely the interests of the dynasties, but also the territorial loyalties of their peoples resisted a close unification. Moreover, the old conflict between the Great Powers of Austria and Prussia barred the road to unity as neither of these two powers was willing to subordinate itself to the other, or to a third power. Lastly, national sentiment to a great extent harked back to the traditions of the Holy Roman Empire and therefore envisaged the new union more as a loose federation of different German and non-German nations than as a real German national State. The old Empire could maintain its supra-national character, its dynastic connexion with almost all other European States, merely through its particularist structure. Even the Prussian statesmen who were the heralds of the national revival did not yet think of constituting Germany as a strictly national State, absolutely independent of other powers. Gneisenau, for example, in 1812 wanted to interest England in the fight against Napoleon by the prospect of large territorial acquisitions in northern Germany, which should then become an integral part of the British Empire and would certainly feel happy under a free constitution. After Napoleon's fall Stein wanted to constitute the German federation under a directorate composed of Austria, Prussia, Bavaria and Hanover. The King of Great Britain in his capacity of King of Hanover would, therefore, have exercised the same influence on German affairs as Prussia or Austria. When the German Confederation was founded at the Congress of Vienna, three foreign rulers signed the pact, and became members for their German territories, namely, the Kings of Great Britain, Denmark and the Netherlands. The pact, moreover, was incorporated in the Act of the Congress of Vienna and thereby placed under the guarantee of all the Great Powers, though this interpretation was later disputed.[1] The Great Powers, therefore, could possibly claim a right of intervention in German affairs. The great jurist Thibaud proposed the elaboration of a common Civil Law for all German States which was a step towards unity, but he also suggested that all the Allied Powers, including England and Russia, should guarantee this codification. In his book on this subject he praised German particularism as a blessing, and said that a full political unity would probably degrade Germany to a state of intellectual inferiority.

The tradition of the old Empire also induced many writers to put forward the suggestion for the incorporation of many countries which had once belonged to the Empire, such as Holland, Belgium, Switzerland, Alsace, and even Burgundy. Some, moreover, went beyond the claim to territories formerly connected with the Empire, and proposed a union of Germany with other

[1] When in 1832 the Assembly of the German Confederation, under the influence of Austria and Prussia, voted severe measures against the movement for political liberty, Palmerston formally protested, referring to that guarantee, and French diplomats spoke in a menacing way. Metternich, however, rejected England's protest. Cf. Alfred Stern, *Geschichte Europas von 1830 bis 1848*, 1921, vol. i, p. 320.

Germanic nations, or the expansion of Germany in the east, and the foundation of German colonies. Germs of the aspirations of later political nationalism, an ardent longing for power and domination were, therefore, not absent in the first half of the nineteenth century.[1] In times of strained relations they manifested themselves in oratorical outbursts, patriotic poetry, or speculations about the great past and future of the nation. But this sentiment was not yet a factor in practical politics. The governments and the bulk of the Conservatives were opposed to an aggressive policy, which seemed to them to imply the danger of strengthening the revolutionary forces, and to threaten the solidarity of the great reactionary powers which was the backbone of the Holy Alliance. Some propagandists for a revolution, indeed, hoped for a war between the reactionary powers, which might lead to their mutual destruction, but these writers had no party behind them. The Liberals naturally detested an aggressive policy because they feared militarism more than anything else.

National sentiment, after the fall of Napoleon, was primarily directed to the winning of political liberty and national unity. Its followers bitterly resented the fact that other nations looked down upon the Germans because of their lack of liberty and unity.[2] The longing for political freedom resulted in revolutionary fermentation and outbursts,[3] and many German radicals hoped that the French would help them to found a German republic by armed force. Many also preferred liberty to unity. Soon after the liberation of Germany from Napoleon's yoke the Napoleonic legend and the cult of the Emperor widely spread again among the German middle class.[4] Many Liberals, how-

[1] Cf. many examples in Charles Andler, *Pan Germanism*, 1915, and *Collection des documents sur le pangermanisme*, 4 vols., 1915-17.

[2] Whether or how far this was really the case need not be discussed here. The resentment in any case was an ideological factor. A fervent patriot, the publisher, Friedrich Perthes, in the 'twenties comments on this sentiment in his correspondence. He tries to refute in detail the widespread view that Germany was in a humiliating position, and mentions that not only among the youth but also among men of knowledge and experience many seem to abandon the national cause in despair, and to console themselves with wine and poetry, science and family life. " The root of the sentiment ", he says, " seems to me the mania for a false national glory which feels dissatisfied as long as Germany does not play a great rôle in Europe, and possibly dominates Europe. These very men, however, would shrink back with horror if they had to face the implications of a political domination over Europe." Cf. C. Th. Perthes, *Friedrich Perthes Leben*, 1857, vol. iii, pp. 273-5.

[3] The German revolutionists were defeated, and mostly fled to Switzerland, where in 1834 they founded with Italian and Polish revolutionaries the society " Young Europe " for the establishment of national republics in their countries, and in the whole of Europe. Nationality was declared sacred, all peoples were to live in freedom. equality and fraternity. Cf. E. und B. Bauer, *Geschichte der constitutionellen und revolutionären Bewegungen im südlichen Deutschland in den Jahren 1831-4*, 1845, vol. iii, p. 358,

[4] Cf. Perthes, p. 281. This sentiment was connected with hatred of England for her rôle in defeating Napoleon. A typical case was Heine's attitude.

ever, realized that the French would not come as unselfish liberators but mainly for reconquering the Rhineland.

The German Revolution of 1848 was an attempt to achieve national unity, liberty and power by peaceful means and in a fraternal spirit towards other nations.[1] Among its leaders were a large number of great historians, eminent lawyers, administrators, and other distinguished men. Nevertheless, the Revolution failed, for various reasons. In spite of the serious wish for good international relations and a reign of justice it everywhere immediately aroused the passions of nationalism. The experience of the French Revolution, which had also started with the promise of fraternity between all nations, repeated itself. The irrational and uncontrollable forces of nationalism arose not only among the Germans but also in the national minorities of Germany and in the neighbouring States, and led to serious frictions which threatened to involve Europe in war.[2] The Revolution, furthermore, awakened forces of political and social radicalism which split the ranks of the friends of liberty. It was finally put down by the armed forces of reaction, especially by the Prussian Army.

The consequences of this catastrophe were almost as fatal as the ruin of the aspirations of the French Revolution through anarchy, aggressiveness and military despotism. In the ten years after the German Revolution more than a million Germans emigrated to America. Many of the best Democrats and Liberals left Germany in despair, and later played a prominent part in the life of the United States.[3] Many others withdrew from politics altogether, while still others began to turn to the right and to set their hope for national unification on the victorious power of Prussian militarism. Bismarck became the heir of this Revolution, as Napoleon had been the heir of the French Revolution.

The hope to achieve national unity by peaceful and humane means had broken down, and the only road now seemed to be war. The idea that Germany could not be unified without resort

---

[1] Cf. the master-work by Veit Valentin, *Geschichte der deutschen Revolution 1848–9*, 2 vols., 1930.

[2] These conflicts mainly arose through the transformation of the old dynastic States into national States. Typical for many frictions was the German-Danish conflict. Under the old regime the duchies Schleswig-Holstein which were predominantly German in language but possessed a considerable Danish minority were under the King of Denmark, who as their Duke was a member of the German Confederation. The rising nationalism in Denmark and Germany, however, wanted to join them firmly with one State only, and this led to two wars which almost resulted in a European conflagration.

[3] Cf. Valentin, vol. ii, p. 552.

to war had already before found followers, but henceforth it spread considerably even in circles not imbued with the spirit of militarism. First of all the question whether Austria or Prussia was to have the hegemony in Germany could hardly be settled without a war. Secondly, a war with one of the other Great Powers seemed to many Germans necessary for breaking the resistance of German particularism. History showed, indeed, that all nations had overcome particularism and had been welded together through great wars. In Germany there was still great antagonism between many of her peoples,[1] and none of them was willing to obtain national unity at the price of submitting to Prussian domination. Other reasons too seemed to make a war unavoidable if national unity was to be achieved, namely, the rivalry between the great foreign powers in which fundamental political principles were involved. Many liberals believed that Germany could be united by a war against Russia, which at that time was the protector of reaction everywhere. Russia certainly could not tolerate the establishment of democracy in Germany, which would have encouraged her own revolutionary forces. During the German Revolution the Prussian Foreign Minister, von Arnim, approached the revolutionary government of France with a plan for a common war against Russia, the liberation of Poland, and the unification of Germany under Prussian hegemony.[2] France, however, did not accept this suggestion. In the Crimean War the Liberals and the Prussian Ambassador, von Bunsen, worked for the same idea, but could not prevail against Bismarck. The Conservatives, of course, abhorred a war with Russia and rather favoured one with France, who was odious to them for her Liberal tendencies. Bismarck later chose this way for uniting the German peoples under Prussian leadership and founding the Empire.

The policy of Bismarck and its effects on German nationalism are too well known to need to be narrated here.[3] Bismarck's success immensely stimulated the rise of an aggressive nationalism. He himself was not in agreement with its wild ambitions, and often disapproved of plans for incorporating the German parts of Austria or the Baltic provinces of Russia. The annexation of territories with a French population in 1871 caused him great misgivings, and he yielded only to the pressure of the General Staff. He also rejected any policy which might bring Germany

[1] Cf. P. A. Pfizer, *Briefwechsel zweier Deutschen*, 1832, p. 323.
[2] Cf. Valentin, vol. i, pp. 538–44.
[3] The history and psychology of German nationalism under Bismarck and William II have been described by me in the book *Nationalgeist und Politik*, 1937, vol. i.

into conflict either with Russia or with England. After his fall German nationalism became ever more extreme under the leadership of the Pan-German League. Its ideology was developed by Treitschke and a host of other German professors and writers, and assumed a particularly intransigent character through the spread of racialism.

23. Heinrich von Treitschke

German nationalism has to a larger degree been created by aspirations of the intelligentsia than that of many other nations and this explains the great rôle of philosophers and historians in its development. These aspirations, however, were widely divergent. Many Liberals put liberty above unity, and regarded every plan of setting up a strong central power for the whole of Germany with suspicion and aversion. In 1848 one of their leaders in Saxony declared they preferred to be free Saxons rather than German slaves. Others believed that first of all unity and strength were necessary and that freedom would follow.

A number of prominent historians proclaimed the mission of Prussia to create a strong united Germany which would also enjoy political freedom.[1] The most conspicuous figure among them was Heinrich von Treitschke (1834-96).[2] He was born in Saxony and his father was an officer in the Saxon Army, who later became a general. His ancestors were Czech Protestants who had emigrated to Saxony after the victory of the Counter-Reformation in Bohemia, and his dark hair and complexion, and other traits, appeared to his friend Hausrath as " unmistakably Slav ". Treitschke himself, though very prejudiced against Slavs, was proud of his forbears and praised the Czechs for having fought the Habsburgs, whom he hated. To his great grief the military career was closed to Treitschke because of his deafness, which he contracted in his youth, and he therefore became a professor and taught history and political science in several universities, and finally in Berlin. In this capacity he had an immense influence

[1] On this school cf. G. Gooch, *History and Historians in the Nineteenth Century*, 3rd ed., 1920, p. 130 ; E. Fueter, *Geschichte der neueren Historiographie*, 1911, pp. 492, 535 ; A. Guilland, *L'Allemagne nouvelle et ses Historiens*, 1899. Many illuminating observations on the German historians were made by Lord Acton. They have been collected in Ulrich Noack, *Geschichtswissenschaft und Wahrheit*, 1935.

[2] Cf. on Treitschke the most instructive chapter in G. Gooch, op. cit., p. 147. The appreciation of Treitschke by Adolf Hausrath is printed in an English version in *Treitschke, His Life and Works*, 1914. Cf. also Th. Schiemann, *Treitschke's Lehr- und Wanderjahre*, 1898. His letters have been edited by Cornicelius, 3 vols., 1913-20. A very useful analysis of Treitschke's thought is given in Ernst Leipprand, *Treitschke im deutschen Geistesleben des 19. Jahrhunderts*, 1935. A survey of English books on Treitschke is in Ernst Leipprand, *Treitschke im englischen Urteil*, 1921.

on the academic youth and the intellectual classes in general. Treitschke was one of the most powerful political writers and speakers in German history. His oratorical gift, in particular, was fascinating and his audiences were completely under his spell. His influence as a writer was hardly less strong. The triumphs which Bismarck won in politics were paralleled and supplemented by those of Treitschke, and their combined effort succeeded in laying the foundation of modern German nationalism.

At first, however, the two men did not see eye to eye in their political plans. Treitschke was a Liberal, though a very conservative one, and for some time he opposed Bismarck's anti-Liberal policy. Later on, he was won over to Bismarck's ideas, and became his most ardent follower. The cause of this conversion was that Treitschke was dominated by the passionate desire for a strong united Germany under Prussian leadership, and was ready to subordinate everything else to its realization.

In 1861 Treitschke wrote a brilliant essay on liberty, in which he said that everything new which this nineteenth century had created was the product of liberalism. His idea of liberty, however, was not that of the French Revolution, which had identified it with equality and had ended in a ghastly despotism. It was the English concept of liberty, based on historical continuity, the leadership of a liberal aristocracy, and municipal self-government, which appeared to him as the ideal. Two years later Treitschke became professor of Political Science at the University of Freiburg. In the whole of southern Germany, and beyond, public opinion was dominated by loyalty to one's small fatherland, under its traditional ruler. The Catholic Church, which had a very strong hold on the people, was naturally opposed to any hegemony of the Protestant power of Prussia in Germany, and stood for a close entente of the small German states with Austria. Besides, liberal and democratic opinions were widespread in southern Germany, and were often connected with strong sympathies for France. All these factors combined to create an atmosphere thoroughly hostile to Prussia, to her traditions and to the idea of her national mission in Germany. This experience filled Treitschke with the deepest indignation. In a letter to Gustav Freytag he wrote that amid this abominable south German particularism it had become perfectly evident to him that the unity of Germany could only be achieved by conquest, and that for this reason Bismarck's policy of extending the power of Prussia was right. Even if Prussia had the very best government, composed of men of the type of Stein and Humboldt, the hatred and jealousy of the south Germans against Prussia would not diminish. To a man, they considered themselves the real Germans, and the north a country half of which was still steeped in barbarity. " Believe me, only the trusty sword of the conqueror can weld together these countries with the North."

In 1864 Treitschke wrote his famous essay on " Federal State and Unitary State ". It was a powerful plea for the unification of Germany under Prussia, and it had a tremendous influence on public opinion. Impressibly he combated all the arguments for the historical decentralization of Germany. His wish was that Prussia should wipe out all the different dynasties and small states, and unite the whole of Germany under her own dynasty. The Germanic Confederation, created by the Congress of Vienna, was not a true union. It was merely a dynastic alliance against the liberty of the people, and it was unable to give Germany a strong and respected position. The idea that it could be transformed into a real unity, and the slogan of organic evolution, put forward by the romanticists, were misleading. A State could be in need of revolutionary energy. Treitschke, further, laid special stress on refuting the argument that German particularism was beneficial to liberty, wealth and culture, and tried to show that only national unification could guarantee their progress. Treitschke's chief grievance, however, was that the German nation had no power and was not respected by other nations. Germany could not rival the great maritime and colonial nations ; but she could at least attain to a respected, though not dominating, position in Europe. For this purpose it was first of all necessary to exclude Austria from Germany. Austria was predominantly a non-German Power ; she had for centuries become ever more estranged from the German nation, and had developed her separate loyalty and traditions. Prussia alone was destined to create German unity. For centuries every great political achievement had been her work, and she herself was the greatest achievement of the German people.

Treitschke, furthermore, investigated in this essay the question whether German unity could not be achieved in the form of a federation, and came to a negative answer. It was a widespread belief that liberty and strength could only be combined in a federation of small states. In the National Assembly of 1848 the extreme Left wanted even to divide the larger German states into small republics, and a school of political thought, brilliantly represented by the liberal historian Gervinus, hoped that all the Great Powers of Europe would be converted into federations.

A small community, however, was unable to fulfil the manifold tasks incumbent on a modern State and must be powerless. The theorists who ignored the historical differences between States forgot the fundamental truth of experience that the nature of the State is firstly power, secondly power and thirdly power. But in order that Prussia might win public opinion and thus increase her power, Treitschke also demanded that she should return to constitutional legality, which Bismarck had violated. "The immense majority of the Germans", he said, "is primarily imbued with liberalism and regards the power of the fatherland as a secondary question." This might be regrettable but could not be overlooked. Treitschke realized that " the name of Prussia sounds odious to the German people ". The movement for national unity had no strong support in the masses and it was doubtful whether the people would ever muster the energy to rise for it. The only road to German unity was that policy which the King of Sardinia and Cavour had used for achieving the unity of Italy, i.e. conquest combined with liberalism.

Meanwhile, in 1862, Bismarck had become the head of the Prussian Government. He immediately entered into sharp conflict with the Liberals, who controlled two thirds of the votes in Parliament, and disregarded constitutional law in breaking their resistance. Treitschke violently denounced him as " the Junker who boasts of blood and iron ". Soon, however, Bismarck realized his boast in three successive wars which resulted in unparalleled triumph and thereby also broke the power of particularism and liberalism. The change of mind shown by Treitschke was shared by a large part of the German middle class. The war against Denmark and its consequences undermined his liberal belief in a policy based on legality and morality, and aroused his hope of national unification by dint of Prussian arms. In 1866 Bismarck offered him a very attractive position, in which he would have had to use his forceful pen for the cause of Prussia. But, though greatly tempted, Treitschke refused, because of qualms caused by the remnants of his liberalism. In a letter he wrote that this statesman seemed to have no inkling of the power of moral forces in the world. But Bismarck knew well the intoxicating power of his policy of blood and iron.

The tremendous transformation of German political mentality through the success of Bismarck's statecraft could be illustrated by many examples. The most consistent defender of the idea of German decentralization, G. G. Gervinus, continued his opposition and rightly prophesied that the establishment of Prussia's paramountcy implied the greatest danger for the peace of Europe and also for internal peace. It could only lead to the revival of despotism, militarism and social radicalism in Europe. Before Bismarck embarked on his policy of realizing a unitary German Government by force, Gervinus declared, hardly anybody was in favour of such a solution. But his success had converted a large number of people to his programme, though this was contrary to the strongest tendency in the German national character.[1] The change was not restricted to politicians and to a large section of public opinion. It also affected the thought of serious scholars on fundamental problems of politics. In some of them, of course, the germs of the new ideas must already have existed before. But political events now induced them to work out and to profess doctrines which previously had been only latent in their minds. A significant case was that of J. H. von Kirchmann, a high Prussian judge, who for his radical convictions had been dismissed by the government and was a prominent politician of the democratic Left. He also published many philosophical books and edited a large series of the works of great philosophers with his commentaries, which for a long time were generally used by students of philosophy. Now, in his commentary on Grotius's *Law of War and Peace*, published in 1869, he showed the greatest scorn for International Law and Grotius's love of peace, and passionately glorified war, on the ground that war was the greatest delight of the Indo-Germanic race, which needed it for the enjoyment of their energies. Morality was not valid for nations. Again and again Kirchmann referred to Bismarck's war of 1866 as a proof of his theses.[2] In 1868 A. Lasson published a book on War and Culture in which he glorified war as a most beneficial factor in cultural evolution.

Treitschke soon became an enthusiastic follower of Bismarck, though he did not go so far in suppressing particularism as Treitschke had desired and left a certain autonomy to the States which had escaped annexation by Prussia. In the policy of winning the masses by granting them political rights, however, Bismarck went much farther than was welcome to Treitschke. The example of Napoleon III had convinced him that the best way of crushing liberalism was the appeal to the masses, and this was the reason of his introduction of manhood suffrage. He even tried to win the

[1] Cf. G. G. Gervinus, *Hinterlassene Schriften*, 1872, pp. 13 f. On Gervinus, cf. Gooch, p. 108.
[2] Cf. the quotations from Kirchmann's book in my book *Nationalgeist und Politik*, vol. i, p. 128. Cf. on Kirchmann as philosopher Moritz Brasch, *Die Philosophie der Gegenwart*, 1888, p. 591.

Socialists, made contact with Lassalle, and after the latter's death made an unsuccessful attempt to get into touch with Marx.

It is not necessary to show here in detail how step by step Treitschke abandoned his liberal principles, and in later life put forward many views which were the exact opposite of his earlier ones. In his famous lectures on Politics, which after his death appeared as a book,[1] in his essays, and lastly in his greatest work, the unfinished *German History*, he developed ideas which became the groundwork of modern German nationalism and had a fatal influence on the mentality of a large part of the German upper and middle classes. True, Treitschke never discarded from his thought a certain residue of his liberal past. Up to 1879 he belonged to the National-Liberal Party and was one of their deputies in the Reichstag. He occasionally pointed out the demoralizing effects of long wars, showed understanding and sympathy for the achievements of other nations, and for a long time was a staunch free trader. The " ridiculous Teutonism " of Jahn and his followers, with their anti-French fanaticism,[2] appeared to him as an aberration, and he also opposed the attempt of " fierce Teutons " to purify the German language of all words of foreign origin. Machiavelli's recognition of the striving for power as the aim of politics, without any further moral justification, seemed to him terrible. In his view power was justifiable by moral aims only. But in their application Treitschke's doctrines were certainly not very different from those of Machiavelli. Prussia's policy of power and prestige was in his eyes always right, while he violently attacked other states if they did the same as Prussia. International Law, morality in politics, humanity in law, political liberty, social equality, the rights of woman, the labour movement, the diffusion of culture among the masses, the Catholic Church were odious to him. The south Germans, the Austrians and other nations he described with great animosity. The rise of Anglophobia and anti-Semitism, too, were largely Treitschke's work.

In most respects Treitschke's views were disapproved by the great majority of German scholars and the intellectuals who were still imbued with liberal ideas. His historical work was subjected to severe criticism and many historians thought that Treitschke was more a political journalist with a great knowledge of history than an impartial historian. In 1872 some leading economists formed the Association for Social Reforms, with a pro-

---

[1] H. von Treitschke, *Politik*, 2 vols., 1897–8.
[2] Treitschke's attitude to France is described in Irmgard Ludwig, *Treitschke und Frankreich*, 1934. It was predominantly hostile.

gramme of research into the condition of the working classes, in order to elaborate proposals for social legislation and thus to decrease social tension. Treitschke soon accused them of favouring socialism, and argued that the attenuation of class differences was not even desirable. Social inequality was sound. Millions had to toil in order to enable a few thousands to govern and to produce culture. This attitude aroused vigorous opposition and most economists joined the Association and co-operated in social research which prepared the ground for many important social and economic reforms.

In 1879 Treitschke began to attack the Jews. At first he emphasized that he was opposed to racial hatred and to any discrimination in civic rights, and that all he wanted was that the Jews should drop their peculiarities and become good Germans. Later, however, his anti-Semitism grew more bitter. It was rightly felt by many that the real object of his campaign was not the Jews, but liberalism,[1] and that the Jews were only used as a means for working up public opinion against its fundamental principles. Among people of cultural standing this campaign was widely condemned and not a single prominent scholar took his side. A public declaration appeared, signed by a large number of eminent personalities, expressing absolute disapproval, and the greatest German scholar, Theodor Mommsen, in several statements blamed Treitschke's attitude and anti-Semitism in general with the greatest indignation and utter contempt.[2] Prince Frederick, the heir to the Throne, declared that anti-Semitism was a disgrace to Germany. Nevertheless, it was eagerly accepted by a part of the students at the universities. Stoecker and other Protestant pastors used it for propaganda among the working class which they tried to capture, though without success. Treitschke, who had always been a pantheist free-thinker and had scoffed at the Churches, now allied himself with this group " for the defence of Christianity ".

Germany had, through Bismarck's policy, become a powerful Empire and in material progress was in the front rank. All those, however, who had harboured the hope that her unification would

---

[1] This is admitted by Leipprand, who shares Treitschke's views. Cf. *Treitschke im deutschen Geistesleben*, pp. 178, 186, where many details about this campaign and the reaction of public opinion are given.

[2] Especially in his letters. Cf. also his judgment in Hermann Bahr, *Der Antisemitismus*, 1894, p. 28. Anti-Semitism, however, never played a great role in German politics before Hitler, though it exercised a certain social influence. The origin, and motives of modern German anti-Semitism are described in Kurt Wawrzinek, *Die Entstehung der deutschen Antisemitenparteien*, 1927.

bring about a great moral and spiritual essor were bitterly disappointed. Jacob Burckhardt had foreseen this from the first and declared that political and cultural pre-eminence were incompatible. His friend, Friedrich Nietzsche, painted the spiritual degeneration of Germany in the most lurid colours, and many others were equally disillusioned. Even Treitschke found that the war of 1870 had destroyed all idealism in Germany, and spoke bitter words about the triumph of vulgarity, materialism and demagogy. The Byzantine flattery devoted to the young Emperor William II appeared to him a symptom of oriental servitude.

Treitschke's most pernicious legacy to our time was the anti-English fanaticism which he developed in his later life, and which had a large share in paving the way for the war of 1914. In his liberal period, Treitschke was an enthusiastic admirer of English liberty and national unity. He praised English parliamentarism and self-government, the English national character and culture. At that time he hated Russia, France and Austria, and the best policy for Germany seemed to him an alliance with Britain. Since the Franco-German War, however, he assumed a hostile attitude towards England. Her neutrality in that war and the widespread English sympathies for France aroused his fury, and England's Oriental policy further increased it. The main factors responsible for his change of sentiment were his abandonment of liberalism, the rise of democracy in Britain, her colonial expansion and the frustration of his ardent longing for a great German colonial Empire. It was clear that this longing could only be realized at the expense of the British Empire. Treitschke already set his hopes on the Boers, whom he wanted to use for ousting the English from South Africa and establishing a German protectorate there. His desire for expansion, however, was not restricted to British possessions. When Bismarck acquired the Cameroons for Germany, Treitschke remarked : " Cameroons ? What are we to do with this sandbox ? Let us take Holland ; then we shall have colonies." In 1876 he had written in a letter that the German Navy would have to win its first laurels by fighting the British Navy, since Britain wished to destroy it. And in his lectures on Politics he expressed the hope that Germany would one day become the greatest naval power. His antagonism to England became a mania, and he now painted a picture of British policy and character which abounded in the most repulsive traits. England he charged with having for centuries stirred up hostility between the nations of the Continent in order to have a free hand for appropriating an immense Empire by mere robbery.

The real cause of Treitschke's wrath, of course, was that Britain stood in the way of Germany's rise to world domination.

24. Pan-Germanism and Racialism in Twentieth-century Germany

In 1891 an association was founded at Frankfurt a.M. for the purpose of propagating a policy of intransigent nationalism, and in 1894 it assumed the name of Pan-German League.[1] The principal founder was Alfred Hugenberg, then a young Prussian official who, in 1909, became the first director of the Krupp concern. The League had never a very numerous membership, but it comprised a considerable number of influential members, such as generals, highly-placed officials, great industrialists, editors of newspapers, professors, and so on. At one time 84 members of the Reichstag belonged to the League. Until 1907 Professor Ernst Hasse was its president, and when he died Heinrich Class succeeded him. The League played a sinister part in German politics by urging a ruthless anti-liberal policy in internal affairs, and unscrupulous and aggressive expansion abroad. It formed the centre of a cluster of nationalist societies like the Navy League, the "Young Germany" League, etc., which together numbered millions of members and were mainly directed or controlled by functionaries of the Pan-German League. One could compare the League to a sort of General Staff of extreme nationalism. Its relations with the government of the Empire were of a curious nature. The League was almost constantly in strong opposition because the government did not sufficiently comply with its demands. No government, indeed, could fulfil the demands of the League without incurring the risk of grave crises and war. Most statesmen responsible for Germany's international policy regarded the League as a nuisance and a danger, and sometimes, when provoked by the League's attacks on their policy, they even rebuked its activities. On the other hand, however, they were well aware that the League was backed by powerful circles, whose wrath they feared to arouse; so they tried to avoid a clash. Moreover, there were always ministers, generals and other high personages who were very favourably disposed towards the League, even when its leaders

[1] Cf. my book *Nationalgeist und Politik*, vol. I., p. 452 ; O. Bonhard, *Geschichte des Alldeutschen Verbandes*, 1920 ; M. S. Wertheimer, *The Pan-German League*, 1924 ; Charles Andler, *Pan-Germanism*, 1915 ; *Collection des documents sur le Pan-Germanisme*, 1915–17 ; *20 Jahre alldeutscher Arbeit und Kämpfe*, 1910 ; H. Class, *Wider den Strom!* 1932 ; Junius Alter, *Nationalisten*, 1930 ; Arnim-Below, *Deutschnationale Köpfe*, 1928.

attacked the official policy. In particular, Admiral Tirpitz, the head of the Admiralty, stood in close relations with the Pan-Germans and employed them for making propaganda on a gigantic scale for naval armaments. The heir to the throne was also particularly friendly to the League.

The ideas which inspired the League were laid down by its president, Professor Hasse, first in his lectures at the University of Leipzig, and then in a work, *Deutsche Politik*, which appeared in numerous parts. Hasse proclaimed that Germany must acquire a great empire, both in Europe and overseas. The expansion of Britain had disturbed the Balance of Power, and implied a denial of equal rights to Germany. True, German trade had made enormous progress in spite of England's colonial monopoly, but it was built on insecure foundations. It depended on the continuance of the " open door " policy by Britain and other nations, and these would certainly enter upon a policy of boycotting German goods, which would be ruinous for Germany and would force her to fight. Hasse, therefore, entirely rejects the " unfortunate " principle of the " open door " and demands that Germany should rather restrict her economic activities to a smaller area exclusively controlled by her. First of all he advocates the formation of a European Customs Union, consisting of Germany, Austria-Hungary, Belgium, Holland, and most of the other small States of Europe. But this union was not to be limited to purely economic aims. The rôle of Germany was to be that of a " protector ". Moreover, she was to acquire large parts of China and Turkey, and in this whole immense area she alone was to exercise influence. Other Pan-German writers have extended this ambitious programme still further, and there were not many parts of the world which were not envisaged by one or the other of them as a sphere of German expansion.

Another typical example of Pan-German mentality is a book by Hasse's successor, Heinrich Class, which appeared in 1912 under the pseudonym Daniel Frymann and under the title *If I were the Emperor*. It ran into many editions and caused a great sensation. Class declares that the situation of the German nation is extremely critical. All classes feel deeply disillusioned and discontented because of the weak and timid policy of the government. Even the Kaiser is accused of an undignified preference for peace and quietude. All Germany's neighbour states increase their spheres of influence, and Germany alone is left empty-handed, though she is in urgent need of expansion. Moreover, the internal situation of Germany is described as a most gloomy and even desperate one. The causes are the rise of the Social Democrats, the demoralizing influence of capitalism and the Jews, and the decay of the middle classes. It is absolutely necessary to abolish the existing manhood franchise, if necessary by violence. The best means to achieve this aim is war, and everybody who loves the German people must long for war. If Germany wins the war, there will be such national enthusiasm that the elections will give the nationalists a majority in parliament, and this must be used for abolishing the democratic suffrage. If, however, Germany loses the war, this would be only a transitory misfortune. Defeat would lead to internal chaos, order could only be restored by a powerful dictator backed by the army, and this too would give an opportunity for restricting the suffrage. In case, however, it should not be possible to bring about a war, the suffrage must be abolished by hook or by crook, possibly by a *coup d'état*. When this is achieved, then the Emperor would have to concede parliamentary government, for the present mode of government is " intolerable ". The programme for the future regime would comprise energetic suppression of " revolutionary activities " (i.e. the Socialists), treatment of the Jews as aliens, the ruthless keeping down of national minorities, restriction of internal migrations, the prohibition of large stores, and most of all, the increase of the army and navy to a maximum. The view that they are merely intended for defence is pitiful and philistine. What Germany wants most urgently is an " active—or to speak frankly—aggressive foreign policy ". The expansion of Germany implies antagonism to England and the only solution is war. Class points out that every educated person in Germany loves and admires England, but not her policy. The industries of the two States have not done each other any real damage and probably never will. After the great conflict, therefore, Germany and England can become sincere friends again. The author also appreciates some good points in France, especially her patriotism and willingness to make sacrifices to military necessities. Nevertheless, Germany's security demands that France must be smashed, that she must cede wide territories to Germany and evacuate the French population so that Germans can be settled there. Belgium and Holland have no right to existence ; they must be incorporated in Germany, although Germans have no reason to welcome this since their populations, through the long rule of the commercial interests, have become completely demoralized and depraved. If they submit voluntarily, their language may perhaps to a certain extent be tolerated, otherwise not. Austria-

Hungary needs a German dictatorship in order to curb the Slavs and Hungarians. As regards Russia, there is no reason for a quarrel. Class, like Hasse, does not grudge Russia her Empire and even advises the Baltic Germans to emigrate if Russia should strangle their nationality. But the Russian hatred of everything German will, he thinks, probably lead to war. The author regards war as an indispensable medicine for the prevention of moral degeneration.

Many other writers have put forward these and similar ideas; they have proclaimed Germany's right to world-domination and indulged in exuberant praise of the moral and political blessings of war. But we need not give further examples as they hardly contribute new ideas to those developed by Treitschke, Hasse and Class.[1]

The Pan-German League concentrated all its efforts on the enhancement of Germany's power. In its ideology power as such appeared as the supreme aim, a view which even Treitschke had declared to be terrible and repulsive when he discussed Machiavelli's philosophy. It was absolutely incompatible with the ethos of Christianity and the cosmopolitan spirit of the classical thinkers and poets of Germany—spiritual forces which still exercised great influence on large sections of the German people. It was Houston Stewart Chamberlain who did most to paralyse this influence by a new cultural nationalism centred on the idea of the immense superiority of the " Aryan race " over all others.[2] This idea had already been propagated by Gobineau and others, but in a form which precluded the chance of any great success. In Gobineau's view the Aryan race was doomed to decay by unavoidable mixture with inferior races, and his outlook was pessimistic. He, moreover, did not credit the Germans with much " Aryan blood " and considered the English to be of better stock. Chamberlain, though of English origin, regarded the Germans as the Chosen People, indulged in denigrations of modern England,[3] and worked out a system of racialism which was much better suited than any other creed to capture the German mind. His

[1] Cf. numerous examples in my book *Nationalgeist und Politik*, vol. I, p. 464; M. Hobohm und P. Rohrbach, *Chauvinismus und Weltkrieg*, 2 vols., 1919; O. Nippold, *der Deutsche Chauvinismus*, 1913.
[2] Cf. this book, p. 62.
[3] Cf. his views on the English character in his *Kriegsaufsätze*, 1941, p. 44. In another essay (p. 24) he revived Fichte's eccentric theory of the unique excellency of the German language and argued that in England not a trace of true culture could reach the people because the language was unfitted for this. The most important task, therefore, was to force the German language upon the whole world. All nations must realize that he who does not know German is an outcast. In another essay he even said that no higher idea could be expressed in the English language.

Pan-Germanism was perhaps even more fanatical and fatal than that of Treitschke, but it was not as ostentatiously political and Prussian, and appealed more to minds interested in cultural problems. Chamberlain's books make on most readers the impression of being written by an encyclopedic mind, by a man deeply versed in every field of culture and learning. He was, indeed, very widely read and had a gift for interpreting his gleanings from history, philosophy, religion, art, and literature so as to confirm racialism. But this imposing and dazzling façade was erected with complete neglect of critical thinking and without real care for truth.[1] Chamberlain, like Treitschke, was a writer of extraordinary power; his style is fascinating and persuasive, and imbued with quasi-religious passion. In his *Foundations of the Nineteenth Century* and in his books on Christ, Goethe, and Kant he tried to show that all great geniuses were true expressions of the Aryan soul, that their teachings were incompatible with the fundamental beliefs of liberalism and democracy, and that the Jews were the worst enemies of the Aryans, the personification of everything mean and perverse. The Emperor Wilhelm II was a close friend of Chamberlain and an enthusiastic believer in his theories, which he propagated with all the means at his disposal. No wonder that Chamberlain succeeded in intoxicating a considerable section of the German intellectuals with an immense pride of race and nationality, and with deep contempt for the " Western ideas " of England and France, which he represented as being largely a product of Jewish capitalism. In this way Chamberlain became the most important pioneer of Hitlerism, and he himself predicted that Hitler would become the " saviour of Germany ".

[1] Cf. ample proofs in my book *Race and Civilization*, 1928.

EPILOGUE

Many readers of this book will expect to find in the last chapter a concise summary of its contents, a recapitulation of its principal theses and practical suggestions of remedies for the evils discussed. The Preface states that the author regards this book as a study in human nature and human society, and this would seem to imply the promise of a theory, of a system of generalizations indicating fundamental tendencies. It has, indeed, been the aim of the author to contribute to the elaboration of such a theory, but he would consider it a grave mistake to attempt to formulate his conclusions in a few sweeping generalizations, while a careful statement of general tendencies would require much more space than present conditions permit. Moreover, since further studies on the subject of nationality will shortly be published by the author it seems that a recapitulation and practical suggestions should be postponed. It may, however, be useful to summarize at least certain negative conclusions, deprecating ways of approach which have proved to be misleading and to add a few other remarks.

The phenomena of nationality form such a perplexing multitude of problems extending over all fields of life and over all times, they are so complicated and evasive that it would be an audacious enterprise to present them in a nutshell. The fundamental fact is national consciousness which in the course of history has assumed many forms, from a vague sentiment of kinship to a distinct striving for national personality and to the ideal of a close community with unlimited solidarity. A developed national consciousness implies a framework of ideas regarding the demarcation, structure, character, and mission of the nation, and on its relations to other nations which constitutes the national ideology. The psychology of national consciousness forms a very complex structure of aspirations, and it appears in the most different forms ; it may be peaceable or pugnacious, progressive or reactionary, tolerant or fanatic.

The first step towards a real understanding must be the working out of an unambiguous and suitable terminology. Most writers on general questions of nationality have disregarded this rule and have operated with terms which have various senses. This resulted in the fact that the writers and the readers soon found themselves landed in a dense fog, which sometimes was not quite unwelcome to those writers. A particular misfortune is the habit of calling all manifestations of national consciousness by the name " nationalism ". In this book nationalism means a specific form of national consciousness centred on superiority, prestige, power and domination. Another case in question is the use of the term " national character ". Most people understand this term as implying an inborn character consisting in a number of instincts, and this leads to the fallacy of racialism, this curse of humanity. Elementary impulses, of course, underlie all human activities, just as man could neither live nor think nor act without the energies produced by the chemical elements in his organism. But it would be as silly to describe Shakespeare's work or the achievements and tendencies of a nation in terms of instincts as to describe it in terms of carbon, hydrogen and oxygen. Nevertheless, the habit of interpreting the aspirations and diversities of nations and the conflicts between them as the outcome of racial dispositions more or less dominates the ideology of all nations. It is the very primitivity of this idea which makes it so popular and irresistible.

The misinterpretation of the word " national character " has induced critics to attack not merely the term, but even the idea that nations show deep-seated differences and thus to fall from one extreme into the opposite. Such diversities certainly exist and have a great influence on the fate of nations. They are rooted in traditions, and in the social structure of the nations and the term " national traditions " would probably be the best substitute available for " national character ". Traditions alone, however, are not necessarily powerful and persistent. They acquire their force as political factors through their connexion with the interests of influential social groups. Most people find it difficult to understand the full significance of traditions for the political life of nations, and, even if they admit their influence, they are usually not able or inclined to give so much time to the study of history as would be required for a real understanding of traditions, which forms one of the most intricate problems of historical research.

The preference for primitive explanations can be observed also in opinions on why aggressive nationalism has gained such power over certain nations though the true interests of the great majority were certainly quite opposed to its aims. Anybody with a knowledge of the mind of the workers and peasants of certain countries, for example, Italy, would find it hard to believe that they were thirsting to sacrifice their lives for the glory and spoils of war. The problem then is : Which sections of the people were primarily responsible? What were their motives? And how were they able to induce other classes to sacrifice everything to aims which obviously were more or less alien to their real wishes? Terrorism and fraud may explain this to a certain degree, but they were certainly not the only factors concerned. Many different answers have been given to those questions. Every political party or social class, every school of history, sociology, or psychology has its own explanation, or inclines to it. Almost all these interpretations, however, mix some truth with a great deal of untruth. They all commit the mistake of oversimplifying matters, and of stressing one factor as the exclusive, or as the paramount cause of nationalism. The most frequent way is that of putting the whole responsibility upon another nation or class than one's own. This book has, I hope, made it clear that nationalism is not the product of one age, nation, class, party, religion or philosophy, but that each has partly contributed to its growth, partly counteracted it, though in very different degrees. In many cases a class, party or school of thought has unconsciously furthered, indeed, the rise of tendencies alien to its aims though sections of certain nations have had a special share in developing nationalism, such as a military caste, the intelligentsia and the younger generation. But germs of nationalism are latent in all strata of society, and when a great crisis arises the national passions may break forth with a power which nobody would have foreseen. The decisive factor is the national ideology which may be compared with a gigantic net in which all classes are inextricably enmeshed while a minority pulls the strings. Moreover, it is the Spirit of the Time which has a paramount influence on the destiny of mankind. Both these forces are the outcome of a constellation of countless factors.

A diagnosis of the causes of nationalism, and of the rise of the spirit of nationality in general, cannot, therefore, be formulated in a few brief sentences. They are both so intimately connected with all branches of life and thought that one could as well attempt to compress the contents of world-history into a few lines. It would, of course, be possible to formulate some general conclusions but they would not convey a real understanding of the problem. Abstract statements, condensing a vast range of observation in the briefest possible form are a delight for the theorist, but their value for the student of nationality is small. The concrete rivalries of nations, or the peculiarities of their traditions and aspirations, can only be understood by a careful study of history in a comparative and sociological spirit.

Similar reasons discourage any attempt to formulate in brief remedies against nationalism. It is now generally recognized that a mere machinery of international organization cannot work if the right spirit is lacking. But how can this spirit be created or strengthened? The proclamation of general principles obviously is not enough. Neither is it sufficient to lay down that nations must be educated towards that spirit, if a practicable plan and an adequate number of qualified educators are not available. The habit of treating such questions in an unrealistic and perfunctory way is bound to lead to failure, disillusionment and cynicism. Education towards world-citizenship, moreover, is not merely a matter for the schools. It is connected with all the great issues of political and economic life, and could only be solved if the leading nations of the world would adopt detailed plans based on identical principles. These remarks may explain why I have withstood the temptation to make practical proposals in a short final chapter.

Nevertheless even negative conclusions of a theoretical kind may have their value for purposes of practical policy. A disease cannot be treated in the right way before its cause has been discovered. Modern medicine could not develop as long as people believed in imaginary causes of illness, for example, evil demons. In the case of nationalism the first step to a practical cure also consists in discarding imaginary causes. The second step, though not the final one, would be a wide appreciation of the real causes. The principal difficulties are the strength of prejudice, egotism, and wishful thinking and the unwillingness of many politicians to adopt complicated plans which can only bear fruit in the future and which are likely to arouse national prejudice and passions.

INDEX

The names of those authors only have been included whose views were discussed or quoted in detail.

Acland, R., 42
Aeneas Silvius, 112
Alsace, 86, 167, 243
America, 182, 229, 231, 236
Animal mind, 17
Anti-Semitism, 265, 275, 403
Arabs, 80, 145
Arbuthnot, J., 27
Augustine, St., 287
Australia, 72, 179
Austria-Hungary, 7, 9, 164, 170, 196, 330

Babylonians, 79
Bacon, F., 303
Bacon, R., 290
Balance of Power, 120, 154, 182
Baltic Germans, 249
Baring-Gould, 57
Barrès, M., 381
Bartholomew Anglicus, 290
Basch, V., 336
Beneš, E., 204
Bentham, 363
Beth, K., 100
Bismarck, 32, 64, 169, 227, 231, 235, 252, 397, 400
Bodin, 298
Bodley, J., 378
Bolingbroke, 313
Bolsheviks, 268
Boniface, St., 115
Boutroux, E., 285
Britain, racialism, 66
Britain, unification, 172, 212
British character and ideology, 42, 50, 68, 213, 362, 379
British Empire, 176
Bryce, J., 237
Bull, John, 27
Bulwer-Lytton, 365
Burke, E., 55, 325
Bury, J., 121
Butler R., 338
Byzantine Empire, 111

Cahun, L., 143
Calvinism, 132
Canada, 178

Capitalism, 253, 264
Capitulations, 146
Carr, E., 34, 97, 275
Carlyle, 367
Caste, 56, 137
Celtic Language, 81, 84, 89, 90
Chamberlain, H. S., 62, 408
Chamberlain, J., 50
Charlemagne, 156
Charles V, 158
Chinese, 72, 77, 94
Chosen people, 20, 102, 305
Christianity and Nationality, 104
Churches, attitude to race, 58
Churches and internationalism, 134
Churches and liberty, 120
Churches and nationality, 107, 109, 122
Civilization and nationality, 24
Class, H., 257, 406
Class-war, 215, 220, 238
Cobden, 369
Coleridge, 366
Collective mentality, 15
Colonial policies compared, 70
Comte, 377
Crimean War, 231
Cromwell, 307
Crusades, 135
Czechs, 81, 89, 97, 118 f., 201, 204, 243

Dante, 83, 289
Darwin, 29
Davies, Trevor R., 153
Defoe, 66
Democracy, 86, 237, 262, 269
Demolins, E., 380
Disraeli, 29, 62, 67, 373
Dubois, P., 290
Dubois-Reymond, 46
Dutch and race, 38

Economics of nationalism, 275
Eisenmann, L., 202
Empires, 153
England, cf. Britain
England, parliament, 212
English Church, 125, 133

English language, 82, 83, 87
English national character, 220
Enlightenment, 310
Erasmus, 295

Feudalism and State, 207
Fichte, 336
Fievée, J., 235
Foreigners, 36, 146, 209, 288
Fouillée, A., 381
France, 31, 68, 70, 161, 165, 209, 213, 298, 374
Francis Joseph I, 199
Frederick II of Prussia, 19, 63, 225
French Church and national character, 126
French language, 81, 330
French Revolution, 252, 323
Freud, S., 17
Froissart, 166, 221

Gandhi, 138, 189
Gentleman, 45
Gentz, F., 328, 355
German ideology and national character, 22, 46, 48, 57, 127, 220, 252
German language, 81, 84, 97, 330, 341
German nationalism, 157, 277, 294
German racialism, 63
German revolution, 1848, 395
Germany, unity, 168, 217
Gervinus, 401
Gibbon, 350
Ginsberg, M., 16, 26
Gioberti, 384
Gladstone, 168, 373
Gneisenau, 227, 393
Gobineau, 62, 378
Goethe, 63, 332
Grattan, 7
Greeks, 80, 92
Gregory VII, 117
Grey, E., 49, 271
Guizot, 376, 379
Gulick, S., 76

Hankins, H., 270
Harnack, A., 113
Harrington, J, 308
Hasse, E., 406
Hayes, C., 5, 34, 149, 384
Hegel, 320, 329, 335, 344
Heiden, K., 260
Helvetius, 45
Henry VIII, 84, 302
Herder, 39, 331
Hinduism, 136

History, teaching, 149
Hitler, 2, 13, 22, 34, 52, 62, 65, 245, 250, 259, 271, 361
Hobbes, 309
Hobson, J. A., 371
Holstein, Baron, 50
Home feeling, 149
Huguenots, 315
Humanism, 292
Humboldt, W., 335
Hume, 39, 44, 327, 363
Hungary, 81, 89, 196

Ibn Chaldun, 25
Immigration, 72
India, 56, 69, 71, 88, 136, 151, 188, 265
Inge, W., 122, 123
Instinct, 16, 411
Intellectuals, 273, 283
International law, 135, 309
Ireland, 55, 67, 84, 89, 104, 110, 175, 240, 243, 391
Islam, 139
Italy, 83, 170, 296

Jaensch, E., 16
Japan, 74
Jaurès, 325
Jews, 14, 54, 58, 64, 79, 92, 147, 243, 344, 403
John of Salisbury, 117, 220, 222, 288
Joseph II, 84
Judaism, 101
Julian, Emperor, 106

Kant, 334
Kautsky, R., 194, 265
King, Bolton, 171
Kirchmann, 401
Kohn, H., 59
Kramar, K., 203

Language and nationality, 78
Laski, H., 191
Law of Nations, 135
League of Nations, 8, 61, 247
Le Bon, G., 16, 381
Leibniz, 334
Leopold II, Emperor, 350
Lessing, 331
Lloyd George, 244
Locke, 312
Louis XIV, 161, 166, 197, 314
Luther, 128

Macartney, C., 144, 247
Macaulay, 365

MacDonald, R., 2
MacDougall, W., 15, 34, 68, 73
Macedonia, 241
Machiavelli, 295, 302, 340
Maistre, J. de, 374
Manin, D., 389
Mannheim, K., 271
Mansergh, N., 391
Maori, 61, 72
Martin, Kingsley, 283, 371
Marx, 23, 238, 263, 353, 369
Masaryk, 203
Mass-psychology, 16
Masterman, J., 114
Matthew Paris, 215, 240, 288
Maurras, Ch., 381
Maynard, J., 194
Maximilian I, Emperor, 294
Mazzini, 7, 34, 384
Meinecke, F., 296
Mercantilism, 276, 306
Meston, Lord, 139
Michelet, 28
Michels, R., 43
Militarism, 47, 76, 223
Mill, J. S., 12
Milton, 308
Minorities, 247
Moltke, H., 46
Mommsen, Th., 403
Montaigne, 301
Montesquieu, 316
More, Th., 338
Motives, types, 18
Mueller, A., 358
Muir, R., 174
Murray, R., 363
Mysticism, 127

Napoleon I, 162, 226, 229, 252, 339, 347, 376, 394
Nation, history of the word, 6, 234, 314; definitions, 5, 11
National character and ideology, 19, 20, 22, 37
National consciousness, analysis, 15, 21
National states, origin, 208
National will, 233
Nationalism, 1, 34, 251; and Religion, 121
Nationality, aspects, 8; Laws, 14; Origin, 31
Natural frontiers, 167
Netherlands, 153, 160
Nicholas II, 232, 253
Nietzsche, F., 47, 131, 360

Normans, 80
Norwegian language, 92
Novalis, 357

Oakesmith, J., 68
Oldham, J., 59
Organism, national, 28
Othello, 60

Pacifism, 292, 309
Palmerston, 369, 371
Pan-German League, 405
Pantheism, 101, 345, 353, 357
Parliaments, 211
Personality, national, 26
Perthes, F., 394
Pestalozzi, 342
Philosophy and national character, 284
Pillsbury, W., 37
Playne, C., 270
Plebiscites, 96, 244
Poles, 200, 248, 321
Pollard, A., 212
Postel, G., 300
Primitive mentality, 271
Protectionism, 185, 276
Proudhon, 376
Prussia, 225
Puritanism, 305

Quakers, 261, 309, 363

Race, 52
Racialism, 53, 239, 378
Rait, R., 81, 127
Ranke, L., 37
Reformation, 117
Religion, 98
Renan, E., 12, 26, 28, 379
Rivarol, 330
Robbins, L., 256
Romans, 80
Romanticism, 86, 353, 355, 362, 386
Roosevelt, Th., 50
Rousseau, 68, 167, 318
Russia, 191

Salisbury, Lord, 46, 49
Sarkar, B. K., 99
Schiller, 332
Schlegel, 356
Scholasticism, 126
Schopenhauer, 360
Scotland, 8, 132, 173
Script and nationality, 93

INDEX

Seeley, J., 177
Seippel, P., 379
Self-determination, 187, 190, 240
Sénart, E., 56
Serbs, 205
Seton-Watson, R. W., 203
Shaftesbury, Lord, 312
Shakespeare, 301, 303
Siegfried, A., 384
Sieyès, 323
Slavs, 88
Smith, Th., 234
Socialists, 23, 263, 266
Sorel, G., 382
South Africa, 69, 71, 179
Southey, 366
Soviet Union, 191
Spain, 153, 160
Spencer, H., 30
Spengler, O., 362
Staël, Madame de, 375
Stalin, 194
State, ideas of, 207, 238, 287 ; range of activities and nationalism, 287 ; size, 154, 242
Steed, H. W., 203
Stephen, Leslie, 365
Stinnes, H., 257
Sulzbach, W., 17
Switzerland, 89, 96
Symbols, 27

Taine, H., 163, 379
Tarde, G., 16
Territory, 146
Thiers, 367
Thomas, St., Aquinas, 115, 289
Thyssen, F., 260
Tocqueville, 185
Towns, 222
Toynbee, A., 14, 58
Tradition, 18
Treitschke, H., 397
Turkey, 142

United States, 73, 75

Voltaire, 317

Wagner, R., 62, 361
Wales, 173
War, 217, 253, 263
Webb, C., 98
Weber, M., 15, 102
Wells, H. G., 122
Welsh language, 84, 91
Wieland, 331
Wilhelm II, 62, 232, 253
William of Malmesbury, 286
Wilson, 75, 237, 244
Wingfield-Stratford, E., 363, 373
Women, position, 105, 107
Wordsworth, W., 367